Marketing
THE CORE

Sixth Canadian Edition

ROGER A. KERIN
Southern Methodist University

STEVEN W. HARTLEY
University of Denver

ARSENIO BONIFACIO
University of Guelph

DONNA DUMONT
Mount Royal University

CAROL BUREAU
Sheridan Institute of Technology and Advanced Learning

Mc
Graw
Hill

MARKETING: THE CORE
Sixth Canadian Edition

The Internet addresses listed in the text were accurate at the time of publication. The inclusion of a Web site does not indicate an endorsement by the authors or McGraw-Hill Ryerson, and McGraw-Hill Ryerson does not guarantee the accuracy of the information presented at these sites.

ISBN-13: 978-1-26-032694-9
ISBN-10: 1-26-032694-2

1 2 3 4 5 6 7 8 9 10 M 27 26 25 24 23 22 21

Printed and bound in Canada.

Care has been taken to trace ownership of copyright material contained in this text; however, the publisher will welcome any information that enables them to rectify any reference or credit for subsequent editions.

Product Director: Rhondda McNabb
Portfolio Manager: Jade Fair
Marketing Manager: Emily Park
Senior Content Developer: Amy Rydzanicz
Portfolio Associate: Tatiana Sevciuc
Supervising Editor: Janie Deneau
Photo/Permissions Editor: Monika Schurmann
Copy Editor: Michael Kelly
Plant Production Coordinator: Tracey Hanson
Manufacturing Production Coordinator: Jason Stubner
Cover and Interior Design: Lightbox Visuals Communication Inc.
Cover Image: Robert Przybysz/Shutterstock
Page Layout: MPS Limited
Printer: Marquis

Author Profiles

Roger A. Kerin is the Harold C. Simmons Distinguished Professor of Marketing at the Edwin L. Cox School of Business, Southern Methodist University in Dallas, Texas. Professor Kerin holds a B.A. (magna cum laude), M.B.A., and Ph.D. from the University of Minnesota. His teaching and research interests lie in marketing planning and strategy, product management, and financial aspects of marketing. Professor Kerin is a frequent participant in executive development programs and is also an active consultant on matters of marketing planning and strategy. Professor Kerin has published and authored several texts and many articles on marketing. He also serves on numerous journal editorial review boards and is currently a member of the Board of Governors of the Academy of Marketing Science.

Steven W. Hartley is Professor of Marketing in the Daniels College of Business at the University of Denver. He holds a bachelor's degree in mechanical engineering, an M.B.A., and a Ph.D. from the University of Minnesota. Dr. Hartley was formerly the chair of the Department of Marketing at the University of Denver and has taught at the University of Colorado, the University of Minnesota, and in several executive development programs. His teaching interests include principles of marketing, marketing research, and marketing planning. Dr. Hartley's research has appeared in many leading marketing publications. He is an active consultant to several prominent U.S. corporations and is active in many professional organizations, including the American Marketing Association, the Academy of Marketing Science, and the Marketing Educators' Association.

Arsenio Bonifacio teaches marketing in the Gordon S. Lang School of Business at the University of Guelph. He applies over 20 years of experience as a marketing executive to the classroom. Arsenio holds an M.B.A. from Wilfrid Laurier University, a B.Sc. from McMaster University, and an Adult Education Certificate from Sheridan College. His career in marketing involved leading teams and initiatives in Canada, the United States, and the United Kingdom. Aside from his teaching, Arsenio is a senior executive at one of Ontario's largest credit unions and is responsible for the organization's member experience.

Donna Dumont is the chair of the Marketing, Entrepreneurship and Social Innovation Department and an Associate Professor of Marketing at Mount Royal University. Donna Dumont obtained her Bachelor of Commerce Degree from the University of Alberta in Edmonton and her Masters of Business Administration from the University of Calgary. Donna has taught both introductory and senior marketing, sales, and entrepreneurial courses in the Bissett School of Business since 1997. Donna has a wide range of sales and marketing experience, including 11 years of work experience in the food industry. She held a variety of marketing and sales positions for Campbell's Soup Company, Kraft General Foods, and Pillsbury Canada Ltd.

Carol Bureau is a Professor of Marketing at the Pilon School of Business at Sheridan College and is also the Program Coordinator for the marketing diploma and degree programs at Sheridan. She is active with student activities, including acting as faculty advisor for the Student Marketing Association, coaching Ontario Colleges Marketing Competition teams, and coordinating internal case competitions. She obtained her M.B.A. from the Ivey Business School at Western University where she worked on several innovative projects, including customer satisfaction measures, selling to the seniors' health care market, telemedicine in Canada, and the development of strategic planning models. Carol graduated with a Bachelor of Business Administration from Wilfrid Laurier University. During the course of her marketing career, she held progressively senior positions in sales and marketing, mainly in the pharmaceutical industry. In addition to teaching, Carol enjoys consulting in her areas of interest, including strategic planning, product launches, and business development.

Brief Contents

Contents

Part 4 Focusing on New and Evolving Areas

Chapter 12 Outbound Marketing Communications 286

Chapter 13 Inbound Marketing Communications 314

Part 5 Putting It All Together

Preface

Welcome to the exciting and dynamic field of marketing! Boosted by technological change, this fast-paced environment continues to quickly evolve, challenging marketers to stay informed and knowledgeable on new marketing approaches, regulations, and ideas. New digital approaches, especially, continue to advance social media marketing, mobile marketing, and customer relationship management programs, as well as in other Internet marketing pathways that may be integrated into offline or online marketing practices.

Real-time marketing and content marketing approaches are used in increasingly creative ways to reach consumers, businesses, and organizations. Conventional marketing approaches reach target markets, and new regulations ensure a smooth transition into this new marketing reality. In all instances, marketing messages compete in a sea of information that floods people's daily lives and challenges marketing programs to be noticed, relevant, and engaging. This marketing reality uses metrics to monitor and measure marketing performance and analytics to reveal insights and areas of improvement.

The sixth Canadian edition of *Marketing: The Core* reflects this new marketing reality with its standard features as well as new elements and content that are designed to engage. There is an expanded focus on digital marketing channels in a chapter called "Inbound Marketing Communications," as well as a focus on financial fluency that has been integrated into the chapters on pricing and strategic planning in a way that students can understand. Each chapter is boosted by new content, examples, and features to ensure the text reflects the very latest online and offline marketing approaches in Canada. There are also articles that focus on the marketing challenges faced during the COVID-19 global pandemic.

The sixth Canadian edition of *Marketing: The Core* returns with its popular magazine-style format that engages with its visual appeal, direct writing style, sound pedagogical features, and fresh new content. Chapter elements include *Chapter Features* and *Chapter Outlines*, which open each chapter, flagging interesting topics and helping students navigate chapter content. Pedagogical elements include *Infographics*, as well as critical-thinking *end-of-chapter* features that help apply and bring the material to life. These elements are in addition to the highly rated chapter-opening vignettes, Marketing NewsFlash boxes, and Focus on Ethics boxes that are all new or updated and interspersed throughout each chapter.

The sixth Canadian edition of *Marketing: The Core* is designed so that students enjoy learning about marketing. It is current. It is real. It reflects marketing in Canada.

Text Organization and Content

Marketing: The Core, Sixth Canadian Edition, is divided into five parts:

Part 1, "Understanding Marketing," looks first at what marketing is and how it creates customer value and customer relationships (Chapter 1). Chapter 2 analyzes the major environmental factors in our changing marketing environment.

Part 2, "Understanding Markets and Their Behaviour," first describes, in Chapter 3, how individual consumers reach buying decisions. Chapter 4 examines the marketing research, and how information about prospective consumers is linked to marketing strategy and decisions. Chapter 5 looks at industrial and organizational buyers and how they make purchase decisions. The process of segmenting and targeting markets and positioning products appears in Chapter 6.

Part 3, "Designing Marketing Strategies and Marketing Mix Elements," covers the four Ps of marketing: product, price, place, and promotion. The product element is divided into two chapters. Chapter 7 looks at the way existing products, services, and brands are managed. Chapter 8 discusses the development of new products and the product life cycle. Pricing is discussed, focusing on the way organizations set prices (Chapter 9). Two chapters address the place aspects of marketing: "Marketing Channels and Supply Chain" (Chapter 10) and "Retailing and Wholesaling" (Chapter 11).

Part 4, "Focusing on New and Evolving Areas," includes revised chapters covering outbound and inbound marketing communications and how to integrate communications to maximize their impact to create community (Chapter 12) and how to leverage digital marketing communications in the promotional mix (Chapter 13). Chapter 14, "Customer Relationship

Management," takes a deeper look into technological innovations that are improving how companies meet consumer needs and grow consumer experience.

Part 5, "Putting It All Together," provides an overview of the strategic marketing planning process that occurs in an organization (Chapter 15) and includes a new marketing plan example in Appendix A.

What's New? Marketing: The Core

The sixth Canadian edition of *Marketing: The Core* builds on the strengths of the previous editions, adding new and exciting elements that make the material even more interactive and engaging. Our authors go to extreme lengths to interview respected Canadian marketers so that content is fresh and accurately reflects current marketing practices. The authors also turn to the teaching environment so that each chapter includes solid pedagogical features that help students learn and faculty teach. The freshness of this new edition is reflected in the following:

- **Enhanced magazine-style format:** The popular magazine-style format returns with its fresh visual appeal, direct writing style, and active-learning techniques that challenge students to understand and enjoy learning about marketing. Many features are included to enhance learning, as noted below.
- **Chapter features and outlines:** Each chapter opens with these elements to highlight newsy features within the chapter and create a path that guides readers through the chapter and its content.
- **New chapter-opening vignettes:** The popular chapter-opening vignettes return with new content that provides a glimpse into real marketing situations, with advice from senior business professionals in Canada. The discussions centre on many exciting brands that will be familiar to students, such as New Era, Toronto Raptors, WestJet, Canada Post, and Hillberg & Berk, as well as many other stellar brands and companies.
- **New Marketing NewsFlash and Focus on Ethics boxes:** These popular features return with new and updated content, meticulously researched to provide perspective on the latest marketing approaches. Examples are Canadian CEOs' response to the COVID-19 global pandemic, the financial services company Questrade's campaign to target a younger market, Mountain Equipment Co-op's corporate social responsibility, and Uber.
- **Sections on metrics, analytics, and big data:** Marketing requires students to understand the metrics

and analytics used by the industry. Sections in the text explain this topic and discuss the issues surrounding big data.
- **Updated sections on forecasting, budgeting, financial analysis, and profit-and-loss statements:** Marketers are involved in forecasting and budgeting, and use financial analyses and profit-and-loss statements to evaluate programs and brand success. These areas are enhanced in the sixth Canadian edition through discussions in the pricing chapter (Chapter 9) and the strategic planning chapter (Chapter 15).
- **Updated marketing plan appendix:** A revised marketing plan example and template has been built into the text. This hypothetical plan was developed in collaboration with Andre Samuels and Cory Snyder of SeeWhy Learning to ensure that it reflects current marketing planning approaches.

Chapter-Specific Additions

In addition to an updated narrative for each chapter and new and updated opening vignettes, Marketing NewsFlash and Focus on Ethics boxes, databoxes, and Infographics, the following topics have been enhanced:

Chapter 1: Marketing Fundamentals

- Role of the marketing function
- The increased importance of corporate social responsibility
- Evolving marketing practices like content, experiential, and influencer marketing
- Marketing regulations and ethical considerations

Chapter 2: The Marketing Environment

- New Statistics Canada infographic on Canada's population
- Generational and ethnic diversity—new generation Z data
- Canadians' use of technology
- The changing household composition
- Updates to regulatory practices in Canada
- The Competition Bureau's *Little Black Book of Scams*
- Real-world example of the steps in a marketing environment scan

Chapter 3: Consumer Behaviour

- Insight into how consumers make difficult decisions
- Consumer trends on decreasing food waste
- The impact of mortgages and growing family debt on consumer spending

Chapter 4: Market Research

- Online metrics and analytics now incorporated into the marketing research process
- Applying research and analytics to respond to a research problem for a Canadian sports team
- Market research sources
- Writing survey questions

Chapter 5: B2B Marketing

- The complexity of B2B marketing
- The risks of cybercrime in Canadian business
- How organizational buying criteria drive big decisions
- The high standards the Government of Canada sets for its suppliers

Chapter 6: Segmentation, Targeting, and Positioning

- Enhanced figure on segmentation strategies: mass, segment, niche, and individualized strategies
- Emphasis on segmentation variables
- Examples of personas
- Updates on the segmentation analytics platform PRIZM5
- Simplified five-step process for segmenting a market
- A quiz and exercise to determine your millennial tribe

Chapter 7: Products and Brands

- Enhanced graphic for the total product concept
- Interbrand's *Best Global Brands* study
- New product mix width, product line length, and product line depth
- The latest packaging trends
- Ipsos' *Most Influential Brands* study
- Building a socially conscious brand

Chapter 8: New Product Development

- Brandspark's *Best New Products* award winners
- Why new products and services fail
- Launching a new product category
- Developing new products in a traditional industry
- The importance of timing in launching a new product
- Successful new Canadian product launches

Chapter 9: Pricing

- Enhanced sections on legal and ethical considerations, including how Canada's Competition Bureau addresses illegal practices
- How companies can disrupt industries through pricing and convenience

Chapter 10: Marketing Channels and Supply Chain

- Supply chain strategies that reduce greenhouse emissions
- The challenges retailers are facing with their distribution models

Chapter 11: Retailing and Wholesaling

- Trends affecting Canadian retailers
- Challenges retailers are facing
- The impact of the COVID-19 pandemic on retailers

Chapter 12: Outbound Marketing Communications

- This chapter emphasizes the paid or outbound areas of the promotional mix
- Internet, mobile and social media are incorporated as tools to communicate the promotional strategy
- The evolution of product placement
- Updated data on advertising expenditures
- Advertising standards in social media

Chapter 13: Inbound Marketing Communications

- This chapter emphasizes the inbound or earned areas of the promotional mix and how to create community
- How to create community on a limited budget
- Online marketing tools
- How social media transformed marketing communications
- Best practices for Facebook, Twitter, YouTube, Instagram, and LinkedIn

Chapter 14: Customer Relationship Management

- Examples of customer relationship management (CRM) as a result of the COVID-19 pandemic
- Enhanced examples of loyalty programs

Chapter 15: Strategic Marketing Planning

This chapter on strategic marketing planning has been placed at the end of the text so that students can gain a greater understanding of marketing before embarking on this more complex topic. The following new content has been included:

- The importance of board diversity
- The importance of innovation
- The importance of strategic partnerships

A Student's Guide to *Marketing: The Core*

Marketing: The Core offers an array of features to help readers learn and apply marketing concepts.

Each chapter opens with a **vignette** on a Canadian marketing situation or program, featuring current facts, real approaches, and tangible examples from interviews with marketers in Canada. **Chapter Features** and **Chapter Outlines** give an overview of the key features and provide an outline of each chapter. Clear and precise **Learning Objectives** help students preview chapter content and study effectively. **Reality Check** questions appear at the end of each vignette.

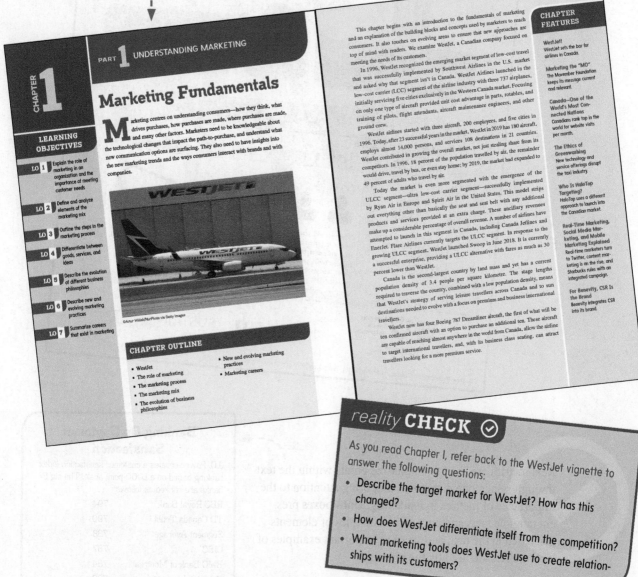

Infographics are used to draw attention to metrics that relate to a topic within the chapter and to help students become familiar with this visual approach to presenting marketing information.

Source: Reducing Food Waste in Ontario (2016) · reproduced with permission from Sustain Ontario.

Real metrics are used to emphasize points within the text through standalone data boxes that bring attention to the importance of metrics in marketing. **Data boxes** present tangible facts and numerical examples of elements discussed in the text, and serve as important examples of how metrics are used by the industry.

Banking On Customer Satisfaction

J.D. Power creates a customer satisfaction index ranking based on a 1,000-point scale. The big 5 banks are ranked as follows:

RBC Royal Bank	794
TD Canada Trust	790
Segment Average	788
CIBC	787
BMO Bank of Montreal	784
Scotiabank	782

Marketing Tips showcase valuable thoughts from real-world marketers that are relevant to the topics discussed in each chapter.

Ask Yourself checkpoints, found near the end of major sections in each chapter, allow students to test their comprehension of the chapter material before moving on.

Marketing NewsFlash boxes provide exciting, current examples of marketing in action, making the material relevant and memorable. **Focus on Ethics boxes** focus on current topics of ethical and social concern. Discussion questions at the end of each box encourage students to apply marketing concepts and critically assess marketing situations.

AdAlyze features give students the opportunity to critically evaluate and dissect the message of an actual print advertisement, helping them understand real-world application.

At the end of each chapter, the **Summary** and list of **Key Terms** help students review the chapter's most important concepts. **Hands On...Apply Your Knowledge** assignments direct students back to the beginning of the chapter to solve a practical marketing scenario. **Chapter Vignette... Activity** challenges students to answer questions that the companies in the vignette will face, which test their understanding of chapter topics and their ability to apply them. **Infographic... Data Analysis** features focus students on relevant metrics and asks them to complete an exercise such as updating the data and analyzing changes.

Award-Winning Technology

McGraw Hill Connect®

McGraw Hill Connect® is an award-winning digital teaching and learning solution that empowers students to achieve better outcomes and enables instructors to improve efficiency with course management. Within Connect, students have access to SmartBook®, McGraw Hill's adaptive learning and reading resource. SmartBook prompts students with questions based on the material they are studying. By assessing individual answers, SmartBook learns what each student knows and identifies which topics they need to practise, giving each student a personalized learning experience and path to success.

Connect's key features also include analytics and reporting, simple assignment management, smart grading, the opportunity to post your own resources, and the Connect Instructor Library, a repository for additional resources to improve student engagement in and out of the classroom.

Application-Based Activities

The Connect Application-Based Activities are highly interactive and automatically graded application- and analysis-based exercises wherein students immerse themselves in a marketing environment, analyze the situation, and apply their knowledge of marketing strategies. Students progress from understanding basic concepts to assessing and solving complex real-world scenarios.

¡SeeIt! Videos

These brief, contemporary videos offer dynamic student-centred introductions, illustrations, and animations to guide students through challenging concepts. Ideal for before class as an introduction, during class to launch or clarify a topic, or after class for formative assessment.

Writing Assignments

The Writing Assignment tool delivers a learning experience to help students improve their written communication skills and conceptual understanding. As an instructor you can assign, monitor, grade, and provide feedback on writing more efficiently and effectively.

Test Builder

Available within Connect, Test Builder is a cloud-based tool that enables instructors to format tests that can be printed or administered within a Learning Management System. Test Builder offers a modern, streamlined interface for easy content configuration that matches course needs, without requiring a download.

Test Builder allows you to:

- access all test bank content from a particular title
- easily pinpoint the most relevant content through robust filtering options
- manipulate the order of questions or scramble questions and/or answers
- pin questions to a specific location within a test
- choose the layout and spacing
- add instructions and configure default settings

Test Builder provides a secure interface for better protection of content and allows for just-in-time updates to flow directly into assessments.

McGraw Hill Connect® + proctorio

Remote Proctoring & Browser-Locking Capabilities

New remote proctoring and browser-locking capabilities, hosted by Proctorio within Connect, provide control of the assessment environment by enabling security options and verifying the identity of the student.

Seamlessly integrated within Connect, these services allow instructors to control students' assessment experience by restricting browser activity, recording students' activity, and verifying students are doing their own work.

Instant and detailed reporting gives instructors an at-a-glance view of potential academic integrity concerns, thereby avoiding personal bias and supporting evidence-based claims.

Instructor Resources

- The **Test Bank,** includes more than 1,400 multiple-choice, true/false, and short answer questions, each categorized according to learning objective, topic, level of difficulty, level of Bloom's taxonomy, and correct answer.
- The highly rated **Instructors' Manual** returns with lecture notes, video cases, supplementary in-class activities, worksheets, handouts, teaching suggestions, online assignments, metrics assignments, as well as answers to questions that are embedded within each chapter. Answers are provided for questions on opening vignettes, Marketing NewsFlash boxes, Focus on Ethics boxes, Ask Yourself checkpoints, and adAlyze and Infographic features.

- **Microsoft® PowerPoint® Slides** incorporate text and high-quality images, including figure slides, product shots, and advertisements. As an aid for instructors who wish to create their own presentations, an **Image Library** containing all visual elements from the text is also available.
- A unique series of 15 contemporary marketing **Video Cases** is available. Each video corresponds to chapter-specific topics that are highlighted within the text. Each video is closed-captioned and is accompanied by a written case, questions and answers, handouts, and teaching suggestions that are in the Instructors' Manual.
- **Alternate Cases, Marketing Advisor** cases, and **Marketing Metrics** cases provide even more opportunities to bring course content to life for students. Cases are accompanied by teaching notes, teaching suggestions, and answers.
- A frequently updated **Author Blog** helps provide instructors with innovative teaching resources to improve student learning, offer timely marketing examples, and help make class preparation time easier.

Effective. Efficient. Easy to Use.

McGraw Hill Connect is an award-winning digital teaching and learning solution that empowers students to achieve better outcomes and enables instructors to improve course-management efficiency.

Personalized & Adaptive Learning

Connect's integrated SmartBook helps students study more efficiently, highlighting where in the text to focus and asking review questions to give each student a personalized learning experience and path to success.

High-Quality Course Material

Our trusted solutions are designed to help students actively engage in course content and develop critical higher-level thinking skills, while offering you the flexibility to tailor your course to meet your needs.

Analytics & Reporting

Monitor progress and improve focus with Connect's visual and actionable dashboards. Reporting features empower instructors and students with real-time performance analytics.

Seamless Integration

Link your Learning Management System with Connect for single sign-on and gradebook synchronization, with all-in-one ease for you and your students.

Impact of Connect on Pass Rates

72.5%
Without Connect

85.2%
With Connect

SMARTBOOK

NEW SmartBook 2.0 builds on our market-leading adaptive technology with enhanced capabilities and a streamlined interface that deliver a more usable, accessible and mobile learning experience for both students and instructors.

Available on mobile smart devices – with both online and offline access – the ReadAnywhere app lets students study anywhere, anytime.

SUPPORT AT EVERY STEP

McGraw Hill ensures you are supported every step of the way. From course design and set up, to instructor training, LMS integration and ongoing support, your Digital Success Consultant is there to make your course as effective as possible.

Learn more about Connect at mheducation.ca

Acknowledgements

We appreciate the time, effort, and insight shared by marketing leaders who shared their expertise and knowledge. Their real-world examples make this book real, practical, and a true reflection of marketing in Canada today. This content is spread across chapter-opening vignettes, Marketing NewsFlash and Focus on Ethics boxes, and chapter content. It brings the content alive and makes a difference to marketing education in Canada. We specifically thank the following people for their contributions:

Richard Bartrem, *WestJet*
J.R. Brooks, *True Buch Kombucha*
Denis Cordick, *AMJ Campbell*
Ken Haqq, *New Era*
Dennis Kwasnicki, *The Paint Channel*
Rachel Mielke, *Hillberg & Berk*
Dion Red Gun, *River Ranche Lodge*
Andre Samuels, *SeeWhy Learning*
Nick Sano, *The Barber's Chair*
Paul Shumlich, *Deepwater Farms*
Cory Snyder, *SeeWhy Learning*
Chris Venter, *IFS*
Jim Wannemacher, *New Era*
Lisa Watts, *Hub Town Brewing Company*
Chris Wilson, *Fuzion Flooring*
Dustin Wright, *Arbor Memorial*

To all the companies who have provided us with images to include in the book, we thank you.

In addition, we extend our appreciation to the reviewers who helped steer the development of this new edition with their comments, feedback, and suggestions:

Raymond Bilodeau, *NAIT*
Michelle Guile, *Sheridan College*
Sheila Moore, *Humber College*
Carolyn Sterenberg, *Mount Royal University*
Erin Whittle, *BCIT*

A special thank you to Carolyn Sterenberg, Marketing Instructor at Mount Royal University, whose assistance in research was invaluable.

We are indebted to the following individuals who helped adapt, critique, and shape the ancillary package for the Canadian market: Ron Currie, *Conestoga College;* Malcolm Howe, *Niagara College;* Sheila Moore, *Humber College;* Maria Vincenten, *Red River College.*

We also extend our gratitude to the people at McGraw Hill for their professionalism, namely Jade Fair (Portfolio Managers), Amy Rydzanicz (Senior Content Developer), Janie Deneau (Supervising Editor), Monika Schurmann (Permissions Editor), and Mike Kelly (Copy Editor), who were invaluable in their attention to detail and moving the process forward.

Finally, we would like to thank our families for their enthusiasm and patient support.

Arsenio Bonifacio and Donna Dumont

Marketing Fundamentals

Marketing centres on understanding consumers—how they think, what drives purchases, how purchases are made, where purchases are made, and many other factors. Marketers need to be knowledgeable about the technological changes that impact the path-to-purchase, and understand what new communication options are surfacing. They also need to have insights into the new marketing trends and the ways consumers interact with brands and with companies.

LEARNING OBJECTIVES

LO 1 Explain the role of marketing in an organization and the importance of meeting customer needs

LO 2 Define and analyze elements of the marketing mix

LO 3 Outline the steps in the marketing process

LO 4 Differentiate between goods, services, and ideas

LO 5 Describe the evolution of different business philosophies

LO 6 Describe new and evolving marketing practices

LO 7 Summarize careers that exist in marketing

©Artur Widak/NurPhoto via Getty Images

CHAPTER OUTLINE

- WestJet
- The role of marketing
- The marketing process
- The marketing mix
- The evolution of business philosophies
- New and evolving marketing practices
- Marketing careers

This chapter begins with an introduction to the fundamentals of marketing and an explanation of the building blocks and concepts used by marketers to reach consumers. It also touches on evolving areas to ensure that new approaches are top of mind with readers. We examine WestJet, a Canadian company focused on meeting the needs of its customers.

In 1996, WestJet recognized the emerging market segment of low-cost travel that was successfully implemented by Southwest Airlines in the U.S. market and asked why that segment isn't in Canada. WestJet Airlines launched in the low-cost carrier (LCC) segment of the airline industry with three 737 airplanes, initially servicing five cities exclusively in the Western Canada market. Focusing on only one type of aircraft provided unit cost advantage in parts, rotables, and training of pilots, flight attendants, aircraft maintenance engineers, and other ground crew.

WestJet airlines started with three aircraft, 200 employees, and five cities in 1996. Today, after 23 successful years in the market, WestJet in 2019 has 180 aircraft, employs almost 14,000 persons, and services 108 destinations in 21 countries. WestJet contributed in growing the overall market, not just stealing share from its competitors. In 1996, 18 percent of the population travelled by air, the remainder would drive, travel by bus, or even stay home; by 2019, the market had expanded to 49 percent of adults who travel by air.

Today the market is even more segmented with the emergence of the ULCC segment—ultra low-cost carrier segment—successfully implemented by Ryan Air in Europe and Spirit Air in the United States. This model strips out everything other than basically the seat and seat belt with any additional products and services provided at an extra charge. These ancillary revenues make up a considerable percentage of overall revenue. A number of airlines have attempted to launch in this segment in Canada, including Canada Jetlines and EnerJet. Flare Airlines currently targets the ULCC segment. In response to the growing ULCC segment, WestJet launched Swoop in June 2018. It is currently a successful enterprise, providing a ULCC alternative with fares as much as 30 percent lower than WestJet.

Canada is the second-largest country by land mass and yet has a current population density of 3.4 people per square kilometre. The stage lengths required to traverse the country, combined with a low population density, means that WestJet's strategy of serving leisure travellers across Canada and to sun destinations needed to evolve with a focus on premium and business international travellers.

WestJet now has four Boeing 787 Dreamliner aircraft, the first of what will be ten confirmed aircraft with an option to purchase an additional ten. These aircraft are capable of reaching almost anywhere in the world from Canada, allow the airline to target international travellers, and, with its business class seating, can attract travellers looking for a more premium service.

CHAPTER FEATURES

WestJet!
WestJet sets the bar for airlines in Canada.

Marketing the "MO"
The Movember Foundation keeps its message current and relevant.

Canada—One of the World's Most Connected Nations
Canadians rank top in the world for website visits per month.

The Ethics of Greenwashing
New technology and service offerings disrupt the taxi industry.

Who Is HaloTop Targeting?
HaloTop uses a different approach to launch into the Canadian market.

Real-Time Marketing, Social Media Marketing, and Mobile Marketing Explained
Real-time marketers turn to Twitter, content marketing is on the rise, and Starbucks rules with an integrated campaign.

For Benevity, CSR Is the Brand
Benevity integrates CSR into its brand.

Before purchasing larger aircraft, WestJet launched WestJet Encore to serve smaller communities and to increase frequency in certain markets. WestJet has also entered into a capacity purchase agreement with Pacific Coastal Airlines to get into even smaller markets to feed the hubs.

Further, WestJet is poised to enter a joint venture arrangement with Delta Airlines and will seek out other, bespoke joint ventures to provide global interconnectivity to its guests.

Product: WestJet has evolved its positioning from its original LCC model. It began with the positioning of a fun, irreverent brand, "taking the job seriously, but not ourselves." WestJet is adding more product and services to better meet the needs of existing customers and has repositioned its brand up the "sophistication curve," providing the same caring experience but adding certain refinements to attract premium and business travellers who each have different wants in their air travel. West-Jet now has business class on some aircraft, is building exclusive lounges, and continues to refine its loyalty program.

Price: WestJet has moved from a low cost strategy to a unit cost strategy. Although it started with an aggressive low pricing strategy, WestJet has now moved to a segmented pricing strategy to better meet its customer needs. The airline utilizes basic pricing, bundle pricing, and premium pricing options for its customers.

Place: WestJet's head office is located in Calgary, Alberta. From 1996 to 1999, the company was privately held; since 1999, WestJet has been publicly traded. The airline was recently purchased by Onex, and it will continue to be headquartered in Calgary.

Promotion: WestJet Airlines uses innovative marketing by giving special gifts and surprises to its customers. Each December, it gives special surprises to its customers or persons in need, calling it the "Christmas Miracle" and uniting loved ones with free tickets offering premium seats. WestJet has earned a lot of goodwill by being constantly involved in corporate social responsibility (CSR) projects and activities, such as when it helped wildfire victims. It also regularly supports community nonprofit organizations by donating trips. West-Jet also uses extensive marketing with continuous campaigns on YouTube where it launches videos regularly to stay connected to its customers and reach a wider audience. WestJet has also added a customer relationship management (CRM) strategy that recognizes loyal users with special awards such as lounge access, free upgrades, and seat selection. It has different loyalty levels depending on flight spending, ranging from teal to silver to gold and to platinum. WestJet's marketing efforts have recognized with the 2019 Airline Strategy Awards marketing award.

In 2018 WestJet rebranded with a new brand positioning and national campaign reflecting its evolution from a point-to-point carrier to a global airline based out of Calgary. The brand-side changes included a refreshed logo, a new tagline (the "Love Where You're Going" slogan), and greater emphasis on the global marketplace. The rebranding video aired on TV during Hockey Night in Canada, as well as on social and digital. WestJet has a presence on Facebook, Twitter, Instagram, and YouTube, as well as a blog.[1]

---

reality **CHECK** ⊘

As you read Chapter I, refer back to the WestJet vignette to answer the following questions:

- Describe the target market for WestJet? How has this changed?
- How does WestJet differentiate itself from the competition?
- What marketing tools does WestJet use to create relationships with its customers?

What Is Marketing?

The good news is that you are already a marketing expert! You perform many marketing activities and make marketing-related decisions every day. For example, would you sell more LG Signature 77-inch 4K OLED TVs at $24,999 or $7,999? You answered $7,999, right? So your experience in shopping gives you some expertise in marketing. As a consumer, you've been involved in thousands of marketing decisions, mostly on the buying and not the selling side.

The bad news is that good marketing isn't always easy. That's why every year thousands of new products fail in the marketplace and then quietly slide into oblivion.

Marketing and Your Career

Marketing affects all individuals, all organizations, all industries, and all countries. This book seeks to teach you marketing concepts—often by having you actually "do marketing"—by putting you in the shoes of a

Are you a marketing expert? If so, what would you pay for this cutting-edge TV?

©Kobby Dagan/VWPics via AP Images

marketing manager facing actual marketing decisions. The book also shows marketing's many applications and how it affects our lives. This knowledge should make you a better consumer and enable you to be a more informed citizen, and it may even help you in your career planning.

Perhaps your future will involve doing sales and marketing for a large organization. Or working for a well-known company—Apple, Ford, Facebook, or General Mills— or a small business that you start. At a minimum, your newfound marketing skills will allow you to better sell your ideas to your employer in any career you choose.

Start-ups and small businesses also offer marketing careers. Small businesses are the source of the majority of new Canadian jobs. So you might become your own boss by being an entrepreneur and starting your own business.

Shortly after leaving Stanford, for example, Elon Musk started and sold a web software company called Zip2. With the proceeds from that business he started another business that merged with another and became PayPal. When PayPal was purchased by eBay, Musk founded another venture called SpaceX, which develops and manufactures space launch vehicles and currently launches satellites and delivers cargo to the International Space Station. Since those initial business start-ups, Musk has also started the electric car company Tesla and a solar power company called SolarCity. In addition, he has started a design competition for a high-speed transportation system called Hyperloop, a not-for-profit artificial intelligence company called OpenAI, and a neurotechnology company called Neuralink. Perhaps your interest in marketing will lead to new business successes like Musk's![2]

The Role of Marketing

> ## marketing TIP
>
> *"We take our job seriously, not ourselves. Our brand expression of personality has changed over the past 23 years to meet the changing needs of our customers."*
>
> – Richard Bartrem, Vice President, Marketing Communications, WestJet

LO 1 The WestJet case illustrates the link between business success and carefully designed product, pricing, distribution, and promotional strategies that meet consumer needs, trends, and expectations. Brands need to be differentiated and marketers are challenged to stay current to ensure that their strategies and messages resonate with customers.

Often students believe marketing only consists of television commercials and advertising. In fact, marketers' ultimate objectives are to drive profits for a company, or if working in the nonprofit sector, to generate revenue and support to fund programs and run operations. Only one aspect of marketing revolves around promotion, with all other elements—including product, price, and place—required to maximize profitability or generate revenue. Marketing is responsible for a large portion of organizational expenses and, conversely, its revenue. Because of this, marketers also need to be financially savvy, be able to create realistic forecasts, dissect a profit and loss statement, and discuss return on investment (ROI) strategies.

Marketing plays an integral function in any business. Figure 1–1 illustrates how a marketing department interacts with other departments in an organization and with society, as well as the impact that external environmental forces can have on marketing strategies. Marketing is intertwined with both internal and external stakeholders.

Within an organization, marketing needs to work cooperatively with other functional areas. Research and development is a main contributor to new product development. Manufacturing produces a company's products, ensuring quality and cost efficiency. Finance monitors sales and costs. Information systems coordinates e-commerce and digital marketing technologies. Human resources ensures that qualified and innovative people are filling roles within the organization. The success of an organization is dependent upon each of these functions cooperating and working collaboratively toward a common vision.

Figure 1–1 also shows the key people, groups, and forces outside the organization that influence its marketing activities. The marketing department is responsible for facilitating relationships, partnerships, and alliances with the organization's customers, its shareholders (or often representatives of nonprofit organizations), its suppliers, and other organizations. Environmental forces involving social, economic, technological, competitive, and regulatory considerations also shape an organization's marketing actions. Finally, an organization's marketing decisions are affected by and, in turn, often have an important impact on society as a whole.

The organization must strike a balance among the sometimes differing interests of these groups. For example, it is not possible to simultaneously provide the lowest-priced and highest-quality products to customers and pay the highest prices to suppliers,

Figure 1–1

A marketing department relates to many people, organizations, and forces. Note that the marketing department both *shapes* and *is shaped by* its relationship with these internal and external groups.

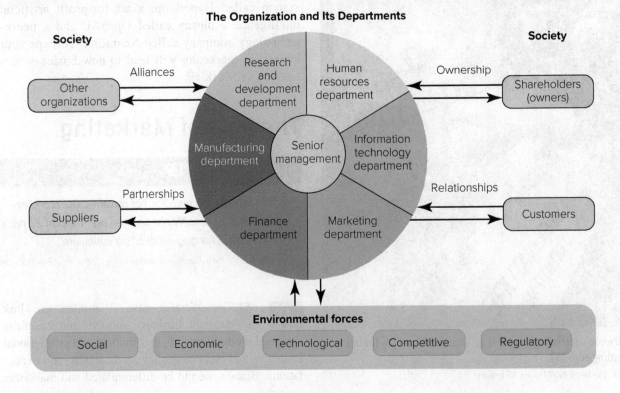

the highest wages to employees, and the maximum dividends to shareholders.

Marketing planning starts with a scan of the environment. External demographic, socio-cultural, economic, technological, competitive, and regulatory forces create opportunities that a company can maximize and threats that a company should minimize.

This chapter works to explain the fundamental principles that guide marketing, dispelling the myth that advertising and marketing are one and the same. In this introductory chapter, the basic marketing principles of meeting customer needs and providing customer value are emphasized; we also provide background on the evolution of business approaches. The marketing process and the concept of target markets are explained, as well as the importance of integrating each element of the marketing mix into programs that address consumer needs. Technological advances are resulting in new and evolving marketing approaches that impact current marketing practices in Canada. Time-tested offline marketing strategies are often supplemented by layers of online digital strategies to better reach consumers. Metrics, analytics, evolving marketing regulations, and ethical considerations are reviewed. Finally, there is a discussion on marketing careers.

Focusing on Customer Needs and Wants

Successful marketing is focused on customer needs and wants and on developing programs that engage consumers and inspire customer loyalty. A **need** occurs when a person feels deprived of basic necessities such as food, clothing, and shelter. A **want** is a need that is shaped by a person's knowledge, culture, and personality. So if you feel hungry, you have a basic need to eat something. Let's say you then want to eat an apple or a frozen pizza snack because, based on your past experience, you know these will satisfy your hunger need. Effective marketing, in the form of creating an awareness of good products at convenient locations, can clearly shape a person's wants. A principal activity of an organization's marketing department is to research its consumers to understand what they need and want, and the forces that shape those needs and wants.

However, consumers do not always know what they want and may not want (or be able) to describe what they need or want. In certain categories, such as fragrances or luxury cars, choices are not entirely rational, but partly based on self-image and emotional attachment to a brand, which can be difficult to articulate.

In situations where children or professionals are the consumers, a child may be unable to express ideas while professionals may not have the time to participate in research. Sometimes, marketers may not be asking the right questions.

The digital world adds another level of complexity to market research. On the one hand, it facilitates the online gathering of information; on the other hand, it introduces new communication platforms that challenge marketers to understand the biases that may exist in this new environment.

There are some general insights about how consumers navigate the online environment that marketers need to consider when developing marketing programs. First, the initial point of contact for consumers with a brand is often online—for example, a corporate website, a promotional microsite, a company blog, one of its social media sites, perhaps a third-party product review site, or even a friend's social media feed. Marketers must therefore understand the role of the online environment in the consumer path-to-purchase and the need to have a solid presence on all these online destinations with information that engages, informs, and motivates. Second, consumers have unlimited opportunities to become informed or distracted. According to Google, online consumers average 20+ touch points for products such as candy bars and 500+ touch points for flights in online consumer purchase paths. This is why effective digital marketing isn't solely about "being there." Everyone is competing for visibility, and as the competitive landscape gets more and more digitally sophisticated, being there becomes less of a competitive advantage. Instead, compelling and unique messaging and creative may be more effective in the long run.[3]

Consider customers who want to purchase a new tablet. Their first stop might be a product review site such as **PCMag.com**. Customers might check out the top ten tablets as rated by the magazine and then narrow down based upon their needs. Customers may want to check out manufacturers' websites (such as **Apple.ca, Samsung.ca,** or **Microsoft.ca**) for more detailed specifications on each tablet. Pricing is a big factor, so customers will often check out several websites (such as **Bestbuy. ca** or **Amazon.ca**) to determine the average prices and also the least expensive option. Customers may then decide to go to the bricks-and-mortar store location to talk to a salesperson and look at and try the tablets. In any case, the connected customer is a much more informed customer.

need
Occurs when a person feels deprived of basic necessities.

want
A need that is shaped by a person's knowledge, culture, and personality.

The Costco.ca site allows customers to easily compare products.
©2005-2020 Costco Wholesale Canada Ltd.

Costco understands this process and ensures that the customer's interaction with its site is seamless by providing reviews, price comparisons, and comprehensive product details.

> *Successful marketing is focused on customer needs and wants and on developing programs that engage consumers and inspire customer loyalty.*

Creating Customer Value

Providing customer value can ensure that customers remain loyal over time. Companies must first create products and services that not only meet customer needs but also provide added value versus the competition. Repeat purchases should be encouraged through marketing programs and incentives that focus on generating repeat purchases.

Marketers must be able to communicate a clear, **customer value proposition**, which conveys the unique combination of benefits received by targeted consumers that will satisfy their needs. These benefits could include quality, price, convenience, delivery, and both before-sale and after-sale service. Walmart's customer value proposition can be clearly described as "everyday low prices for a broad range

customer value proposition
The unique combination of benefits received by targeted buyers that will satisfy their needs; includes quality, price, convenience, delivery, and both before-sale and after-sale service.

of products that are always in stock in convenient locations." Marketers work diligently to deliver this value by carefully managing each element of the marketing mix (product, price, place, and promotion) so that this value is evident to consumers who in turn purchase or use the products.

Creating products with added value is often achieved through a combination of (1) product design, (2) pricing strategies, and (3) service elements. For example, Walmart focuses on the lowest price, Mountain Equipment Co-op focuses on providing the best products, PUR Gum highlights its natural ingredients and health benefits, and Pizza Pizza (with its award-winning app for mobile ordering) highlights its fast purchase and delivery service as added-value elements for its consumers. Let's examine Amazon to find out how it balances product design, pricing, and service levels to create meaningful products with added value.

Mountain Equipment Coop very simply highlights product quality in this ad.

Mountain Equipment Co-op/Wasserman + Partners

Amazon is an online brand that presents customers with outstanding value through a searchable database of well-priced products that are peer-rated and reviewed. It also recommends related products and tracks delivery dates through timely e-mails—design, price, and service all rolled into one. Customized e-mails are sent out to its database of customers to encourage loyalty through special offers, featured products, and the announcement of new releases. Amazon's consistent value proposition continues to result in strong business metrics. It dominates online retailing, evidenced by its ranking as #3 on the National Retail Federation's top 100 list.[4] In 2017, Amazon Prime shipped more than 5 billion items worldwide, with over 100 million items available for free two-day shipping.[5] Amazon added further value to its brand in Canada with Amazon Prime membership, which, for an annual $79 fee or monthly $7.99 fee, provides members with free shipping on millions of items, unlimited photo storage, award-winning movies and TV shows through Prime Video, and access to exclusive deals.[6]

Appealing to Target Markets

In a competitive marketplace, companies cannot satisfy everyone's needs with a single product, and so products are designed to appeal to specific groups of consumers. Marketing follows the principle that with limited funds, it is better to channel resources toward consumers who are most interested in purchasing a product, rather than target everyone and squander funds on those who have may have little interest. A **target market** can be formally defined as the specific group (or segment) of existing and potential consumers to which marketers direct their marketing efforts. Marketers ensure that each element of the marketing mix appeals to the characteristics of the target market.

Coordinating the Marketing Mix

LO 2 The elements of the **marketing mix**—known as the 4 Ps: product, price, place, and promotion—are all controllable factors that need to be carefully managed by marketers to ensure that they are well-coordinated and that each appeals to the distinct characteristics of the target market. There is no point in having an amazing product if consumers cannot find it at the retail stores they frequent or online through a search. If the product is priced too high for the target market, it will be unaffordable; if it's priced too low, it will simply portray the wrong image. If marketers promote a product on TV, but the target market rarely watches TV, instead spending time online, then the message will not be received. In all instances, marketers need to understand what makes their consumers tick, what they desire, and how best to communicate with them. This information is often clarified by market research on consumer behaviour to help determine how marketing efforts can be designed or modified to meet the needs of the target market. Marketers use this information to improve marketing programs and coordinate each element of the marketing mix. These elements are all included in a brand's annual marketing plan where details for each element of the marketing mix are outlined, together with the required budgets and profit and loss statements for the brand. Chapter 15 provides more details on this area.

The elements of the marketing mix can be simply described as follows:

1. **Product**: All the attributes that make up a good, a service, or an idea to satisfy the customer need, including product design, features, colour, packaging, warranty, and service levels.

2. **Price**: What is exchanged for a product, including the expected regular retail or sale price.

3. **Place**: The way in which your product gets to the consumer, including the distribution channels, retail formats, and merchandising used to sell a product.

4. **Promotion**: The tools needed to communicate with consumers about a product, including advertising, public relations, sales promotion, direct response, event marketing, sponsorship, online approaches, and personal selling.

> *Marketers need to understand what makes their consumers tick.*

We now look at how Halo Top ice cream, the cult brand and Instagram sensation, hit the Canadian market in 2018 with promises of less sugar, fewer calories, *and* more protein than your usual pint while delivering the satisfaction of eating real ice cream.

target market
The specific group or segment(s) of existing and potential consumers to which marketers direct their marketing efforts.

marketing mix
The 4 Ps—product, price, place, and promotion.

product
Attributes that make up a good, a service, or an idea, including product design, features, colour, packaging, warranty, and service levels.

price
What is exchanged for a product, including the expected regular retail or sale price.

place
Distribution channels, retail formats, and merchandising used to sell a product.

promotion
Communication tools needed to inform consumers about a product, including advertising, public relations, sales promotion, direct response, event marketing, sponsorship, online approaches, and personal selling.

Halo Top's target market was male and female adults willing to pay a premium to indulge in ice cream with less guilt while meeting their goal to eat healthier. The company was able to successfully break into the Canadian dairy market by partnering with a co-packer to produce and distribute its products in the Canadian market.

The packaging is smart. Each tub comes with a gold-rimmed lip and cleverly designed message underneath, telling you to "Stop When You Hit The Bottom" or declaring "I'm Cold, Let's Spoon." The real draw, however, is that each pint has just 80 to 100 calories per 125ml serving, far fewer than regular ice cream. With more air whipped into the product, the texture is decidedly lighter, but the flavour variety offers something a lot of brands don't. Halo Top cuts back on the sugar by using three different sweeteners: Stevia (a low-calorie natural sweetener), erythritol (natural sugar alcohol), and cane sugar. In a comparison of Halo Top Vanilla Bean and Häagen-Dazs Vanilla, Halo Top has just 80 calories, 2.5g fat, 5g protein, and 15g carbs, while Häagen-Dazs has 290cal, 18g fat, 5g protein, and 26g carbs.[7]

Halo Top tapped into the science of flavour, starting with how our taste buds work. A study published in the *Journal of Dairy Science* proved we're actually pretty terrible at detecting the difference in fat levels in things like ice cream. Fat content could vary as much as 4 percent, and participants were none the wiser, and while that doesn't sound like a lot, it helps save around 154 calories per pint. So, Halo Top uses only the lower-fat parts of the ingredients that add a rich texture, like milk and eggs. And one more thing: Halo Top is obviously cold, which works in its favour. Cold has a numbing effect on your taste buds, so not as much sweet is actually needed.[8]

At first, Halo Top avoided a traditional media approach, relying on word-of-mouth and social media to spread the word about its lower-calorie ice cream, which tops out at 360 calories per pint. Then it began facing increased competition and stepped up its marketing.

Halo Top's success has been due, in large part, to social media. Justin Woolverton founded the company in 2011, but *AdAge* says it wasn't until 2016 that sales jumped a shocking 2,500 percent.[9] That was, in part, thanks to a rave review in *GQ* written by a journalist who embarked on a mission to eat nothing but Halo Top for ten days. Not only did he survive to tell the tale, but he lost weight...and bought a couple more pints of chocolate after finishing off 50 pints.

His story went viral on social media, and that kicked off Halo Top's popularity. Since then, Halo Top has stayed true to the idea behind the company. You'll see some television ads, sure, but Woolverton says all marketing is done in-house. Ads are spread out among Facebook, Twitter, and Instagram, and success came just in time, too. The boom happened when the company was running out of cash. After spending hundreds of thousands in design and development, resorting to high-interest loans and maxing out credit cards, the company almost folded instead of taking off.

In August 2017, the gay dating app Grindr took another step into broadening Halo Top's online presence. Grindr launched a companion lifestyle site, Into, with the hopes of attracting companies that wanted to put their advertising dollars into a site that would help them reach the LGBTQ community. Two organizations jumped on board immediately: FX's show *American Horror Story: Cult* and Halo Top. *AdWeek* says scrolling ads for the two brands featured heavily in the site's launch, with Into showrunners hoping they were going to lead the way for other advertisers who wanted to reach a new market that might not be as heavily catered to by other sites and publications.[10]

Since then, competition has heated up a bit, with mainstream brands and grocers bringing out somewhat similar products. Halo Top has responded with new products, including non-dairy varieties and low-calorie ice cream pops. It also opened its own scoop shops in California.

It is important to note that, over time, marketers gather extensive information on their target markets, being able to identify purchase motivation that goes beyond age and gender into behavioural and psychological motivation, which are important determinants in many purchases. In this way, marketers define their target markets in more complex terms, including elements such as likes, dislikes, motivation, interests, and concerns.

Halo Top ice cream in the Canadian market.
©Kirk McKoy/Los Angeles Times via Getty Images

The digital reality has made the marketing mix more complex. Marketers realize that each element now has many layers that need to be managed, no easy task in the online environment. A product, for example, now has many faces: offline in stores and online on corporate websites, on blogs, on promotional microsites, on apps, and on social media sites where marketers carefully monitor and join conversations to engage consumers. This is made even more complex by the different technical requirements needed for websites to render appropriately on different mobile devices.

The Marketing Process

LO 3 The **marketing process** involves (1) identifying consumer needs, (2) managing the marketing mix to meet these needs, and (3) reaching potential consumers or the market (see Figure 1–2). The marketing process requires that marketers understand their customers and apply strategic, analytical, and creative-thinking skills. Throughout the cycle, marketers constantly evaluate program success, recommending and implementing changes to strengthen efforts. Let's consider Amazon Prime and how this process works.

Amazon Prime was created to offer regular Amazon customers the ability to have free two-day delivery on an unlimited number of products, with no minimum order size. Shoppers prefer to have free shipping when purchasing online, but many sites have minimum order sizes or longer shipping times. Amazon provides additional value to the membership by also including access to streaming movies and television shows through Prime Video, unlimited music streaming, unlimited reading on any device, and unlimited photo storage, all for one membership fee. The price is for Amazon Prime is $79 CDN per year or $7.99 per month to provide value to the customer.[11] The average Canadian online shopper spends $2,000 annually, resulting in potentially high shipping charges.[12] Amazon offers a 30-day free trial, after which time the customer is charged the annual fee. The free trial eliminates barriers to trial and allows customers to see the value prior to spending any money. Shipping has consistently been a key differentiator within the customer decision-making process online. A survey from Morgan Stanley shows that nearly 80 percent of consumers would buy more online if e-commerce firms offered free shipping. It also stated that consumers value free shipping and delivery above all other e-commerce service offerings.[13] Amazon Prime is available online, on the **Amazon.ca** site, where the customer is already shopping. Customers also receive an offer to purchase Amazon Prime at checkout, once they have seen their shipping charges for the order in their shopping cart.[14]

marketing process
The process of (1) identifying consumer needs, (2) managing the marketing mix to meet these needs, and (3) realizing profits.

Figure 1–2
The Marketing Process

Organization's marketing department

Discover consumer needs by researching what consumers' needs are

Concepts for products

Satisfy consumer needs by designing a marketing program having the right combination of:
- Product
- Price
- Promotion
- Place

Information about needs

Products, services, ideas

Potential consumers: The market

Amazon Prime has been communicated using simple and clear messaging, through e-mail promotion (to existing Amazon customers), through online promotion (on its site), and through social media. Globally, there are 100 million paid Prime members.[15]

Marketers are ultimately responsible for generating company profits (or revenues and support for nonprofit organizations), and marketing programs are designed with this end in mind. Formally, **marketing** is described as the process through which goods and services move from concept to the customer. It includes the coordination of four elements called the 4 Ps of marketing, to identify, select, and develop a product; determine its price; select a distribution channel to reach a customer's place; and develop and implement a promotional strategy.[16]

Exchange is the trade of things of value between buyers and sellers so that each benefits. In simple terms, the trade is money for a product or service. However, there is more to exchange than just money—customers may provide referrals to a tutoring service or to a fitness club in return for discounts or additional services. A consumer may volunteer time with a nonprofit organization such as the Heart and Stroke Foundation, which in return may satisfy the consumer's need to support the cause. In the online environment, exchange is often more complex. In many instances, websites may not be selling a product at all but instead providing free information or a service that drives traffic to their website, where advertising is used to help pay for the service. The numbers of page views to the website and data on its demographics are used to sell this advertising space and generate revenue for the website. Many news websites, such as **Macleans.ca**, and web portals, such as **Google.ca** and **Canada.com**, fall into this category.

> *The marketing process requires that marketers understand their customers and apply strategic, analytical, and creative-thinking skills.*

What Can Be Marketed?

LO 4 In marketing, the term *product* encompasses goods, services, and ideas. These products can all be marketed to encourage people to buy something or, as in the case of ideas, to encourage support.

A **good** is a product that is tangible—you can touch it and own it. Examples are a can of Red Bull or a pair of Adidas running shoes. Adidas running shoes are tangible products that are marketed in different styles and colours, sold at a premium price, merchandised in sporting goods and shoe stores, and promoted with ads and social media with a focus on performance and style. Adidas achieves publicity through the sponsorship of athletes and sporting events. Adidas repeats its message across all forms of social media and demonstrates the value of its shoes on its YouTube channel.

A **service** is an intangible product you cannot touch. It does not result in something you can own. A physiotherapy session, a vacation, or going to a movie are examples of services. When you watch a movie at Cineplex Entertainment, marketers have worked to ensure the experience encourages you to return. Movie selection, theatre layout, seating, loyalty programs, and concession items have all been carefully selected and designed with the comfort and needs of the target market in mind. The Cineplex-Scotiabank SCENE loyalty rewards program has been created with rewards that encourage customers to return to Cineplex Entertainment theatres time after time to collect points and receive benefits such as discounted concession items, free movies, or discounted dining.[17]

Ideas can also be marketed. An **idea** is a concept that typically looks for support. An example is Mothers Against Drunk Driving (MADD) Canada. MADD Canada's mission is "to stop impaired driving and to support victims of this violent crime." Statistics show that on average, up to four Canadians are killed every day by impaired drivers. MADD increases the awareness of the impact of impaired driving through campaigns such as Project Red Ribbon, when millions of red ribbons are sold each year. It has been estimated that almost 43,000 lives have been saved through the efforts of MADD and its awareness campaigns.[18] Another example is the Movember Foundation campaign that asks men to grow moustaches in November to support men's health initiatives. For about this campaign, see the Marketing NewsFlash box, "Marketing the 'Mo.'"[19]

> *Ideas can also be marketed.*

Marketing the "Mo"

As the seasons change to winter, it is inevitable that we see our male colleagues, friends, and family growing facial hair that lasts for a full month's time.

The Movember Foundation was started in Australia in 2004 by two friends. What started as an idea to bring the moustache back in fashion has dovetailed into a fundraising campaign for men's health. Those two friends were able to entice 30 of their friends to grow moustaches in 2003 for no money. They then thought about the potential power of this platform and subsequently formalized Movember. The Movember Foundation focuses on four specific issues: prostate cancer, inactivity, testicular cancer, and mental health.

It is a fairly simple idea: Men grow moustaches during the month of November and have friends and family sponsor their endeavour. What evolved from this simple idea has been historic!

In 2007, Movember was launched in Canada. Since its inception, the Movember campaign in Canada has raised approximately $700 million, with the peak in 2012 with over $40 million in donations that year. In fact, the Movember Foundation is one of the largest investors in men's health in the world. Movember has created its own language and culture. "Mo," "Mo Bro," "Mo Sista," and "Mo Mentor" are just a few of the terms

that supporters are quite familiar with. Advice about how to grow a "Mo" and how to eat with a "Mo" is shared on the foundation's website. The 2019 campaign slogan was "Whatever you grow will save a bro."

As Movember celebrated its tenth anniversary in Canada in 2019, donations were down. Movember Canada is trying to move beyond the moustache. The moustache is still a major part of the brand, but it has expanded into men's mental health and suicide prevention. There is less focus on the moustache logo and more focus on stopping men from dying too young.

To further the cause, Movember has partnered with corporations including Visa, the NHL, Harley-Davidson, and GoodLife Fitness to introduce MOVE. MOVE encourages donations for individuals who commit to MOVE-ing every day during the month of November. This expands participation beyond growing a moustache.

Part of the reason that the moustache is no longer at the forefront of the campaign is the popularity of the campaign itself. Moustaches have become more popular over the last decade, particularly among younger men. Movember is credited for having driven that trend. Men grew the moustache, tried it, and kept it.

Wanting to extend its message beyond the month of November,

Movember Canada has recognized April as Testicular Cancer Awareness Month, with a #knowthynuts campaign. This campaign is meant to encourage men to complete their own self-exams to ensure early detection of testicular cancer, a type of cancer most common in younger men.

The campaign has also expanded into September, focusing on men's mental health for World Suicide Prevention Day on September 15, 2019. The campaign of "Be a man of more words" is meant to shed light on the stigma of men's mental health.

Movember is a month-long opportunity for participants to outwardly show their support for men's health, generating conversation, exchange of knowledge, and ultimately donations to the Movember Foundation. ●

Questions

1. How do not-for-profits stay relevant?

2. How do partnerships help spread a nonprofit organization's message?

Many successful marketers today launch products with layers of goods, services, and ideas to connect with consumers. For example, you may decide to purchase a new smartphone. You select an iPhone from Apple. This smartphone comes with 32 GB of storage, weighing 130g, and is 7 mm thick and 4.7 inches long (*product*). Once you begin to use your phone, you download songs using iTunes. You also like to shop, so you sign up for Apple Pay so that you can use your iPhone to pay for purchases (*services*).

What Is a Market?

The term **market** is used in marketing to describe potential consumers who have both the willingness and the ability to buy a product. Importantly, just being willing to buy a product does not constitute a market. For example, the Nintendo Wii is a gaming console that has been targeted to families. The Wii has a multitude of action games, such as those in its Super Mario/Luigi franchise, as well as interactive games that simulate bowling, golf, baseball, and boxing. Although the Wii is used by kids, kids are not considered to be the product's market because they do not have the money or the physical means to buy the product. The market would consist of parents with children up to their teenage years.[20]

The Wii touches on an interesting marketing issue: Sometimes the market, target market, and consumers are different groups of people, and marketers need to decide on a balance of whom should be targeted with their programs. While the market for the Nintendo Wii is parents with children, the marketing also needs to focus on the children, who may exert some influence over their parents. Therefore, we see that the target market for the product includes both children and parents. Finally, the consumers of the product, in this case the users, are mainly the children, not the parents, and marketers need to ensure that the product is designed with their abilities and interests in mind, without overlooking the parents, who are the main decision-makers in the purchase process.

market
Potential consumers with both the willingness and the ability to buy.

production orientation
Focusing organizational efforts on the manufacture of goods.

sales orientation
Focusing organizational efforts on selling as many products as possible.

marketing orientation
Focusing organizational efforts to collect and use information about customers' needs to create customer value.

relationship marketing
When organizations create long-term links with customers, employees, suppliers, and other partners to increase loyalty and customer retention.

The Evolution of Business Philosophies

LO 5 Marketing was not always the driving force in business philosophy. Until the 1930s, businesses were in the **production orientation** stage. This stage focused on manufacturing, which until the Industrial Revolution, was not a widespread phenomenon. Manufactured goods tended to sell, regardless of their quality, because they were in short supply. Consumer needs were not a priority. It was during this era that the Ford Motor Company introduced the assembly line, manufacturing cars in a fast and efficient way. The second stage, from the 1930s to the 1960s, was the **sales orientation** stage. This stage focused on selling as many products as possible. The market had become more competitive, production had become more efficient, and products were in abundance. Companies started to hard-sell to make a profit, and consumer needs were still not a major consideration. As the marketplace became more competitive, businesses developed more-sophisticated approaches. In the 1960s, consumer needs became more important, and the marketing concept became the focus of businesses. The **marketing orientation** stage focuses on the idea that an organization should strive to satisfy the needs of consumers while also trying to achieve an organization's goals. An organization that has a marketing orientation focuses its efforts on continuously collecting information about customers' needs, sharing this information across departments, and using it to create customer value.

Marketing has evolved from a discipline with a short-term focus on transactions to one that now also focuses on building long-term customer relationships. This **relationship marketing** stage sees organizations considering the lifetime value of their customers and striving to offer better services, along with higher-quality products to encourage long-term relationships with customers. Over the last few years, relationship marketing has included a greater use of social media, and an increased focus on customer relationship management and corporate social responsibility to create meaningful relationships. These approaches emphasize customer retention and ongoing customer satisfaction rather than short-term transactions. Organizations carefully collect and use information on customer interests to develop relationships with customers and retain their loyalty. Businesses recognize that improved customer relationships can result in increased customer loyalty, improved customer

Figure 1–3
The evolution of business philosophies

retention levels, and greater profits for an organization. (Figure 1–3 summarizes this evolution of business philosophies.)

Database technology has surfaced as a tool that facilitates relationship marketing by putting a focus on **customer relationship management (CRM)** for the marketing industry. This approach is rooted in the knowledge that it is less expensive to service and maintain current customers than to constantly acquire new ones. CRM identifies a firm's most-valued customers and builds programs to appeal to their needs. It systematically identifies what will lead to customer satisfaction and profitable brand loyalty. It is often facilitated by CRM software and databases. Formally, CRM is defined as the process of building and developing long-term customer relationships by delivering customer value and satisfaction.[21]

We can look to the Canadian retail industry to better understand CRM and to find out how it is applied. In its simplest form, CRM involves the occasional customer e-mail about upcoming sales or advanced notice of new product launches. In a more advanced state, it includes sophisticated customer loyalty programs that reward continued purchases and usage. Air Miles is an example of a widely recognized and sophisticated CRM program that partners with brands to provide members with rewards.

Retailers use CRM loyalty programs to help secure a greater **share of wallet** from their customers. Share of wallet refers to the percentage of a customer's purchases that a company has in a specific product category. They use loyalty cards to track individual purchases and then correlate the data with offers and incentives to determine what works best. Offers are then customized to meet their purchase habits. Pioneers of CRM in Canada include Hudson's Bay with its HBC Rewards card and President's Choice/Shoppers Drug Mart with its PC Optimum card.

Advanced CRM considers **customer lifetime value** and what offers will keep customers loyal over their lifetime. Customer lifetime value refers to the potential sales that will be generated by a customer if that customer remains loyal to that company for a lifetime. Let's look at a simple example. If a pregnant woman buys prenatal vitamins at a store that uses CRM tracking software, such as through its loyalty cards, in time she may start receiving coupons for diapers, baby food, and tips on infant nutrition; her prenatal purchase has triggered sophisticated computer programs to recognize her eventual need for baby products. As this woman's needs evolve, and as the children get older, the offers may change to include over-the-counter medications for toddlers or school supplies for youths. This is one of the ways that companies can use CRM to encourage customer loyalty. CRM is covered in more detail in Chapter 14.

Finally, **corporate social responsibility (CSR)** has become an important part of the relationship marketing stage, with companies realizing that consumers want to be associated with companies that share their values and interests. CSR is a concept where organizations voluntarily consider the well-being of society and the environment by taking responsibility for how their businesses impact consumers, customers, suppliers, employees, shareholders, communities, the environment, and society in general. In this manner, CSR programs become part of a brand's fabric and help to build long-term relationships and solidify brand connections with consumers. The apparel company Benevity provides an excellent example of CSR being integrated into the brand itself (see the Marketing NewsFlash box, "Benevity— Making CSR the Brand!").[22]

CSR initiatives can range from the simple to the complex and typically include one of three approaches. In its simplest forms, CSR can involve (1) the sponsorship and/or spearheading of community programs and (2) the sponsorship and/or involvement in fundraising initiatives for charitable organizations. In its most advanced form, CSR is used (3) as a business

---

customer relationship management (CRM)
The overall process of building and maintaining profitable customer relationships by delivering superior customer value and satisfaction.

share of wallet
The percentage of a customer's purchases that a company has in a specific product category.

customer lifetime value
The potential sales that will be generated by a customer if that customer remains loyal to that company for a lifetime.

corporate social responsibility (CSR)
When organizations voluntarily consider the well-being of society by taking responsibility for how their businesses impact consumers, customers, suppliers, employees, shareholders, communities, the environment, and society in general.

Benevity—Making CSR the Brand!

We are, a *mighty force* for collective impact.

We Are We | &benevity

Benevity, Inc.

Corporate social responsibility (CSR) initiatives can often seem as though they were an afterthought or an add-on to corporate strategy. For Benevity, CSR is its brand!

Certified B Corporations are businesses that meet the highest standards of verified social and environmental performance, public transparency, and legal accountability to balance profit and purpose. Benevity Inc., a certified B Corporation, was co-founded in 2008 by CEO Bryan de Lottinville and a group of tech innovators as a platform that enables companies to engage their employees and customers around social responsibility and community investment. Benevity's ultimate goal and vision is for there to be no need for a separate category of B Corporations, "because every company will pursue hybrid goals of profit and purpose."

Benevity is the global leader in corporate social responsibility and employee engagement software, including online giving, matching, volunteering, community investment, and purpose-driven actions. Many of the world's most iconic brands rely on

Benevity's award-winning cloud solutions to power corporate "Goodness" programs that attract, retain, and engage today's diverse workforce by connecting people to the causes that matter to them. With software that is available in 17 languages to an employee base of 12 million users around the world, Benevity has processed $4 billion in donations and 23 million hours of volunteering time to over 230,000 charities worldwide. Benevity currently sits at around 600 employees, with a customer base of more than 600 clients spanning large, global enterprises like Microsoft, Coca-Cola, Google, and Honda.

"By engaging more people, more often in Goodness—no matter where they are located—companies can make their CSR programs and purpose-driven initiatives more experiential and inclusive for everyone, strengthening employee engagement and retention," says de Lottinville.

"With the addition of mobile, our clients now have another way to empower their people to support causes they care about, which in turn helps to create a workplace

culture distinguished by meaning, engagement, and a passion to make the world better," he adds. "It's an essential and logical next step in the evolution of our platform."

The socially concerned consumer is alive and well across the globe. A recent Nielsen study showed that 55 percent of global online consumers were willing to pay more for products from companies that were socially responsible. The likelihood of embracing social responsibility is even greater in Asia Pacific, Latin America, and the Middle East/Africa. Canada is only the launching pad for Benevity's impactful strategy. ●

Questions

1. What strategies do you believe that Benevity should focus on to remain relevant?

2. Do you believe that Benevity is a fad, or is it here to stay?

philosophy of an organization that implements socially responsible business practices to positively impact the community at large (for one example, see the Infographic about UPS in Canada).

Loblaw Companies Limited is another excellent example of a company that has demonstrated a commitment to give back to the community and operate in a responsible manner. Loblaw's CSR strategy has three pillars: sourcing, environment, and community. Responsible sourcing targets many components of the supply chain for Loblaw, from the working conditions of suppliers' employees, to the elimination of concerning ingredients from products, to a priority

focus on informative labelling. The environmental pillar targets waste reduction by decreasing the use of plastic shopping bags (12 billion to date) and donating perishable food. With a focus on energy efficiency, Loblaw was able to reduce its carbon footprint by 26.1 percent since 2011. Community giving at Loblaw includes the donation of $77 million to local charities and not-for-profits through the President's Choice Children's Charity and the Shoppers LOVE. YOU initiatives. Loblaw donated $5 million to the Canadian Red Cross to support residents affected by the Fort McMurray, Alberta, wildfires. The addition of Shoppers Drug Mart to the Loblaw portfolio

Infographic

Canada 2019 by the numbers

619 young adults graduated from UPS driver safety training through the UPS Road Code Program.

$398,083 in The UPS Foundation grants.

1,200+
UPS Access Point® locations
are increasing customer convenience and reducing unnecessary trips by providing centralized locations for customers to pick up packages across Canada.

113,703 Volunteer hours
from UPS employees, families and friends in Canada. Global Goal: 20 Million volunteer hours by the end of 2020.

278 Drivers
UPS Circle of Honour drivers with 25 years or more of accident-free driving.

1,277 vehicles
in our alternative fuel and advanced technology fleet in 2019.

1,000 Trees
were planted across Canada through 2019 to help offset emissions and improve lives as part of the UPS Global Forestry Initiative.

$1.1+ Million
in total charitable contributions to the United Way in Canada.

$100,000
In community grants to over 140 different charitable organizations.

Responsible sourcing is a key pillar of Loblaw's CSR strategy.
©Valentino Visentini/Alamy Stock Photo

expanded its definition of community to include accessible health care. To this end, Loblaw has implemented in-store wellness programs and has supported the expansion of the role of pharmacists in disease screening and awareness.[23]

Many organizations now include CSR components in their business plans, issuing annual CSR reports and CSR plans to ensure they live up to their directives. Loblaw has published an annual corporate social responsibility report every year since 2007. *Maclean's* magazine has partnered with Sustainalytics, a leading organization in sustainability analytics, to determine Canada's top 50 socially responsible companies by reviewing their environmental, social, and governance approaches to business. Its latest report points out that best-in-class organizations perceive CSR as fundamental to the fabric of their organizations. Among the organizations that rank highly on the *Maclean's* Top 50 Social Responsible Companies 2015 are Telus and Pepsico. Recognized in the telecom/electronics category, Telus's data centres consume 80 percent less power than a typical data centre. Telus is also a major sponsor of We Day, and through its employee volunteer program called "Telus Days of Giving," over 337,000 volunteer hours have been invested in communities across Canada.[24] Pepsico was recognized in the food and beverage category for reducing water usage by 40 percent at its manufacturing plants and being the first in Canada to adopt all-electric, green-powered delivery trucks.[25]

greenwashing
The deceptive use of marketing practices to give the impression that a good, service, or organization is environmentally friendly.

Loblaw Community Giving in 2018

Charitable donations	$77 million
President's Choice Children's Charity	granted $54 million to feed and educate kids about nutrition
Food drives	8.5 million pounds of food
Pharmicists administered vaccines and injections	1.6 million

Procter & Gamble provides another great example of CSR. Pampers has partnered with UNICEF since 2006 to battle maternal and neonatal tetanus (MNT) in underprivileged areas. This partnership has funded 300 million vaccines, protecting 100 million mothers and babies around the world.[26]

Unfortunately, a few companies have taken advantage of the environmental movement by deceptively positioning products as being green, when in fact they do little to help the environment. This has given rise to the term **greenwashing**, which refers to the deceptive use of marketing practices to imply that a good, service, or organization is environmentally friendly. Dawn dish soap has come under fire in the past due to its claims that "Dawn helps save wildlife." All the while, triclosan, an antibacterial agent declared toxic to aquatic life, is an ingredient in the dish soap. Procter & Gamble

Procter & Gamble partners with UNICEF to support tetanus vaccinations in underprivileged areas.

©Newscast Online Limited/Alamy Stock Photo

New and Evolving Marketing Practices

societal marketing concept

Marketing programs that focus on the consumer *and* the well-being of society.

LO 6 Marketing today focuses on meeting short-term consumer needs and generating immediate company profits, as well as the long-term viability and sustainability of a business through the transparent connections it makes with its business partners and by creating meaningful customer relationships and community initiatives. Many new tools are now available for marketers to communicate organizational approaches and product benefits. In this section, we review some of the latest new and evolving marketing practices.

Some of the recent marketing approaches include customer relationship management programs and corporate social responsibility (as already discussed), with evolving areas including (1) digital marketing, including content marketing, mobile marketing, and social media marketing; (2) augmented reality; (3) experiential marketing; (4) influencer marketing; (5) partnership marketing; (6) metrics and analytics; and (7) new marketing regulations and ethical considerations.

Digital Marketing

The backdrop to new and evolving marketing approaches is the rapid adoption of Internet technology by our society, with consumers and businesses having access to lower-priced computers, multiple mobile devices, high-speed Internet connections, and cloud computing. In addition, many free online services are available, such as e-mail, online search, cloud file storage, and social media platforms.

Digital technology has changed consumer behaviour, with many people using smartphones and tablets to stay connected with friends, family, and work throughout the day and to get media updates on their areas of interest. In 2019 there were over 33 million subscribers to mobile devices in Canada.[29] Wireless services have become an integral part of Canadians' lives. Whether to stay in touch with family and friends, consume content, or work while on the move, wireless services have become indispensable for most Canadians. More Canadians have mobile phones (90 percent) than

maintains that it is complying with current regulatory requirements in Canada.[27] The Canadian Marketing Association provides a number of resources on how to market environmentally friendly products to help reduce unethical business practices. Its website at **www.the-cma.org** includes green tips and information on best practices.

The marketing community is also putting an increased focus on the well-being of society and the environment in its marketing programs. It is commonplace to now see marketing initiatives that focus on the consumer and the well-being of society, an approach described as the **societal marketing concept**. One of the pioneers of societal marketing is The Body Shop. The Body Shop was started on the belief that only natural ingredients should be used in products and that those products should not be tested on animals. Back in 1976, this was a very original business strategy. Since that time, The Body Shop has supported a range of causes including human rights, environmental protection, and fair and ethical trade. In 2016, The Body Shop launched the Limited Edition "Change" Hemp Hand Protector. The packaging was developed by a world-renowned street artist named Eine, and the product sports a strong message of CHANGE on the label. A portion of the revenue from each unit sold is donated to The Body Shop Foundation to support a range of projects dedicated to improving the planet, oceans, people, and animals.[28]

Digital marketing provides many online communication tools.

©3dm1983/Dreamstime.com/GetStock.com

landlines (41 percent), while approximately one-third of Canadian households rely exclusively on wireless services. People in Canada are among the most connected in the world, spending over 157 minutes per day online. Online video viewing is particularly high, with Canadians logging an average of 25 hours per month watching online videos. Social networking is also very popular, with people increasingly accessing social networks on mobile devices.[30]

Device Reach in Canada, U.S., and U.K.

	Population	Desktop	Mobile (Smartphone & Tablet)
Canada	27.6 MM	87%	82%
U.S.	217.6 MM	83%	91%
U.K.	42.0 MM	75%	89%

The widespread use of digital technology in Canada is the most important trend impacting how marketers do business. Digital technology has changed the path-to-purchase and drives how consumers gather information, connect with each other and businesses, and purchase products. The amount of time consumers spend on the Internet has changed significantly over the last few years, prompting marketers to increasingly use digital marketing approaches to reach consumers. **Digital marketing** is an approach that uses electronic means to reach consumers, whether this be through computers, gaming devices, out-of-home electronic screens, or mobile devices such as smartphones and tablets.

Digital marketing includes many stellar online tools, such as display advertising, affiliate marketing, search engine marketing, search engine optimization, pay-per-click advertising, mobile marketing, e-mail marketing, and social media marketing. An example of an integrated digital marketing campaign can be seen with Starbucks. Starbucks is heavily invested in social media with record-breaking engagement with its Facebook, Twitter, and Instagram platforms. Starbucks has tried to maximize its mobile interactions with customers by encouraging mobile payments, which decrease the time that a customer

Starbucks is serious about its customers' ideas!
©FotograFFF/Shutterstock

stands in line. With over 200,000 ideas submitted to the My Starbucks Idea website, Starbucks successfully implements crowdsourcing to show its customers that it values their suggestions.[31] Among the key strategies laid out by the company were the continued focus on Starbucks's app-based rewards program, which hit the 17.2 million 90-day active user mark and is growing 14 percent year over year. Digital initiatives like its rewards program look to cater to a "digitally savvy" customer base that expects higher levels of convenience and a more personalized experience. Starbucks's digital initiatives drove a third of its 6 percent comparable store sales increase during Q3 of 2019.[32]

Content Marketing Integral to the success of any digital marketing campaign is the concept of **content marketing**, when brands or companies publish blogs, investing in resources to produce unique content and paying for content-related ads. When you think of examples of content marketing done right, Hubspot is always on the list. In addition to creating a free tool as a growth hacking strategy, Hubspot has used content marketing by writing in-depth blog posts about the issues its visitors care about; adding content upgrades such as e-books to its blog posts; creating an educational and content sharing hub (Inbound.org), which gets 321,000 visitors each month and provides a great opportunity to promote its certification and partnership programs; and creating videos for Facebook and using LinkedIn to send traffic to those videos.

Charmin, the toilet paper brand, created an app for its customers called Sit or Squat. Charmin built a social media campaign around this unique app to get the word out about its products.

The app allows users to check the toilets around their local area to find out whether they are clean. The

digital marketing
Using digital technology to reach consumers through computers, gaming devices, out-of-home electronic screens, or mobile devices such as smartphones and tablets.

content marketing
Creating and sharing expertise, information, or branded content that is designed to inform and engage with tools such as research papers, e-books, infographics, how-to videos, blogs, webinars, e-newsletters, case studies, and events that can readily be found with search engines.

Charmin Sit or Squat campaign.
©2020 PROCTER & GAMBLE

idea behind this is that if they are clean, people can feel free to sit, but if they aren't clean, then they may want to squat. This silly app was the perfect way to connect with customers about a real problem they face that is relevant for the brand to address.

One reason why this app and the resulting campaign is so effective is that it gets people talking. The app idea may seem silly, but it is, at its core, still useful and relevant to consumers who would be using Charmin's products. The app is also interactive, which allows consumers to take part in the content experience themselves.[33]

Mobile Marketing **Mobile marketing** is a major disruption that continues to intensify. It includes both smartphones and tablets. Successful marketers must embrace the channel and focus on the importance of seamless, user-friendly experiences on mobile. Over 80 percent of mobile time is dominated by app consumption. M-commerce (buying and selling) is predicted to be the number-one use of mobile, with mobile payments and watching video a close second and third.[34]

Display and search are the most popular forms of mobile advertising, but branded content shows the most potential for future growth. Location data is at the core of mobile, but marketers expect the Internet of Things marketing applications to drive mobile growth by 2022. The current challenges in mobile marketing are the lack of data and how to measure the effectiveness of the investment.

Retail and entertainment lead the way in innovative use of mobile. Amazon was cited as the most innovative brand in mobile retail best practices by the Mobile Marketing Association. Amazon is one of the first organizations to embrace mobile commerce with a mobile-optimized site, consistent design across apps and mobile sites, easy repeat purchases, prominent call-to-action, one shopping basket across all platforms, predictive search, and spelling correction. Starbucks achieved second place in innovative mobile recognition in its overall brand use with its mobile payment, notifications, loyalty program, free downloads, and easy order/pay/pickup. Facebook Messenger was recognized in third place for gaining mass use quickly and giving scale to user-generated live video.[35]

Looking to the future, it is expected that branded content will continue to be the focus of mobile marketing. Over the next year, marketers are focusing on mobile web display advertising and mobile search, with significantly fewer marketers prioritizing loyalty schemes and mobile coupons. It is expected that screens and devices will increasingly become better suited for

> **mobile marketing**
> A set of practices that enables organizations to communicate and engage with their audiences in an interactive and relevant manner through any mobile device or network.

Mobile marketing reaches people on their personal devices.
©Marcel De Grijs/Dreamstime.com

consuming longer-form content, and mobile-optimized websites will be the norm. By 2022, the Internet of Things and smart home technologies are expected to double in importance. Use of mobile wallets and virtual reality technology is also expected to increase significantly over the next five years.[36]

Social Media Marketing

Social media, with its ability to interact with consumers, often in real time, through social networks such as Facebook, YouTube, Google+, Twitter, LinkedIn, Instagram, Snapchat, TikTok, Pinterest, and blogs, has added a new dimension to relationship marketing, making it more immediate and interactive. Social media is formally defined as a form of online media that allows members to create their own network of friends and contacts to share comments, articles, opinions, videos, and images as a form of self-expression. Social media provides consumers with the ability to interact with marketing messages by posting comments that are visible to all. This open environment encourages companies to be more transparent and interactive in their communications.

Social media marketing is when brands reach out to consumers online through social media networks. Brands can take various approaches with social media. A brand can place ads on social networks that accept advertising to increase awareness and can hire social media community managers to deploy social media programs and to monitor, measure, and respond to questions, comments, and inquiries. Social media marketing allows the brand to authentically connect with its audience on a personal level, humanizing the brand. While the popularity of social networks can rapidly change due to the ease with which consumers gravitate to different platforms, the most popular social networks in Canada today are Facebook, LinkedIn, Instagram, Twitter, and Snapchat, among numerous other niche social networks.[37]

With more than 97 million fans on Facebook, Coca-Cola dominates as a leader in social media marketing. What is interesting is that Coca-Cola is not very active on its Facebook page, posting once per month and sometimes even less frequently. The company is able to do this because it has such a strong brand identity and perhaps doesn't need the constant engagement with customers on social media. Very few brands have such strong brand equity that this lack of engagement wouldn't matter.[38]

Nike provides an excellent example of a very active brand on social media. While its numbers are not as high as Coca-Cola, Nike has fairly strong consumer engagement. With several Facebook pages, one for Nike Corporation and others focused on dedicated areas of business (for example, Nike Football and Nike Golf), Nike's fan bases range from the lower millions on some pages to over 42 million on the Nike Football page. The dedicated sports pages are normally updated daily, while the corporate site is updated less often. Postings will typically attract a few thousand likes, thousands of shares, and a few hundred comments. Nike also benefits from athletes who tweet and post content about Nike, creating even more interest and offering Nike even more content.[39]

Augmented Reality

Augmented reality (AR) is a relatively new technology combining things in the real world with computer-generated information. It allows people to enjoy experiences that are often more immersive than the real world alone offers.

Ford wanted to stay competitive in the Canadian sport utility vehicle (SUV) market and knew doing so meant reaching out to a younger-than-average demographic. It worked with Snapchat to make an AR filter related to its EcoSport mini-SUV that featured, inside Snapchat, a true-to-life 3D model of the car. Users could position and scale the car anywhere in their immediate environment, discovering both the internal and exterior aspects of it. Ford did not publish sales figures linked to this campaign, but it was the first AR vehicle marketing campaign in the Canadian market. That fact helped both media outlets and the public realize the car company is not afraid to take chances to reach its audience.[40]

Experiential Marketing

Marketers often embed experiential marketing approaches within their marketing programs to create buzz and, in many cases, a focal point for social media programs. **Experiential marketing** is an approach where marketers create fun and memorable opportunities for consumers to directly interact with a brand.[41] The consumers (and the company) will spread the word about their experience through social media. This approach can build awareness and generate word-of-mouth buzz and other forms of publicity for the brand. The brand goes from being passive to actively interacting with the target market. A brand can follow a number of approaches with experiential marketing, often using a combination of public relations, event marketing, and promotions to break through the clutter of competing marketing messages.

social media
A form of online media that allows members to create their own network of friends and contacts to share comments, articles, opinions, videos, and images as a form of self-expression.

social media marketing
Reaching out to consumers online through social media networks.

experiential marketing
Creating opportunities for consumers to directly interact with brands.

In the future, experiential marketing is expected to evolve and become more sophisticated. The mainstream use of virtual reality creates an additional platform for customer interaction. Pop-ups are an effective tool to reach niche customers by setting up in very specific locations. Nike launched the SNKRS XPRESS, a remodelled streetcar, outfitted with its newest models of sport and running shoes. The streetcar travelled the streets of Toronto and other North American cities during the 2016 NBA All-Star Game. Customers could try on and ultimately buy the new shoe styles during the 25-minute trip around Toronto.[42]

Inventive outdoor marketing will interact with customers in a more engaging way. Lego has been successful installing Instagram-ready bus stop displays, where customers can superimpose themselves into a Star Wars scene, choosing the "dark side" or the "light side," and posting to Instagram using the hashtag indicating their choice.[43] The integration of live streaming also adds another touch point. Companies such as Nestlé have utilized Periscope, a video-streaming service from Twitter, to stream real customer experiences with their products. Periscope will automatically post a link to the video from the customer's Twitter account, extending its reach. Nestlé was the first to use Periscope, focused on its Drumstick ice cream product, with its #FirstDayofSummer campaign. The campaign generated more than 5,000 views and more than 50,000 hearts (indicating approval) in just over 12 hours.[44]

Influencer Marketing

Influencer marketing plays a major role in all types of modern marketing. But businesses are no longer limited to major celebrities and names that everyone knows when deciding to work with an influencer. Micro-influencers have found their niche in social media marketing to convert leads, connect with audience members, and boost brand awareness. Micro-influencers are social media promoters with a smaller, niche following (typically, thousands to tens-of-thousands of followers). Although they have fewer followers, their followers have a higher level of engagement. Also, they are considered "average" or "everyday" people, so their followers are more likely to trust their opinions or recommendations. True influence is in engagement rates measured by clicks, subscribes, and ultimately purchases.[45]

Partnership Marketing

Partnership marketing has gained momentum over the last few years with companies providing customers with added value through complementary promotional offers. The intent of **partnership marketing** is to create formal associations between brands that will result in incremental business for both brands that could not have been achieved separately. Partnership marketing, also referred to as *affinity marketing,* is rooted in the idea that brands with similar customers can combine marketing expertise and use each other's strengths to build brand awareness and incremental revenue streams among a larger audience. The challenge lies in finding appropriate partners, setting realistic goals, tracking results, and aligning partnership goals with business objectives.[46]

Brand partnerships (sometimes referred to as *co-branding*) can manifest themselves in many ways. Nutella has mastered the brand partnership by integrating its delicious hazelnut and chocolate spread as a key ingredient in the product offerings of its partners. Rather than being satisfied as a take-home spread from the grocery store, Nutella has partnered with Tim Hortons to offer a Nutella doughnut, as well as

partnership marketing
The creation of formal associations between brands that will result in incremental business for both brands that could not have been achieved separately.

The faster way to earn SCENE points

Get 5 FREE movies† when you open a bank account with a SCENE®* debit card. Plus, earn SCENE points on all your everyday purchases.

Learn more at www.scotiabank.com/scene

You're richer than you think.® Ⓢ **Scotiabank**®

*® Registered trademark of The Bank of Nova Scotia.
*® Registered trademark of SCENE IP LP, used under license
*Visa Int. / Licensed User
*Interac, Interac Flash and Pay in a flash are trademarks of Interac Inc. The Bank of Nova Scotia is authorized user of the trademarks.
*Conditions and limitations apply. For new chequing account customers only. When you open a new SCENE-eligible bank account and get a SCENE ScotiaCard® debit card, you will receive 5,000 SCENE points on your SCENE membership account after you have set up a pre-authorized payroll deposit or 2 pre-authorized debits (PAC), or 2 pre-authorized debits (PAD), on 1 PAC/PAD. Your automatic payroll or PAD/PAC must be set-up and clear your account within 60 days of opening your Eligible Account. All pre-authorized transactions must clear the eligible account at least once per month in order to qualify. 1,000 SCENE points will be added to your SCENE membership account at month end in the month that your pre-authorized transactions were set-up. The remaining 4,000 SCENE points will be added no later than 2-3 statement cycles after your pre-authorized transaction(s) are set up. The Eligible Account must be open and in good standing at the time of payout. SCENE members can redeem 1,000 points for a free General Admission movie ticket. This offer does not apply to existing SCENE-eligible Scotiabank account holders. This offer cannot be duplicated or combined with any other offer. Scotiabank may withdraw or change this offer at any time without notice.

A strategic alliance between Scotiabank and Cineplex Entertainment created the SCENE loyalty card.

Used with permission of Bank of Nova Scotia

Nutella-filled pastries. Nutella has also partnered with Longo's grocery store chain in Ontario, with pop-up kitchens making crepes with Nutella filling.[47]

Another form of partnership marketing, with a longer-term focus, is the **strategic alliance**. This involves long-term arrangements between companies with similar values and objectives that extend beyond short-term promotional offers into long-term business agreements. An example of a strategic alliance exists with the SCENE loyalty movie rewards program where Cineplex Entertainment and Scotiabank formed a long-term arrangement to benefit both companies. SCENE members collect points when purchasing Cineplex Entertainment tickets or concession items. Points can be redeemed for free movies or snacks. Scotiabank Visa credit card holders earn additional points when paying with their Scotiabank Visa card. There are over 7 million SCENE members, many of them between the ages of 18 and 34, a much-desired demographic for the banking industry.[48]

Metrics and analytics provide important measures of performance.
©triloks/iStock/Getty Images

Metrics and Analytics

The Canadian business world is a performance-based culture that uses metrics and analytics to improve programs and deliver better results. A key role of the marketer is to collect and analyze metrics to make better brand decisions. Digital technology has resulted in a deluge of data that challenges marketers to interpret and manage. Easy-to-use software gathers the data, sorts it into actionable areas for increased focus and analysis, and flags elements that require immediate attention. Robust paid analytics platforms can be provided by companies such as IBM and Salesforce with their analytics platforms, or through free metrics platforms such as Google Analytics and Social Mention.

Metrics and analytics software can measure and track online sales and drill down into the origin of each sale. It can also measure website interactions such as unique visitors, time on site, page views, returning visitors, newsletter signups, and digital downloads. It can measure the effectiveness of online advertising campaigns, as well as the impact of social media programs. In the social media sphere, for example, analytics platforms can collect data that measure online buzz,

identify positive and negative sentiment, and point to online brand advocates. It can flag online conversations about a brand, keep an eye on competitor sentiment, and track topics of interest, whether they are on blogs, social networks, video-sharing sites, photo-sharing sites, or the websites of mainstream media. Importantly, this data can be combined with a marketer's costing information so that financial insights can determine costs per click, costs per conversion, costs per interaction, and ultimately, the return on investment (ROI) of specific programs.

In the offline marketing world, metrics and analytics are also important, again pointing to performance. Routine metrics are measured against marketing plan targets and look at elements such as sales, market share, profit margins, and profit levels. Program-specific metrics analyze specific marketing programs and measure performance against benchmarks and targets. These metrics can include elements such as ROI, awareness levels, ad recall, sales conversions, coupon redemption rates, contest entries, or media mentions, depending on the task at hand.

Metrics refers to numeric data that are collected and grouped to track performance. It is often presented in spreadsheets and dashboards, so it is easy to understand and interpret. **Dashboards** visualize data using graphs, charts, and numbers so that the data is easy to use and understand. **Analytics** refers to the process of taking metrics data and applying smart thinking and technology to gain actionable insights that can help make better business decisions. An analytics platform helps answer questions and provides customer insights, and predicts patterns that can improve marketing performance. Analytics can help segment customers, plan and forecast, manage risk, and take corrective action.

Marketers are challenged to use metrics and analytics to better understand how to build better customer relationships. Metrics, analytics, and types of data are covered in more detail in Chapter 4.

Marketing Regulations and Ethical Considerations

In Canada, regulations are put in place to safeguard people, communities, and the environment from businesses that may not have their well-being in mind. These regulations can take many forms, such as pollution-emission thresholds, water safety guidelines, food and safety regulations, advertising standards, competitive guidelines, and telemarketing regulations, just to name a few. The Government of Canada sponsors a website that collects and distributes information on product recalls in Canada. It can be accessed at **http://healthycanadians.gc.ca/.**

Consumer privacy is a growing concern for Canadians. Security breaches have occurred at companies such as Facebook, Google, and other leading brands and have led consumers to become concerned about their confidential online data. Privacy regulations have been enacted with increased fines to improve data privacy. An example of one of the most significant cases of online personal information security breach in Canada is that of LifeLabs in British Columbia and Ontario in 2019. LifeLabs is Canada's largest health care lab-testing firm, and the personal health information of nearly 15 million Canadians was stolen in a ransomware cyberattack. LifeLabs claimed it paid the hackers off to get the data back and said in an open letter to consumers that information including "names, addresses, emails, logins, passwords, date of birth, health care numbers and lab test results" was taken. LifeLabs offered one year of identity theft and dark web monitoring insurance to compensate those affected by the breach. Emerging technologies can help with these security challenges. New identity management or know your customer solutions are being developed that can improve security, reduce fraud, and improve insight about customers across multiple devices.

The evolution of digital technology has forced marketing associations and government bodies to revise and update legislation and implement new guidelines. New laws now protect consumers' rights to privacy and provide strict guidelines that marketers need to follow. Anti-spam legislation has also been put in place to regulate e-mail marketing practices, while do-not-track policies have been created for online behavioural advertisers to use. In addition, new industry associations and regulatory bodies have surfaced to control the wireless industry in Canada so that its marketing practices are ethical, legal, and transparent. Chapter 2 reviews in more detail the regulations that govern marketing in Canada, and the Focus on Ethics box, "The Ethics of Greenwashing," offers a case study of one current ethical issue in marketing today.[49]

CANADIAN MARKETING ASSOCIATION

CMA

The Canadian Marketing Association provides excellent resources for marketers.
Used with permission of Canadian Marketing Association

In addition to government regulations, many companies, industries, and professional associations have guidelines and codes of ethics that provide direction to employees and members on areas that are considered unacceptable. The Canadian Marketing Association (CMA) is the professional body for the marketing industry, and its guidelines, codes of ethics, and educational programs help shape marketing in Canada. The CMA provides input on legislative issues such as Canada's anti-spam legislation (CASL) and digital advertising do-not-track guidelines. The CMA has dealt with policy issues concerning telemarketing regulations, electronic commerce, and consumers' right to privacy. It has hundreds of corporate members, including major financial institutions, insurance companies, manufacturers, publishers, retailers, charitable organizations, agencies, relationship marketers, and those involved in e-business and digital marketing.

The CMA has a code of ethics by which all members must comply. Its purpose is to encourage high marketing standards that are honest, truthful, accurate, fair, and professional. The code of ethics covers topics such as accurate representations, truthfulness in marketing communications, price claims, fulfillment practices, privacy, marketing to children, and marketing to teenagers. It also provides direction on direct marketing practices, sales promotion, public relations, and media usage. Navigate to the CMA code of ethics on its website at **www.the-cma.org** to review the details in this important document.

The CMA website also contains a wealth of information for marketers with practical guides, best practices, white papers, case studies, news releases, job postings, and information on its educational courses and conferences. CMA student memberships are available at significantly discounted prices for students who are enrolled full-time in Canadian post-secondary education.

> *The CMA website also contains a wealth of information for marketers.*

The Ethics of Greenwashing

Natural, organic, and recyclable options are increasingly demanded by millennials and Gen Z-ers. A 2019 study by *Harvard Business Review* found that brands that were marketed as sustainable were growing faster than traditional competitors. This has led to the increased use of buzzwords such as "sustainable," "eco-friendly," and "green" to try to highlight the ecological advantages of products or services. Hospitality as well as food and beverage companies often focus on promoting achievements in saving water and electricity or reducing greenhouse gas emissions either directly or along their supply chain. This option is provided to hotel customers with the option of not changing your bedding or towels on a daily basis.

To respond to their customers, companies that decide to participate in "Green Marketing" tend to be under constant scrutiny by consumers. Sadly, these initiatives hailed publicly as sustainable often just act as a smokescreen to divert public attention from business activities that remain, at their core, harmful to the planet. This heightened public sensitivity means that more and more firms get caught in their use of fluffy marketing terms and advertisements that paint them in a greener light than their activities merit. The confusion and deception felt by consumers who are victims of greenwashing can lead to decreased brand loyalty and a loss in brand equity.

More than ever, the next few years will be crucial for companies to stay true to their environmental policies and messaging. A shift toward a circular economy, one in which not only are products are made from recycled and recyclable substances but also consumers are actively educated, encouraged, and assisted to re-use materials, is inevitable for any business that wants to be a true driver for positive change.

According to a publication by the *Cambridge Institute for Sustainability Leadership,* the tourism industry is responsible for about 5 percent of current greenhouse gas emissions. With numbers of travellers and hotel rooms booming, this number is set to increase by 130 percent by 2035.

Due to the heavy investments needed to update existing locations and inherently low profit margins compared to other industries, hotels and restaurants have been rather slow in adopting sustainable business practices. By 2050, hotels will need to reduce emissions per key by 90 percent to be in line with the Paris Climate Agreement. Public and political pressure on the sector is rising to implement drastic changes in coming years.

A worldwide gold standard for sustainable tourism in Canada is the Fogo Island Inn in Newfoundland. Rather than a mere hotel, Zita Cobb and her team have created a social enterprise with the inn at the heart of it—a revolutionary business project that effectively saved a community that once stood on the brink of extinction. The hotel is effectively owned by the community; all profits fund micro-lending projects, including greenhouse workers who supply the restaurant, and workshops where furnishings are fashioned by local artists, some of whom run painting, still-life drawing, or found-object collage workshops at the inn. Five stunning, light-filled studios have been built for artists to seek inspiration from nature at its most dramatic. In construction of the hotel, locally sourced, sustainable building materials were chosen

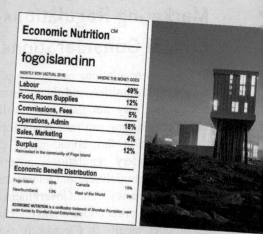

Fogo Island Inn

whenever possible; the entire steel frame is well insulated; rainwater from the roof is collected for use in toilets, laundry, and kitchen appliances; and wood-fired boilers and solar panels are used for hot water and underfloor heating. The result is a building that manages to stand out, yet remains distinctly of its Newfoundland home. Though it fulfills the role excellently, it's much more than a luxury stay; the inn stands as a statement of the revival of an entire cod-fishing community, previously left behind by industrial modernization.

Zita Cobb sums up her vision beautifully:

> But I really think it has a lot to do with the fact that, as humans, we're trying to ask better questions—and one of those better questions is—what is a better relationship between business and community? And how do we use business in a way that strengthens the most important things, like nature and culture? So I think that it's a good sign, it's a signal, that we're just better aware. ●

Questions

1. What are the ethical considerations surrounding greenwashing?

2. Do you think that hospitality industry and hotels like the Fogo Island Inn will ultimately win?

Economic Nutrition CM		
fogo island inn		
NIGHTLY STAY (ACTUAL 2018)		WHERE THE MONEY GOES
Labour		49%
Food, Room Supplies		12%
Commissions, Fees		5%
Operations, Admin		18%
Sales, Marketing		4%
Surplus Reinvested in the community of Fogo Island		12%

Economic Benefit Distribution

Fogo Island	65%	Canada	19%
Newfoundland	13%	Rest of the World	3%

ECONOMIC NUTRITION is a certification trademark of Shorefast Foundation, used under license by Shorefast Social Enterprises Inc.

ask YOURSELF

1. What are the stages in the evolution of business philosophies?

2. What are the key components of a relationship marketing orientation?

3. In your own words, explain mobile marketing?

4. What is CSR?

Marketing Careers

LO 7 Getting a job is usually a lengthy process, and it is exactly that—a process that involves careful planning, implementation, and evaluation. The starting point is to get an education and, while studying, to create a network of business professionals to contact upon graduation. Creating this network can be done through summer jobs, co-op placements, and internships. Network with guest speakers who may visit your school, involve yourself in on-campus clubs, and participate in volunteer opportunities. Have you created a promotional plan, a research report, or a marketing plan in your classes? Throughout your education, gather samples of your work as a demonstration of your knowledge and abilities. All of these methods provide opportunities to meet professionals in the marketing field and gain exposure to the marketing discipline. Despite these strengths, you still need to market yourself.

The process of getting a job involves the same activities that marketing managers use to develop and introduce products and brands into the marketplace. The only difference is that you are marketing yourself, not a product. Start by conducting a personal SWOT analysis. SWOT analyses are used by business to assess themselves and develop strategies. (See Chapter 15 for more information on SWOT analysis.) Ensure that you understand your strengths and what differentiates you from the competition. Conversely, what areas do you need to improve to increase your chances in the job market—these are your weaknesses. Consider how you are currently perceived and how you want to be perceived.

What opportunities exist in the marketing field? As in any field, it is somewhat dependent on the strength of the economy, but entry-level marketing jobs exist for college and university graduates. Entry-level positions exist in sales, marketing, and promotions in a variety of fields. Job titles vary from company to company, but typical jobs include marketing coordinators, marketing analysts, marketing assistants, sales representatives, and account coordinators. These entry-level jobs usually include on-the-job training, liaison with other departments within the company, exposure to marketing program development, and the potential to move up within the organization. Areas of growth are in promotions and digital marketing services. Opportunities exist in creating your own business, as well as working in small, medium, and large organizations in the private sector, in the non-profit sector, or in the government. In the private sector, marketers are required in consumer marketing and in the business-to-business market.[50]

What threats exist? Are there certain industries that are cutting back? Do other job candidates possess sought-after skills?

Once you have completed this research, create a game plan. Select a target market—those job opportunities that match your goals and strengths. Now, create the marketing mix or 4 Ps to position your personal brand to that target market. The *product* is you and the skills, experience, and competencies that you have to differentiate your personal brand. *Price* is the salary range you are seeking. *Promotion* is communicating with potential employers electronically, in writing, or in person. *Place* focuses on where you will interact with employers—online, career fairs, or through your career centre.

Be sure to also bookmark Canadian marketing job-search websites and to track job postings. Examples of

Job Seekers

Employers

Career Resources

Professional Development

Marketing Job Bank
Your Canadian Marketing Career Resource Centre

The Canadian Marketing Association has a job bank that can be used by its members.
Used with permission of Canadian Marketing Association

sites that have job postings include **www.iabcanada .com**, **www.strategyonline.ca**, **www.the-cma.org**, **www .mediajobsearchcanada.com**, and more general job search sites such as **www.workopolis.com** and **www.indeed.ca**.

Students wanting to get into the marketing field need to be analytical, be able to work with others, be capable of working in teams, and have strong communication skills in both written and verbal contexts. They must be competent with technology, be able to problem-solve, and not hesitate to drill down into data analysis. As a marketer, you need to keep your finger on the pulse of the consumer. This requires you to stay current and to be intellectually curious. Marketers need to read online web portals, blogs, newspapers, and magazines; follow social media sites; attend conferences and webinars;

surf the Internet, watch TV, and listen to the radio; and absorb the trends that are evolving in society and around the world. Publications such as *Strategy* magazine (**www.strategyonline.ca**), *Canadian Business* (**www .canadianbusiness.com**), and *Maclean's* magazine (**www .macleans.ca**) are highly recommended, as is subscribing to the *eMarketer* (**www.emarketer.com**) online newsletter. Daily newspapers such as the *Globe and Mail* (**www.globeandmail.com**) and *National Post* (**www .nationalpost.com**) are good up-to-date sources of business and marketing news.

Marketing is an exciting area where change is the norm and being able to rise to the challenge is imperative. Learn the fundamentals through education and apply your knowledge by working in the industry.

An airline that treats people like people.

WESTJET
Love Where You're Going

1. *Who is the target market for this WestJet ad?*
2. *Why do you think this ad was so appealing to WestJet's target market?*

• The role of marketing is to focus on consumer needs and to generate revenue, profits, or support for an organization.

• Successful marketing focuses on customer needs and wants and developing programs that engage consumers and inspire customer loyalty.

 • The marketing mix, also known as the 4 Ps, consists of product, price, place, and promotion.

• Product refers to all the attributes that make up a good, a service, or an idea. Product elements include areas such as product design, product features, colour, packaging, warranty, and service levels.

• Price refers to what is exchanged for a product, including the expected regular retail or sale price.

• Place is the way in which your product gets to the consumer, including the distribution channels, retail formats, and merchandising used to sell a product.

• Promotion refers to the tools needed to communicate with consumers about a product, including advertising, public relations, sales promotion, direct response, event marketing, sponsorship, online approaches, and personal selling.

 • The marketing process follows three main steps: (1) identifying consumer needs, (2) managing the marketing mix to meet consumer needs, and (3) realizing revenues or profits.

 • A product in marketing can be a good, a service, or an idea. A good is a product you can touch and own. A service is a product that is intangible that you cannot touch. An idea is a concept that typically looks for support.

LO 5 • The evolution of marketing has progressed from a production orientation stage, to a sales orientation stage, to a marketing orientation stage, and finally to a relationship marketing stage.

• Important areas of the relationship marketing stage are customer relationship management (CRM) and corporate social responsibility (CSR).

LO 6 • New and evolving marketing practices have surfaced in the areas of (1) digital marketing, including content marketing, mobile marketing, and social media marketing; (2) augmented reality; (3) experiential marketing; (4) influencer marketing; (5) partnership marketing; (6) metrics and analytics; and (7) new marketing regulations and ethical considerations.

• The Canadian Marketing Association (CMA), the professional body for the marketing industry, responds to legislative issues and sets guidelines on responsible marketing practices.

LO 7 • The starting point to a marketing career is to get an education and, while studying, to create a network of business professionals to contact upon graduation. Careers exist in sales, market research, advertising, promotions, marketing analytics, and brand management.

• The process of getting a job involves the same activities that marketing managers use to develop and introduce products and brands into the marketplace. The only difference is that you are marketing yourself, not a product.

key terms and concepts... **A REFRESHER**

analytics	idea	production orientation
content marketing	market	promotion
corporate social responsibility (CSR)	marketing	relationship marketing
customer lifetime value	marketing mix	sales orientation
customer relationship management (CRM)	marketing orientation	service
customer value proposition	marketing process	share of wallet
dashboards	metrics	social media
digital marketing	mobile marketing	social media marketing
exchange	need	societal marketing concept
experiential marketing	partnership marketing	strategic alliance
good	place	target market
greenwashing	price	want
	product	

Marketing Mix Assignment WestJet has experienced success segmenting its market as the brand evolves. Review the opening vignette on WestJet and then brainstorm on a new marketing mix for its premium customer segment that includes new forms of content marketing, social media marketing, mobile marketing, and partnership marketing. Outline the new marketing mix under the headings Product, Price, Place, and Promotion.

This chapter's opening vignette examines WestJet's approach to marketing. Brainstorm in groups the idea of evolving WestJet into an international carrier. What new products would you consider? Would CSR be part of your plan?

Review the Infographic that details information on corporate citizenship for UPS Canada in 2019. What is your favourite brand or company? Does it participate in any corporate social responsibility (CSR) initiatives? Research your favourite brand or company and document its CSR investments. Are you surprised by this brand or company's significant support or perhaps lack of support for CSR initiatives? Does this make a difference to you?

The Marketing Environment

LEARNING OBJECTIVES

LO 1 Explain the importance of an environmental scan and how it is used to improve marketing programs

LO 2 Describe the elements of an environmental scan and summarize the trends affecting each area

LO 3 Outline the current demographic and socio-cultural influences that affect marketing approaches

LO 4 Explain how changes in the economic environment influence consumer purchase behaviour

LO 5 Discuss the technological developments shaping current marketing practices

LO 6 Describe the different forms of competition and the regulatory forces that shape the marketing industry

LO 7 List the steps in an environmental scan

T he impact of the external environment is a key component of the strategic planning process for most companies. This chapter focuses on understanding the marketing environment and how it provides marketers with direction on the development and marketing of new products, as well as the successful marketing of current products. We start by looking at the very rapid change in the external business environment for Canada Post. Canada Post is a Crown corporation, responsible for the delivery of letter mail and parcels to Canadians.

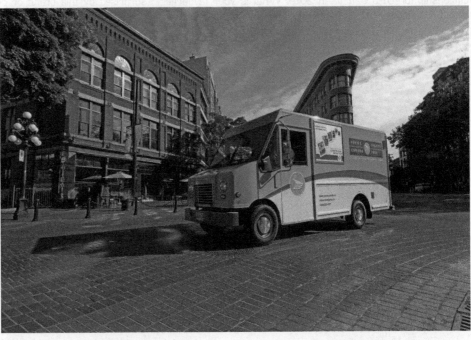

Used with permission of Canada Post Corporation

CHAPTER OUTLINE

- Canada Post
- Marketing environment
- Demographic and socio-cultural forces
- Economic and technological forces
- Competitive and regulatory forces
- Steps in an environmental scan

Nothing has had more impact on Canada Post's business over the last few years than a monumental change in consumer behaviour, choice, and preferences. When was the last time you mailed a letter? Well, 42 percent of Canada Post's revenue still comes from letter mail delivery, but Canadians mailed 2.4 billion fewer pieces of mail in 2018 than they did in 2006. Annual volume declines of 5 or 6 percent have been common over the last few years. What happens to a company when its major revenue stream is affected by such a significant external threat?

Let's look at the range of external factors that Canada Post needs to consider, now and going forward, to be successful:

Demographic factors: The number of homes in Canada continues to grow each year. From Canada Post's perspective, the number of postal addresses has grown to 16.4 million. That means more homes to deliver mail to.

Canada Post does not receive taxpayers' money, but it has an obligation to provide mail delivery to all postal addresses in Canada. The increase in the number of addresses puts a significant strain on the company's profitability.

Socio-cultural factors: Between 2007 and 2018, the volume of letter mail per address declined by 44 percent. This places significant pressure on Canada Post's finances. Less mail but more homes to deliver to means less revenue, but higher costs; this does not add up to a successful future.

However, the same Internet that is eroding the mail business is driving Canada Post's highest growth, which is in its parcels business. Consumers are gravitating toward online shopping. About 76 percent of Canadian households shop online. Every year, consumers are shopping online more often, and buying items of greater variety and higher value.

And when Canadians do spend money online, they want a sense of control over the delivery of purchases—they want accurate shipping costs provided at checkout, with precise shipping times, and they want to be able to track purchases throughout the delivery cycle so they always know where their order is.

Economic factors: Canadian spending levels are somewhat volatile, up one month and down the next. Consumers are still a bit nervous about spending too much. However, higher growth in spending has been seen on items such as clothing and shoes. By 2023, it is estimated that Canadians will spend $55 billion online.

Statistics Canada has estimated that only 17 percent of Canadian businesses are selling online. This number will grow rapidly in the short term. To avoid falling behind other markets, the push is on for Canadian companies to set up e-commerce platforms for their businesses.

Technological factors: Canadians are more likely to have access to the Internet than people in any other G20 country. In fact, 87 percent of Canadian households are connected to the Internet, and the majority of Canadians have access to high-speed Internet. As a result, there has been a steady movement to e-billing and online banking, which has drastically reduced the volume of mail.

Distribution is also impacted by technology with drones now being used in delivery.

CHAPTER FEATURES

Canada Post Capitalizes on E-commerce Trend
Changes in the external environment shape the future of Canada Post.

Statistics Canada—Demographic Trends
Canada's population is aging and being impacted by an ever-changing ethnic mosaic.

Millennials versus Generation Z
Marketers need to recognize the differences between generations.

Ethnic Shoppers
Canadian companies are focused on meeting the needs of ethnic consumers.

Technology Is Evolving Rapidly
Technological advances keep marketers on their toes.

The Little Black Book of Scams
The Competition Bureau helps consumers recognize and ultimately avoid scams.

The impact of the digital movement is evident in the advertising field as well. Over the last ten years, digital advertising has grown tenfold while physical direct mail has decreased.

In a digital world, Canada Post has a major challenge to remain relevant and profitable, given that 42 percent of its revenue comes from paper bills, statements, and letters, and another 17 percent comes from direct mail advertising.

Competitive factors: By law, Canada Post has a monopoly to deliver letters. But the parcel delivery business is another story. There, Canada Post faces stiff competition. Companies that are larger on a global scale, such as Amazon, FedEx, and UPS, are investing in Canada. Barriers to entry have historically been high in the national parcel delivery business since broad distribution networks and sophisticated tracking technology have been required, and brand recognition has been important to customers. Other Canadian companies are also competing for more business. There are also emerging or potential threats, such as Uber.

Finally, e-commerce retailers themselves are eager to reduce their delivery costs, using such initiatives as ship-from-store or promoting in-store pickup of online orders. In this tough business environment, Canada Post grew to become the one of the country's top parcel company in 2017 (by revenue). It is also the majority owner of Purolator, the second-largest parcel company.

Regulatory factors: Mail delivery in Canada is regulated under the *Canada Post Corporation Act*. All other delivery is not regulated.

The Government of Canada has recognized the importance of keeping Canadians connected and has developed the Digital 150 plan, which includes investments in making high-speed Internet available in all areas of the country, and providing support to small businesses to help them integrate digital technology into their businesses.

Canada Post's transformation

Canada Post considered all of these factors and the impact that they have on its business. With traditional mail volumes declining at a steady pace, it needed to reinvent its business for the digital age. Canada Post's growth strategy centres on two of its three business units: parcels and direct marketing.

With the current and future growth of e-commerce, Canada Post decided to focus on parcel delivery and improving the end-to-end customer experience. Excellent customer service anchors this success. Canada Post works to integrate its services into retailers' websites to provide a seamless customer experience from purchase (providing accurate shipping rates), through sorting and shipping (providing tracking of the parcel), and finally to delivery (on time, secure, and convenient).

As a major distributor in the shopping delivery business, Canada Post has amassed data about the purchasing behaviour of Canadians. While respecting privacy laws that protect individuals' information, Canada Post's e-commerce team offered GROW workshops to entrepreneurs that provided valuable insight into industry trends, shoppers' preferences, shipping options, and marketing strategies.

A case in point where Canada Post is adapting to its changing environment is the publication of *Incite* magazine, which highlights the best direct marketing from around the world. *Incite* is a content marketing publication published quarterly and is free for customers. In relation to marketing, direct mail has been replaced by direct media where all channels converge around the consumer. The digital and physical worlds are working together using immersive technology, and Canada Post is highlighting some of the most innovative and successful campaigns.

Canada Post

Winnipeg has the most cottage owners per capita in Canada. They also love their Internet, but cottage country in Manitoba is too remote for traditional connectivity. Another interesting fact about Winnipeg is that it is known as the mosquito capital of Canada. The Rogers Rocket Hub offers wireless high-speed Internet, but there was little awareness of either the brand or the product among cottagers. To tackle both problems, Rogers targeted Winnipeggers with direct mail just before the first long weekend of cottage season. The self-mailer was wrapped in real mosquito netting with the message, "Going to the cottage? Don't forget to pack the net." Rogers' call volume increased by 200 percent. This mailing was a case of relevance in action—going beyond a person's name on a brochure, envelope, or leaflet and recognizing what resonates and motivates in a specific region.

It seems as though Canada Post has e-commerce all wrapped up![1]

reality **CHECK** ⊘

As you read Chapter 2, refer back to the Canada Post vignette to answer the following questions:

- Which major environmental changes have impacted Canada Post?

- What new services do you think that Canada Post should offer to continue to meet customer needs?

The Marketing Environment

LO 1 Marketers and consumers do not function in a vacuum, and marketers understand that successful marketing programs must reach out and address changes and new opportunities in the marketplace. In the Canada Post example highlighted in this chapter's opening vignette, the combination of a significant decline in the use of letter mail, but an increasing number of postal addresses to deliver to, created a big threat to the continued profitability of Canada Post. Simultaneously, an increase in e-commerce spending created an opportunity for increasing its parcel delivery business. However, with competitors such as UPS, FedEx, and other national parcel delivery companies providing excellent customer service, Canada Post needed to understand the customer's needs for rapid delivery, parcel tracking, and instant shipping charge quotations. This resulted in a remodelled parcel delivery service that met the needs of the online shopper.

Marketers constantly monitor the marketing environment with a view to capitalizing on new opportunities and curtailing potential threats that may challenge their businesses. In short, marketers scan the marketing environment in six key areas: (1) demographic forces, (2) socio-cultural forces, (3) economic forces, (4) technological forces, (5) competitive forces, and (6) regulatory forces. This chapter looks at developments in these areas, providing a variety of examples that demonstrate how noting and responding to these changes can result in more-effective marketing programs.

The environmental scan is an important tool that is part of the strategic planning process and is part of

Canada Post has two-thirds of the online delivery business in Canada.

Used with permission of Canada Post Corporation

the situation (SWOT) analysis that organization's conduct on a regular basis. The external environment must be considered along with the organization's internal strengths and weaknesses.

> *Successful marketing programs must reach out and address changes and new opportunities in the marketplace.*

Situation (SWOT) Analysis

The essence of **situation analysis** is taking stock of where the firm or product has been recently, where it is now,

situation analysis
Taking stock of a firm's or product's past performance, where it is now, and where it is headed.

SWOT analysis
The assessment of how well an organization or brand is servicing its businesses and target markets by evaluating its internal strengths and weaknesses, and its external opportunities and threats.

environmental scan
The process of continually acquiring information on events occurring outside an organization to identify trends, opportunities, and threats to a business.

demographics
The statistical data on a population according to characteristics such as gender, age, ethnicity, income, education, and occupation.

and where it is headed in terms of the organization's marketing plans and the external forces and trends affecting it. An effective summary of a situation analysis is a **SWOT analysis**, an acronym describing an organization's appraisal of its internal **S**trengths and **W**eaknesses and its external **O**pportunities and **T**hreats.

The SWOT analysis is based on an exhaustive study of four areas that form the foundation upon which the firm builds its marketing program:

- Identify changes and trends in the organization's industry.
- Analyze the organization's current and potential competitors.
- Assess the organization itself, including available resources.
- Research the organization's present and prospective customers.

The task is to translate the results of the SWOT analysis into specific marketing actions that will help the firm grow. The ultimate goal is to identify the *critical* strategy-related factors that impact the firm and then build on vital strengths, correct glaring weaknesses, exploit significant opportunities, and avoid disaster-laden threats.

An Environmental Scan

LO 2 An **environmental scan** is the process of continually acquiring information on events occurring outside an organization to identify external trends, that are opportunities or threats to a business. Marketers use this knowledge to ensure that goods, services, and ideas are relevant and meaningful, using an environmental scan to define the opportunities and threats to their existing business. An environmental scan is often the first step in developing a more extensive SWOT analysis. A SWOT analysis (**S**trengths, **W**eaknesses, **O**pportunities, and **T**hreats) is discussed in more detail in Chapter 15, but in simple terms, it involves assessing how well a company is servicing its businesses and/or consumers by assessing an organization's internal strengths and weaknesses, as well as its external opportunities and threats (from an environmental scan). This information is then used to set the future direction for a business and to lay the groundwork for competitive

marketing programs. An environmental scan looks at six key external areas, namely demographic forces, socio-cultural forces, economic forces, technological forces, competitive forces, and regulatory forces.

An Environmental Scan of Today's Marketplace

What trends might affect marketing in the future? A firm conducting an environmental scan of the marketplace might uncover a number of key trends—from the growing popularity of brand advocates, to the increasing application of virtual reality and augmented reality, to the surging scrutiny regarding the collection and use of consumer data.[2] These trends affect consumers and the organizations that serve them. Trends such as these are described in the following discussion of the six environmental forces.

Demographic Forces

LO 3 The statistical study of populations is referred to as **demographics**. It looks at characteristics of a group of people, such as gender, age, ethnicity, income, education, and occupation. Marketers can access demographic information through Statistics Canada and through surveys and external databases. It is important for marketers to clearly understand changes that are occurring in the demographic arena to ensure that marketing efforts are well placed and opportunities are not overlooked.

Statistics Canada provides demographic data through its census information, which is collected every five years. The latest Census of Canada occurred in 2016 (with the next scheduled for 2021), and it shows that the Canadian population is aging, contains diverse generations, is settling in large cities, and is ethnically mixed.[3] We look at these trends and identify their impact on marketing efforts.

An Aging Population The 2016 Census of Canada shows that Canada is populated by approximately 35.2 million people. There has been a significant growth in the population over the age of 65. For the first time in census history, the population over the age of 65 (5.9 million) outnumbers children under 14 (5.8 million). In addition, seniors represent 16.9 percent of the population, a 20 percent increase from 2011.[4] By 2038, it is estimated that there will be more than 10 million Canadians over the age of 65. This represents a growth of 75 percent over the 20-year period of 2015 to 2035 (see Figure 2–1).

Figure 2–1

Population aged 0 to 14 years and 65 years and older, 1998 to 2018 (estimates) and 2019 to 2038 (projections), Canada

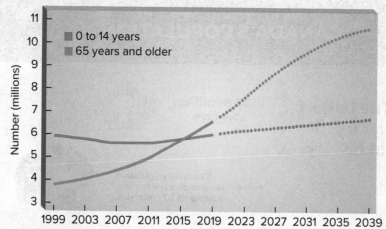

Source: Data from 1998 to 2018 are population estimates. Data for 2019 to 2038 (shown in the graph as dotted lines) are population projections taken from *Population Projections for Canada (2013 to 2063), Provinces and Territories (2013 to 2038)* (91-520-X). **Source(s):** Tables 17-10-0005-01 and 17-10-0057-01.

Figure 2–2 provides an overview of Canada's population in 2019. Canada's population growth was the highest of the G7 countries, up more than half a million people to 37.6 million.

Government agencies and marketers are taking note of these demographic changes and determining the needs of the aging market. Hospitals, for example, are reviewing the need for more orthopedic surgeons to conduct joint replacement surgeries; the health care industry is reviewing its home support service policies; and marketers of personal care items are creating more products for an older population, such as face creams that reduce the signs of aging, medicines such as Tylenol Arthritis Pain to relieve painful joints, and a large variety of vitamins and herbal supplements to maintain health.

Diverse Generations

A generation is a group of people who are bound together by similar events that they experienced as they grew up. Marketers note four main generational groups of consumers: baby boomers, generation X, generation Y (or millennials), and generation Z. The definitions as to when these generations start and stop vary by publication and researcher. Keep in mind that although the specific birth dates are inconsistent depending on the source, the characteristics of each generational group are still consistent and relevant.

Baby boomers are the generation of people born between 1946 and 1965.[5] There are 13 million baby boomers in Canada, accounting for 35 percent of the population, of which half are seniors aged 65 and older.[6]

Baby boomers are redefining the concept of aging with a keen interest in health and an active self-image. Many boomers act and feel many years younger. Baby boomers are generally well educated and culturally diverse. Boomers have been known to be brand-loyal customers.

There are many lifestyle decisions to be made for baby boomers: They will have more leisure time; they will probably downsize their homes; and they will have to deal with an increasing number of health issues over time. Marketers have noted these changes in lifestyle and are developing products that address these needs, such as larger smartphone screens, educational vacations, and luxury retirement homes.[7]

Baby boomers increasingly use digital technology to communicate with others and conduct research. A report conducted by Media Technology Monitor concludes that baby boomers in Canada are adopting new technology, although at a slower pace than younger Canadians: 67 percent of boomers use smartphones compared with 88 percent for younger Canadians. When it comes to connectivity, 75 percent of baby boomers connect to the Internet with their devices versus 92 percent of younger Canadians.[8]

Generation X is the group of people born after the baby boomers, between 1966 and 1980. In Canada, this generation numbers 7.3 million, accounting for 20 percent of the population.[9] This generational cohort is smaller than the baby boomers or generation Y cohorts. These consumers are highly educated, most of them have children, and most are employed (mainly full time).[10] They are more likely to have household incomes higher than $100,000 per year. Nearly one quarter (23 percent) of gen X respondents reported not being born in Canada. The high earning power of generation X allows them to be more experimental with technology. As a result, 90 percent own a smartphone, two-thirds

baby boomers
Generation of people born between 1946 and 1965.

generation X
People born between 1966 and 1980.

Figure 2–2
Canada's aging population

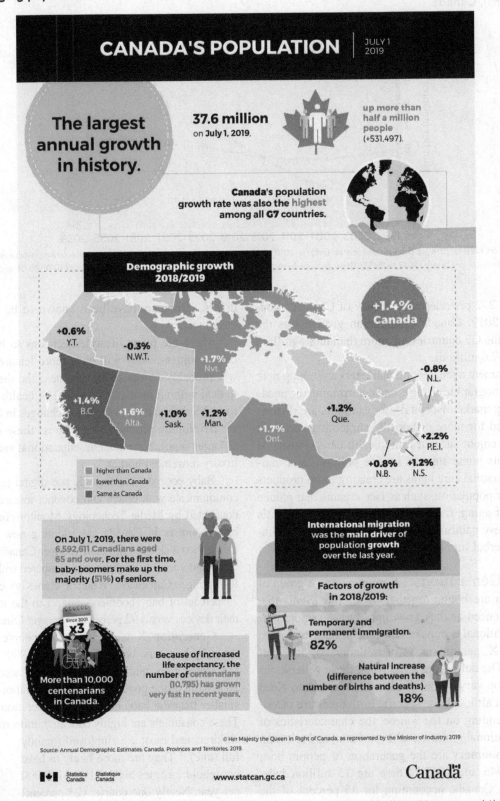

CANADA'S POPULATION | JULY 1 2019

The largest annual growth in history.

37.6 million on July 1, 2019.

up more than half a million people (+531,497).

Canada's population growth rate was also the highest among all **G7** countries.

Demographic growth 2018/2019

+1.4% Canada

+0.6% Y.T.
-0.3% N.W.T.
+1.7% Nvt.
-0.8% N.L.
+1.4% B.C.
+1.6% Alta.
+1.0% Sask.
+1.2% Man.
+1.7% Ont.
+1.2% Que.
+2.2% P.E.I.
+0.8% N.B.
+1.2% N.S.

higher than Canada
lower than Canada
Same as Canada

On July 1, 2019, there were 6,592,611 Canadians aged 65 and over. **For the first time, baby-boomers make up the majority (51%) of seniors.**

Since 2001 x3

More than 10,000 centenarians in Canada.

Because of increased life expectancy, the number of centenarians (10,795) has grown very fast in recent years.

International migration was the **main driver** of population **growth** over the last year.

Factors of growth in 2018/2019:

Temporary and permanent immigration. **82%**

Natural increase (difference between the number of births and deaths). **18%**

© Her Majesty the Queen in Right of Canada, as represented by the Minister of Industry, 2019

Source: Annual Demographic Estimates: Canada, Provinces and Territories, 2019.

Statistics Canada   Statistique Canada   www.statcan.gc.ca   Canadä

Source: Statistics Canada, "Canada's Population, July 1 2019," September 30, 2019, accessed January 2020 at https://www150.statcan.gc.ca/n1/pub/11-627-m/11-627-m2019061-eng.htm.

own a tablet, and 84 percent own a laptop. They are also more likely to own wearable technology, with 21 percent owning a Fitbit. They tend to be knowledgeable consumers, searching for good value in their purchases. They like to use the Internet to make purchases. They prefer to use the same brand rather than try new ones. Once

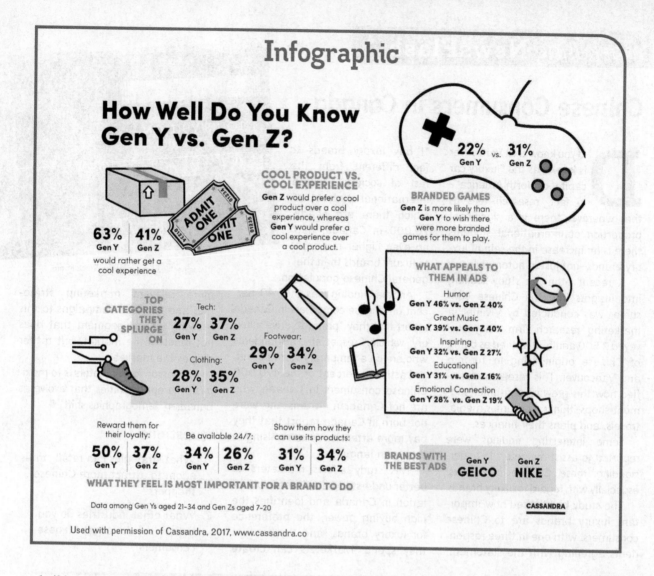

Infographic

How Well Do You Know Gen Y vs. Gen Z?

22% vs. **31%**
Gen Y   Gen Z

BRANDED GAMES
Gen Z is more likely than Gen Y to wish there were more branded games for them to play.

COOL PRODUCT VS. COOL EXPERIENCE

Gen Z would prefer a cool product over a cool experience, whereas Gen Y would prefer a cool experience over a cool product.

63% | **41%**
Gen Y | Gen Z
would rather get a cool experience

TOP CATEGORIES THEY SPLURGE ON

Tech:
27% | **37%**
Gen Y | Gen Z

Footwear:
29% | **34%**
Gen Y | Gen Z

Clothing:
28% | **35%**
Gen Y | Gen Z

WHAT APPEALS TO THEM IN ADS

Humor
Gen Y 46% vs. Gen Z 40%

Great Music
Gen Y 39% vs. Gen Z 40%

Inspiring
Gen Y 32% vs. Gen Z 27%

Educational
Gen Y 31% vs. Gen Z 16%

Emotional Connection
Gen Y 28% vs. Gen Z 19%

Reward them for their loyalty:
50% | **37%**
Gen Y | Gen Z

Be available 24/7:
34% | **26%**
Gen Y | Gen Z

Show them how they can use its products:
31% | **34%**
Gen Y | Gen Z

BRANDS WITH THE BEST ADS
Gen Y **GEICO**
Gen Z **NIKE**

WHAT THEY FEEL IS MOST IMPORTANT FOR A BRAND TO DO

Data among Gen Ys aged 21–34 and Gen Zs aged 7–20

CASSANDRA

you build a relationship with generation X consumers, they remain loyal. They are less prone to materialism and extravagance than baby boomers. Generation X is becoming a key influence in the market.[11]

Generation Y or **millennials** is the group of people born between 1981 and 2000. These are mostly children of baby boomers. They number 9.6 million and account for 27 percent of the Canadian population.[12] Music, video games, sports, and computer purchases are key products developed to meet the needs of this demographic group. In time, this generation is expected to become as influential as their baby boom parents. Generation Y is often casually referred to as the millennials. The millennials are highly influenced by Internet technology and are moulding society with their effortless integration of digital technology in all aspects of their lives.[13]

Generation Z is the group of people born in 2001 and beyond. They were born into an online world with social media, extensive connectivity, and multiple devices. They do not know what life is like without technology. They believe they can change the world and expect to work longer and harder in order to become successful. They are frugal and do not buy premium brands. They comparison-shop and actively critique online. They are used to getting things from social media and technology whenever and wherever they want, resulting in less patience and expecting immediate gratification.[14] In Canada, they number 8.1 million and account for 18 percent of the population.[15] See the nearby Infographic for a comparison of the some of the purchasing preferences of generation Y and generation Z.

Each of these four generations has very different tastes, consumption patterns, and attitudes. For each generation, marketers need to develop distinct marketing programs, products, and services. For example, each of these generations uses the media quite differently, and marketers have to carefully select which communication tools should be used. Canada Post is focusing on those consumers who purchase over the

generation Y
People born between 1981 and 2000. This generation is also referred to as *millennials*.

millennials
People born between 1981 and 2000. This generation is also referred to as *generation Y*.

generation Z
People born in 2001 and beyond.

Chinese Consumers in Canada

©Imaginechina Limited/Alamy Stock Photo

Did you know that Vancouver is known as the "luxury car capital of North America"? In fact, research tells us that wherever there is a significant proportion of international students there is an increase in the sale of luxury brands—not just in automobiles.

A recent ethnicity study looking into insights into the Chinese consumer was conducted by Vivintel, a marketing research firm. They surveyed 2,500 adults identified as being of Chinese origin living in Toronto and Vancouver. This research identified how this growing consumer segment shops, thinks, consumes media, travels, and plans their finances.

Some interesting findings were reported to assist marketers in understanding these Chinese consumers, especially with regard to luxury brands.

The study highlighted how important luxury brands are to Chinese consumers, with one in three respondents agreeing with the statement, "I buy luxury brands to feel different from the rest of society. Chinese international students, of which there are nearly 70,000 in Canada, had an even higher response to luxury brands than the general Chinese population.

Another finding was that 40 percent of Chinese consumers in Canada report that they "prefer to drive a luxury vehicle," especially respondents who are on a temporary work permit.

Lastly, 53 percent of the 490,000 Chinese consumers in Canada who are not Canadian citizens and were not born in Canada report that they pay more attention to advertising in their own language.

This study allows marketers to better understand the Chinese population in Canada and identifies the high buying power, the preference for luxury brands, and the amount they spend. Marketers can create more relevant marketing strategies and targeted campaigns to this growing market segment that does not react to the market, but rather shapes the market.

The lesson for marketers is to maximize the opportunities that evolve as Canadian demographics shift. ●

Questions

1. What strategies can retail stores adopt to attract more Chinese shoppers?

2. What other industries do you believe should target Chinese consumers?

Internet, which means focusing on meeting the needs of the millennials and generation X consumers.

Big-City Growth   Canada experienced its largest growth rate in its history in July 2019, with its population up 1.4 percent, or more than a half-million people, the fastest growing country in the G7. Figure 2–2 highlights the growth in each province and territory, with Nunavut and Ontario leading the way at 1.7 percent, followed closely by Alberta at 1.6 percent. (Newfoundland and Labrador and the Northwest Territories experienced reduced population.)[16] Boosted by immigration, big cities continue to grow faster than rural areas, with the cities in Western Canada growing more rapidly. Calgary grew by 14.6 percent, Edmonton increased 13.9 percent, and Saskatoon and Regina saw growth rates of 12.5 and 11.8 percent, respectively. There is a significant concentration of the Canadian population (three in five Canadians) living in Ontario and Quebec, two-thirds of the population live close to the Canadian border, and 35.5 percent of the population live in Toronto, Montreal, and Vancouver.[17]

Ethnic Diversity   Canada prides itself on being a multicultural country. Recent surveys from Statistics Canada show that 83 percent of the nation's growth between 2018 and 2019 was due to the arrival of immigrants and non-permanent residents. Canada admitted the highest number of immigrants in Canadian history, including nearly 30,000 Syrian refugees. Non-permanent residents experienced the highest increase in history as well, growing 171,536 in 2018/2019. While also fuelled by rapid growth in asylum claimants, this gain was mainly led by an increase in the number of work and study permit holders. Temporary immigration assists Canada in meeting its labour market needs.[18] By 2036, the largest increase in immigration will be from Asia (44.8 percent of immigrants in 2011 to over 55 percent of immigrants in 2036), and a decrease in immigration will be seen from Europe (from 31.6 percent in 2011 to between 15.4 and 17.8 percent in 2036).[19]

The increase in immigration has reinforced the linguistic diversity of Canada. Immigrant languages (those other than English, French, the Indigenous languages, and sign languages) are spoken at home by 7.3 million Canadians. The main immigrant languages are Mandarin, Cantonese, Punjabi, Spanish, Tagalog, and Arabic.[20]

This multicultural mix creates an interesting array of opportunities for marketers. In fact, many companies in Canada have recognized the potential impact of multicultural marketing strategies. Specific ethnic groups have their own particular interests and habits, which can be addressed in unique ways. Pepsi launched its "Get Hyped for Cricket" campaign targeted to the South Asian community. Companies such as Rogers Communications have risen to this challenge, offering a diverse list of multicultural programming—Canadians can watch Polish, Korean, Arabic, and Cantonese programming, just to mention a few.[21] The Marketing NewsFlash box, "Chinese Consumers in Canada," discusses how marketers are working to meet the needs of Canada's growing diversity.[22]

World Markets The world's population has reached over 7.7 billion people, with Africa and Asia accounting for over 75 percent of the population. China is home to 1.4 billion people, 18.5 percent of the world's population. India is home to almost 1.4 billion people, or 18.5 percent of the population.[23] Canada ranks number 39 on the list of most populous countries in the world. One of the major opportunities for future expansion is into foreign markets. The sheer size of these countries presents an enormous opportunity for growth.

> *Canada prides itself on being a multicultural country.*

Changing Household Composition In Canada, the composition of households has changed significantly. For the first time, the dominant household structure is the one-person household, surpassing couples with children.

Five Largest Countries (population in millions, as of 2019)

China	1,431.3
India	1,360.1
United States	328.1
Indonesia	269.3
Pakistan	214.6

This shift has been driven by an aging population, an increase in the economic independence of Canadians, and an increase in separation/divorce rates. In addition, Canada has seen a growth in the number of couples living without children, the number of common-law relationships, the number of same-sex couples, and the number of multi-generational families.[24]

Socio-cultural Forces

Socio-cultural trends are more difficult to pinpoint than demographic changes. It is not easy to identify societal and cultural shifts in attitudes or to track newly evolving trends. Socio-cultural changes tend to be gradual, over a prolonged period of time, and are sometimes very subtle. Statistical data is not as readily available in these areas, but marketers observe changes in society and conduct research to identify evolving trends and opportunities. Sometimes, identifying these trends involves consumer research; other times, it involves a keen eye and good intuition.

When we discuss **socio-cultural forces**, we are referring to cultural values, ideas, and attitudes that are learned and shared among a group of people. It also includes society's morals and beliefs that are demonstrated through behaviour common among a socio-cultural group. Canadians are known to be fair and inclusive. Canadian society is diverse, and Canadians value a good quality of life, access to education, health care, clean air and water, work–life balance, and the availability of social programs, Marketers monitor changes in these areas in order to capitalize on new opportunities with their marketing programs. Most recently, marketers are responding to socio-cultural changes as they relate to communications, food, health, shopping, entertainment, and the environment.[25]

Media

DEVICE CONNECTIVITY Consumers' widespread use of the Internet, and their ability and desire to access it numerous times throughout the day and on multiple devices, is changing the way marketers relate and communicate with consumers, and how people communicate and interact with each other—impacting socio-cultural norms within our society. In Canada today, we find a society that increasingly relies on electronic communication rather than face-to-face interaction.

Research from Internet analytics company comScore reveals that electronic devices play different roles throughout the day: A typical consumer starts the day at home checking messages and e-mails on a smartphone or tablet. At work, the consumer uses a desktop or laptop computer,

socio-cultural forces
Cultural values, ideas, and attitudes, as well as society's morals and beliefs.

and in the evening, tablets dominate.[26] In a survey by Media Technology Monitor, it was found that 51 percent of the time, people are watching television and accessing the Internet simultaneously.[27]

The proliferation of devices and connectivity means that many shoppers will access information about a product from social networks, product reviews, and online stores on mobile devices. This has coined the term **showrooming**, the practice of using mobile devices in store to check competitive online product reviews and prices and to then purchase the cheaper product online. Best Buy enacted a lowest price policy to combat showrooming. Best Buy guaranteed it would match the price of local and online retailers, so consumers would be encouraged to buy while in the store. Recently, reverse showrooming has become popular. Consumers tend to do a lot of research on a product before heading to the store, and then, armed with all the information they need, they prefer purchasing from the store.[28]

SOCIAL MEDIA Social media is no longer only a platform for people to stay in touch with friends. Social media sites allow consumers to express their opinions about products, to conduct research before making a purchase, and to communicate directly with companies. Marketers must use social media to speak to consumers. Brands need to have Facebook pages, Instagram accounts, Twitter feeds, and YouTube channels to build relationships with customers and manage their brand in an open communication forum. Facebook engages consumers with ads and offers, Twitter connects with newsworthy updates and by responding to customer questions, and YouTube is used for posting engaging videos, brand advertising, and how-to content.[29]

An Insights West study indicates that the social networks most used by Canadians are Facebook, YouTube, Twitter, and Pinterest (see Figure 2–3). Facebook usage continues to grow faster than other social networks. YouTube and Instagram are also increasing in usage, while Twitter, Google +, and Pinterest are declining. A study by Forum Research focused on the generational differences in social media usage. This study showed that the usage of Facebook is highest in the 18 to 34 age group and then decreases with age. LinkedIn is most popular with generation X, and its use is growing. Twitter is used most frequently by millennials.[30]

TV AND VIDEO VIEWING Canadians are highly engaged with TV and video viewing. While this data are changing rapidly, when it comes to TV, Canadians currently watch over 27 hours per week of television, though this number has been steadily declining over the last few years. The younger viewers are watching less than the average (19.7 hours), while older viewers are watching

Figure 2–3
Canadian social media usage statistics

Weekly Social Media Usage x Age

	18 to 34			35 to 54			55+		
	2019	2017	2016	2019	2017	2016	2019	2017	2016
facebook	86% ▲	82%	81%	85% ▲	73%	72%	76% ▲	61%	66%
YouTube	75% ▼	80%	74%	69%	68% ▲	51%	50% ▲	32%	30%
Instagram	65% ▲	54%	44%	37% ▲	26% ▲	16%	21% ▲	10% ▲	6%
Twitter	29% ▼	41%	38%	33%	30%	29%	24% ▲	16%	13%
Pinterest	18% ▼	24%	26%	22%	19%	24%	19%	16%	15%
LinkedIn	19%	19%	14%	20% ▲	15%	13%	10%	12%	10%
snapchat	37%	38% ▲	25%	8% ▼	11% ▲	5%	3% ▲	1%	2%
reddit	32% ▲	23% ▲	8%	8% ▲	5%	5%	3% ▲	0%	1%
tumblr	5%	7%	10%	3% ▼	6%	4%	<1%	1%	1%

Source: Insights West, "2019 Canadian Social Media Insights," June 2019, accessed January 18, 2020, at https://www.insightswest.com/wp-content/uploads/2019/06/Rep_IW_CDNSocialMediaInsights_June2019.pdf, p. 9.

42 hours per week.[31] This is at least partially due to online streaming of content. "Cord cutters" are people who decide to cancel TV cable or satellite and focus on online viewing. A recent study by the Convergence Consulting Group estimated that approximately 200,000 Canadians cancel their traditional TV service annually, and this number has been growing by about 80 percent each year.[32]

When it comes to online content, Canadians spend the majority of their time on television programming, news, music, and games.[33] Canadian Netflix subscriptions have now surpassed 5 million.[34] The video-streaming market has expanded to meet consumer demand: Bell has launched Crave TV; Apple TV is available; and many Canadians illegally access the Netflix U.S. content by using a VPN (virtual private network) blocker. The ability of streaming services to provide entire seasons for viewing on-demand is promoting a new form of viewing, **binge viewing** (popular among the 18- to 34-year-old demographic). This is where consumers watch episodes of complete or partial seasons over a few days. **Social TV** is an industry term that refers to viewers watching live TV while adding comments on social networks. Social conversations about television are increasing with Canadians, with the majority using Facebook.[35]

Canada study confirmed that two-thirds of Canadians are making an effort to buy local Canadian products.[39] There has been steady growth in the demand for products to meet specific dietary requirements, such as gluten-free, lactose-free, and sugar-free (diabetic) foods. This market is expected to be worth $645 million by 2020.[40] Thousands of products have been launched in the "food intolerance" segment. Companies such as Glutino focus only on gluten-free products, but even private brands, such as the Compliments label from Sobey's, carry a wide range of fresh and processed gluten-free options.

Gluten-free foods have become mainstream.
Used with permission of Sobeys Capital Incorporated

Ethnic foods will continue to be popular with Canadians and in fact have become mainstream. Most supermarket chains have ethnic food aisles with Asian, South American, European, and Caribbean products. When it comes to ethnic foods, consumers in Canada are exposed to a wide variety of international meals from friends, families, restaurants, and multicultural communities. This variety trickles down to the foods people enjoy and wish to purchase. Marketers note these trends and develop products geared to evolving palates. Examples are Patak's, which markets a full line of Indian sauces in mainstream supermarkets, and Club House, with its blends of spices and seasonings that include Thai, Greek, Cajun, and Indian Masala varieties.

Food Consumption Canadians are increasingly concerned with what they eat. The rise in chronic diseases in Canada has focused attention on the need for healthier food choices. As a result, there has been increased pressure put on food suppliers, the industry, and the government to ensure transparent labelling. Consumers want to have clarity around the definitions of food claims, such as "low-fat" and "fat-free," and they want to be aware of the health implications of the food they are purchasing.[36] Even Kraft Dinner has eliminated artificial preservatives and colours.[37]

Consumers are switching from processed fruits and vegetables to fresh products. This trend has caused a shift in the frozen food segment, with marketers focusing on the freshness and nutrient value of their frozen products.[38] In an effort to eat healthier and fresher food, Canadians are also buying local. A Business Development Bank of

Consumers are demanding more prepared food and ready-to-eat meals. But they are not looking for frozen dinners or fast-food takeout; they want a variety of fresh and delicious meals. This trend is referred to as home meal replacement (HMR), and it is currently estimated to be a $2.4 billion business in Canada. Consumers look to grocery stores for a broad selection of healthier HMR options. Chains such as Loblaw have added hundreds of new, fresh dishes across its locations in Canada. The HMR segment is now the fastest-growing grocery segment, with customers choosing the convenient fresh meal options over fast-food restaurants.[41] We also see a recent influx of gourmet meal delivery services that deliver fresh ingredients and recipes to your door for you to cut, chop, and cook. These services can provide very specialized vegan, gluten-free, or otherwise customized meals, decreasing shopping time, while providing the healthy and fresh options that consumers want. Easy, fresh, convenient, and customized—that is what Canadians want!

Attitude and Roles of Men and Women

One of the most notable cultural changes has been in the attitudes and roles of men and women in the marketplace. Some companies are moving away from traditional gender norms to avoid gender stereotypes. Disney has removed gender labels from its Halloween costumes. Fashion leader Zara introduced a line of ungendered clothing which includes sweatshirts, T-shirts, trousers, and shoes, and Calvin Klein introduced fragrance CK2 for women and men. Gender-neutral advertising is also becoming more common. Jaden Smith recently modelled Louis Vuitton's new women's line with three female models, and one of Diesel's advertising campaigns uses the tagline, "This ad is gender neutral."[42]

With a large aging population, there is an ever-increasing consumer interest in maintaining and improving health. This interest includes healthy eating and exercise, as well as living an holistic lifestyle. This trend is particularly influential for baby boomers. Statistics Canada estimates that by 2036, 25 percent of Canadians

Fitbit monitors activity, eating, and sleep patterns.
©Kelvin Wong/Shutterstock

will be over 65, and so this trend is expected to continue for many years to come.[43]

Companies are responding to this shift in the socio-cultural environment by modifying their products to make them healthier and by creating new products and services that address concerns related to health, nutrition, obesity, and associated medical conditions. This interest in healthy living extends into a variety of sectors, such as technology, food, pharmaceuticals, clothing, and travel. These sectors are developing products and applications that address these trends. One very successful example is the Fitbit, a wristband activity tracker that monitors your movements, sleeping patterns, and heart rate. The Fitbit app for your smartphone or tablet tracks your data on a dashboard, and its connectivity allows users to challenge friends to fitness competitions and to track performance. Apple offers 43,000 health care apps, with thousands also available for Android devices, resulting in a dilemma for doctors who are asked by patients to recommend apps to improve health.[44] Several companies, including Akira, Equinoxe, and Ask the Doctor, have launched virtual health care apps that allow you to consult with a Canadian doctor using mobile or Internet technology. For travellers, the opportunities for health and medical tourism are growing. Tourism can range from spas to health-focused cruises to "medical tourism." Medical tourism refers to Canadians travelling abroad for medical treatment.[45] More than 52,000 Canadians travel out of the country annually to avoid long wait times for medical care and to have access to treatments not readily available in Canada.[46]

> *There is an ever-increasing consumer interest in maintaining and improving health.*

One of the most significant changes stemming from the socio-cultural interest in health, fitness, and nutrition is the Canadian Children's Food and Beverage Advertising Initiative (CAI). Introduced in 2007, this

Diesel is making changes to appeal to women as well as men.
Source: Diesel

directive was voluntarily created by some of Canada's largest food and beverage companies to restrict children's advertising messages to healthy choices. Today, CAI consists of 17 members that promote healthier dietary choices for children under 12 years of age. The initiative is monitored by Advertising Standards Canada. Monitoring includes traditional TV, radio, Internet, and print advertising, as well as word-of-mouth promotions, company websites or microsites, and ads placed in elementary schools. Campbell Company, Danone, General Mills, Kellogg, McDonald's, Parmalat, and Post all focus on more nutritious choices in child-directed ads, while Coca-Cola, Kraft, Ferrero, Hershey, Nestlé, Mars, Mondelez, PepsiCo, Unilever, and Weston Bakeries have committed to not advertising their products to children under 12.[47]

Ethical Consumption Canadians show a keen interest in being less wasteful by making choices that do not negatively impact the environment and by supporting businesses that adhere to ethical business practices. Canadians are among the most likely to recycle, more likely to buy used or preowned goods, and more likely to use their own bags in a store than consumers in other countries.[48] Green consumers are those buyers who consider the environmental impact of every purchase they make. However, with a variety of environmental certifications, eco-labelling options and numerous products making green claims, Canadians are confused and skeptical at the point of purchase. Retailers have adopted "green" aisles in their stores to highlight their eco-friendly products and to capture green customers in a focused shopping environment.[49]

In order to avoid the green product confusion that currently exists, the industry is being advised to collaborate and standardize the claims being made. For companies without their own green certification program, there are several independent bodies that have created standards for green, environmental, and ethically

The Fairtrade Canada logo help consumers identify green /environmental/ethical products.

©Fairtrade Canada. This Mark appears on products which have been independently audited and adhere to international standards of Fairtrade.

produced claims. Once a product has been reviewed and meets the required standards, it can bear the logo of the certifying organization.[50]

As more information is accessible regarding a company's business practices, Canadians are willing to make decisions and support companies that adopt responsible and ethical practices. Sixty percent of Canadians consider themselves "ethical consumers," while 75 percent say they will pay more for products that are ethically produced.[51] Considering the amount of information that is readily available to consumers through social media and other sources, companies need to be fully transparent and aware of their ethical practices. Canadian companies such as Canadian Tire have put a framework in place to ensure a positive impact on the environment throughout their business operations.[52]

Economic Forces

LO 4 The **economy** is another area in an environmental scan that marketers need to consider. The ability of a consumer to purchase a product is what interests marketers, and with the global economy being interconnected, this area has become even more difficult for businesses to forecast. When the economy experiences a significant downward turn, consumer confidence wanes, resulting in delayed or cancelled purchases of unnecessary or higher-priced items. An economic downturn can also result in lower household income, again negatively impacting consumers' ability and desire to purchase. If people become unemployed, for example, they will likely defer the purchase of a new car and concentrate purchases on life's necessities. Conversely, an upswing in the economy can result in greater confidence and an increase in spending power.

Canadian consumer confidence is starting to stabilize. However, Canadians are cautious in their spending, focusing on paying down debt. Canadians still like to splurge when they have a few extra dollars, resulting in an increase in spending on dining out, clothing, and home and garden.[53]

economy
The collective income, expenditures, and resources that affect the cost of running a business or a household.

macroeconomic forces

The state of a country's economy as a whole as indicated by its growth rates, inflation rates, unemployment rates, and consumer confidence indexes.

gross domestic product (GDP)

The total dollar value of all goods and services produced in a country within a specified time period.

inflation

When the cost to produce and buy products and services gets higher as prices rise.

recession

A time of slow economic activity with two consecutive periods of negative growth.

interest rates

The amount charged as a fee for borrowing money, normally expressed as a percentage per year.

unemployment rate

Measures the share of the labour force that is not working.

microeconomic forces

The supply and demand of goods and services and how this is impacted by individual, household, and company decisions to purchase.

gross income

Total amount of money made in one year by a person, household, or family unit, including taxes.

Marketers need to recognize how the economy affects the purchase behaviour of their target markets. Some products, such as camping gear, thrive in a poor economy, with consumers wanting to take less-expensive and close-to-home vacations. While new automobile sales will decline in a poor economy, services such as automobile repair thrive.[54]

The economy consists of macroeconomic forces and microeconomic forces. **Macroeconomic forces** refer to the state of a country's economy as a whole. Indicators of strength and weakness should be on marketers' radar screens so that they can react quickly to changes that affect their consumers. A country's key economic indicators are its economic growth rate (usually measured by the change in gross domestic product), its inflation rate, and its unemployment rate. Consumer confidence is also an important indicator of the economy's health, showing how people feel about their long-term economic prospects.

A country's **gross domestic product (GDP)** is the total dollar value of all goods and services produced in a country within a specified time period. GDP is normally a fairly accurate indicator of the economic health of a country.[55]

Another key economic indicator is **inflation**, a period when the cost to produce and buy products and services gets higher as prices rise. From a marketing standpoint, if prices rise faster than consumer income, consumer purchasing power decreases.

A **recession** is a time of slow economic activity with two consecutive periods of negative growth. During recessions, production levels decline, unemployment levels rise, and many consumers have less money to spend. At these times, consumers tend to focus their spending on life's necessities.

Interest rates can affect consumer spending. If interest rates are high, people may lean toward saving money and earning higher interest. Conversely, when interest rates are low, people may be more inclined to spend and borrow money.[56]

Unemployment rate measures the share of the labour force that is unemployed. When unemployment is high, spending can decline due to the uncertainty of future income.

A country's business cycle fluctuates between different levels of growth depending on the state of the economy, international economic factors, and global pressures. Marketers keep apprised of a country's key economic indicators—economic growth rate, inflation rate, and unemployment rate—to understand whether to expect a downturn or upswing in the economy. Based upon the projected economic climate, marketers may adjust marketing programs to maximize business results.

Microeconomic forces directly refer to the supply and demand of goods and services and how this is impacted by individual, household, and company decisions to purchase. A marketer needs to be alerted as to how these areas affect consumer buying power. Here are some terms you need to know (see Figure 2–4):

- **Gross income:** This is the total amount of money made in one year by a person, household, or family unit, including taxes.
- **Disposable income:** This is the after-tax income that consumers have left for spending and savings. Typical ongoing purchases are for rent, clothing, and transportation. If taxes rise at a faster rate than income, consumers have less disposable income with which to pay the bills.
- **Discretionary income:** This is the after-tax income a consumer has left after paying for necessities such as food, shelter, and clothing. This income is used for discretionary purchases that are not deemed a necessity. Examples include going to a movie, eating at a restaurant, or going on vacation.

Technological Forces

LO 5 Changes in how consumers use technology must be understood by marketers. Marketers need to know not only what new inventions are coming on the scene but also how consumers are integrating technology into their lives.

Technological forces refer to inventions or innovations that stem from scientific or engineering research. Each new wave of technology can replace existing products, and companies need to be aware of technological changes to ensure that products do not become obsolete.

Technological change is the result of research, so it is difficult to predict. Some of the most dramatic technological changes occurring now, however, include the following:

- Artificial intelligence capabilities will impact many marketing functions, including sales, retailing, and customer service.

Figure 2–4
Three levels of consumer income

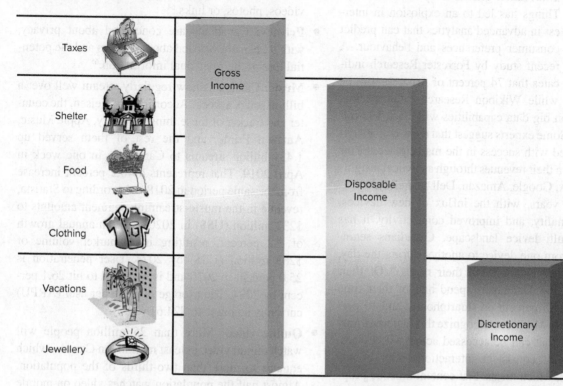

Taxes
Shelter
Food
Clothing
Vacations
Jewellery

Gross Income

Disposable Income

Discretionary Income

- Automation will become prevalent in products ranging from autonomous cars, to delivery drones, to robots in the home and office.
- The Internet of Things (IoT) will become a reality as digital assistants such as Amazon's Alexa allow easy connectivity to all electronic devices.
- Wearable technology will take many new forms, from biometric monitors related to fitness and well-being, to visual displays for information and training, to exoskeletons to enhance personal mobility.

Some of these trends in technology are already being realized in today's marketplace. IBM, for example, has partnered with **Salesforce.com** to use artificial intelligence to enhance Salesforce's customer service software. Amazon recently began delivery by automated drone in the United Kingdom. LG recently introduced a "connected" refrigerator that can track food expiration dates and respond to voice commands. Other technologies, such as IBM's Watson, Slack's new software, and Apple Pay, are likely to replace or become substitutes for existing products and services such as customer service representatives, e-mail, and plastic credit cards and money.[57]

Today, technologies have advanced to allow computer chips to be placed in almost anything and to be connected to a network almost anywhere. This network of products embedded with connectivity-enabled electronics has come to be known

disposable income
Balance of income left after paying taxes; income that is used for spending and savings.

discretionary income
Money that consumers have left after paying taxes and buying necessities.

technological forces
Inventions from science or engineering research.

Marketers are challenged to keep up with technological advances.

©manaemedia/iStock Editorial/Getty Images Plus

Internet of Things (IoT)
The network of products embedded with connectivity-enabled electronics.

as the **Internet of Things (IoT)**. The information generated by the Internet of Things has led to an explosion in interest in advanced analytics that can predict consumer preferences and behaviour. A recent study by Forrester Research indicates that 74 percent of firms want to be "data-driven," while Wikibon Research estimates that expenditures on big data capabilities will reach $92 billion by 2026. Some experts suggest that the use of analytics is associated with success in the marketplace. Firms that have grown their revenues through analytical insights include Netflix, Google, Amazon, Dell, and eBay.[58]

In recent years, with the influx of new devices, better functionality, and improved connectivity, it has become a multi-device landscape. Canadians seamlessly move from one device to another during the day, based upon their location and their needs.[59] Of their time spent online, Canadians spend half of their time on computers, 35 percent on smartphones, and 15 percent on tablets.[60] Marketers recognize this and must now create content that can be accessed across all devices. Consumers want consistent interactions with brands across devices, which means that content must be properly adapted and maximized for each device. Equally important is the need to understand online consumer behaviour.[61]

> *Marketers need to know how consumers are integrating technology into their lives.*

Let's look at some of the latest data on Canadians' use of technology that marketers need to note:

- **Internet access:** Internet usage is high in Canada, with 96 percent of Canadian households having Internet access.[62]
- **E-commerce:** Online spending reached $65 billion in 2019 and is expected to grow to $108 billion in 2023. Eighty percent of Canadians shopped online in 2019. Forty percent of Canadians plan to buy more domestically in the coming year. Sixty percent of online purchases in Canada are made by 18 percent of online shoppers.[63]
- **Cloud-based services:** "The cloud" simply refers to web services and storage that reside on the Internet, rather than on a local computer. Examples of cloud-based services are Google Apps (used for mail, documents, messaging), Blogger for blog creation, Dropbox for document storage, Google Analytics

or Salesforce.com for online measurement, and Facebook, YouTube, Instagram, and Twitter to share videos, photos, or links.[64]

- **Privacy:** Canadians are concerned about privacy, with 92 percent worried about hackers and the potential loss of their personal information.[65]
- **Music:** Canadians now regularly stream well over a billion songs a week. According to Nielsen, the counter and tracker of these things, Spotify, Apple Music, Amazon Prime, and the rest of them served up 1.431 billion streams to Canadians in one week in April 2019. That represents a 40.2 percent increase from the same period in 2018.[66] According to Statista, revenue in the music-streaming segment amounts to $232 million (US$) in 2020, with an annual growth of 3.2 percent, resulting in a market volume of $263 million (US$) by 2024. User penetration is 25.0 percent in 2020 and is expected to hit 26.1 percent by 2024. The average revenue per user (ARPU) currently amounts to $24.61 (US$).[67]
- **Online video:** More than 25 million people will watch digital video at least monthly in Canada, which equates to more than two-thirds of the population. Almost half the population watches video on mobile devices, and there were 16.5 million smartphone video viewers in Canada in 2019. YouTube is the leading digital video platform in Canada, but over-the-top (OTT) services are becoming popular destinations, as well. Netflix accounts for the bulk of OTT viewing, but other services like Amazon Prime Video and homegrown services like Crave have gained significant subscribers. TV shows and movies are the primary types of content for video, but sports is also a key category. Sportsnet Now, TSN Direct, and international streamer DAZN have expanded their programming to meet a growing appetite for streaming live sports.[68]
- **Computers:** Despite the increased usage of new devices (smartphones and tablets), computers, including desktops and laptops, still account for 87 percent of Internet traffic.[69]
- **Smartphones:** Ownership of smartphones is rapidly increasing in Canada, where smartphone penetration has reached 90 percent and continues to climb. Smartphones are used for everything on the go, with usage including taking photos, messaging, social networking, watching videos, listening to music, conducting searches, using apps, and playing games.[70]
- **Mobile payments:** Canada is among a top tier of countries where proximity mobile payments have become a common method of transacting in retail stores. Built on a solid installed base of contactless

terminals nationwide, the ability to tap and pay with a card or phone has become the norm. There will be 6.8 million mobile payment users in Canada by the end of 2019, or 21.0 percent of the population. That's up 13.1 percent from last year, the culmination of a near fivefold increase since 2014.[71]

The last two decades have seen disruptive technological change that is altering our lives. The way we shop, communicate, pay, and entertain ourselves has evolved dramatically.

marketing TIP

"Ubiquitous and always-connected smart devices have rendered old-fashioned paper-based mail, and Canada Post's exclusive privilege to deliver it, far less meaningful."

– Deepak Chopra, president and CEO, Canada Post

Competitive Forces

LO 6 Another important element in an environmental scan is competition. This puts a focus on **competitive forces** that consumers can examine to satisfy a need. There are various types of competition, and each company must consider its present and potential competitors when designing its marketing strategy. Determining a product's main competitors can be done in a number of ways. Large organizations often purchase research data from companies such as the Nielsen Company or comScore to obtain competitive market share data and to identify general industry trends and market growth patterns. Smaller companies may prefer to reduce their expenditures in this area, instead relying on competitive information obtained from salespeople, suppliers, customers, and retailers.

One of a marketer's primary concerns is to monitor the competitive activity of products that compete head-to-head with its brands. Any changes made by a major competitor in areas of product, price, place, and promotion are routinely noted, and detailed analyses are conducted to determine the impact on business results. These head-to-head competitors are called **direct competitors** and refer to very similar products sold in the same category. Examples are Coke versus Pepsi in the cola category and Nike versus Adidas in the running shoe category.

Marketers also understand that consumers do not function in a vacuum and often make choices between products that do not directly compete in the same category. Marketers therefore also look (a little less intently) at **indirect competitors**, those products that compete for the same buying dollar but in a slightly different category. For example, while Pepsi may focus on Coke, they should not ignore Canada Dry ginger ale, A&W root beer, or San Pellegrino water because these indirect competitors also compete for consumers wanting to purchase carbonated beverages.

Marketers need to be intimately familiar with competitive products and try to anticipate competitive moves in the marketplace. When analyzing the competitive environment, a marketer needs to review all major competitors, present and future. More attention is given to those that can directly impact a marketer's business. Apart from understanding direct and indirect competitors, marketers need to have a clear understanding of the competitive nature of the industry in which they function and factor this into an environmental scan. If, for example, there

competitive forces
Alternative products that can satisfy a specific market's needs.

direct competitors
Similar products sold in the same category.

indirect competitors
Products competing for the same buying dollar in a slightly different but related category.

Direct and indirect competitors must be considered in the soft drink category.

©Jill Braaten/McGraw-Hill Education

Figure 2–5
Types of competition

Monopoly
One firm
Example: regional
electricity companies

Oligopoly
Few firms
Example: airlines

**Monopolistic
Competition**
Many Firms,
Similar Products
Example: Running Shoes

**Perfect
Competition**
Many firms,
identical products
Example: apple farmers

monopoly

When only one
company sells in a
particular market.

oligopoly

Type of competition
that occurs when a
few companies control
a market.

**monopolistic
competition**

Type of competition
where a large number
of sellers compete
with each other, offer-
ing customers similar
or substitute products.

are very few competitors, a marketer will consider changes among competitors to be significant, while in a situation where numerous competitors and undifferentiated products exist, changes may be viewed differently. Figure 2–5 shows the four basic types of competition as identified by economists.

At one end of the competition spectrum is a **monopoly**. A monopoly exists when there is only one company selling in the market. Monopolies are legal in Canada but they are carefully monitored by the Competition Bureau to ensure that consumers are not charged excessive prices. Examples of monopolies in Canada are regional electricity companies.

The second point in the continuum is an **oligopoly**, which occurs when a few companies control a market. In Canada, this situation exists with network providers that control the telecommunications industry. Companies such as Bell, Telus, and Rogers dominate the market. Because there is limited competition, it is thought that prices are usually higher because companies want to protect their profits. Marketers who function in an oligopoly need to be acutely aware of competitive moves and particularly changes in price.

The third type of competition is **monopolistic competition**. This is when a large number of sellers compete with each other, offering customers similar or substitute

products. Marketers need to know that in this instance, branding plays an important role, as does product differentiation and added-value activities to draw consumers to the product. Being in touch with consumer needs

What type of competition typifies the hotel industry—monopoly, oligopoly, monopolistic competition, or perfect competition?

©Digital Vision/Alamy Stock Photo

and adjusting the marketing mix to meet those needs is crucial for long-term survival. The market for running shoes is a good example. This market is dominated by major brands such as Nike, Adidas, New Balance, and Reebok, as well as many less-popular brands. The result is that when it comes to buying running shoes, consumers are presented with a wide array of options. Marketers in this category need to keep the competitive nature of this market top-of-mind when marketing products.

The fourth type of competition is **perfect competition**, when there are many sellers with nearly identical products and little differentiation. Companies that deal in commodities—that is, products such as grains, vegetables, or rice—often function in an environment where perfect competition exists. In this instance, marketers need to know that pricing plays a key role in securing business, and that the focus will be on cost reduction in every element of the business.

ask YOURSELF

1. *What is the difference between a consumer's disposable and discretionary income?*

2. *What type of competition is found in the gasoline industry?*

3. *What are the indirect competitors to Monster energy drinks?*

Regulatory Forces

The final area involved in an environmental scan relates to **regulations**, which are restrictions placed on marketing practices by government and industry associations. These regulations are put in place to protect consumers from unscrupulous business practices, to set acceptable standards of practice, and to encourage fair competition. Marketers need to clearly understand all the legal and ethical guidelines that affect their business practices and to retain legal guidance as needed to ensure that their practices are legal. Ethical business practices should also be followed to avoid consumer backlash and negative publicity.

Below we review the key regulatory groups and regulations that affect marketing practices in Canada. It is worth noting that regulations are updated and changed by these groups as needed to meet changing business practices. Marketers are strongly advised to check these associations regularly for updates and changes, and to consult with a marketing lawyer to ensure practices are both legal and ethical.

The key groups that regulate marketing practices in Canada are the Competition Bureau, Advertising Standards Canada (Ad Standards), the Canadian Radio-television and Telecommunications Commission (CRTC), the Canadian Marketing Association (CMA), and the Office of the Privacy Commissioner of Canada (OPC). In addition to these general regulatory bodies, the Canadian Wireless Telecommunications Association (CWTA) and the Mobile Marketing Association (MMA) provide specific guidance on mobile marketing practices, and the Digital Advertising Alliance of Canada (DAAC) oversees online behavioural advertising. Marketers also need to review other regulatory bodies and associations specific to their industry, as well as those that have jurisdiction in other countries, provinces, or states where they conduct business.

Competition The Competition Bureau is an independent law-enforcement agency tasked to ensure that the market in Canada is competitive and innovative. In this manner, people in Canada can benefit from fair prices, product choice, high-quality services, and a reduction in fraudulent business practices. It is responsible for the administration and enforcement of the *Competition Act,* the *Consumer Packaging and Labelling Act,* the *Textile Labelling Act,* and the *Precious Metals Marking Act,* just to name a few areas of responsibility.

The Canadian Anti-Fraud Centre (CAFC) is managed jointly by the RCMP, the Ontario Provincial Police (OPP), and the Competition Bureau to reduce marketing fraud. The CAFC maintains a website, **www.antifraudcentre.ca**, with up-to-date data on fraudulent marketing schemes and an area for consumers to report scams. These scams use various communication tools

perfect competition
Type of competition where there are many sellers with nearly identical products and little differentiation.

regulations
Restrictions placed on marketing practices by government and industry associations.

The Competition Bureau can levy hefty fines.
Competition Bureau Canada

The Little Black Book of Scams

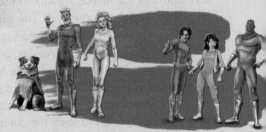

Fraud Fighters - The Little Book of Scams
Competition Bureau Canada

Scams are a big business. They can come to you in many different ways—mail, online, or over the phone. It is estimated that in 2019, Canadians lost $100 million to scams. As technology infiltrates our lives, the ease of carrying out a scam also increases. The Competition Bureau of Canada is taking this seriously and is focused on ensuring Canadians are aware of these dangers. "The Little Black Book of Scams" was first published in 2012, and with the continual influx of new types of scams, the book is available online and is updated regularly. The latest update was in 2018 and included versions in eight different languages as well as new and improved scams. What type of cons should Canadians be aware of? Here are just a few:

Internet scams most commonly take the form of phishing e-mails. Have you ever received an e-mail from your bank asking you to click on a link to its website and re-enter your personal information? This is phishing! Phishers may send millions of copies of the same e-mail, and all they need is for a few to respond to make it worth their efforts.

Dating and romance scams netted almost $22.5 million from Canadians in one year. Online dating has become the norm for many singles. It is estimated that at least 20 percent of online dating profiles are fake. The scam begins when a person meets someone wonderful online, and after ongoing communication, they ask for money and then disappear.

Identity theft cost Canadians $21.2 million in one year (2018). It happens when a fraudster uses online methods (phishing or spyware) or offline methods (stealing mail or going through trash) to find enough information about you to steal your identity and turn your life upside down. Fraudsters can make purchases, empty bank accounts, get credit cards in your name, and even get a passport.

Tax scams are a growing problem and cost Canadians over $5 million a year. Many immigrants and seniors are targeted by scammers pretending to be the Canada Revenue Agency. People new to Canada or the elderly are threatened with jail or fines if they don't pay their "taxes." The scammers ask for personal information that they can then use for identity theft or for payment by iTunes gift cards or untraceable money transfers.

Follow these tips to protect yourself:

- Protect your personal details and only give out personal information to people you know and trust.
- Don't send money to anyone that you don't know, and never pay fees to claim prizes or obtain a job.
- Never reply to spam e-mails or open attachments from any suspicious e-mails.
- Install security software on your computer.
- If you think you have been the victim of a scam, act immediately to limit your damages and report it to the appropriate authority.

"The Little Black Book of Scams" can be downloaded from the Competition Bureau website at **www.competitionbureau.gc.ca.** ●

Questions

1. Do you think the number of scams and cons will continue to rise in Canada? Why or why not?

2. Many consumers are unaware of the frequency of scamming in Canada. How can social media help increase awareness of these practices?

---

such as mail, e-mail, the Internet, and the telephone to take advantage of unsuspecting people. The Competition Bureau regularly updates its publication of "The Little Black Book of Scams," which highlights the wide range of scams that exist (see the Focus on Ethics box, "The Little Black Book of Scams").[72]

The Competition Bureau also reviews mergers and acquisitions and prohibits deceptive business practices that include, among others, price fixing among competitors, predatory pricing by large competitors to run small companies out of business, and bid rigging among competitors to inflate prices on government contracts. Prohibited pricing practices to lure consumers include bait-and-switch advertising, fraudulent advertising claims, and misleading pricing practices such as double ticketing. Bait-and-switch advertising refers to the practice of advertising a low-priced product (bait) to lure consumers into a store and then, because the product is not made available in large quantities, selling these consumers higher-priced products (switch). In 2014, the *Competition Act* was amended to include new areas that relate to Canada's anti-spam legislation making it an offence to include false or misleading information in electronic messages.

Failure to abide by Competition Bureau rules can result in fines and jail time. False and/or misleading representations to sell products can result in orders by the Competition Bureau for companies to publish corrective notices, stop the prohibited practice, pay administrative costs, and pay restitution to purchasers. In addition, the Competition Bureau has the legal clout to levy hefty fines on individuals and/or companies. To find out more about the Competition Bureau, and to see a complete list of its regulations and recent rulings, visit its website at **www.competitionbureau.gc.ca**.

Advertising Advertising Standards Canada (Ad Standards) is a self-regulatory non-profit body supported by advertising, media, and marketing companies with the purpose of setting and regulating standards of professional practice in the advertising industry. The industry has agreed to abide by its leadership, code, process, and rulings. Ad Standards sets and regulates advertising guidelines, monitored through a consumer complaint process. A single complaint will trigger a review of advertising placed in the Canadian media, with the eventual withdrawal of the ad if changes are required and not made. Ad Standards also provides advice and pre-clearance services for advertisers.

Ad Standard's jurisdiction does not carry over into the legal arena. It does not levy fines or engage in legal proceedings. Instead, it relies on industry compliance to ensure that ads contravening its guidelines, the Canadian Code of Advertising Standards (or the Code), cease to air. Deceptive and fraudulent advertising, although covered under the Code, is also scrutinized by the Competition Bureau, which can levy fines and take legal action if necessary.

The Code has a comprehensive set of guidelines designed to encourage truthful, fair, and accurate marketing communications. It covers 14 areas, as shown in Figure 2–6, that address issues such as comparative advertising, accuracy, safety, decency, and advertising to children. These guidelines are updated as required with a detailed list of guidelines available at **www .adstandards.ca**.[73]

Do Not Call List The Canadian Radio-television and Telecommunications Commission (CRTC) is another government agency that sets guidelines and enforces a clear set of regulations on Canadian businesses. The areas most relevant to marketing are the *Broadcasting Act*, the *Telecommunications Act*, the Wireless Code, the Do Not Call List, and particular areas of Canada's anti-spam policy.

The *Broadcasting Act* and the *Telecommunications Act* set guidelines for broadcast standards, and in 2013, the CRTC created the Wireless Code, a mandatory code of conduct for all wireless service providers.

Navigate to adstandards.ca to review guidelines and reports on advertising in Canada.

Advertising Standards

Figure 2–6
Advertising Standards Canada—The Code

Advertising Standards Canada (Ad Standards) encourages truth in advertising through a code that provides guidelines under these areas:

- Accuracy and clarity
- Disguised advertising techniques
- Price claims
- Bait and switch
- Guarantees
- Comparative advertising
- Testimonials
- Professional or scientific claims
- Imitation
- Safety
- Superstitions and fears
- Advertising to children
- Advertising to minors
- Unacceptable depictions and portrayals

Details can be found on the Ad Standards website at www.adstandards.ca.

Reprinted with permission from Advertising Standards Canada.

The CRTC adjudicates on the cross-media ownership of media companies to ensure that a single media organization or conglomerate does not overpower local markets. It also approves broadcast licences for TV and radio stations and sets guidelines on the broadcast of Canadian content. In addition, the CRTC sets limits on the number of minutes of advertising permitted hourly on TV. While it does not directly regulate the content of ads, primarily an Ad Standards concern, it does oversee the advertising of alcohol beverages and works with Ad Standards on issues related to advertising to children.

The CRTC also has jurisdiction over the national **Do Not Call List (DNCL)**. The DNCL gives consumers the ability to elect to not receive telemarketing calls on cellphones and landline phones by registering their phone numbers. Registration keeps these numbers in the DNCL for five years, after which consumers must re-register. Telemarketers are required by law to subscribe to the DNCL and to not call the numbers in its database.

There are five exemptions to the DNCL: registered charities, newspaper subscriptions, political parties/candidates, market research companies, and companies where business has been conducted in the last 18 months. Failure to comply with the DNCL can result in fines of up to $1,500 for an individual and up to $15,000 for a corporation for each violation. A major challenge for the CRTC is the onslaught of call centres located outside of Canada. The resolution of many of these cases required the cooperation of international regulators.[74] You can read more about the CRTC at www.crtc.gc.ca.

Marketing The Canadian Marketing Association (CMA) guides the practices of the marketing industry through its Code of Ethics and Standards of Practice. It is mandatory for all members to abide by these policies, which are clearly outlined on the CMA website at www.the-cma.org. This website provides marketers with numerous practical guides on topics such as native advertising, anti-spam legislation, digital marketing, privacy compliance, telemarketing, promotional contests, fundraising, marketing lists and data, and marketing to children and teenagers.[75]

> *The Canadian Marketing Association (CMA) guides the practices of the marketing industry.*

Mobile The Canadian Wireless Telecommunications Association (CWTA) provides resources on the wireless industry in Canada. It deals with the government on issues related to cellular phones, personal communication devices, text messaging, and wireless and mobile satellite carriers, and represents companies working in that space. Its website provides useful statistics on the industry as well as regulations that control the sector.[76] The CWTA introduced common short code (CSC) guidelines to regulate the industry's use of text messaging. This includes outlining protocols to ensure that all messaging is permission-based, allowing customers to immediately opt-out by using the keyword STOP. To read more about mobile marketing regulations, go to Chapter 13. Updates on CSC regulations can be found at www.cwta.ca and www.txt.ca.[77]

The Mobile Marketing Association (MMA) is a global association that sets standards and guidelines, and shares best practices on mobile marketing. The MMA has over 800 members and is represented in nearly 50 countries. It has a resource centre for marketers; publishes a code of conduct, a best practices guide, and privacy policy templates; and sets standards for mobile messaging, mobile advertising, and mobile promotions. You can read more about the MMA at www.mmaglobal.com.[78]

Do Not Call List (DNCL)

Gives customers the ability to elect to not receive telemarketing calls on cellphones and landline phones by registering the numbers of their communication devices.

Privacy The collection of personal data by private sector companies is governed by the *Personal Information Protection and Electronic Documents Act* (PIPEDA). Personal information includes age, name, social status, ID numbers, income, ethnicity, opinions, comments, evaluations, purchase habits and disputes, credit records, loans, medical information, employee files, and disciplinary actions. It does not include employee information such as name, title, address and telephone number. These acts are periodically updated, and guidelines and reports can be found on the Office of the Privacy Commissioner of Canada's website at **www.priv.gc.ca**.

Federal legislation for the private sector falls under PIPEDA and is reviewed by the government every five years to ensure that it remains current and actionable in the light of new technologies. Many provinces and territories have their own privacy legislation similar to PIPEDA and have specific requirements pertaining to health care as well as the banking and credit sectors.[79]

PIPEDA requires organizations to obtain consent from individuals for the collection, use, and disclosure of information, including video surveillance. It also stipulates that information must be safely stored and security breaches must be communicated to consumers.

PIPEDA and the Canadian Marketing Association require businesses to regularly review their privacy policies, to appoint a privacy policy officer, and to collect only necessary information. In the online environment, privacy policies must be clearly posted on all websites and detail the type of personal information that is collected, how it is collected, how it is used and protected, whether information is disclosed to outside parties, and whether the company complies with Canadian privacy legislation and anti-spam laws.

Individuals can table complaints on privacy issues directly to an organization's privacy officer as well as to the Office of the Privacy Commissioner of Canada. If the Office of the Privacy Commissioner of Canada finds an individual or organization knowingly contravened PIPEDA, this can be processed through the courts and result in penalties of up to $100,000. Due to the rapid changes in digital marketing practices, PIPEDA is under constant pressure to update its legislation, and therefore, marketers are strongly advised to be well-versed in the latest privacy regulations and fines, and to check the website of the Office of the Privacy Commissioner of Canada at **www.priv.gc.ca**, and the Canadian Marketing Association website at **www.the-cma.org**, for updates and guidelines. The most recent updates prohibit the use of automated computer programs in the unauthorized collection of e-mail addresses to comply with Canada's anti-spam policy. PIPEDA is constantly under pressure to include amendments that relate to evolving digital marketing practices.[80]

Spam Canada's anti-spam legislation (CASL) came into effect in July 2014 to protect consumers and businesses from unwanted commercial electronic messages (CEMs), including messages to e-mail addresses, social networking accounts, and text messages sent to a cellphone. In 2015, additional legislation was put in place to protect individuals from the installation of computer programs and mobile apps without their prior consent and knowledge. **Spam** refers to the dissemination of unsolicited electronic messages to recipients.

CASL is enforced by the CRTC, the Competition Bureau, and the Office of the Privacy Commissioner of Canada. Contravening CASL can be costly. Administrative monetary penalties for businesses reach as high as $10 million per violation for businesses, with fines of up to $1 million per violation for individuals. An online spam-reporting centre is available at **fightspam.gc.ca** for businesses, organizations, and consumers to file complaints on unsolicited CEMs and those containing false and misleading information.[81]

CASL requires the following conduct with respect to electronic messaging:

- Must have opt-in consent.
- Must include accurate sender information, subject line information, and content.
- Must not be altered and sent to another destination without consent.
- Must include an unsubscribe mechanism.
- Online promotions must not be false or misleading.
- Restrictions on the unauthorized collection of email addresses through automated computer programs.
- Computer software cannot be installed on an electronic device without explicit consent.
- Personal information cannot be collected by unlawfully accessing a computer.

Nonetheless, various exemptions exist, such as those for registered charities that are conducting fundraising, political parties, immediate family members, and legitimate interactions between organizations and its employees. Exemptions also exist for legitimate

Canada's anti-spam legislation is enforced by the CRTC, the Competition Bureau, and the Office of the Privacy Commissioner of Canada.

©Comstock/Jupiterimages

business inquiries, quotes, applications, complaints, warranties, recalls, and safety or security issues. Since this legislation is relatively new and its legal interpretation is still evolving, marketers are strongly advised to become compliant with the anti-spam legislation, to obtain legal advice on their use of CEMs, and to check the CMA website for updates. The CMA advises marketers to obtain expressed opt-in consent from all business relationships so that they are in compliance with the new CASL law.[82]

Online Behavioural Advertising

Online **behavioural advertising (OBA)** refers to the tracking of consumers' online browsing activities in order to deliver online ads that correspond to their browsing interests.[83] OBA works by storing a text file (called a *cookie*) in a computer's web browser to track which websites are visited by the browser. It then predicts interests and serves ads that meet these interests.

The Digital Advertising Alliance of Canada (DAAC) was formed to ensure that consumers were aware of OBA and could opt out of the collection and use of OBA data on their devices. In 2013, the DAAC announced its AdChoices program, a self-regulatory framework that guides online behavioural advertising in Canada, making it consistent with existing privacy laws in Canada and aligned with similar self-regulatory programs in the U.S., Europe, and Australia. AdChoices asks behavioural advertisers to follow a set of OBA principles and use a standardized triangular blue OBA icon next to OBA ads and websites where such data is begin collected. Viewers can click on the icon to learn more and opt out, if they so choose. Advertising Standards Canada monitors program participants for compliance and accepts consumer complaints about OBA as part of the Canadian AdChoices program.[84]

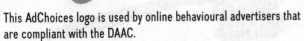

This AdChoices logo is used by online behavioural advertisers that are compliant with the DAAC.

Used with permission of Digital Advertising Alliance of Canada

Steps in an Environmental Scan

LO 7 Environmental scans are conducted routinely by marketers, often with the help of other departments in an organization to ensure that products and marketing approaches stay relevant and resonate with consumers. An environmental scan will often be conducted annually as part of the marketing planning process, but marketers should be monitoring changes and developments in each area on an ongoing basis.

Here is a quick checklist and a step-by-step guide:

Step 1: Collect the facts and identify trends.

- **Gather data and information.**
  The starting point is to gather accurate and relevant information on all areas of an environmental scan (see Figure 2–7).

- **Conduct competitive reviews.**
  Delve deeper into the competition and conduct a rigorous review of the marketplace to determine competitive practices and new approaches in each area of the marketing mix (product, price, place, and promotion). Understand consumer triggers and their connectivity to a brand by putting on your consumer's hat and visiting stores to review competitive products and to speak to sales representatives. Read product reviews and industry research reports.

- **Cluster information into facts and trends.**
  Gather and sort the information you have gathered into facts and trends for each area of the marketing environment scan. Capture this information in a simple table that can be easily understood, such as that shown in Figure 2–8 for Canada Post.

  Note: Some information may fall into more than one area in a marketing environment scan. The information should be repeated as necessary to ensure adequate focus.

Figure 2–7
Information sources for an environmental scan

Factors in an Environmental Scan	Sources of Information
Demographic • Shifts in age, gender, ethnicity, rural or urban populations, family status, home ownership, family life cycle, education, occupation	• Euromonitor reports (www.euromonitor.com) • Statista (www.statista.com) • Statistics Canada (www.statcan.gc.ca)
Socio-cultural • Evolving attitudes, values, shopping habits, usage of technology, cultural norms, product consumption	• Alliance for Audited Media (www.auditedmedia.com) • Blogs and social media • Euromonitor reports (www.euromonitor.com) • Forrester Research (www.forrester.com) • GFK Group (www.gfk.com) • Interactive Advertising Bureau of Canada (iabcanada.com) • Ipsos Canada (www.ipsos.ca) • Leger (www.leger360.com.) • News sources: use Google News (news.google.ca) or newspaper sites, for example, *Globe and Mail* (www.globeandmail.com), *National Post* (www.nationalpost.com), *New York Times* (www.nytimes.com) • Numeris (numeris.ca) • Pew Research Center (www.pewresearch.org) • Solutions Research Group (www.srgnet.com) • *Strategy* magazine (strategyonline.ca) • Statista (www.statista.com)
Economic • Changing discretionary and disposable income levels, economic growth, inflation, unemployment rates	• Bank of Canada (www.bankofcanada.ca) • Euromonitor reports (www.euromonitor.com) • Major banks publish reports on the Canadian economy • News sources: use Google News (news.google.ca) or newspaper sites, for example, *Globe and Mail* (www.globeandmail.com), *National Post* (www.nationalpost.com), *New York Times* (www.nytimes.com) • Organization for Economic Cooperation and Development (OECD) (www.oecd.org) • Statistics Canada (www.statcan.gc.ca) • Statista (www.statista.com)
Technological • Technological inventions and innovations that impact business	• Euromonitor reports (www.euromonitor.com) • GFK Group (www.gfk.com) • Industry Canada (www.ic.gc.ca) • News sources: use Google News (news.google.ca) or newspaper sites, for example, *Globe and Mail* (www.globeandmail.com), *National Post* (www.nationalpost.com), *New York Times* (www.nytimes.com) • Trade magazines
Competitive • Change in the competition's marketing mix—product, price, place, and promotion—as well as changes in the structure of the industry	• Blogs and social media • Competitors' websites • comScore reports (www.comscore.com) • *eMarketer* (www.emarketer.com) • Industry association websites • Industry Canada (www.ic.gc.ca) • Nielsen Canada reports (www.ca.nielsen.com) • News sources: use Google News (news.google.ca) or newspaper sites, for example, *Globe and Mail* (www.globeandmail.com), *National Post* (www.nationalpost.com), *New York Times* (www.nytimes.com) • Product reviews and industry research reports • SEDAR (www.sedar.com) or EDGAR (www.sec.gov/search/search.htm) • *Strategy* magazine (strategyonline.ca) • Statista (www.statista.com) • Trade publications and industry articles • Visit retailers and see what the competition is doing • World Advertising Research Center (WARC) (www.warc.com)

(Continued)

Figure 2–7 (Continued)

Factors in an Environmental Scan	Sources of Information
Regulatory • Evolving federal and provincial legislation and industry association guidelines	• Advertising Standards Canada (www.adstandards.ca) • Canadian Marketing Association (www.the-cma.org) • Canadian Radio-television and Telecommunications Commission (www.crtc.gc.ca) • Competition Bureau (www.competitionbureau.gc.ca) • Industry association websites • Euromonitor reports (www.euromonitor.com) • Government of Canada (www.canada.gc.ca) • Law firms and consultants: Gowlings (www.gowlingwlg.com), Deloitte (www2.deloitte.com) • Office of the Privacy Commissioner (www.priv.gc.ca)

Step 2: Determine the impact that this fact/trend will have on the business.

• **Set business objectives.**
Based upon your analysis and the state of your current business, determine business objectives.

• **Analyze the external trends to determine their impact.**
Determine the impact (positive or negative) that each trend will have on the business.

Step 3: Brainstorm, evaluate, and implement ideas to meet business objectives.

• **Brainstorm.**
Brainstorm ideas that address the facts, trends, and business objectives. All reasonable ideas should be considered at this point as they will be screened down to a few actionable elements in the subsequent step.

• **Evaluate and implement alternatives.**
Evaluate the realistic alternatives against the business objectives and select those that are worthwhile and can be implemented.

For greater clarification, review the marketing environmental scan for Canada Post (Figure 2–8). Canada Post monitors its external environment regularly, so it has been able to determine which external factors are changing and which will have an impact on its business.

Canada Post was discussed in this chapter's opening vignette. After gathering data and information on the market and competition, Canada Post identified potential opportunities and determined the approach it wanted to take.

Figure 2–8
Impact of an environmental scan—Canada Post

Factors in an Environmental Scan	STEP 1 Facts and Trends Collect the facts and identify trends in each category.	STEP 2 Determine Impact Analyze each external trend to determine its impact on the business.	STEP 3 Ideas for Implementation Brainstorm, evaluate, and implement ideas to meet business objectives.
Demographic factors	• Significant increase in the number of postal addresses in Canada.	• Additional costs to deliver to more addresses.	• Grow the parcel business to increase revenue. • Maximize automated sorting of letter mail to manage costs per address.
Socio-cultural factors	• People are mailing fewer letters. • Online shopping has taken off with the majority of Canadians. • When Canadians order products online, they want control over their purchases.	• Decrease in revenue from letter mail. • An increase in online shopping means more available parcel delivery business.	• Ensure Canada Post delivery is an option upon online checkout. • Offer an excellent customer experience—accurate shipping rates, delivery options, fast and efficient delivery, tracking of the package along its journey, and if necessary, easy returns. • Open "parcel pickup" stores with drive-thru parcel pickup

(Continued)

Figure 2–8 (*Continued*)

Factors in an Environmental Scan	STEP 1 Facts and Trends Collect the facts and identify trends in each category.	STEP 2 Determine Impact Analyze each external trend to determine its impact on the business.	STEP 3 Ideas for Implementation Brainstorm, evaluate, and implement ideas to meet business objectives.
			and change rooms to allow the customer to try on clothes purchased online and return them immediately if needed.
Economic factors	• Canadians spend $39 billion online annually. • Only 13 percent of Canadian businesses are currently selling online.	• Parcel business could grow even further if more Canadian businesses sold products online.	• Collect customer data from parcel delivery. • Help retailers with bricks-and-mortar stores implement ship-from-store solutions. • Increase the number of new retailers selling online by helping them with their e-commerce startup and integrate Canada Post's technology into their websites. • Introduce Canada Post E-Commerce Innovation Awards to recognize retailer success and identify promising start-ups to nurture and grow to the next level.
Technological factors	• There is widespread access to high-speed Internet service in Canada. • Increase in e-billing. • Digital advertising is growing, and the use of physical direct mail advertising is declining.	• Potential decrease in revenue from direct mail promotions. • Decrease in revenue from letter mail.	• *Smartmail*—help businesses better target their customers for direct mail promotion. • Offer help with post-campaign analysis. • Conduct *"Science of Activation"* research to reinforce the value of direct mail in the promotional mix. • *Epost* for the management of online bill payments.
Competitive factors	• Parcel delivery business is quite competitive with three key competitors: Purolator, FedEx, and UPS. • Emerging competition from regional/local competitors for parcel delivery. • Barriers to enter the national parcel delivery business are high due to the required infrastructure.	• Canada Post has a comprehensive delivery infrastructure in place to compete effectively in the parcel delivery market.	• Create a competitive e-commerce parcel shipping business by providing excellent customer experience for the retailer and customers.
Regulatory factors	• Letter mail monopoly in Canada falls under the *Canada Post Corporation Act.* • Consumer prices for letter mail are determined by regulation. • Government of Canada is investing in the expansion of digital connectivity and digital commerce.	• Canada Post is responsible for the delivery of mail to all Canadian addresses. • Future increases in e-commerce and demand for parcel delivery.	• Working with government-appointed review panel to determine the best path forward to serve Canadians while keeping Canada Post financially self-sufficient.

LO 1 • An environmental scan is the process of continually acquiring information on events occurring outside an organization to identify external trends that are opportunities or threats to a business.

LO 2 • Elements in an environmental scan include demographic factors, socio-cultural factors, economic factors, technological factors, competitive factors, and regulatory factors.

LO 3 • Demographics is the statistical data about a population according to characteristics such as gender, age, ethnicity, income, education, and occupation.

• Socio-cultural forces look at cultural values, ideas, and attitudes, as well as society's morals and beliefs.

 LO 4 • Economic forces consider macro and micro environmental factors. These forces reflect the state of the overall economy as well as the ability of consumers to spend.

 LO 5 • Technological forces relate to scientific inventions and innovations that may impact the running of a business and influence consumer behaviour and interactions.

 LO 6 • Competitive forces refer to direct and indirect competitors as well as the competitive nature of the market in which they function.

• Regulatory forces are the restrictions placed on businesses, products, or services by the government or industry associations.

LO 7 • Steps in a marketing environment scan involve (1) collecting the facts and identifying trends, (2) determining the impact that these facts/trends will have on the business, and (3) brainstorming, evaluating, and implementing ideas.

key terms and concepts... **A REFRESHER**

baby boomers
binge viewing
competitive forces
demographics
direct competitors
discretionary income
disposable income
Do Not Call List (DNCL)
economy
environmental scan
generation X
generation Y
generation Z

gross domestic product (GDP)
gross income
indirect competitors
inflation
interest rates
Internet of Things (IoT)
macroeconomic forces
microeconomic forces
millennials
monopolistic competition
monopoly
oligopoly
online behavioural advertising (OBA)

perfect competition
recession
regulations
showrooming
situation analysis
social TV
socio-cultural forces
spam
SWOT analysis
technological forces
unemployment rate

hands-on... **APPLY YOUR KNOWLEDGE**

Focus on demographic factors. The Marketing NewsFlash box, "Chinese Consumers in Canada," focused on the research of Chinese Canadians and their influence on the luxury goods market in Canada. There are many articles that have been written on the topic of ethnic marketing. Do some research on the topic and choose a company that has adopted ethnic marketing strategies. Outline its strategies and tactics. Has it been successful? What should the company do next?

This chapter's opening vignette examines the massive changes made at Canada Post based upon the changes taking place in the external environment. Assume that you are a marketing manager for UPS or FedEx. How would you respond to these changes and better compete?

Research new products that have been introduced in the automotive industry. Use recent data from Canadian newspapers (*National Post, Globe and Mail*), as well as other reputable business sources such as *Canadian Business, Maclean's*, and the DesRosiers Automotive Consultants website (**www .desrosiers.ca**).

Review the "How Well Do You Know Gen Y vs. Gen Z?" Infographic. If you were an automobile manufacturer, what impact would this information have on the following:

- The products that you develop to target each generational group
- The way that you communicate with each group

CHAPTER **3**

Consumer Behaviour

Understanding how consumers make decisions is an important goal for marketers. Although the consumer decision-making process is similar for most purchases, the time spent moving through the process varies among the complexity of the solution. Furthermore, there are some needs that are not really considered until consumers move through different life events.

Used with permission of Arbor Memorial.

As the senior director, marketing communications for Arbor Memorial, Dustin Wright has the challenging role of marketing an unsought consumer product (discussed in more detail in Chapter 7). Although a necessary part of the journey in life, celebrating a life is a personal experience that may be difficult for many to discuss with others. Each person's life is unique, so the creation of memorials, funerals, and experiences that truly reflect a loved one needs to be managed with compassion and care.

Considered by Deloitte as one of Canada's Best Managed Companies in 2018, 2019, and 2020, Arbor Memorial opened its first cemetery in 1947. The company had a strong sense of purpose as it provided personalized memorials in Canada. In a parkland setting, Arbor Memorial offered Canadians of all backgrounds caring, professional support for their end-of-life needs. As the business grew, ultimately expanding to include funeral homes, Arbor Memorial maintained its commitment to the highest standards of quality and attentive personal service.

When asked about marketing an unsought product, Wright shares, "Consumers make purchases to either derive pleasure or avoid pain. Our funeral and cemetery professionals help families during a very difficult time. The advice and guidance provided helps families celebrate the life of their loved one." With solid advice, price is not a driving factor of the consumer decision-making process in the funeral homes industry.

When a loved one passes, Canadians struggle with the information search. They are not certain where to start and unsure of what to ask. Wright suggests, "Marketers need to understand all the decisions consumers need to make and help them make them." Despite a strong, well-thought-out marketing strategy, Wright has to continue to adapt to a transforming industry. Over a trillion dollars in wealth will be transferred to the next Canadian generation in over ten years. And the recipients have different beliefs and behaviours than their parents.

Traditional funerals now compete with transfer services and direct cremation. The topic of how to honour a loved one may be polarizing. "Canadians may be driven by religiosity, have a desire for legacy, or both." Family and religion that traditionally drove ceremony is evolving, making the marketing strategy complex. "There are approximately 87 decisions to be made when making final arrangements (i.e., funeral and cemetery) for a loved one," explains Wright. "As consumer behaviour changes, organizations have to adapt."[1]

CHAPTER OUTLINE

- Difficult decisions for the next generation
- Consumer purchase decision process
- Situational influences on consumer decisions
- Psychological influences on consumer behaviour
- Socio-cultural influences on consumer behaviour

Consumer Purchase Decision Process

LO 1 Whether you are purchasing toothpaste or a new laptop for school, behind the visible act of making a purchase lies an important decision process. The stages that a consumer passes through when making choices about which products and services to buy is the **purchase decision process**. This process has five stages, as shown in Figure 3–1: problem recognition, information search, evaluation of alternatives, purchase decision, and post-purchase behaviour. Although technology has not changed the core elements of the process, the introduction of online and mobile technology has allowed consumers to make faster and more informed decisions.

A consumer's involvement in the purchase decision process varies based on the complexity of the decision. The time spent in each stage will depend on various factors, including what is being purchased. Access to information makes decision-making a lot easier for Canadians, and access to credit makes purchasing items easier as well. This has put Canadians in a challenging situation where they are now laden with debt due to purchasing items they have no room to store.[2]

Furthermore, businesses make decisions that follow a similar purchase decision process when considering products and services from suppliers. Chapter 5 looks at marketing to organizations in detail, including the different approaches required due to the magnitude of the decisions needed.

Problem Recognition: Perceiving a Need

Problem recognition, the initial step in the purchase decision, occurs when a person realizes that the difference between what he or she has and what he or she would like to have is big enough

to actually do something about it. The problem can be solved or the need can be met by purchasing a good or a service.[3] The process may be triggered by a situation as simple as finding no milk in the refrigerator. It could be more tenuous for a college or university student realizing his wardrobe is not in style with his classmates. Furthermore, problem recognition can be as complex as purchasing a new laptop computer to excel in studies. In marketing, advertisements, salespeople, or peers activate the consumer purchase decision process by highlighting the shortcomings of existing products and services. Consider smartphone advertisements that have stimulated problem recognition by emphasizing maximum use from one device.

Information Search: Seeking Value

After recognizing a problem, consumers begin to search for information about what product or service might satisfy the newly discovered need. First, they may scan their memory for knowledge of or previous experiences with products or brands. This action is called *internal search*. For frequently purchased products such as shampoo and conditioner, an internal search may be all a consumer needs. If the decision is more complex, however, a consumer may undertake an *external search* for information.[4] An external search is beneficial when a consumer lacks experience with or knowledge about a product, the risk of making a bad decision is high, and the cost of gathering information is low. The primary sources of external information are *personal sources*, such as relatives and friends who the consumer trusts; *public sources*, including various product-rating organizations such as *Consumer Reports* or government agencies; and *marketer-dominated sources*, such as information from sellers that includes advertising, company websites, salespeople, and point-of-purchase displays in stores.

During their daily lives, consumers engage with multiple screens, which adds additional content to their information search.[5] This additional information allows

purchase decision process
Stages that a buyer passes through when making choices about which products or services to buy.

Figure 3–1
Purchase decision process

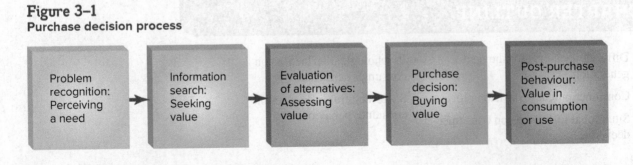

| Problem recognition: Perceiving a need | Information search: Seeking value | Evaluation of alternatives: Assessing value | Purchase decision: Buying value | Post-purchase behaviour: Value in consumption or use |

Infographic

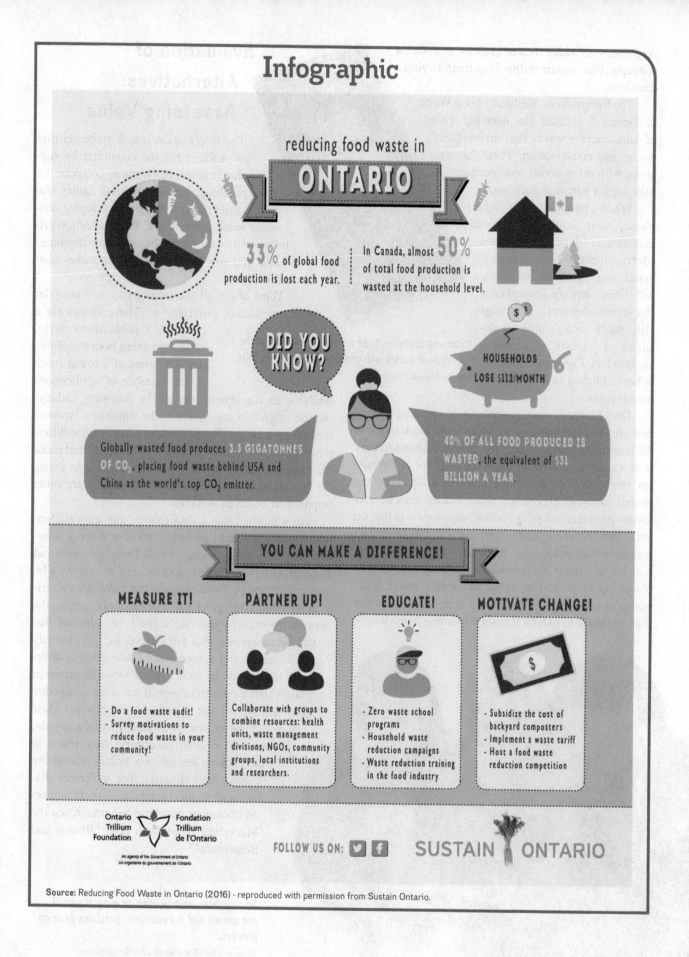

reducing food waste in

ONTARIO

33% of global food production is lost each year.

In Canada, almost **50%** of total food production is wasted at the household level.

DID YOU KNOW?

HOUSEHOLDS LOSE $112/MONTH

Globally wasted food produces **3.3 GIGATONNES OF CO₂**, placing food waste behind USA and China as the world's top CO₂ emitter.

40% OF ALL FOOD PRODUCED IS WASTED, the equivalent of $31 BILLION A YEAR.

YOU CAN MAKE A DIFFERENCE!

MEASURE IT!
- Do a food waste audit!
- Survey motivations to reduce food waste in your community!

PARTNER UP!
Collaborate with groups to combine resources: health units, waste management divisions, NGOs, community groups, local institutions and researchers.

EDUCATE!
- Zero waste school programs
- Household waste reduction campaigns
- Waste reduction training in the food industry

MOTIVATE CHANGE!
- Subsidize the cost of backyard composters
- Implement a waste tariff
- Host a food waste reduction competition

Ontario Trillium Foundation

Fondation Trillium de l'Ontario

An agency of the Government of Ontario
Un organisme du gouvernement de l'Ontario

FOLLOW US ON:

SUSTAIN ONTARIO

Source: Reducing Food Waste in Ontario (2016) - reproduced with permission from Sustain Ontario.

consumers to make better choices and factor concepts like sustainability into their buying decisions.

The Infographic, "Reducing Food Waste in Ontario," reflects the evolving views of consumers towards the environment, waste, and consumption. These factors along with other social considerations may impact purchase decisions.

When purchasing a smartphone, your information search may include friends and relatives, advertisements for smartphones, brand and company websites, and stores carrying smartphones (for demonstrations). You might also study comparable evaluations of various smartphones as found in *Consumer Reports*, either published in hard copy or found online.

Samsung continues to be a strong competitor in the smartphone market with offerings like the Galaxy S10+.
©robtek/Shutterstock

Once you have your smartphone, you will experience how mobile technology has added new behaviours to the consumer purchase decision process. *Showrooming* is an example of how all organizations, not just retailers, must integrate online mechanisms to optimize the overall customer experience. Since consumers can now review products and prices online, organizations that do not seamlessly incorporate online tools and technologies into their marketing, sales, and customer service efforts will be at a distinct competitive disadvantage. Online marketing is critical to small and medium-size businesses as consumers in Asia and North America have a high tendency to exhibit this showrooming behaviour.[6]

Evaluation of Alternatives: Assessing Value

The information-search stage clarifies the problem for the consumer by suggesting criteria, or points to consider, for the purchase; providing brand names that might meet the criteria; and developing consumer value perceptions. What selection criteria would you use in buying a smartphone? Would you use price, features, or some other combination?

Think about all the factors you may consider when evaluating smartphones. These factors are a consumer's *evaluative criteria*, which represent both the objective attributes of a brand (such as the number of applications available on the iPhone versus the Samsung Galaxy) and the subjective ones (such as the status of a business executive owning a iPhone) you use to compare different products and brands.[7] Firms try to identify and make the most of both types of evaluative criteria to create the best value for consumers. These criteria are often emphasized in advertisements.

For a product like a smartphone, the information-search process would probably involve visiting wireless providers such as Rogers and Telus, checking out these providers' websites, and talking to friends who own smartphones. Consumers often have several criteria for comparing products. For example, among the evaluative criteria you might think of, suppose that you focus on two that are crucial for you, namely pixel density and screen size. These criteria determine the brands in your *evoked set*—the group of brands that a consumer would consider acceptable from among all the brands in the product class of which he or she is aware.[8] In this example, your two evaluative criteria may result in an evoked set of two brands (Samsung Galaxy and iPhone). For a further discussion about brands and their impact on consumer purchase behaviour, see the Marketing NewsFlash box, "Brands and Behaviour."[9]

Smartphones have become an integral part of our society and the consumer purchase decision process.
©Darrenbaker/Dreamstime.com/GetStock.com

Brands and Behaviour

Bose and Spotify partnered on a project to engage millennials.

©Mark Kelly/Alamy Stock Photo

Consumer decisions are influenced by a number of factors. One of the psychological influences on decisions is the brand loyalty developed through learning. Corporate logos help consumers form strong perceptions of organizations. Consumers like to align themselves to brands that reflect their own self-concepts and self-images.

Along with learning, consumers are psychologically influenced by lifestyle. For example, it is suggested that millennials would rather rent than own. Unlike previous generations that look to home ownership as a milestone, millennials tend to put off purchasing homes and see home buying as an investment. The high cost of entry and the potential for a highly leveraged position are common reasons why millennials put this purchase off.

Understanding how brands drive consumer behaviour in consumer cohorts like millennials will help make marketers more effective. If millennials would rather not tie up their funds in huge purchases, it's no wonder why companies like Bose are winning millennials over. Millennials are independent and value quality. Bose has approached them with a strategy that emphasizes the firm's high-quality sound production, which millennials are willing to pay a premium for. Furthermore, confident in its technology, Bose took the time to understand millennials and partnered with Spotify, a digital music service frequented by millennials. Together, Bose and Spotify co-produced videos that educated the audience on sound and music production. These mini-documentaries are appealing to millennials, and the companies cross-marketed the series on their respective websites. ●

Questions

1. What associations come to mind with respect to Bose and Spotify?

2. As a consumer, give examples of brands that elicit positive associations with you and those that elicit negative associations with you.

Purchase Decision: Buying Value

Having examined the alternatives in the evoked set, you are almost ready to make a purchase decision. Three choices remain: the chosen brand, from whom to buy, and when to buy. The choice of which wireless provider to buy from will depend on such considerations as the provider's location, your past experience buying from the provider, and the return policy.

Deciding when to buy is frequently determined by a number of factors. For instance, you might buy sooner if one of your preferred brands is on sale or its manufacturer offers a rebate. Other factors, such as the store atmosphere, pleasantness of the shopping experience, salesperson persuasiveness, time pressure, and financial circumstances, could also affect whether a

By using kiosks or purchasing tickets online, moviegoers can avoid the traditional lineups at the theatre.

Used with permission of Cineplex

purchase decision is made or postponed. If your decision is the latest Samsung Galaxy, you may decide to buy it from Telus because it offers unlimited nationwide calling as an added incentive.

Technology has enabled the process of gathering information, evaluating alternatives, and making buying decisions. The addition of this technological dimension to the consumer purchase decision process can accelerate the process because it puts information at consumers' fingertips.

Effects of Mobile Technology on Purchase Behaviour Mobile devices are not only popular consumer purchases, they are enablers of the consumer purchase decision. Mobile devices have allowed the purchase decision to evolve by making the information-search and purchase-decision stages easier. The younger and future consumer expects an online presence from companies and uses technology to research products, voice opinions, and express needs.[10]

Mobile devices have empowered consumers a great deal and caused companies to take notice. Best Buy uses a variety of strategies to successfully retain customers in its stores, even those that exhibit showrooming behaviour.[11] Cineplex Entertainment has leveraged mobile technology to enhance the consumer experience. When choosing a movie at the theatre, tickets can be purchased online at your home computer, at the box office, or at an on-site kiosk. Cineplex Mobile offers an easy-to-use service for moviegoers to purchase tickets online.

Cognitive dissonance is the anxiety or tension felt after a purchase.
©noppawan09/Shutterstock

Post-purchase Behaviour: Value in Consumption or Use

After buying a product, the consumer compares it with his or her expectations and is either satisfied or dissatisfied. A company's sensitivity to a customer's consumption experience strongly affects the value a customer perceives after the purchase. Studies show that satisfaction or dissatisfaction affects consumer communications and repeat-purchase behaviour. Satisfied buyers tell three other people about their experience. Dissatisfied buyers complain to nine people![12] Furthermore, mobile technology allows buyers to share complaints and dissatisfaction in a more timely manner with even more reach.

In response, some companies are hiring employees to exclusively monitor sites such as Twitter and interact with unsatisfied customers right on the site. They are beginning to realize that the voice of the consumer on the web is very powerful. Consumers who are not finding satisfaction when a problem occurs may take matters into their own hands online. If a company were to Google its name followed by the word "sucks," it will find a large number of hits that consist of negative stories about consumers' experiences with its products. Other consumers are venting their frustrations on Twitter and Facebook. Progressive companies use this feedback as an opportunity to link up with these disgruntled customers and resolve the problems.

Often, a consumer is faced with two or more highly attractive alternatives, such as choosing between an iPhone and a Samsung Galaxy. If you choose the Samsung Galaxy, you may think, "Should I have purchased the iPhone?" This feeling

involvement
Personal, social, and economic significance of a purchase to the consumer.

of post-purchase psychological tension or anxiety is called *cognitive dissonance*. To alleviate it, consumers often attempt to applaud themselves for making the right choice. So, after purchase, you may seek information to confirm your choice by asking friends questions like, "What do you think of my new smartphone?" or by reading ads of the brand you chose. You might even look for negative features about the brand you didn't buy. Firms often use ads or follow-up calls from salespeople in this post-purchase stage to assure buyers that they made the right decision. It is important for firms to address consumer feelings of dissonance as it impacts their satisfaction and loyalty levels.[13]

Involvement and Problem-Solving Variations

LO 2 Depending on the purchase decision, consumers may not engage in the five-step purchase decision process in the same manner. They may skip or minimize one or more steps depending on the level of **involvement** required. The level of involvement that a consumer has in a particular purchase depends on the personal, social, and economic consequences of that purchase to the consumer.[14] Items such as soft drinks or toothpaste may have such a low level of involvement for consumers that they may skip or minimize one or more steps in the process. But consumers may do just the opposite for a high-involvement purchase like a computer or an automobile.

High-involvement purchase occasions typically have at least one of three characteristics: The item to be purchased is expensive; it is bought infrequently; or it could reflect on one's social image. For these occasions,

Figure 3–2
Comparison of problem-solving variations

Characteristics of Purchase Decision Process	Range of Consumer Involvement Low ←——————→ High		
	Routine Problem-Solving	Limited Problem-Solving	Extended Problem-Solving
Number of brands examined	One	Several	Many
Number of sellers considered	Few	Several	Many
Number of product attributes evaluated	One	Moderate	Many
Number of external information sources	None	Few	Many
Time spent searching	Minimal	Little	Considerable

consumers engage in extensive information search, consider many product attributes and brands, form attitudes, and participate in word-of-mouth communication. Marketers who sell high-involvement products such as cars, homes, and computers must understand the information-gathering and evaluation process of consumers. Researchers have identified three general variations in the consumer purchase process based on consumer involvement and product knowledge. Figure 3–2 summarizes some of the important differences between the three problem-solving variations.[15]

Routine Problem-Solving
For products such as table salt and milk, consumers recognize a problem, make a decision, and spend little effort seeking external information and evaluating alternatives. The purchase process for such items is virtually a habit and typifies low-involvement decision-making. Routine problem-solving is typically the case for low-priced, frequently purchased products. An example is a consumer who stops by Tim Hortons on her way to work and purchases a coffee and a bagel. She doesn't ponder the potential benefits of going to a Second Cup or specialty coffee store even though they are all on her way to work. Marketers strive to attract and maintain habitual buying behaviour by creating strong brand relationships with the consumer.

Limited Problem-Solving
Limited problem-solving is characterized by low consumer involvement but significant perceived differences among brands. For example, a consumer loves Activia yogourt but switches to BioBest yogourt, not out of dissatisfaction but just out of a desire to try something new. The consumer may have spent a moderate amount of time evaluating the available brands in the store before selecting BioBest. With limited problem-solving behaviour, consumers rely on past experience more than external information, but they may pay attention to new varieties shown in advertising and point-of-purchase displays. Marketers of leading brands should focus on getting consumers to shift to routine problem-solving behaviour by dominating shelf space and running advertisements that remind consumers of the benefits of their brands. Consumers might use limited problem-solving when choosing a pair of jeans, deciding on a restaurant for dinner, and making other purchase situations in which they have little time or effort to spend researching options.

Consumers might use limited problem-solving when choosing a restaurant for dinner.

©Iofoto/Dreamstime.com/GetStock.com

Extended Problem-Solving In extended problem-solving, each of the five stages of the consumer purchase decision process is used in the purchase, including considerable time and effort on external information search and identifying and evaluating alternatives. Several brands are in the evoked set, and these are evaluated on many attributes. Extended problem-solving exists in high-involvement purchase situations for items such as automobiles, houses, and financial investments.

Consumer Purchase Decision Process Influencers

Whether decisions require routine, limited or extended problem-solving, a company's marketing mix influences the consumer purchase decision process. Figure 3–3 shows how the marketing mix and other influences play a role in decisions. The decision to buy a product can be impacted by important situational, psychological, and socio-cultural influences. These influences are discussed throughout the remainder of this chapter.

Situational Influences on Consumer Decisions

LO 3 Often, the purchase situation will affect the purchase decision process. Five *situational influences* have an impact on your purchase decision process: the purchase task, social surroundings, physical surroundings, temporal effects, and antecedent states.[16]

1. The *purchase task* is the reason for engaging in the decision in the first place. Information searching and evaluating alternatives may differ depending on whether the purchase is a gift, which often involves social visibility, or for the buyer's own use. For example, some consumers may be frugal shoppers when it comes to purchasing products for themselves, but may spend lavishly if the product is a gift for a friend.

2. *Social surroundings*, including the other people present when a purchase decision is made, may also affect what is purchased. For example, Paco Underhill, a behavioural research consultant, has shown that when two women shop together, they spend more time in the store shopping than they would if they were alone.[17]

3. *Physical surroundings* such as decor, music, and crowding in retail stores may alter how purchase decisions are made. Crowding, for example, is a two-edged sword. When consumers see a throng of people in the Apple Store, they may be eager to enter the store to be part of the experience. On the other hand, some people may be turned off because they don't like shopping in a crowded environment.

4. *Temporal effects*, such as time of day or the amount of time available, will influence where consumers have breakfast and lunch and what is ordered.

Figure 3–3
Influences on the consumer purchase decision process

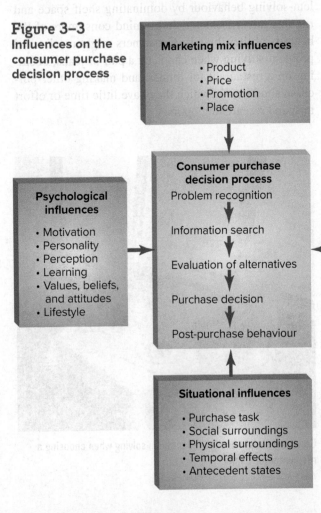

Marketing mix influences
- Product
- Price
- Promotion
- Place

Psychological influences
- Motivation
- Personality
- Perception
- Learning
- Values, beliefs, and attitudes
- Lifestyle

Consumer purchase decision process
Problem recognition
Information search
Evaluation of alternatives
Purchase decision
Post-purchase behaviour

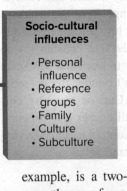

Socio-cultural influences
- Personal influence
- Reference groups
- Family
- Culture
- Subculture

Situational influences
- Purchase task
- Social surroundings
- Physical surroundings
- Temporal effects
- Antecedent states

Infographic

WHAT DO WE KNOW ABOUT **HOMEOWNERSHIP** AND **MORTGAGE DEBT** IN CANADA?

HOMEOWNERSHIP IS INCREASING IN CANADA

60% 1999 / 63% 2016

In 2016, **63%** of Canadian families owned their homes, up from **60%** in 1999.

Homeownership is on the rise largely because of population aging, as **older people** are more likely to own their homes.

THE PROPORTION OF FAMILIES WHO HAVE PAID OFF THEIR HOUSE IS DECREASING

Between 1999 and 2016, the proportion of homeowners who had paid off their mortgage declined, from **46%** to **43%**.

Without population aging, the proportion would have declined from **46%** in 1999 to **36%** in 2016. This is because older people are more likely to have paid off their houses.

MOST FAMILIES WITH A MORTGAGE HAVE A FIXED MORTGAGE RATE

Type of mortgage

Fixed 74%

Variable 21%

Combination 5%

MORTGAGE DEBT IS RESPONSIBLE FOR THE MAJORITY OF THE INCREASE IN TOTAL FAMILY DEBT[1]

Between 1999 and 2016, mortgage debt accounted for **84%** of the total increase in family debt.

Between 2012 and 2016, **100%** of the increase in the debt of families was due to mortgage debt while consumer debt remained constant.

The median mortgage debt among families with a mortgage **doubled** in real terms **between 1999 and 2016**.

1999 $91,900

2016 $180,000

Source: Uppal, Sharanjit. 2019. "Homeownership, mortgage debt and types of mortgage among Canadian families". *Insights on Canadian Society*. August. Statistics Canada Catalogue no. 75-006-X.

[1] The numbers are expressed in constant 2016 dollars. Families include individuals living together who are related and one-person families (i.e., individuals living alone or with non-relatives).

Statistics Canada / Statistique Canada

www.statcan.gc.ca

Canadä

Source: Statistics Canada (2019), retrieved from https://www150.statcan.gc.ca/n1/pub/11-627-m/11-627-m2019054-eng.htm

---

5. Finally, *antecedent states*, which include the consumer's mood or the amount of cash on hand, can influence purchase behaviour and choice. As shown in the Infographic, "What Do We Know about Homeownership and Mortgage Debt in Canada," Canadians are incurring more debt. How someone perceives their financial situation may positively or negatively influence their ability to spend.

Psychological Influences on Consumer Behaviour

LO 4 Psychology helps marketers understand why and how consumers behave as they do. In particular, concepts such as motivation and personality; perception; learning; values, beliefs, and attitudes; and lifestyle are useful for interpreting buying processes and directing marketing efforts. Although every consumer is a unique individual, common factors can cause similar behaviours.

Motivation and Personality

Motivation and personality are two familiar psychological concepts that have specific meanings and marketing implications. They are both used frequently to describe why people do some things and not others.

Motivation   **Motivation** is the energizing force that stimulates behaviour to satisfy a need. Because consumer needs are the focus of the marketing concept, marketers try to arouse these needs.

An individual's needs are boundless. People have physiological needs for basics such as water, food, and shelter. They also have learned needs, including esteem, achievement, and affection. The late psychologist Abraham Maslow developed a theory that characterized needs and arranged them into a hierarchy. He argued that people take

motivation
Energizing force that stimulates behaviour to satisfy a need.

Figure 3–4
Maslow's hierarchy of needs

> Self-actualization needs: Fulfillment of ambitions and hopes
>
> Esteem needs: Status, respect, prestige
>
> Social needs: Friendship, belonging, love
>
> Safety needs: Freedom from harm, financial security
>
> Physiological needs: Food, water, shelter

care of their lower-level needs first and then are motivated to satisfy their higher-level needs. Figure 3–4 shows Maslow's hierarchy of needs, which contains the following five need classes:[18]

1. *Physiological needs* are basic to survival and must be satisfied first. A fast-food advertisement featuring a juicy hamburger attempts to activate the need for food.

2. *Safety needs* involve self-preservation and physical well-being. Smoke detector and burglar alarm manufacturers focus on these needs. Michelin combines security with parental love to promote tire replacement for automobiles.

3. *Social needs* are concerned with love and friendship. Dating services such as eHarmony and fragrance companies try to arouse these needs.

Shopping malls like the West Edmonton Mall host various consumers with different purchase decision motivations.

©Fallsview/Dreamstime.com

4. *Esteem needs* are represented by the need for achievement, status, prestige, and self-respect. Using the TD Aeroplan Infinite card and shopping at Holt Renfrew appeal to these needs. Sometimes, firms try to arouse multiple needs to stimulate problem recognition.

5. *Self-actualization needs* involve personal fulfillment. For example, travel providers offer specialized educational and exotic trips to enhance a consumer's life experience.

While Maslow believed that needs were innate, studies have found that social culture contributes to our identification of these needs. Therefore, it is critical for marketers to first understand our consumer needs in order to satisfy them.[19]

Personality **Personality** refers to a person's character traits that influence behavioural responses. Although numerous personality theories exist, most identify key traits such as assertiveness, extroversion, compliance, dominance, and aggression, among others. Research suggests that compliant people prefer known brand names and use more mouthwash and toilet soaps. In contrast, aggressive types use razors, not electric shavers; apply more cologne and after-shave lotions; and purchase signature goods such as Gucci, Yves St. Laurent, and Donna Karan as an indicator of status.[20]

Personality characteristics are often revealed in a person's *self-concept*, which is the way people see themselves and the way they believe others see them. Marketers recognize that people have an actual self-concept and an ideal self-concept. The actual self refers to how people actually see themselves. The ideal self describes how people would like to see themselves. Marketers appeal to these two self-images in the products and brands a person buys, including automobiles,

Dove Men+Care products appeal to the trend of men concerned about body image and grooming.

©Editorial Image, LLC/Alamy Stock Photo

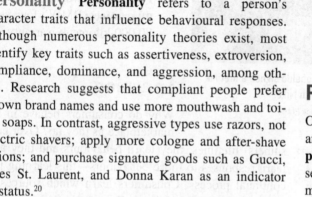

home appliances and furnishings, magazines, clothing, grooming products, and leisure products, and in the stores where a person shops. The use of attractive models in ads for grooming products appeals to a person's ideal self-concept. Men are becoming more concerned about their self-concept when it comes to body image and grooming. Unilever has responded to this trend by introducing a line of grooming products for men called Dove Men+Care.

> *Research suggests that compliant people prefer known brand names and use more mouthwash and toilet soaps.*

Perception

One person sees a Porsche as a mark of achievement; another sees it as showing off. This is the result of **perception**—that is, the process by which an individual selects, organizes, and interprets information to create a meaningful picture of the world.

Selective Perception The average consumer operates in a complex, information-rich environment. The human brain organizes and interprets all this information with a process called *selective perception*, which filters the information so that only some of it is understood or remembered or even available to the conscious mind. *Selective exposure* occurs when people pay attention to messages that are consistent with their attitudes and beliefs and ignore messages that are inconsistent. Selective exposure often occurs in the post-purchase stage of the consumer decision process, when consumers read advertisements for the brand they just bought. It also occurs when a need exists—you are more likely to "see" a McDonald's advertisement when you are hungry rather than after you have eaten a pizza.

Selective comprehension involves interpreting information so that it is consistent with your attitudes and beliefs. A marketer's failure to understand this can have disastrous results. For example, Toro introduced a small, lightweight snow-blower called the Snow Pup. Even though the product worked, sales failed to meet expectations. Why? Toro later found out that consumers perceived the name to mean that Snow Pup was a toy or too light to do any serious snow removal. When the product was renamed Snow Master, sales increased sharply.[21]

Selective retention means that consumers do not remember all the information they see, read, or hear, even minutes after exposure to it. This affects the internal and external information-search stage of the purchase decision process. This is why furniture and automobile retailers often give consumers product brochures to take home after they leave the showroom.

Perceived Risk Consumers' beliefs about the potential negative consequences of a product or service strongly affect their purchasing decisions. **Perceived risk** represents the anxieties felt because the consumer cannot anticipate the outcomes of a purchase but believes that there may be negative consequences. Examples of possible negative consequences concerning snowboarding are the price of the product (Can I afford $400 for a snowboard?) and the risk of physical harm (Is snowboarding more dangerous than alpine skiing?). Some products such as hair colouring lend themselves to perceived risk. There is always the fear that the hair colouring may not turn out to the consumer's satisfaction. Perceived risk affects the information-search step of the purchase decision process: The greater the perceived risk, the more extensive the external search is likely to be.

Recognizing the importance of perceived risk, smart marketers develop strategies to make consumers feel more at ease about their purchases. Strategies and examples of firms using them include the following:

In 2016, Cristiano Ronaldo signed a lifetime endorsement deal with Nike.
©Islandstock/Alamy Stock Photo

- **Obtaining seals of approval:** The Good Housekeeping seal that appears on many brands.
- **Securing endorsements from influential people:** Nike's products endorsed by athletes like LeBron James and Cristiano Ronaldo.
- **Providing free trials of the product:** Samples of perfume offered at Hudson's Bay.
- **Providing illustrations:** Photos of different colours and hairstyles on Clairol Canada's website.
- **Providing warranties and guarantees:** BMW's four-year, 80,000-kilometre warranty.[22]

Learning

Why do consumers behave in the marketplace as they do? Over consumers' lifetimes, they learn behaviours and they also learn responses to those behaviours—this learning is a continual process. Consumers learn which sources to use for information about products and services, which evaluative criteria to use when assessing alternatives, and how to make purchase decisions. **Learning** refers to those behaviours that result from repeated experience and reasoning.

Behavioural Learning *Behavioural learning* is the process of developing automatic responses to a type of situation built up through repeated exposure to it. Four variables are central to how one learns from repeated experience: drive, cue, response, and reinforcement. A *drive* is a need, such as hunger, that moves an individual to action. A *cue* is a stimulus or symbol that one perceives.

perceived risk
Anxiety felt when a consumer cannot anticipate possible negative outcomes of a purchase.

learning
Behaviours that result from repeated experience or reasoning.

New BMW vehicles like this one have a four-year, 80,000-kilometre warranty.
©Thampapon/Shutterstock

> *Consumers familiar with one product will often transfer their feelings to others that seem similar—whether the similarity is in a brand name or in the shape and colour of the packaging.*

A *response* is the action taken to satisfy the drive, and a *reinforcement* is the reward. Being hungry (a drive), a consumer sees a cue (a billboard), takes action (buys a hamburger), and receives a reward (it tastes great!). If what the consumer experiences upon avoiding a stimulus is favourable (I don't feel sick now!), then *negative reinforcement* has occurred. Behavioural learning plays a major role in consumer decision-making—in this case, causing the consumer to avoid the behavioural response rather than repeat it.

Marketers use two concepts from behavioural learning theory. *Stimulus generalization* occurs when a response brought about by one stimulus (cue) is generalized to another stimulus. Using the same brand name to launch new products is one common application of this concept, as when the makers of Tylenol followed up their original pain reliever with Tylenol Cold, Tylenol Flu, Tylenol Sinus, and others. Consumers familiar with one product will often transfer their feelings to others that seem similar—whether the similarity is in a brand name or in the shape and colour of the packaging. Are you familiar with President's Choice Cola or Costco's Simply Soda? They use red cans, similar in colour to Coca-Cola cans—this is stimulus generalization in action!

Stimulus discrimination refers to one's ability to perceive differences among similar products. Consumers may do this easily with some groups of products, such as automobiles. But in many cases, such as low-involvement purchases, advertisers work to point out the differences. For example, consumers' tendency to perceive all light beers as being alike led to Budweiser Light commercials that distinguished between many types of lights and Bud Light.

Cognitive Learning

Consumers also learn without direct experience—through thinking, reasoning, and mental problem solving. This type of learning, called *cognitive learning*, involves making connections between two or more ideas or simply observing the outcomes of others' behaviours and adjusting your own accordingly. Firms also influence this type of learning. Through repetition in advertising, messages such as "Advil is a headache remedy" attempt to link a brand (Advil) and an idea (headache remedy) by showing someone using the brand and finding relief.

In the competitive soft drink market, companies may choose to package their colas in red cans similar to other brands.
©Akkaranant/Dreamstime.com

Brand Loyalty

Learning is also important to marketers because it relates to habit formation. Developing habits means that a consumer is solving problems (such as what to do when she's hungry) routinely and consistently, without much thought. Not surprisingly, there is a close link between habits and **brand loyalty**, which is a favourable attitude toward and consistent purchase of a single brand over time. Brand loyalty results from positive reinforcement. If a consumer is satisfied with a product, he reduces his risk and saves time by consistently purchasing that same brand.

Values, Beliefs, and Attitudes

Values, beliefs, and attitudes play a central role in consumer decision-making.

Attitude Formation

An **attitude** is a "learned predisposition to respond to an object or class of objects in a consistently favourable or unfavourable way."[23] Attitudes are shaped by our values and beliefs, which we develop in the process of growing up. For example, we speak of core values, including material well-being and humanitarianism. We also have personal values, such as thriftiness and ambition. Marketers are concerned with both, but focus mostly on personal values. Personal values affect attitudes by influencing the importance assigned to specific product attributes, or features. Suppose thriftiness is one of your personal values. When you evaluate cars, fuel economy (a product attribute) becomes important. If you believe a specific car has this attribute, you are likely to have a favourable attitude toward it.

brand loyalty
Favourable attitude toward and consistent purchase of a single brand over time; the degree of target market commitment toward a brand over time that results in varying levels of purchase commitment.

attitude
Tendency to respond to something in a consistently favourable or unfavourable way.

Beliefs also play a part in attitude formation. In consumer terms, **beliefs** are one's perception of how a product or brand performs on different attributes. Beliefs are based on personal experience, advertising, and discussions with other people. Beliefs about product attributes are important because, along with personal values, they create the favourable or unfavourable attitude the consumer has toward certain products and services.

Attitude Change Marketers use three approaches to try to change consumer attitudes toward products and brands, as shown in the following examples:[24]

1. *Changing beliefs about the extent to which a brand has certain attributes.* To reduce consumer concern that Aspirin use causes an upset stomach, Bayer Corporation successfully promoted the gentleness of its Extra Strength Bayer Plus Aspirin.

2. *Changing the perceived importance of attributes.* Consumers up to now were divided on the number of hours of sleep required for good health. Recent articles in the media are changing consumers' perceived importance of required hours. The Mayo Clinic, for example, recommends seven to nine hours of sleep for adults.[25] Sleep Country Canada emphasizes in its commercials the importance of getting a good night's rest and how Sleep Country can help the situation by providing a mattress that can improve the quality of sleep.

3. *Adding new attributes to the product.* Colgate-Palmolive included a new antibacterial ingredient, triclosan, in its Colgate Total Toothpaste and spent $100 million marketing the brand. The result? Colgate Total Toothpaste is now a billion-dollar-plus global brand.

Lifestyle

Lifestyle is a way of living that reflects how people spend their time and resources (activities), what they consider important in their environment (interests), and how they think of themselves and the world around them (opinions). The analysis of consumer lifestyles, called *psychographics*, has produced many insights into consumer behaviour. For example, lifestyle analysis has proven useful in segmenting and targeting consumers for new and existing products and services. One of the most psychographic systems is the VALS system from Strategic Business Insights.[26] The VALS, which stands for "values and lifestyles," identifies eight interconnected categories of adult lifestyles based on a person's self-orientation and resources. *Self-orientation* describes the patterns of attitudes and activities that help a person reinforce his or her social self-image. Three patterns have been uncovered, which are oriented toward principles, status, and action. A person's resources range from minimal to abundant and include income, education, self-confidence, health, eagerness to buy, intelligence, and energy level. Each of these categories exhibits different buying behaviour and media preferences.

VALS is an American-based system, and the psychographics of Americans differ significantly from those of Canadians. When some market researchers have tried to use American values and lifestyles to describe Canadians, they have not succeeded. For Canadian insights, marketers can turn to one of the leading firms in marketing and analytical services: Environics Analytics. Through its PRIZM5 segmentation system, Environics Analytics has segmented the Canadian population into a variety of data points, including demographics, lifestyles, and values. Figure 3–5 provides an example of segments in the Canadian population that rank high on attending professional basketball games. Although these segments have unique characteristics, there are similar

Figure 3–5
PRIZM5 segments that attend professional basketball games

Source: ©2017 Environics Analytics; PRIZM is a registered trademark of Claritas, LLC and used with permission.

traits among them that create a larger target market for products and services related to basketball.

As part of the PRIZM5 system, Environics Analytics provides exceptional insight into 68 segments of the Canadian population. For example, it describes a specific segment of the population as Grads & Pads—number 38 on the 68-rung socio-economic ladder. These individuals are described as young, well-educated individuals living near post-secondary education institutions who like to stay active skiing and working out at health clubs. While this generalized description may not describe every individual in the segment, it provides an overall theme of the expected consumer behaviour of the individuals living in postal codes associated with that segment.[27]

Environics Analytics is one of the leaders in consumer segmentations. The sample segments described earlier fall into much broader socio-economic categories, and life-stage groups continue to change with every new Canadian census. Figure 3–6 provides examples of the broader socio-economic categories of the PRIZM5 segmentation system. By using the key drivers of demographics, lifestyles, and values, Environics Analytics creates added-value tools for marketers to understand consumer behaviour and markets anywhere in Canada.

Figure 3–6
Examples of PRIZM5 cluster categories

Segment Code	Cluster Category	Brief Description
UI	Urban Elite	The most affluent Canadian households belong to Urban Elite, the social group that ranks at the top of several demographic measures: income, home value, and educational achievement. With their university degrees and positions as executives and professionals, these middle-aged and older residents tend to live in fashionable homes in big-city neighbourhoods and close-in suburbs.
SI	Suburban Elite	The households in Suburban Elite represent the most upscale suburban social group, characterized by middle-aged and older families living in single-family homes. One socio-economic rung down from Urban Elite, these Canadians have university and college educations, and hold service-sector and white-collar jobs.
EI	Exurban Elite	Exurban Elite consists of the wealthiest households outside the nation's metropolitan sprawl, beyond the suburbs but within reasonable commutes to city jobs. The residents in this exurban group tend to be married, middle-aged and older couples and families who live in comfortable homes and hold a mix of white-collar, blue-collar, and service-sector jobs. With their large families of school- and college-aged children, households here have high rates of enjoying team and winter sports, golfing, boating, community theatre, and all types of exhibitions: craft, cottage, fitness, gardening, pet, and home.
U2	Urban Upscale Diverse	Generally found in Toronto, Vancouver, and Montreal, the Urban Upscale Diverse group consists of four mostly middle-income segments with high concentrations of immigrants, especially from Asia, Europe, Central America, and the Middle East. Their households are a mix of middle-aged and older couples and families, with children in their late teens and twenties. Many residents inhabit a bi-cultural world, with nearly a third speaking a language at home other than English or French.
S2	Suburban Younger	The four Suburban Younger segments contain family-filled households where most maintainers are under 45 years old. Because the adults in this group have varying educational backgrounds—from high school to university degrees—and many having only recently entered the labour force, household income levels range from upscale to lower-middle, earned from a broad mix of jobs. But most families can afford to own their homes, typically recently built singles, semis, and row houses.
E2	Exurban Middle-Aged	The Exurban Middle-Aged group represents the nation's middle-aged, mostly midscale couples and families living in Canada's growing exurban communities. In these mixed households—the families feature children of all ages—parents holding college diplomas or less work at a range of blue-collar, white-collar, and service-sector jobs; their average incomes allow them to own single-family homes built after 1980. With their neighbourhoods located outside the nation's big cities, the cost of living is lower than average, and residents pursue active, outdoorsy lifestyles.
U3	Urban Young	Home to the nation's youngest residents, Urban Young consists of households with maintainers who are typically under 45 years old. With many just entering the workforce, these university-educated singles and couples earn a range of incomes—from upper-middle to lower-middle income—from their white-collar and service-sector jobs. Without the financial obligations of a family, they're able to rent decent apartments in older, downtown neighbourhoods and lead a hip, progressive lifestyle.

Source: ©2017 Environics Analytics; PRIZM is a registered trademark of Claritas, LLC and used with permission.

Socio-cultural Influences on Consumer Behaviour

LO 5 Socio-cultural influences, which evolve from a consumer's formal and informal relationships with other people, also have an impact on consumer behaviour. These include personal influence, reference groups, family, culture, and subculture.

Personal Influence

A consumer's purchases are often influenced by the views, opinions, or behaviours of others. Two aspects of personal influence are important to marketing: opinion leadership and word-of-mouth activity.

Opinion Leadership Individuals who have social influence over others are called **opinion leaders**. Opinion leaders are more likely to be important for products that provide a form of self-expression. Automobiles, clothing, and club memberships are products affected by opinion leaders, but appliances usually are not.[28]

A small percentage of adults—from influential community leaders and business executives to movie stars—are opinion leaders. Identifying, reaching, and influencing opinion leaders is a major challenge for companies. Some firms use sports figures or celebrities as spokespersons to represent their products, such as singer Kelly Clarkson for Citizen watches.

Word of Mouth People influencing each other during conversations is called **word of mouth**. Word of mouth is perhaps the most powerful information source for consumers, because it typically involves friends or family who are viewed as trustworthy.

Companies like Citizen use celebrities as spokespeople to represent its products and influence consumer decision-making.
Source: Citizen Watch Company of America

The power of personal influence has prompted firms to make efforts to increase positive and decrease negative word of mouth.[29] For instance, "teaser" advertising campaigns are run in advance of new-product introductions to stimulate conversations. Other techniques such as advertising slogans, music, and humour also heighten positive word of mouth. On the other hand, rumours about McDonald's (worms in hamburgers) and Corona Extra beer (contaminated beer) have resulted in negative word of mouth, none of which was based on fact. Overcoming negative word of mouth is difficult and costly. Firms have found that supplying factual information, providing toll-free numbers for consumers to call the company, and giving appropriate product demonstrations also have been helpful.

The term *buzz marketing* refers to a brand becoming popular as a result of people talking about it to friends and neighbours. Another way that a company can create buzz is by hiring an outside agency. Word-of-mouth agencies such as Matchstick specialize in product-seeding programs. Product seeding consists of hiring people to talk up a brand to others. The Word of Mouth Marketing Association (WOMMA) has issued ethical guidelines on product seeding, including the guideline that brand

opinion leaders
Individuals who have social influence over others.

word of mouth
People influencing each other in personal conversations.

focus on Ethics

Social Issues and Consumer Behaviour

One of the most powerful forms of marketing is a natural activity: talking. Telling others your opinion about products and brands. Word-of-mouth marketing is an extraordinary tool for marketers to use to promote their brands, and technology has enabled word-of-mouth promotions, allowing social media to create a forum with mass reach.

In a study involving cultural industries that create, produce, and commercialize anything from musical performances to video games, it was found that professional commentators had a more positive influence on buying decisions than the comments made by ordinary consumers. These opinion leaders have an influence in the future buying decisions of Canadians. When Canadians use online group-buying sites, Internet advertising and electronic word of mouth have a positive influence on consumers.

Being extremely impactful to the future economy as a generation, marketers need to better understand what drives the millennials to word of mouth and loyalty. One key driver to the purchases of millennials is social issues like the environment; millennials reward brands with this focus through word of mouth and loyalty.

Based in Regina, Saskatchewan, tentree International is a company that catches a millennial's attention. It commits to ten trees planted for every product purchased, whether that be directly from its online store, or from one of its over 300 retail partners. By planting millions of trees, tentree is providing employment, protecting wildlife, restoring eco-systems, and educating locals, as well as providing wood for fuel, cooking, and building in impoverished areas. tentree also has partnerships across the world to help

Used with permission of tentree International

identify areas that can benefit from planting trees. ●

Questions

1. How does the impact that tentree International makes to the environment and communities across the world influence your decision to purchase clothing from this company?

2. When you consider buying a large ticket item, how much do you consider social issues in your purchase decision?

---

representatives must always disclose their relationship to the brand when promoting it to others.

> ❝ *Product seeding consists of hiring people to talk up a brand to others.*

The power of word of mouth has been magnified through online marketing. The online version of word of mouth is called *viral marketing*. This includes the use of messages that consumers pass along to others through online forums, social networks such as Facebook and Twitter, chat rooms, bulletin boards, blogs, and e-mails. These messages can be positive or negative. Companies are now recognizing the value of social media platforms such as Twitter and Facebook, and are monitoring messages so that they can respond to consumers quickly. The Focus on Ethics box, "Social Issues and Consumer

Behaviour," considers the impact of social issues for some consumers' purchasing habits.[30]

Reference Groups

A **reference group** is a group of people who influence a person's attitudes, values, and behaviours. For example, you might consider your family or the other students in your school as a reference group. Other examples of reference groups are movie stars and sports celebrities. Reference groups affect consumer purchases because they influence the information, attitudes, and aspiration levels that help set a consumer's standards. Reference groups have an important influence on the purchase of luxury products but not of necessities—reference groups exert a strong influence on the brand chosen when its use or consumption is highly visible to others.[31]

reference group
A group of people who influence a person's attitudes, values, and behaviour.

Consumers have many reference groups, but three groups have clear marketing implications:

- **Membership group:** One to which a person actually belongs, including fraternities and sororities, social clubs, and family. Such groups are easily identifiable and are targeted by firms selling insurance, insignia products, and vacation packages.

- **Aspiration group:** One that a person wishes to be a member of or wishes to be identified with. An example is a person whose dream it is to play in the NHL. Brands such as Gatorade and Nike frequently rely on spokespeople or settings associated with their target market's aspiration group in their advertising.

- **Dissociative group:** One that a person wishes to maintain a distance from because of differences in values or behaviours.

Family Influence

Family influences on consumer behaviour result from three sources: consumer socialization, passage through the family life cycle, and decision-making within the family or household.

family life cycle
A family's progression from formation to retirement, with each phase bringing distinct needs and purchasing behaviours.

Consumer Socialization The process by which people acquire the skills, knowledge, and attitudes necessary to function as consumers is *consumer socialization*.[32] Children learn how to purchase by interacting with adults in purchase situations and through their own purchasing and product usage experiences. Research demonstrates that children show signs of brand preferences as early as age 2, and these preferences often last a lifetime. This knowledge prompted Time Inc. to launch *Sports Illustrated for Kids*. The brand of toothpaste, laundry detergent, or soft drink used in your home will very likely influence your brand choice when you purchase these items for yourself.

Family Life Cycle Consumers act and purchase differently as they go through life. The **family life cycle** concept describes the distinct phases that a family progresses through from formation to retirement, each phase bringing with it identifiable purchasing behaviours.[33] Today, the traditional family—married couples with children—constitute just over 26 percent of all Canadian households. Nearly 30 percent are households without children.[34]

Young single consumers' buying preferences are for nondurable items, including prepared foods, clothing, personal care products, and entertainment. They represent a significant target market for recreational travel, automobile, and consumer electronics firms. Young married couples without children are typically more affluent than young singles because usually both spouses are employed. These couples exhibit preferences for furniture, housewares, and gift items for each other. Young marrieds with children are driven by the needs of their children. These families make up a sizable market for life insurance, various children's products, and home

The late Steve Jobs co-founded Apple, built it into the world's leading tech company, and led a mobile computing revolution with wildly popular devices such as the iPod, iPhone, and iPad that connected different generations of a family.

left: ©Aflo Foto Agency/Alamy Stock Photo; right: ©Paul Sakuma, File/AP Photo/The Canadian Press

furnishings. Single parents with children are the least financially secure type of households. Their buying preferences are usually affected by a limited economic status and tend toward convenience foods, child care services, and personal care items.

Middle-aged married couples with children are typically better off financially than their younger counterparts. They are a significant market for leisure products and home improvement items. Middle-aged couples without children typically have a large amount of discretionary income. These couples buy better home furnishings, status automobiles, and financial services. Persons in the last two phases—older married and older unmarried—make up a sizable market for prescription drugs, medical services, vacation trips, and gifts for younger relatives.

Families may influence the decisions made by their family members.

©gilaxia/iStock/Getty Images Plus

Family Decision-Making A third family-based influence on consumer decision-making occurs in the context of the relationship dynamics of the household. Two decision-making styles exist: spouse-dominant and joint decision-making. With a joint decision-making style, most decisions are made by both husband and wife. Spouse-dominant decisions are those for which either the husband or the wife has more influence in the purchase decision. Research indicates that wives tend to have the most say when purchasing groceries, children's toys, clothing, and medicines. Husbands tend to be more influential in home and car maintenance purchases. Joint decision-making is common for cars, vacations, houses, home appliances and electronics, medical care, and long-distance telephone services. As a rule, joint decision-making increases with the education of the spouses.[35]

> *Even though women are often the grocery decision makers, they are not necessarily the purchaser. Husbands do about one-half of food shopping.*

Roles of individual family members in the purchase process are another element of family decision-making. Five roles exist: information gatherer, influencer, decision maker, purchaser, and user. Family members assume different roles for different products and services.[36]

Furthermore, since 70 to 80 percent of consumer purchasing is done by the buying power of influence of women, men's clothing stores may choose to advertise in women's magazines such as *Chatelaine* and *Redbook*. Even though women are often the grocery decision makers, they are not necessarily the purchaser. Husbands do about one-half of food shopping. Increasingly, preteens and teenagers are the information gatherers, influencers, decision makers, and purchasers of products and services items for the family, given the prevalence of working parents and single-parent households. Children and teenagers directly influence billions of dollars in annual family purchases. These figures help explain why, for example, Johnson & Johnson, Apple, Kellogg, P&G, Sony, and Oscar Mayer, among countless other companies, spend billions annually in media that reach preteens and teens.[37]

Culture and Subculture

LO 6 **Culture** refers to the set of values, ideas, and attitudes that are learned and shared among the members of a group. Thus, we often refer to Canadian culture, American culture, or Japanese culture. Describing Canadian culture may be difficult due to the diversity in the nation, but many could agree that Canadians are individuals who are polite and fair. Canadians value politeness and feel uncomfortable in situations of conflict. It is a balance of pride and humility. This generalization does not stem to all Canadians, and inaccurate perceptions of Canada were addressed by Molson

culture
A set of values, ideas, and attitudes that are learned and shared among the members of a group.

subcultures
Subgroups within a larger culture that have unique values, ideas, and attitudes.

through its "rant ad" beer commercials in 2000.[38]

Subgroups within the larger, or national, culture with unique values, ideas, and attitudes are referred to as **subcultures**. Subcultures can be defined by regions, by demographic groups, or by values. The most prominent types of subcultures are racial and ethnic, and many of these exist within the Canadian mosaic of people. French, German, Italian, Chinese, and Ukrainian subcultures are the ones we see most in Canada, and they make up nearly 40 percent of the Canadian population. Each one exhibits unique buying patterns and socio-cultural behaviours.

Canada's outlook on ethnicity is that cultural and ethnic groups are welcome to continue with their traditions, languages, and values. Canada is a nation of many faces, and people have been immigrating here continually over many decades. A person may regard herself as Italian, yet never have been to Italy—her grandparents may have immigrated here many years ago. If Italian customs have been maintained by the family, she may behave much like a recently arrived Italian. Some countries encourage immigrants to join the mainstream national culture, while diversity is encouraged in Canada.

Our ethnic composition, and the philosophy that we take toward it, has led to the creation of many ethnic neighbourhoods in our cities. As our population becomes more diverse, people immigrating here bring foods from their native lands. Canadians do not have a lot of native food and preparation styles, so the country has been particularly welcoming of cuisine from around the world. Immigration has had a major influence on Canada's food market, both in the many restaurants and in food items available from all corners of the globe. Not only food consumption is affected by immigration but also many cultural events have become mainstream, and many local happenings are the result of a tradition or celebration brought here by some new Canadians.

Examples of Canadian Subcultures There are almost 10 million French-speaking Canadians in this country, about 30 percent of the population.[39] By far, the largest majority of them live in the province of Quebec. Research shows that French-speaking Quebecers do exhibit different consumption behaviour than the rest of Canada.[40] For example, when asked what is important to them, Quebecers are more likely than other Canadians to say "enjoying life" and "seeking happiness." French Canadians, more so than English Canadians, are more likely to believe

that everybody should be free to do their own thing. Quebecers are also more willing to pay higher prices for convenience and premium brands. Some people feel that French Quebec can be characterized by a set of values that are traditional, consistent, and relatively static, but changes are evident. While values are still strong regarding family life and having children in a marriage, the use of birth control is rising, and the marriage rate is below the national average.

Canada's Diverse Consumers

Identifiable Ethnic Group

Canadian	32%
English	18%
French	14%
Scottish	14%
Irish	13%
German	10%
Italian	5%
Chinese	5%
North American Indian	4%
East Indian	4%
Other	52%

Note: Respondents identified with more than one ethnic group, so percentages add up higher than 100 percent.

Source: "Canada," Central Intelligence Agency, The World Factbook website, accessed October 2019 at https://www.cia.gov/library/publications/the-world-factbook/attachments/summaries/CA-summary.pdf.

French Quebecers are members of a Canadian subculture who are cautious about new products and often postpone trying something new until they see that the product has proven itself. They exhibit brand loyalty, but they will switch brands if offered a special. French Quebecers are less likely to buy grocery items on impulse, and are increasingly calculating in their food purchases. Some grocery chains have responded to this characteristic by offering more discount coupons, weekly specials, and money-saving tips. Quebecers like things that please the senses. For example, they like fine restaurants and fine wines. Quebecois women are also very fashion-conscious, and upscale brands such as Prada and Lancome sell well in Quebec. This desire for beauty helps explain why campaigns for anti-wrinkle products are even more successful in Quebec than in the rest of Canada.[41]

While the province of Quebec has the highest percentage of alcohol drinkers and the most-relaxed drinking laws in Canada, it also has the lowest percentage of excessive drinkers and the fewest alcohol-related problems. French Quebecers are big buyers of lottery tickets and more likely to subscribe to book clubs, but they make fewer long-distance phone calls. They travel less, whether for business or pleasure. More French Quebec adults hold life insurance policies, but they are less likely to have a credit card. They also tend to use the services of credit unions (*caisses populaires*) rather than banks. Marketers must realize that certain products and other elements of the marketing mix may have to be modified in order to be successful in French Quebec. In addition to cultural differences, there are other issues that marketers must address. Commercial advertising to children is prohibited, and greater restrictions exist for alcohol advertising. Provincial regulations also require that labels and packages must be both English and French, while storefront signage must be in French, not English. Good investigation and analysis of this market is a requirement for all companies wishing to do business in this province.

Chinese New Year celebrations take place in Vancouver each year and have become an integral part of the city's cultural fabric.

©Richard Lam/The Canadian Press

Another Canadian subculture and one of the largest and fastest-growing visible minorities in Canada's population is Chinese, with 40 percent residing in Toronto and 31 percent in Vancouver. The average Chinese household spends $63,500 each year, slightly higher than the Canadian average of $58,500. In general, these consumers are relatively young, educated, and affluent. They tend to spend their money on home furnishings, automobiles, kids' education, high-tech gadgets, travelling, and gifts. They like to do business within their own communities and prefer media in their own languages. They have strong allegiance to brands and are very family-oriented. Because they live in close-knit communities, word of mouth is very important to them.[42]

Chinese-Canadians have a preference for luxury vehicles, and many car dealerships see them as good potential customers for new cars. In general, they tend to eat out at restaurants more than the average Canadian, and there has been significant growth in the number of Chinese restaurants in Canada, and particularly in Vancouver and Toronto, over the past ten years. For these, and a number of other factors, many marketers cater to the Chinese market as they see them as being good prospective customers.

Global Cultural Diversity

Canada has become increasingly multiethnic and multicultural, making it one of the most diverse countries in the world. Different countries take different approaches to admitting immigrants and integrating them into society. Canada's approach is often referred to as a mosaic, meaning that people who come to the country from another are welcome to maintain their cultural identities and customs—the belief is that this will create a situation where all Canadians can learn from the rich variety of over 200 cultures that make up the citizenry of the country. This environment works to increase Canadian companies' sensitivity and orientation toward other cultures, so the transition to global activities and relationships is facilitated.

Just as marketers must be sensitive to subcultures in Canada, they must appreciate the cultural differences of people in other countries if they want to market products and services to them. A necessary step in this process is **cross-cultural analysis**, which involves the study of similarities and differences among consumers in two or more nations or societies.[43] A thorough cross-cultural analysis involves an understanding of and an appreciation for the values, customs, symbols, and language of other societies.

cross-cultural analysis
Study of similarities and differences among consumers in two or more societies.

Values A society's values represent socially preferable modes of conduct or states of existence that tend to persist over time. Understanding and working with these aspects of a society are important factors in global marketing. For example, consider the following:[44]

- McDonald's does not sell hamburgers in its restaurants in India because the cow is considered sacred by almost 85 percent of the population. Instead, McDonald's sells the McMaharajah: two all-mutton patties, special sauce, lettuce, cheese, pickles, onions on a sesame-seed bun.

- Germans have not been overly receptive to the use of credit cards such as Visa or MasterCard, nor to the idea of borrowing to purchase goods and services. The German word for "debt," *Schuld*, is the same as the German word for "guilt."

Customs

customs
Norms and expectations about the way people do things in a specific country or culture.

Customs are what is considered normal and expected about the way people do things in a specific country or culture. Clearly, customs can vary significantly from country to country. Some customs may seem unusual to Canadians. Consider, for example, that in France, men wear more than twice the number of cosmetics that women do, and that the Japanese consider slurping their food to be a sign of approval and appreciation to the chef.

The custom of giving token business gifts is popular in many countries where they are expected and accepted. However, bribes, kickbacks, and payoffs offered to entice someone to commit an illegal or improper act on behalf of the giver for economic gain is considered corrupt in most cultures. The widespread use of bribery in global marketing has led to an agreement among the world's major exporting nations to make bribery of foreign government officials a criminal offence.

The Organisation for Economic Co-operation and Development (OECD) is an international body whose goal is to foster democratic government and a market-driven economy. With its global reach, OECD addresses issues of general interest to its members and affiliates. Corruption has become an issue of major importance in the past decade, and the OECD has taken action to set guidelines and procedures for preventing international bribery and corruption. Canada has adopted the OECD's anti-corruption convention and has made bribery of foreign public officials a criminal offence.[45]

Bribery paid to foreign companies is another matter. In France and Greece, bribes paid to foreign companies are a tax-deductible expense!

Coca-Cola executives learned valuable lessons when they used the Eiffel Tower and the Parthenon in global advertising campaigns.

(left) ©Wam1975/Dreamstime.com/GetStock.com; (right) ©Bcbounders/Dreamstime.com/GetStock.com

Cultural Symbols

Cultural symbols are objects, ideas, or processes that represent a particular group of people or society. Symbols and symbolism play an important role in cross-cultural analysis because different cultures attach different meanings to things. By cleverly using cultural symbols, global marketers can tie positive symbolism to their products and services to enhance their attractiveness to consumers. However, improper use of symbols can spell disaster. A culturally sensitive global marketer will know the following:[46]

- North Americans are superstitious about the number 13, and Japanese feel the same way about the number 4. *Shi*, the Japanese word for "four," is also the word for "death." Knowing this, Tiffany & Company sells its fine glassware and china in sets of five, not four, in Japan.

- "Thumbs-up" is a positive sign in Canada. However, in Russia and Poland, this gesture has an offensive meaning when the palm of the hand is shown, as AT&T learned. The company reversed the gesture depicted in ads, showing the back of the hand, not the palm.

Cultural symbols stir up deep feelings. Consider how executives at Coca-Cola's Italian office learned this lesson. In a series of advertisements directed at Italian vacationers, the Eiffel Tower, Empire State Building, and the Tower of Pisa were turned into the familiar Coca-Cola bottle. However, when the white marble columns in the Parthenon that crown Athens's Acropolis were turned into Coca-Cola bottles, the Greeks were outraged. Greeks refer to the Acropolis as the "holy rock," and a government official said the Parthenon is an "international symbol of excellence" and that "whoever insults the Parthenon insults international culture." Coca-Cola apologized for the ad.[47]

Language

Global marketers should know not only the basics of the native tongues of countries in which they market their products and services but also the subtleties and unique expressions of the language. For example, Pepsi found that Spanish-speaking people in Argentina tend to pronounce the soft drink as Pecsi rather than Pepsi. Pepsi responded by launching a successful marketing campaign that temporarily used the spelling Pecsi rather than Pepsi on billboards in Argentina. The brand name Pepsi was never really legally changed, but humorously altered for the period of the campaign.[48]

About 100 official languages exist in the world, but anthropologists estimate that at least 3,000 different languages are actually spoken. There are 11 official languages spoken in the European Union,

The Nestlé Kit Kat bar influences teens in Japan through its translated meaning.
©CB2/ZOB/WENN/Newscom

and Canada has two official languages (English and French). Seventeen major languages are spoken in India alone.

English, French, and Spanish are the principal languages used in global diplomacy and commerce. However, the best language with which to communicate with consumers is their own, as any seasoned global marketer will agree. Language usage and translation can present challenges. Unintended meanings of brand names and messages have ranged from the absurd to the obscene, as in the following examples:

- When the advertising agency responsible for launching Procter & Gamble's successful Pert shampoo in Canada realized that the name means "lost" in French, it substituted the brand name Pret, which means "ready."

- The Vicks brand name common in North America is German slang for sexual intimacy; therefore, Vicks is called Wicks in Germany.

Experienced global marketers use **back translation**, where a translated word or phrase is retranslated back into the original language by a different interpreter to catch errors.[49] IBM's first Japanese translation of its "Solution for a small planet" advertising message yielded "Answers that make people smaller." The error was caught by back translation and corrected. Sometimes, unintended translations can produce favourable results. Consider Kit Kat bars marketed by Nestlé worldwide. Kit Kat is pronounced "kitto katsu" in Japanese, which roughly translates to "I will win." Japanese teens eat Kit Kat bars for good luck, particularly when taking crucial school exams.[50]

cultural symbols
Objects, ideas, or processes that represent a particular group of people or society.

back translation
Retranslating a word or phrase back into the original language by a different interpreter to catch errors.

McMillennials

While enjoying a Big Mac™ for lunch in Squamish, British Columbia, a McDonald's customer may wonder if the experience she is enjoying is similar in other locations. Hopping on a plane and travelling to the East Coast, the customer will generally have a consistent experience at a McDonald's in Halifax.

Offering this level of consistency among all its locations is one of the strengths of McDonald's and why its brand is considered among the Top 10 global brands. Maintaining this consistency can pose a challenge with a company with over 1,400 stores in Canada. This can also get costly as innovation is needed to service future generations of customers.

According to *UCLA Magazine*, the millennial demographic is now larger than the baby boomer demographic. Marketers need to understand how to appeal to their desire for high-end brands and technology. Furthermore, millennials seem to be drawn to products from companies that have similar social and political

values. Millennials are comfortable testing new technology and enjoy receiving content in small chunks. Millennials seem to shy away from old business models and look to models that embrace digital technology. Moreover, millennials view shopping as a sport, leading retailers to adopt a more experienced-based marketing strategy.

Interpreting what future generations need and want is a challenge. However, making bold moves to change the way traditional business is done is something McDonald's is a pioneer for across the world. For Canadians, McDonald's Canada has introduced a solution that will appeal to millennials who embrace utility. Self-service kiosks and table delivery is now available for individuals who choose not to stand and wait for their food. Furthermore, additions to the menu will allow for custom-made burgers. The 1,400 stores in Canada receiving this innovation will cost approximately $200,000 each to refit. By marketing to millennials

The McDonald's kiosk and other innovations may appeal to millennials.
©Tribune Content Agency LLC/Alamy Stock Photo

who embrace digital technology, this can attract a new generation of brand-loyal consumers who value a consistent experience as well as a consistent product. With the future Generation Z being influenced by friends and family, McDonald's and other companies need to establish an online presence and excellent customer experience. ●

Questions

1. How are your consumer behaviours similar to the generalizations describing millennials?

2. How will McDonald's kiosks impact your decision to go to McDonald's?

Successful marketers understand the differences and similarities in consumers. They draw together commonalities and segment their audience into groups that will find their products and services appealing. By keeping current with the changing trends in consumer values and attitudes, marketers can stay in sync with their audiences. See, for example, the Marketing NewsFlash box, "McMillennials."[51]

ask **YOURSELF**

1. *What are the two primary forms of personal influence?*

2. *What challenges do marketers face when marketing to ethnic subcultural groups?*

LUV GOES A LONG WAY.

With 65 Southwest cities across the country, we're pretty good at long-distance relationships.

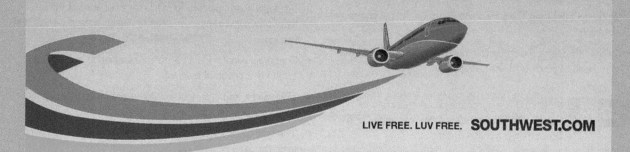

LIVE FREE. LUV FREE. **SOUTHWEST.COM**

Source: Southwest Airlines Co.

1. *What type of consumer involvement is required when choosing an airline ticket?*
2. *Describe the consumer purchase decision process as it relates to purchasing an airline ticket.*

Summary... JUST THE FACTS

 1 • The first stage of the purchase decision process is problem recognition where the consumer perceives a need.

- The second stage is the information search where the consumer seeks value in the potential purchase options.

- The third stage is the evaluation of alternatives where the consumer assesses the value of each option.

- In the fourth stage, the consumer executes the purchase decision.

- In the fifth stage, the consumer determines the value of the purchase in post-purchase behaviour.

 2 • Consumer purchase decisions range in complexity. This creates three variations of the consumer purchase decisions.

- Routine problem-solving, such as purchasing tissues when you have a cold, requires little effort.

- Limited problem-solving may occur when consumers compare and decide upon different brands, such as for refreshments.

- Extended problem-solving routinely involves time and consideration in each of the five distinct stages of the consumer purchase decision process. Purchasing electronics usually requires extended problem-solving.

 3 • There are five situational influences that impact the consumer purchase decision process.

- The reason for engaging in the decision in the first place is called the purchase task. Why you are making the purchase may determine how much you plan on spending.

- Social surroundings, including who else is present in the process, also have an impact on the decision process.

- Another situational influence is the physical surroundings during the process. A store that is busy may have a positive or negative effect on the consumer.

- When the purchase is being made is a temporal effect, and the momentary mood or antecedent state of the consumer also affects the process.

 4 • The main psychological influences affecting consumer behaviour are motivation and personality; perception; learning; values, beliefs and attitudes; and lifestyle.

- Motivation is the energizing force that causes consumers to satisfy a need, while personality and character traits influence behavioural responses.

- Perception is important to marketers because of the selectivity of what a consumer sees or hears, comprehends, and retains.

- Consumers learn from repeated experience, and brand loyalty is a result of learning.

- The values and beliefs of a consumer create their learned predisposition or attitudes toward a product.

- The consumers' lifestyle identifies how they plan to spend their time and resources.

 5 • The consumer purchase-decision process can be affected by personal influence, reference groups, and family influences.

- Personal influence can be seen in opinion leadership and word-of-mouth activity. These are normally created by individuals with social influence. Personal influence can also take the form of reference groups.

- Family influences on consumer behaviour include where the family is in its family life cycle and how decisions are made within the household.

 6 • Culture is the set of values, ideas, and attitudes that are learned and shared among the members of a group.

- There are subgroups within larger cultures that have unique values, ideas, and attitudes. These subgroups are called subcultures.

- Both culture and subculture influence consumer behaviour as these values permeate through situational, psychological, and socio-cultural influences.

key terms and concepts... A REFRESHER

attitude	culture	perceived risk
back translation	customs	perception
beliefs	family life cycle	personality
brand loyalty	involvement	purchase decision process
consumer behaviour	learning	reference group
cross-cultural analysis	motivation	subcultures
cultural symbols	opinion leaders	word of mouth

Unsought Product Purchase Assignment Arbor Memorial helps Canadians commemorate the lives of their loved ones.

Review the consumer decision-making process and outline how a difficult decision to choose Arbor Memorial may be made.

chapter vignette... **ACTIVITY**

The vignette at the beginning of the chapter explores consumer behaviour with an unsought product. The chapter also discusses the various influences affecting whether a consumer purchases a particular product. In your class, work individually or within a group and consider the consumer purchase decision process when working with an organization like Arbor Memorial. After listing the steps, identify which situational, psychological, and socio-cultural influences might affect your decision.

infographic... **DATA ANALYSIS**

The Infographic entitled "Reducing Food Waste in Ontario" discusses how consumers and organizations can reduce food waste. Discuss how a consumer who believes in the importance in reducing food waste may have a different consumer decision making process than someone who is not as concerned with this social issue.

The Infographic entitled "What Do We Know about Home Ownership and Mortgage Debt in Canada?" illustrates how consumer debt is increasing. Discuss how increasing consumer debt may impact the consumer decision-making process.

Market Research

Market research, metrics, and analytics are tools used by marketers to gather data and obtain insights to make fact-based decisions easier and more accurate. Today, forward-thinking organizations use these tools and foster a culture of measurement, analytics, and continuous improvement by investing in technology, partnerships, and people. The goal is to manage data and to discern patterns, correlations, and insights that are actionable and provide a competitive edge. This chapter focuses on these tools, explaining their purpose and how they are used in this era of big data.

Deepwater Farms

CHAPTER OUTLINE

- Deepwater Farms
- Market research process
- Types of research, metrics, and analytics

The food industry has experienced increased challenges as the world's population continues to grow, and as urban sprawl reduces farm land. There is also an increasing demand for farm-to-table fresh food and fish. An entrepreneurial student, Paul Shumlich, together with his co-founder Kevin Daniels, recognized this opportunity while still in university, and the two of them leveraged their research skills to build an innovative new business, Deepwater Farms, a Calgary-based aquaponics farm.

There has never been so much access to data as there is in today's society. Deepwater Farms grows local, sustainable fresh leafy greens and sea bass. "Currently there's no year-round provider. There's no high-quality source. So, we just saw a gap between restaurants looking for high-quality, sustainable local ingredients and being able to provide that year-round in consistently high volumes," Shumlich says.

Aquaponics is a combination of aquaculture, which is growing fish and other aquatic animals, and hydroponics, which is growing plants without soil. Aquaponics uses these two processes in a symbiotic combination in which plants are fed the aquatic animals' discharge or waste. In return, the vegetables clean the water that goes back to the fish. Along with the fish and their waste, microbes play an important role in the nutrition of the plants. These beneficial bacteria gather in the spaces between the roots of the plant and convert the fish waste and the solids into substances the plants can use to grow. The result is a perfect collaboration between aquaculture and gardening.

The appeal of aquaponic farming is its reduced uses of water, space, and labour. Today, almost a third of commercial fish stocks are overharvested at biologically unsustainable levels. Moreover, population growth and demand are still outpacing supply. This represents an opportunity for sustainable food production systems like aquaponics, with benefits including a lack of pesticides, herbicides, and chemical fertilizers. The system enables both protein (e.g., fish) and vegetables to be grown from a single integrated system that operates 24/7, 365 days a year.

The demand to grow local has been significant. One study suggests that 50 percent of respondents were prepared to pay 10 percent more for locally grown foods, with one-third prepared to pay 25 percent more. Today, Deepwater Farms's clients are the chefs and staff at fine-dining restaurants who share the same values associated with high-quality and sustainable local ingredients. This commitment has been critical to the early success of Deepwater Farms. Shumlich notes, "We are so proud that so many of our clients are now listing us on their menu. This is a true sign that we are a partner, not just a supplier." In order for Deepwater Farms to grow its local market, the company meets monthly with every chef in the city until they place their first order, and then meet with them every month to ensure they are satisfied. "This is a small community of people, so their success is our success. These relationships are what will drive our local growth."

Calgary has proven to be an optimal market for Deepwater Farms to build its business in because it meets the key market criteria of a large and affluent population that imports 95 percent of its fish. Though Canada exports over $5 billion (US$) of fish, different varieties of freshwater fish are imported to Canada, including trout, tilapia, catfish, salmon, and carp. In Calgary, Deepwater Farms's main competition is imported products from California, Arizona, and Mexico. This is because aquaponic farming is a small, but rapidly growing business that is driven by demand for food security, reduced access to fresh water and land, and increasing consumer demand for locally grown food.

Deepwater Farms's mission is to bring the farm closer to people and people closer to their food. While their first commercial sale happened in February 2018 with the sale of aquaponic kale to fine-dining restaurants that put a focus and high value on local, farm-stable, high-quality ingredients, recently, a new 10,000 sq. ft. warehouse farm opened with room to expand to tens of thousands of fish. In the past two years, the company has tripled its fish production and doubled its plant production. Deepwater Farms wants to build farms all over the world and improve the food system by localizing production and bringing people closer to their food, so they have a better understanding of what's in it and the impact it has.[1]

The Role of Marketing Research

Let's (1) look at what marketing research is, (2) identify some difficulties with it, and (3) describe the five steps marketers use to conduct it.

What Is Marketing Research?

marketing research
The process of defining a marketing problem and opportunity, systematically collecting and analyzing information, and recommending actions.

Marketing research is the process of defining a marketing problem and opportunity, systematically collecting and analyzing information, and recommending actions.[2] Although imperfect, marketers conduct marketing research to reduce the risk of—and thereby improve—marketing decisions.

The Challenges in Doing Good Marketing Research

LO 1 Whatever the marketing issue involved—whether discovering consumer tastes or setting the right price—good marketing research is challenging. For example:

- Suppose your firm is developing a product that is completely new to the marketplace, and you are charged with estimating demand for the product. How can marketing research determine if consumers will buy a product they have never seen, and never thought about, before?
- Understanding why consumers purchase some products often requires answers to personal questions. How can marketing research obtain answers that people know but are reluctant to reveal?
- Past purchase behaviours may help firms understand the influence of marketing actions. How can marketing research help people accurately remember and report their interests, intentions, and purchases?

Marketing research must overcome these difficulties and obtain the information needed so that marketers can assess what consumers want and will buy.

The Five-Step Market Research Approach

LO 2 Effective market research is not left to chance. A systematic approach ensures that market research is done thoroughly, that all elements are considered, and that results are accurate. The Saskatchewan Roughriders, based out of Regina, contracted Insightrix Research to better understand its target

Saskatchewan Roughriders: Using Analytics to Fill Mosaic Stadium

©Cal Sport Media/Alamy Stock Photo

The Saskatchewan Roughriders have a long and storied history, starting in 1910 as the Regina Rugby team and continuously playing some sort of football for the last 110 years. The Roughriders are community owned and located in the second-smallest professional sports market in North America, only slightly larger than Green Bay, Wisconsin. This Canadian Football League (CFL) team is based in Regina, Saskatchewan, but has fans throughout Saskatchewan and Canada. These fans are known as "Rider Nation," and they fill the stands with their green and white jerseys and watermelon hats at home and away games.

In 2017 the team was moving into the brand new Mosaic Stadium and wanted to better understand its fans, especially the younger demographics. Miriam Johnson, director of marketing for the Saskatchewan Roughriders, summed it up this way:

> As we prepared for significant change in our game-day environment and potentially the perception of our brand with the move to new Mosaic Stadium, we needed to have a better understanding of what our baseline measurement was prior to the move.

Enter Insightrix Research, a Saskatchewan-based research company that starts "with a research approach that looks beyond the superficial to uncover people's true motivations and opinions." To get these insights, Insightrix uses a tool called SaskWatch, which is a panel of over 15,000 people from Saskatchewan that they can poll at any time about any issue.

Once the (1) *problem* of understanding the various segments of the market was identified, the team went to work designing a (2) *research plan* that utilized the SaskWatch panel.

In doing the exploratory research, Insightrix realized that sports is a highly intangible and personalized service—each participant, spectator, or fan receives a unique set of benefits from their participation, and the sport product is inconsistent and unpredictable. With this knowledge in hand, Insightrix developed a series of questions (3) *collect the relevant information* utilizing the SaskWatch panel. To confront the sector-specific characteristics mentioned above, specialist segmentation approaches (unique to professional sports supporters) were adopted by Insightrix.

Emphasis was placed on the importance of a sport fan's values (ranging from "I bleed green" to "I do not care about the team") along with the number of games fans watch every season. The segments identified were further analyzed to understand demographics, thoughts and feelings, purchase behaviour, and general sports viewership.

Once the (4) *findings* were developed, the complex linkages between the Roughriders supporters' motives (for example, winning, entertainment, or self-image) and their loyalty and behaviour were uncovered. This assisted the team in understanding the actual demographics and motivations of its fans, as opposed to preconceptions or stereotypes. This, in turn, assisted and informed the Roughriders to (5) *take marketing actions* to better facilitate and encourage engagement with Saskatchewan residents and be better prepared to help fans create positive memories during special situations, like watching the game in the new Mosaic Stadium.

The Roughriders found this experience to be so positive that the organization now uses SaskWatch regularly to monitor success of game-day promotions and the overall satisfaction of the fans. The ongoing success of this research motivated the Roughriders to create a position on the staff for a CRM programmer analyst to use market research and analytics to measure customer satisfaction and make recommendations to the organization. Johnson concluded:

> What we anticipated leveraging for measurement (demographic) wasn't what we ended up using due to the consistent results and, instead, utilized the level of fan to segment the province to show areas of potential growth as we move forward. ●

Questions

1. Why did the Roughriders decide to conduct research with Insightrix?

2. What key performance indicators (KPIs) did the Saskatchewan Roughriders use to measure the success of its promotions?

market and assist in marketing decisions, especially as the team was moving into a brand new, large stadium. The organization wanted to better understand how the team is perceived by Saskatchewan residents, especially among younger demographics. The Roughriders aimed to identify different segments within its fan base to understand how it engages with both the team itself and with the Rider brand overall. Insightrix was able to reach out to Saskatchewan residents through SaskWatch®, the largest Saskatchewan-based online research panel, which currently numbers over 15,000 Saskatchewan residents as dedicated members. You can read more about this research project in the Marketing NewsFlash box, "Saskatchewan Roughriders: Using Analytics to Fill Mosaic Stadium," which demonstrates market research in practice.[3]

Let's look at the basic five-step approach that is commonly used to conduct market research studies. It is worth noting that not all research projects require qualitative and quantitative studies (steps 3 and 4). In many instances, qualitative research can suffice, while in others, quantitative studies are required for greater certainty.

Figure 4–1 shows this sequence of steps, and in the next few pages, we will discuss these steps in detail.

objectives
Specific, measurable, and achievable goals.

measures of success
Criteria or standards used in evaluating proposed solutions to the problem.

ask YOURSELF

1. *What are the three types of market research?*
2. *What steps are included in the five-step market research process?*

Step 1: Define the Problem/ Issue/Opportunity

The first step in the market research process is to clearly define the problem, issue, or opportunity, and to clarify the research objectives. This is often posed as a question that needs to be answered. Most market researchers would agree with the saying that "a problem well-defined is half-solved," but defining a problem is a difficult task. Most market research issues stem from poorly defined problems and objectives that are vague and unclear: If objectives are too broad, the problem may not be tangible; if the objectives are too narrow, the value of the research may be questionable. Market researchers spend considerable time precisely defining marketing problems and clarifying research objectives in formal proposals that clearly describe the research task and its approach. **Objectives** are specific, measurable, and achievable goals that the decision maker seeks to achieve. Common research objectives are to discover consumer needs and wants, and to determine why a product is not selling.

Identify Possible Marketing Actions

Effective decision makers develop specific **measures of success**, which are criteria or standards used in evaluating proposed solutions to the problem. Different research outcomes, based on the measure of success, lead to different marketing actions.

Marketing researchers know that defining a problem is an incredibly difficult task. If the objectives are too broad, the problem may not be researchable. If they

Figure 4–1
The basic market research process

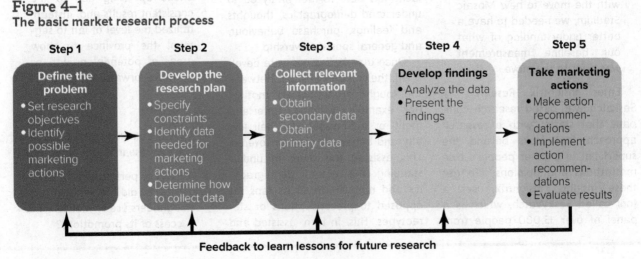

Feedback to learn lessons for future research

are too narrow, the value of the research results may be seriously diminished. This is why marketing researchers spend so much time defining a marketing problem precisely and writing a formal proposal that describes the research to be done.[4]

Using the Saskatchewan Roughrider scenario as an example, the team was moving to a larger, brand new stadium and contracted Insightrix to better understand its fan base and target market and the potential opportunities for growth. This was the basis of the problem and its research objectives.

Step 2: Develop the Research Plan

The second step in the market research process is to identify which approach will be taken to complete the project. This includes identifying what information is needed, how it will be collected, and whether a sampling plan is needed. Let's look at these three areas.

Information Requirements

Often, market research studies collect data that is interesting but not relevant to the task at hand. Marketers need to avoid this situation because it is time-consuming, confusing, and costly. In the Saskatchewan Roughriders situation, Insightrix was contracted to conduct a survey with Saskatchewan residents to understand how the team is perceived by Saskatchewan residents, especially among younger demographics. The Roughriders aimed to identify different segments within its fan base to understand how they engage with both the team itself and with the Roughriders brand overall.

Collection Methods

When determining the way in which data will be collected, methodology, cost, efficiency, and accuracy of results are important considerations. As a result, it is important to have a data collection plan. There are mathematical considerations and operational issues that the researcher must consider. Determining how to collect the data is often as important as actually collecting the data. Researchers can consider whether available pre-existing data is sufficient to answer the research question or whether they need to conduct their own research using a variety of data collection methods, such as in-depth personal interviews, focus groups, telephone surveys,

personal questionnaires, or mail surveys. The Internet also provides numerous online tools that facilitate the gathering of information. Surveys can be easily completed online, and online communities and online bulletin boards can also be used to provide additional data.

To ensure that accurate answers are obtained, researchers carefully select research methodologies that encourage honesty. The method chosen is critical to obtaining accurate results. In the case of the Saskatchewan Roughriders, the organization contracted Insightrix to reach out to Saskatchewan residents through SaskWatch, the largest Saskatchewan-based online research panel, which currently numbers 15,000 Saskatchewan residents as dedicated members.

Canadian market researchers rely on their training, expertise, and judgment to make appropriate methodology decisions. They can also turn to their professional association, the Marketing Research and Intelligence Association, for resources and training.

Sampling

Sampling is another important factor in research design. A researcher's sampling plan identifies who is to be sampled, how large the sample should be, and how the sample will be selected. Rarely does a research project involve a complete census of every person in the research population, because this is time-consuming and costly. Therefore, market researchers use smaller samples that are representative of the population being surveyed. **Sampling** is the process of gathering data from a subset of the total population, rather than from all members of that particular group.

> **sampling**
> The process of gathering data from a subset of the total population rather than from all members of that particular group.

Rarely does a research project involve a complete census of every person in the research population, because this is time-consuming and costly.

A properly selected sample should be representative of the population being researched; however, unless the entire population can be included, sampling errors can occur. Increasing the sample size can help decrease sampling error, but the larger the sample size, the higher the cost.

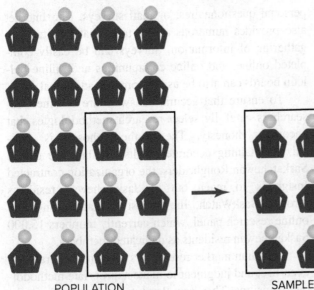

POPULATION → SAMPLE

A properly selected sample should be representative of the population being studied.

Other factors that may impact research design are the timelines for the research to be completed and the budget. Currently, a number of market researchers are debating the validity of online market research studies, questioning whether online samples are valid because they exclude respondents who are not online. In reality, all research methodologies have advantages and disadvantages. Market researchers always need to understand the limitations of the methodology they select.

There are two basic sampling techniques: probability and non-probability sampling. **Probability sampling** involves precise rules to select the sample so that each element of the population has a specific known chance of being selected. For example, if your university wants to know how last year's 1,000 graduates are doing, it can put their names into a bowl and randomly select 100 names to contact. The chance of being selected (100 out of 1,000, or 1 in 10) is known in advance, and all graduates have an equal chance of being contacted. This procedure helps to select a sample (100 graduates) that should be representative of the entire population (the 1,000 graduates), and allows conclusions to be drawn about the population being researched.

Non-probability sampling involves the use of arbitrary judgment by the market researcher to select a sample so that

the chance of selecting a particular element of the population is either unknown or zero. If your university decided to talk to 100 of last year's graduates, but only selected those who lived closest, many graduates would be excluded. This would introduce a bias, tainting the representativeness of the sample and its ability to draw accurate conclusions.

It is worth noting that the researcher may decide to follow non-probability sampling when time and budgets are limited, or for exploratory research purposes when conclusions are mostly directional and may require further research. In general, market researchers use data from such non-probability samples with caution. The data can provide valuable information, but the results need to be viewed carefully as they may not accurately represent the population being researched.

In the case of the example involving the Saskatchewan Roughriders and Insightrix, they carefully set quotas by age and gender to make sure the survey respondents mirrored the Saskatchewan provincial population.

ask YOURSELF

1. *How do research objectives relate to marketing actions?*

2. *What are the differences between probability and non-probability sampling?*

3. *Which type of sampling did Insightrix and the Saskatchewan Roughriders utilize?*

Step 3: Collect Relevant Information

LO 3 Collecting enough relevant information to make a rational, informed marketing decision sometimes simply means using your knowledge to decide immediately. At other times it entails collecting an enormous amount of information at great expense.

Figure 4–2 shows how the different kinds of marketing information fit together. **Data**, the facts and figures related to the project, are divided into two main parts: secondary data and primary data. **Secondary data** are facts and figures that have already been recorded prior to the project at hand. As shown in Figure 4–2, secondary data are divided into two parts—internal and

probability sampling

Selecting a sample so that each element of a population has a specific known chance of being selected.

non-probability sampling

Selecting a sample so that the chance of selecting a particular element of a population is either unknown or zero.

data

The facts and figures related to the project that are divided into two main parts: secondary data and primary data.

secondary data

Facts and figures that have already been recorded by a third party.

Figure 4–2
Sources of information

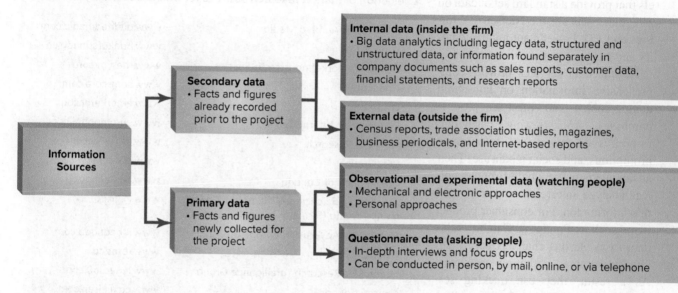

external secondary data—depending on whether the data come from inside or outside the organization needing the research. **Primary data** are facts and figures that are newly collected for the project. Figure 4–2 shows that primary data can be divided into observational data, questionnaire data, and other sources of data.

marketing TIP

"In today's data-driven economy, market research is about speed more than it ever has been before. The need for faster, cheaper, and better research is changing the marketing landscape."

– Raj Manocha, EVP, Delvinia

Secondary research may be followed up by primary research such as focus groups or research with online communities and bulletin boards to further probe attitudes and opportunities.

Secondary Data

An overview of information sources of secondary data can be seen in Figure 4–2. This data comes in two forms: external data and internal data. *Internal data* exists within a company and can include data derived from data analytics, or simpler approaches that review basic sales reports, profitability data, and costing information. *External data* comes from published sources outside the organization.

Secondary Data: Internal The internal records of a company generally offer the most easily accessible marketing information. These internal sources of

secondary data may be divided into two related parts: (1) marketing inputs and (2) marketing outcomes.

Marketing input data relate to the effort expended to make sales. These range from marketing budget reports, which include advertising expenditures, to salespeople's call reports, which describe the number of sales calls per day, who was visited, and what was discussed.

Marketing outcome data relate to the results of the marketing efforts. These involve accounting records on shipments and include sales and repeat sales, often broken down by sales representative, industry, and geographic region. In addition, e-mails, phone calls, and letters from customers can reveal both complaints and what is working well.[5]

Secondary Data: External Published data from outside the organization are external secondary data. Statistics Canada publishes a variety of useful reports. Best known is the 2016 Census, which is the most recent count of the Canadian population that occurs every five years. These surveys contain detailed information on Canadian households, such as the number of people per household and the age, sex, race/ethnic background, income, occupation, and education of individuals within the household. Marketers use these data to identify characteristics and trends of ultimate consumers.

Several marketing research companies pay households and businesses to record all their purchases using a paper or electronic diary. Such *syndicated panel* data economically answer questions that require consistent data collection over time, such as, "How many times did our customers buy our products this year compared to

primary data
Data that is original and specifically collected for a project.

last year?" Examples of syndicated panels that provide a standard set of data on a regular basis are the Nielsen TV ratings and J.D. Power's automotive quality and customer satisfaction surveys.

Some data services provide comprehensive information on household demographics and lifestyle, product purchases, TV viewing behaviour, responses to coupon and free-sample promotions, and social media use. Their advantage is that a single firm can collect, analyze, interrelate, and present all this information. For consumer product firms such as Procter & Gamble, sales data from various channels help them allocate scarce marketing resources. As a result, they use tracking services such as IRI's InfoScan to collect product sales and coupon/free-sample redemptions that have been scanned at the checkout counters of supermarket, drug, convenience, and mass merchandise retailers.

Finally, trade associations, universities, and business periodicals provide detailed data of value to marketing researchers and planners. These data are often available online and can be identified and located using a search engine such as Google or Bing.

Statistics Canada, the federal government's statistical agency, publishes a wide variety of useful reports, such as census data that includes information on the number of people per household and their age, gender, ethnic background, income, occupation, and education. Statistics Canada also publishes a wide range of other statistical reports that are used by businesses across the country. These reports include information on the following:

- Economic indicators
- International trade
- Culture and leisure
- Agriculture
- Tourism and travel
- Manufacturing
- Government
- Environment
- Justice and crime
- Health

Figure 4–3
A selection of market research sources for online secondary data

Alliance for Audited Media	www.auditedmedia.com
Bank of Canada	www.bankofcanada.ca
Canadian Marketing Association	www.the-cma.org
comScore	www.comscore.com
eMarketer	www.emarketer.com
Euromonitor International	www.euromonitor.com
Forrester Research	www.forrester.com
GFK Group	www.gfk.com
Government of Canada	www.canada.gc.ca
Innovation, Science and Economic Development Canada (formerly Industry Canada)	www.ic.gc.ca
Interactive Advertising Bureau of Canada	www.iabcanada.com
Ipsos Canada	www.ipsos.ca
Leger, The Research Intelligence Group	www.leger360.com
Nielsen Canada	www.ca.nielsen.com
Numeris	www.numeris.ca
Organisation for Economic Co-operation and Development (OECD)	www.oecd.org
Pew Research Center	www.pewresearch.org
SEDAR	www.sedar.com
Solutions Research Group	www.srgnet.com
Statista	www.statista.com
Statistics Canada	www.statcan.gc.ca
World Advertising Research Center	www.warc.com

Worth Noting
Your library may have access to various online databases that can assist with research projects. Examples of these databases are Business Source Complete, CBCA Business, Canadian Newsstand, Conference Board of Canada, Factiva, LexisNexis Academic, Mergent Online, Proquest, Scott's Canadian Business Directory, and ThompsonOne.

A list of online secondary research sources is detailed in Figure 4–3. These sources are often posted online. Marketers can read interesting articles, view snapshots of research projects, download full reports, or read synopses of research studies. Examples include third-party organizations that audit magazine and newspaper circulation or the popularity of TV shows. Similarly, competitive market share data is available for marketers to purchase to help track competitive activity.

ask YOURSELF

1. What are some of the online tools available to market researchers?

2. What are the advantages and disadvantages of secondary data?

Primary Data

LO 4 In a research project, a general rule is to first obtain secondary data followed by detailed, proprietary primary data. This sequencing is because secondary data is lower in cost and easier to obtain than primary data. Secondary data can also help illuminate further data requirements. These advantages of secondary data must be weighed against its disadvantages, namely that (1) the secondary data may be out of date, (2) the definitions or categories may not be right for the project, and (3) the data may not be accurate or specific enough for the study. Primary data is data that is original and specifically collected for the project at hand. Let's review the primary sources of information.

Focus Groups

A popular qualitative research technique is the focus group. A **focus group** is an informal interview session in which six to ten people are brought together in a room with a moderator to discuss topics surrounding the market research problem. The moderator poses open-ended questions and encourages individuals to discuss the issues. Often, focus group sessions are watched by observers and are videotaped. Participants are always informed that they are being observed and/or taped and asked for permission to do so.

> " *A popular qualitative research technique is the focus group.*

In-Depth Interviews

Another qualitative research technique used to obtain primary data involves the use of in-depth interviews. **In-depth interviews** are detailed individual interviews where a researcher discusses topics with an individual at length in a free-flowing conversation in order to discover information that may help solve a marketing problem. Sometimes, these interviews can take a few hours, and they are often recorded with respondents' consent.

Online Research Communities

A relatively new qualitative research tool used by marketers to gain feedback on marketing approaches is the online research community. **Online research communities** involve the use of consumer groups, brought together privately in an online environment, to answer questions, respond to ideas, and collaborate with researchers in real time. This approach uses vocal consumers, often in high-involvement categories, such as sports and entertainment, or other areas where consumers are passionate about their products, such as chocolate and baby food. These consumers provide feedback to researchers in a private online environment where only the marketers, researchers, and respondents are privy to the conversations. Typically, this approach invites consumers to join an online community on a specific topic in return for interesting and lively debate, thought-provoking ideas, and a small stipend for their time. An online community is managed by a research company to ensure that the community is engaged and continues to be interested in the topic. Participants can be gathered from a variety of sources such as website visitors, consumer lists, or company databases. The community involves regular two-way communication visible to all within the community, is managed by a researcher, and can involve 200 to 300 people depending on the need. Multinational brands often maintain large global communities to help answer their marketing questions.

Online Research Bulletin Boards

Another new research tool available to researchers is the online research bulletin board. **Online research bulletin boards** are private online forums where respondents can post their responses to questions. They are static website locations where questions are posted online, and respondents are asked to comment on ideas. Only those with access to the bulletin board

What form of research is a focus group?
©Marmaduke St. John/Alamy Stock Photo

focus group
A qualitative research technique where a small group of people (usually six to ten) meet for a few hours with a trained moderator to discuss predetermined areas.

in-depth interviews
Detailed interviews where a researcher questions an individual at length in a free-flowing conversational style in order to discover information that may help solve a marketing problem.

online research communities
The use of consumer groups, brought together privately in an online environment, to answer questions, respond to ideas, and collaborate with researchers in real time.

online research bulletin boards
Private online static forums, without real-time dialogue, where respondents can post their responses to questions posed by researchers.

are privy to the posted questions and responses. While online bulletin boards may not provide researchers with the depth of information available through an online community, they are easier to manage and administer.

Social Listening

The growth in social media and its ability to influence consumers has given rise to a new exploratory research technique, *social listening*, which monitors public online consumer conversations and images on social media sites such as social networks, blogs, and public forums. The metrics derived from social listening can measure positive and negative sentiments, popularity scores, and message reach, the levels of conversation, and buzz and crisis monitoring. Social listening research can take the form of qualitative or quantitative information depending on the parameters of the study.[6]

> *Social listening raises an important ethical issue.*

Pizza Hut Canada has used social listening extensively and has been able to make product strategy decisions based on the results. In the past, Pizza Hut has used social media to post different product images and then track the response and conversation around each image. The one that received the largest response was used in its ads. In another case, Pizza Hut was monitoring social media in the U.K. and noted that customers believed that the new "Triple Treat" box was too big for one person. Using this information, when the "Triple Treat" was launched in Canada, Pizza Hut

observational research
Obtained by watching how people behave, in person or by using a machine to record the event.

Pizza Hut uses social listening to make product strategy decisions.
©simon evans/Alamy Stock Photo

emphasized sharing the pizza with friends and family, thereby avoiding the negative feedback seen in the U.K.[7]

Social listening raises an important ethical issue: While participants in social networks realize many of their comments and pictures are publicly posted, they may not be aware that their conversations may be monitored and used for research purposes. Social networks are required to have privacy policies that protect consumer data from being kept and misused by third parties, and marketers need to abide by these laws.

Further research can be conducted using quantitative research through observational and/or questioning techniques. The main advantage of quantitative research is that it is designed to be statistically accurate and it is less open to interpretation. The main disadvantage of quantitative research is that it is far more costly and time-consuming to collect than qualitative or secondary research. The primary quantitative research techniques include (1) observational research, (2) surveys/questionnaires, and (3) experiments (see Figure 4–4).

Observational Research

Observational research is obtained by watching how people behave, either in person or by using a machine to record events. While observational research can be qualitative if small sample numbers are recorded, large samples are used for reports such as those provided by Nielsen with its Homescan program. With Homescan, panellists scan the barcodes on products that they purchase each week.[8] Other examples of observational research can be in the form of the social listening research mentioned earlier, as well as web-tracking software such as Google Analytics, which measures website traffic, unique visitors, page views, time on site, and referring sites. Observational research can also be done in person, with researchers observing elements such as consumer interaction with a salesperson. Observational research tools are both useful and flexible, but they can be costly and unreliable when dependent upon human observation, which can at times report different conclusions after watching the same event.

> *Market researchers have to make important trade-offs to balance costs against the expected quality of information.*

Surveys

Surveys are used to gather quantitative information. Survey questions can be standardized in the form of a **questionnaire** and asked to a large

Figure 4–4
Quantitative research: Comparing techniques

Technique	Examples	Advantages	Disadvantages
Observational research	• Homescan • Google Analytics • Personal observations of consumer interactions • Social listening	• Reflect actual behaviour • Highly accurate when collected by machines • Mechanical observations reduce interviewer bias • Appropriate when respondents cannot clearly articulate opinions	• Do not indicate why consumers behave as they do • Do not provide data on attitudes and opinions • Different researchers may interpret behaviour differently • May require further explanation • Ethical questions exist around privacy issues
Surveys/ Questionnaires	• Personal interviews • Central location interviews such as mall-intercepts • Mail questionnaires • Telephone interviews • Internet surveys	• Can ask numerous questions • Questions are standardized • Questions can be administered via mail, telephone, the Internet, or in person • Personal interviewers can often probe for more in-depth answers	• Results can be biased by the methodology • Results can be influenced by the interviewer • Can be expensive and time-consuming
Experiments	• Test markets • Simulated test markets • Lab experiments	• Researchers can change key variables and measure results in a controlled setting • Can avoid costly failures by allowing marketers to modify marketing programs prior to full launch • Can provide a more accurate reflection and predictor of consumer behaviour since people are behaving more naturally	• Can be expensive and time-consuming • Results can be difficult to interpret • Actual test markets may be visible to the competition • Difficult to find a representative sample

representative sample to obtain accurate data. These surveys can be conducted in person, on the telephone, by mail, or through the Internet, with each method having limitations.

In choosing from these alternatives, market researchers have to make important trade-offs to balance costs against the expected quality of information. Personal interviews have the major advantage of enabling interviewers to ask probing questions and get reactions to visual materials. However, this approach is very costly. Mail surveys are not used very often anymore. They are less costly but have low response rates and are usually biased because those most likely to respond have had positive or negative experiences. Telephone interviews allow respondents to be probed but they are increasingly difficult to complete due to call-display features and respondents' reluctance to participate. Internet surveys are restricted to respondents that have the technology, but this approach is becoming an increasingly popular method of gathering information. Figure 4–5 summarizes the advantages and disadvantages of different survey approaches.

Increasingly, marketing researchers have begun to use *online surveys* (e-mail and Internet) to collect primary data. The reason: Most consumers have an Internet connection and an e-mail account. Marketers can embed a survey in an e-mail sent to targeted respondents. When they open the e-mail, consumers can either see the survey or click on a link to access it from a website. Marketers can also ask consumers to complete a "pop-up" survey in a separate browser window when they access an organization's website. Many organizations use this method to have consumers assess their products and services or evaluate the design and usability of their websites.

The advantages of online surveys are that the cost is relatively minimal and the turnaround time from data collection to report presentation is much quicker than the traditional methods discussed earlier. However, online surveys have serious drawbacks: Some consumers may view e-mail surveys as "junk" or "spam" and

questionnaire
Obtaining information by posing standardized questions through surveys that can be conducted in person, through the mail, on the telephone, or through the Internet.

Figure 4–5
Advantages and disadvantages of survey techniques

Survey Technique	Advantages	Disadvantages
Personal interview	• Can probe for detailed responses • Can demonstrate marketing programs • Can result in high levels of accuracy	• Time-consuming • Expensive • Interviewers can bias responses
Telephone survey	• Can be conducted quickly and cheaply • Computerized techniques allow for randomized calling • Appropriate when data is needed quickly	• People are reluctant to participate • Low response rates • Call-display features screen-out calls • Increasing number of people with no home phone • Interviews are limited to five to ten minutes • Interviewers can bias responses • Questionable representativeness of samples
Mail survey	• No interviewer bias • Useful for national surveys • If using a panel, can track changes over time • Can be affordable if part of a syndicated or omnibus survey	• Lengthy time-lag for data collection • Low response rates • Questionable data accuracy • Inability to probe respondents
Internet survey	• No interviewer bias • Can be conducted quickly and cheaply • Efficient for electronic data collection • High Internet penetration can lead to good sampling • Can easily target customer databases • Useful for national surveys • If using a panel, can track changes over time • Can be affordable if part of a syndicated or omnibus survey	• Difficult to verify respondents' identity • Questionable data accuracy due to anonymity • Inability to probe respondents • Some debate over sample representativeness

syndicated studies
A hybrid of primary and secondary research whereby the cost of a research study is shared among clients and made available at a price to interested parties.

may either choose to not receive them (if they have a "spam blocker") or purposely or inadvertently delete them, unopened. For Internet surveys, some consumers have a "pop-up blocker" that prohibits a browser from opening a separate window that contains the survey; thus, they may not be able to participate in the research. For both e-mail and Internet surveys, consumers can complete the survey multiple times, creating a significant bias in the results. This is especially true for online panels. In response, research firms such as SurveyMonkey have developed sampling technology to prohibit this practice.[9]

The foundation of all research using questionnaires is developing precise questions that get clear, unambiguous answers from respondents.[10]

Also, time needs to be taken to ensure that survey questions are well-written so that answers will properly address research questions. Check out Figure 4–6 for hints on how to write better survey questions.

Researchers can reduce the costs of proprietary questionnaires by joining established syndicated studies that are conducted by well-respected research conglomerates. **Syndicated studies** are a hybrid of primary and secondary research conducted by a research company, spreading the cost across many clients to reduce the price. These studies are routinely conducted with extensive panels of consumers to determine trends.

Surveys can gather data from a large number of consumers.

Figure 4–6
Mistakes to avoid when writing survey questions

1. Leading or loaded questions
Questions designed to make a person think in a specific way.
Avoid: Some people say that the food at XYZ restaurant is fantastic, what do you think? (You have already put a positive impression in the mind of the respondent.)
Better: What do you think about the food at XYZ restaurant?

2. Non-specific questions
Questions that cannot be clearly understood.
Avoid: Do you watch Netflix regularly? (What is regularly? This term can have different meanings to different people.)
Better: How often do you watch Netflix?

3. Missing options
Potential answers are missing.
Solutions:
o Conduct a pre-test to determine potential responses.
o Include "Other (please specify)" as an option.

4. Asking two questions at one time
Questions that ask two things but the respondent can only provide one answer.
Avoid: What is the fastest and least expensive Internet provider?
Better: What is the least expensive Internet provider? What is the fastest Internet provider?

5. Confusing wording
Questions that include acronyms, industry jargon, or any other language that may be unfamiliar to the respondent.
Avoid: Do you own an iOS smartphone?
Better: Do you own an iPhone?

marketing TIP

"With automation, and access to consumer panels, brands can now gather customer opinions in a matter of hours, giving them the ability to react in real time and implement the feedback they receive."

– *Raj Manocha, EVP, Delvinia*

Formally, a survey **panel** includes a large sample of respondents that voluntarily complete questionnaires on a regular basis so that researchers can assess changes in behaviour and attitudes. An **omnibus survey** also includes the voluntary participation of respondents in routine surveys, allowing individual marketers to add a small number of questions to an existing survey to receive cost-effective data in response to their questions.

Ipsos conducts omnibus surveys with homeowners, parents, teens, and separate provincial online omnibus surveys, even providing an overnight omnibus survey for next-day results.

Experiments Experiments are the third quantitative research approach used in market research. It involves measuring changes in consumer behaviour over time to determine reactions to new product introductions or new promotional offers. A marketing **experiment** involves changing a variable involved in a purchase to find out what happens. Ideally, the researcher changes just one element, usually one of the factors in the marketing mix, and keeps the other variables constant.

Experiments can be conducted either in contrived environments that mimic real-life situations, known as *simulated* test markets, or *in-market* through real-time in-field tests where the product/promotion is actually sold in a limited location and monitored for success during a specific time period. Contrived, simulated experiments use computer simulations to predict consumer behaviour. Marketers typically input marketing mix variables and rely on complex forecasting programs to determine potential success levels. Formally, a **test market** is an in-market localized approach, or short-term online destination, used to test the success of promotional offers, new services, or new product launches.

Test markets can provide a more realistic evaluation of product or promotional success than other research options. However, test markets are time-consuming, costly, and visible to the competition. In

panel
A large sample of respondents that voluntarily complete questionnaires on a regular basis so that researchers can assess changes in behaviour and attitudes.

omnibus survey
The voluntary participation of respondents in routine research surveys that allow marketers to add a small number of questions to an existing survey to receive cost-effective data.

experiment
In marketing, changing a variable involved in a customer purchase to find out what happens.

test market
An in-market localized approach, or short-term online destination, used to test the success of promotional offers, new services, or new product launches.

terms of promotional offers, Internet marketers routinely test pay-per-click advertising campaigns, alternative online consumer offers, and the design of various website landing pages. For new products, large companies often use test markets to determine whether consumers will buy new products or brands, or shop at a new store concept. There are several cities in Canada that are used regularly as test markets for a variety of different products/services. McDonald's Chicken McNuggets and Tim Hortons Dark Roast coffee were tested in London, Ontario. Test cities tend to be under 1 million in population and need to be similar culturally to the rest of the country, with a variety of socio-economic backgrounds represented. Other frequent test markets in Canada are Edmonton, Alberta, and Barrie, Ontario.[11]

Step 4: Develop Findings

LO 5 Mark Twain once observed, "Collecting data is like collecting garbage. You've got to know what you're going to do with the stuff before you collect it." So, marketing data have little more value than garbage unless they are analyzed carefully and translated into information and findings, Step 4 in the marketing research approach.

After data has been collected, it has to be compiled, analyzed, and summarized so that it can be turned into actionable information. The researcher must know how to analyze the data and what tools to use. There are many statistical packages that can make this task easier. Market researchers face the challenge of synthesizing and simplifying pages of data into dashboards as well as individual charts with relevant observations and conclusions that can help marketers address business problems, challenges, and opportunities.

In the Roughriders and Insightrix example, the detailed analysis addressed the complex linkages between the Roughriders supporters' motives (e.g.,winning, entertainment, or self-image) and their loyalty and behaviour. It also assisted the team in understanding the actual demographics and motivations of its fans, as opposed to preconceptions or stereotypes. This in turn assisted and informed the Roughriders to better facilitate and encourage engagement with Saskatchewan residents and be better prepared to help fans create positive memories during special situations, like watching a game in the new Mosaic Stadium.

Hear more about the brand research employed by the Saskatchewan Roughriders in the *Lessons Learned in Marketing* podcast by Phoenix Group.

key performance indicators (KPIs)
Types of metric that are used to evaluate performance.

market share
The percentage of sales volume for a product, relative to the entire sales volume of the category in which it competes; ratio of a firm's sales to the total sales of all firms in the industry.

Metrics

As introduced in Chapter 1, *metrics* refers to numeric data that is collected and grouped to track performance. Metrics are often presented in spreadsheets and dashboards to make the data easy to understand and interpret. *Dashboards* visualize data and **key performance indicators (KPIs)**, using graphs, charts, and numbers, so numerical information tells a story that is insightful, easy to use, and understand.

Metrics data can come from a variety of sources, such as tracking data from websites, social media pages, call centre interactions, online ads, app downloads, webinars, and subscribers, as well as sales, costs, profits, and competitive and market growth data. Metrics data can measure elements such as revenue, market share, profit margins, buzz, sentiment, engagement, response rates, awareness levels, brand loyalty, retention rates, and a brand development index. Metrics data can point to return on investment, customer lifetime value, brand advocates, and sales conversion rates. Figure 4–7 describes a few rules that marketers can use to ensure that the metrics selected are relevant, measurable, and actionable.

Figure 4–8 provides a snapshot of key metrics that marketers often use to analyze performance. Importantly, companies frequently identify their specific metrics requirements and their key performance indicators to track and evaluate business results. (See also the Infographic from Source Approach titled "The 25 Amazon Product Search Ranking Factors.") Metrics are selected based on company protocols, normally based on the results needed to achieve business objectives. Marketers are often advised to use no more than five to seven key metrics to make the data focused, clear, and actionable.

Let's look at brand health metrics as an example of how metrics are used. Two key drivers are market share and brand development index. **Market share** is the

Figure 4–7
Rules of marketing metrics

Metrics should be easy to understand.	The metrics you are monitoring should make sense to those collecting the data and those using the data. They should also be understood across the organization.
Metrics should be available on a regular basis.	Marketers should focus on data that is available regularly and can be tracked from one time period to the next.
Metrics should be actionable and impact the business.	Seeing a metric decrease by 10 percent is important information to have and tells you that something is impacting your business. However, if you can't determine why this decrease happened or take any action to improve that metric, then the metric alone is not valuable.

percentage of sales volume for a product, relative to the entire sales volume of the category in which it competes. A car brand sold in Canada, for example, may have a market share of 17 percent, meaning that 17 percent of all car sales in Canada are attributed to this brand. This is a useful metric when tracked over time and compared to competitive market share levels.

Brand development index (BDI) shows how well a brand's sales are developed in a region relative to the region's population size. It is the percentage of total brand sales in a particular region relative to the percentage of the country's population in that region. This is a useful metric when trying to determine regional growth opportunities for a brand. For example, let's assume that the same car brand has 30 percent of its sales in Ontario. However, 38.5 percent of Canada's population

is in Ontario.[12] The BDI is calculated by dividing 30 percent by 38.5 percent to achieve a BDI of 77.9. Regions with a BDI below 100 may have an opportunity for growth, while regions with a BDI greater than 100 could be seen as doing very well, with less opportunity for significant future growth.

> **brand development index (BDI)**
> An index that shows how well a brand's sales are developed in a region relative to the region's population size.

ask YOURSELF

1. Why are metrics so important to an organization?
2. What metrics would you use to measure a Facebook campaign?

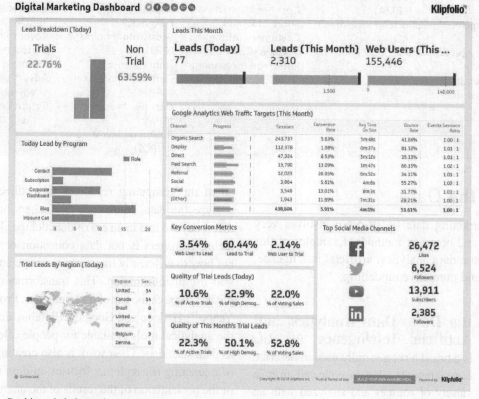

Dashboards help marketers visualize metrics.
Klipfolio Inc.

Figure 4–8
Key marketing metrics

Website	E-commerce	Online Ad Campaigns	Social Media	E-mail Programs
Visits	Purchases	Reach	Demographics	Sent and delivery rates
Unique visitors	Purchase frequency	Impressions	Followers	Open rates
Returning visitors	Average order value	Engagement	Views	Forward rates
Page views	Returns	Dwell time	Comments	Click-through rates
Time on site	Churn rates	Search/display overlap	Likes/unlikes	Bounce rates
Traffic sources	Complaints	Conversions	Post reach	Subscribe rates
Referrals	Customer satisfaction	Cost per click (CPC)	Shares	Unsubscribe rates
Bounce rates	Customer acquisition costs	Cost per thousand views (CPM)	Sentiment	Complaints
Return on investment (ROI)	Conversion rates	Click-through rates (CTR)	Engagement	E-mail revenue
	Customer lifetime value (CLV)	Cost per conversion (CPC)	Conversion rates	Lead generation
	Shopping cart abandonment	Keywords	Churn rate	Return on investment (ROI)
	Customer service calls	Return on investment (ROI)	Visitor frequency	
	Product reviews		Return on investment (ROI)	
	Return on investment (ROI)			

Brand Health	Financial	Customer Relationship Management (CRM)	Offline Ad Campaigns	Public Relations
Sales	Sales/revenue	Prospects and leads	Awareness	Interviews
Growth rates	Cost of goods sold	Conversion rates	Recall (aided and unaided)	Press releases
Market share	Gross margins	Retention rates	Share of voice	Journalist inquiries
Awareness levels	Profit margins	Churn rates	Clarity of communication	Events and conferences
Brand loyalty	Marketing expenditures	Engagement	Memorable elements	Share of voice
Brand trial rates	Earnings before income and taxes (EBITA)	Cost per acquisition (CPA)	Reach	Impressions
Repeat purchase rates	Return on investment (ROI)	Cost per interaction	Frequency	Audience
Brand development index (BDI)		Share of wallet	Gross rating points (GRP)	Reach
Category development index (CDI)		Customer lifetime value (CLV)	Impressions	Coverage
Profitability trends		Return on investment (ROI)	Cost per impression (CPI)	Message impact
Return on investment (ROI)			Cost per thousand (CPM)	Mentions
			Return on investment (ROI)	Advertising value equivalency (AVE)
				Return on investment (ROI)

Analyze the Data

Analyzing marketing data today often involves very sophisticated and complex methods. Examples of this include big data, data analytics, artificial intelligence, data mining, and predictive modelling.

Big Data, Data Analytics, and Artificial Intelligence

Big data is a broad term generally used to describe large amounts of data collected from a variety of sources and analyzed with an increasingly sophisticated set of technologies. **Information technology** includes all of the computing resources that collect, store, and analyze the data. Marketing researchers have observed that today we live in an era of data deluge. The challenge facing managers is not data collection or even storage but how to efficiently transform the huge amount of data into useful information. This transformation is accomplished through the use of data analytics. Products such as Yahoo!'s Hadoop and Google's Bigtable are examples of the analytical tools available for people often referred to as data scientists. Their work is also creating a new field of marketing research that focuses on *data visualization*, or the presentation of the results of the analysis.

Today, marketers obtain data from many sources such as barcode scanners at checkout counters, online

information technology
Includes all of the computing resources that collect, store, and analyze data.

Infographic

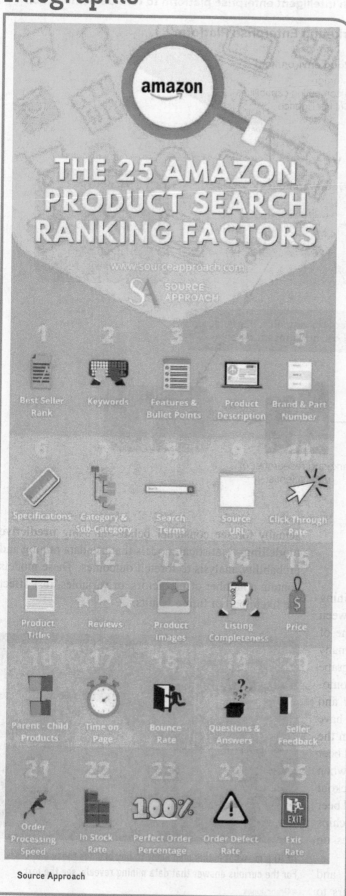

THE 25 AMAZON PRODUCT SEARCH RANKING FACTORS

www.sourceapproach.com

SA SOURCE APPROACH

1	2	3	4	5
Best Seller Rank	Keywords	Features & Bullet Points	Product Description	Brand & Part Number

6	7	8	9	10
Specifications	Category & Sub-Category	Search Terms	Source URL	Click Through Rate

11	12	13	14	15
Product Titles	Reviews	Product Images	Listing Completeness	Price

16	17	18	19	20
Parent - Child Products	Time on Page	Bounce Rate	Questions & Answers	Seller Feedback

21	22	23	24	25
Order Processing Speed	In Stock Rate	Perfect Order Percentage	Order Defect Rate	Exit Rate

Source Approach

tracking software on computers and tablets, and usage histories on your telephone. In fact, the growth of the Internet of Things (IoT) now allows data collection from almost any device a consumer might use. Marketing managers use a combination of data, technology, and analytics to convert the data into useful information that answer marketing questions and lead to effective marketing actions. An organization that accomplishes this successfully is often referred to as an *intelligent enterprise*.[13]

As shown in Figure 4–9, the elements of an intelligent marketing enterprise platform interact to facilitate the work of the marketing researcher or data scientist. The top half of the figure shows how big data are created through a sophisticated communication network that collects data from internal and external sources. These data are stored, organized, and managed in databases. Collectively, these databases form a data warehouse. Data storage (and computing) may also take place in "the Cloud," which is simply a collection of servers accessed through an Internet connection. Large databases are also subject to *artificial intelligence* platforms that undertake reasoning and common sense tasks to allow computers to "behave" intelligently. IBM, Tesla, and Amazon, for example, are using artificial intelligence to operate Watson, guide self-driving cars, and make purchase recommendations, respectively.[14]

As shown at the bottom of Figure 4–9, data analytics consists of several elements. Marketers use computers to specify important marketing queries or questions and to access the databases in the warehouse (or the Cloud). Analytical tools are used to organize and manipulate the data to identify any managerial insights that may exist. The results are then presented using tables and graphics for easier interpretation. When accessing a database, marketers can use sensitivity analysis to ask "what if" questions to determine how hypothetical changes in product or brand drivers—the factors that influence the buying decisions of a household or organization—can affect sales.

Traditional marketing research typically involves identifying possible drivers and then collecting data. For example, we might collect data to test the hypothesis that increasing couponing (the driver) during spring will increase trials by first-time buyers (the result).

Figure 4–9

How marketing researchers and managers use an intelligent enterprise platform to turn data into action

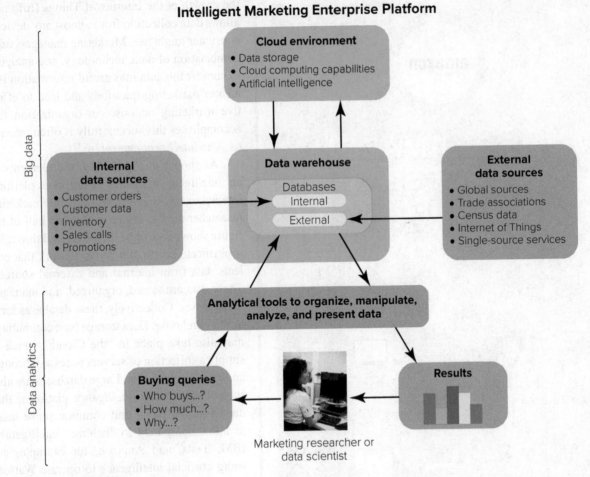

Intelligent Marketing Enterprise Platform

Cloud environment
- Data storage
- Cloud computing capabilities
- Artificial intelligence

Internal data sources
- Customer orders
- Customer data
- Inventory
- Sales calls
- Promotions

Data warehouse
Databases
Internal
External

External data sources
- Global sources
- Trade associations
- Census data
- Internet of Things
- Single-source services

Analytical tools to organize, manipulate, analyze, and present data

Buying queries
- Who buys...?
- How much...?
- Why...?

Results

Marketing researcher or data scientist

Big data

Data analytics

photo: ©Todd Warnock/Lifesize/Getty Images

Data Mining and Predictive Modelling

In contrast, **data mining** is the practice of examining large databases to find statistical relationships between consumer purchasing patterns. Some of these are common sense: Since many consumers buy peanut butter and grape jelly together, why not run a joint promotion between Skippy peanut butter and Welch's grape jelly? But would you have expected that men buying diapers in the evening sometimes buy a six-pack of beer too? Supermarkets discovered this when they mined purchase data from checkout scanners. So they placed diapers and beer near each other, then placed potato chips between them—and increased sales on all three items!

Refinements in data mining and data analytics now permit marketers to actually foresee consumer behaviour using **predictive modelling**—statistical models that use data mining and probability analysis to foretell outcomes. These models contain a number of predictors, or variables, that affect the likelihood of future results.

data mining
The processing of large amounts of data using sophisticated software to find insightful correlations and patterns that lead to better business decisions.

predictive modelling
Based on statistical models that use data mining and probability analysis to foretell outcomes.

At 10 p.m., what is this man likely to buy besides these diapers? For the curious answer that data mining reveals, see the text.

©Brent Jones

No More Personal Secrets: The Downside of Data Mining and Predictive Modelling

Amazon, Google, Yahoo!, eBay, YouTube, reputation.com, . . . yes . . . and Facebook and Twitter, too! The common denominator for all these is their sophisticated data mining techniques that reveal an incredible amount of personal information about almost anyone. *Time* journalist Joel Stein, using both online and offline sources, discovered how easily outsiders could find his U.S. Social Security number and then found a number of other things about himself—some correct, some not.

For example, his data mining effort revealed that he likes hockey, rap, rock, parenting, recipes, clothes and beauty products, and movies. He makes most of his purchases online, averaging only $25 per purchase. He uses Facebook, LinkedIn, Pandora, and StumbleUpon. He bought his house in November, which is when his home insurance is up for renewal. His dad's wife has a traffic ticket.

And some sources predicted that he is an 18- to 19-year-old woman! For the record, Mr. Stein is not a teen, and he is a male.

OK, OK, sometimes data mining and predictive modelling errors occur!

These data are collected in many ways—from tracking devices on websites; to apps downloaded on a smartphone, PC, or tablet device that reveal a user's contact list and location; to techniques that aggregate data from multiple online sources.

These personal details have huge benefits for marketers, but do they invade a consumer's privacy? Data mining and predictive modelling now enable companies to target individual consumers and facilitate the design of personalized product offerings. This involves using not only demographics such as age and gender but also "likes," past buying habits, social media used, brands bought, TV programs watched, stores visited, and so on. ●

Protecting your personal data...
©Rawpixel.com/Shutterstock

Questions

1. What are some of the sources of data mining that you use regularly online that may be capturing your personal information?

2. Go to www.ghostery.com and find out what companies are grabbing your data when you visit a website?

As an example, Target has used data mining to identify 25 products that, when bought together or over time, predict a woman's likelihood of being pregnant as well as her child's expected due date. To determine the probability of pregnancy, a woman's purchase patterns, coupled with available demographic data, are linked to published baby registries. Predictive modelling shows that certain items are purchased in the first trimester, others in the second trimester, and still others in the third trimester, including the baby's due date. For good measure, the buying of blue or pink blankets indicates a high probability of the child's gender. Armed with this knowledge, Target is able to send product ads and coupons to mothers-to-be appropriate for each stage in her pregnancy.[15]

For how much data mining and predictive modelling can reveal about you and your purchasing behaviour and a look at the ethical issues involved, see the Focus on Ethics box.[16]

Analytics

Analytics refers to the process of taking metrics data and applying smart thinking and technology to gain actionable insights that can help make better business decisions. An analytics platform helps give a picture as to where the company is today, answers questions, provides customer insights, and predicts patterns that can improve marketing performance. Analytics can help segment customers, plan and forecast, manage risk, and take corrective action. It may start by mining data, analyzing the information, modelling the data to predict outcomes, and visualizing data with dashboards that appear in reports.

Let's look at two of the main categories of big data analytics: descriptive and predictive.

Descriptive Analytics

Descriptive analytics focus on *what has happened.* It is the simplest and most common form of analytics. Web analytics, social analytics, and RFM (recency, frequency, and monetary value) analysis are descriptive.

Web analytics is the measurement and analysis of website data, looking at elements such as visits, unique visitors, page views, time on site, traffic sources, referrals, and bounce rate. Google Analytics is an example of an excellent, free web analytics tool.

Social analytics gains insights from social media interaction and social listening. Social media interactions, such as followers, views, comments, likes/ unlikes, reach, shares, engagement, sentiment, conversion rates, and churn rate, are analyzed to determine the level of interaction with customers and the success of marketing programs on social platforms. **Social listening** pays attention to real-time public conversations on social networks to discover trends as well as common themes, attitudes, topics, and areas of interest. Social analytics can measure social media campaign performance, assess message resonation and amplification, determine a brand's buzz level, and gauge sentiment toward a brand through words or images. It can identify key influencers, brand advocates, and opinion leaders, and it can interact in real time with consumers.

There are many free and paid social analytics tools. Examples include Hootsuite, which provides a basic, free social analytics tool, as well as a more-robust paid platform for businesses, and Salesforce Marketing Cloud, which is a paid social media analytics platform. Visit **www.hootsuite.com** and **www.salesforce.com/marketingcloud** to see details about these services.

An example of how big data analytics is used can be seen with **RFM analysis** (recency, frequency, and monetary value analysis). This approach can use automated software to classify customers on the basis of how recently products were purchased (recency), how often products were purchased (frequency), and the dollar value of the transactions (monetary value). Customers are scored using these attributes and then automatically ranked so that organizations can segment the market and tailor offers to different categories of consumers. Let's think about how strategies can be created for specific segments. For customers who have purchased recently, who purchase frequently, and who spend at a high level, a company will want to create offers for these customers that will keep them coming back and keep them loyal. For customers who have purchased recently, who purchase frequently, but who spend at a low level, a company will want to keep them coming back but to increase the value of their purchases.

Non-profit organizations often use RFM analyses to target people most likely to make donations. Customer relationship management (CRM) loyalty programs use these analyses to segment customers. Loyalty programs such as those from Shoppers Drug Mart and Loblaw use loyalty cards to collect ongoing customer purchase data, and then use data-mining techniques to customize offers based on past purchases. In this way, RFM analysis can be descriptive in that it captures data and then categorizes customers based on that data; it can also be predictive by determining the factors that drive purchases and link these factors to future behaviour, which allows offers to be made based upon past behaviour.[17]

Predictive Analytics

Predictive analytics combines data from varied sources to reveal patterns that are modelled to predict *what might happen* in the future. For example, data can be combined from CRM databases, social media analytics, marketing program metrics, customer service databases, and purchased data to reveal groupings of customers with common attitudes and purchase patterns. This information can then be used to predict future consumer behaviour and to customize offers for specific groupings. Data mining refers to the processing of large amounts of data using software to find insightful correlations and patterns that lead to better business decisions.

Various companies provide data management and analytics services. Salesforce.com and IBM are examples, providing top-quality services that help transform data into actionable insights. Salesforce.com uses cloud-based platforms to help companies manage and use data from e-mail, mobile, social media, customer service, sales, and CRM interactions. IBM has business intelligence products that allow users to collaborate, analyze, model, plan, and create reports. It has predictive analytics products that use statistical algorithms and data-mining techniques to predict outcomes, and it has performance management products that create integrated systems to increase performance. Leading-edge data management and analytics companies deal with these areas to help improve an organization's performance.[18]

ask YOURSELF

1. What are the challenges of big data?
2. What is an RFM analysis and how can it improve ROI?

Step 5: Take Marketing Actions

Once the data has been analyzed, the researcher will discuss the results with a marketing manager and prepare a report to communicate the research findings. The report will include recommendations that address the marketing problem and research objectives. It is important to understand that marketing data and information have little value unless translated into findings and recommendations that lead to marketing action. Managers generally prefer clear, concise reports where key findings are highlighted within dashboards and individual charts, graphs, and tables of data.

In the Saskatchewan Roughriders example, the recommendations were to focus on differentiating Roughriders fans by the level of engagement versus demographics. It assisted the team in understanding the actual demographics and motivations of its fans, as opposed to preconceptions or stereotypes, to grow the brand in future. These recommendations were actionable in marketing messages and promotions.

Evaluate the Results

Evaluating results is a continuing way of life for effective marketing managers. There are really two aspects of this evaluation process:

- *Evaluating the decision itself.* This involves monitoring the marketplace to determine if action is necessary in the future. For the Saskatchewan Roughriders, are the new promotions successful in engaging the fans? If this strategy has been successful, the Roughriders should use SaskWatch regularly to monitor success of game-day promotions and the overall satisfaction of the fans.

- *Evaluating the decision process used.* Was the marketing research and analysis used to develop the recommendations effective? Was it flawed? Could it be improved for similar situations in the future? The Saskatchewan Roughriders and Insightrix must be vigilant in looking for ways to improve the analysis

and results—to learn lessons that might apply to future marketing research efforts.

Again, systematic analysis does not guarantee success. But, as in the case of the Saskatchewan Roughriders, it can improve a firm's success rate for its marketing decisions.

The Future of Market Research

In today's world of big data, marketers have extensive information on consumers, the competition, and the market. This information can come from secondary sources or primary sources and is used to help marketers make fact-based decisions. Technology is facilitating the gathering and sifting of this information, using analytics platforms to flag issues and highlight opportunities for marketers. Market research projects are sometimes needed to reveal further insights, and these projects increasingly use the Internet to discern attitudes and opinions.

The future of market research sees a continued growth in online market research approaches as well as the increased use of analytics platforms to help manage big data and obtain insights. Organizations are expected to increasingly invest in technology and training programs that will help marketers to focus on meaningful, actionable data. Organizations will come to realize that actionable data and data-savvy employees are among their most valuable assets and will invest in these areas.

> *The future of market research sees a continued growth in online market research approaches as well as the increased use of analytics platforms to help manage big data and obtain insights.*

ask YOURSELF

1. In the marketing research for the Saskatchewan Roughriders, what is an example of (a) a finding and (b) a marketing action?
2. In evaluating marketing actions, what are the two dimensions on which they should be evaluated?

Ethically and legally, marketers and market research practitioners will need to keep consumers' privacy top-of-mind. Privacy laws in Canada require businesses to comply with the *Personal Information Protection and Electronic Documents Act* (PIPEDA) as well as Canada's anti-spam legislation (CASL). You can read more about these areas in Chapter 2 where marketing regulations are discussed in detail. Marketers are well advised to check the latest privacy legislation and anti-spam laws in Canada at the Canadian Marketing Association's (CMA) website at **www.the-cma.org,** the CASL website at **http://fightspam.gc.ca,** and the Office of the Privacy Commissioner of Canada at **www.priv.gc.ca.** Legal marketing experts should be consulted to ensure that market research practices are legal.

Market researchers are also well advised to visit the website of the Marketing Research and Intelligence Association (MRIA) of Canada at **http://mria-arim.ca,** a not-for-profit association that represents all aspects of the market intelligence and survey research industries, including social research, competitive intelligence, data mining, insight, and knowledge management. It provides education for market researchers, publishes a market research magazine, and provides a wealth of information to its members.

summary... JUST THE FACTS

 LO 1
- Marketing research is done because it reduces risk by providing the vital information to help marketing managers understand the wants and needs of consumers and translate them into marketing actions.

LO 2
- Marketing researchers engage in a five-step decision-making process to collect information that will improve marketing decisions. The first step is to define the problem, the second step is to develop the research plan, the third step is to collect the relevant information, the fourth step is to develop findings from the marketing research data collected, and the fifth step is to take marketing actions.

LO 3
- Secondary data have already been recorded prior to the start of the project and primary data is collected specifically for the project.

 LO 4
- Marketing researchers observe people electronically using Nielsen people meters to measure TV viewing behaviour, ask questions using questionnaires, utilize panels to see if behaviours change, and experiments to measure the effect of marketing variables.

 LO 5
- Market research, metrics, and analytics are used by marketers to help gather data and obtain insights. Metrics use numeric data to track performance. Analytics applies smart thinking and technology to metrics data to gain action-able insights.

key terms and concepts... A REFRESHER

brand development index (BDI)
data
data mining
descriptive analytics
experiment
focus group
in-depth interviews
information technology
key performance indicators (KPIs)
market share
marketing research

measures of success
non-probability sampling
objectives
observational research
omnibus survey
online research bulletin boards
online research communities
panel
predictive analytics
predictive modelling
primary data

probability sampling
questionnaire
RFM analysis
sampling
secondary data
social analytics
social listening
syndicated studies
test market
web analytics

hands-on... APPLY YOUR KNOWLEDGE

Market Research Assignment The course you are completing may require you to submit a report on the marketing of a product. Navigate your way to the online research sources identified in Figure 4–3 to review and collect secondary data on your product, the industry it competes in, and its target market. Summarize and source your findings with bullet points for future reference.

chapter vignette... ACTIVITY

This chapter's opening vignette examines how Deepwater Farms is reinventing farming with aquaponics. Applying the marketing research process, what are some potential new products that Deepwater Farms should expand into. What are the key sources of secondary data that they should consider? Review the company's website at www.deepwaterfarms.com.

infographic... DATA ANALYSIS

Review the Infographic about "The 25 Amazon Product Search Ranking Factors." If you were an entrepreneur selling running shoes on Amazon, what impact would this information have on how you sell your product on Amazon? What research data would you want to collect?

LEARNING OBJECTIVES

LO 1 Identify the distinguishing characteristics of industrial, reseller, government, and non-profit markets and how they are measured

LO 2 Describe the importance of content marketing to business-to-business (B2B) marketers

LO 3 Explain which key characteristics of organizational buying make the process different from consumer buying

LO 4 Describe how buying centres and buying situations influence organizational purchasing

LO 5 Outline the process of business segmentation

LO 6 Explain the growing importance of and the approaches to online buying for industrial, reseller, and government markets

B2B Marketing

Business partners that make business better are assets to organizations. Not only can good business partners enhance performance, they can help companies to react to changing market conditions. Strong B2B marketing also helps potential business partners market appropriately to their prospective clients.

©Naruedom Yaempongsa/Shutterstock

Used with permission of IFS.

Operating in over 40 countries and providing solutions for well-known companies like Pepsi and Saab, IFS understands the importance of B2B marketing. The company develops and delivers enterprise software for customers around the world. IFS solutions enable customers to enhance business performance.

Founded in 1983, IFS has grown to over 3,500 employees and supports more than 10,000 customers worldwide. The IFS network of local offices facilitates on-site

CHAPTER OUTLINE

- Applications for success
- The nature and size of organizational markets
- Measuring industrial, reseller, government, and non-profit markets
- Characteristics of organizational buying
- The organizational buying process and the buying centre
- Business market segmentation
- Online buying in organizational markets

support. IFS develops and sells software solutions supported by strong professional services individuals like Chris Venter. The project director gets involved in after-sales implementations of IFS solutions to create a lasting business relationship between IFS and its clients.

Buying centres in an organization make decisions on potential purchases. With the complexity and impact to the business that IFS solutions provide, users and influencers normally play a key role in the buying process. Users utilize the software while influencers have the specialized knowledge of what is being purchased. "It is important for me to be available to the users and influencers in an organization," shares Venter. "Not only do I want the solution to meet the client's immediate needs, I want to be able to anticipate future needs that we can solve."

In order to thrive, organizations need to make good business decisions. IFS has pioneered component-based service management and enterprise resource planning (ERP) software. ERP information systems help managers make decisions by aggregating company data. This creates a huge opportunity for IFS to continue to build its customer base.

When asked about the size of IFS's target market, Venter offers this advice: "To be successful in B2B marketing, it is important to focus and develop understanding around a few industries that you can develop expertise in." IFS focuses on a few core industries. Choosing which industries to pursue is facilitated by the North American Industry Classification System (NAICS), and focusing on core industries allows marketers to become more relatable, to communicate with buzzwords, and essentially, to begin prospective relationships.

In 2013, Seaspan Marine Transportation, a prominent marine transportation company operating along the West Coast of North America, selected IFS applications to support its shipbuilding materials requirements. (More details about Seaspan can be found in the Marketing NewsFlash, "New Seaspan Ships to Span Sea.") Alluding to the complexities of shipbuilding, Venter explains, "You need to be able to order an anchor in advance. You don't want parts of the ship too early or too late. You want it ready when it is time for installation."

Not only does IFS promote its solutions, it in turn uses its own solutions. It is currently undergoing a transformational change ensuring that its own infrastructure is powered by its own solutions. Venter believes that "organizations that use their own solutions have more credibility and trust among the industries they serve." And he is a key individual building that credibility and trust among IFS and its partners.[1]

CHAPTER FEATURES

Supplying Applications for Success
How IFS helps its partners deliver their complex solutions on time.

The Importance of Vigilance
Understanding the risks of cybercrime in Canadian business.

Helping Feed the World
Canada is in the top 10 of exporters of agricultural products.

New Seaspan Ships to Span Sea
How organizational buying criteria drives big decisions.

Leading by Example
The Government of Canada sets high standards for its suppliers.

Part of Our World
How does Canada's largest company fare on the global stage?

Marketing Mishaps in the Global Economy
Explore the perception of different cultures on marketing plans.

reality CHECK ⊘

As you read Chapter 5, refer back to the IFS vignette to answer the following questions:

- How does specializing in particular industries facilitate B2B marketing for IFS?
- Why is the professional services sales support that Mr. Venter provides critical to the B2B marketing effort?

The Nature and Size of Organizational Markets

LO 1 Effective marketers have a clear understanding of buying behaviour. Effective business marketers also have an understanding of organizational markets. Also referred to as business-to-business (B2B) marketing, **business marketing** is the marketing of products to companies, governments, or non-profit organizations for use in the creation of goods and services that they then produce and market to others.[2] Many firms engage in business marketing, so it is important to understand the buying behaviour of organizational buyers, as it differs from consumer buying behaviour. Marketing plans are important as road maps for firms selling industrial products, just as they are for companies that sell consumer products. Chapter 15 describes marketing plans in greater detail.

Organizational buyers are those manufacturers, wholesalers, retailers, and government agencies that buy goods and services for their own use or for resale. For example, these organizations buy computers and smartphones such as the BlackBerry for their own use. Manufacturers buy raw materials and parts that they reprocess into the finished goods they sell, and wholesalers and retailers resell the goods they buy without reprocessing them. Organizational buyers include all buyers in a nation except ultimate consumers. These organizational buyers purchase and lease large volumes of equipment, raw materials, manufactured parts, supplies, and business services. They often buy raw materials and parts, process them, and sell them. This upgraded product may pass through several different organizations (as it is bought and resold by different levels of manufacturers, distributors, wholesalers, and retailers) before it is purchased by the final organizational buyer or final consumer. So the total purchases of organizational buyers in a year are far greater than those of ultimate consumers.

marketing TIP

"To be successful in B2B marketing, it is important to focus on and develop understanding around a few industries that you can develop expertise in."

– Chris Venter, project director, IFS

According to Industry Canada, there are a variety of industries that a business can sell to, including construction, manufacturing, wholesale trade, retail trade, and public administration. Organizational buyers are divided into four different markets: industrial, reseller, government, and non-profit markets.[3]

Industrial Markets

Industry Canada also notes there are over 2.4 million business locations in Canada. These *industrial firms* in some way reprocess a product or service they buy before selling it again to the next buyer. For example, there are many suppliers that sell to car companies. Although the consumer purchases one consumer product (i.e., the car), the automobile company purchases parts from many suppliers just to make that one car. There are suppliers for such parts as steering wheels, brakes, doors, tires, seats, and so on. The business market involves more purchases and dollars than the consumer market.

The importance of services in Canada today is emphasized by the composition of the industrial markets. Primary industries (e.g., agriculture, fishing, mining, and forestry), utilities, manufacturers, and construction firms sell physical products. The service market sells diverse services such as legal advice, auto repair, and dry cleaning, and includes organizations such as finance, insurance, and real estate businesses; transportation, communication, and public utility firms; and non-profit associations. Furthermore, there are over 1.1 million small businesses in Canada defined as having fewer than 100 employees.[4]

Organizational buyers make purchases on a larger scale than consumers.

©Auremar/Dreamstime.com/GetStock.com

Reseller Markets

Wholesalers and retailers that buy physical products and sell them again without any reprocessing are *resellers*. In Canada, there are over 200,000 retailers and over 65,000 wholesalers. Some of the largest Canadian-owned retailers in Canada include Loblaw, Alimentation Couche-Tard, Empire Company Limited (Sobeys), Metro, Shoppers Drug Mart, and Canadian Tire. This chapter focuses on how resellers act as organizational buyers and make decisions on which products they choose to carry.

Government Markets

Government units are the federal, provincial, regional, and municipal agencies that buy goods and services for the constituents that they serve. With a spending budget of over $280 billion in 2013, the federal government is a major customer, possibly the largest in Canada. To hold itself accountable, it created an online database to explain where taxpayer dollars are going.[5] In addition to specialized purchases for the military, government agencies also buy almost everything that regular consumers buy, from toilet paper to chewing gum to cars for federal prisons, hospitals, and schools. At the federal government level, the bulk of the purchasing is done by Public Works and Procurement Canada. Provincial and municipal governments typically have government departments that do the buying for them. In addition, hundreds of government departments, agencies, and Crown corporations (owned by the government on behalf of the people of Canada) such as CBC, VIA Rail, and the Royal Canadian Mint purchase supplies and services to operate. An example of a company that has been selected during the government procurement process is Bombardier. Over the years, it has produced regional aircraft, business jets, mass transportation equipment such as subways and passenger rail vehicles, and recreational equipment. Many of its sales are to governments. See also the Marketing NewsFlash, "New Seaspan Ships to Span Sea," for another example of organizational buying and governments.[6]

Because of the nature and size of business markets, it is critical for organizations to be diligent with how their organizations are protected. Information held by these organizations can be targeted by criminals. As seen in the Infographic, "Cybercrime and Canadian Businesses, 2017," businesses spent $14 billion to prevent, detect, and recover from cybersecurity incidents.

Car manufacturers are part of the industrial market.
©Bill Pugliano/Stringer/Getty Images

Non-profit Organizations

Organizations that operate without having financial profit as a goal, and which seek to provide goods and services for the good of society, are called *non-profit organizations*. They are also known as charitable organizations, and some 83,000 of them are registered with the Canada Revenue Agency.[7] Tax advantages make it beneficial for this type of organization to register with the federal government.

You are probably familiar with many non-profit organizations. Were you a member of the Boy Scouts or Girl Guides? Have you participated in a Canadian Cancer Society run or marathon? Have you been asked for a donation to the United Way? Hospitals, arts organizations, cultural groups, and some research institutes can be classified as non-profit organizations. In your school, you may have a foundation office that raises money for student awards and aid; this too is a non-profit organization. In the past, marketing in these organizations has been limited, but increasingly

Helping Feed the World	
Canada is in the top 10 of exporters of agricultural products.	
1. European Union	6. Indonesia
2. United States	7. Thailand
3. Brazil	8. Australia
4. China	9. India
5. **Canada**	10. Argentina

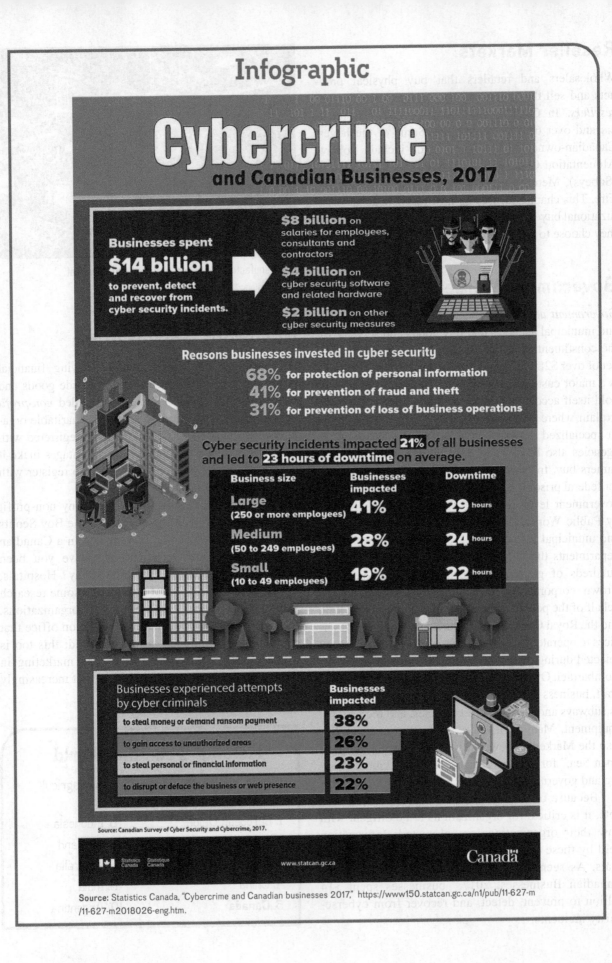

Cybercrime
and Canadian Businesses, 2017

Businesses spent
$14 billion
to prevent, detect and recover from cyber security incidents.

$8 billion on salaries for employees, consultants and contractors

$4 billion on cyber security software and related hardware

$2 billion on other cyber security measures

Reasons businesses invested in cyber security

68% for protection of personal information
41% for prevention of fraud and theft
31% for prevention of loss of business operations

Cyber security incidents impacted **21%** of all businesses and led to **23 hours of downtime** on average.

Business size	Businesses impacted	Downtime
Large (250 or more employees)	**41%**	**29** hours
Medium (50 to 249 employees)	**28%**	**24** hours
Small (10 to 49 employees)	**19%**	**22** hours

Businesses experienced attempts by cyber criminals	Businesses impacted
to steal money or demand ransom payment	**38%**
to gain access to unauthorized areas	**26%**
to steal personal or financial information	**23%**
to disrupt or deface the business or web presence	**22%**

Source: Canadian Survey of Cyber Security and Cybercrime, 2017.

Statistics Canada / Statistique Canada

www.statcan.gc.ca

Canada

Source: Statistics Canada, "Cybercrime and Canadian businesses 2017," https://www150.statcan.gc.ca/n1/pub/11-627-m/11-627-m2018026-eng.htm.

they are adopting the same types of marketing techniques that other business firms employ, and with good success. As purchasers, this sector of business buys a wide array of goods and services to conduct their operations.

Measuring Industrial, Reseller, Government, and Non-profit Markets

The measurement of industrial, reseller, government, and non-profit markets is an important first step for a firm interested in determining the size of one, two, or all of these markets in Canada and around the world. This task has been made easier with the **North American Industry Classification System (NAICS)**.[8] The NAICS provides common industry definitions for Canada, Mexico, and the United States, which facilitate the measurement of economic activity in the three member countries of the United States-Mexico-Canada Agreement (USMCA). The NAICS replaced the Standard Industrial Classification (SIC) system, a version of which had been in place for more than 50 years in the three USMCA member countries. The SIC neither permitted comparability across countries nor accurately measured new or emerging industries. Furthermore, the NAICS is consistent with the *International Standard Industrial Classification*

of All Economic Activities, published by the United Nations, to help measure global economic activity.

The NAICS groups economic activity to permit studies of market share, demand for goods and services, competition from imports in domestic markets, and similar studies. The NAICS designates industries with a numerical code in a defined structure. A six-digit coding system is used. The first two digits designate a sector of the economy, the third digit designates a subsector, and the fourth digit represents an industry group. The fifth digit designates a specific industry and is the most detailed level at which comparable data is available for Canada, Mexico, and the United States. The sixth digit designates individual country-level national industries. Figure 5–1 presents an abbreviated breakdown within the Arts, Entertainment, and Recreation sector (code 71) to illustrate the classification scheme.

North American Industry Classification System (NAICS)
Provides common industry definitions for Canada, Mexico, and the United States.

Figure 5–1
NAICS breakdown for the Arts, Entertainment, and Recreation sector: NAICS code 71 (abbreviated)

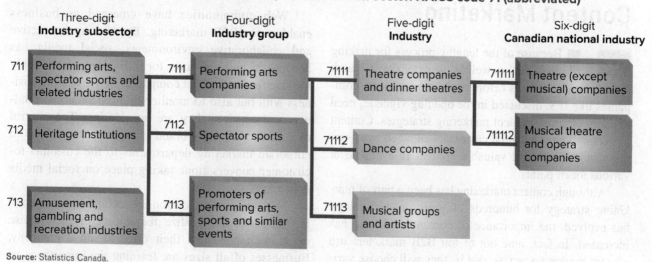

Source: Statistics Canada.

New Seaspan Ships to Span Sea

©Darryl Dyck/The Canadian Press

In May 2019, Prime Minister Justin Trudeau announced that up to 16 new Coast Guard ships would be built at Seaspan's Vancouver shipyards. The new ships will be used for a variety of missions, including offshore search and rescue, and are part of Canada's National Shipbuilding Strategy. With a Canadian Coast Guard vessel as a backdrop, the Prime Minister stated that the government would spend $15.7 billion on these new ships.

Seaspan is an association of Canadian companies that are primarily involved in shipbuilding services and coastal marine transportation in Western North America. Its supply chain management department is responsible for all supply-chain-related activities on behalf of the member group of companies. Supply chain activities include demand planning, negotiation, distribution management, and logistics. Logistics involves transportation, order processing, inventory management, and warehousing.

Along with Seaspan, Canada's National Shipbuilding Strategy involved the Irving Shipyards in Halifax. Seaspan and Irving were selected in 2011 to be responsible for building new vessels for the Coast Guard and Navy.

The Prime Minister also alluded to Quebec's Davie Shipyard to potentially be added to the national strategy. When the Davie Shipyard announcement was made, Seaspan's vice president, Tim Page raised concerns that a third supplier could impact the resource investments made in the Vancouver shipyard.

Although Seaspan currently employs 1,200 employees at its Vancouver shipyards, the Canadian government believed alternative options were needed. Trudeau noted that the Irving and Seaspan shipyards did not have the capacity to complete the fleet renewal on their own. This is an example of how important supply chain management is in an organization and how demands on a supply chain may require purchasers to look for alternatives. It also highlights how the ability to conform to an organization's buying criteria of meeting required delivery schedules are critical in B2B marketing. ●

Questions

1. Other than the size of the $15.7 billion purchase, what other organizational buying characteristics does the Government of Canada display in this example?

2. How can Seaspan use the experience of the Prime Minister's announcement when negotiating future government contracts?

Content Marketing

LO 2 Because of the lengthy process for making decisions, as well as the extensive research required by businesses before decisions are made, companies like IFS, discussed in the opening vignette, need to adopt effective content marketing strategies. Content marketing keeps potential customers engaged by ensuring that relevant and valuable content is available at various touch points.

Although content marketing has been a part of marketing strategy for hundreds of years, as technology has evolved, the importance of content marketing has increased. In fact, nine out of ten B2B marketers use content marketing tactics; that is, they will choose various ways to reach their target audience, including social media, e-newsletters, videos, and research reports.

Web communities have emerged as business enablers for B2B marketing. By creating interactive and collaborative environments, social media has become the go-to resource for B2B customers, not only to share feedback about companies they are doing business with but also to monitor discussions about products and services they are considering. The control of a B2B company's brand is rapidly changing from corporate marketing departments to the customer-to-customer conversations taking place on social media networks.

Not surprisingly, customers recognize their growing influence and realize the impact of their praise or, more importantly, their criticism on a company. Businesses of all sizes are learning the importance of listening, rather than preaching, in order to acquire and retain their customers. Customers using social media are not interested in vague and impersonalized advertising and sales pitches.

This new environment creates big challenges but also incredible opportunities for B2B sales. Sales professionals can no longer completely rely on traditional e-mail and cold-calling campaigns. Companies like Contently offer companies content marketing solutions to help keep business customers engaged.

Working with Contently allows business sales professionals to gain timely and relevant insights about their customers as well as engage at a very deep and personal level—two huge boons to the B2B sales process. Thanks to social media monitoring and conversation, individuals within the organization have the ability to champion the identity of their corporate brand.

Social media is just one tactic in content marketing. In 2013, Xerox was recognized for its content marketing thought leadership as it expanded into the health care industry. The HealthBiz Decoded website was launched by Xerox and filled with articles from Xerox subject matter experts and other freelance journalists. The end result is a digital magazine that hosts videos and infographics to enhance the content. It is a subtle but effective strategy for Xerox to show it is not just a copier company; it is a company that is an effective service provider. Recently, Xerox has worked with the technology solutions company Contently to help rebrand itself.[9]

B2B marketers can engage audiences to act by implementing an effective content marketing strategy, so companies may now spend approximately a quarter of their marketing budgets on getting content marketing right for their audience. Since technology and talent are now readily available to most organizations, there is tremendous value to a company to get its message right and keep it relevant.

Not only has technology allowed businesses to reach other businesses through a variety of channels, it has provided the opportunity for regular feedback. By tracking usage and views, B2B marketers can adjust content accordingly to make information for clients more and more relevant.[10]

Characteristics of Organizational Buying

LO 3 Organizations are different from individuals in the way they purchase goods and services, so buying for an organization is different from buying for yourself and your family. In both cases, the objective in making the purchase is to solve the buyer's problem—to satisfy a need or want. Unique objectives and policies of an organization put special constraints on how it makes buying decisions. Understanding the characteristics of organizational buying is essential in designing effective marketing programs to reach these buyers. Key characteristics of organizational buying are listed in Figure 5–2 and discussed next.[11]

Figure 5–2
Key characteristics of organizational buying behaviour

Characteristics	Dimensions
Market characteristics	• Demand for industrial products is derived. • The number of business customers is typically small, and their purchase orders are typically large.
Product or service characteristics	• Products or services are technical in nature and purchased on the basis of specifications. • Many goods purchased are raw or semi-finished. • Heavy emphasis is placed on delivery time, technical assistance, and postsale service.
Buying process characteristics	• Technically qualified and professional buyers follow established purchasing policies and procedures. • Buying objectives and criteria are typically spelled out, as are procedures for evaluating sellers and their products or services. • There are multiple buying influences, and multiple parties participate in purchase decisions. • There are reciprocal arrangements, and negotiation between buyers and sellers is commonplace. • Online buying over the Internet is widespread.
Marketing mix characteristics	• Personal selling to organizational buyers is used extensively, and distribution is very important. • Advertising and other forms of promotion are technical in nature. • Price is often negotiated, evaluated as part of broader seller and product or service qualities, and frequently affected by quantity discounts.

Derived Demand

derived demand

Demand for industrial products and services driven by demand for consumer products and services.

inelastic demand

Demand for products does not change because of increases or decreases in price.

Consumer demand for products and services is affected by their price and availability and by consumers' personal tastes and discretionary income. By comparison, industrial demand is derived. **Derived demand** means that the demand for industrial products and services is driven by, or derived from, demand for consumer products and services, as demonstrated in Figure 5–3. For example, the demand for Weyerhaeuser's pulp and paper products is based on consumer demand for products like newspapers, Domino's "keep warm" pizza-to-go boxes, FedEx packages, and disposable diapers. Derived demand is often based on expectations of future consumer demand. For instance, Whirlpool purchases parts for its washers and dryers in anticipation of consumer demand, which is affected by the replacement cycle for these products and by consumer income. Another example of derived demand is the car industry. Demand for auto parts is driven by new car sales. Magna International Inc., a Canadian company based in Aurora, Ontario, is Canada's largest automobile parts manufacturer, and one of the country's largest companies.

Figure 5–3
Direct versus derived demand

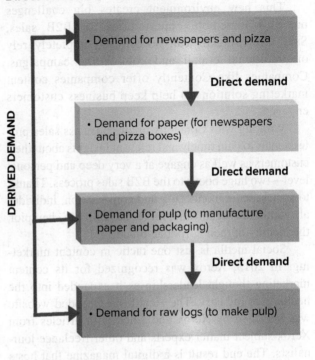

DERIVED DEMAND

- Demand for newspapers and pizza

Direct demand

- Demand for paper (for newspapers and pizza boxes)

Direct demand

- Demand for pulp (to manufacture paper and packaging)

Direct demand

- Demand for raw logs (to make pulp)

Inelastic Demand

Inelastic demand means that regardless of whether there is an increase or decrease of the price of a B2B product, customers will buy the same quantity. For example, if

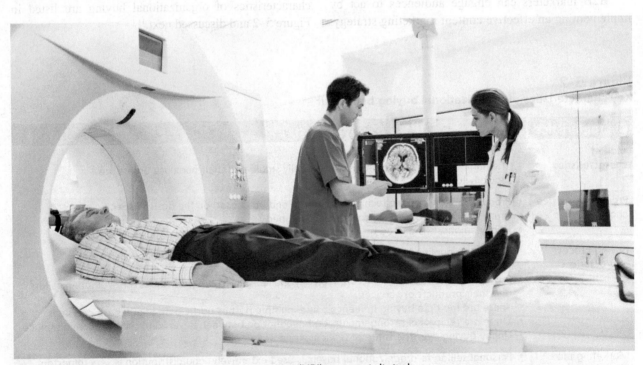

The number of potential buyers of magnetic resonance imaging (MRI) scanners is limited.

©alvarez/Vetta/Getty Images

the price of brake pads goes up, a car manufacturer will still order the same quantity. A single business product, such as a brake pad, is only one of many parts that go into making the final product, and is only a minor portion of the price of the car.

Fluctuating Demand

Small changes in demand for consumer products can result in large increases or decreases in demand for the facilities and equipment needed to make the consumer product. This is referred to as **fluctuating demand**. A product's life expectancy also has a bearing on this type of demand. For example, business products such as large machinery are purchased infrequently. Demand for such products can be high one year when they are wearing out but low in the following year if the old machinery is operating satisfactorily.

Size of the Order or Purchase

The size of the purchase involved in organizational buying is typically much larger than that in consumer buying. The dollar value of a single purchase made by an organization often runs into the millions of dollars. For example, in 2009, the Toronto Transit Commission (TTC) received approval to spend $1.2 billion to purchase 204 new streetcars from Bombardier. The following year, Bombardier sold 186 new subway cars to the Toronto Transit Commission (TTC) for a value of $390 million.[12]

With so much money at stake, most organizations place constraints on their buyers in the form of purchasing policies or procedures. Buyers must often get competitive bids from at least three prospective suppliers when the order is above a specific amount, such as $5,000. When the order is above an even higher amount, such as $50,000, it may require the review and approval of a vice president or even the president of the company. Knowing how the size of the order affects buying practices is important in determining who participates in the purchase decision and makes the final decision, as well as the length of time required to arrive at a purchase agreement.

Number of Potential Buyers

Firms selling consumer products or services often try to reach thousands or millions of individuals or households. For example, your local supermarket or bank probably serves thousands of people, and Kellogg tries to reach millions of Canadian households with its breakfast cereals and probably succeeds in selling to a third or half of these in any given year. In contrast, firms selling to organizations are often restricted to far fewer buyers. Bombardier Aerospace can sell its Challenger business jets to a few thousand organizations throughout the world, and B.F. Goodrich sells its original equipment tires to fewer than ten car manufacturers.

Bombardier markets to organizational buyers such as the Toronto Transit Commission (TTC). In 2010, Bombardier sold 186 new subway cars to the Toronto Transit Commission (TTC) for a value of $390 million.

(left): ©Peter Power/The Globe and Mail/The Canadian Press; (right): ©njene/Shutterstock

Organizational Buying Objectives

Organizations buy products and services for one main reason: to help them achieve their objectives. For business firms, the buying objective is usually to increase profits through reducing costs or increasing sales. 7-Eleven buys automated inventory systems to increase the number of products that can be sold through its convenience stores and to keep those products fresh. Nissan Motor Company switched its advertising agency because it expects the new agency to devise a more effective ad campaign to help it sell more cars and increase sales. To improve executive decision-making, many firms buy advanced computer systems to process data.

The objectives of non-profit firms and government agencies are usually to meet the needs of the groups they serve. Thus, a hospital buys a high-technology diagnostic device to serve its patients better. Understanding buying objectives is a necessary first step in marketing to organizations.

> *Understanding buying objectives is a necessary first step in marketing to organizations.*

Organizational Buying Criteria

Consumers use criteria when purchasing a product. Businesses also use criteria in their purchasing: They specify *organizational buying criteria*, which are detailed specifications for the products and services they want to buy and the characteristics of the suppliers that will supply them. When suppliers are selected, their products and their firm's characteristics are evaluated using these criteria. The following lists some of the most commonly used criteria:

- Price
- Ability to meet the quality specifications required
- Ability to meet the required delivery schedules
- Technical capability
- Warranties and claims policies
- Past performance on previous contracts
- Production facilities and capacity

Many organizational buyers today are transforming their buying criteria into specific requirements that are communicated to suppliers. This practice, called *reverse marketing*, means that organizational buyers are attempting to work with suppliers to make their products, services, and capabilities fit the buyer's needs. Working closely and collaboratively like this with suppliers also helps build buyer–seller relationships and leads to supply partnerships. Companies such as Tim Hortons will work with external partners to build stores and host events.

Fear in Organizational Buying Behaviour

It's important at this point to examine the role of emotion in the organizational buying process. Emotions drive human behaviour and are the engines that propel people forward to reach their goals.

According to one author, B2B buying decisions are usually driven by one emotion—fear. Specifically, B2B buying is all about minimizing fear by eliminating risk. There are two distinct types of risk. There is organizational risk, typically formalized and dealt with in the buying process, and then there is personal risk, which is unstated but remains a huge influencing factor in organizational buying. For example, a buyer who chooses to deal with the same trusted supplier for many years is minimizing fear by eliminating organizational risk. Personal risk is explained by the buyer who chooses not to work with a new supplier even if that potential supplier's products offer better value. The buyer may fear that the latter may not produce a quality product, for example, and the buyer fears being reprimanded and thus may fear working with new suppliers to avert any risk. Humans do not always make rational decisions. In fact, some decisions are made irrationally. People use shortcuts, gut feel, emotions, beliefs, instincts, and habits to reach decisions. Consumer research found this out long ago, but for some reason, many people refuse to accept that the same mechanisms are at play in the business world.[13]

Buyer–Seller Relationships and Supply Partnerships

Another distinction between organizational and consumer buying behaviour lies in the nature of the

Leading by Example

As of December 2012, there were over 1.1 million businesses in Canada. With over 98 percent of these organizations having less than 100 employees, businesses cannot overlook the opportunity to work with small businesses as either buyers or sellers.

The Government of Canada purchases over $16 billion worth of goods and services from various businesses each year. These purchases are made on behalf of the various federal agencies and departments that help run our country. Given the size of the Canadian government, leveraging its purchasing power allows the Government of Canada to receive great value from its purchases. Furthermore, contracts flow through Public Services and Procurement Canada once costs for goods and services exceed $25,000. This makes the organizational buying process more fair and structured.

In fact, the Government of Canada has made it easier for businesses to sell to it by breaking down its buying procedure. It clearly articulates its organizational buying behaviour and prepares businesses for future bidding opportunities. The Government of Canada strives to makes its process accessible and fair while promoting competition among the different businesses it interacts with.

Being one of the largest purchasers in Canada, the Government of Canada is also practising green procurement; that is, federal departments and agencies consider environmentally responsible procurements by identifying green goods and services as well as the companies that supply them. These programs include the ECOLOGO® Certification program, which outlines criteria and life-cycle-based standards, and EnerGuide, which promotes energy efficiency. ●

©REB Images/Blend Images LLC

Questions

1. As a small business in Canada, what do you believe would be the pros and cons of selling products and services to the Government of Canada?

2. Knowing the green procurement practices of the Government of Canada, what steps do you believe small businesses need to take with respect to the production of their goods and services?

---

relationship between organizational buyers and suppliers. Specifically, organizational buying is more likely to involve complex and lengthy negotiations concerning delivery schedules, price, technical specifications, warranties, and claims policies. These negotiations can last for more than a year.

Reciprocal arrangements also exist in organizational buying. Reciprocity is an industrial buying practice in which two organizations agree to purchase each other's products and services. Governments frown on reciprocal buying because it restricts the normal operation of the free market. However, the practice exists and can limit the flexibility of organizational buyers in choosing alternative suppliers. The Focus on Ethics box, "Leading by Example," has more about government buying practices with respect to environmental standards.[14]

Fear may cause organizational buyers to make irrational decisions they will regret.

©Tetra Images/Alamy Stock Photo

supply partnership
Relationship between a buyer and supplier that adopt mutually beneficial objectives, policies, and procedures.

organizational buying behaviour
Process by which organizations determine the need for goods and then choose among alternative suppliers.

Because of the need to ensure that both buyer and seller perspectives are understood and addressed, buyer–seller relationships develop into supply partnerships in some cases. These partnerships are long-term relationships built on transparency and understanding.[15] A **supply partnership** exists when a buyer and its supplier adopt mutually beneficial objectives, policies, and procedures for the purpose of lowering the cost or increasing the value of products and services delivered to the ultimate consumer. For example, Sarmazian Brothers, an Ontario flooring retailer, partners with companies that are market leaders in flooring to enhance its offering.

ask YOURSELF

1. *What is derived demand?*

2. *A supply partnership exists when*
   _____.

The Organizational Buying Process and the Buying Centre

LO 4 Organizational buyers, like consumers, engage in a decision process when selecting products and services. **Organizational buying behaviour** is the decision-making process that organizations use (1) to establish the need for products and services, and (2) to identify, evaluate, and choose among alternative brands and suppliers. There are important similarities and differences between the two decision-making processes. To better understand the nature of organizational buying behaviour, we first compare it with consumer buying behaviour. We then describe a unique feature of organizational buying: the buying centre.

Stages in the Organizational Buying Process

As shown in Figure 5–4, the five stages that a student might use in buying a smartphone also apply to organizational purchases. However, comparing the two right-hand columns in Figure 5–4 reveals some key

Figure 5–4
Comparing the stages in a consumer and organizational purchase decision process reveals subtle differences

Stage in the Buying Decision Process	Consumer Purchase: Smartphone for a Student	Organizational Purchase: Camera for a Smartphone
Problem recognition	Student doesn't like the features of the cellphone now owned as compared to the features of a smartphone and desires to purchase one.	Marketing research and sales departments observe that competitors are improving the quality of cameras on their new models, which will be purchased from an outside supplier.
Information search	Student uses past experience and that of friends, ads, the Internet, and magazines to collect information and uncover alternatives.	Design and production engineers draft specifications for the camera. The purchasing department identifies suppliers of cameras.
Evaluation of alternatives	Alternative smartphones are evaluated on the basis of important attributes desired in a smartphone, and several stores are visited.	Purchasing and engineering personnel visit with suppliers and assess facilities, capacity, quality control, and financial status. They drop any suppliers not satisfactory on these factors.
Purchase decision	A specific brand of smartphone is selected, the price is paid, and the student leaves the store.	They use quality, price, delivery, and technical capability as key buying criteria to select a supplier. Then they negotiate terms and award a contract.
Post-purchase behaviour	Student re-evaluates the purchase decision, and may return the smartphone to the store if it is unsatisfactory.	They evaluate the supplier using a formal vendor-rating system and notify the supplier if the camera does not meet their quality standard. If the problem is not corrected, they drop the firm as a future supplier.

differences. For example, when a smartphone manufacturer buys digital cameras for its smartphones, more individuals are involved, supplier capability becomes more important, and the post-purchase evaluation behaviour is more formal. The buying decision process of an organization purchasing cameras for smartphones is typical of the steps made by organizational buyers.

The Buying Centre: A Cross-functional Group

For routine purchases with a small dollar value, a single buyer or purchasing manager often makes the purchase decision alone. In many instances, however, several people in the organization participate in the buying process. The individuals in this group, called a **buying centre**, share common goals, risks, and knowledge important to purchase decisions. For most large multi-store chain resellers, such as 7-Eleven convenience stores, the buying centre is very formal and is called a *buying committee*. However, most industrial firms or government units use informal groups of people or call meetings to arrive at buying decisions.

A firm marketing to industrial firms and government units must understand the structure, technical, and business functions represented, and the behaviour of the buying centre. One researcher has suggested four questions to provide guidance in understanding the buying centre in these organizations:[16]

- Which individuals are in the buying centre for the product or service?

Formal presentations to buying centres are part of the organizational buying process.

©PhotoAlto sas/Alamy Stock Photo

- What is the relative influence of each member of the group?
- What are the buying criteria of each member?
- How does each member of the group perceive the potential supplier, its products and services, and its salespeople?

People in the Buying Centre Who makes up the buying centre in a given organization depends on the specific item being bought. Although a buyer or purchasing manager is almost always a member of the buying centre, individuals from other functional areas are included, depending on what is to be purchased.[17]

In buying a million-dollar machine tool, the president (because of the size of the purchase) and the production vice president would probably be members. For key components to be included in a final manufactured product, a cross-functional group of individuals from research and development (R&D), engineering, and quality control are likely to be added. For new word-processing software, experienced office staff who will use the equipment would be members. Still, a major question in understanding the buying centre is finding and reaching the people who will initiate, influence, and actually make the buying decision.

> *A major question in understanding the buying centre is finding and reaching the people who will initiate, influence, and actually make the buying decision.*

Roles in the Buying Centre Researchers have identified five specific roles that an individual in a buying centre can play (see Figure 5–5).[18] In some purchases, the same person may perform two or more of these roles.

Buying Situations and the Buying Centre The number of people in the buying centre largely depends on the specific buying situation. Researchers who have studied organizational buying identify three types of buying situations, called **buy classes**. These buy classes vary from the routine reorder, or *straight rebuy*, to the

buying centre
Group of people in an organization who participate in the buying process.

buy classes
Three types of organizational buying situations: straight rebuy, modified rebuy, or new buy.

Figure 5–5
Roles in the buying centre

Users are the people in the organization who actually use the product or service, such as office staff who will use new word-processing software.

Influencers affect the buying decision, usually by helping define the specifications for what is bought. They usually have specialized knowledge. The information systems manager would be a key influencer in the purchase of a new computer network.

Buyers have formal authority and responsibility to select the supplier and negotiate the terms of the contract. The purchasing manager probably would perform this role in the purchase of a computer network.

Deciders have the formal or informal power to select or approve the supplier that receives the contract. Whereas in routine orders the decider is usually the buyer or purchasing manager, in important technical purchases it is more likely to be someone from R&D, engineering, or quality control. The decider for a key component being included in a final manufactured product might be any of these three people.

Gatekeepers control the flow of information in the buying centre. Purchasing personnel, technical experts, and office staff can all help or prevent salespeople (or information) from reaching people performing the other four roles.

completely new purchase, termed *new buy*. In between these extremes is the *modified rebuy*.[19]

- **Straight rebuy:** Here the buyer or purchasing manager reorders an existing product or service from the list of acceptable suppliers, probably without even checking with users or influencers from the engineering, production, or quality control departments. Office supplies and maintenance services are usually obtained as straight rebuys.

- **Modified rebuy:** In this buying situation, the company is purchasing a product that it has experience purchasing, such as new laptops for salespeople, but it wants to change the product specifications, price, delivery schedule, or supplier. The changes usually mean involving users, influencers, and/or deciders in the buying decision—more input than would be necessary for a straight rebuy.

- **New buy:** In this situation, the company is buying the product or service for the first time. This purchase involves greater potential risk and is more complex than other buying situations. The buying centre is larger, comprising people representing those parts of the organization having a stake in the new buy. In 2013, the Government of Canada awarded a $15 million contract to ARUP Canada Inc. for a new St. Lawrence Bridge in Montreal. Under the contract ARUP Canada Inc. was to provide engineering and coordination services for the new bridge.[20]

Figure 5–6 summarizes how buy classes affect buying centre tendencies in different ways.[21]

B2B Market Segmentation

LO 5 Chapter 6, "Segmentation, Targeting, and Positioning," focuses primarily on the consumer market. Here we focus on the business market. Consumer market segmentation groups consumers into groups that have common needs and respond similarly to marketing programs. The process of segmenting business markets divides markets based on type of customer, size, buying situation, customer location, and benefits sought. By applying market segmentation concepts to groups of business customers, a marketer can develop a strategy that best suits a particular segment's needs.

Figure 5–6
How the buying situation affects buying centre behaviour

Buying Centre Dimension	Buy-Class Situation		
	Straight Rebuy	Modified Rebuy	New Buy
People involved	1	2–3	Many
Decision time	Short	Short	Long
Problem definition	Well-defined	Minor modifications	Uncertain
Buying objective	Low-priced supplier	Low-priced supplier	Good solution
Suppliers considered	Present	Present	New/present
Buying influence	Purchasing agent	Purchasing agent and others	Technical/operating personnel

Type of Customer

The NAICS codes discussed earlier provide a useful tool for identifying business target markets. For example, Steelcase, a major producer of office furniture, segments its customers into ten industries, including banking, higher education, hospitality, and health care.

Size of Customer

Many B2B marketers divide their potential market into large and small accounts, using separate distribution channels to reach each segment. For example, marketers may develop one strategy to reach Fortune 500 corporations, which have complex purchasing procedures, and another strategy for small firms where decisions are made by one or two people. American Express provides information and assistance for small business owners with its Small Business Services unit, which is dedicated exclusively to the success of small business owners and their companies.

Type of Buying Situation

B2B marketers can divide their potential market by the three types of buy classes: new buy, modified rebuy, and straight rebuy. We recognized in the buy-class discussion above that a new buy is significantly different from a straight rebuy in several important respects. Consequently, a business seller might well segment its market into the three buy-class categories.

Customer Location

The product manager might segment on the basis of region or actual location of the potential customer. Firms located in a metropolitan area might receive a personal sales call, whereas those outside this area might be contacted by telephone.

Benefits Sought

The market may also be segmented on the basis of benefits sought. Xerox may decide to focus on firms looking for quality products and good customer service as opposed to those looking simply for lower prices.

---

ask YOURSELF

1. What one department is almost always represented by a person in the buying centre?

2. What are the three types of buying situations or buy classes?

Online Buying in Organizational Markets

LO 6 Organizational buying behaviour and business marketing continue to change with the use of the Internet and e-commerce. Due to the rising competition, organizations are learning from their successes and adapting to their failures. Scale allows organizations to vastly outnumber consumers in terms of both online transactions made and purchase volume.[22] In fact, organizational buyers account for about 80 percent of the total worldwide dollar value of all online transactions. Organizational buyers in North America will account for about 60 percent of these purchases. Almost all small business reportedly make purchases online.

Prominence of Online Buying in Organizational Markets

Online buying in organizational markets is prominent for three major reasons.[23] First, organizational buyers depend heavily on timely supplier information that describes product availability, technical specifications, application uses, price, and delivery schedules. This information can be conveyed quickly online. The Internet has altered one aspect of B2B purchasing: Buyers have much more knowledge at their fingertips about the seller's product than in the past. Second, web-based technology has been shown to substantially reduce buyer order-processing costs. At General Electric, online buying has cut the cost of a transaction from $50 to $100 per purchase to about $5. Third, business marketers have found that web-based technology can reduce marketing costs, particularly sales and advertising expenses, and broaden their potential customer base for many types of products and services. For these reasons, online buying is popular in all three kinds of organizational markets. For example, airlines order over $400 million in spare parts from the Boeing Company website each year.

> *At General Electric, online buying has cut the cost of a transaction from $50 to $100 per purchase to about $5.*

Online buying can assume many forms. Organizational buyers can purchase directly from suppliers. For instance, a buyer might acquire a dozen desktop photocopiers from **Xerox.ca**. This same buyer might purchase office furniture and supplies online through a reseller, such as Staples at **staples.ca.** Increasingly, organizational buyers and business marketers are using e-marketplaces and online auctions to purchase and sell products and services.

E-marketplaces: Virtual Organizational Markets

A significant development in organizational buying has been the creation and growth of online trading communities, called **e-marketplaces**, that bring together buyers and supplier organizations.[24] These online communities go by a variety of names, including portals, exchanges, and e-hubs, and make possible the real-time exchange of information, money, products, and services. Globally, the number of e-marketplaces for businesses is extensive.

E-marketplaces can be independent trading communities or private exchanges. Independent e-marketplaces typically focus on a specific product or service, or serve a particular industry. They act as a neutral third party and provide an online trading platform and a centralized market that enable exchanges between buyers and sellers. Independent e-marketplaces charge a fee for their services and exist in settings that have one or more of the following features:

- Thousands of geographically dispersed buyers and sellers
- Frequently changing prices caused by demand and supply fluctuations
- Time sensitivity due to perishable offerings and changing technologies
- Easily comparable offerings between a variety of suppliers

Well-known independent e-marketplaces include PaperExchange (paper products), PlasticsNet (plastics), Altra Energy (electricity, natural gas, and crude oil), and FarmTrade (agricultural products). Small business buyers and sellers, in particular, benefit from independent e-marketplaces. These e-marketplaces offer suppliers an economical way to expand their customer base and reduce the cost of purchased products and services.

Large companies tend to favour private exchanges that link them with their network of qualified suppliers and customers. Private exchanges focus on streamlining a company's purchase transactions with its suppliers and customers.

Like independent e-marketplaces, they provide a technology trading platform and central market for buyer–seller interactions.

Large firms such as IBM, General Motors, and Toyota have formed private exchanges. Some, such as IBM and GE, have mandated that their suppliers must deal with them primarily through online exchanges. These private exchanges provide tremendous cost savings through the elimination of periodic negotiations and routine paperwork.

Ariba is an e-marketplace that connects one million businesses. Ariba's global membership includes buyers and suppliers from a variety of industries. It was originally set up as a one-stop solution to specifically meet the e-procurement needs of the natural resource industry.[25]

The growth of virtual B2B interactions has not limited face-to-face interactions, however, particularly in the global business community. The Marketing NewsFlash box, "Marketing Mishaps in the Global Economy," looks at some common mishaps to avoid when working with international business partners.[26]

Part of Our World

As of March 31, 2020, Royal Bank of Canada was Canada's largest company, but only the 99th largest in the world, by market capitalization. The top five global companies by market capitalization are shown below.

	Market Value
1. Saudi Aramco	$1,602 billion
2. Microsoft	$1,200 billion
3. Apple	$1,113 billion
4. Amazon.com	$971 billion
5. Alphabet	$799 billion

Online Auctions in Organizational Markets

Online auctions have grown in popularity among organizational buyers and business marketers. Many e-marketplaces offer this service. Two general types of auctions are common: a traditional auction and a reverse auction.[27] Figure 5–7 shows how buyer and seller participants and price behaviour differ by type of auction. Let's look at each auction type more closely to understand the implications of each for buyers and sellers.

In a **traditional auction**, a seller puts an item up for sale and would-be buyers are invited to bid in

marketing NewsFlash

Marketing Mishaps in the Global Economy

There is a heightened sense of formality in Japanese interaction. When doing business in Japan, your suitability with respect to conducting business will be assessed during a first meeting. It is important to maintain a sense of professionalism and be aware of the host country's customs. Offending a professional from another country could affect your business relationship.

In Japanese society, the bow is used when meeting, when getting attention, to show gratitude, to express sympathy, or as an apology. In Western society, handshakes were more the norm. Now, cultural norms are being revisited as physical distancing and mask-wearing becomes more and more prevalent in North America.

The diversity of our world offers interesting challenges in business. What some cultures deem as humorous may be quite offensive to others. Marketers blunder if the differences between cultures are not taken seriously.

When doing business in Japan, the exchanging of business cards involves a degree of ceremony. The card is seen to represent the individual, so it should be treated with respect. Before travelling to Japan, ensure that you have ample cards

and have one side translated into Japanese. Include your position within the company on it. Invest in a carrying case to store cards and keep this in an easy-to-access location. When exchanging cards, offer your card, with the Japanese side up, with both hands. Ensure that there is no barrier between you and the recipient, such as a table, chair, or plant. When accepting a card, always use two hands as this shows deference.

The Japanese like dealing with quiet, sincere, and compromising individuals. Extroverts are seen as brash and arrogant. Early on in negotiations, remain humble, indirect, and non-threatening. Silence is considered a virtue. If things go quiet when doing business in a meeting, don't panic. Reflection is taking place. Silence may be also be accompanied by the closing of the eyes. Never interrupt or break the silence.

Some marketing mistakes that have happened in the past include Nike's release of women's leggings in New Zealand that had a pattern that resembled a Samoan tattoo. The international company did not realize that the tattoo was reserved

Presenting business cards with two hands is normal business practice in Japan.
©Phillip Jarrell/Getty Images

for men. Nike was made aware of its error and pulled the product.

North Americans are comfortable with slang phrases. So comfortable that Coors launched a cool campaign entitled "Turn It Loose." Unfortunately, the phrase, which was intended to infer releasing inhibitions and having fun, did not translate that way in Spanish-speaking markets as the translation was "suffer from diarrhea." ●

Questions

1. Can you think of other customs that a businessperson should be aware of in doing business in other countries?

2. What are some ways you can prepare for meetings or discussions with business people from other countries?

---

competition with each other. As more would-be buyers become involved, there is an upward pressure on bid prices. Why? Bidding is sequential—that is, bidders bid in order, one at a time. Prospective buyers observe the bids of others and decide whether to increase the bid price. The auction ends when a single bidder remains and "wins" the item with its highest price. Traditional auctions are frequently used to dispose of excess merchandise. For example, Dell Computer sells surplus,

refurbished, or closeout computer merchandise at its **dellauction.com** website.

A reverse auction works in the opposite direction from a traditional auction. In a **reverse auction**, a buyer communicates a need for a product or service and would-be suppliers are invited to bid in competition with each other. As more would-be suppliers

> **reverse auction**
> Occurs when a buyer communicates a need for something and would-be suppliers bid in competition with each other.

Figure 5–7
How buyer and seller participants and price behaviour differ by type of online auction

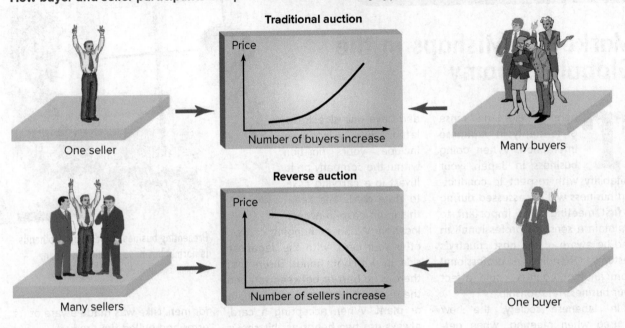

Traditional auction

One seller → Price / Number of buyers increase ← Many buyers

Reverse auction

Many sellers → Price / Number of sellers increase ← One buyer

become involved, there is a downward pressure on bid prices for the buyer's business. Why? Like traditional auctions, bidding is sequential and prospective suppliers observe the bids of others and decide whether to decrease the bid price. The auction ends when a single bidder remains and "wins" the business with its lowest price. Reverse auctions benefit organizational buyers by reducing the cost of their purchases. As an example, General Electric, one of the world's largest companies, has its own Global eXchange Services unit, which runs online reverse auctions for the company. It claims that it saved $780 million on the purchase of $6 billion worth of products and services.[28]

Clearly, buyers welcome the lower prices generated by reverse auctions. Some suppliers also favour the reverse auction process because it gives them a chance to capture business that they might not have otherwise had because of a longstanding purchase relationship between the buyer and another supplier. On the other hand, suppliers argue that reverse auctions put too much emphasis on prices, discourage consideration of other important buying criteria, and threaten supply partnership opportunities.[29]

ask **YOURSELF**

1. *What are e-marketplaces?*

2. *How do traditional auctions and reverse auctions affect bid prices?*

LO 1
- Organizational buyers are divided into four different markets:
  - Industrial firms reprocess a product or service and then sell it.
  - Resellers buy physical products and sell them without reprocessing them.
  - Government units at the federal, provincial, regional, and municipal levels purchase goods and services to help serve their constituents.
  - Non-profit organizations purchase products and services to help their organizations serve the good of society as opposed to a financial goal.
- The North American Industry Classification System (NAICS) is a convenient starting point to begin the process of measuring business markets.

LO 2
- Content marketing keeps potential customers engaged by ensuring that relevant and valuable content is available at various touch points.

 LO 3
- Key differences between the business and consumer buying processes include demand characteristics, number of potential buyers, buying objectives, buying criteria, size of the order or purchase, buyer–seller relationships and partnerships, and multiple buying influences within companies.

 LO 4
- The buying centre is a group of people in an organization that participate in the buying process.

- The buying centre usually includes a person from the purchasing department and possibly representatives from R&D, engineering, and production, depending on what is being purchased. These people can play one or more of five roles in a purchase decision: user, influencer, buyer, decider, or gatekeeper.
- The organizational purchasing process is influenced by the extent of the buying situation:
  - A straight rebuy is a routine purchase that may not involve any users or influencers.
  - A modified rebuy would involve users and influencers since there is a change to the specifications of the original purchase.
  - A new buy will be more complex and involve more people in the buying centre.

 LO 5
- The process of segmenting business markets divides markets based on type of customer, size, buying situation, customer location, and benefits sought.
- By applying market segmentation concepts to groups of business customers, a marketer can develop a strategy that best suits a particular segment's needs.

LO 6
- Online buying is prevalent in industrial, reseller, and government markets.
- Globally, the number of e-marketplaces for businesses is extensive, and online auctions are commonly used by organizational buyers and business marketers.

key terms and concepts... **A REFRESHER**

business marketing
buy classes
buying centre
derived demand
e-marketplaces

fluctuating demand
inelastic demand
North American Industry Classification System (NAICS)
organizational buyers

organizational buying behaviour
reverse auction
supply partnership
traditional auction

hands-on... **APPLY YOUR KNOWLEDGE**

B2B Marketing Differences In the opening vignette, Chris Venter discusses the importance of being able to provide good solutions for his partners in a team environment. In particular, for larger purchases and key partnerships, decisions need to be made by a committee as opposed to an individual. Review the opening vignette and identify other differences in the organizational-buying purchase-decision process that need to be considered in B2B marketing.

Strategic partnerships are critical to the success of many businesses. This chapter's opening vignette describes how IFS marketing helped build a partnership with Seaspan Marine Transportation. At the end of the vignette, consider the question about the individuals involved when businesses rely on their suppliers to meet the needs of their customers. Relate this to the concept of the buying centre and the different roles of individuals outlined in this chapter.

infographic... **DATA ANALYSIS**

The Infographic in this chapter, "Cybercrime and Canadian Business, 2017," outlines the amount spent by companies to protect against cybersecurity incidents. Review recent articles to identify companies that may have been impacted by cybercrime and discuss whether you believe Canadian companies are winning or losing this struggle.

Segmentation, Targeting, and Positioning

Market segmentation, target markets, and product positioning are the foundations of marketing practices. We turn to Dion Red Gun, founder of River Ranche Lodge, and director for Indigenous Tourism Alberta. We asked Dion to describe how proper customer segmentation, targeting, and messaging can drive business in the tourism industry. We then explore these concepts in more detail throughout the chapter.

River Ranche Tourism

CHAPTER OUTLINE

- River Ranche Lodge
- Market segmentation
- Segmentation strategies
- Target markets and personas
- Segmentation analytics
- Steps in market segmentation
- Product positioning

Indigenous tourism is one of the fastest growing sections of the tourism industry, and it provides opportunities to promote greater cultural understanding while increasing Indigenous peoples' capacity and economy. Indigenous Tourism Alberta (ITA) encourages and promotes authentic Indigenous tourism that showcases the unique and immersive experiences offered by its members.

There is still some resistance and skepticism from the Indigenous community about commodifying their culture and history, but Chief Lee Crowchild, chief of the Tsuut'ina Nation southwest of Calgary, said perspectives are changing. "We talk about tourism, about the economic benefits behind it. But more importantly, we talk about what it means for us to move our identity forward. We're saying this is our land, we're still here, we're not invisible. We're not the showcase Indians of the '60s and '50s, we're the real people of the land. We have lots of things to show you. And more importantly, we have a lot of things to teach you."

As part of this wave of Indigenous tourism growth across the country, Dion Red Gun has pushed to preserve the stories and traditions by sharing them with those outside the community. "That's why I'm very determined to lead a good path forward, and hopefully I'll lead a good path for the grandchildren; share the same stories that were passed down to me as close as I can to how I'm connected to the land," said Red Gun.

Dion Red Gun is sharing the land and stories with global travellers who are interested in visiting his River Ranche Lodge on the northern plains of Alberta. His dream is to educate Albertans and all visitors about the culture of his people. He hopes that travellers leave with a greater understanding of the Indigenous way of life moving forward.

The business started as a fly fishing outfitter with teepees and then moved to a lodge with cabins in 2006. River Ranche Tourism was recognized as a destination fly fishing lodge with primarily American clients for seasonal river activities and visiting sites significant to Siksika. The former facilities, with a lodge, four cabins, and a boat storage barn, were off the grid with solar power. Remote teepee campsites along the Siksika Bow River Valley were also part of the resort. In 2013, flooding literally washed the business down the river. Dion Red Gun had to overcome both business and personal obstacles to rebuild the business.

The new lodge overlooks the Bow River and is nestled within one of the largest intact Cottonwood riverine ecosystems in Western Canada. It features four double occupancy rooms adjoining the main lodge area, where there is ample room for dining and socializing. Visitors can learn both about the outdoors and the Blackfoot culture. Outdoor enthusiasts will enjoy the fly fishing, kayaking, birding, and cross-country skiing excursions. Cultural activities can include a Blackfoot teepee camp stay, Blackfoot elder storytelling, and a tour of the Siksika Reserve, where Blackfoot historical sites are abundant. Packages can include homemade meals, which feature authentic Indigenous cuisine. Those seeking cultural experiences will learn from Siksika Elders who share their knowledge of healing and wellness. Through the

Majorville Medicine Wheel Journey through Siksika lands, Elders and members share the interpretation of the stones, dances, stories of the dancing regalia, and significant sites important to the Siksika. Guests can end their days of outdoor adventure on the large deck, enjoying a campfire or relaxing in the hot tub watching spectacular sunsets. The lodge's central location allows them to offer clients trips to sites such as Head-Smashed-In Buffalo Jump and Blackfoot Crossing Historical Park, and they are currently seeking partnerships to extend trips into southeastern Alberta and the Badlands.

The current largest consumer segment of River Ranche Lodge is outdoors enthusiasts and cultural spirituality seekers; however, their activities are gaining more attention with their endeavours to utilize the Blackfoot Crossing Historical Park and traditional territory and wellness programs.

Dion Red Gun worked with a university marketing class to assist him in identifying more potential segments for his lodge. Some of the segments that River Ranche Lodge has identified as potential clients are:

- Outdoor lovers
- Fly fishing enthusiasts
- Kayakers/canoers
- Cross-country skiers
- Birding groups
- Corporate clients for retreats and team-building
- International vacationers
- Yoga practitioners
- Crafters
- Family members wishing to reunite
- Plant and herb naturalists
- Community members for community meetings
- School children for cultural experiences
- Youth for camps
- University students—writer's retreat

What does the River Ranche Lodge have to offer these target groups? For the outdoor enthusiasts, the unique location along the Bow River offers world-class fly fishing and is located within one of the largest intact Cottonwood riverine ecosystems in Western Canada. For the segments interested in an authentic cultural experience, River Ranche Lodge is partnered with Indigenous Tourism Alberta, Travel Alberta, and the Indigenous Tourism Association of Canada to participate in tours with other partners in Alberta. It also has a close relationship with the Siksika community and its Elders to share their stories and traditions.

What were the overall implications of this new segmentation to the marketing plan for the River Ranche Lodge? When River Ranche Lodge expanded its target market to include more segments, the lodge found it was able to minimize the seasonality of the business. It also found further opportunities to partner with other businesses and organizations to offer an unique experience to its customers.

Dion Red Gun summarizes the importance of the segmentation and clearly identifying the target market for his business: "Indigenous peoples who are striving to improve and provide experiences for global travellers must be prepared for obstacles at the local level," advises Dion. "Know who your target market is and never give up on your journey to provide high-quality products and services in order to achieve success."[1]

Segmentation, Targeting, and Positioning

Segmentation, targeting, and product positioning are fundamental concepts that are central to how marketers run their businesses and market their products. These concepts are intertwined and work together to create and reinforce a product's image to its consumers and to the market in general.

A market segmentation analysis allows marketers to identify which segments could be a focus, where gaps in the market exist, and where future opportunities may lie. Having a clear position in the market allows more focused and consistent communication with customers in a meaningful way. Marketers are careful to consistently reinforce a product's image by ensuring that all elements of the marketing mix are well coordinated to reflect the product's positioning and target market needs and wants.

> *Segmentation, targeting, and product positioning are fundamental concepts that are central to how marketers run their businesses and market their products.*

River Ranche Lodge uses these approaches to ensure that its product features and marketing programs are relevant and focused to meet the needs of its target audience. In such a competitive marketplace, this approach helps River Ranche Lodge maintain a competitive edge.

Market Segmentation

LO 1 The concepts of market segmentation, target markets, and product positioning are based on three important facts. First, consumers have a range of different needs, and a single product cannot satisfy everyone. Second, companies have limited amounts of money, which needs to be spent efficiently and effectively on consumers who are most likely to purchase the product. Third, marketers need to have clear consumer insights on their target markets in terms of product needs, price expectations, purchase habits, and the communication tools most used.

In simple terms, a market segment is a piece of the market. In the marketing world, there are two main market segments: the consumer market and the business market. The **consumer market** consists of goods, services, and ideas that a person can purchase or support for his or her own personal use. The **business market** involves products that are purchased either to run a business or to be used as a component in another good or service. How a product is classified depends on its usage. Let's look at an example to clarify this point. A person buys an iPad in order to connect on social networks, surf the Internet, stream music, upload photos, and watch movies for entertainment. A company buys its salespeople iPads so that they can make better customer presentations and more easily access head-office files. The products are exactly the same. In the first instance, the iPad is a consumer product for personal use; in the second instance, the iPad is a business product for assisting salespeople. There are many other similar examples, but it is important to understand that many products are tailored specifically for one market or the other, and not necessarily both. Heavy machinery used for landscaping is not a consumer product, and a comic book is not a business product.

Formally, **market segmentation** involves aggregating prospective buyers into groups that have common needs and respond similarly to marketing programs. These groups are relatively homogeneous and consist of people who are fairly similar in terms of their consumption behaviour, attitudes, and profiles.

There is normally more than one firm vying for the attention of prospective buyers in a market. This results in marketers following a strategy of **product differentiation** to position their products apart from the competition in the eyes of consumers so that they appear distinct from competitive offerings. It is important to note that product differentiation does not mean a product has to be better than the competition. Marketers position their products as best they can to meet the needs of their target consumers. Sometimes, this may mean adding a unique feature; other times, it may mean creating a unique image or a better price.

consumer market
Goods, services, and ideas that a person can purchase, use, or support for personal use.

business market
Products that are purchased either to run a business or to be used as a component in another product or service.

market segmentation
The aggregation of prospective buyers into groups that have common needs and respond similarly to marketing programs.

product differentiation
Positioning a product to a target group so that it appears distinct from competitive offerings.

Forms of Market Segmentation

LO 2 There are a number of different approaches companies can take to segment the market. Whether a company is in the business-to-business market or the consumer market, it can follow one of these four strategies: a mass marketing strategy, a segment marketing strategy, a niche marketing strategy, or an individualized marketing strategy (see Figure 6–1).

Mass Marketing This approach exists in a limited capacity today due to the competitiveness of the market and the need for marketers to specifically address consumer needs with their offerings. A **mass marketing** strategy is when a product with broad appeal is widely marketed to the entire market with no product or marketing differentiation at all. Examples can be found in the utilities area, with items such as natural gas being marketed to all consumer groups with no variation from either a product or marketing perspective. Other examples can be found in the fruits and vegetables market with products such as broccoli, radishes, and spring onions also being sold indiscriminately to all target groups. Today, there are few products that ascribe to a mass marketing approach. With the influx of data and the range of technology to communicate with consumers, it makes it more practical for a brand to better profile consumers and engage them through more-focused messaging.

Segment Marketing This form of market segmentation is the most common form of segmentation, followed by companies such as River Ranche Lodge, discussed in this chapter's opening vignette. Segment marketing involves the marketing of a wide range of different products and brands to specifically meet the needs of an organization's varied target markets. Examples of this approach can be seen in competitive industries that are dominated by large organizations, such as the food business, car industry, and smartphone

What segmentation strategy is used to market these products?
©filmfoto/Getty Images

market, just to name a few. For example, in the car industry, companies such as General Motors market cars, trucks, sport utility vehicles, crossovers, and minivans under a wide range of brands and models. Well-known General Motors brands include Cruze, Camaro, Yukon, Sierra, Equinox, and Corvette, as well as its premium Cadillac brand with its luxury vehicles such as the Escalade. These brands are created and marketed to appeal to different market segments in the automobile market—all owned and marketed by General Motors.

Let's look at the laundry detergent category for additional clarity and examine Procter & Gamble's (P&G) brand approach to market segmentation. If we look at laundry detergent in general, there are products that appeal to different demographic and behaviouristic groups. For example, there are detergents that are superior at cleaning your clothes, detergents that are gentle on clothing, and detergents that make your clothing smell great. When P&G started making laundry detergent, it was a "one size fits all" product. Tide was the first "heavy-duty synthetic detergent" available on the market. Mass marketing approaches were used to promote and sell the original Tide. Using the slogan "oceans of suds," Tide became the top-selling laundry detergent. Over time, this strategy shifted to a segmented approach, with P&G launching multiple

mass marketing
Marketing a product with broad appeal to the entire market without any product or marketing differentiation.

Figure 6–1
Companies can take different approaches to market segmentation

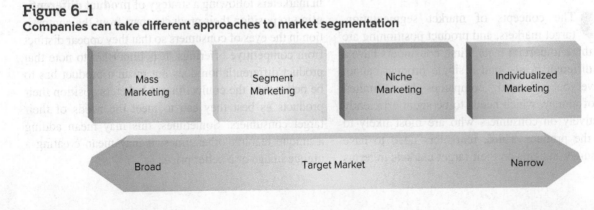

Mass Marketing | Segment Marketing | Niche Marketing | Individualized Marketing

Broad   Target Market   Narrow

laundry detergent brands with an assortment of product offerings under each brand. Tide focuses on consumers who want superior cleaning; Ivory Snow focuses on families who want a gentle detergent for their children's clothing; and Gain focuses on consumers who want their clothes to smell great. Through the development of innovative new products, P&G has expanded into even more targeted segments, including products for consumers who are energy conscious, consumers who want whiter clothes, and consumers who want products without added fragrance, just to name a few.

> *A segment marketing strategy is also followed by companies in the business-to-business market.*

Each product not only caters to the specific product needs of distinct target markets but also has its own marketing program to ensure that each target group's needs are properly met. If you look at the packages for these products, they reflect different target market interests and needs. Ivory Snow, for example, has soft pink packaging with images of hearts to reflect its gentle formulation. Tide has bright packaging featuring a bull's-eye and bright orange colour to boldly stand out on the shelf. Gain is packaged in a bright green package with whimsical images of flowers, reflecting the focus on product fragrance.[2]

As discussed in Chapter 5, a segment marketing strategy is also followed by companies in the business-to-business market, using variables such as the type of customer, size of customer, location of customer, type of buying situation, or benefits sought. An example can be seen in the food-service industry. French's ketchup and mustard are well-known in the Canadian consumer market, but French's also has an ingredient business, selling its products to food manufacturers and restaurants. Many fast-food restaurants provide small, individual 9g ketchup packages to customers with their meal. A fast-food chain may order the ketchup from its head office to supply to its many restaurants. The head office may order pallets of 40 boxes with 1,500 ketchup packages in each box, and then distribute the boxes to its restaurants. French's may also have a poultry processor as a customer. This poultry processor uses ketchup in the seasoning for its chicken wings that it sells to customers in the frozen-food section at grocery stores. This poultry processor's specification would take into account the volume of ketchup it requires, the taste of the ketchup, how it is used in the manufacturing process, and packaging. Since this customer requires hundreds of gallons of ketchup annually, and all processing is done in one location, it orders 330-gallon stackable totes of the ketchup. These totes provide the volume needed by the poultry processor, and the totes can be easily stacked and stored at the plant. In these two examples, French's is segmenting its customers by the type of customer (restaurant versus food manufacturer). Another key segmentation variable is benefits sought. The fast-food chain requires individual packets that can be easily distributed to its individual restaurants, while the poultry processor requires large volumes that can been easily stored.[3]

Niche Marketing The market segmentation strategy where a company restricts its efforts to marketing a limited product line to a narrow but profitable single segment of the market that is of marginal interest to major competitors is called **niche marketing**.[4] Staying within the car industry and laundry detergent market, we look at the Tesla Motors car brand and

niche marketing
Marketing a limited product line to a narrow but profitable segment of the market that is of marginal interest to major competitors.

Brands such as Heinz and French's follow a segment marketing strategy in their food-service businesses.
(left) ©Andrew Francis Wallace/Toronto Star via Getty Images, (right) ©Rosenfeld Images Ltd/Science Source

individualized marketing

One-to-one marketing that involves customizing offers and, in some cases, products to fit individual needs.

Eco-Max laundry detergent to see niche marketing approaches. Tesla Motors is an independent car company headquartered in California that manufactures and markets electric vehicles only. Its first car, a Roadster, was launched in 2008; today, it also markets a Model S sedan, a cyber-truck, and a Model X sport utility vehicle that compete with high-end car manufacturers such as BMW and Mercedes, but it restricts its offerings to only the niche elec-tric-vehicle category. Tesla products are not sold through dealerships, but instead through a small number of exclusive Tesla stores, some located in upscale shopping malls.[5]

Eco-Max laundry detergent is an example of a product that started out using a niche marketing approach. Eco-Max was initially launched to consumers in 2007 by Prism Care Corporation, a company focused on replacing toxic cleaning products with natural non-toxic and effective formulations. Its products are made from "100% plant-based ingredients that are biodegradable, renewable and sustainable." Eco-Max has focused on consumers who are eco-conscious and want products that are safer to use, as well as being safe for the environment.[6]

Crown Outdoor and Tactical, a family-owned business located in Calgary, has been in the surplus business for the last 65 years. It has provided uniforms, mortars, firearms, tents, torpedos, and camouflage nets to cadets, military, and paramilitary. It also provides

What segmentation strategy is used by Eco-Max with its laundry detergent?

Used with permission of Prism Care Corporation

the above as fabulous props and treasures to the film industry. The company supplied props to such shows and movies as *Reverent, Wynonna Earp, Fargo, Brokeback Mountain*, and many more. Some entertainers who have visited Crown Outdoor and Tactical in Calgary are Cher, Radiohead, Dwight Yoakam, Jann Arden, Slipknot, Erika Eleniak, Michelle Williams, Marilyn Manson, the late Heath Ledger, Tom Hardy, and Calgary's own k.d. lang. However, the COVID-19 pandemic that began the spring of 2020 has necessitated that the business move to more online sales. Crown also supplies an emergency food supply kit with 56 meals that lasts for 25 years that retails for $200. A very well-defined niche market indeed.[7]

Individualized Marketing

New technology has boosted individualized marketing as a segmentation option for marketers. **Individualized marketing** can also be called one-to-one marketing with "segments of one," and it involves customizing products to fit individual needs.[8] It is important to differentiate between individualized segmentation and individualized marketing communication. With the wide-scale use of technology and collection of customer data, messages and offers are regularly being customized for target audiences. But with individualized market segmentation, product and service offerings are also customized to meet individual needs.

Marketers are rediscovering today what previous generations knew running a general store a century ago. Every customer is unique, has particular wants and needs, and requires special care from the seller. Efficiencies in manufacturing and marketing during the past century made mass-produced goods so affordable that most customers were willing to compromise their individual tastes and settle for standardized products. Today's Internet ordering and flexible manufacturing and database marketing techniques have facilitated individualized market segmentation by making it easier to tailor goods and services to suit individual customer needs.

Consider Coca-Cola with its "Share a Coke" campaign where customers can find their own names or other popular titles.

For the campaign, 1,000 of the country's most popular names, all written in the beverage's distinctive script, replaced the Coca-Cola logo on bottles of Coca-Cola, Diet Coke, and Coke Zero. In 2015, the campaign

Coca-Cola's "Share a Coke" Campaign

©Chayut Orapinpatipat/Shutterstock

also included a limited-edition release of Cherry Coke, and the nearly 25 million personalized 500ml bottles featured new names, including Calvin, Maddy, Leo, Maya, Meagan, Keith, Nancy, and Dillon. The company worked with a research firm to have the names cover approximately 90 percent of the population. For those Canadians whose name didn't make a bottle, Coca-Cola provided an opportunity for people to customize their own mini-can at select large events across the country, or create a virtual bottle online and share it via their social media feeds. The first "Share a Coke" campaign in 2014 was one of its most successful programs of all time, with total sales up 6 percent, new customers increased by 5 percent, and overall brand health scores boosted by 8 percent.[9]

> *Every customer is unique, has particular wants and needs, and requires special care from the seller.*

The key to successful product differentiation and market segmentation strategies lies in finding the ideal balance between satisfying a customer's individual wants and being able to do this profitably.

Target Market Profiles and Personas

Segmentation Variables in Consumer Markets

LO 3 Marketers need to understand what makes their consumers tick, what they desire, and how best to communicate with them. A *target market* is the specific group or segment(s) of existing and potential consumers to which marketers direct their marketing efforts.

Developing an accurate **target market profile** is crucial to the success of all marketing initiatives as it drives decisions about the product's marketing mix and the product's positioning in the market. Markets are segmented using four variables: (1) geographics, (2) demographics, (3) psychographics, and (4) behaviouristics. Figure 6–2 clearly outlines these four variables.

Often, students wonder why it is important to identify all these variables when describing a target market. If consumers are buying chewing gum, what is the relevance of their income level or where they live? In fact, usually only a few elements in a target market profile are the main determinants in why a consumer purchases a product. Nonetheless, all variables need to be included in the target market profile as this profile is used in other marketing areas. If elements are missing, crucial errors can be made. For example, a target market profile is used extensively when creating advertising programs. The consumer insights are used to help develop campaigns that speak to the target group, and media is bought against the specific target market data such as age, income, location, interests, and media habits.

Geographics A **geographics** descriptor of a target market looks at where a target market lives, using variables such as country, region, province, city size, and population density, such as urban, suburban, or rural. Marketers often find that Canadians differ in terms

target market profile
A description of the target market that contains specific information about the target group in four areas: geographics, demographics, psychographics, and behaviouristics.

geographics
Where a target market lives, using variables such as country, region, province, city size, and population density, such as urban, suburban, or rural.

Who is the target market for e-scooter rentals?

©hanohiki/Shutterstock

of needs or preferences based on where they live. An example is a product such as the Lime e-scooter rental company, which is geared toward urban dwellers. The target market for this scooter mainly resides in city centres. In Canada, Lime piloted in Waterloo, Ontario, in 2018, and currently operates only in the city centres of Calgary, Edmonton, and Montreal, where its scooters can be located through a smartphone app and

Figure 6–2
Examples of typical target market variables in Canadian consumer markets

Target Market Profiles		
Categories	**Variables**	**Typical Breakdowns**
Geographics (Where does the target market live and work?)	Region	Atlantic; Quebec; Ontario; Prairies; British Columbia
	City or census metropolitan area (CMA) size	Under 5,000; 5,000–19,999; 20,000–49,999; 50,000–99,999; 100,000–249,999; 250,000–499,999; 500,000–999,999; 1,000,000–3,999,999; 4,000,000+
	Density	Urban; suburban; rural
Demographics (What is the basic census-type information on the target market as a whole?)	Age and family composition	Infant; under 6; 6–11; 12–17; 18–24; 25–34; 35–49; 50–64; 65+
	Gender	Male; female
	Marital status	Single or equivalent; married or equivalent
	Income	Under $24,999; $25,000–$34,999; $35,000–$49,999; $50,000–$74,999; $75,000–$99,999; $100,000–$149,999; $150,000+
	Occupation	Professional; managerial; clerical; sales; blue collar; white collar; student; retired; housewife; unemployed
	Education	Some high school; high school graduate; completed college or university; completed post-graduate studies
	Ethnic background	Country of origin
	Home ownership	Own home; rent home
Psychographics (What are the prevailing attitudes, values, interests, habits, and approaches to life that this target market shares?)	Personality traits	Social; compulsive; extroverted; introverted; intuitive; analytical; judgmental
	Lifestyle values and approaches	Rigid; disciplined; discontented; fearful; confident; positive; optimistic; energetic; resentful; dependent; negative; caring; materialistic; conformist; adventurous; independent; sharing
	Leisure activities, hobbies, and interests	Politics; music; sports; the arts; entertaining; fashion; gaming; health and fitness; travel; food; gardening; cars; movies; arts and crafts; the environment
	Media habits	Internet; newspaper; magazine; TV; radio; out-of-home
	Technology usage	Desktop computer; laptop; tablet; smartphone; TV; tech-savvy; tech-naive
Behaviouristics (How does this target market use and interact with the product?)	Main occasion for product use	Leisure; recreation and socializing with friends; professional and work situations; medical and personal care, home care, family care, etc.
	Main product benefit sought	Entertainment; self-improvement; fashion; fun; personal status; performance; specific product features such as taste, nutritional value, speed, etc.
	Primary and secondary product usage	Specific main usage and secondary usage of the product. (For example, the main usage of a cereal may be as a nutritious start to the day, but its secondary usage may be as a baking ingredient.)
	Frequency of use	Multiple times throughout the day; daily; weekly; monthly; every few months; biannually; annually
	Frequency of purchase	Daily; weekly; monthly; every few months; biannually; annually
	Product usage rate	Light user; medium user; heavy user
	Product usage status	Non-user; ex-user; prospect; first-time user; regular user
	Product loyalty status	None; some; medium; strong

accessed with a one-time registration that allows members to rent scooters by the minute. You must be a minimum of 18 years old to rent the scooters. There is no set drop-off location, which is one of the complaints of the service with the nuisance of scooter-dumping on sidewalks and street corners. Lime has hired 30 people in Montreal, called the "Tidy Squad," whose duties include rounding up scooters and reminding riders how to behave, and Montreal has introduced a by-law that mandates that the company remedy incidents of unlawfully parked scooters within two hours on weekdays. Another problem is safety; during the first two weeks of e-scooters in Calgary, there were 60 injuries reported to the city's urgent care centres and emergency rooms. More than 150,000 unique users took scooters for a spin over 915,000 times in four months in Calgary in 2019. Lime reports that half of one percent of scooter rides results in injuries.[10]

How do the target markets for Rogers Communications and Fido differ?

©JHVEPhoto/Shutterstock

Demographics

One of the easiest factors to determine is the *demographics* profile of a target market. This includes identifying ranges for age, gender, family composition, income, occupation, education, ethnic background, and home ownership for the main target market. This information can be identified through a company's market research information and other secondary data sources, such as Statistics Canada. An example of where demographics plays a leading role in a target market profile is with the Centrum vitamin brand. Centrum formulates and markets many of its products based on age and gender requirements. Centrum Men 50+ is formulated for men over 50 years of age; Centrum Women 50+ is formulated specifically to meet the needs of women over 50 years of age. There are also formulations for women and men under 50. Centrum Junior is focused on children between the ages of 4 and 12, and Centrum Prenatal is for women who are pregnant.[11]

Demographic and Geographic Profile: *Canadian Living* Magazine

Gender	Men/women	28%/72%
Age	Principal target	35–64 years
Income	Average annual household income	$85,976
Geography	Ontario	50%

Psychographics

Psychographics is one of the most difficult variables to identify for marketers. It involves understanding consumers' attitudes to life, values, personalities, general interests, opinions, media usage, technology preferences, and activities. This information is generally based on the primary research that marketers conduct to gather insights on their consumers. Image-based products gear much of their marketing efforts around these psychographic variables. The fragrance industry, for example, relies heavily on psychographics, as do many soft drink companies. Reflect for a minute on Coca-Cola, positioned as a traditional, refreshing soft drink rooted in old-fashioned Americana. Now think of Pepsi-Cola, marketed as the energetic cola for those with a youthful attitude to life. The products may vary only slightly in taste, but their target markets differ considerably in attitudes, interests, and opinions. Coca-Cola and Pepsi-Cola use psychographics as main variables in their marketing efforts.

Behaviouristics

Behaviouristics directly refers to how and why consumers buy and use products. It is one of the most important target market variables as it can direct the product's positioning in the market and can drive the main marketing communication messages of the brand, as well as promotional ideas and areas for new product development.

Behaviouristics looks at why consumers buy a product, the expected product benefits, how a product is used, how frequently they buy, where they buy, and whether consumers are brand loyal in their purchase behaviour. Database marketing analytics can collect data on consumer purchases and over time identify

psychographics
Understanding consumers' attitudes to life, values, personalities, general interests, opinions, and activities.

behaviouristics
How and why consumers buy and use a product, including the desired product benefits, how frequently they buy, where they buy, and whether consumers are brand loyal in their purchase behaviour.

what triggers consumer purchases as well as how loyal customers are. Primary research can help uncover why consumers purchase a product, what products benefits are most important, and how the product is used. Secondary data such as Nielsen data can provide industry data regarding where products are most frequently purchased.

Companies in the telecommunications industry often use behaviouristics to market to different customer groups with completely separate companies and brands. Rogers Communications, for example, owns Fido, which is used to market cheaper plans with no contracts to younger consumers who want basic talk, text, and social media access. Similarly, Bell owns Virgin Mobile, and Telus owns Koodo Mobile to market to a hip, younger, budget-conscious crowd. How and why these consumers use their phones and the benefits they desire are key drivers in these marketing efforts. *Brand loyalty* refers to the favourable attitudes that a consumer has over time toward a brand that result in varying levels of purchase commitment to the brand. Marketers strive toward having highly committed, brand-loyal consumers as this helps insulate their brands from competitive marketing practices and a rapidly changing marketing environment.

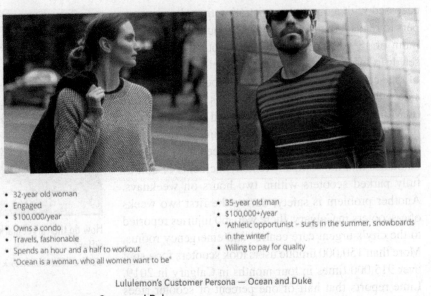

- 32-year old woman
- Engaged
- $100,000/year
- Owns a condo
- Travels, fashionable
- Spends an hour and a half to workout
"Ocean is a woman, who all women want to be"

- 35-year old man
- $100,000+/year
- "Athletic opportunist – surfs in the summer, snowboards in the winter"
- Willing to pay for quality

Lululemon's Customer Persona — Ocean and Duke

Lululemon personas: Ocean and Duke

Lululemon Athletica

ask YOURSELF

1. *Market segmentation involves aggregating prospective buyers into groups that have two key characteristics. What are they?*

2. *What is the difference between psychographics and behaviouristics?*

personas

Character descriptions of a typical customer in the form of fictional character narratives, complete with images that capture the personalities, values, attitudes, beliefs, demographics, and expected interactions with a brand.

Personas

Personas are character descriptions of a brand's typical customers. Personas bring target market data alive by creating fictional character narratives, complete with images, in one-page descriptions or snapshots that capture the personalities, values, attitudes, beliefs, demographics, and expected interactions of a typical user with a brand. Personas take target market research data and simplify and synthesize it, adding a few fictional details, such as name and image, so that human traits and characteristics become memorable for marketers. Well-defined personas usually include information on gender, age, interests, hobbies, education, goals, jobs, influencers, media usage, technology preferences, fears, concerns, drivers, and delights and interactions with a brand. They may capture a "day in the life of" a typical user. A branded product may have more than one persona: a primary persona on the typical main consumer, and a secondary persona that captures the profile of other, less important groups who should not be overlooked. Lululemon Athletica has developed two personas for its athleisure wear, as displayed in the images below.

Segmentation Analytics

LO 4 Marketers need to be aware that research companies can provide general data on the size and growth of markets, as well as general consumer and lifestyle trends, to assist in segmentation analysis. Data can be purchased from companies such as Nielsen or Euromonitor, which show trends, market size, competitive products, market share, and future prospects for industries. Euromonitor, for example, provides data on over 200 product categories in over 200 countries.[12]

Other segmentation analytics companies provide segmentation data on a more granular basis to pinpoint information on population clusters that assists marketers. These companies, such as Environics Analytics, Pitney

Bowes, and SuperDemographics, analyze populations and create market segments and detailed data to help marketers target specific groups with high levels of accuracy.

Environics Analytics is a highly respected marketing and analytical services company. It helps Canadian companies turn demographic, lifestyle, and behavioural data into customer insights, strategy, and results. Its PRIZM5 segmentation system slices the Canadian population into 68 lifestyle segments, such as Cosmopolitan Elite, Electric Avenues, Les Chics, and Lunch at Tim's, based on common demographics, lifestyles, interests, and values. Its data synthesizes information from the latest census with Environics' demographic projections, as well as its research on social values and consumer behaviour. This data gives users the ability to review information on what consumers are purchasing, what they enjoy doing, and their attitudes to life. Data funnels down to the granular postal code level where a breakdown of the population for a single postal walk is available. This is particularly useful for database marketing campaigns where postal code information triggers a host of data that assists companies in their targeting and segmentation efforts. This information helps guide marketing campaigns and media strategies.[13]

The Infographic, "The Six Key Tribes of Millennials," is the result of a major national survey of Canadian millennials, those born between 1980 and 1995. Social values research is necessary because, although millenials can share common experiences and aspirations as befits their stage in live, they cannot be lumped by demographic characteristics such as age, gender, region, or socioeconomic status. The study explored their social values with a focus on their life goals and what it means to be an adult. The research also explored their career aspirations, work experience, and political and social engagement. Some key findings were that fewer than half of Canadian millennials say they have enough money to live the kind of life they want, that most want a good balance between work and personal life, and that one in four millennials are actively engaged in a cause or issue.[14]

Pitney Bowes PSYTE HD also provides granular segmentation data through its segmentation system, which results in 57 unique lifestyle clusters. Postal code detail helps marketers discover untapped markets, finesse the targeting of their marketing campaigns, launch new products in appropriate markets, design cost-effective mailing and sampling programs, streamline retail offerings, and select the most profitable locations for new stores, restaurants, and retail developments.[15]

Infographic: The Six Key Tribes of Millennials

Lone Wolves

Engaged Idealists

Bros and Brittanys

Diverse Strivers

Critical Counterculturists

New Traditionalists

Environics Research

What Is Pickleball and Why Do People Love It?

©ZUMA Press Inc/Alamy Stock Photo

These are two very interesting questions about the fastest growing sport in North America—a sport that has been adopted by the silent generation and baby boomers as they retire and have a lot of spare time on their hands. Canadian snowbirds play this interesting game outdoors in RV parks and condo complexes in the southern U.S. or indoors at recreation centres throughout Canada.

Pickleball is very popular with seniors because it is fast-paced and low-impact, and anyone who has played any racquet sports can quickly catch on. The game is a combination of tennis, badminton, and ping pong played on a badminton-sized court with wooden paddles and hard wiffle balls. There are a few rules to learn, but most people can start playing within minutes of deciding it might be fun. It is fun and very social as it is almost always played as doubles, and usually people rotate through a bracket, exchanging courts and partners each short match.

Pickleball in North America has grown over 650 percent since it started to really catch on in the Sunbelt states around 2009, according to the U.S. Pickleball Association. (There is such a thing and a Canadian one too.) Global Newswire reported that pickleball equipment sales were anticipated to continue growing at almost 9 percent year over year for the next decade. This is where Bryan Banerd of Vernon, British Columbia, comes into the story. Shortly after picking up a racquet in 2012, Bryan realized that pickleball was going to be the next big thing, so he opened Pickleball Depot to supply Canadians with equipment. What started as an online pickleball equipment retailer soon became the largest pickleball multi-brand retailer and wholesaler in Canada. The growth of the sport soon had the company spinning off a new division, Apex Pickleball, to manufacture affordable equipment for the Canadian market with an ultimate goal of sharing the joy of pickleball with a wider audience.

Pickleball Depot has a chain of distributors throughout Canada and a super-efficient distribution team out of locations in Kelowna and Vernon B.C. Bryan's daughter Cara has taken over the day-to-day operations of the company, leaving Bryan to follow his passion of playing pickleball and coming up with new and innovative ideas for Pickleball Depot.

Pickleball has traditionally been a sport played by retired baby boomers, but Pickleball Depot and Pickleball Canada are working hard to reach other segments in the market. Returning snowbirds are creating pickleball leagues and offering lessons in recreation centres, gyms, and abandoned tennis courts across Canada, and Pickleball Depot is ready with affordable equipment to make the sport accessible to all. ●

Questions

1. What are some things that the pickleball community can do to appeal to a younger demographic?

2. How might social media be used to promote the sport?

Manifold Data Mining is another reputable service provider in the segmentation analytics area. It too provides data down to the postal code level. It uses census data as well as statistics from Citizenship and Immigration Canada, Health Canada, Industry Canada, Bank of Canada, real estate boards and companies, provincial ministries of health, Numeris Canada, and Manifold proprietary databases.[16] The Marketing NewsFlash box, "What Is Pickleball and Why Do People Love It?" examines how one company takes advantage of segmentation analytics.[17]

Students are advised to visit the websites of these two analytics companies to review samples of the rich data that is available for marketers. While Internet sites can change, the following websites currently provide a solid understanding of what data is available from these companies:

● Navigate to the PRIZM5 section of the Environics website at **www.environicsanalytics.ca/prizm5** and enter a postal code to review an overview of the cluster information.

● Navigate to the Consumer Lifestyle Clusters information at the Manifold Data Mining website at **manifolddatamining.com/data/consumer-lifestyle-clusters/** to review their description of the consumer lifestyle down to six-digit postal codes.

Steps in Market Segmentation

LO 5 Segmenting a market and selecting target markets is an integral part of the overall marketing planning process (see the section on the planning phase of the marketing plan in Chapter 15). This section focuses on the process of market segmentation and target market selection. As part of the marketing plan, target market decisions and actions will be evaluated as part of the objective setting and evaluation phases.

A marketer needs to combine strong analytical skills, sound strategic thinking, an understanding of the consumer, a vision on where the market is heading, and how this all fits with the company's direction. The process of segmenting a market for both the consumer market and business-to-business market is divided into six steps, which can be seen in Figure 6–3.

1. *Identify consumer/customer needs and common characteristics in the market.* This should be done from a consumer/customer perspective, looking at what drives the category and what future trends are evolving. Marketers should be able to easily identify common interests and evolving trends by analyzing what products currently exist in the category, which areas of the market are expanding and shrinking, and where consumer/customer interests lie. Looking to other countries sometimes provides interesting ideas on where potential future interests may lie. At this point, marketers will turn to market research studies and analytics data to see what the facts reveal. Database analyses may reveal some interesting facts about purchase patterns and point to segments that had not been considered. Sometimes, marketers may need to conduct further market research to clarify questions.

Figure 6–3
The six-step process for segmenting a market

> **Steps in Market Segmentation**
>
> 1. Identify consumer/customer needs and common characteristics in the market.
> 2. Cluster common consumer/customer variables to create meaningful market segments.
> 3. Estimate the size and feasibility of each segment.
> 4. Identify the segment(s) to be targeted.
> 5. Take actions with marketing programs to reach the segment(s).
> 6. Monitor and evaluate the success of these programs compared with objectives.

2. *Cluster common consumer/customer variables to create meaningful market segments.* A marketer needs to stand back from the market and look for clusters of products and gaps in the market that point to common consumer/customer interests, usage patterns, and prevailing attitudes. New areas of interest should not be overlooked as these may point to evolving segments. These clusters will identify the segments that exist in the market. Sometimes there is overlap between segments, and other times the segments are not well-defined, but this is generally a reflection of the consumers/customers, who can be fickle and non-committal.

Segmentation analytics companies, as noted earlier, can provide marketers with data on market clusters, which, combined with marketing analytics, can help reveal profitable new approaches and opportunities. Companies may use its own data from customer relationship management (CRM) databases that group consumers by purchase behaviour and monetary value to a company. Software can run an *RFM analysis* (recency, frequency, and monetary value) to rate customers on how *recently* products were purchased (recency), how *often* products were purchased (frequency), and the *dollar value* of the transactions (monetary value). Customers are then scored and rated to create segments that organizations use to tailor offers and marketing messages. Non-profit organizations frequently use RFM analyses to target those most likely to make donations, while CRM loyalty programs use loyalty cards to collect customer purchase data to then customize offers.

It is very important during this step to review the market from a consumer/customer perspective and not from a product perspective. For example, if we continue to review the laundry detergent market, we may group products into those that contain bleach and establish this as a segment. The segment is in fact better defined, and more meaningful to marketers, when identified as appealing to adults who want to fight tough stains.

Laundry detergent customers can be grouped into potential segments based upon their attitudes, needs, and demographic profile. Three possible market segments are shown in Figure 6–4.

3. *Estimate the size and feasibility of each segment.* Based on external data analysis and/or the use of segmentation analytics data, the size of the segment needs to be estimated. The marketer is then tasked with forecasting the sales potential for this segment, which should also consider anticipated competitive reactions.

Figure 6–4
Identifying consumer clusters

Consumer Clusters Example: Laundry Detergents		
Consumer Cluster	**Cluster Attributes**	**Product Examples**
Clean Fanatics	Adults with families Want clothes to continue to look like new Stain removal is important Family-oriented	Tide
Scent Lovers	Want fresh-smelling clothes Cleaning is important	Gain
Gentle and Purists	Family-oriented Prefer gentle and pure products Want soft clothes Focused on baby clothes and other fine washables	Ivory Snow

4. *Identify the segment(s) to be targeted.* A target market segment must be selected carefully. Marketers should use the following criteria select a target market:

- **Market size:** The estimated size of the segment is an important factor in deciding whether it's worth going after. Is the segment large enough to generate expected sales levels? Is the segment manageable so that the marketing budget is sufficient to support marketing initiatives?

- **Expected growth:** Although the size of the market in the segment may be small now, perhaps it is growing significantly or is expected to grow in the

Marketers segment the market to more effectively and more efficiently reach their target markets.

©mstanley/Shutterstock

future. For example, the market for environmentally friendly laundry detergents was very small a decade ago, but has grown significantly. Tide Coldwater was launched to meet the needs of this segment, far before the market potential had been reached.

- **Competitive position:** Is there a lot of competition in the segment now, or is there likely to be in the future? The less the competition, the more attractive the segment is.

- **Compatibility with the organization's objectives and resources:** Will targeting this segment be consistent with overall company objectives, including sales and profit objectives, market share targets, as well as corporate social responsibility initiatives and new business focus?

- **Cost of reaching the segment:** A segment that is inaccessible to a firm's marketing actions or if the cost of reaching that segment is too great, it should not be pursued.

5. *Take actions with marketing programs to reach the segment(s).* Once a target market has been selected, a marketing plan needs to be developed and implemented. Essential decisions need to be made regarding the marketing mix (product, price, place, and promotion) that are consistent with the needs and wants of the target market. Specific objectives should be set to define success for the programs. Objectives should be evaluated regularly, and plans should be adapted accordingly.

6. *Monitor and evaluate the success of these programs compared with objectives.* Marketers often work with financial analysts to determine the sales forecasts, costs, and profits realized in comparison with the cost and sales projections outlined in Steps 3 and 5 of the segmentation process. Chapter 9 reviews budgeting and profit-and-loss statements.

Positioning

LO 6 One of the central elements in marketing is product positioning. Marketers position products in the market to appeal to certain target groups and to present a particular impression relative to the competition. **Product positioning** refers to the impression of the branded product you want to establish in consumers' minds relative to their needs and also in contrast to the competition. Companies generally use a combination of factors to position their products, always leading with the elements that are real; to differentiate the product; and to create long-term, memorable impressions with consumers. In this way, there are three basic factors, or combinations of factors, that tend to surface in product positioning:

1. *Image.* Products are often positioned as leaders, contenders, or rebels in the market, also taking on characteristics such as trusted, prestigious, or thrifty. TSN, for instance, positions itself with the "Champions Live Here" image to solidify its place as the leader in sports broadcasting.[18]

2. *Product attribute.* Products with features that differentiate them from the competition are often positioned on this platform, bringing product claims to the forefront. The fast-food restaurant Subway, for example, positions itself as having healthy and fresh sandwiches.

3. *Price.* Products with brand parity and little product differentiation may position themselves on a price platform. Retailers such as Walmart position themselves as offering the lowest retail prices ("Everyday low prices") to support its image in the market.

Marketers create positioning statements to clearly and simply outline the positioning of a product in the market. These statements are used to crystallize the image for marketers so that they can design a marketing mix that aligns with the product's positioning. This is very important; otherwise, the product may present a confusing image to consumers who will refrain from buying it. A **positioning statement** is a formalized statement that identifies the image a branded product represents in the market and what sets it apart from the competition. A positioning statement is generally included in a brand's annual marketing plan and its relevant strategic documents. It is important for all functional areas in a company to understand a product's positioning, as it drives activities throughout the organization.

> " *Positioning statements are simple, clear, and focused.*

Positioning statements are simple, clear, and focused. They average a short paragraph and identify four elements: (1) the target market and need, (2) the branded product name, (3) the category in which the product competes, and (4) the brand's unique attributes and benefits (what sets the product apart from the competition and meets customer needs). Positioning statements should take the following format:

> *For (target market) who desire (target market need), (brand) is the (product category) that offers (product benefits).*

product positioning
The impression of the product you want to establish in consumers' minds relative to their needs and the competition.

positioning statement
A formalized statement that identifies the image a branded product represents in the market and what sets it apart from the competition.

How is Volvo positioned in the automobile market?
©Paceman/Shutterstock

repositioning
Changing the place a product occupies in consumers' minds relative to competitive products to more accurately meet consumer needs.

positioning maps
Visual representations of how products in a category are positioned in consumers' minds; also known as *perceptual maps*.

The positioning statement for Volvo could be:

For upscale families who desire a care-free driving experience, Volvo is a premium-priced automobile that offers the utmost in safety and dependability.

This positioning statement directs Volvo's marketing strategy and focuses its product development efforts, such as the inclusion of side door airbags in its automobiles. The statement also directs Volvo's marketing communications message. Volvo advertising stresses safety and dependability—the two benefits that are the basis of its "Volvo for life" slogan.

Repositioning

Companies rarely change a product's positioning but do so when long-term changes in consumer attitudes or opinions of the brand require a shift in the brand's image to more accurately meet consumer needs and to reflect how it fits their lifestyle and needs. **Repositioning** is often implemented in stages over time with a refresh of a brand and the elements of its marketing mix. Many recent examples can be found in the fast-food industry, as restaurant chains struggle to keep up with changing tastes and emerging competitive threats.

McDonald's Experience of the Future stores feature self-ordering kiosks that give customers more choice in their experience.

©S and S Imaging/Shutterstock

McDonald's is a good example of a repositioning effort from a dated, stale brand to one willing to adjust to consumer's changing needs. This resulted in an increased sales and an increased stock price while investing in new technology initiatives, customer experiences, and corporate responsibility. McDonald's achieved this transformation through restaurant redesigns, menu updates, and a global restructuring. The company focused on better ingredients such as chicken without antibiotics and cage-free eggs. McDonald's Canada was the first company in Canada to serve Canadian beef from certified sustainable farms and ranches, beginning with its Angus line-up. It was one of the first to serve all-day breakfast and saw great success with its value menus. McDonald's is also embracing new technologies with its kiosk ordering platform, its mobile order and pay app, and its delivery system through Uber Eats or SkipTheDishes. McDonald's is listening to its customers, and its goal is to be Canada's favourite place to eat and drink. It is also working to gain a greater share of the food-service beverage market.[19]

Increased competition in the burger/fast-food restaurant business has resulted in a change in positioning for A&W. The restaurant needed to expand its target audience to a younger customer base. Based on customer insights from the 25- to 44-year-old target market, A&W has differentiated itself with the quality of its ingredients, reducing packaging, and increasing "authenticity" with actor-free ads to "keep it real." It was the first fast-food restaurant to serve Beyond Meat plant-based burgers in Canada. Menu changes also included using only chicken that was antibiotic-free and hens that were only vegetarian-fed to produce quality eggs. This repositioning, based on changing customer needs, has created a unique and differentiated place in the fast-food restaurant market that has resulted in sales and market share.[20] For another example of repositioning, see the Marketing NewsFlash box, "Not Your Parents' Financial Services—Questrade."[21]

Positioning Maps

Positioning maps, also known as *perceptual maps*, are visual representations of how products or product groups are positioned within a category to consumers/customers. Positioning maps can visually represent categories within a market or, more specifically, product and brand offerings within a category. Positioning maps are useful tools for marketers as they can reveal gaps in the market where consumers may be underserved, while also highlighting the competitive nature of the category.

Not Your Parents' Financial Services—Questrade

Questrade ad to reinforce positioning

Questrade

Questrade is Canada's largest independent online brokerage. Doing business from Toronto since 1999, Questrade has over $10 billion in assets under management and is Canada's fastest-growing online brokerage. Questrade has been deemed the top pick for best overall online brokerage in Canada by the award-winning Young and Thrifty Personal Finance Blog, and it has been named eight times as one of the best-managed companies in Canada. Questrade grew by over 50,000 accounts in 2019 due to its very low fees, easy-to-use app, and targeted advertising at the millennial generation.

The ad campaign that ran from 2019 into the 2020s questions the entire value proposition of the financial services industry and is threatening the industry's entire business model. The ads focus on a new mom who dumps her financial advisor because she can't support both her new child and a financial advisor, or the couple who isn't satisfied with ten minutes of attention per year from their financial planner. Questrade has designed its products and services around a growing disconnect between financial services fees and the value that they provide.

Questrade services are created and designed for the millennial generation who are comfortable with technology and the concept of utilizing technology to manage their money. Questrade has two options for investors, depending on their time to spend and their comfort with investing. The first is self-directed investing where the user can invest in a variety of financial products with very low fees. To assist self-directed account holders with managing their accounts, Questrade has just partnered with a New Brunswick start-up, Passiv. Passiv provides wealth management tools for self-directed investors and is now available free to all Questrade investors.

"Building wealth is not always simple, but with a tool like Passiv, Questrade can make it much easier," says Edward Kholodenko, president and CEO, Questrade. "The partnership with Passiv builds on our commitment to provide unique, innovative, and cost-efficient online services to our customers, so Canadians can achieve their financial goals faster and, ultimately, keep more of their money."

The second option for Questrade investors is Questwealth Portfolios, intelligent, lower-fee portfolios managed by experts utilizing a strategy of creating portfolios with specific goals for investors with less time and knowledge. Realizing that the millennial segment was much more concerned about social issues than their baby boomer parents, Questrade created socially responsible portfolios that invest in ethical and clean businesses while still embracing the same financial goals.

Understanding the millennial generation has helped Questrade become a Canadian success story, winning numerous awards, ranking highest among comparable companies, and syncing its values with those of its target market. Questrade partners with other Canadian companies to offer new services and gives back to the community by partnering with Canadian food banks. ●

Questions

1. How did millennials' attitudes about financial strategies help Questrade position its brand?

2. How can a financial service such as Questrade create an emotional connection with the customer?

A key to positioning a product or brand effectively is discovering the perceptions in the minds of potential customers by taking three steps:

1. *Identify the important attributes for a product or brand class.* One might rush to immediately identify price as a key variable, but often this is a less important feature, evaluated by consumers once a short list of attributes on which they initially evaluate a purchase are identified. Let's make this clear with two examples. First, in the laundry detergent market, scent and strength might be key attributes used by families evaluating different product offerings (price would come into play later in the purchase decision). In the second example, we can look at beverages. Research reveals the key attributes adults use to judge various

Figure 6–5
A positioning map to suggest a strategy for positioning beverages

photo: ©McGraw-Hill Education

drinks are nutrition and children's drinks versus adult drinks, as shown by the two axes in Figure 6–5.

2. *Discover how target customers rate competing products or brands with respect to these attributes.* Continuing with the beverage example, the factors of nutrition and adult/child–focused drink can be used objectively to evaluate products in the category. Figure 6–5 shows where beverages are placed on the positioning map and how one is positioned against another. It plots milk, tea, sports drinks, fruit juices, and soft drinks relative to each based on nutritional value and whether they are appropriate for adults or children. For these key elements, we can see diet drinks are geared to adults, while milkshakes appeal to children.

3. *Discover where the company's product or brand is on these attributes in the minds of potential customers.* With a focus on chocolate milk, Figure 6–5 shows that it is viewed as mainly a children's drink with moderate nutritional value. The makers of chocolate milk could consider repositioning themselves as an adult drink to expand their business.

ask YOURSELF

1. What is product positioning and what is the purpose of a positioning statement?

2. Why do marketers use positioning maps?

A&W

1. What psychographic interests can you determine about the target market from this ad?

2. What behavioural insights can you determine about the target market from this ad?

LO 1 • Market segmentation involves aggregating prospective buyers into groups that have common needs and respond similarly to marketing programs.

• In the marketing world, there are two main market segments: (1) the consumer market and (2) the business market.

LO 2 • There are four different market segmentation strategies: mass marketing, segment marketing, niche marketing, and individualized marketing.

LO 3 • Marketers define their target markets by looking at four main variables: (1) geographics, (2) demographics, (3) psychographics, and (4) behaviouristics.

• Geographics looks at where a target market lives, such as a country, region, province, city size, and population density, such as urban, suburban, or rural.

• Demographics includes identifying ranges for age, gender, family composition, income, occupation, education, ethnic background, and home ownership.

• Psychographics involves understanding consumer attitudes to life, values, personalities, general interests, opinions, and activities.

• Behaviouristics looks at why consumers buy a product, the product benefit, how and when the product is used, and whether consumers are brand loyal in their purchase behaviour. Usage rate also plays a role in this information.

• Personas are character descriptions of a product's typical customers in the form of fictional character narratives, complete with images that capture the personalities, values, attitudes, beliefs, demographics, and expected interactions of a typical user with a brand.

LO 4 • Segmentation analytics analyzes market segments and provides data to help target specific groups with high levels of accuracy.

• Segmentation analytics data clusters consumers into lifestyle segments and provides information that details geographics, demographics, psychographic, and behaviouristic data by postal code, defined shopping areas, or neighbourhood.

LO 5 • Segmenting the market involves six steps that require strong analytical skills, sound strategic thinking, an understanding of the consumer, a vision on where the market is heading, and how this all fits with the company's direction.

• The six market segmentation steps start with identifying customer needs and common characteristics in the market, and continues by clustering consumer variables to create meaningful segments, estimating the size and feasibility of each segment, and finally identifying the target segment(s), taking marketing actions to reach the segment(s), and monitoring and evaluating the success of these programs compared with objectives.

LO 6 • Product positioning refers to the image of a branded product in the consumers' minds relative to the competition.

• Marketers create positioning statements to clearly and simply outline the positioning of a product.

• Repositioning includes a shifting of the product image and adjusting its marketing mix to more accurately meet consumer needs.

• Positioning maps are otherwise known as perceptual maps. They visually represent how products or product groups are positioned within a category to consumers.

behaviouristics
business market
consumer market
geographics
individualized marketing
market segmentation

mass marketing
niche marketing
personas
positioning maps
positioning statement
product differentiation

product positioning
psychographics
repositioning
target market profile

Target Market and Personas Assignment Go to one of the segmentation analytics websites outlined in the text. Enter in your postal code to come up with a profile of the consumer who lives in your neighbourhood or select a consumer profile you find interesting. Create a persona for this consumer with an image of the consumer and a description, including gender, age, interests, hobbies, education, goals, jobs, influencers, media usage, technology preferences, fears, and concerns.

This chapter's opening vignette examines how River Ranche Lodge segments its target audience for both the Canadian and international market. Using the information in the vignette, as well as your own research, create a positioning map similar to Figure 6–5 for River Ranche Lodge.

Review the Infographic that shows the six unique tribes based on the social values of millennials. Complete the quiz at **https://environicsresearch.com/insights/canadian** **-millennials-quiz/** to determine what tribe you are in. Use an organization previously discussed in this chapter and determine how that organization should market to your tribe.

Products and Brands

Managing the marketing mix is no easy task, and this chapter explores the areas that marketers consider when managing products and brands. Rachel Mielke, the CEO and founder of Hillberg & Berk, is responsible for creating and building this socially conscious national brand from making jewellery in her spare time to ten retail locations across Western Canada, with plans to soon expand into the United States.

Hillberg & Berk, Flagship Store, Regina, SK, 2015

CHAPTER OUTLINE

- Hillberg & Berk—building a brand
- Types of products
- The total product concept
- Product lines and mixes
- Consumer and business products
- Branding
- Types of brands

Growing up, Rachel Mielke didn't have a lot of special jewellery; it was just too expensive. She made her first necklace at 23 for a trip and liked how it made her feel special. She graduated with a marketing major from the University of Regina in 2003, regularly making jewellery for herself and her girlfriends in her spare time. After selling several thousand dollars' worth of jewellery at a weekend trade show in 2003, Mielke opened Urban Pearl Accessories. Rachel decided to rebrand to Hillberg & Berk because she felt that Urban Pearl was too specific to jewellery, and it also gave the impression that she may only make jewellery featuring pearls. She wanted a name that didn't box her in and could potentially represent other products outside of jewellery in the future. She also felt that Urban Pearl didn't have a long-term, timeless feel. It suited her business as a young woman starting out, but didn't feel right for the business she endeavoured to build. Four years later, she changed the name to the more upscale Hillberg & Berk, honouring her great grandmother (Hilda Bergman) and her dog (a miniature pinscher named Berkeley). Hillberg & Berk (H&B) does feel timeless and could represent anything, but that can be a shortcoming. It can be hard for people to remember when they first hear it, some people equate it with a professional firm given the "name & name" format (lawyers, accountants, etc.), and people can struggle with the spelling, although the shortened H&B moniker helps with those concerns. In 2008, she appeared on *Dragons' Den*, and W. Brett Wilson invested in her and her company. He is still involved in the business as an investor and consultant.

Mielke founded Hillberg & Berk in 2007 by creating designs intended to be "modern and timeless, practical and functional" that are crafted from sterling silver, Swarovski crystals, gemstones, and Hillberg & Berk's signature Sparkle Balls™, which inspired Hillberg & Berk's top-selling Sparkle Collection. Prices are considered accessible, with many pieces priced at under $150 and intricate designs featuring semi-precious gemstones at upwards of $450.

Mielke saw entrepreneurship as a platform to create change and sought to empower women through design, creating pieces that evoke a positive feeling for women while giving back to the community. Rachel and her team have travelled the world for inspiration, but the heart of the brand still beats firmly in Rachel's hometown of Regina, Saskatchewan, where the majority of Hillberg & Berk's jewellery is designed and produced. Local production also helps keep things sustainable. Quality materials, such as sterling silver, ensure that Hillberg & Berk pieces will last a lifetime, and leftover silver is re-melted and fashioned into new designs.

In 2014, Saskatchewan's Lieutenant Governor commissioned Hillberg & Berk to make a brooch for Her Majesty Queen Elizabeth II. The floral design featured Madagascar tourmaline, a freshwater pearl, and pave set diamonds. Since receiving the brooch, Her Majesty has been photographed wearing it several times. In 2017, Hillberg & Berk was chosen to design a second brooch for Her Majesty Queen Elizabeth II, which also was gifted to her on behalf of the people of Canada to celebrate her Sapphire Jubilee. Hillberg & Berk has also been popular with a wide range of celebrities, and the brand has collaborated with various other retail brands and well-known individuals.

Hillberg & Berk remains successful due to its strong brand image as a socially conscious women's advocate. The company is consistent and thoughtful in the products it produces, its promotions, and the partnerships it creates. Mielke created a brand of jewellery that women find both aspirational and attainable. Along the way, Rachel has seen the business through some pretty unique successes, including a showing at the Oscars, partnerships with Olympic athletes such as Tessa Virtue, and two designs commissioned for Her Majesty Queen Elizabeth II. She has sought trail-blazers and change-makers as the faces of her campaigns and tells their story through these campaigns. A couple of recent cases (or faces) are Ashley Callingbull, the first Canadian and Indigenous woman to win Ms. Universe, the face of the 2017 and 2018 collections, and Gayle Tzemach Lemmon, a celebrated journalist and fellow at the Council on Foreign Relations, the face of the Aurora Lux Collection in 2013. Rachel hopes that by making visible these stories of resilience, she can show her customers what empowerment looks like at its most beautiful, inspiring them to take power over their own life stories.

Her energy comes from a desire to support women through design and to re-create those "I feel special" moments—just like the one she had at 23—for women who want to feel beautiful and put together, whether for special occasions or everyday life. "What makes something like Sparkle so special is that it's a product you can wear casually, every day, or to the fanciest events. It's so transitional," she says. "I think we make some of the most beautiful product in the world at an affordable price point."

H&B runs campaigns and collaborates with various organizations, including Look Good Feel Better, the Canadian Breast Cancer Foundation, and the YWCA. On its website, a section entitled "Empowering Women" profiles three women who represent resilience, determination, and ambition, and who have effected real change in the world. "It's the 'why' of why we all come to work at the beginning of the day and why we're passionate about what we do. . . . It's bigger than just making beautiful jewelry. . . . I want the legacy [of Hillberg & Berk] to be that we helped women realize that there are no boundaries."

But Mielke insists she's not growing the company for growth's sake. For her, business is still a platform effecting social change. Since 2007, Hillberg & Berk has donated over $10 million in cash and product to a variety of charitable organizations that educate, inspire, and provide opportunities to women in Canada and globally. Rachel has also funded several scholarships for women through her alma mater, the University of Regina, and she recently established a collective of jewellery makers in Myanmar by providing meaningful work for women who would not otherwise have safe and reliable jobs. Her activism occurs on a micro-level, too; it wouldn't be uncommon to see her giving away her jewellery— sometimes from around her own neck or wrists—to people she meets randomly or to those deserving a pick-me-up. There are other stories like these, all of which fall under the umbrella of "Share Your Sparkle," a catchphrase turned hashtag turned way of life, established after Hillberg & Berk launched its now-iconic sub-brand, Sparkle, in 2009. "Sparkle is about sharing our light and love with the world, then having women go out and feel confident wearing the product. They can then pass that [Sparkle] on to other women."

As for the company's future, Rachel wants to go global. "We thought, how can we become the best in the world at something? And thinking about who we are at the core of our company, we thought, we can be the best in the world at championing and supporting women through our entire supply chain."[1]

---

reality CHECK ⊘

As you read Chapter 7, refer back to this vignette on Hillberg & Berk to answer the following questions:

- Describe Hillberg & Berk in terms of its core, actual, and augmented product offerings.
- Review the elements of a good brand name and evaluate the strength of the Hillberg & Berk brand name.

Types of Products

LO 1 One of the key functions of marketing lies in managing and developing products and brands that meet the needs of their target markets. As discussed in Chapter 1, in marketing, a *product* is a good, a service, or an idea, consisting of a bundle of tangible and intangible attributes. Tangible attributes include physical characteristics such as colour or sweetness, and intangible attributes include those aspects of a product that can't be "touched," such as how a piece of jewellery from Hillberg & Berk makes you feel.

Products are available in both the online and offline environment. In the offline environment, examples of products are laundry detergents, cars, or the services provided by a hairdresser. In the online world, examples are search engines such as Google, online gaming websites, and music stores such as iTunes. It is important to realize that with the widespread use of the Internet today, most offline products develop a strong web presence. The first point of contact for consumers with a brand is often online at a company website or on its Facebook page. Hillberg & Berk has both a strong offline and a strong online presence, with almost 79,000 followers on Facebook, 60,000 followers on Instagram, 6,600 followers on Twitter, and 2,300 followers on Pinterest. These are used to share information, and the e-commerce website is another distribution outlet.

Products are divided into three main categories: (1) non-durable goods, (2) durable goods, and (3) services. A **non-durable good** is an item that does not last and that is consumed only once, or for a limited number of times. Examples of non-durable goods are food products and fuel. A **durable good** is a product that lasts for an extended period of time and encompasses items such as appliances, automobiles, and computers. A *service* is an intangible activity, benefit, or satisfaction, such as banking, conducting an online search, using cloud-based software to create websites or blogs, visiting a doctor, taking a vacation, going to a movie, or taking a course. Canada has a strong service-based economy with services accounting for approximately 71 percent of its gross domestic product (GDP).[2]

In the service industry, it is useful to distinguish between a company's primary service and its supplementary services. An airline's primary service may be providing flights from one location to another, but it also offers supplementary services such as food and drink, magazines, airport lounges, and in-flight entertainment. Supplementary services often allow products to differentiate their offerings from the competition while also adding value to consumers. Common supplementary services for products can include product updates, free delivery, and payment terms as well as complimentary consultations, order-taking, and sales assistance. Companies also offer free trials, online

What type of product is being marketed by MADD?
MADD Canada

support services, complimentary webinars, and elements such as free subscriptions as added-value services to its customers. For more about how customer service is adapting to changing times, see the Infographic, "The Evolution of Customer Service."

Many products cannot be defined as "pure goods" or "pure services" but are in fact hybrids—a combination of goods and services to offer a more competitive product to consumers. Many goods are augmented with intangible services such as warranties, websites, and online support. Services also use goods to ensure a more complete offering to consumers. For example, a theatre provides an entertainment experience, but it also provides the customer with a booklet about the show; a travel agency that books travel also provides glossy catalogues of potential destinations. Importantly, the online environment is giving rise to new **virtual services** that exist onlyonline and have no form of physical person-to-person interaction or tangible component. Travel sites, online gaming sites, and online analytics are examples of virtual services.

As companies look at what they bring to market, there is a range from the tangible

non-durable good
An item that does not last and is consumed only once, or for a limited number of times.

durable good
An item that lasts over an extended number of uses.

virtual services
Services that exist only online and have no person-to-person interaction.

Figure 7–1
The service continuum

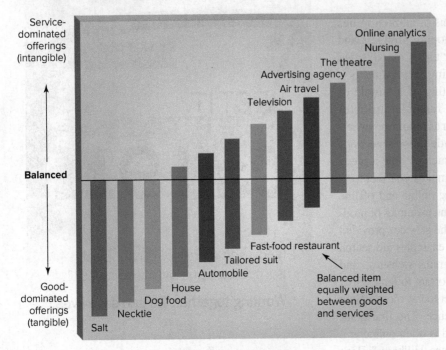

Service-dominated offerings (intangible)

Balanced

Good-dominated offerings (tangible)

Online analytics
Nursing
The theatre
Advertising agency
Air travel
Television
Fast-food restaurant
Tailored suit
Automobile
House
Dog food
Necktie
Salt

Balanced item equally weighted between goods and services

Online services often provide potential customers with free limited online trials or time-sensitive downloads as a means of testing out the service.

Inconsistency Delivering services is challenging because the quality of a service is dependent on the people who provide it, and it can therefore differ in consistency. Quality can vary with each person's capabilities, experience, motivation, and even personality. One day, a restaurant may have wonderful service, and then the next day, it may have a very disappointing showing. Similarly, you may have a very enjoyable stay at one location of a Hilton hotel, but then have a terrible experience at another due to the varying standards of the staff at its locations. Companies try to overcome the inconsistent delivery of services by training employees on how to deliver a consistent quality experience.

Online products are often able to overcome issues of inconsistency through standardized software, consistent website interfaces, and reliable Internet servers that limit service disruptions.

Inseparability A third difference between services and goods, and related to problems of consistency, is inseparability. In most cases, the consumer cannot (and does not) separate the deliverer of the service from the service itself. For example, the quality of a spa and its facilities might be excellent, but if you are not satisfied with the massage that you received or if it took too long to be registered and brought into the facility, this immediately reflects poorly on the spa.

Inventory In many instances, the inventory of services is more complex than that of goods due to the nature of services. Inventory problems exist because services cannot necessarily be stored and accessed when in demand. For example, in the instance of sporting events,

to the intangible, or goods-dominant to service-dominant. This is defined as the **service continuum** and is demonstrated in Figure 7–1 where the services continuum for a number of products is shown. Online analytics, nursing, and going to the theatre are examples of intangible, service-dominated offerings, while salt, neckties, and dog food are goods-dominated offerings. Fast-food restaurants are in the middle of the service continuum, offering a combination of both tangible and intangible goods and services; the food is the tangible good, while the courtesy, cleanliness, speed, and convenience are the intangible services they provide.

The Uniqueness of Services

There are four unique elements to services: intangibility, inconsistency, inseparability, and inventory. These four elements are referred to as the *four Is of services*.

Intangibility Services are intangible; that is, for the most part, they cannot be held, touched, or seen before a purchase. In contrast, before purchasing a physical good, a consumer can touch a box of laundry detergent, kick a car tire, or sample a new beverage. Services tend to be more performance-oriented and, as experiences, cannot generally be tried before purchase. Free trials are often provided to overcome this drawback. To help consumers assess and compare services, it is important for marketers to demonstrate the benefits of using the service. A spa may highlight a virtual tour of its facilities as well as include testimonials from customers to help the consumer evaluate the service.

Many products cannot be defined as 'pure goods' or 'pure services' but are in fact hybrids—a combination of goods and services to offer a more competitive product to consumers.

Infographic

The Evolution of Customer Service

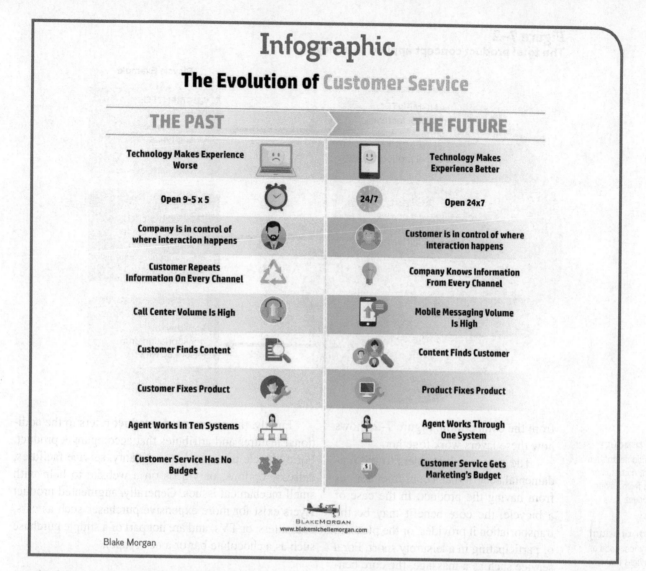

THE PAST			THE FUTURE
Technology Makes Experience Worse			Technology Makes Experience Better
Open 9-5 x 5		24/7	Open 24x7
Company is in control of where interaction happens			Customer is in control of where interaction happens
Customer Repeats Information On Every Channel			Company Knows Information From Every Channel
Call Center Volume Is High			Mobile Messaging Volume Is High
Customer Finds Content			Content Finds Customer
Customer Fixes Product			Product Fixes Product
Agent Works In Ten Systems			Agent Works Through One System
Customer Service Has No Budget		$1	Customer Service Gets Marketing's Budget

BLAKEMORGAN
www.blakemichellemorgan.com

Blake Morgan

unsold tickets cannot be stored and sold at a later date; therefore, they represent lost revenue. Online services can often be stored and accessed at a later date, as evident with online virus scans that can be run as needed. Similarly, online movies are often configured to be conveniently viewed on-demand to suit viewers.

In the service industry, issues arise due to fluctuating demand throughout the day and the difficulty in assessing the requirements needed to service customers at peak times. **Idle production capacity** is expensive and arises when a service is available when there is little demand. Idle production capacity is formally defined as a situation when the supply of a service exceeds its demand. To deal with this issue, the service industry often uses part-time employees who are paid an hourly wage and are scheduled to work shifts. This is clearly demonstrated in a grocery store setting where the number of cashiers varies depending on the time of day and day of the week. The number of cashiers at 2:30 p.m. during the week will be far fewer than the number of cashiers available at noon on a Saturday due to the number of people shopping at these times.

Product Elements

The Total Product Concept

LO 2 Marketers view products as having three different layers: the core product layer, the actual product layer, and the augmented product layer. The more complex and expensive the product, the more intricate the layers used to differentiate the product

idle production capacity
When the supply of a service exceeds its demand.

Figure 7–2
The total product concept applied to a bicycle

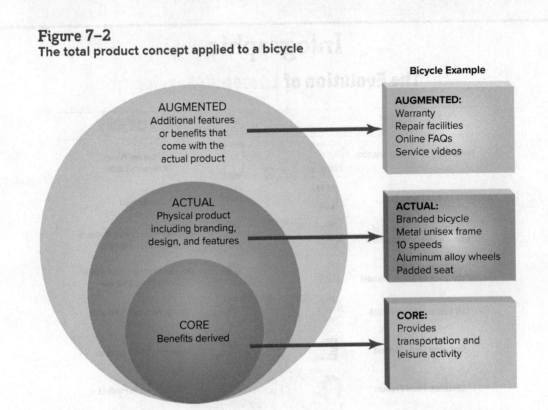

Bicycle Example

AUGMENTED
Additional features or benefits that come with the actual product

ACTUAL
Physical product including branding, design, and features

CORE
Benefits derived

AUGMENTED:
Warranty
Repair facilities
Online FAQs
Service videos

ACTUAL:
Branded bicycle
Metal unisex frame
10 speeds
Aluminum alloy wheels
Padded seat

CORE:
Provides transportation and leisure activity

core product
The fundamental benefit that a consumer derives from having the product.

actual product
The physical good or the services that a consumer purchases.

augmented product
The additional features and attributes that accompany a product.

from the competition. Figure 7–2 shows how these layers work together.

The **core product** refers to the fundamental benefit that a consumer derives from having the product. In the case of a bicycle, the core benefit may be the transportation it provides, or the pleasure of participating in a leisurely sport. For a service such as a massage, the core benefit may be the relaxation it provides.

The **actual product** is the physical good or the service that a consumer purchases when buying a product. It includes the product's branding, design, and features. With a bicycle, a consumer purchases a piece of equipment, directly associated with a brand name, design, and features. With a massage, the actual product is the massage itself and the time spent having a trained and expert massage therapist relax a client's muscles. In this instance, one may think that branding has no role to play. On the contrary, in the case of a massage, the brand becomes either the name of the massage therapist or the organization providing massage services.

Marketers view products as having three different layers: the core product layer, the actual product layer, and the augmented product layer.

Finally, the **augmented product** refers to the additional features and attributes that accompany a product. For a bicycle this may be a warranty, service facilities, delivery options, or videos on a website to help with small mechanical issues. Generally, augmented product layers exist for more expensive purchases such as cars, computers, or TVs, and are not part of a simple purchase such as a chocolate bar or a newspaper.

Packaging and Labelling

Marketers need to pay close attention to a product's packaging and labelling, as well as the logos it uses to communicate its brand positioning to consumers. For many products, the packaging and labels are an integral part of the product; for other products (such as online products), there may be no packaging at all and their websites become a form of packaging, central to communicating the brand elements to consumers. Packaging can be a key source of competitive advantage since along with providing functional benefits, packaging can communicate information about the product and reinforce the brand image.

Function First and foremost, packaging has functional benefits. It allows a product to be conveniently used, allows for better storage, protects a product that is fragile, improves product quality, provides a safety function, makes a product easier to use, and makes a product more efficient to transport. Take, for example, the influx of squeeze bottles for condiments such as ketchup, mayonnaise, relish, and even jams, making them more convenient to use. From a safety

Packaging that highlights the product and its purpose.
Frito-Lay North America

perspective, over-the-counter medications use safety seals and tamper-resistant containers, and best-before dates are provided for meat, dairy, and other perishable food products.

Communication Packaging and labelling also serve as platforms from which to communicate detailed product information, offers, directions on usage, nutritional content, and other packaging requirements needed to meet legal obligations. Take, for example, these chips that have packaging that highlights both the product and its purpose. What an excellent way to communicate your product features by showing them directly to the customers!

Brand Image Packaging and labelling decisions are of paramount importance to a product's success, and marketers work hard to ensure that designs clearly reflect a product's positioning, its brand equity, and its image, which have all been nurtured over time. In 2020 and beyond, expect brands to take a more comprehensive approach to their packaging design—and to use their packaging as an opportunity to tell their brand story, communicate their

key messaging, and build a deeper connection with their ideal customers. Online, packaging has to carry more weight due to the lack of a storefront experience. Branded packaging is especially important for subscription boxes, where the box itself becomes the only representation of the brand since the contents feature other brands and

FabFitFun is a monthly subscription box of products from the beauty, fashion, fitness, wellness, home, and tech sectors.
©ZUMA Press, Inc./Alamy Stock Photo

Oasis Juice with new paper straw packaging.

Lassonde Industries Inc.

product line

A group of similar products that are closely related because they satisfy a similar need and are directed at the same general target market.

Companies are constantly reviewing the competitive landscape and making adjustments to ensure that their connections with consumers remain strong. Marketers must consider the balance between making a customer connection and other challenges, including handling environmental concerns, managing health and safety issues, and monitoring packaging costs. The Marketing NewsFlash box, "Packaging the Brand," describes some of the latest packaging trends that are driving product sales by listening to customer needs and wants.[4]

Product Lines and Product Mixes

LO 3 Marketers often manage groups of products that are closely related under an umbrella product line and brand name. A **product line** is a group of similar products that are closely related because they satisfy a similar need and are directed at the same general target market. Examples of a product line can be seen by examining Coca-Cola's product offerings. Coca-Cola Canada offers six product lines: soft drinks, waters, juice drinks, sports drinks, dairy products, and iced teas. Its soft drink line, for example, includes Coca-Cola (and its different varieties), Sprite, and Fresca.[5]

Looking to the service industry, online and offline products in this sector can also be grouped into product lines. The services offered by the Hospital for Sick Children, for example, can be grouped into three main product lines based on usage: in-patient hospital care, out-patient physician services, and medical research. Looking to the digital arena, the product lines for a digital brand such as Google can also be grouped into product lines based on usage. For example, one of Google's product lines consists of advertising services for businesses that wish to reach consumers through online

products. In this case, the packaging is a key component of the brand itself.

Another example is the craft beer industry, where competition is increasing and the awareness of individual brands is quite low. The number of breweries in Canada has grown to over 1,100, driven by an influx of very small, low-volume producers. In this industry, branding plays an important role in getting customers to choose a specific brand of craft beer. Customers tend to sample a variety of craft beers, and since cans and bottles are usually sold separately, this is quite easy to do. However, this is not the only challenge, as customers generally do not remember the names of the beers. These facts are driving many craft breweries to focus on creating distinctive packaging and impactful brand names to catch people's attention and be remembered. In another beverage sector, Oasis Juice, headquartered in Quebec, is responding to environmental concerns by testing paper straws in its new innovative single-serve tetra juice pack.[3]

The product mix for Procter & Gamble consists of baby, feminine, and family care; beauty; fabric and home care; and health and grooming product lines.

(Always): ©Keith Homan/Shutterstock; (Bounce): ©Keith Homan/Shutterstock; (Tide): ©Roman Tiraspolsky/Shutterstock; (Head & Shoulders): ©Robson90/Shutterstock; (Old Spice): ©Keith Homan/Shutterstock

Packaging the Brand

As customers walk down the aisle of the grocery store, scroll through the offerings on Amazon, or unpack a package delivered to their door, the first thing they will see is the product packaging. Packaging provides a myriad of functions and can be almost as important to the consumer as the product itself. A brand's packaging must not only be pleasing to the eye but also protect the product, communicate brand values and detailed product information, and align with the customers' attitudes around waste and the environment. According to Kristen Karzarian of *Packaging Strategies,* "2019 seemed to be a year of refining," as consumers demanded more choices in packaging that allowed for decreasing waste and increasing reuse. As we move into the 2020s, shopping is changing, and packaging is evolving right along with it.

Packaging provides the marketer with the opportunity to catch the attention of the consumer and convey the image and positioning of the brand. With the increase in online shopping, packaging has become even more important as a protector of the goods as well as a communicator of the brand message. If the media is the message, then the packaging illustrates the brand's commitment to social responsibility by the design and materials chosen for its packaging. Major brands are investing in package innovation to reduce waste, eliminate plastics, and reuse materials while supporting their brand values and building brand equity along the way. Here are a few examples of interesting trends:

• **Packaging that tells a story:** We know that humans are hard-wired to take in and remember stories much more easily than facts or lists, so packaging that tells a story will be much more memorable and persuasive. It is important for all brands to utilize storytelling in their packaging, but it is vital for products that are distributed predominantly online. E-commerce products can't be seen, touched, or smelled, so the story must be used to evoke the emotions to build a connection with the consumer. The increase in subscription boxes illustrates the importance of the unboxing experience to the online shopper, providing an opportunity for brands to use a story to support their key messaging and build a lasting connection with their customers.

• **Sustainable packaging:** Consumers are demanding that product packaging can be reduced, reused, or recycled. It is no longer good enough for packaging to be recyclable; it must be made of recycled material or at least be reusable. The onus is more and more on the product manufacturers to be responsible for disposal and reuse of packaging materials; this has led to many innovations in this area, including, labelling products that do not use recycled materials; using recyclable, compostable, and edible substrates to create packaging; increasing the use of paper in place of plastic packaging for products like beer; and using easily reusable materials, such as glass and aluminium, for consumable products like water and pop.

"As we dive deeper into the climate crisis, one of the biggest challenges for designers and clients in the next years—even decades—will be to find ecological, plastic-free packaging alternatives to current materials," says 99designs designer Obacht.

Dalston's Soda Co.

• **What you see is what you get:** Using transparent packaging can be an attractive way to show off the product while building trust in your brand. This type of packaging lets the colour and quality of the product shine through and provides a message of authenticity that the market today is looking for. New transparent labels that are easily removed make this tactic easier than ever.

• **Personalized packaging:** Digital printing makes it much easier to create personalized packaging. There are various levels of personalizing, from adorning your Bud Light can with the colours of your favourite team, finding a Coca-Cola can with your name on it, or having your face on a bag of Frito-Lay chips. Recent studies have shown that 61 percent of consumers feel more positive about a brand when its messages are personalized, and 20 percent of millennials look for products that are personalized.

Understanding your customers and their attitudes, values, and desires will help you build packaging that not only communicates but also builds your brand equity by delivering products intact, reducing returns, and demonstrating your commitment to social responsibility. ●

Questions

1. Which packaging trend do you believe will have the most lasting influence?

2. Give an example of how packaging builds brand equity.

Figure 7-3
Reviewing the Procter & Gamble Canada product mix

PRODUCT MIX FOR PROCTER & GAMBLE

← Width of Product Mix →

↕ Product Line Length

Beauty	Baby, Feminine, and Family Care	Fabric and Home Care	Health and Grooming
• Hair Food	• Always	• Bounce	• Align
• Head & Shoulders	• Bounty	• Cascade	• Braun
• Herbal Essence	• Charmin	• Dawn	• Clearblue
• Ivory	• Pampers	• Downy	• Crest
• Olay	• Tampax	• Febreze	• Gillette
• Old Spice		• Gain	• Metamucil
• Pantene		• Ivory Snow	• Oral-B
• Secret		• Mr. Clean	• Pepto-Bismol
		• Swiffer	• Scope
		• Tide	• Venus
			• Vicks
			• ZzzQuil

product mix
All the product lines marketed by a company.

product mix width
The number of different product lines offered by a company.

product line length
The total number of products or brands in a product line.

product line depth
The assortment of different versions of each product sold within its product lines.

consumer products
Products purchased for their personal use by the ultimate consumer.

business products
Products that are purchased either to run a business or to be used as a component in another product or service.

ads. This product line currently includes Google search/display ads, YouTube ads, AdSense, analytics, and app campaigns.[6]

Most organizations offer a **product mix**, which consists of all the product lines marketed by a company. While one can slice and analyze a company's product mix in many different ways depending on the depth of analysis required, it is often helpful to drill down into the product mix by looking at product lines and the products within each line.

A more in-depth analysis can then be conducted to pinpoint the specific products within each line, as shown in Figure 7-3. The **product mix width** refers to the number of different product lines offered by the company. For Procter & Gamble (P&G), the product mix width is four. The **product line length** refers to the number of product or brands in the product line. Using Figure 7-3, we can see that there are eight products listed in the beauty product line. Therefore, P&G Canada's beauty product line length is eight. The **product line depth** refers to the number of different versions of each product sold within its product lines. For example, Dawn dish detergent has approximately 18 different versions offered. Visit the Procter & Gamble website at **www.pg.ca** and examine its

product mix width, product line length, and product line depth.[7]

ask YOURSELF

1. What is included in the total product concept?

2. What benefits can be derived from a brand's packaging and labelling?

Consumer and Business Products

LO 4 Products are classified as either consumer or business products depending on their usage. **Consumer products** are purchased by the ultimate consumer for their personal use, while **business products** (also called *industrial goods* or *organizational products*) are purchased either to run a business or to be used as a component in another product or service. In many instances, the differences are obvious: Monster Energy drinks and the Ontario Science Centre are examples of consumer products, while a cement mixing truck is primarily a business product. Some products, however, are both consumer and business products depending on their usage. A Canon printer can be classified as a consumer product when purchased as a final product for personal use, or it can be classified as a business product when purchased by an organization to help run a business. Consumer and business products consist of numerous types of products, as explained below.

Consumer Products

The consumer market consists of four different categories of products: convenience, shopping, specialty, and unsought. These items differ in terms of the amount of effort that a consumer puts into making a purchase, and how often the items are purchased.

Convenience products are inexpensive items that a consumer purchases frequently with minimal shopping effort. If the product does not meet expectations, there is little risk because the product is inexpensive and easy to purchase. Examples of convenience products are bread, gum, or items purchased from a vending machine. **Shopping products** are items for which the consumer comparison-shops, assessing the attributes and prices of different products and brands. These types of products require a greater investment of shopping time, are more expensive than convenience products, and require a greater assurance of purchase satisfaction. Examples are jeans, airline tickets, and electronic items such as smartphones or tablets. **Specialty products** are items that require considerable time and effort to purchase. They tend to be more expensive branded products in a category that are needed for special occasions. They include specialty brands and require high purchase satisfaction. Examples of specialty products include a Rolex watch or taking a cruise with Norwegian Cruise Lines. **Unsought products** are items that the consumer either does not know about or is not interested in purchasing.

The manner in which a consumer product is classified depends on the individual. One person may view

Rolex watches are specialty products.

©Papin Lab/Shutterstock

a camera as a shopping product and quickly visit a couple of stores before deciding on a brand to purchase. A friend, however, may view a camera as a specialty product, looking for a high-end camera for her photography hobby. This may result in extensive shopping at high-end camera shops for a specific type of camera. It is important to understand that although many products are clearly separated into one category or another, people in varying stages of life will classify products differently. Figure 7–4 generally compares the different types of consumer products and how their marketing mixes may vary depending on the type of product.

Figure 7–4
Classification of consumer products

	Type of Consumer Product			
	Convenience	**Shopping**	**Specialty**	**Unsought**
Purchase behaviour of consumers	• Frequent purchases • Little time and effort spent shopping	• Occasional purchases • Needs to comparison-shop	• Infrequent purchases • Needs time to search and purchase	• Very infrequent purchases • Some comparison-shopping
Brand loyalty of consumers	• Aware of brand, but will accept substitutes	• Prefers specific brands, but will accept substitutes	• Very brand loyal • Will not accept substitutes	• Will accept substitutes
Product examples	• Newspapers, chocolate bars, soft drinks, and bread	• Cameras, TVs, briefcases, and clothing	• Wedding dresses, luxury items such as Rolex watches	• Insurance products, such as life and disability insurance
Price	• Inexpensive	• Fairly expensive	• Usually very expensive	• Varies
Place (distribution)	• Widespread; many outlets	• Large number of outlets	• Very limited distribution	• Often limited distribution
Promotion (communication)	• Emphasis on price, availability, and awareness	• Emphasis on differentiation from competitors	• Emphasis on uniqueness of brand and status	• Emphasis on awareness

> *Products are classified as either consumer or business products depending on their usage.*

Business Products

A major characteristic of business products is that their sales are often the result of *derived demand*; that is, sales of business products frequently result (or are derived) from the sale of consumer products. For example, as consumer demand for Ford cars (a consumer product) increases, Ford may increase its demand for paint-spraying equipment (a business product). Business products may be classified as production goods and services, or support goods and services.

Production Goods and Services

Items used in the manufacturing process that become part of the final product are production goods and services. These can include raw materials, such as grain or lumber, or component parts, such as door hinges used by Ford in its car doors.

Support Goods and Services The second class of business products is support goods and services, which are items used to assist in producing other goods and services. These include the following:

- *Installations* such as buildings and fixed equipment.
- *Accessory equipment* such as tools and office equipment and is usually purchased in small-order sizes by buyers.
- *Supplies* such as stationery, paper clips, and brooms.
- *Services* are intangible activities needed to assist a business in its operations and in producing its goods and services. This category can include transportation services, maintenance and repair services, and advisory services such as tax or legal counsel. This may also include online analytics to monitor website traffic, the creation of a website to support a business, or the use of an e-mail database to send out newsletters.

Branding

LO 5 A **brand** is a name, phrase, symbol, or design uniquely given by a company to identify its product(s) and to distinguish the product(s) from the competition. Brand names and logos are often created in tandem, designed to visually represent the brand to consumers and to build brand recognition. Over the long term, the support that goes into marketing a brand results in strong brand associations and a certain degree of consumer loyalty. This creates **brand equity**, which is formally described as the value of a brand that results from the favourable exposure, interactions, associations, and experiences that consumers have with a brand over time.

Developing and nurturing a brand is an important factor in the marketing of a product. This involves creating a new brand name or selecting a name that already exists in a company's arsenal. A brand also needs to be supported with marketing activity, starting with creating its logo and designing its packaging (if relevant) and website, as well as developing new products and promotions to engage users and bring revenues and profits into the company. Research needs to be conducted periodically to help determine trends and requirements, while metrics and analytics are needed to determine success and areas of improvement.

Ipsos Reid annually conducts its Most Influential Brands study, which looks at "key dimensions that define and determine the most influential brands in Canada," including leading edge, trustworthy, presence, corporate citizenship, and engagement.[8] Ipsos conducts its own research and, with input from advertising agencies and associations as well as consumers, determines this annual influential brand study and rankings.

Let's look at these brand elements in more detail:

- **Trustworthiness:** This is considered the most important element for a brand. It encompasses the consistently dependable image that consumers have for a brand and fosters their ongoing confidence in recommending it to others.

- **Engagement:** Brands that engage consumers encourage brand loyalty by creating interactions, so consumers can learn more about a brand and ultimately share it with others.

- **Leading edge:** Brands that stand out are often unique, innovative, and forward-thinking. Their approach tends to be edgy and somewhat different, and stands as a benchmark for other brands.

- **Corporate citizenship:** Brands that are caring have the ability to connect with consumers by instilling pride.

- **Presence:** Brands need to have a high profile with consumers and stand out from the crowd. These brands make a statement about themselves and the people that use them. Often these brands have many advocates that support them.

Ipsos's top ten most influential brands in Canada in 2019 were as follows:

1. Google
2. Amazon
3. Facebook
4. Microsoft
5. Apple
6. YouTube
7. Netflix
8. Samsung
9. Walmart
10. Visa

> *Brand equity is the result of considerable marketing investment and needs to be protected.*

Google is topping the list for the eighth consecutive year, while Amazon and Facebook are tied for second. From this report, Ipsos confirmed that Google is considered an innovative brand that has transformed the way we look for information and is a leader in the exploration for innovative new technology. Google is a brand that focuses on users and their needs, which has resulted in strong scores across the influence, leading-edge, and trustworthiness indices.

Interbrand's Top 10 Global Brands		
Ranking	Brand	Brand Value ($ million)
1	Apple	234,241
2	Google	167,713
3	Amazon	125,263
4	Microsoft	108,847
5	Coca-Cola	63,365
6	Samsung	61,098
7	Toyota	56,246
8	Mercedes-Benz	50,832
9	McDonald's	45,362
10	Disney	44,352

Brands influence generations differently. Boomers take more of a traditional view of brands and like the brands that they grew up with, rating brands such as the CBC, Visa, and Canadian Tire higher. Gen Xers gravitate toward both online and offline brands with a mix of preferences, including Facebook and Amazon. Millennials embrace the digital age with Google, Netflix, Amazon, YouTube, Facebook, and Apple. Generation Z comes of age and finds technology brands such as Instagram and Snapchat most influential.[9]

Many large, well-entrenched brands are often marketed around the world and have become global brands. **Global brands** tend to enjoy strong brand equity due to their hefty marketing budgets and well-recognized trademarks. Starting in 2000, Interbrand has conducted an annual study on global brands with publicly available financial records. To be included in this brand study, a brand needs to meet certain criteria: 30 percent of its revenues need to be from outside its home country; it must be present in Asia, Europe, North America, and emerging markets; it must have publicly available financial records; it must have future profit growth expectations; and it must have a public profile and awareness levels outside its own marketplace. Interbrand's Best Global Brands 2019 identified Apple, Google, Amazon, Microsoft, and Coca-Cola as the top five global brands in the world (see table above). Its ratings look specifically at a brand's competitive strength, the role it plays in the purchase decision, and its financial performance.[10]

global brands
Brands that are sold in a variety of international markets and that enjoy wide recognition in these markets.

Brand Strategies

Brands are classified as either individual brands or family brands, depending on whether the name has been extended to cover more than one product category. An **individual brand** is when a company uses a brand name solely for a specific product category. Two examples are the Tide brand name, used by Procter & Gamble only for laundry detergent, and Twitter, used solely for the micro-blogging social networking site.

A **family brand** is when a company uses a brand name to cover a number of different product categories. The brand name Crest, although initially used only for toothpaste, is now used by Procter & Gamble for toothpaste, dental floss, mouthwash, and teeth-whitening products. Crest extended the use of the brand name and used it to market other products; we call this a **brand extension**. Sony, Nike, and Microsoft are also examples of a family brand, where the company name is also the brand name, and all product categories launched by the company are using the corporate name. A **sub-brand** uses both the family brand name and its own brand name. This is a common strategy in the automobile industry. For example, Porsche successfully markets its higher-end Porsche Carrera and its lower-end Porsche Boxster, with both products benefiting from the quality and performance associated with the Porsche name.

The advantage of using an established family brand name for new goods or services is that brand equity is quickly transferred from the flagship brand to the new product, thus saving the company the marketing funds needed to build up this brand equity from scratch. A disadvantage of using a family branding approach is that if the new product does not live up to the image of the flagship brand, or does not share in its values, then the brand equity built up over time can be eroded for all products under this family brand name.

Protecting Brands—Patents, Trademarks, and Copyright

Brand equity is the result of considerable marketing investment and needs to be protected. Patents, copyrights, and trademarks are used to protect products, brands, and processes from unethical infringement and illegal use. **Patents** are used to legally protect new technologies, or improvements on products or processes. They provide a time-limited, legally protected, exclusive right to make, use, and sell an invention. Patents serve as a reward for ingenuity.[11] In Canada, patents currently protect owners for a period of 20 years after the patent is filed, providing that maintenance fees are paid during this time. After 20 years, the patent then becomes available to the market.

Copyrights are used to legally protect original written works, sound recordings, or forms of communication from being copied by others. It covers music, literature, and performances. In Canada, a copyright is protected for a lifetime plus 50 years.[12]

Trademarks are used by people or organizations to protect brand images, names, slogans, and designs from usage by others.[13] Trademarks are limited to a period of ten years from the date of registration, but can be renewed by their owners to maintain their investment. A trademark legally protects a brand name and its related logo, colours, fonts, and various combinations that exist for use in a particular category and in a part of the world. If trademarks are to be used in foreign countries, the owner is wise to register an international application. Companies hold separate trademarks for each version of a brand name and its associated graphics and logo. For a brand to be trademarked, a company first conducts a trademark search to ensure that the trademark is not already owned by another company. If the trademark is available and not challenged, then the brand and its associated design and logos can be legally registered in the company name. Care must be taken to renew these trademarks as required to ensure that they do not expire. Information on trademarks in Canada can be found at the Canadian Intellectual Property Office website at **www.cipo.ic.gc.ca**. Here you can easily conduct a search of the trademark database and its

Proctor & Gamble has used a family branding approach to leverage the brand equity of Crest across a range of products.

2020 Procter & Gamble

#Protectyourbrand

With the rapid uptake in social media usage and the subsequent popularity of digital marketing tools, brands need to be even more vigilant about protecting their intellectual property and ultimately protecting brand equity. With over 2.45 billion monthly users of Facebook, 330 million active Twitter users, and 359 million domain names registered globally, the world of social media and the Internet can be challenging for marketers. Dell, for example, currently manages 26 pages/groups on Facebook and 34 Twitter feeds. In the past, the protection of trademarks and copyrights was fairly straightforward, but with companies supporting dozens of different social media sites, websites, and tweets throughout any given day, there are many questions to be asked:

- Does my company have rights to the social media usernames, hashtags, and domain names that are needed to promote the company's products?
- How can my company monitor social media for trademark infringement?
- Are trademark policies clearly outlined on the social media sites my company uses?

Cybersquatting is the registering of an Internet name with the intent of profiting on another company's name or defaming the company. Domain names using a trademark are protected in Canada by the Canadian Internet Registration Authority (CIRA), and complaints are resolved through the CIRA Domain Name Dispute Resolution Policy (CDRP) for .ca domain names. For example, if someone had registered a domain name who did not have any rights to the trademarked name, the rights to the domain name reverted back to the company that owned the trademark. Sometimes organizations pay to secure back their domain with some of the most expensive recorded being CarInsurance.com at $49.7 million, Insurance.com at $35.6 million, VacationRentals.com at $35 million, PrivateJet.com at $30.18 million, and most recently, Voice.com at $30 million.

Companies are more frequently focusing on the value of a branded hashtag in their social media marketing campaigns. Hashtags can quickly spread globally, and since hashtags can be used by anyone, including competitors, they can create positive or negative viral discussions about a brand. Marketers are now including hashtags in their brand strategy, which begs the question: Can hashtags be protected so that marketers can manage their brand messages? Trademarking hashtags can be hit and miss, with fewer than 50 percent of hashtags meeting the criteria for trademarking, so a company called Twubs lets people register hashtags in case there are legal issues in the future.

The question is whether a hashtag has evolved further so that it functions as a hashtag trademark—or a "tagmark." The answer is an unequivocal yes. In both Canada and the U.S., hundreds of tagmarks have been registered by some of the world's biggest consumer products companies and some of the smallest start-ups. Hashtag-related claims have emerged in a number of trademark infringement lawsuits. To quote the Trademarks Office, "the addition of the # symbol or equivalent word to a clearly descriptive trademark will not render it registrable. . . . [E]ach trademark must be examined based on its own merit and trademarks consisting of, or

Reckitt Benckiser has registered a hashtag for its Mucinex brand of cough and cold products.

Mucinex and the Mr. Mucus character are trademarks of Reckitt Benckiser LLC. Used with permission.

containing, the hash symbol or word 'hashtag' will always be examined on a case by case basis."

In Canada, not only do we have guidance from the Trademarks Office, we also can see from reviewing the trademarks register that many hashtag marks have been successfully registered. A good example of this is Toronto-based influencer platform Hashtag Paid Inc. This company has successfully registered the trademark "#paid" in association with advertising agency services and advertising and business management consultancy services, among other things. The hashtag #paid illustrates how brands have developed a distinctive hashtag to be used as an identifier and a registrable mark. The world of hashtag trademarks continues to evolve, and the law is playing catching up. We can expect that the number of hashtags being used and applied for as trademarks will increase as businesses start relying more heavily on social media as sales platforms and increase the scope of their branding efforts to incorporate the use of hashtags as identifiers of their offerings.

On social media sites such as Twitter, Instagram, and Facebook, usernames are assigned on a first-come, first-served basis and cannot be reserved. Therefore, someone could take your trademark as a username, and unless they are misleading people to believe that they are affiliated with your business, nothing can be done. For example, if someone other than Coca-Cola registers cocacola as a username and then posts information about competitive products, which is then confusing to viewers and may be harmful to the Coca-Cola brand, Coke may have the grounds to submit a trademark infringement claim.

In the case of trademark protection on social media, prevention is the best policy. It is also recommended that companies develop clear policies on how to deal with each potential source of infringement. Here are some tips to protect your brand in social media:

1. Protect company names, logos, slogans, and brand names using trademarks.
2. Consult a professional regarding the need for and use of trademarks and copyright in social media.
3. Use defensive registration by registering all trademark domain names and usernames (including common misspellings) up front.
4. Create trademark use guidelines to ensure that the company is consistent in its use of trademarks, preventing confusion.
5. Regularly conduct searches (or hire a professional watching service), not only to detect potential trademark infringement, but to monitor potential defamation and to be aware of how your brand is being perceived.
6. Claim your trademarks as usernames as soon as possible.

Marketers must include social media in their intellectual property strategy to maximize as well as protect their brand messaging and brand equity. ●

Questions

1. It is important for companies to monitor social media for trademark infringement. Can you suggest how this could be done?

2. While companies and brands have faced issues with cybersquatting, celebrities have as well. What is the main motivator for cybersquatters?

---

registered trademarks. The Canadian Intellectual Property Office provides information on which trademarks are registered, when they were registered, and who owns the trademark.

Protecting your brand trademark has become even more important and more challenging in an increasingly online environment. Read the Focus on Ethics box, "#Protectyourbrand," for more details and examples of how companies are struggling to keep up with their brands on social media.[14]

Brand Loyalty

Just how much do consumers like and insist on a particular brand? Will they choose another if their first choice is not available, or will they insist on finding their brand? These are brand loyalty decisions. The degree of attachment that consumers have to a particular brand tells a marketer about their brand loyalty. Brand loyalty refers to the favourable attitudes that a consumer has over time toward a brand that result in varying levels of purchase insistence and commitment to the brand. Brand loyalty varies by product and from person to person. Marketers strive to have highly committed, brand-loyal consumers as this helps insulate their brand from competitive marketing practices.

Scrabble protected its trademark from online knock-offs.

©The McGraw-Hill Companies, Inc./Jill Braaten

Consumers that readily switch brands depending on price generally have very little brand loyalty. Consumers with a stronger brand attachment may have some brand loyalty but may easily brand-switch if the brand is not available. A brand's most loyal consumers will insist on purchasing their brand of choice and will postpone a purchase if the brand is not available. Most people have different degrees of brand loyalty depending on the product, brand, or category. Consider the products you purchase, and determine where you have strong brand loyalty and where you have very little.

> *Marketers work to associate brands with specific personality traits and to help consumers make emotional connections with their brands.*

What keeps consumers loyal to their favorite product brands

3: Product consistency (size, taste, quality, etc.) **65%**

4: Customer service **56%**

5: Easy shopping experience (shopping, check out, returns) **55%**

2: Value for money **66%**

6: Selection/ product assortment **55%**

1: Product quality **74%**

7: Pricing **54%**

Respondents who said these factors were very or extremely important in earning and keeping their loyalty to a brand

Source: The truth about customer loyalty, KPMG International, 2019

Consumers reveal what keeps them coming back.
The truth about customer loyalty, KPMG International, 2019

Brand Personality

Marketers recognize that brands offer more than product recognition and identification. Successful brands take on a **brand personality** of their own—a set of human characteristics associated with the brand.[15] Research shows that consumers often associate particular human personality traits with certain brands and prefer those whose personalities are most appealing. For example, Pepsi-Cola is seen as being youthful in spirit and exciting, while Dr. Pepper is viewed as being unique and non-conformist. The traits often linked to Harley-Davidson are masculinity, defiance, and rugged individualism. Millward-Brown conducted a study of 500,000 people globally to determine how brands were aligned with personality traits. There were some cultural and regional differences that were noted. The most successful brands in Canada were described as "creative" and "in control." Brand personalities described as "different" were not as successful in Canada.[16] Through marketing and promotion, marketers work to associate brands with specific personality traits and to help consumers make emotional connections with their brands.

Brand Names

When we say Xbox, iPad, Duracell, Porsche, Coke, or Nike, we typically do not think about how companies determined these brand names. Selecting a successful brand name can be a long and sometimes expensive process. Companies can spend thousands of dollars developing and testing a new brand name. Here are some key points to consider when determining a good brand name:

- **The name should suggest the product benefits.** This is demonstrated by brand names such as

Easy-Off (oven cleaner) and Chevrolet Spark (electric car), both of which clearly describe the product's benefits. Care should be taken to review how the brand name translates into other languages to avoid future pitfalls.

- **The name should be memorable, distinctive, and positive.** A number of new brands have been introduced over the last few years with distinctive brand names such as iPad, Xbox, Twitter, and Google. All these names are very distinctive and were entirely unique and unknown when first introduced. Today, these brand names have high awareness in Canada and enjoy very strong brand recognition.

- **The name should fit the company or product image.** Brand names such as Duracell or Eveready clearly suggest that these products provide reliable and long battery life. Twitter expresses the short conversations (tweeting) that can occur on this platform of 140 characters.

- **The name should have the ability to be legally protected.** A brand name must be "trademarkable" to protect a company's investment. If the brand name is too generic, or the trademark is owned by another company, the proposed brand name cannot be trademarked. Increasingly, brand names also need a corresponding website address, which can complicate name selection, as there are close to 360 million domain names registered globally.[17] An example that made international headlines was that of **MikeRoweSoft.com**. A 17-year-old teenager in Victoria, British Columbia, named Mike Rowe, set up this website for his graphic design business. He thought that since his name was Mike Rowe, it would be humorous to add Soft to the end and have an interesting play on words. Once Microsoft became aware of the site, it quickly sent a letter to Mike Rowe demanding that the website be shut down immediately due to trademark infringement. In what has now become a page in Internet history, Mike Rowe eventually settled the lawsuit for an Xbox and a few games.[18] This case was a pioneer in the cybersquatting (registering an Internet name with the intent of profiting on another company's name) world, and on average, 3,400

> **brand personality**
> A set of human characteristics associated with a brand.

cybersquatting cases are filed annually, with continued growth over the last few years.[19]

- **The name should be simple.** The brand names iPad, Xbox, Twitter, and Google are all simple names to spell and remember. This makes them more memorable and helps build brand equity.

What type of brand is Mastercraft?

Used with permission of Canadian Tire Corporation

Types of Brands

LO 6 There are three types of brands: (1) manufacturer's brands, (2) private-label brands, and (3) generic brands.

A **manufacturer's brand** is one that is owned and produced by the manufacturer. Gravol (dimenhydrinate is the name of the drug) is the manufacturer's brand created by Church & Dwight and sold to drugstores throughout Canada. Church & Dwight invested considerable resources, time, and money into the development and marketing of the brand. When Gravol was launched in Canada, it was protected by a patent, but as mentioned earlier, a patent is restricted to a limited number of years, currently over 20 years in Canada. Once a patent expires, other manufacturers can produce a similar product. Church & Dwight has subsequently launched brand extensions with naturally sourced ingredients, as well as additional formats to extend the life of Gravol as a manufacturer's brand.

A **private-label brand**, otherwise known as a store brand, is owned by a retailer that contracts its manufacturing out to major suppliers and then sells the product at its own retail stores, under its own store-brand name. Often these products are manufactured in the same factories as the manufacturer's brand. Private-label products are very popular in Canada, with 20 percent of shopping dollars spent on private-label products. This is higher than the global average. Canadian customers believe that private-label products are good alternatives to manufacturer's brands, offering good quality and good value.[20] A private-label brand provides a retailer with the opportunity to offer its customers a less expensive alternative to a manufacturer's brand. Private-label products are generally sold at prices 25 to 30 percent lower than manufacturer's brands. Because these store brands do not have to pay high listing fees and they have lower marketing costs, retailers often make more profit on private-label brands. This is an incentive to invest in the development of more private-label products.[21]

Examples of private-label products are Life brand, available at Shoppers Drug Mart; Selections and Irresistibles brands at Metro; and Mastercraft at Canadian Tire.

> *A private-label brand provides a retailer with the opportunity to offer its customers a less expensive alternative to a manufacturer's brand.*

A **generic brand** has no branding at all and is sometimes produced as a cheap alternative to a manufacturer's brand and to a private-label branded product. A generic brand is typically named using the main product ingredient, with its main point of difference

---

manufacturer's brand
A brand owned and produced by the manufacturer.

private-label brand
Otherwise known as a store brand, a brand owned by a retailer that contracts its manufacturing to major suppliers, and then sells the product at its own retail stores, under its own store-brand name.

generic brand
A product that has no branding and is produced as a cheap alternative to a manufacturer's brand and to branded private-label products.

being price. Generic products most commonly found in the pharmaceutical industry. Once the patent has expired for a prescription medication, many generic versions are created and sold to pharmacies by generic drug manufacturers such as Apotex Inc. or Novopharm. Once a generic is available, these cheaper versions are often substituted by pharmacists for the branded medicines when a prescription is filled. This can save governments, insurance companies, and consumers substantial sums of money. Although a less expensive alternative to other branded products, a generic product lacks the brand equity and product recognition that is enjoyed by both a manufacturer's brand and branded private-label products.

Outside of the pharmaceutical industry, generic products can often be found at various retail outlets such as dollar stores where select products with no associated brand names are sold. Dollarama stores, for instance, sell plastic clogs that are direct knock-offs of Crocs but have absolutely no branding at all.

1 • A product is a term used in marketing to designate non-durable goods, durable goods, and services that are marketed. Some products are a combination of both goods and services.

• There are four unique elements to services: intangibility, inconsistency, inseparability, and inventory. These four elements are referred to as the four Is of services.

LO 2 • The total product concept includes the core product, the actual product, and the augmented product.

LO 3 • Product mix is the combination of product lines managed by a company. The product mix width refers to the number of different product lines offered by the company. The product line length refers to the number of product or brands in the product line. The product line depth refers to the number of different versions of each product sold within its product lines.

 • Consumer products are classified into convenience products, shopping products, specialty products, and unsought products.

• Business products are classified into production or support goods. Production goods include raw materials and components parts, while support goods include installations, accessory equipment, supplies, and services.

LO 5 • A brand is a name or phrase used to identify a product and to distinguish it from the competition. Brand equity is the result of the positive experiences consumers have with the brand over time and results in brand loyalty.

• Trademarks are used to legally protect brands, patents are used to protect unique processes, and copyrights are used to protect the written or spoken word.

LO 6 • Companies may restrict a brand name for use with a single product line, thus using an individual brand, or may extend a brand name to encompass a number of different product categories, resulting in the creation of a family brand and, in some instances, sub-brands.

• Brands are categorized as manufacturer's brands, private-label brands, and generic brands.

actual product
augmented product
brand
brand equity
brand extension
brand loyalty
brand personality
business products
consumer products
convenience products
copyrights
core product

durable good
family brand
generic brand
global brands
idle production capacity
individual brand
manufacturer's brand
non-durable good
patents
private-label brand
product line
product line depth

product line length
product mix
product mix width
service continuum
shopping products
specialty products
sub-brand
trademarks
unsought products
virtual services

Branding Assignment In groups, pick a favourite company. Gather information on that company and its brands from the Internet, including the company's website and social media. Describe the product mix width as well as the product line length and depth. Choose one of the company's brands. Brainstorm with your group ways in which the company could improve brand equity and increase brand loyalty.

Hillberg & Berk has developed a socially conscious national brand from scratch. Carefully review the opening vignette and conduct your own research. Outline the strengths and weaknesses of Hillberg & Berk and list the external factors currently impacting the brand. What external opportunities and threats should Hillberg & Berk be most concerned about in the future?

Review the Infographic, "The Evolution of Customer Service," that highlights the future of customer service. Compare and contrast the evolution of customer service from the past to the future. Is there anything else you would add? Write a short analysis of your findings.

New Product Development

LEARNING OBJECTIVES

LO 1 Explain the concept of the product life cycle and the elements involved in each stage

LO 2 Describe the ways that product life cycles can be extended

LO 3 Differentiate between different types of new products

LO 4 Describe the adoption curve of new products

LO 5 Detail each step in the new product development process

This chapter looks at new products and how they are developed, launched, and managed over time. J.R. Brooks, co-owner of True Büch, an innovative Canadian company, describes the development of True Büch Kombucha and the creation of a whole new product category in Canada.

True Büch Kombucha

CHAPTER OUTLINE

- True Büch Kombucha
- The product life cycle
- Product life cycle strategies
- Types of new products
- The adoption curve

- Why new products succeed or fail
- Approaches to new product development
- The new product development process

Louisa and Conrad Ferrel (husband and wife) were travelling in Asia when they discovered kombucha for the first time and became hooked on its health benefits. When they returned home, they started brewing kombucha and offering it to friends and family members to try. On the side of their 9-to-5 corporate jobs, they sold their kombucha at farmers' markets as a fun hobby. Both Louisa and Conrad had jobs in accounting, but they wanted to pursue something they were passionate about. What they truly desired was an opportunity to enrich the health and happiness of consumers; their focus was to help communities they cared about and impact the planet positively. Conrad moved to the business full time and convinced Louisa to also do so by promising her they would donate a portion of profits to community projects they cared about.

The founders rented commercial kitchen space in a curling club in Alberta that provided them with enough space to start brewing more kombucha. This made True Büch the first commercial kombucha brewer in Alberta. Today, True Büch's mission is to "make the most delicious probiotic drinks for people looking to add a healthy boost to their daily lives." It aims to be the local market leader for kombucha while having a minimal impact on the environment, supporting its employees, and investing a portion of the proceeds into non-profit projects that the company are passionate about. True Büch makes environmental- and community-conscious business decisions that are showcased through producing a gut-healthy product that is brewed truthfully and authentically. Most importantly, its kombucha is craft-brewed in small batches with high-quality and organic ingredients. Recently, True Büch was named as one of the Top New Growth Companies by *Maclean's* and *Canadian Business*, making it the first kombucha company on this Startup 50 ranking.

After starting out as a draught provider of kombucha, for operational and environmental reasons, True Büch has recently increased focus on the production of single-serve bottles. To offset a portion of the impact of each bottle, it donates to eight community partners year-round, which includes working to offset carbon emissions with Bullfrog Power and planting 1,000 trees a year with TreeEra. In addition, production is currently 10,000 to 12,000 bottles per week, with a target to increase to 30,000 to 50,000 in 18 months. The kombucha must also be kept refrigerated. True Büch kombucha's flavour profile is less vinegary and more palatable than other brands. It is slightly carbonated and contains mostly organic ingredients that are mainly locally sourced. The main ingredient (tea) is from Naked Leaf, which True Büch secures from a local supplier. It makes new flavours every single month by draught and continuously tests new ones. True Büch also has released single-serve collaboration bottles with retail partners, including Freson Bros., Sunterra, and Community Natural Foods.

Kombucha is a quickly growing and evolving category. As recently as 2018, you could only find it in health food stores, and now it's in pretty much every grocery store across the country and most 7-Eleven's. That said, the company considers health-conscious, middle-income and above people, aged 20 to 50, to be the target market. Internal metrics show that the majority of its customers are female who also fit that description.

True Büch carefully considers new product introductions in its organization. Initially, the company conducts some informal market research on trends in health foods and botanicals that are gaining popularity. It also has someone in the brewery who leads flavour development and creates new products based on seasonal flavours that are available and new teas from suppliers. From there, True Büch conducts taste tests as a team and performs shelf-life testing before deciding to offer a flavour as a new product. This is continually ongoing for draught flavours so it can continually offer something different with draught.

One of its most popular and successful promotions is with Mealshare, in which anytime someone buys or refills a bottle of the flavour of the month, True Büch donates a meal to a youth in need. This pairs with the ongoing flavour development, and retailers fully support the program because they like the cause and know that their customers seek it out to participate in the program.

True Büch had a competitive first-mover advantage, being the first company to offer draught kombucha commercially in Western Canada. Having relatively no direct competitors, the company was able to grow very quickly and set prices at the rate desired. However, this has since changed, and in summer 2015, its first local competitor came out with a very different taste and process. Today, there are at least eight small brewers in Alberta and over three national brewers in Canada, along with three to four international competitors coming into the market. Some companies in this space include GT'S Kombucha, RISE Kombucha, Master Brew Kombucha, and Brew Dr. Kombucha.

True Büch is aware that the industry is becoming saturated and wants to stay at the forefront of the market. To do so, True Büch must consider the larger market dynamics. As individuals are becoming more health conscious, companies are promoting their products' wellness benefits. Indirect competitors that provide healthier products, such as tea, matcha drinks, turmeric drinks, water, and milk alternatives, are becoming stronger. The carbonated soft drinks category is declining in popularity, while bottled water has grown 6.2 percent. Research suggests that tea is the second-most consumed beverage, after water.

Kombucha is a fizzy, fermented, non-alcoholic tea. It provides benefits to one's digestive system through probiotics, enzymes, and amino acids. Kombucha contains antioxidants that fight free radicals (molecules that can damage cells); studies suggest it can kill bacteria and may help prevent diseases. Kombucha is created by fermenting organic tea and organic cane sugar with a symbiotic culture of bacteria and yeast (SCOBY). The SCOBY is made up of good bacteria and is fully organic and compostable. The SCOBY turns the cane sugar into good bacteria (like probiotics and enzymes) by feeding on it, but kombucha will still have traces of remaining sugar in it (approximately 5 to 7 grams per 8-ounce serving). To create authentic kombucha, it should not be pasteurized; when it is, it loses its naturally occurring probiotic content.

As part of their growth strategy, the Ferrels partnered with Zenabis Ltd. (Zenabis), a licensed producer of cannabis located in Vancouver. Zenabis quickly became a leader in the cannabis industry and is one of the largest cannabis producers in the world based on growing capacity. The company is currently awaiting edible legalization in Canada to start creating and distributing infused cultured tea beverages with CBD (not THC). The strategy is to leverage True Büch's expertise of cultured teas and align with Zenabis' expertise of cannabis to penetrate the new, growing infused food market.

Both this acquisition and the goal to grow its core Kombucha business aggressively introduces numerous strategic challenges and decisions. With True Büch's tight-knit family of co-workers, it is worried that plans for expansion may disrupt its family dynamic in the workplace when bringing on new employees. The biggest challenge faced by expansion is maintaining the quality and values they pride themselves on.[1]

reality CHECK ✓

As you read Chapter 8, refer back to the True Büch Kombucha opening vignette to answer the following questions:

- What type of innovation is True Büch Kombucha: a minor innovation, a continuous innovation, or a radical innovation?
- What stage in the product life cycle is True Büch in: introductory, growth, maturity, or decline?
- Considering the adoption curve (Figure 8-6), which group of consumers is True Büch targeting with its CBD-infused Kombucha drinks: innovators, early adopters, or the early majority?

The Product Life Cycle

LO 1 The concept of the **product life cycle** describes the stages that a new product goes through, starting with its initial introduction into the marketplace and moving through to the stages of growth, maturity, and decline. The concept of the product life cycle is used by many marketers to help manage a product from its initial launch through to its eventual decline. Marketers try to manage products so that they extend the time until the decline stage or, perhaps, so they don't reach the decline stage at all. This is done by changing, updating, and repositioning products to meet evolving consumer needs and competitive challenges.

While all products follow this same product life cycle, products in the online and technology areas often experience shorter cycles that require frequent product updates to stay competitive. We see this frequently with social media sites such as Facebook, Pinterest, and Twitter, which frequently add new features for its users, as well as new tools for marketers.

Figure 8–1 traces the curve of a product life cycle by plotting a product's sales and profits over time. The curves change in response to the competitive environment and to consumers' demand for the innovation.

Initially, during the introduction stage, a product experiences minimal sales that are growing slowly, minimal or nonexistent profits, and very few competitors. Over time, propelled by marketing programs and product demand, a product moves into a period of rapid growth, and profit increases. As the competition becomes more severe, consumers are presented with competitive products, which cause a product's sales and profits to flatten out and eventually, if not addressed by a marketer, decline. The length of each stage in the product life cycle depends on the product, the category, and how it is being marketed.

A more detailed example of how products are marketed through their life cycles can be seen in the smartphone category. Apple launched the original iPhone in 2007, and it has changed the product's features, services, pricing, and marketing over time to stay relevant and competitive against Samsung, Google, LG, Motorola, and the variety of other smartphone manufacturers that have entered the market (see Figure 8–2). In 2007, the original iPhone was revolutionary. At that time, the smartphone market was focused mainly on the corporate market, and features focused on e-mail and work-related functions. The iPhone changed all that. While the typical smartphone functions were still available, the iPhone had a large colourful screen and touch features that eliminated the external keyboard. Apple targeted the consumer market rather than only the corporate segment. Initially, the Apple operating system was fairly basic and features were limited. Over time, the market became more competitive, with companies like Samsung introducing new models and features at a rapid pace. Throughout its growth phase, Apple continued to improve its features,

> **product life cycle**
> The stages that a new product goes through, starting with introduction and evolving into growth, maturity, and decline.

Apple's iPhone continuously introduces new features and models to keep it relevant and competitive.
©NYC Russ/Shutterstock

Figure 8–1
Product life cycle

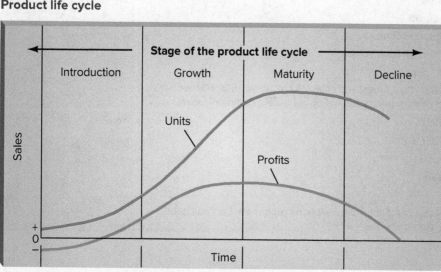

Figure 8–2
Apple iPhone product life cycle

Apple's iPhone—Managing the Product Life Cycle (PLC)		
Product	**Product Description**	**Price (US$)**
2007: Original iPhone	• One model • 4, 8, 16 GB • 3.5" multi-touch screen • 2 megapixel camera • iOS 3 • No apps	$499–$599
2008/2009: iPhone 3 • iPhone 3G • iPhone 3GS	• Two models • 8, 16, 32 GB • 3.5" multi-touch screen • 2–3 megapixel camera • iOS 3 • Grew from 500 to 50,000 apps • NEW: App Store; faster; less battery usage, ability to cut, copy, and paste text; visual voicemail; parental controls; photo geotagging; voice dialing; landscape keyboard	$199–$299
2010/2011: iPhone 4 • iPhone 4 • iPhone 4S	• Two models • 8, 16, 32, 64 GB • 3.5" multi-touch screen • 5–8 megapixel camera • iOS 4/5 • Grew from 225,000 to 360,000 apps • NEW: Stainless steel design, dual-core processor, location-based systems, iCloud, Facetime, iBooks, HD video, and iMessage	$199–$399
2012/2013: iPhone 5 • iPhone 5 • iPhone 5S • iPhone 5C	• Three models • 8, 16, 32, 64 GB • 8 megapixel camera • 4" multi-touch screen • iOS 6/7 • Grew from 700,000 to 900,000 apps • NEW: Passbook, improved Maps app, A7 chip provides two-times faster performance, fingerprint sensor, larger screen	$199–$399
2014/2015: iPhone 6 • iPhone 6 • iPhone 6 Plus • iPhone 6S • iPhone 6S Plus	• Four models • 32, 64, 128 GB • 8–12 megapixel camera • 4.7"–5.5" multi-touch screen • 1.3 million apps • NEW: Faster A8/9 processing chips, HD 4K video (6S), 3D touch (6S), improved iSight camera, Apple Pay, near-field communication	$199–$499
2016: iPhone 7 • iPhone 7 • iPhone 7 Plus	• Two models • 32, 128, 256 GB • 12 megapixel camera • 4.7" screen • iOS 10 • NEW: Water resistant, no headphone jack (new EarPods headphones), stereo speakers	$649

Apple's iPhone—Managing the Product Life Cycle (PLC)		
Product	**Product Description**	**Price (US$)**
2017: iPhone 8 • iPhone 8 • iPhone 8 Plus	• 32, 64, 128, 256 GB • 12 megapixel camera • iOS 11 • NEW: Glass and aluminum design, Retina HD displays, A11 Bionic Chip, new single & dual cameras with support for portrait lighting, optimized for augmented reality, Super Retina Display, TrueDepth camera system, Face ID	$699-$999+
2018: iPhone X • iPhone XR • iPhone XS • iPhone XS Max	• 64, 128, 256 GB • iOS 11 • NEW: Super Retina OLED display; improved scratch, splash, and water resistance; 12 megapixel dual camera system; TrueDepth camera system; faster Face ID; wider stereo sound; dual SIM support; A12 Bionic Chip	$749-$1,099+
2019: iPhone 11 • iPhone 11 • iPhone 11 Pro • iPhone Pro Max	• 32, 64, 128, 256 GB • 12 megapixel camera • iOS 11 • NEW: Liquid Retina HD display; dual 12 megapixel ultra-wide and wide cameras; 12 megapixel front-facing camera; 4K video at up to 60fps; A13 bionic processor; up to 5 hours more battery life; stronger, matte-finish glass enclosure	$699-$999+

such as camera quality, memory, screen size, faster performance, and touch sensors. In addition, Apple placed a significant focus on the development of exclusive apps and services to increase the functionality of its devices. The number of apps available for the iPhone has exceeded 2 million, and Apple has provided services such as iCloud, iBooks, Apple Pay, iMessages, and location-based services.

At launch, Apple focused on generating awareness and demand for the iPhone. Advertising showcased the elegance of the iPhone, which was so different from the existing genre of smartphones. As the functionality of the iPhone improved during the growth phase, Apple used advertising to highlight its unique features and the evolution of the Apple App Store. Up to this point, Apple wanted to convince customers that they needed an iPhone. As the iPhone settles in to the maturity phase, ads now focus on confirming that the iPhone is an integral part of life, reinforcing to consumers that they have made the right decision by selecting the iPhone. This message is validated by the continuing evolution of differentiating features such as 5G and 3D depth sensing.

In the following sections, we look at each stage of the product life cycle in more detail to appreciate how marketers use this concept to manage their products profitably (see Figure 8–3). The product life cycle concept is used by marketers in many different ways. It is most often used to help manage products or brands and, in some instances, to analyze an industry in general.

Introduction Stage

The introduction stage of the product life cycle occurs when a product is first introduced to its intended target market. During this period, profits are minimal typically due to three things: (1) slow sales growth, (2) high product development costs, and (3) high levels of marketing spending needed to launch the new product. The key marketing objective during this stage is to create consumer awareness and to stimulate trial (or the first purchase) of the new product.

This stage is characterized by little competition and a lack of consumer awareness about the product. Radical new categories or technological innovations also come with the added challenge of having to educate consumers on the existence and relevancy of the category itself. In many cases, the money spent on advertising and promotion is focused on developing demand for the product class rather than just the brand, since there are few competitors established in the market. The other elements of the marketing mix are also carefully crafted to ensure that they are in step with the product launch and its consumers.

During the introduction stage, pricing can be high or low. A high initial price is called a price skimming strategy and is used by companies to help recover research and development costs. This approach takes advantage of the price insensitivity of innovators and early adopters. The price skimming strategy is very common in the electronics market, with products such as 4K Smart

Figure 8–3
Managing the stages of the product life cycle

Stage in Product Life Cycle	Introduction	Growth	Maturity	Decline
Competition	Few competitors exist	More competitors enter the market	Many competitors in the market	Reduced competition, with some competitors leaving the market
General marketing objective	Awareness	Product differentiation	Brand loyalty	Product rationalization
Product	Focus on a new product or brand	Introduce more features	Ensure full product line is available and innovative with new ideas	Retain only best sellers or discontinue
Price	Use a skimming or penetration strategy	Prices are slowly reduced	Price discounts are used frequently	Very low prices
Place (distribution)	Limited distribution	Distribution is increased	Full distribution is achieved	Distribution is reduced
Promotion (communication)	Focus on building awareness with advertising	Emphasize points of difference versus the competition	Focus on pricing and sales promotion	Only minimal promotion, if any
Profit	Minimal profits, if any	Increased profits that reach their maximum	Maximized profits that level off	Decreasing and minimal profits

TVs and smartphones being launched at high prices to recover costs and then lowering their prices to attract a larger, more price-sensitive market. If a company uses a low price to enter the market, this is referred to as a penetration pricing strategy and is used to encourage rapid acceptance of an innovation or to combat a competitive threat. Pricing strategies are discussed in greater detail in Chapter 9.

Distribution can often be a challenge during the introduction stage of the product life cycle because channel members may be hesitant to carry a new product that is unproven. Listing fees may also present themselves as an expensive proposition for marketers, who often experience retailers charging to recover the costs and risks of listing, shelving, and merchandising a new product in stores.

> *Distribution can often be a challenge during the introduction stage of the product life cycle because channel members may be hesitant to carry a new product that is unproven.*

Looking at the iPhone during its introductory stage, it was launched at a high price, and Apple has focused on continuous innovation to protect its brand value and pricing.[2]

Growth Stage

The growth stage of the product life cycle sees an increase in competition and a rapid rise in sales and profits. The market is flooded with competing brands that thrust a category and its products into the forefront. This results in new consumers being enticed into the category and a resultant increase in sales.

In this competitive arena, marketers focus their programs on differentiating products from competitive offerings. New features are added to original designs, and product proliferation often occurs. Pricing levels are generally lowered to become more competitive and distribution increases. Promotion at this stage becomes more product-specific, with advertising playing a key role in focusing consumers toward particular brands. Profits often reach their peak at this stage due to more focused promotion and a decline in development and production costs. Marketing objectives focus on product differentiation.

The Instant Pot electric pressure cooker provides an excellent example of the growth stage. Introduced in 2010, it had a slow but steady growth during the introductory phase, but word of mouth from social media and influential bloggers created an explosive rise in demand for the versatile multi-cooker. Designed by a small Canadian-based company, Instant Brands, the device became the single largest-selling item on Amazon by 2017. Robert Wang, an IT expert who lost his job in telecom, introduced the product to solve a problem he experienced in his two-income family—cooking a quick and healthy dinner after work and getting takeout food less. He was looking to invent an automated cooking machine that was an all-in-one cooking product that could assist you in putting dinner on the table in 30 to 40 minutes. Based on consumer input, he wanted to invent a device that performed the functions of multiple devices to reduce an already overcrowded kitchen. He also wanted to build a community on Facebook, with one of the official pages having over 5.5 million followers who regularly share recipes. Today, it is still a bestseller with a cult following, introducing different versions of the Instant Pot and other innovative small appliances.[3]

> *The maturity stage of the product life cycle is characterized by a slowdown of sales growth and profit.*

Maturity Stage

The maturity stage of the product life cycle is characterized by a slowdown of sales growth and profit. Competitors are well-established, and fewer new consumers enter the market. Marketing focuses on holding or gaining market share by continuing to differentiate the product and building on existing customer loyalty. Profits level off at this stage, often due to price competition. A major consideration in a company's strategy in this stage is to control overall marketing costs by improving promotional and distribution efficiency.

The maturity stage is generally the longest stage in the product life cycle, with marketers focusing efforts to ensure that the product does not go into decline. Marketers use short-term promotional tactics such as consumer promotions to encourage consumers to purchase the product. Product innovation can also become a priority as marketers try to reposition products in the market and revamp product lines to be more competitive and relevant to consumers' needs. The purpose of this renewed focus on innovation is to try to take the product back into the growth or early maturity stages of the product life cycle, as we have seen with products such as the iPhone.

Numerous well-established products are in the maturity stage of their product life cycles; examples include Heinz Ketchup, Hellmann's Mayonnaise, M&M's, and Kraft Dinner (KD). What do marketers of these products do to maintain product relevancy in these categories and to stop them from going into decline? Packaging changes, product modifications, and extended-usage approaches are often used to keep them relevant.

Decline Stage

The decline stage of the product life cycle occurs when sales and profits steadily decline over time. Frequently, a product enters this stage when products become obsolete due to technological innovation or changes in consumer needs. Downloadable music files replaced CDs, video streaming replaced DVDs, and laptops/tablets have replaced desktop computers.

Products in the decline stage tend to take a disproportionate share of management and financial resources relative to their future value. As a result, a company follows one of two strategies to deal with a declining product. It will either **delete** the product or **harvest** the product. Deletion is when a product is discontinued. Normally, decisions to discontinue a product are not taken lightly as there can be residual customers who still use this product. Harvesting is when a company keeps the product but reduces marketing support in an attempt to reap some minor profits at this stage in the life cycle.

delete
When a company discontinues a product.

harvest
When a company keeps a product but reduces marketing support in an attempt to reap some minor profits.

Length of the Product Life Cycle

The length of a product life cycle varies according to the industry, the competition, technological innovation, and approaches to marketing the product. There is no set timeframe for a product to move through its life cycle. Generally, consumer products have shorter life cycles than business products. For example, some new consumer food products, such as FritoLay's Baked Lay's potato chips, move from the introduction stage to maturity quickly. The availability of mass communication vehicles informs consumers quickly and shortens life cycles. Technological change shortens product life cycles as product innovation replaces

KD has launched additional varieties and formats.

(all images) ©Helen Sessions/Alamy Stock Photos

existing products. For example, smartphones have largely replaced digital cameras in the amateur photography market. Other products, such as Heinz ketchup, have extended product life cycles that have continued for years, driven by marketing approaches that keep the product relevant.

Shape of the Product Life Cycle

The generalized life cycle shown in Figure 8–1 does not always apply to all products. Figure 8–4 shows four product life cycle curves that apply to different types of products. These products and their life cycles can be categorized into four main areas: high-learning products, low-learning products, fashion products, and fad products.

A **high-learning product** is one where there is an extended introductory period due to the significant efforts required to educate customers on the usage and benefits of the product. Movie-streaming services are an example of such a product. A switch to online movie streaming from DVD or blu-ray was a real shift in thinking for many consumers who were a bit slow to understand the advantages of the new technology, how to use it, and what to do with their old DVDs and video rental memberships. It also required consumers to overcome issues of insufficient bandwidth, the necessity to use a computer or other device (prior to the introduction of SMART TVs), and the fact that few movie titles were initially offered for streaming. It took considerable time for consumers and the industry to fully adopt this technology, resulting in an extended introductory period for movie streaming services.

In contrast, a **low-learning product** has a short introductory stage in the product life cycle. In these instances, the benefits of purchasing these products are self-evident and very little learning is required. An example of a successful low-learning product is the Apple Watch, which required little education on behalf of consumers. Consumers trusted the Apple brand and were familiar with its touch technology from use of the Apple iPhone.

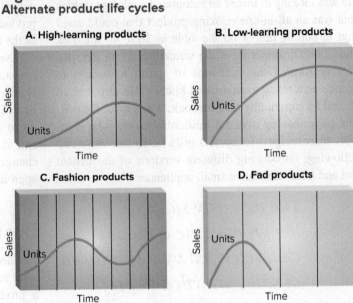

Figure 8–4
Alternate product life cycles

A. High-learning products
B. Low-learning products
C. Fashion products
D. Fad products

The product life cycle for a **fashion product** is cyclical. The length of the cycle will vary, but it is relatively short, going from introduction to decline, generally within a two- to three-year period, only to resurface again a few years later. Life cycles for fashion products most often appear in men's and women's footwear and apparel. Whether we like it or not, fashion trends such as bell bottom pants, crop tops, and leggings have gone away only to come back again years later.

A **fad** refers to a product with a very short product life cycle. It typically experiences immediate rapid growth, followed by an equally rapid decline, with no real maturity stage at all. These products tend to be novelties, such as the Pet Rock craze and Pokémon Go. Children's toys often fall into this category.

marketing TIP

"We're constantly monitoring the trends on health foods and botanicals that are gaining popularity to create new flavours for consumers."

- J.R. Brooks , co-owner, True Büch Kombucha

ask YOURSELF

1. What are the four stages in the product life cycle? How do they differ in terms of sales and profits?

2. How do high-learning and low-learning products differ?

3. What is the shape of the product life cycle for a smartphone in today's marketplace?

Product Life Cycle Strategies

LO 2 It is important for a firm to manage its products through their life cycles, profitably extending and prolonging their relevance in the market. Product life cycles can be extended in a number of ways, namely by (1) modifying the product, (2) modifying the market, (3) repositioning a product, and (4) introducing a new product. It is important to realize that a combination of these approaches is most often used to keep products fresh and relevant.

Modifying the Product

Product improvements and line extensions are often used by marketers to ensure that products remain competitive and address new trends in the market.

Product Improvements Examples can be seen in the food industry, where marketers are addressing consumers' demand for healthier foods. For example, Tropicana juices responded to consumers' demand for functional foods by introducing the Tropicana Essentials Probiotic line, and Beyond Meat responded to the demand for more plant-based products.[4]

Line Extensions Some of the most successful and long-lasting brands use line extensions to extend their product life cycles. They also include innovative marketing approaches to stay relevant to consumers. A **line extension** is the term used when a new item is added to an already existing product line, such as Cheerios

Procter & Gamble utilizes a line-extension strategy for Tide laundry detergent.
©Roman Tiraspolsky/Shutterstock

adding Chocolate Peanut Butter Cheerios to its already well-established Cheerios product line. To capitalize on the green trend, Procter & Gamble introduced Tide Coldwater (for cold-water washing) and Tide Free & Gentle (free of dyes and perfumes).[5]

Modifying the Market

There are three key market modification strategies. Companies may decide that their current product is under-represented with certain consumer groups and may see an opportunity to target these consumers. In addition, marketers may try to increase a product's use within its existing customer group, which is an especially useful strategy where there is strong brand loyalty. Lastly, a company may develop new uses for a product, extending its utility to the customer.

> **line extension**
> The addition of a new item to an already existing product line.

Finding New Customers Marketers are often cautious and somewhat reluctant to follow this approach as it can be an expensive proposition that yields few results. Harley-Davidson has tailored a marketing program to encourage women to take up biking, thus doubling the number of potential customers for its motorcycles.

A *Canadian Business* special report, Canadian Brand Top 40, highlighted the results of the Reputation Institute survey of Canadians and how they rate their brands. The survey of Canadians ranks brands based on reputation (defined as the trust, admiration, good feeling, and overall esteem of its products), its performance, its products and services, innovation, workplace, governance, citizenship, and leadership.

Christie keeps its product lines fresh with new items and marketing campaigns.
©Keith Homan/Shutterstock

McCain Foods focuses on natural ingredients in its products and a consistent brand message.

McCain® Foods Limited

The top three Canadian brands were identified as (1) Tim Hortons, (2) WestJet, and (3) McCain Foods. McCain Foods embodies a humble, unpretentious image and is one of Canada's most reputable brands. It has basically the same logo as it had when the company was founded in 1956. It was started in New Brunswick by a family descended from potato farmers. McCain Foods is a remarkably consistent company when it comes to its messaging and brand values. Survey respondents agreed with the characterization of the McCain Foods brand as friendly, straightforward, and simple. In 2010, it moved towards more natural ingredients in its products and continues that today.[6]

Increasing a Product's Use This approach encourages more frequent usage of a product by existing customers. It is typically used by products with a strong and loyal customer base. It has been a strategy of Campbell Soup Company. Because soup consumption rises in the winter and declines during the summer, the company now advertises more heavily in warm months to encourage consumers to think of soup as more than a cold-weather food. Similarly, the Florida Orange Growers Association advocates drinking orange juice throughout the day rather than for breakfast only.

Creating a New Use Situation Finding new uses for an existing product is not a simple task, because many products do not lend themselves to this approach. This has been a strategy used by Rice Krispies cereal by promoting its use as a baking ingredient for Rice Krispie Squares. Follow the links at **www.kelloggs.ca** to see the extended usage recipes used to market Rice Krispies.

Another example is Arm & Hammer baking soda, which is sold as a baking ingredient but is also marketed as a product that eliminates odours, unblocks sinks, and cleans various household items. The Marketing NewsFlash box, "Underwear—Who Knew?" looks at how two new Canadian companies created successful new products in existing traditional industries.[7]

Repositioning a Product

Once a product has reached its maturity stage, it often needs an injection of newness to focus the market on the product and to provide it with a renewed competitive advantage. This can be achieved through repositioning the product to meet changing consumer needs, to react to a competitor's move, or to improve the value offered to the consumer.

Based on consumer interest in the classic flip phone, Motorola launched a brand-new foldable Android smartphone with the same general form factor, but it replaces the T9 keypad and small LCD with a 6.2-inch foldable plastic OLED panel and the Android 9 Pie operating system. Instead of turning a modern-sized phone into a smaller tablet, it turns a conventional-sized smartphone into something much smaller and more pocketable. It was launched in January 2020 with a cost of $1,499.[8]

Motorola razr is an updated version of the flip phone.

©DecaStock/Alamy Stock Photo

Underwear—Who Knew?

Knix Wear

Which two successful Canadian companies are two of the top three most-successful companies to ever pitch on *Dragons' Den* and have at least one X in their names?

If you guessed Knix Wear and SAXX, you would be correct, and even though both companies pitched new and improved underwear to the Dragons, only Knix Wear got a deal. Both companies have gone on to be Canadian success stories by developing innovative products in a very traditional industry that hadn't seen any innovation for decades.

In 2015, after creating some buzz in the underwear biz, Knix Wear decided to create an innovative, versatile wireless bra. Based on its research, the company learned that most women had owned 17 different bras, wore them a month between hand-washings, and found them to be mostly uncomfortable. With this knowledge in hand and with high-tech design tools and fabrics, the 8-in-1 Evolution Bra was born. The team at Knix had two problems to solve. The first was to validate the concept: even though it had tested the design thoroughly with over 50 testers of all shapes and sizes, it still needed to prove that the market was

ready for a completely new concept. Secondly, it needed financing to do its first production run. Enter Kickstarter, a crowd-funding platform that allows a start-up to validate a concept by letting average people invest in a product that they find attractive. The magnitude of the investment indicates the potential demand in the market for this new product. Within a couple of months, the 8-in-1 Evolution Bra became the most-funded fashion product in the history of Kickstarter, raising over $1.1 million from 13,642 investors, proving that women were definitely looking for something new in bras.

The story of SAXX Underwear is also very interesting, with many twists and turns along the way. Trent Kitsch, founder of SAXX, tells a story of being on a fishing trip in a clammy ocean suit and wondering why there wasn't a way for men to be "more comfortable down south." Trent, relying on his personal experience as an athlete, he developed the BallPark Pouch™—a patented 3D, hammock-shaped pouch that keeps everything in place, thanks to breathable mesh panels that prevent skin-against-skin friction and no exposed stitching for chafe-free comfort. Trent questioned the status quo of the industry like only a start-up can. Even though SAXX didn't get a deal on *Dragons' Den*, Trent sold $30,000 worth of underwear the next day, and the company was launched.

Knix Wear founder Joanna Griffiths has continued to build Knix Wear by listening to her customers and adding more products to both the bra and underwear lines. In 2019, Knix Wear was estimated to have over $5 million in revenue, and word on the street was that it was looking for venture capital to take on Victoria's Secret in the lingerie market. Since the beginning, the Knix Wear brand has made extraordinary products for ordinary people. The brand uses real people of all shapes and sizes on its website and relies heavily on reviews since, until recently, all sales had been were online. Trent Kitsch sold SAXX for $50,000, and it is still innovating and growing. SAXX is now partnering with a major Canadian advertising company to take on the American market. It goes to show that innovation in even the most traditional of industries can prove successful if you can solve a problem. ●

Questions

1. What product life cycle strategy are Knix Wear and SAXX examples of?

2. Why do you think these companies were so successful?

3. Where is Knix Wear and SAXX in their product life cycles?

UNDERWEAR RE-INVENTED

// Experience the BallPark Pouch for friction-free support.

SAXX Underwear

Introducing a New Product

Adding a new product to a line can provide the focus that a mature product needs, bringing it back in the product life cycle to either the growth or early maturity stage. Apple has done this successfully by regularly introducing new versions of its iPhones, iPads, and computers with updates to its technology and design. Regardless of the type of product, new products have a greater chance of success if they provide meaningful benefits to its target market.

Drivers of Product Success
When it comes to new products, the 2020 BrandSpark Canadian Shopper Study reviewed the opinions and attitudes of over 48,000 respondents in Canada. The study tells us that consumers want value for their money. Convenience plays a lesser role in shopping decisions. Shoppers like trying new products and are willing to pay more if the new product is better than what is currently available.[9]

minor innovations
Minor product modifications that require no adjustments on behalf of the consumer.

The BrandSpark Best New Products Awards of 2020 echo the drivers for product success. These annual awards include the opinions of over 16,000 consumers on new products in the consumer packaged-goods industry (health and beauty, food and beverage, and household care). The winning products all provide good value and are seen as innovative in their categories. In the health and beauty segment, Neutrogena Hydro Boost Body Gel Cream Fragrance Free won in the body lotion category for delivering the benefits of a moisturizer with no fragrance. In the food and beverage segment, Sabra Avocado Toast was recognized in the Grab-and-Go Meal for its healthy meal convenience.[10]

ask YOURSELF

1. What approaches can be used to extend a product's life cycle?

2. Christie's developed Fudge Covered Oreos. What strategy was used to extend the product life cycle for Oreos?

New Products
Types of New Products

LO 3 New products are the lifeblood of a company, helping to make products relevant and to bring future revenues into the company. There are many types of new products, ranging from a slight product modification to a more radical innovation. How new products are categorized depends on the degree of newness involved, and how much time a consumer needs to learn to use the product. Based on these factors, we classify innovations as (1) minor innovations, (2) continuous innovations, and (3) radical innovations (see Figure 8–5).

Minor innovations refer to minor product modifications that require no adjustments on behalf of the consumer. Consumers do not need to be educated on how to use the product. Colgate Max Fresh KnockOut is an example of a minor innovation. The extra features in the new toothpaste do not require buyers to learn new behaviours, so effective marketing for a product like this is focused on generating awareness for the new innovation.

> *New products are the lifeblood of a company, helping to make products relevant and to bring future revenues into the company.*

Best New Product Award Winners

Product	Category
Neutrogena Hydro Boost Body Gel Cream Fragrance Free (body lotion)	Health and beauty products
Batiste Bare Dry Shampoo (dry shampoo)	
Sensodyne Rapid Relief (toothpaste)	
Robitussen Honey (cough syrup)	
Beyond Meat Burger (plant-based burger)	Food and beverage products
Siggi's Yogurt (yogurt)	
Triscuit Woven with Chia Seeds Rosemary & Jalapeno (crackers)	
Sabra Avocado Toast (grab-and-go meal)	
Milk-Bone Wonder Bones (dog food/treat)	Household products
Finish In-Wash Dishwasher Cleaner (dishwasher cleaner)	
Downy Wrinkleguard Fabric Conditioner (fabric enhancer)	
Airpods Pro (noise-cancelling earbuds)	

Figure 8–5
Degree of product innovation

	Minor Innovation	Continuous Innovation	Radical Innovation
Definition	Requires no new learning by consumers	Changes consumer's normal routine but does not require totally new learning	Requires new learning and consumption patterns by consumers
Examples	New and improved toothpaste or detergent	Swiffer WetJet; wearable technology	Amazon Alexa or Google Home; self-driving cars; 3D printers
Marketing emphasis	Gain consumer awareness and wide distribution	Advertise points of difference and benefits to consumers	Educate consumers through advertising, product trial, and personal selling; public relations can play a major role

Continuous innovations refer to new products that include more than just a minor product improvement but do not require radical changes in consumer behaviour. Continuous innovations are not as common and require extensive product development by a company. Marketers must invest in marketing communication programs to launch these innovative products and to communicate their benefits to consumers. Electric cars are an example of a continuous innovation. While consumers drive an electric car in a similar manner to gasoline-powered vehicles, there are some points of difference that require education and communication, such as shorter driving ranges, the availability of charging stations, and the uncertainty around the cost of operating an electric vehicle.[11]

Radical innovations are the least common form of innovation. They involve the introduction of a product that is entirely new to the market. The success of these products is often dependent on the education of the consumer, usually through advertising and/or public relations efforts.

Drones are an example of radical innovation. Drones are unmanned aircraft that were originally developed for use in war to surprise and attack the enemy. Unlike the remote control aircraft that came before them, drones can operate somewhat autonomously. Drones combine technology such as GPS, cameras, controllers, computer programming, and radio-frequency or WiFi communication. Now, drones are disrupting the way business is done in many industries. The commercial use of drones has evolved for package delivery, agriculture monitoring, real estate development, news coverage, law enforcement, and simply for entertainment. Drones represent an exciting convergence of several cutting-edge technologies. Regulators are struggling to keep pace. The significant potential dangers of flying drones, as well as privacy concerns, are creating an urgent need for the development of rules to govern drone use.[12]

For a look at some other radical innovations that may be trending over the next few years, see the Infographic, "Top 5 Tech Trends for 2020."

The Adoption Curve

LO 4 The success of a new product and how quickly it is adopted by consumers is demonstrated in Figure 8–6, which shows the adoption curve. The **adoption curve** takes the point of view that some consumers are more ready than others to buy a product innovation. North American research (statistics vary across the world) shows that 2.5 percent of the population are innovators who are the first to purchase new products; 13.5 percent are considered early adopters, another group that will accept a new offering sooner rather than later. In the middle of the pack are

continuous innovations
New products with more than just a minor product improvement, but that do not require radical changes by the consumer.

radical innovations
New products that involve the introduction of a product that is entirely new and innovative to the market.

adoption curve
The sequential diffusion and acceptance of an innovation into the market by consumers.

Drones, which are unmanned aircraft, are an example of radical innovation.

©Doxieone Photography/Getty Images

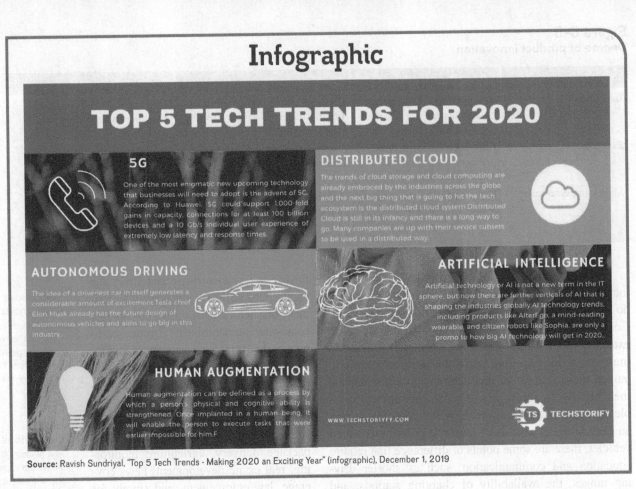

TOP 5 TECH TRENDS FOR 2020

5G

One of the most enigmatic new upcoming technology that businesses will need to adopt is the advent of 5G. According to Huawei, 5G could support 1,000-fold gains in capacity, connections for at least 100 billion devices and a 10 Gb/s individual user experience of extremely low latency and response times.

DISTRIBUTED CLOUD

The trends of cloud storage and cloud computing are already embraced by the industries across the globe and the next big thing that is going to hit the tech ecosystem is the distributed cloud system. Distributed Cloud is still in its infancy and there is a long way to go. Many companies are up with their service subsets to be used in a distributed way.

AUTONOMOUS DRIVING

The idea of a driverless car in itself generates a considerable amount of excitement. Tesla chief Elon Musk already has the future design of autonomous vehicles and aims to go big in this industry.

ARTIFICIAL INTELLIGENCE

Artificial technology or AI is not a new term in the IT sphere, but now there are further verticals of AI that is shaping the industries globally. AI technology trends, including products like AlterEgo, a mind-reading wearable, and citizen robots like Sophia, are only a promo to how big AI technology will get in 2020.

HUMAN AUGMENTATION

Human augmentation can be defined as a process by which a person's physical and cognitive ability is strengthened. Once implanted in a human being, it will enable the person to execute tasks that were earlier impossible for him.F

WWW.TECHSTORIYFY.COM

TS **TECHSTORIFY**

Source: Ravish Sundriyal, "Top 5 Tech Trends - Making 2020 an Exciting Year" (infographic), December 1, 2019

the early and late majority, each comprising approximately 34 percent of the population. Once accepted by the innovators and early adopters, the adoption of new products moves on to the early majority and late majority, who respond to the product being well-established in the market and are influenced by the purchase habits of their peers. Another 16 percent of the population are the laggards, who are either reluctant or late purchasers of the innovation and may in fact never purchase it.[13]

For any product to be successful it must be purchased by innovators and early adopters. Often, marketers spend a lot of effort involving innovators and early adopters with their new product prior to launch. These consumers are the opinion leaders in a particular product category, and so their experiences can play an integral role in future demand for the product. Marketers then try to move the product from the innovators and early adopters through to the early majority so as to quickly reap the benefits of increased sales and profits as soon as possible. In this manner, marketers design marketing programs to target these specific groups in different ways and separately focus their marketing programs on the demographic and psychographic needs and interests of these target groups. There are several types of barriers that can deter a consumer from adopting a new

product. Common reasons are usage barriers (the product is not consistent with existing usage habits), value barriers (there is no incentive to change), risk barriers (the existence of physical, economic, or social risks if the product is purchased), and psychological barriers (cultural or image differences).[14]

A new product currently struggling to move along the adoption curve is the electric car. Electric cars have earned less than 1 percent of global automobile sales. A usage barrier exists because prospective buyers believe these cars are not compatible with existing driving habits. Contributing to this belief is the lack of charging stations across Canada and the perception that electric cars have very short travelling ranges. Second, there is also a value barrier. Consumers have not recognized the superiority of electric cars over vehicles with internal combustion engines. Third, a risk barrier exists due to buyer uncertainty about the actual cost of owning an electric-powered car. This has been an even greater issue since gasoline prices have stabilized.[15]

Another industry that is looking for rapid uptake and adoption is virtual health care. Read about the experience of Telus in the Marketing NewsFlash box "Timing Is Everything—Virtual Health Care during a Pandemic."[16]

Figure 8–6
The adoption curve

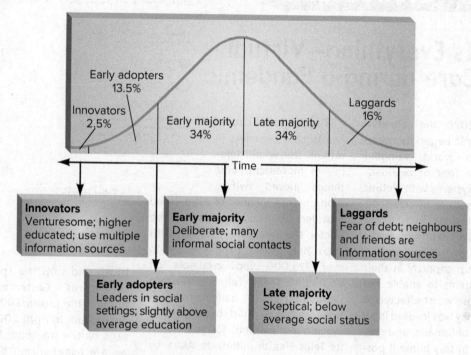

1. *Describe the three types of product innovation and explain which ones are most common.*

2. *What type of innovation are electric cars?*

3. *How does the adoption curve apply to the diffusion of new products in the marketplace?*

New Product Development

Developing and launching new products is an expensive undertaking with a high risk of failure. Research costs are high, and the time and effort spent on developing prototypes and marketing materials are extensive. We are familiar with successful new products and brands such as Google, Xbox, Twitter, and iPad, yet research has shown that only 15 to 50 percent of new products are successful. Success rates vary between industries, with consumer products experiencing the highest failure rates.[17]

Product failure can result in expensive product write-offs and a lack of future credibility in the market. Hundreds of thousands of dollars are often at stake. It is important at this point to remember that new products become successful over time and that marketers work to finesse these new products with upgrades and improvements that better meet consumer needs and expectations. However, many product launches also fail for reasons spanning from an insignificant point of difference to an inadequate market distribution strategy (see Figure 8–7). There are many examples of product failure, even from very large companies. New Coke is the textbook example of a new product launch gone wrong. Introduced in April 1985 and rapidly removed from the market in July 1985, Coke failed to understand the intense loyalty of its customers for the original Coke brand.[18]

The costs to an organization for poor quality can be staggering and include the labour, materials, and other expenses to fix the problem—not to mention the lost sales, profits, and market share that usually result. Consider self-balancing scooters, commonly referred to as "hoverboards." After gaining widespread attention with the media, as well as popularity with teens, hoverboards made by a variety of manufacturers were found to catch fire or explode. Needless to say, hoverboard sales suffered greatly as a result.[19]

In order to avoid expensive product failures, companies can use a number of different approaches when developing new products. These range from providing clear strategic direction to creating particular company structures to instituting rigorous product development processes. We look at these areas in more detail in the sections that follow.

Timing Is Everything—Virtual Health Care during a Pandemic

Telus Health

In March 2020, the coronavirus pandemic began its sweep across the world, bringing with it the fear of overloading health care systems with victims of the worst symptoms of COVID-19. After learning lessons from China and Italy, Canadian health care providers in each province worked diligently to open up capacity in their overcrowded systems to enable the treatment of those worst affected. A state of emergency was invoked in all of the provinces of Canada, and residents were told to stay home if possible and to maintain a two-metre buffer zone between themselves and others to reduce the spread of the virus. This new normal created challenges for medical practices: how could patients receive care without leaving home? It turns out there was a solution that had been around for decades but never wholeheartedly adopted: virtual health care.

It is not as if telemedicine is new; it has been used in the sparsely populated Canadian North and on NASA space missions since the 1960s, but it never quite caught on. Even though research by the Canadian Medical Association showed that 69 percent of people would use virtual visits for at least some of their medical visits, the growth in virtual medical appointments has never quite reached its potential. There seemed to be a number of reasons for the slow adoption of virtual health services: the provincial health services were hesitant to reimburse for virtual visits, patients and doctors were reluctant to embrace a practice that wasn't face to face, and older patients weren't comfortable with the technology required for a virtual visit.

The pandemic caused health care providers to rethink the whole telehealth movement, and things moved swiftly. Along with a number of established providers like Equinoxe and Ask the Doctor, the number of mobile health apps has grown exponentially to over 325,000 apps available on app stores today. Telus, a Western Canada-based telecommunications company, had been preparing for this moment for years with its Telus Health Initiatives. Akira by TELUS Health has been used by benefits providers to their members for a number of years and seemed to be a good urgent care solution for minor issues, prescription refills, and lab test requisitions. The growth of virtual health services was slowly growing, but there was no trigger for mass adoption of the services until 2020.

The COVID-19 pandemic in 2020 changed everything. Government health providers like Alberta Health Services changed gears and encouraged medical practitioners to provide virtual visits and compensated them accordingly. Telus was prepared for this eventuality and introduced Babylon by TELUS Health to the citizens of Alberta in partnership with Alberta Health Services. Babylon is a free health care app that allows patients to check symptoms, consult with doctors, and access health care records. Babylon also uses AI to assist doctors in triaging and diagnosing their patients. The governments of British Columba and Alberta are encouraging people to use this app during the pandemic in order to reduce travel and stop the spread of the coronavirus. Costs are covered through the provincial health insurance plans. In April 2020, the message on the site read, "Please note we are experiencing high demand for consults and are doing our best to serve all of our patients as soon as possible."

This shows how important it is to have a new product development strategy within every organization. Marketers need to be on top of external trends to ensure that new product concepts not only consider those external opportunities but also exploit internal company strengths. Being prepared helps, but being in the right place at the right time is the secret. ●

Questions

1. Many patients are now trying out virtual health apps that they would have been hesitant in the past to try? Do you think this will be a permanent change to the way health care is delivered?

2. Can you think of any other products or services that flourish in time of emergencies?

3. Can you think of other health care innovations that are needed to deal with large-scale pandemics?

Figure 8–7
Avoiding new product failure

Why New Products and Services Fail	
Issue	**Potential Solution**
Insignificant point of difference	• Determine a distinctive and meaningful point of difference for the target audience. • Conduct research with consumers and monitor competitors' products/activities.
Incomplete new concept definition	• Identify consumer insights and clearly define the product's features and benefits. • Develop a clear positioning.
Insufficient market attractiveness	• Identify a target market (with a need) that is large enough and has growth potential to support the product.
Poor execution of the marketing mix	• Ensure the 4 Ps—product (including brand name and package), price, promotion, distribution—are aligned and attractive to consumers. • Focus on gaining sufficient distribution to access consumers.
Bad timing	• Launch products when consumers are eager to purchase. • Monitor market conditions and competitor actions.

Approaches to New Product Development

Strategic Direction From a strategic point of view, companies can follow different approaches to growth (see Figure 8–8). It is somewhat dependent on the degree of risk and investment that companies are willing to take. The most common forms of growth take either a market penetration or product development slant, focusing on current consumers with promotional tactics (market penetration) or looking to develop a new product for these current consumers (product development). Higher-risk considerations include either a market development or diversification strategy, taking the more expensive approach of either targeting new markets with current products (market development) or moving into new arenas with totally new products (diversification). More information about these strategies is included in Chapter 15.

Company Structure Companies use different structures to encourage innovation. Some companies, such as True Büch, use internal teams and external customers to help get successful new products to consumers. Many companies use a cross-functional team-based approach that includes representation from many departments across an organization, including marketers, regulatory experts, product developers, quality assurance specialists, and sales.

> *New product development success ultimately requires the expertise of people with different specializations.*

Other companies may follow a more focused approach by centralizing product development responsibilities with one person (new product development manager) or to a full department. In other organizations, new product development is included in the role of the general marketer. In some instances, new venture teams are used to concentrate on all innovation projects for the company, which could include new products, new processes, or new business ventures.

Regardless of the formal structure, new product development success ultimately requires the expertise of people with different specializations and from varied backgrounds to ensure that the best product ideas are developed. These experts are either fully involved in the process from the start, or brought in along the way to contribute to the journey.

Product quality has hampered the commercial potential of hoverboards. Sales plummeted after product safety issues were discovered.
©B Christopher/Alamy Stock Photo

Figure 8–8
Strategic approaches to growth

Markets	Products	
	Current	New
Current	**Market Penetration**	**Product Development**
	Finding ways to make current products appeal to current customers	Reaching current customers with a new product
New	**Market Development**	**Diversification**
	Reaching new customers with a current product	Reaching new customers with a new product

The New Product Development Process

LO 5 In order to avoid expensive product failures, companies will use rigorous product development processes to minimize the risk. The **new product development process** includes the seven steps shown in Figure 8–9 and summarized in Figure 8–10, Today, many organizations use a formal Stage-Gate® process that focuses on the collection of data and analysis at each step in the process to determine whether the results are successful enough to justify proceeding to the next stage. If results cannot be improved, the project doesn't proceed to the next step, and product development is halted.[20]

Step 1: New Product Development Strategy
Having a clear definition and understanding of what you are trying to achieve with product innovation is one of the most important building blocks in the new product development process. A **new product development strategy** involves setting the new product strategic direction for the company as a whole, as well as the precise objectives for the innovation at hand. There must be consistency between the two.

An example can be seen with Apple and an interview with its CEO, Tim Cook, in 2018. He highlighted Apple's new product philosophy as coming down to two questions: Did we make a good product? Did we enrich people's lives? The company has faith that this strategy leads to results over the long haul. Apple now focuses on fewer ideas to things that matter. It wants to make products that give people the ability to do things they couldn't do before. Apple starts projects years before they come out, and it takes the time to get them right and patience

to wait until something is great, producing category-redefining products such as wireless AirPods, the Apple Watch, and the latest iPhone with facial recognition and high-quality cameras. Apple was recognized as the World's Most Innovative Company in 2018.[21]

True Büch is a company built on a foundation of innovation, and its goal is to concentrate on the ongoing development of new flavours that follow trends in health foods and botanicals that are gaining popularity.

Step 2: Idea Generation
Once the purpose and direction for the product development project is clarified, the second step of **idea generation** comes into play. Ideas can be generated from a number of sources and in a number of different ways. Ideas can come from inside or outside the company, depending on the organization's approach to new product development. Brainstorming sessions can be utilized, which focus on participants coming up with new ideas for the project at hand. It is important for these brainstorming sessions to include individuals who are creative, have varied experiences, and have differing areas of expertise. This should stimulate a more varied and interesting pool of ideas.

Brainstorming sessions can result in a host of interesting ideas, but for this approach to work, participants must be willing to share their most ridiculous or boring ideas with the group. Participants need to be open-minded, energetic, flexible, and willing to build on each other's ideas. Often, companies hire an outside moderator, skilled in these types of sessions, to promote creativity sessions that render results. Brainstorming is a key technique used by the founders of True Büch Kombucha to determine new flavours created.[22]

Cross-functional teams reduce new product development time.
©Rawpixel.com/Shutterstock

new product development process
Sequence of steps that a firm takes to develop a new product idea and take it to market.

new product development strategy
Setting the new product strategic direction for the company as a whole, and the precise objectives for the project at hand.

idea generation
Developing a pool of new product ideas.

Figure 8–9
Steps in the new product development process

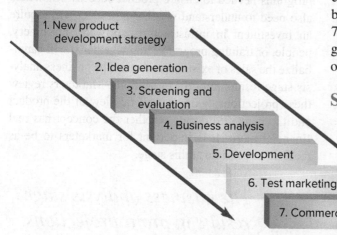

1. New product development strategy
2. Idea generation
3. Screening and evaluation
4. Business analysis
5. Development
6. Test marketing
7. Commercialization

discovering that some children thought the pods were candy and tried to eat them. How successful has Tide Pods been for P&G? After its first year, the product garnered a 73 percent share of the "unit dose" segment of the detergent market on estimated sales of $500 million—making it one of the company's most successful product launches![23]

Step 3: Screening and Evaluation
The third stage of the new product development process, **screening and evaluation**, attempts to reduce the array of product ideas down to a manageable list of promising concepts. Ideas are initially screened internally by the new product development team, which eliminates ideas that do not meet the objectives, as well as those that are clearly not technically feasible. The short list of ideas is then further developed by the product development team into concepts. A concept is a more detailed idea, written in consumer terms, with enough detail for consumers to fully understand. Consumers are presented with a short descriptive paragraph and an accompanying visual, which could be a sketch, mock-up, or promotional piece. They are then asked for feedback.

Concept tests are external evaluations of the new product idea, rather than the actual product itself. Several key issues are addressed during concept testing, such as how the customer perceives the product, who would use it, and how it would be used. The purpose of these evaluations is to get feedback on the strengths and weaknesses of the concepts and to

> **screening and evaluation**
> Reduces the list of ideas down to a list of promising concepts.
>
> **concept tests**
> External evaluations of a new product idea, rather than the actual product itself.

Valuable input can be obtained from customers and suppliers. Sales or purchasing personnel can talk to their customers to pinpoint unmet needs. Customers also feed their suggestions into companies through customer service and social media channels. Many companies invest in consumer research, focused on coming up with new product ideas. This input should be considered for future product development. Customers are the ones using a company's product, and they have a good understanding of potential improvements.

P&G spends billions of dollars each year on product research and development. A significant additional investment is made in consumer research, with an eye to generating ideas for product innovation. In 2012, with a $150-million marketing budget, P&G launched Tide Pods. Tide Pods are a revolutionary three-chamber liquid dose of Tide that cleans, fights stains, and brightens. Following its successful launch, P&G redesigned its packaging after

Figure 8–10
Elements in each stage of the new product development process

Stage of Process	Purpose of Stage	Marketing Information and Methods Used
New product development strategy	Identify new-product development focus that meets company objectives	Company objectives; SWOT analysis of company/product/brand
Idea generation	Brainstorm new ideas	Ideas from employees, co-workers, and consumers
Screening and evaluation	Evaluate product ideas and develop concepts	Internal evaluation of technical requirements, external concept tests
Business analysis	Identify the product's features and its marketing strategy, and make financial projections	Product's key features and anticipated marketing mix; assessment of production, legal, and profitability issues
Test marketing	Test the product and marketing strategy in the marketplace on a limited scale (if necessary)	Test marketing in defined areas
Development	Create the prototype and test it internally at the company and externally with consumers	Internal company assessments and external tests on product prototypes
Commercialization	Launch and fully market the product in the marketplace	Implement all areas of the marketing mix; possible regional rollout

Procter & Gamble's new Tide Pods launch shows how it has improved both planning and implementation by involving consumers earlier in its innovation activities.
©McGraw-Hill Education/Mike Hruby

understand what further modifications are required. Concept tests will result in some concepts being eliminated and others surfacing as more-promising opportunities that require further investigation.

True Büch Kombucha conducts taste tests and shelf-life testing to determine which products to produce and introduce into the market.[24]

Step 4: Business Analysis

After the concept tests have determined which product, or line of products, are strong new product candidates, the **business analysis** step is necessary. This involves determining financial projections on bringing the new product to market and selling it in the future. Typical financial projections for a new product cover a three-year period and often look five years into the future.

At this point in the new product development process, marketers are checking the commercial viability of the new product. This requires strong analytical skills and the ability to understand the dynamics of the market. Marketers need to initially establish the positioning of the product in the market and what marketing elements are needed for a successful launch. The new product is also studied to determine whether it can, and should, be protected with a patent, trademark, or copyright. A marketer must also be able to anticipate competitive reactions and foresee target market needs.

The business analysis step requires marketers to determine market share projections, price points, cost parameters, special discounts, distribution requirements,

business analysis
Financial projections on the impact of bringing the new product to market and selling it in the future.

development
The new product idea is turned into a prototype for further consumer research and manufacturing tests.

test marketing
Offering a new product for sale on a limited basis in a defined geographic area to assess its success.

research needs, and all the marketing communication programs needed to ensure product success. Marketers also need to understand whether a product will require an investment in infrastructure, software, machinery, people, or training programs, and whether it will cannibalize the sales of existing products. The business analysis stage results in profit projections. Marketers review these projections, taking a realistic view of the product and the market to decide whether the concept has real financial merit. It is important for marketers to be as realistic as possible at this stage.

> ❝ *The business analysis stage results in profit projections.*

If the product can meet sales, profit, and market share targets, then the new product development process will continue to the next step. If not, marketers may reassess the concept, going back to consumers to conduct further research. This is usually the last checkpoint before significant resources are invested in creating a prototype, a full-scale operating model of the product.

Step 5: Development

New product ideas that survive the business analysis step proceed to actual **development**, turning the idea into a prototype for further consumer research and manufacturing tests. This step is considerably complex, involving laboratory and consumer tests to ensure that the product consistently meets legal and quality control requirements. Manufacturing trials are also conducted to eliminate manufacturing problems and to reduce costs.

This step can be time-consuming, with some products requiring extensive testing before they can be safely brought to market. Pharmaceutical products, children's toys, cars, and food products are examples that fall into this category.

The advantage of the development step is that it allows marketers to take actual product prototypes into consumer research or show them to potential buyers. This provides a platform to probe preliminary sales strategies with key accounts or marketing ideas with consumers.

Step 6: Test Marketing

Test marketing involves offering a product for sale on a limited basis in a defined geographic area. This test is done to determine whether consumers will actually buy the product, and to what extent. Marketers may use this opportunity to test different marketing approaches to support the product.

> *To minimize the risk of financial failure, many companies use regional rollouts.*

There are several cities in Canada that are used regularly as test markets for a variety of different products/services. Test-marketing is often conducted in cities such as London, Ontario; Edmonton, Alberta; and Barrie, Ontario. Test cities tend to be under 1 million in population and need to be similar culturally to the rest of the country, with a variety of socio-economic backgrounds represented, making them representative of Canada in general. Using tracking systems by firms such as Nielsen, marketers can try to correlate local advertising campaigns to in-store purchases by using data from store scanners. McDonald's Chicken McNuggets and Tim Hortons® Dark Roast coffee were tested in London, Ontario, before being launched throughout Canada.[25]

The main drawbacks of test markets are that they are expensive to conduct, and they immediately alert the competition. Competitors can easily sabotage test markets by altering their own pricing and marketing support to render the test market unsuccessful. These issues are so real that many marketers do not embark on test markets, relying instead on research to provide good direction for a full product launch.

Technology is assisting marketers by creating simulated test markets through a number of software programs. An emerging trend uses virtual reality testing to allow marketers to present consumers with a range of experiences such as simulated store environments. Ipsos is an example of a reputable market research firm that conducts simulated test marketing services for its clients.

Step 7: Commercialization

Commercialization is the step when the new product is brought to market with full-scale production, sales, and marketing support. Companies proceed very carefully at the commercialization stage because this is the most expensive stage for most new products. To minimize the risk of financial failure, many companies use regional rollouts, introducing the product sequentially into geographic areas of the country to allow production levels and marketing activities to build gradually. Grocery product manufacturers and some telecommunication service providers are examples of firms that use this strategy.

Marketing plays a crucial role in the success of a new product, and marketers need to intimately understand their consumers and what is important to their purchase decisions. Each element of the marketing mix needs to be carefully crafted to help make a new product successful.

commercialization
When the new product is brought to market with full-scale production, sales, and marketing support.

ask YOURSELF

1. *What are the main reasons that new products fail?*

2. *What occurs in the screening and evaluation step of the new product development process?*

3. *What is the purpose of the business analysis step in the new product development process?*

4. *What are the advantages and disadvantages of a test market?*

McDonald's Chicken McNuggets and Tim Hortons® Dark Roast coffee were tested in London, Ontario.
Tim Hortons®

LO 1
- Product life cycles are the stages that a new product goes through from its initial introduction through to growth, maturity, and decline.
- The shape of a product life cycle varies depending on the industry, the competition, technological innovation, and the marketing of the product.

LO 2
- Product life cycles can be extended through various marketing techniques that encourage new and current users to keep purchasing the product and to use it in new ways.
- Extending a product life cycle can be done by following one or a combination of these approaches: (1) modifying the product, (2) modifying the market, (3) repositioning a product, and (4) introducing a new product.

LO 3
- There are many types of new products, ranging from slight product modifications, to more innovative changes, to the more radical innovations that we see in the market. We term these minor innovations, continuous innovations, and radical innovations.

LO 4
- The adoption curve shows the sequential diffusion and acceptance of an innovation into the market by consumers. It categorizes people into five groupings: innovators, early adopters, early majority, late majority, and laggards.

LO 5
- The new product development process follows seven steps: (1) new product development strategy, (2) idea generation, (3) screening and evaluation, (4) business analysis, (5) development, (6) test marketing, and (7) commercialization.

key terms and concepts... A REFRESHER

adoption curve
business analysis
commercialization
concept tests
continuous innovations
delete
development

fad
fashion product
harvest
high-learning product
idea generation
line extension
low-learning product

minor innovations
new product development process
new product development strategy
product life cycle
radical innovations
screening and evaluation
test marketing

hands-on... APPLY YOUR KNOWLEDGE

New Product Development Assignment Review this chapter's opening vignette on True Büch Kombucha and gather additional information about this and other products in this category by going online to visit brand websites and social media sites. Also, review the latest news in this category. Present your ideas on how the online environment can be used to market True Büch Kombucha to consumers.

chapter vignette... ACTIVITY

This chapter's opening vignette explains the development and launch of True Büch Kombucha. True Büch used brainstorming as an important technique to come up with some of the initial ideas for its kombucha flavours. Conduct a brainstorming session with a group of fellow students and come up with a list of at least 15 different ideas for future products for True Büch Kombucha.

infographic... DATA ANALYSIS

Review the Infographic titled "Top 5 Tech Trends for 2020." Pick an industry that you are interested in. Research some of the latest innovations impacting that industry. What specific consumer need/challenge do you believe is addressed by this innovation? How is innovation in the industry impacted by the top tech trends? What are further opportunities for innovation in the industry, utilizing new, developing technology?

Pricing

L aws and regulations are in place to protect consumers and promote fair pricing. Price fixing, deceptive pricing, predatory pricing and price discrimination are prominent considerations businesses should be aware of.

©Parilov/Shutterstock

CHAPTER OUTLINE

- Cutting prices
- Nature and importance of price
- General pricing approaches
- Estimating demand and revenue
- Determining cost, volume, and profit relationships
- Pricing objectives and constraints
- Setting a final price

Stanley Cup champions, television personalities, and C-suite business executives all try to take care of their appearance. As far back as the Roman Empire, short haircuts were a requirement for legionaries. When a good barber or hairstylist is found, most clients show long-term loyalty if they receive great service and a quality result.

The Barber's Chair specializes in men's hairstyles and promotes a modern experience. Nick Sano, owner of The Barber's Chair, shares, "Although men's hairstyles are oftentimes considerably less complicated than women's hairstyles, both men and women deserve service and style."

Sano describes men's hairstyles as being more versatile today. Short, long, textured, and coloured, the latest trends for hairstyles are endless. However, finding the trend that looks best can be challenging. With age, style, and fashion sense playing a large part in which hairstyle suits each individual, the professionals at The Barber's Chair share expertise and guidance to ensure clients have the modern touch.

"This is not your grandfather's barber shop," explains Sano. Years of training have allowed the stylists to suit facial features and personal style. The experienced team of professionals provides personal attention and concern for their clients.

The experience provided by the organization's hairstyling professionals seems over and above what a traditional barber shop will offer. Even with additional features and benefits, The Barber's Chair uses at-market pricing for its clients. "We realize that men's hairstyles are more diverse and liberated than ever before, with long hair being just as acceptable as short styles, and colour being used for visual appeal rather than a practical function for covering greys," says Sano. "We know we add value to our clients' experience, so we want to price fairly and earn repeat business." The Barber's Chair long-term focus shows its understanding of customer lifetime value (discussed in more detail in Chapter 14).

The experience provided by The Barber's Chair helps address the unique elements of service (discussed in more detail in Chapter 8). Sano illustrates the element of inseparability as clients travel across the Canada to be served by him. "I have had clients travel across Canada for an appointment with me," shares Sano. His ability to provide a consistent, quality result makes his services sought after.

The Competition Act prohibits the practice of price discrimination—that is, different prices charged to different customers for the same or very similar goods. When asked about men's and women's hairstyles, Sano shares, "We will cut a man's or woman's hair at The Barber's Chair, but we let them know that we specialize in men's hairstyles." That way, everyone receives the same service and same price. Treating people fairly and providing quality results has served this business well for the past 25 years.[1]

CHAPTER FEATURES

Cutting Prices
How a barber uses pricing strategies to stay competitive in the marketplace.

Growing Food Prices
Rising food prices have an impact to the consumer.

Highlighting the Value of Services
H&R Block offers Canadians free online tax preparation software to help highlight the value of its tax experts.

Fixing Prices to Save Bread
Learn how Canada's Competition Bureau addresses illegal practices like price fixing.

Uber Profitable
Exploring how Uber has disrupted the transportation industry through pricing and convenience.

reality CHECK ⊘

As you read Chapter 9, refer back to this opening vignette to answer the following questions:
- Why do you believe The Barber's Chair is using at-market pricing?
- What services do you believe clients will make extra efforts to receive service from a particular provider?

Nature and Importance of Price

LO 1 The price paid for goods and services goes by many names. You pay *tuition* for your education, *rent* for an apartment, *interest* on a bank credit card, and a *premium* for car insurance. Your dentist or physician charges you a *fee*, a professional or social organization charges *dues*, and airlines charge a *fare*. And what you pay for clothes or a haircut is termed a *price*.

Price has many implications for marketing. Beyond it being a key element of the 4 Ps of the marketing mix, marketers need to know how pricing impacts their target markets, competitors, and demand.

What Is a Price?

From a marketing viewpoint, *price* is the money or other considerations, including other goods and services, exchanged for the ownership or use of a product. For example, Wilkinson Sword could exchange some of its knives for advertising that promotes its razor blades. This practice of exchanging goods and services for other goods and services rather than for money is called barter. Barter transactions account for billions of dollars annually in domestic and international trade.

For most products, money is exchanged. Generally, consumers focus on purchasing necessities first. Prices for necessities increase with inflation. As seen in the Infographic, "2019 Food Pricing Forecasts," certain foods can increase drastically over time. When prices of necessities rise, consumers have less to spend on other products. Furthermore, how much money is paid is not always consistent with the list, or quoted, price because of discounts, allowances, and extra fees. While discounts, allowances, and rebates make the effective price lower, other marketing tactics raise the real price. One pricing tactic is to use "special fees" and "surcharges." This practice is driven by consumers' zeal for low prices combined with the ease of making price comparisons online. Buyers are more willing to pay extra fees than a higher list price, so sellers use add-on charges as a way of having the consumer pay more without raising the

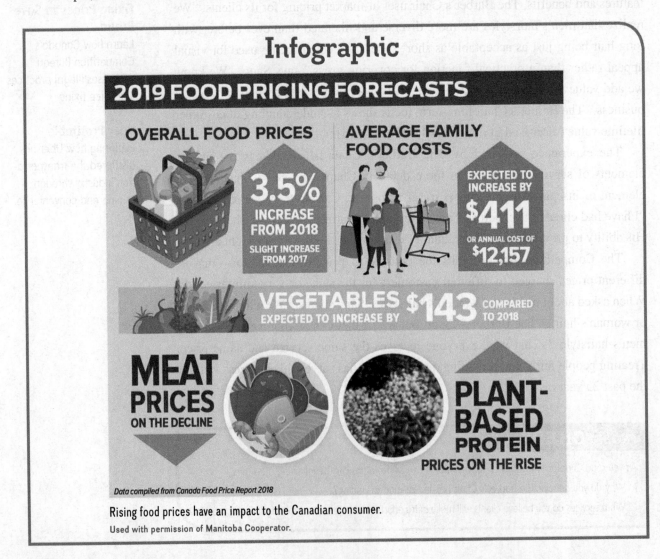

Infographic

2019 FOOD PRICING FORECASTS

OVERALL FOOD PRICES
3.5% INCREASE FROM 2018
SLIGHT INCREASE FROM 2017

AVERAGE FAMILY FOOD COSTS
EXPECTED TO INCREASE BY **$411**
OR ANNUAL COST OF **$12,157**

VEGETABLES EXPECTED TO INCREASE BY $143 COMPARED TO 2018

MEAT PRICES ON THE DECLINE

PLANT-BASED PROTEIN PRICES ON THE RISE

Data compiled from Canada Food Price Report 2018

Rising food prices have an impact to the Canadian consumer.

Used with permission of Manitoba Cooperator.

Figure 9–1
The price of three different purchases

Price Equation				
Item Purchased	**Price**	**= List Price**	**– Incentives and Allowances**	**+ Extra Fees**
New car bought by an individual	Final price	= List price	– Rebate – Cash discount – Old car trade-in	+ Financing charges + Special accessories + Destination charges
Term in university bought by a student	Tuition	= Published tuition	– Scholarship – Other financial aid	+ Special activity fees
Merchandise bought from a wholesaler by a retailer	Invoice price	= List price	– Quantity discount – Cash discount – Seasonal discount – Functional or trade discount	+ Penalty for late payment

list price. Consider this when you purchase a cellphone. Examples of such special fees may include a "system licensing charge" or "911 emergency service access charge" that increase the monthly cellphone bill. You may also encounter an environmental surcharge on new tires and batteries for cars in some provinces.

The different factors that increase or decrease the price are put together in a *price equation*, which is shown for several different products in Figure 9–1.

Suppose that you decide you want to buy a Bugatti Veyron, the world's fastest production car, which can move you from 0 to 100 km/h in 2.5 seconds, with a top speed of 422 km/h. The Veyron has a list price of $2.5 million, but you want the clear-coat paint option, so it will cost an extra $430,000. An extended warranty will add an additional $70,000 to the cost. However, if you put $500,000 down now and finance the balance over the next year, you will receive a rebate of $50,000 off the list

price. For your 2016 Honda Civic DX 4-door sedan that has 100,000 kilometres and is in fair condition, you are given a trade-in allowance of $5,000. Assume another $300,000 for additional taxes and charges. Finally, your total finance charge at an annual interest rate of 5 percent over a five-year period is $378,640.[2]

Applying the price equation (as shown in Figure 9–1) to your purchase, your final price is as follows:

$$
\begin{aligned}
\text{Final price} &= \text{List price} - (\text{Incentives} + \text{Allowances}) \\
&\quad + \text{Extra fees} \\
&= \$2{,}500{,}000 - (\$500{,}000 + \$50{,}000 \\
&\quad + \$5{,}000) + (\$430{,}000 + \$70{,}000 \\
&\quad + \$300{,}000 + \$378{,}640) \\
&= \$3{,}173{,}640
\end{aligned}
$$

Are you still interested in buying this car? If so, put yourself on the waiting list.

Consider all the costs when purchasing items like the Bugatti Veyron.
©culture-images GmbH/Alamy

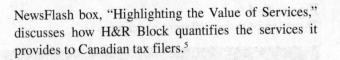

Price as an Indicator of Value

value
The ratio of perceived benefits to price.

profit equation
Profit = total revenue - total cost.

From a consumer's standpoint, price is often used to indicate value when it is compared with the perceived benefits of a product or service, such as quality, durability, and so on. Specifically, **value** is the ratio of perceived benefits to price,[3] or

$$\text{Value} = \frac{\text{Perceived benefits}}{\text{Price}}$$

This relationship shows that for a given price, as perceived benefits increase, value increases. If you can purchase a medium or a large pizza for $13.99, which pizza would you choose? Would having more pizza to eat be more valuable? Many marketers often engage in the practice of *value pricing*—increasing product or service benefits while maintaining or decreasing price. McDonald's understands the importance of price to consumers and launched its McValue® Menu which has evolved into Value Picks®. McDonald's Extra Value Meal combinations show how lowering prices can increase the value of to a consumer.

Marketers must be careful when using price as an indicator of value. For example, for many consumers, a low price would imply poor quality, and ultimately, poor perceived value. This is particularly true for services. For example, what would be your perception of a dentist who charges only $25 for a checkup and cleaning, when the average dentist charges between $150 and $200? Consumers make comparative value assessments, so it is important for marketers to know what their competitors are charging.

In a survey of home-furnishing buyers, 84 percent agreed with the statement, "The higher the price, the higher the quality." In turn, firms may use high prices to signify high quality.[4] For example, Kohler introduced a walk-in bathtub that is safer for children and the elderly. Although priced higher than conventional step-in bathtubs, it has proven very successful because buyers are willing to pay more for what they perceive as the benefit of extra safety. The Marketing

McDonald's increases value to consumers by reducing the overall price of food items purchased in a combo.
©Steve Stock/Alamy Stock Photo

NewsFlash box, "Highlighting the Value of Services," discusses how H&R Block quantifies the services it provides to Canadian tax filers.[5]

Price in the Marketing Mix

Pricing is a critical decision made by a marketing executive because price has a direct effect on a firm's profits. This is apparent from a firm's **profit equation**:

$$\text{Profit} = \text{Total revenue} - \text{Total cost}$$
$$= (\text{Unit price} \times \text{Quantity sold}) - \text{Total cost}$$

What makes this relationship even more complicated is that price affects the quantity sold, as illustrated with demand curves later in this chapter, because the quantity sold sometimes affects a firm's costs because of efficiency of production, price also indirectly affects costs. Thus, pricing decisions influence both total revenue (sales) and total cost, which makes pricing one of the most important decisions marketing executives face.

> *Pricing decisions influence both total revenue (sales) and total cost, which makes pricing one of the most important decisions marketing executives face.*

General Pricing Approaches

LO 2 A key to a marketing manager's setting a final price for a product is to find an "approximate price level" to use as a reasonable starting point. Four common approaches to helping find this approximate price level are demand-oriented, cost-oriented, profit-oriented, and competition-oriented approaches (see Figure 9–2). Although these approaches are discussed separately below, some of them overlap, and an effective marketing manager will consider several in searching for an approximate price level.

Highlighting the Value of Services

The value of professional services and advice is difficult to quantify. A financial professional's recommendation may save consumers money; however, the knowledge, conversation, and expertise involved in that recommendation may be difficult for a consumer to value. H&R Block's unique pricing strategy with its online tax software helps it showcase the value of its tax experts.

Historically, there are numerous quotations and discussions about the certainty, dread, or complexity of taxation. In Canada, taxpayers search for options and evaluate alternatives for filing their personal and business taxes by their respective April deadlines. Whether they are students, professors, business professionals, or retired, Canadians who seek help for tax preparation services have a number of different options. After careful evaluation of their alternatives, Canadians remain loyal to only a few of them. Tax preparers who have discovered the correct strategy for effective pricing have realized the lifetime value of their clients.

Value involves a relationship with perceived benefits and price, and effective marketers use this to their advantage. In H&R Block's case, the value of the company's tax experts is seen through the exceptional services they provide their clients. H&R Block manages tax preparations services across more than 1,100 offices across Canada. The company's headquarters is in Calgary, Alberta, and it has had experience with Canadian tax returns for over 50 years.

What makes the organization successful and sustainable is its ability to see trends in its industry and act on them. There are approximately 11 million do-it-yourself tax filers among the 28 million Canadians tax filers. As technology helps enable the process of tax filing, it is important for H&R Block to provide services that offer perceived benefits in a technology-rich environment.

Todd McCallum, vice president, products and services encapsulates the strategy: "Our 100% free guarantee is now available to users of our online and download tax software. We believe if Canadians want to file their own taxes—whether doing them online or with downloadable desktop software—they should be able to do so for free. And while there are other programs that claim to be free, we believe we are the only provider in Canada whose free is 100 percent guaranteed across all provinces, in English and French."

By providing free online tax software, H&R Block provides a service to do-it-yourselfers who believe they

H&R Block helps Canadian tax filers through over 1,100 offices across the country.
Used by permission of H&R Block

can complete their taxes on their own. In addition to the free service are options for do-it-yourselfers that include having H&R Block tax experts review the returns prior to filing. H&R Block has thus enhanced the value of tax experts by showcasing the perceived benefits for Canadians that include the benefit of potential for more accurate and better returns. ●

Questions

1. Given your experience with taxes and your stage in life, would you choose H&R Block's free online software or tax preparation service? Why?

2. Can you think of a product in a different industry that may offer a service for free in order to increase the value of the product?

Demand-Oriented Approaches

Demand-oriented approaches emphasize factors underlying expected customer tastes and preferences more than such factors as cost, profit, and competition when selecting a price level.

Skimming Pricing A firm introducing a new product can use *skimming pricing*, setting the highest initial price that those customers really desiring the product are willing to pay. These customers are not very price-sensitive because they weigh the new product's

Figure 9–2
Four approaches for selecting an approximate price level

Demand-oriented approaches	Cost-oriented approaches	Profit-oriented approaches	Competition-oriented approaches
• Skimming • Penetration • Prestige • Odd-even • Target • Bundle • Yield management	• Standard markup • Cost-plus	• Target profit • Target return on sales • Target return on investment	• Customary • Above, at, or below market • Loss leader

price, quality, and ability to satisfy their needs against the same characteristics of substitutes. As the demand of these customers is satisfied, the firm lowers the price to attract a more price-sensitive segment. Thus, skimming pricing gets its name from skimming successive layers of "cream," or customer segments, as prices are lowered in a series of steps.

In early 2003, many manufacturers of flat-screen TVs were pricing them at about $5,000 and using skimming pricing because many prospective customers were willing to buy the product immediately at the high price. Generally, prices of flat-screen TVs have dropped over time; however, retailers of TVs featuring new technology or larger screens continue to use skimming pricing.

Penetration Pricing   Setting a lower, more affordable, initial price on a new product to appeal immediately to the mass market is *penetration pricing*, the exact opposite of skimming pricing. This strategy makes sense when consumers are price-sensitive; Nintendo consciously chose a penetration strategy when it introduced the Nintendo Wii, its popular video game console. It continues to use the strategy with Nintendo Wii U.

Nintendo used penetration-pricing strategy to introduce its Wii video game console and its Wii U home console, and its Nintendo Switch (shown here).

©Kazuhiro Nogi/AFP/Getty Images

In addition to offering the potential to build sales, market share, and profits, penetration pricing discourages competitors from entering the market because the profit margin is relatively low. Furthermore, if the costs to produce drop because of the accumulated volume, competitors that enter the market will face higher unit costs, at least until their volume catches up with the early entrant. Walmart comes to mind when one thinks about penetration pricing. The same holds true for the very successful chain Dollarama, which is constantly increasing its number of stores in Canada.

In some situations, penetration pricing may follow skimming pricing. A company might price a product high in the early stages of the product life cycle to attract price-insensitive consumers. After the company has earned back the money spent on research and development and introductory promotions, it uses penetration pricing in the later stages of the product life cycle to appeal to a broader segment of the population and increase market share.[6]

Prestige Pricing   Although consumers tend to buy more of a product when the price is lower, sometimes the reverse is true. If consumers are using price as a measure of the quality of an item, a company runs the risk of appearing to offer a low-quality product if it sets the price below a certain point. *Prestige pricing* involves setting a high price so that quality- or status-conscious consumers are attracted to the product and buy it. Rolls-Royce cars, Chanel perfume, and Cartier jewellery have an element of prestige pricing in them and may not sell as well at lower prices than at higher ones.[7]

The higher the price of a prestige product, the greater the status associated with it and the greater its exclusivity, because fewer people can afford to buy it. Unlike products such as flat-panel TVs, which have decreased in price over the product life cycle, prices of prestige products remain high throughout the product life cycle.

An example of prestige pricing is the All Day Heels® collection of women's high-heeled shoes developed by

Canadian retailer Ron White. This fashionable line of women's shoes combines elegance as well as comfort. The All Day Heels collection is set at a high price that matches its superior quality. The shoes provide arch support, built-in cushioning materials, and thin lightweight insoles made of Poron, a flexible high-tech elastic polymer developed by NASA.

Price Lining

Often, a firm that is selling not just a single product but a line of products may price them at a number of different specific pricing points, which is called *price lining*. For example, a discount department store manager may price a line of women's dresses at $59, $79, and $99. In some instances, all the items may be purchased at the same cost and then marked up to different percentages to achieve these price points, based on colour, style, and expected demand. In other instances, manufacturers design products for different price points, and retailers apply approximately the same markup percentages to achieve the three price points offered to consumers.

Odd-Even Pricing

If you are in hardware store, you may see a mitre saw for $399.99. In a grocery store, you may find Windex glass cleaner for $2.97. These firms are using *odd-even pricing*, which involves setting prices a few dollars or cents under an even number. The presumption is that consumers see the mitre saw as priced at "something over $300" rather than "about $400." The effect this strategy has is psychological: $399.99 *feels* significantly lower than $400—even though there is only one cent difference. There is some evidence to suggest this does work. However, research suggests that overuse of odd-ending prices tends to mute its effect on demand.[8]

Target Pricing

Manufacturers will sometimes estimate the price that the ultimate consumer would be willing to pay for a product. They then work backward through markups taken by retailers and wholesalers to determine what price they can charge for the product. This practice, called *target pricing*, results in the manufacturer deliberately adjusting the composition and features of a product to achieve the target price to consumers.

Bundle Pricing

A frequently used demand-oriented pricing practice is *bundle pricing*, which is the marketing of two or more products in a single "package" price. For example, Air Canada offers vacation packages that include airfare, car rental, and hotel. Bundle pricing is based on the idea that consumers value the package more than the individual items. This is due to benefits received from not having to make separate purchases as well as increased satisfaction from one item in the presence of another. Bundle pricing often provides a lower total cost to buyers and lower marketing costs to sellers.[9]

Yield Management Pricing

Have you ever been on an airplane and discovered the person next to you paid a lower price for her ticket than you paid? Annoying, isn't it? But what you observed is *yield management pricing*, the charging of different prices to maximize revenue for a set amount of capacity at any given time.[10] Airlines, hotels, and car rental firms engage in capacity management by varying prices based on time, day, week, or season to match demand and supply.

Cost-Oriented Approaches

With cost-oriented approaches, a price is more affected by the cost side of the pricing problem than the demand side. Price is set by looking at the production and marketing costs and then adding enough to cover direct expenses, overhead, and profit. The chapter-opening vignette about Be Sweet Inc. highlights the importance of managing production and marketing costs.

Standard Markup Pricing

In order to make a profit, firms sell their products at a price that exceeds their costs of producing or sourcing the items and the costs of marketing them. Conventionally, the difference between the selling price of an item and its cost is referred to as the **markup**, and this is normally expressed as a percentage. Markup is also often referred to as gross margin.

Manufacturers commonly express markup as a percentage of cost, which is the difference between selling price and cost, divided by cost. This is also referred to as *standard markup*. Manufacturers use this approach because they are concerned most of the time with costs.

> **markup**
> The difference between selling price and cost, usually expressed as a percentage of cost.

Airlines use yield management pricing to help fill empty seats.
©Claudio zaccherini/Shutterstock

Figure 9–3
Markup examples

Markup Table Based on Selling Price		
	$	%
Selling price	$75.00	100%*
– (minus) Cost	$60.00	80%
= (equals) Markup	$15.00	20%

Markup Table Based on Cost		
	$	%
Selling price	$72.00	120%
– (minus) Cost	$60.00	100%**
= (equals) Markup	$12.00	20%

* Price is always 100 percent when markup is relative to price.

** Cost is always 100 percent when markup is relative to cost.

Parties who buy and resell products—for example, wholesalers and retailers—are nearly always dealing with selling prices. They often express markup as a percentage of price, which is the difference between selling price and cost, divided by the selling price. Using the same markup percentage for both of the above approaches will result in a different selling price (see the example in Figure 9–3).

Consider the example of a product that is produced by a manufacturer and sold to a wholesaler, who in turn sells it to a retailer, who then sells it to a consumer. The product will be subjected to a series of markups as shown below:

Manufacturer's cost:	**$50.00**
Markup % (based on manufacturer's cost):	40%
Markup $:	$20.00
Selling price to wholesaler:	**$70.00**
Wholesaler cost:	**$70.00**
Markup % (based on selling price to retailer):	15%
Markup $:	$12.35
Selling price to retailer:	**$82.35**
Retailer cost:	**$82.35**
Markup % (based on retailer selling price):	35%
Markup $:	$44.34
Retailer selling price:	**$126.69**

This may surprise you to find out that a product costing $50 to produce can end up costing a consumer more than twice that much when bought at a retailer, but this is not unusual. It is important to remember that markup is necessary at each stage so that companies involved can cover their costs of purchasing the item, can pay to market it to the next stage in the distribution channel, and can generate some profit. The markups shown would be representative of some items such as designer furniture.

This percentage markup varies depending on the type of retail store (such as furniture, clothing, or grocery) and on the product involved. High-volume products usually have smaller markups than do low-volume products. Supermarkets such as Loblaws and Sobeys mark up staple items such as sugar, flour, and dairy products 10 to 25 percent, whereas they mark up discretionary items such as snack foods and candy 25 to 47 percent. These markups must cover all expenses of the store, pay for overhead costs, and contribute something to profits. For supermarkets, these markups, which may appear very large, can result in only a 1 percent profit on sales revenue.

Cost-Plus Pricing Many manufacturers, professional services, and construction firms use a variation of standard markup pricing. *Cost-plus pricing* involves summing the total unit cost of providing a product or service and adding a specific amount to the cost to arrive at a price. Cost-plus pricing is the most commonly used method to set prices for business products.[11] Increasingly, however, this method is finding favour among business-to-business marketers in the service sector. For example, the rising cost of legal fees has prompted some law firms to adopt a cost-plus pricing approach. Rather than billing business clients on an hourly basis, lawyers and their clients agree on a fixed fee based on expected costs plus a profit for the law firm. Many advertising agencies now use this approach. Here, the client agrees to pay the agency a fee based on the cost of its work plus some agreed-on profit.[12]

Profit-Oriented Approaches

A company may choose to balance both revenues and costs to set price using profit-oriented approaches. These might involve either setting a target of a specific dollar volume of profit or expressing this target profit as a percentage of sales or investment.

Target Profit Pricing When a firm sets an annual target of a specific dollar amount of profit, this is called *target profit pricing*. For example, if you owned a picture frame store and wanted to achieve a target profit of $7,000 in the coming year, how much would you need to charge for each frame? Because profit depends on revenues and costs, you would have to know your costs and then estimate how many frames you would sell. Let's assume, based on sales in previous years, you expect to frame 1,000 pictures next year. The cost of your time and materials to frame an average picture is $22, while your overhead expenses (rent, manager salaries, and so on) are $26,000. Finally, your goal is to achieve a profit of $7,000. How do you calculate your price per picture?

$$\text{Profit} = \text{Total revenue} - \text{Total costs}$$
$$= (\text{Pictures sold} \times \text{Price/picture})$$
$$- [(\text{Cost/picture} \times \text{Pictures sold})$$
$$+ \text{overhead cost}]$$

Solving for price per picture, the equation becomes:

$$\text{Price/picture} = \frac{\text{Profit} + [(\text{Cost/picture} \times \text{Pictures sold}) + \text{overhead costs}]}{\text{Pictures sold}}$$

$$= \frac{\$7,000 + [(\$22 \times 1,000) + \$26,000]}{1,000}$$

$$= \frac{\$7,000 + \$48,000}{1,000}$$

$$= \$55 \text{ per picture}$$

Clearly, this pricing method depends on an accurate estimate of demand. Because demand is often difficult to predict, this method has the potential for disaster if the estimate is too high. Generally, a target profit pricing strategy is best for firms offering new or unique products, without a lot of competition. What if other frame stores in your area were charging $40 per framed picture? As a marketing manager, you'd have to offer increased customer value with your more expensive frames, lower your costs, or settle for less profit.

Target Return-on-Sales Pricing Firms such as supermarkets often use *target return-on-sales pricing* to set prices that will give them a profit that is a specified percentage—say, 1 percent—of the sales volume. This pricing method is often used because of the difficulty in establishing a benchmark of sales or investment to show how much of a firm's effort is needed to achieve the target.

Items on a supermarket shelf may be priced using target return-on-sales pricing.
©MBI/Alamy Stock Photos

Target Return-on-Investment Pricing Firms such as General Motors and many public utilities use *target return-on-investment pricing* to set prices to achieve a return-on-investment (ROI) target, such as a percentage that is mandated by its board of directors or regulators. For example, a hydro utility may decide to seek 10 percent ROI. If its investment in plant and equipment is $50 million, it would need to set the price of hydro to its customers at a level that results in $5 million a year in profits. The importance of achieving ROI estimates will be explored later in this chapter.

Competition-Oriented Approaches

Rather than emphasize demand, cost, or profit factors, a company's approach may be based on an analysis of what competitors are doing.

Customary Pricing For some products where tradition, a standardized channel of distribution, or other competitive factors dictate the price, *customary pricing* is used. Candy bars offered through standard vending machines have a customary price of a few dollars, and a significant departure from this price may result in a loss of sales for the manufacturer. Hershey typically has changed the amount of chocolate in its candy bars depending on the price of raw chocolate, rather than vary its customary retail price so that it can continue selling through vending machines.

Above-, at-, or below-Market Pricing The "market price" of a product is what customers are generally willing to pay, not necessarily the price that the firm sets. For most products, it is difficult to identify a specific market price for a product or product class. Still, marketing managers often have a subjective feel for the competitors' price or the market price. Using this benchmark, they then may deliberately choose a strategy of *above-*, *at-*, or *below-market pricing*. The Focus on Ethics box found later in this chapter, "Fixing Prices to Save Bread," discusses the impact of below-market pricing strategy.

> *Among watch manufacturers, Rolex takes pride in emphasizing that it makes one of the most expensive watches you can buy—a clear example of above-market pricing.*

Among watch manufacturers, Rolex takes pride in emphasizing that it makes one of the most expensive watches you can buy—a clear example of above-market pricing. Manufacturers of national brands of clothing such as Christian Dior and retailers such as Holt Renfrew deliberately set higher prices for their products than those seen at The Bay.

Large mass-merchandise chains such as Hudson's Bay generally use at-market pricing. These chains are often seen as establishing the going market price in the minds of their competitors. They also provide a reference price for competitors that use above- and below-market pricing.

In contrast, a number of firms use below-market pricing. Walmart positions itself this way. Manufacturers of generic products and retailers that offer their own private brands of products ranging from peanut butter to shampoo deliberately set prices for these products about 8 to 10 percent below the prices of nationally branded competitive products such as Skippy peanut butter or Pantene Pro-V shampoo.

Some video game consoles may be sold at a loss in order to create profit from the video games.
©charnsitr/Shutterstock

Loss-Leader Pricing Retailers sometimes deliberately sell commonly used products, such as paper towels, soft drinks, and facial tissues, at very low prices to attract consumers who, the retailer hopes, will also buy other, regularly priced merchandise. The downside to loss-leader pricing is that some consumers move from store to store, making purchases only on those products that are loss leaders. This purchasing pattern, called cherry-picking, effectively foils the strategy underlying loss-leader pricing—to attract customers who will also buy products with healthier profit margins. For example, video game consoles may be sold at a loss to create the opportunity to profit from high-margin video games.

ask YOURSELF

1. *What products and brands would consider prestige pricing?*
2. *What is the difference between skimming and penetration pricing?*
3. *What is odd-even pricing?*

Estimating Demand and Revenue

LO 3 Creating the correct price for a product begins the process of forecasting. With the product's price known, marketers try to determine the extent of customer demand for it given their marketing efforts and the efforts of their competitors. Once an estimate for demand is known, marketing executives must translate this information to an estimate of revenues the firm expects to receive.

Rolex watches are priced above market.
©Lertsnim/Dreamstime.com/GetStock.com

The Importance of Accurate Forecasting

The forecasts created by the marketing department impact decisions made in other areas of an organization, including production and finance. Inaccurate information and poor estimates can be detrimental to the profitability of a marketing campaign. Similar to market research, both quantitative and qualitative analysis are used to make projections for an organization. Still, a forecast is still an estimate, so given the importance of the estimate, research continues to identify methodologies that can help marketers forecast more accurately.[13]

Forecasting Methods There are various methods that can be used to forecast. For our introductory purposes, consider the four broad categories of qualitative methods, regression methods, multiple equation methods, and time-series methods. Qualitative methods involve market experts coming to consensus using non-quantitative means to achieve projections. Regression methods link the forecast to a number of other variables through an equation. Multiple equations related to one another can also be used to forecast. Finally, time-series methods assume that the variable being forecast is affected by time.[14]

Profit and Loss Accurate profit and loss statements help organizations measure financial performance. The statement summarizes the revenues, costs, and expenditures outlined in a particular time frame and helps organizations project their ability for achieving future cash flow. For marketers, it is one of the best tools to gauge the success of a given marketing campaign or initiative.[15]

Return on Investment (ROI) With profit and loss capturing the performance of a given campaign, return on investment (ROI), or return on marketing investment (ROMI), evaluates the dollars invested in the initiative. When investing in a marketing campaign, marketers are essentially "risking" capital to achieve a desired result. The profit achieved from their initiatives in comparison to what was invested results in the return on marketing investment. Since this model assumes that an infinite number of customers are available to the firm, additional measures such as return on customer (ROC) are being explored to help marketing departments measure campaigns more accurately.[16]

$$\text{return on investment (\%)} = \frac{(\text{gain attributable to investment} - \text{cost of investment})}{\text{cost of investment}}$$

If a marketing investment of $10,000 in additional advertising and promotion was directly related to an increase in profits of $20,000, then the return on investment would be 100 percent.

$$\text{return on investment} = \frac{(\$20,000 - \$10,000)}{(\$10,000)} = 100\%$$

Fundamentals of Estimating Demand

Demand for a product or service can be estimated in different ways. An organization can study the marketplace by reviewing historical results from its sales and its competitors' sales. An organization can also conduct tests to gauge the demand of its product. In 1986, *Newsweek* decided to conduct a pricing experiment at newsstands in 11 cities. In one city, newsstand buyers paid $2.25. In five other cities, newsstand buyers paid the regular $2.00 price. In another city, the price was $1.50, and in the remaining four cities it was only $1.00. By comparison, the regular newsstand price for a competing magazine, *Time*, was $1.95. Why did *Newsweek* conduct the experiment? According to a *Newsweek* executive, "We wanted to figure out what the demand curve for our magazine at the newsstand is."[17]

Unfortunately, forecasting is challenging as the marketplace for different products and services continues to change. Amazon, Netflix, and Uber have disrupted their respective industries by making it easier for the consumer to purchase the products and services they need. These companies learned from previous disruption as access to information on the Internet made print-based media fall in demand. In December 2012, *Newsweek* published its last print edition and is now under new management with goals to grow the brand in the digital age.[18]

The last print issue of *Newsweek* was due to laws of demand.
©Kristoffer Tripplaar/Alamy Stock Photo

The Demand Curve A **demand curve** shows the number of products that will be sold at a given price. Demand curve D1 in Figure 9–4A shows the newsstand demand for *Newsweek* under the pricing conditions when it still offered a print version. Note that as price falls, more people decide to buy and unit sales increase. But price is not the complete story in estimating demand. Economists emphasize three other key factors:

1. *Consumer tastes:* These depend on many factors, such as demographics, culture, and technology. Because consumer tastes can change quickly, up-to-date marketing research is essential. For example, although older readers prefer paper books, research finds it is easier for them to read from electronic tablets.[19]

2. *Price and availability of similar products:* The laws of demand work for one's competitors, too. Consider *Newsweek* in its print format again. If the price of *Time* magazine falls, more people will buy it. Fewer people will buy *Newsweek* since *Time* is considered by economists to be a substitute for *Newsweek*. In 2012, other online magazines were considered substitutes, so if their prices fell or their availability increased, the demand for a product (*Newsweek* magazine, in this case) would fall. The result was *Newsweek* magazine moving online.

3. *Consumer income:* In general, as real consumer income (allowing for inflation) increases, demand for a product also increases. More disposable income allows for additional purchases that are not necessarily necessities. In 2015, Canada's inflation rate was 1.5 percent.

The first of these two factors influences what consumers *want* to buy, and the third affects what they can buy. Along with price, these are often called *demand factors,* or factors that determine consumers' willingness and ability to pay for goods and services. It is often very difficult to estimate demand for new products, especially because consumer likes and dislikes are often so difficult to read clearly. (See the Marketing NewsFlash box, "Uber Profitable," to find out how Uber used factors impacting demand to become a successful company.)[20]

Movement along versus Shift of a Demand Curve Demand curve D1 in Figure 9–4A shows that as the price is lowered from $2.00 to $1.50, the quantity demanded increases from 3 million ($Q1$) to 4.5 million ($Q2$) units per year. This is an example of a *movement along a demand curve* and assumes that other factors (consumer tastes, price and availability of substitutes, and consumer income) remain unchanged.

Figure 9–4
Illustrative demand curves for *Newsweek*

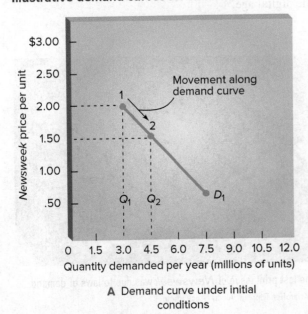

A Demand curve under initial conditions

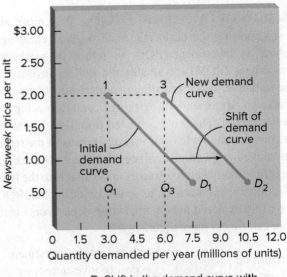

B Shift in the demand curve with different conditions

Uber Profitable

When Travis Kalanick and Garrett Camp had trouble hailing a cab in 2008, their experience led to an idea that evolved into a transportation network company. Today, Uber offers a number of services that challenge the taxi industry. One of its services, UberX, offers low-cost options for reaching destinations. By linking individuals that need a ride with individuals that can offer a ride, Uber created an opportunity to avoid the issues Kalanick and Camp had years ago.

Uber fills a need and creates an experience in our busy, overscheduled lives. In order to help, consumers find a ride at the touch of an app; Uber requires satisfactory background checks as well as other criteria for its drivers. Uber imposes specific requirements on the vehicles in its fleet, but does not own any of the vehicles. This model allows Uber to offer rides to consumers at significantly competitive prices compared to taxi drivers.

Uber is available in Ontario, Quebec, and Alberta, and has been a target for protests and legal actions around the world. In Toronto, the

UberX was legally able to operate in early 2016. This decision followed a controversial debate that lasted for months. Toronto City Council reduced regulations for taxis while asking Uber to raise its base fare.

The ability to operate a taxi cab is limited to individuals that own licences. Taxi licences are so coveted that they are passed on from generation to generation. However, when UberX was introduced in Toronto, the price competition that arose created concerns. Taxi licences in Toronto fell from $360,000 to below $100,000 in 2014.

Because of the disparity between what Uber charged and what Toronto taxi drivers traditionally charged, Toronto City Council had to pass certain rules to create a more fair and more competitive landscape. The rules included compensation for taxi-plate owners who were impacted in a negative way by Uber.

Uber was able to create this disruption by understanding the relationship between the allocation of drivers and the liquidity of riders. Prior to the convenience offered by

Uber has changed the way consumers obtain transportation.

©Mr.Whiskey/Shutterstock

Uber, there were not enough drivers for the impatient supply of riders. The Uber app offers convenience and communications to make more connections between drivers and riders, allowing Uber to better understand and manage demand. ●

Questions

1. Should companies like Uber be permitted to disrupt their respective industries?

2. What other companies can you think about that created disruptions like Uber in their industries? How did they use demand, pricing, and convenience to their advantage?

What if some of these factors change? For example, if advertising causes more people to want *Newsweek*, newsstand distribution is increased, or if consumer incomes rise, then the demand increases. Now the original curve, *D*1 (the blue line in Figure 9–4B), no longer represents the demand; a new curve must be drawn (*D*2). Economists call this a *shift in the demand curve*—in this case, a shift to the right, from *D*1 to *D*2. This increased demand means that more *Newsweek* magazines are wanted for a given price: At a price of $2, the demand is 6 million units per year (*Q*3) on *D*2 rather than 3 million units per year (*Q*1) on *D*1.

While print magazine were still in demand, what price did *Newsweek* select after conducting its experiment? It kept the price at $2.00. However, through expanded newsstand distribution and more aggressive

Tipping Etiquette	
Restaurants	15% on the total bill before tax 20% for exceptional service
Hairdressers, manicurists, aestheticians, and taxi drivers	10% minimum is common

advertising, *Newsweek* was later able to shift its demand curve to the right and charge a price of $2.50 without affecting its newsstand volume.

Price Elasticity of Demand

Marketing managers must also pay attention to *price elasticity*, a key consideration related to the product's demand curve. Price elasticity refers to how sensitive consumer demand and the firm's revenues are to changes in the product's price.

A product with *elastic demand* is one in which a slight decrease in price results in a relatively large increase in demand, or units sold. The reverse is also true: With elastic demand, a slight increase in price results in a relatively large decrease in demand. Marketing experiments on products that are price-sensitive, such as cola, coffee, and snack foods, show them often to have elastic demand. So marketing managers may cut prices to increase the demand, the units sold, and total revenue for one of these products, depending on what competitors' prices are. The demand for many consumer products is elastic—think jeans, DVDs, and car stereos.

One major factor influencing the elasticity of demand is the availability of substitute products. If consumers can easily find close substitutes for a good or service, the product's demand tends to be elastic.

In contrast, a product with *inelastic demand* means that slight increases or decreases in price will not significantly affect the demand, or units sold, for the product. Products and services considered as necessities, such as hydro or going to the dentist, usually have inelastic demand. What about gasoline for your car? Will an increase of a few cents per litre cause you to drive fewer kilometres and buy less gasoline? No? Then you're like millions of other consumers, which is why gasoline has inelastic demand. This means that an increase of a few cents per litre may have a relatively minor impact on the number of litres sold, and may actually increase the total revenue of the gasoline producer. Inelastic demand is usually a relatively short-term phenomenon. Consumers, when they are faced with high prices for something they have to have, will seek out an alternative, and/or producers will see an opportunity to develop a new product. A hybrid car is, in some ways, a producer's response to high gas prices. Or maybe you could learn to love the bus!

Another example of inelastic demand is when buyers are less price-sensitive when the product they are buying is unique or is high in quality and prestige. In this case, consumers perceive that the high price means more quality and the demand for that product will not suffer very much. In some cases, a higher price may result in higher sales, which results in the demand curve actually sloping upwards.

The ability to access product information online has changed the elasticity of demand for some products. In the past, a consumer's choice when considering buying a product was limited to the number of bricks-and-mortar stores available. Now, there are many more choices of suppliers to choose from. The large number of suppliers competing with each other has led to lower prices on products that were once available only in stores. The availability of different suppliers online combines to create more products with elastic demand.

Fundamentals of Estimating Revenue

While economists may talk about "demand curves," marketing executives are more likely to speak in terms of "revenues generated." Demand curves lead directly to an essential revenue concept critical to pricing decisions: **total revenue**. As summarized in Figure 9–5, total revenue (*TR*) equals the unit price (*P*) times the quantity sold (*Q*). Using this equation, let's recall our picture frame shop and assume our annual demand has improved so that we can set a price of $100 per picture and sell 400 pictures per year. So,

$$TR = P \times Q$$
$$= \$100 \times 400$$
$$= \$40,000$$

This combination of price and quantity sold annually will give us a total revenue of $40,000 per year. Is that good? Are you making money, making a profit? Total revenue is only part of the profit equation that we saw earlier:

$$\text{Total profit} = \text{Total revenue} - \text{Total cost}$$

The next section covers the other part of the profit equation: cost.

Figure 9–5
Total revenue concept

Total revenue (TR) is the total money received from the sale of a product. If

  TR = Total revenue
  P = Unit price of the product
  Q = Quantity of the product sold
Then
  TR = P × Q

ask YOURSELF

1. What is loss leader pricing?

2. What are three demand factors other than price that are used in estimating demand?

3. What is the difference between movement along a demand curve and a shift in a demand curve?

Determining Cost, Volume, and Profit Relationships

LO 4 While revenues are the monies received by the firm from selling its products or services to customers, costs or expenses are the monies the firm pays out to its employees and suppliers. Marketing managers often use break-even analysis to relate revenues and costs, topics covered in this section.

The Importance of Controlling Costs

Understanding the role and behaviour of costs is critical for all marketing decisions, particularly pricing decisions. Many firms go bankrupt because their costs get out of control, causing their total costs to exceed their total revenues over an extended period of time. This is why sophisticated marketing managers make pricing decisions that balance both their revenues and costs. Three cost concepts are important in pricing decisions: **total cost**, **fixed cost**, and **variable cost** (Figure 9–6).

Break-Even Analysis

LO 5 Marketing managers often employ an approach that considers cost, volume, and profit relationships, based on the profit equation. **Break-even analysis** is a technique that analyzes the relationship between total revenue and total cost to determine

Figure 9–6
Total cost concept

Fixed cost (FC) is the sum of the expenses of the firm that are stable and do not change with the quantity of product that is produced and sold. Examples of fixed costs are rent on the building, executive salaries, and insurance.

Variable cost (VC) is the sum of the expenses of the firm that vary directly with the quantity of product that is produced and sold. Examples are the direct labour and direct materials used in producing the product. Variable cost expressed on a per unit basis is called *unit variable cost (UVC)*.

$$TC = FC + VC$$

Total cost (TC) is the total expense incurred by a firm in producing and marketing the product. Total cost is the sum of fixed cost and variable cost.

profitability at various levels of output. The *break-even point (BEP)* is the quantity at which total revenue and total cost are equal. Profit comes from any units sold after the BEP has been reached. In terms of the definitions in Figure 9–6,

$$BEP_{Quantity} = \frac{Fixed\ cost}{Unit\ price - Unit\ variable\ cost}$$

Calculating a Break-Even Point Consider again your picture frame store. Suppose that you wish to identify how many pictures you must sell to cover your fixed cost at a given price. Let's assume demand for your framed pictures has increased, so the average price customers are willing to pay for each picture is $100. Also, suppose your fixed cost (*FC*) has grown to $28,000 (for real estate taxes, interest on a bank loan, and other fixed expenses) and unit variable cost (*UVC*) for a picture is now $30 (for labour, glass, frame, and matting). Your break-even quantity (BEP_{Quantity}) is 400 pictures, as follows:

$$BEP_{Quantity} = \frac{Fixed\ cost}{Unit\ price - Unit\ variable\ cost}$$

$$= \frac{\$28,000}{\$100 - \$30}$$

$$= 400\ pictures$$

The bolded row in Figure 9–7 shows that your break-even quantity at a price of $100 per picture is 400 pictures. At less than 400 pictures, your picture frame store incurs a loss, and at more than 400 pictures it makes a profit. Figure 9–7 also shows that if you could double your annual picture sales to 800, your store would make a profit of $28,000—the row shaded in brown in the figure.

Figure 9–8 shows a graphic presentation of the break-even analysis, called a *break-even chart*. It shows that total revenue and total cost intersect and are equal at a quantity of 400 pictures sold, which is the break-even point at which profit is exactly $0. You want to do better? If your frame store could double the quantity sold annually to 800 pictures, the graph in Figure 9–8 shows that you can earn an annual profit of $28,000, as shown by the row shaded in brown in Figure 9–7.

total cost
Total expenses incurred by a firm in producing and marketing a product; total cost is the sum of fixed cost and variable costs.

fixed cost
Firm's expenses that are stable and do not change with the quantity of product that is produced and sold.

variable cost
Sum of the expenses of the firm that vary directly with the quantity of products that is produced and sold.

break-even analysis
Examines the relationship between total revenue and total cost to determine profitability at different levels of output.

Figure 9–7
Calculating a break-even point for a picture frame store

Quantity of pictures sold (Q)	Price per picture (P)	Total revenue (TR) = (P × Q)	Unit variable cost (UVC)	Total variable cost (TVC) = (UVC × Q)	Fixed cost (FC)	Total cost (TC) = (FC + TVC)	Profit = (TR − TC)
0	$100	$0	$30	$0	$28,000	$28,000	−$28,000
200	100	20,000	30	6,000	28,000	34,000	−14,000
400	100	40,000	30	12,000	28,000	40,000	0
600	100	60,000	30	18,000	28,000	46,000	14,000
800	100	80,000	30	24,000	28,000	52,000	28,000
1,000	100	100,000	30	30,000	28,000	58,000	42,000
1,200	100	120,000	30	36,000	28,000	64,000	56,000

Figure 9–8
Break-even analysis for a picture frame store

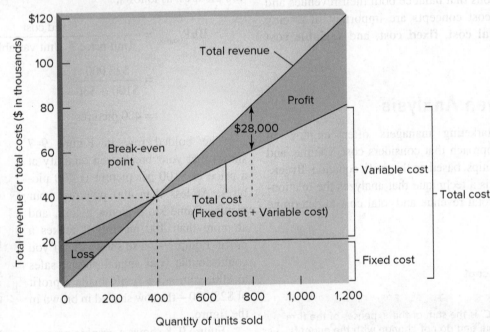

Applications of Break-Even Analysis

Because of its simplicity, break-even analysis is used extensively in marketing, most frequently to study the impact on profit of changes in price, fixed cost, and variable cost. The mechanics of break-even analysis are the basis of the widely used electronic spreadsheets such as Microsoft Excel that permit managers to answer hypothetical "what if" questions about the effect of changes in price and cost on their profit.

Pricing Objectives and Constraints

LO 6 With such a variety of alternative pricing strategies available, marketing managers must consider the pricing objectives and constraints that will impact their decisions. While pricing objectives frequently reflect corporate goals, pricing constraints often relate to conditions existing in the marketplace.

Identifying Pricing Objectives

Pricing objectives specify the role of price in an organization's marketing and strategic plans. To the extent possible, these pricing objectives are carried to lower levels in the organization, such as in setting objectives for marketing managers responsible for an individual brand. These objectives may change, depending on the financial position of the company as a whole, the success of its products, or the segments in which it is doing business. H. J. Heinz, for example, has specific pricing objectives for its Heinz ketchup brand that vary by country.

Profit Three different objectives relate to a firm's profit, which is often measured in terms of return on investment (ROI). These objectives have different implications for pricing strategy. One objective is *managing for long-run profits*, in which a company—such as many Japanese car or TV set manufacturers—gives up immediate profit in exchange for achieving a higher market share. Products are priced relatively low compared to their cost to develop, but the firm expects to make greater profits later because of its high market share.

A *maximizing current profit* objective, such as for a quarter or year, is common in many firms because the targets can be set and performance measured quickly. North American firms are sometimes criticized for this short-run orientation.

A third profit objective is a *target return* objective that occurs when a firm sets its price to achieve a profit goal (such as 20 percent for return on investment), usually determined by its board of directors. These three profit objectives have different implications for a firm's pricing objectives.

Another profit consideration for firms such as movie studios and manufacturers is to ensure that those firms in their channels of distribution make adequate profits. For example, Figure 9–9 shows where each dollar of your movie ticket goes. The 51 cents the movie studio gets must cover its profit plus the

> **pricing objectives**
> Expectations that specify the role of price in an organization's marketing and strategic plans.

Figure 9–9
Where each dollar of your movie ticket goes

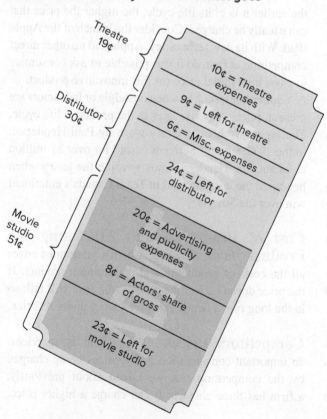

Theatre 19¢
10¢ = Theatre expenses
9¢ = Left for theatre

Distributor 30¢
6¢ = Misc. expenses
24¢ = Left for distributor

Movie studio 51¢
20¢ = Advertising and publicity expenses
8¢ = Actors' share of gross
23¢ = Left for movie studio

photo: ©Francis Vachon/The Canadian Press

cost of making and marketing the movie. Although the studio would like more than 51 cents of your dollar, it settles for this amount to make sure theatres and distributors are satisfied and willing to handle its movies.

Sales

As long as a firm's profit is high enough for it to remain in business, an objective may be to increase sales revenue, which will in turn lead to increases in market share and profit. Cutting the price on one product in a firm's line may increase its sales revenue but reduce those of related products. Objectives related to sales revenue or unit sales have the advantage of being translated easily into meaningful targets for marketing managers responsible for a product line or brand.

Market Share

Market share is the ratio of the firm's sales to those of the industry (competitors plus the firm itself). Companies often pursue a market share objective when industry sales are relatively flat or declining. For example, the cola market is declining, but Coke wants to keep its market share by retaining its piece of a dwindling pie. Although increased market share is a primary goal of some firms, others see it as a means to increasing sales and profits.

Adopting a market share objective does not always imply low price. The lowest-priced brand rarely has the highest market share. Tropicana orange juice, French's mustard, and Heinz ketchup are market share leaders and are all premium-priced. Brands such as these retain their market share positions because they offer value to consumers.

Volume

Many firms use volume, the quantity produced or sold, as a pricing objective. These firms often sell the same product at several different prices, at different times, or in different places in an attempt to match customer demand with the company's production capacity. Using volume as an objective can sometimes be misleading from a profit standpoint. Volume can be increased by using sales incentives (lowering prices, giving rebates, or offering lower interest rates). By doing this, the company chooses to lower profits in the short run to sell its product quickly. For example, a new health club might focus on getting a certain number of people to join by lowering its membership prices and accepting less profit, at first.

Survival

In some instances, profits, sales, and market share are less important objectives of the firm than mere survival. Air Canada has struggled to attract passengers with low fares and aggressive promotions to improve the firm's cash flow. This pricing objective has helped Air Canada to stay alive in the competitive airline industry.

Social Responsibility

A firm may forgo higher profit on sales and follow a pricing objective that recognizes its obligations to customers and society in general. Gerber supplies a specially formulated product free of charge to children who cannot tolerate foods based on cow's milk.

Identifying Pricing Constraints

Factors that limit the range of price a firm may set are **pricing constraints**. Consumer demand for the product clearly affects the price that can be charged. Other constraints on price vary from factors within the organization to competitive factors outside it.

Demand for the Product Class, Product, and Brand

The number of potential buyers for a product class (cars), product (sports cars), and brand (Bugatti Veyron) clearly affects the price a seller can charge. So does whether the item is a luxury, like a Bugatti Veyron, or a necessity, like bread and a roof over your head.

Newness of the Product: Stage in the Product Life Cycle

The newer the product and the earlier it is in its life cycle, the higher the price that can usually be charged. Consider the launch of the Apple iPad. With its new technology, Apple had no other direct competition at first, so it was possible to ask consumers to pay a high initial price for this innovative product.

Sometimes, such as when nostalgia or fad factors are present, prices may rise later in the product's life cycle. The legendary hockey jersey worn by Paul Henderson in the 1972 Summit Series was sold for over $1 million at an auction. Henderson was wearing the jersey when he scored the winning goal in Team Canada's emotional win over the Soviets.[21]

Cost of Producing and Marketing the Product

In the long run, a firm's price must cover all the costs of producing and marketing a product. If the price doesn't cover these costs, the firm will fail; so in the long run, a firm's costs set a floor under its price.

Competitors' Prices

When a firm sets its prices, an important consideration is the prices being charged by the competition. As we talked about previously, a firm has three choices: It can charge a higher price, the same price, or a lower price than its competitors. Each choice conveys a message to customers. For example, e-readers such as Amazon's Kindle and the Sony Reader were developed as single-function devices, meant solely for use as a reader. The iPad, on the other hand, is a multi-function appliance that allows the user to surf the Internet as well as use it as a reader. Because the e-readers made by Sony and Amazon have a limited use, they were forced to drop their prices dramatically when the iPad came on the scene.[22] Amazon has gone on to develop its own multi-function device, introducing the Kindle Fire in November 2011, which includes Internet, video, app, and gaming functionality to go along with its reader. Amazon's price for its Kindle Fire is significantly lower than the iPad, a strategy to reach consumers who are price-sensitive.

A high price signifies that the firm believes its offering represents a higher value in comparison to competing products—value being quality, brand image, benefits and unique features offering extra benefits, or something as simple as instant availability. Sony is known as a firm that typically prices higher than most of its competitors. Consumers wanting quality will pay a higher price.

Charging the same price as the competition means that the firm is relying on some aspect other than price to position and differentiate its products in the minds of customers—that differentiation may be a unique attribute, widespread availability, or an intensive marketing campaign. Thinking again of consumer electronics, Panasonic, JVC, and Sharp are examples of manufacturers whose prices are close for similar products. Consumers typically buy these brands on the basis of some unique attribute of the product, or because they prefer to deal with a specific retailer.

Lower prices can be a challenge, but many firms rely on this strategy. From the company standpoint, lower prices can mean lower profits on each sale, which may need to be offset by larger volume sales. In addition, larger volumes can result in production efficiencies and lower costs. Less well-known brands and some of the larger manufacturers such as RCA use this strategy. For consumers, the lower prices often mean forgoing some aspect such as quality or brand image.

Canadian hockey legend Paul Henderson, who scored the game-winning goal during the 1972 Summit Series against the Soviet Union, holds his original 1972 Team Canada sweater.

©Nathan Denette/The Canadian Press

The decision to charge a certain price is impacted by marketing and pricing objectives. If winning market share is an objective, lower prices may be the solution. If being perceived as the "best brand" is an objective, higher prices may be part of the answer. Being known as a *market leader* based on pricing is a title that could be ascribed to firms using either strategy.

Charging prices in line with the competition earns firms the title of *market follower*. This is a conscious choice of many smaller firms manufacturing and selling similar or often the same products. Emphasis is shifted away from price to some other aspect of the marketing mix.

There are occasions where other objectives override any consideration of competitor pricing, such as selling off discontinued models or time-sensitive items (summer-vacation packages, for example).

Legal and Ethical Considerations

Deciding on a final price is a complex process. In addition to the considerations we have just presented, there are laws and regulations that also play a role in the price decision. We will look at four of the most prominent considerations.

Price Fixing When competitors collaborate and conspire to set prices, they agree to increase, decrease, or stabilize a price for their benefit. This is called *price fixing,* and it is illegal—the *Competition Act* prohibits this practice. The *Competition Act* consists of federal regulations governing most business conduct in Canada. Price fixing usually occurs where price is the most important factor in the marketing mix. Twelve global airlines that ran a cargo price-fixing cartel for years were hit with fines totalling $1.1 billion by European Union regulators. The European Commission slapped Air Canada with the third-smallest fine at $29.2 million. In Canada, Hershey Canada was fined $4 million in its role in a price-fixing chocolate cartel.[23]

More recently, grocery chains were under investigation for price fixing. The Focus on Ethics box, "Fixing Prices to Save Bread" discusses the what happened.[24]

Fixing Prices to Save Bread

Buying groceries is routine for many Canadians; however, regularly checking the bill may not be a practice all Canadians undertake. Fortunately, Canada's Competition Bureau is looking out for the best interests of Canadians and recently identified a number of Canadian grocery chains and bakeries that conspired to fix the price for more than 10 years.

Businesses use different pricing strategies to remain competitive with one another and generate a profit. The costs to produce goods generally increases with inflation; however, the different bakeries and retailers were colluding to increase the prices of bread at the same rate and time. This is an unfair and illegal practice.

Unfortunately, this instance of price fixing is not the only one Canadians have observed in recent years. A few years ago, one of the largest confectionery and snack companies around the world was accused of deceptive pricing practices. In 2013, Hershey Canada was fined $4 million for its role in a price-fixing chocolate cartel. The six-year investigation found that

Hershey was guilty of conspiring, agreeing, or arranging to fix prices in the Canadian chocolate industry in 2007. Hershey Canada cooperated with the Competition Bureau's investigation involving a class action lawsuit resulting in Cadbury Adams Canada Inc., Nestlé Canada Inc., Mars Canada Inc., and Hershey Canada Inc. agreeing to pay more than $23 million to settle.

In a statement, John Pecman, commissioner of competition, said, "Price-fixing is a serious criminal offence, regardless of whether it is in the chocolate confectionary market or any other industry."

Most Canadians would not think of trusted organizations like Loblaws, Wal-Mart Canada, Sobeys, and Metro could be involved in a price-fixing scheme. They were just willing to pay for their groceries as the price of bread increased by at least $1.50 between 2001 and 2015. ●

A number of major grocery chains were found guilty of price fixing.
©Ingram Publishing/SuperStock

Questions

1. If a company such as Loblaw's can be accused of deceptive pricing practices, what other companies could as well? Give an example from your own experience where you encountered deceptive pricing practices.

2. Price fixing is a key concern for the Competition Bureau. Figure 9–10 highlights four deceptive pricing practices. Which of the four do with you feel is the most unethical and unlawful? Give reasons.

Price Discrimination If different prices are charged to different customers for the same or very similar goods and the same terms, *price discrimination* has occurred. The *Competition Act* prohibits this, but in order for a firm to be charged with the offence, there has to be evidence of a "practice" of price discrimination—that is, that it is not just a one-time or occasional event.

Deceptive Pricing Price offers that mislead the consumer are considered *deceptive pricing*, and this is prohibited under the *Competition Act*. Figure 9–10 shows the most common deceptive pricing practices. Many companies across the country have been accused of deceptive pricing, but it can be difficult to police and the laws are hard to enforce. Often, regulators rely on

the ethical standards of those making and publicizing pricing decisions. The Canadian Code of Advertising Standards provides guidelines for various aspects of promotion, and pricing is one of these; advertising industry members are expected to follow this Code and to self-regulate (ensure that they and their colleagues adhere to the Code).

An example of deceptive pricing is menswear retailer Grafton-Fraser Inc. The retailer agreed to pay a $1.2 million penalty to settle an advertising case regarding misleading sale prices. The Competition Bureau found that Grafton-Fraser had significantly inflated the regular price of certain garments sold in its stores, resulting in an overstatement of the savings to consumers when these garments were on sale. The retailer joins other

Figure 9–10
Most common deceptive pricing practices

Deceptive Practice	Description
Bait and switch	A firm offers a very low price for a product (the bait), and when consumers come to purchase it, they are persuaded to buy a more expensive product (the switch). Uses techniques such as downgrading the advertised item or not having it in stock.
Bargains conditional on other purchases	A firm advertises "buy one, get one free" or "get two for the price of one." If the first items are sold at the regular price, this is legal. If the price for the first items is inflated for the offer, it is not.
Price comparisons	Advertising "retail value $100—our price $85" is deceptive if a substantial number of stores in the area are not using the $100 price—in other words, if it is not the "going price." Advertising "below manufacturer's suggested list price" is deceptive if no sales occur at the manufacturer's list price. Advertising that the price is reduced 50 percent is deceptive if the item was not offered for sale at the higher price for a substantial previous period of time.
Double ticketing	When more than one price tag is placed on an item, it must be sold at the lower price; this practice is not illegal, but the law requires that the lower price be charged.

merchants, including Suzy Shier, Sears Canada Ltd., and Forzani Group Ltd., that the Competition Bureau found were inflating an item's regular price and thereby overstating the savings of the sale price. Grafton-Fraser, the bureau found, was tagging garments with both a regular and a sale price; however, the items did not sell "in any significant quantity or for any reasonable period of time at the regular price," the Bureau said. Grafton-Fraser runs stores across the country that operate under several names, among them Tip Top Tailors, George Richards Big & Tall, and Grafton & Co.[25]

Predatory Pricing Charging a very low price for a product with the intent of undercutting competitors and possibly driving them out of the market is called *predatory pricing*. After the competitors have been driven out, the offending firm raises its prices. If a company can genuinely operate more efficiently than others, and this lets them offer its products at a lower price, should this be classified as predatory pricing? No! It's not easy to prove that the intent of the lower price is to eliminate a competitor, and that the prices set are unreasonably and artificially low, so there are many more charges of predatory pricing than there are convictions.

Global Pricing Strategy

Global companies face many challenges in determining a pricing strategy as part of their worldwide marketing effort. Individual countries, even those with free trade agreements, may place considerable competitive,

political, and legal constraints on the pricing flexibility of global companies. For example, Walmart was told by German antitrust authorities that the prices in its stores were too low, relative to competitors, and faced a fine for violating the country's trade if the prices weren't raised![26]

Pricing too low or too high can have dire consequences. When prices appear too low in one country, companies can be charged with dumping, a practice subject to severe penalties and fines. **Dumping** occurs when a firm sells a product in a foreign country below its domestic price or below its actual cost. A recent trade dispute involving U.S. apple growers and Mexico is a case in point. Mexican trade officials claimed that U.S. growers were selling their red and golden delicious apples in Mexico below the actual cost of production. They imposed a 101 percent tariff on U.S. apples, and a severe drop in U.S. apple exports to Mexico resulted. Later negotiations set a price floor on the price of U.S. apples sold to Mexico.[27]

When companies price their products very high in some countries but competitively in others, they face a grey market problem. A **grey market**, also called *parallel importing*, is a situation where products are sold through unauthorized channels of distribution. A grey market comes about when individuals buy products in a lower-priced country from a manufacturer's authorized retailer, ship them to higher-priced countries, and then sell them below the manufacturer's

dumping
Occurs when a firm sells a product in a foreign country below its domestic prices or below its actual cost.

grey market
Situations where products are sold through unauthorized channels of distribution.

suggested retail price through unauthorized retailers. Many well-known products have been sold through grey markets, including Olympus cameras, Seiko watches, and Mercedes-Benz cars. Parallel channels are not strictly illegal in Canada, but there are mounting legal challenges to them. Parallel importing is legal in the United States. It is illegal in the European Union.[28]

Setting a Final Price

LO 7 The final price set by the marketing manager serves many functions. It must be high enough to cover the cost of providing the product *and* meet the objectives of the company. Yet it must be low enough that customers are willing to pay it. But not too low, or customers may think they're purchasing an inferior product. Confused? Setting price is one of the most difficult tasks the marketing manager faces, but four generalized steps are useful to follow.

Step 1: Select an Approximate Price Level

Before setting a final price, the marketing manager must understand the market environment, the features and customer benefits of the particular product, and the goals of the firm. A balance must be struck between factors that might drive a price higher (such as a profit-oriented approach) and other forces (such as increased competition from substitutes) that may drive a price down.

Marketing managers consider pricing objectives and constraints first, and then choose among the general pricing approaches—demand-, cost-, profit-, or competition-oriented—to arrive at an approximate price level. This price is then analyzed in terms of cost, volume, and profit relationships. Break-even analyses may be run at this point, and finally, if this approximate price level "works," it is time to take the next step: setting a specific list or quoted price.

Step 2: Set the List or Quoted Price

A seller must decide whether to follow a one-price or flexible-price policy.

One-Price Policy A *one-price policy* involves setting one price for all buyers of a product or service. For example, when you buy a product at Walmart, you are offered the product at a single price. You can decide to buy it or not, but there is no variation of the price under the seller's one-price policy. Some retailers such as Dollarama married this policy with a below-market approach and used to sell mostly everything in their stores for $1! Dollarama has added more products at prices ranging from $1.25 to $4.

Flexible-Price Policy In contrast, a *flexible-price policy* involves setting different prices for products and services depending on individual buyers and purchase situations in light of demand, cost, and competitive factors. Dell Computer adopted flexible pricing as it continually adjusts prices in response to changes in its own costs, competitive pressures, and demand from its various personal computer segments (home, small business, corporate, and so on). "Our flexibility allows us to be [priced] different even within a day," says a Dell spokesperson.[29]

> *Is it any wonder that 60 percent of prospective car buyers dread negotiating the price?*

Dollarama previously used a one-price policy.
©Paul Chiasson/The Canadian Press

Flexible pricing is not without its critics because of its discriminatory potential. For example, car dealers have traditionally used flexible pricing on the basis of buyer-seller negotiations to agree on a final price. Is it any wonder that 60 percent of prospective car buyers dread negotiating the price?

Step 3: Make Special Adjustments to the List or Quoted Price

LO 8 When you pay $2 for a bag of M&Ms in a vending machine or receive a quoted price of $15,000 from a contractor to renovate a kitchen, the pricing sequence ends with the last step just described: setting the list or quoted price. But when you are a manufacturer of M&M candies and sell your product to dozens or hundreds of wholesalers and retailers in your channel of distribution, you may need to make a variety of special adjustments to the list or quoted price. Wholesalers also must adjust list or quoted prices they set for retailers. Three special adjustments to the list or quoted price are discounts, allowances, and geographical adjustments.

Discounts *Discounts* are reductions from list price that a seller gives a buyer as a reward for some activity of the buyer that is favourable to the seller. Four kinds of discounts are especially important in marketing strategy: quantity, seasonal, trade (functional), and cash.[30]

- **Quantity discounts:** To encourage customers to buy larger quantities of a product, firms at all levels in the channel of distribution offer quantity discounts, which are reductions in unit costs for a larger order. For example, an instant photocopying service might set a price of 10 cents a copy for 1 to 24 copies, 9 cents a copy for 25 to 99, and 8 cents a copy for 100 or more. Because the photocopying service gets more of the buyer's business and has longer production runs that reduce its order-handling costs, it is willing to pass on some of the cost savings in the form of quantity discounts to the buyer.

- **Seasonal discounts:** To encourage buyers to stock inventory earlier than their normal demand would require, manufacturers often use seasonal discounts. A firm such as Toro that manufactures lawn mowers and snow blowers offers seasonal discounts to encourage wholesalers and retailers to stock up on lawn mowers in January and February and on snow blowers in July and August—months before the seasonal

Toro uses seasonal discounts to stimulate consumer demand and smooth out seasonal manufacturing peaks and troughs.
©Daniel Acker/Bloomberg via Getty Images

demand by ultimate consumers. This enables Toro to smooth out seasonal manufacturing peaks and troughs, thereby contributing to more-efficient production. It also rewards wholesalers and retailers for the risk they accept in assuming increased inventory carrying costs and gives them the benefit of having supplies in stock at the time they are wanted by customers.

> *Although the manufacturer may suggest trade discounts, the sellers are free to alter the discount schedule depending on their competitive situation.*

- **Trade (functional) discounts:** To reward wholesalers and retailers for marketing functions they will perform in the future, a manufacturer often gives trade, or functional, discounts. These reductions off the list or base price are offered to resellers in the channel of distribution on the basis of where they are in the channel and the marketing activities they are expected to perform in the future.

  Traditional trade discounts have been established in various product lines such as hardware, food, and pharmaceutical items. Although the manufacturer may suggest trade discounts, the sellers are free to alter the discount schedule depending on their competitive situation. Suppose that a manufacturer quotes prices in the following form:

  List price − $100, less 30/10/5

  The first number in the percentage sequence (in this example, 30/10/5) always refers to the retail end of the channel, and the last number always refers to the wholesaler or jobber closest to the manufacturer in the channel. The trade discounts are simply subtracted one at a time. This price quote shows that $100 is the manufacturer's suggested retail price:

- For the retailer, 30 percent of the suggested retail price ($100 × 0.3 = $30) is available to cover costs and provide a profit;
- Wholesalers closest to the retailer in the channel get 10 percent of their selling price ($70 × 0.1 = $7); and
- The final group of wholesalers in the channel (probably jobbers) that are closest to the manufacturer get 5 percent of their selling price ($63 × 0.05 = $3.15).

Thus, starting with the manufacturer's retail price and subtracting the three trade discounts shows that the manufacturer's selling price to the wholesaler or jobber closest to the manufacturer is $59.85 (see Figure 9–11).

- **Cash discounts:** To encourage retailers to pay their bills quickly, manufacturers offer them cash discounts. Suppose that a retailer receives a bill quoted at $1,000, 2/10 net 30. This means that the bill for the product is $1,000, but the retailer can take a two percent discount ($1,000 × 0.02 = $20) if payment is made within 10 days and send a cheque for $980. If the payment cannot be made within 10 days, the total amount of $1,000 is due within 30 days. It is usually understood by the buyer that an interest charge will be added after the first 30 days of free credit.

Retailers provide cash discounts to consumers as well, to eliminate the cost of credit granted to consumers. These discounts take the form of discount-for-cash policies.

Allowances Allowances—like discounts—are reductions from list or quoted prices to buyers for performing some activity.

- **Trade-in allowances:** A new car dealer can offset the list price of that new Toyota Camry by offering you a trade-in allowance of $500 for your old Honda. A trade-in allowance is a price reduction given when a used product is part of the payment on a new product. Trade-ins are an effective way to lower the price a buyer has to pay without formally reducing the list price.
- **Promotional allowances:** Sellers in the channel of distribution can qualify for promotional allowances for undertaking certain advertising or selling activities to promote a product. Various types of allowances include an actual cash payment or an extra amount of "free goods" (as with a free case of pizzas to a retailer for every dozen cases purchased). Frequently, a portion of these savings is passed on to the consumer by retailers.

Geographical Adjustments Geographical adjustments are made by manufacturers or even wholesalers to list or quoted prices to reflect the cost of transportation of the products from seller to buyer. The two general methods for quoting prices related to transportation costs are FOB origin pricing and uniform delivered pricing.

- **FOB origin pricing:** FOB means "free on board" some vehicle at some location, which means the seller pays the cost of loading the product onto the vehicle that is used (such as a barge, railroad car, or truck). FOB origin pricing usually involves the seller's naming the location of this loading as the seller's factory or warehouse (such as "FOB Montreal" or "FOB

Figure 9–11
How trade discounts work

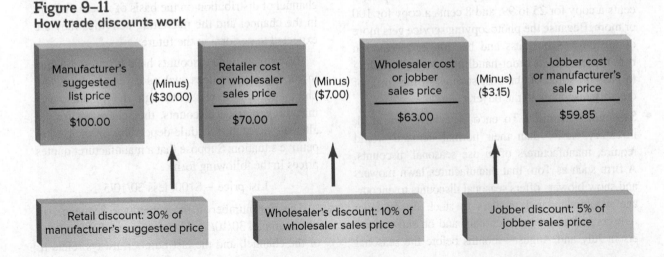

factory"). The title and ownership to the goods passes to the buyer at the point of loading, so the buyer becomes responsible for picking the specific mode of transportation, for all the transportation costs, and for subsequent handling of the product. Buyers furthest from the seller face the big disadvantage of paying the higher transportation costs.

- **Uniform delivered pricing:** When a uniform delivered pricing method is used, the price the seller quotes includes all transportation costs. It is quoted in a contract as "FOB buyer's location," and the seller selects the mode of transportation, pays the freight charges, and is responsible for any damage that may occur because the seller retains title to the goods until delivered to the buyer.

Step 4: Monitor and Adjust Prices

Rarely can a firm set a price and leave it at that. As you have learned, there are many constraints that affect setting prices, and the firm has objectives that it also takes into account. Things change both in the external business environment and within the firm itself; as a result, prices need to be reviewed and revised if necessary. A key activity is the monitoring of competitor activity, legislative changes, economic conditions, and—the ultimate measure—consumer demand! These factors, and their potential impact on the firm's ability to achieve its marketing goals, have to be examined and action taken when necessary.

ask **YOURSELF**

1. Why would a seller choose a flexible-price policy over a one-price policy?

2. What is the purpose of (a) quantity discounts and (b) promotional allowances?

$29.⁹⁵* student pricing.

Keep more money in your pocket.

When you file with your taxes with H&R Block, you keep more money in your pocket. You'll also get great pricing, the best refund possible and a free SPC† card.

For more information, speak to an H&R Block Tax Professional today.

12345 Your Street
Enter City Name, Province
Office Phone: (123) 456-7890
Email: hrblock.12345@hrblock.ca

© H&R Block Canada, Inc.
* $29.95 valid for student tax preparation only. To qualify, student must present either (i) a T2202a documenting 4 or more months of full-time attendance at a college or university during the applicable tax year or (ii) a valid high school Id card. Students pay $79.99 for Complex/Premier return. Expires 12/31/14. Valid only at participating locations.
†SPC Card available at participating locations in Canada only. Offers may vary, restrictions may apply. For full terms see www.spccard.ca

H&R BLOCK®

hrblock.ca | 800-HRBLOCK (472-5625)

Used with permission of H&R Block

---

1. *What pricing strategies has H&R Block used in this advertisement?*

2. *How does the ad make you feel about working for or with this company?*

LO 1
• Price is the money or other considerations exchanged for the ownership or use of a product or service.

• Price typically involves money and the amount exchanged can be different from the list or quoted price because of allowances and extra fees.

• When reviewing the perceived benefits of a good or service, price is used as an indicator of value by consumers.

 LO 2
• Four general approaches for finding an approximate price level for a product or service:

• Demand-oriented pricing approaches stress consumer demand and revenue implications of pricing and include eight types: skimming, penetration, prestige, price lining, odd-even, target, bundle, and yield management.

• Cost-oriented pricing approaches emphasize the cost aspects of pricing and include two types: standard and cost-plus pricing.

• Profit-oriented pricing approaches focus on a balance between revenues and costs to set a price and include three types: target profit, target return-on-sales, and target return-on-investment pricing.

• Competition-oriented pricing approaches emphasize what competitors or the marketplace are doing and include three types: customary; above-, at-, or below-market; and loss-leader pricing.

 LO 3
• A demand curve shows the maximum number of products consumers will buy at a given price and for a given set of (a) consumer tastes, (b) price and availability of other products, and (c) consumer income.

• The price elasticity of demand relates to the reaction of consumer demand and a firm's revenue when a price changes.

 LO 4
• Marketers need to understand the total revenue and total costs when considering pricing decisions as they will determine their ability to generate an appropriate profit.

 LO 5
• Break-even analysis shows the relationship between total revenue and total cost at various quantities of output for given conditions of price, fixed cost, and variable cost.

• The break-even point is where total revenue and total cost are equal.

 LO 6
• Pricing objectives, which specify the role of price in a firm's marketing strategy, may include pricing for profit, sales revenue, market share, unit sales, survival, or some socially responsible price level.

• Pricing constraints such as demand, product newness, costs, competitors, other products sold by the firm, and the type of competitive market restrict a firm's pricing range.

 LO 7
• In setting a final price, Step 1 is to set an approximate price level.

• Setting the list or quoted price is Step 2.

• Step 3 involves making special adjustments to prices through discounts and allowances.

• Finally, Step 4 requires marketers to monitor and adjust prices.

 LO 8
• Geographical adjustments to price reflect the cost of transportation.

• Organizations can reward buyers by offering discounts such as quantity discounts or seasonal discounts that also work in favour of the seller.

• When buyers perform an activity, they can sometimes receive allowances or reductions to listed or quoted prices.

key terms and concepts... **A REFRESHER**

break-even analysis	markup	total revenue
demand curve	pricing constraints	value
dumping	pricing objectives	variable cost
fixed cost	profit equation	
grey market	total cost	

hands-on... **APPLY YOUR KNOWLEDGE**

Pricing Your Services Review the Marketing NewsFlash box about H&R Block. Consider that you are the individual offering similar professional services and review the textbook section on break-even analysis. Determine how many hours you would have to work in order to break even if your annual fixed costs for your professional practice were $12,000 annually and variable costs for an hour of work were $25 dollars on average.

Chapter Vignette... ACTIVITY

Effective marketing requires individuals with a variety of skill sets. Although creativity is an important skill in this discipline, the ability to analyze figures and data is critical in developing marketing strategy. Review this chapter's vignette about The Barber's Chair, and the importance of key marketing calculations for developing an appropriate pricing strategy. In your class, work with a group to estimate the price of a new product to be used by a barber. Complete break-even analyses and return-on-investment calculations to determine the demand required to achieve your new product goals.

Infographic... DATA ANALYSIS

The Infographic from Canada Food Price Report illustrates rising food prices. Consider other foods or products you have recently purchased and determine by what percentage their price has increased over the past 5, 10, and 20 years.

LEARNING OBJECTIVES

LO 1 Explain what is meant by a marketing channel and the value created by intermediaries

LO 2 Distinguish among traditional marketing channels, electronic marketing channels and different types of vertical marketing systems

LO 3 Describe factors that marketing executives consider when selecting and managing a marketing channel

LO 4 Discuss supply chain and logistics management and how they relate to marketing strategy

Marketing Channels and Supply Chain

In order to compete with corporate and contractual marketing systems, independent retailers rely on quality intermediaries for support. An effective marketing channel provides retailers with the inventory of products they need to keep their customers satisfied. In short, good supply chains and marketing channels are critical to getting customers what they need when they need it.

Used with permission of Fuzion Flooring.

CHAPTER OUTLINE

- Strategic use of marketing channels
- Nature and importance of marketing channels
- Channel structure and organization
- Vertical marketing systems
- Channel choice and management
- Logistics and supply chain management

Logging multiple travel miles as he sources manufacturers in China, South Korea and Europe, Chris Wilson still finds a way to keep himself grounded. He has to. His business is flooring distribution.

Becoming the fastest-growing business in an old, mature industry was not an easy task. But strategic planning, years of experience and excellent execution allowed Fuzion Flooring to catch the eye of the Business Development Bank of Canada (BDC). As the vice president of operations of Fuzion Flooring, Wilson oversees the distribution of flooring products to retailers and commercial contractors across Canada. "We were thrilled when we were invited into BDC's Growth Accelerator Program," explains Wilson. "Having that investment meant we could develop the right channel strategy to meet the needs of our retail partners."

Overseeing 115,000 square feet of warehouse space in Ontario and over 40,000 square feet in Calgary has given Wilson a strong appreciation for supply chain and logistics. His company is focused on having the right products at the right time for customers. As Fuzion Flooring serves a lot of local retailers as well as dealers across Canada, hundreds of orders are picked daily in the warehouses for delivery and for pickup.

The company is a specialty merchandise merchant wholesaler and a leader in its business. The showroom in the head office invites retailers and designers to peruse the vast number of products that have been "crafted to stand the test of time. Wilson believes products that meet the value equation (discussed in more detail in Chapter 9) will lead to satisfied retailers who in turn will continue to represent Fuzion Flooring's products.

The well-lit showroom has an inviting look and feel, but is not open to the general public. The rationale for this decision highlights the importance of channel design considerations and satisfying buyer requirements. Opening a showroom to the public could create a vertical conflict (as noted in later in this chapter).

Wilson's 30 years of experience in the flooring industry has given him sage understanding of the potential conflict and necessary care required when designing a marketing channel. "In order to survive in the flooring business in Canada, a company has to find a way to do business with as many people as possible without causing channel conflict." Disintermediation occurs when a channel member (i.e., manufacturer) bypasses another member (i.e., distributor) and sells directly to a retailer or consumer. Being aware of potential channel conflict and avoiding it has served Fuzion Flooring well over the years.

Fortunately for Fuzion Flooring, major channel disruptions don't seem to occur in the flooring industry. "It has traditionally and continues to be a three-step process from manufacturer to distributor, distributor to retailer, and retailer to consumer," shares Wilson. This indirect channel is core to Fuzion Flooring's business; however, the organization is always looking for new channels. "Although distribution is the same," reminisces Wilson, "manufacturers used to anchor the business." The need to be more meaningful to diverse geographic markets and less reliant to manufacturers led distributors to start developing their own in-house private-label brands.

Fuzion Flooring is proud of its innovation. It has designed all of its flooring in Canada for various Canadian markets and created engineered hardwood collections that have redefined wood craftsmanship. It is also a company striving for sustainability and acting in an environmentally responsible manner. All products and raw materials are sourced from suppliers recognized for sustainability, safety, and responsible natural resource consumption.[1]

reality CHECK ⊘

As you read Chapter 10, refer back to the Fuzion Flooring vignette to answer the following questions:

- As a retailer, choosing the right supplier is critical to meeting your customers' needs. What has Fuzion Flooring done and not done to ensure that retailers consider them as a strong partner?
- Fuzion Flooring stores its private warehouse in its supply chain. How do you believe the private warehousing strategy impacts its other key logistical functions, including transportation, order processing, and inventory management?

Nature and Importance of Marketing Channels

LO 1 Reaching potential buyers is a critical part of successful marketing. Buyers benefit from well-structured and efficient distribution systems. The route to do this is direct in some cases and indirect in others.

Getting the product to the consumer is another key component of the marketing mix. In order to ensure an established place for consumers to acquire the product or service, marketers need to understand the distribution and supply chain aspects of bringing a product to market. Good marketers understand the value of the supply chain to perform the activities required to deliver a good or service to customers.

marketing channel
The set of individuals or firms involved in the process of making a product available.

intermediaries
Individuals or firms performing a role in the marketing channel, involved in making a product available.

What Is a Marketing Channel?

You see the results of distribution every day. You may have purchased Lay's potato chips at Mac's convenience store, a book through **chapters.indigo.ca**, or Levi's jeans at Hudson's Bay. Each of these items was brought to you by a marketing channel of distribution, or simply a marketing channel. A **marketing channel** consists of individuals and firms involved in the process of making a product or service available.

Marketing channels can be compared with a pipeline through which water flows from a source to an endpoint. Marketing channels make possible the flow of goods from a producer, through **intermediaries**, to a buyer. There are several types of intermediaries, as shown in Figure 10–1. Intermediaries go by various names and perform various functions. Some intermediaries actually purchase items from the producer, store them, and resell them to buyers. For example, Nestlé Canada produces Aero chocolate bars and sells them to wholesalers. The wholesalers then

Figure 10–1
Terms used for marketing intermediaries

Term	Description
Middleman	Another name for intermediary
Agent or broker	Any intermediary with legal authority to act on behalf of another channel member (for example, a manufacturer)
Wholesaler	Any intermediary who sells to other intermediaries, usually to retailers—this term usually applies to intermediaries who deal in consumer goods
Retailer	An intermediary who sells to consumers
Distributor	A general term used to describe intermediaries who perform a variety of functions, including selling, maintaining inventories, extending credit, and others—usually used for those in business markets
Dealer	A general term that can mean the same as a distributor, a retailer, or a wholesaler

Figure 10–2
How intermediaries minimize transactions

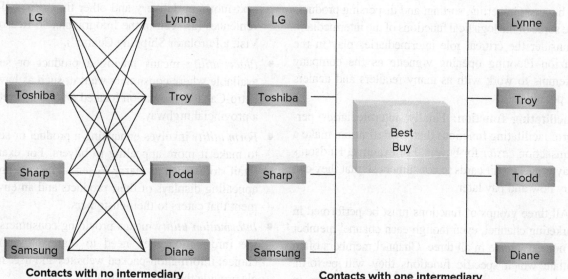

Contacts with no intermediary
4 producers × 4 buyers = 16 contacts

Contacts with one intermediary
4 producers + 4 buyers = 8 contacts

sell the bars to independent convenience and grocery stores, which in turn sell them to consumers. Other intermediaries, such as brokers and agents, represent sellers but do not actually ever own the products; their role is to bring a seller and buyer together. Real estate agents are examples of this type of intermediary.

Value Is Created by Intermediaries

Few consumers appreciate the value created by intermediaries; however, producers recognize that intermediaries make selling goods and services more efficient because the intermediaries minimize the number of sales contacts necessary to reach a target market. Figure 10–2 shows a simple example of how this comes about in the flat-panel TV market. Without a retail intermediary

(such as Best Buy), LG, Toshiba, Sharp, and Samsung would each have to make four contacts to reach the four consumers shown, who are in the target market. When Best Buy acts as an intermediary, each producer has to make only one contact, reducing the number of industry transactions from 16 to 8, which reduces producer costs.

Functions Performed by Intermediaries

Intermediaries make possible the flow of products from producers to ultimate consumers by performing three basic functions (see Figure 10–3).

- **Transactional function:** Intermediaries perform a transactional function when they buy and sell goods or services. But an intermediary such as a wholesaler also performs the function of sharing risk with the producer when it stocks merchandise in anticipation of sales. If the stock is unsold for any reason, the intermediary—not the producer—suffers the loss.

Figure 10–3
Marketing channel functions performed by intermediaries

Type of Function	Activities Related to Function
Transactional function	• *Buying:* Purchasing products for resale • *Selling:* Contacting potential customers, promoting products, and seeking orders • *Risk-taking:* Assuming business risks in the ownership of inventory
Logistical function	• *Selection:* Putting together a selection of products from several different sources • *Storing:* Assembling and protecting products at a convenient location • *Sorting:* Purchasing in large quantities and dividing into smaller amounts • *Transporting:* Physically moving a product to customers
Facilitating function	• *Financing:* Extending credit to customers • *Marketing information and research:* Providing information to customers and suppliers, including competitive conditions and trends

- **Logistical function:** The logistics of a transaction involve the details of preparing and getting a product to buyers. Gathering, sorting, and dispersing products are some of the logistical functions of the intermediary. Consider the critical role intermediaries play in the Fuzion Flooring opening vignette as the company attempts to work with as many retailers and dealers as possible.

- **Facilitating function:** Finally, intermediaries perform facilitating functions that, by definition, make a transaction *easier* for buyers. For example, Hudson's Bay issues credit cards to consumers so that they can buy now and pay later.

All three groups of functions must be performed in a marketing channel, even though each channel member may not participate in all three. Channel members often negotiate which specific functions they will perform. Sometimes disagreements result, and a breakdown in relationships among channel members occurs. This happened when Pepsi-Cola's bottler in Venezuela switched to Coca-Cola. Given the intermediary's logistical role—storing and transporting Pepsi to Venezuelan customers, in this case—Pepsi-Cola either had to set up its own bottling operation to perform these marketing channel functions, or find another bottler, which it did. Since then, Pepsi has continued to improve its bottling procedures to control costs in difficult years and a challenging market.[2]

Consumer Benefits from Intermediaries

Consumers also benefit from the actions of intermediaries. Having the goods and services you want, when you want them, where you want them, and in the form you want them is the ideal result of marketing channels. In more specific terms, marketing channels help create value for consumers through these five utilities: time, place, form, information, and possession.

Purolator adds value by offering time utility to customers.

©Ron Bull/Toronto Star via Getty Images

- *Time utility* refers to having a product or service when you want it. For example, Purolator provides next-morning delivery and other time-oriented conveniences (as seen in the Infographic, "6 Reasons to Visit a Purolator Shipping Centre").

- *Place utility* means having a product or service available where consumers want it, such as having a Petro-Canada gas station located on a long stretch of a provincial highway.

- *Form utility* involves enhancing a product or service to make it more appealing to buyers. For example, retail stores such as Harry Rosen and Roots provide appealing displays of their products and an environment that caters to their customers.

- *Information utility* means providing consumers with the information they need to make an informed choice; information-packed websites and user manuals provide this type of utility.

- *Possession utility* involves efforts by intermediaries to help buyers take possession of a product or service, such as providing various ways for payment to be made for a product—by credit card, debit card, cash, or cheque.

ask YOURSELF

1. What is meant by a marketing channel?
2. What are the three basic functions performed by intermediaries?

Channel Structure and Organization

LO 2 A product can take many routes on its journey from producer to buyer, and marketers search for the most efficient route from the many alternatives available. As you'll see, there are some important differences between the marketing channels for consumer goods and those for business goods.

Marketing Channels for Consumer Goods and Services

Figure 10–4 shows the four most common marketing channel configurations for consumer goods and services. It also shows the number of levels in each marketing channel—that is, the number of intermediaries between

a producer and ultimate buyers. As the number of inter-mediaries between a producer and buyer increases, the channel is viewed as increasing in length. The producer → wholesaler → retailer → consumer channel is longer than the producer → consumer channel.

Channel A in Figure 10–4 represents a *direct channel* because a producer and ultimate consumers deal directly with each other. Many products and services are distributed this way. A number of insurance companies sell their financial services using a direct channel and branch sales offices. M&M Food Market, the Canadian frozen food retail chain, offers an online store and retail outlets. Because there are no intermediaries with a direct channel, the producer must perform all channel functions.

The remaining three channel forms are *indirect channels* because intermediaries are inserted between the producer and consumers and perform numerous channel functions. Channel B, with a retailer added, is most common when the retailer is large and can buy in large quantities from a producer. Packaged goods companies such as Procter & Gamble use this channel with large retailers such as Loblaws and Sobeys. These retailers buy in sufficient quantities to make it cost-effective for a producer to deal with only a retail intermediary. Adding a wholesaler in channel C is most common when the wholesaler sells to small retailers, such as independent convenience stores and small grocery stores that do not buy enough to warrant a producer selling to these retailers directly. Channel C is most common for low-cost, low-unit value items that are frequently purchased by consumers, such as candy, confectionary items, and magazines. For example, Mars sells its line of candies to wholesalers in case quantities; wholesalers can then break down (sort) the cases so that individual small retailers can order in boxes of much smaller quantities.

Channel D, the most indirect channel, is employed when there are many small manufacturers and many small retailers and an agent is used to help coordinate a large supply of the product. Mansar Products, Ltd., is a Belgian producer of specialty jewellery that uses agents to sell to wholesalers, which then sell to many small retailers.

Marketing Channels for Business Goods and Services

The four most common channels for business goods and services are shown in Figure 10–5. In contrast with channels for consumer products, business channels typically are shorter and rely on one intermediary or none at all because business users are fewer in number,

Figure 10–4
Common marketing channels for consumer goods and services

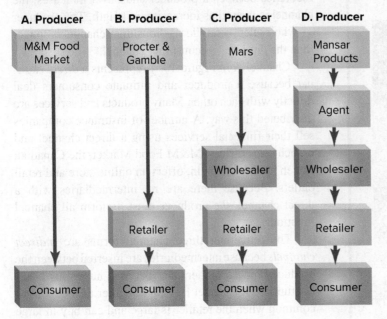

and require hands-on expertise in terms of installation or use. Bombardier and Airbus Industries would be other examples.

Channels B, C, and D are indirect channels with one or more intermediaries to reach industrial users. In channel B, an *industrial distributor* performs a variety of marketing channel functions, including selling, stocking, and delivering a full product assortment and financing. In many ways, industrial distributors are like wholesalers in consumer channels. Caterpillar relies on industrial distributors to sell and service its construction and mining equipment in almost 200 countries.

Channel C introduces another intermediary, an agent, who serves primarily as the independent selling arm of producers and represents a producer to industrial users. For example, Stake Fastener Company, a producer of industrial fasteners, has an agent call on industrial users rather than employing its own sales force.

Channel D is the longest channel and includes both agents and distributors. For instance, Culligan, a producer of water treatment equipment, uses agents to call on distributors who sell to industrial users.

tend to be more concentrated geographically, and buy in larger quantities. For these reasons, business channels can be served directly or by a limited number of intermediaries.

Channel A, represented by IBM's large, mainframe computer business, is a direct channel. Firms using this kind of channel maintain their own sales force and perform all channel functions. This channel is employed when buyers are large and well-defined, the sales effort requires extensive negotiations, and the products are of high unit value

electronic marketing channels
Channels that use the Internet to make goods and services available to consumers or business buyers.

Electronic Marketing Channels

The marketing channels that we have just discussed for consumer and business goods and services are not the only routes to the marketplace. Advances in electronic commerce have opened new avenues for reaching buyers and creating customer value.

Interactive electronic technology has made possible **electronic marketing channels**, which employ the Internet to make goods and services available to consumers or business buyers. A unique feature of these channels is that they can combine electronic and traditional intermediaries to create time, place, form, information, and possession utility for buyers.[3]

Figure 10–6 shows the electronic marketing channels for books (**Amazon.ca**), travel reservation services (**Travelocity.ca**), and personal computers (**Dell.ca**). Are you surprised that they look a lot like common marketing channels? An important reason for the similarity resides in the channel functions detailed in Figure 10–3. Electronic intermediaries can and do

Figure 10–5
Common marketing channels for business goods and service

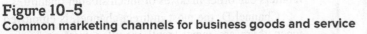

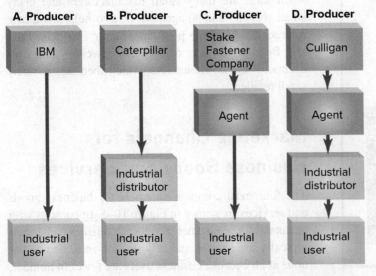

Figure 10–6
Examples of electronic marketing channels

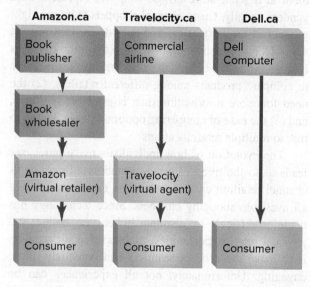

Amazon.ca	Travelocity.ca	Dell.ca
Book publisher	Commercial airline	Dell Computer
Book wholesaler		
Amazon (virtual retailer)	Travelocity (virtual agent)	
Consumer	Consumer	Consumer

perform transactional and facilitating functions effectively and at a relatively lower cost than traditional intermediaries because of efficiencies made possible by information technology. However, electronic intermediaries are incapable of performing elements of the logistical function, particularly for products such as books and automobiles. This function remains with traditional intermediaries or with the producer, as seen with Dell and its direct channel.

Many services are distributed through electronic marketing channels, such as travel services marketed by **Travelocity.ca**, financial securities by Royal Bank, and insurance by Metropolitan Life. Software, too, can be marketed this way. However, many other services, such as health care and auto repair, still involve traditional intermediaries.

Coke distributes Canada Dry soft drinks to stores in Canada.
©Bradcalkins/Dreamstime.com/GetStock.com

Multiple Channels and Strategic Alliances

In some situations, producers use **dual distribution**, an arrangement whereby a firm reaches different buyers by employing two or more different types of channels for the same basic product. For instance, GE sells its large appliances directly to home and apartment builders but uses retail stores, including Walmart, to sell to consumers. In some instances, firms pair multiple channels with a multibrand strategy. This is done to minimize cannibalization of the firm's family brand and to differentiate the channels. For example, Hallmark sells its Hallmark greeting cards through Hallmark stores and select department stores, and its Ambassador brand of cards through discount and drugstore chains.

A recent development in marketing channels is the use of *strategic channel alliances*, whereby one firm's marketing channel is used to sell another firm's products.[4] An alliance between Canada Dry and Coke is a case in point. Coke distributes Canada Dry soft drinks to stores in Canada. Strategic alliances are popular in global marketing, where the creation of marketing channel relationships is expensive and time-consuming. For example, General Mills and Nestlé have an extensive alliance that spans 70 international markets from Brazil to Poland to Thailand.

Multichannel Marketing to the Online Consumer

Consumers and companies populate two market environments today. One is the traditional marketplace, where buyers and sellers engage in face-to-face exchange relationships in an environment characterized by physical facilities (stores and offices) and mostly tangible objects. The other is the *marketspace*, an Internet/web-enabled digital environment characterized by "face-to-screen" exchange relationships and electronic images and offerings.

The existence of multiple market environments has benefited consumers tremendously. Today, consumers can shop for and purchase a wide variety of products and services in either market environment. Many consumers now browse and buy in multiple environments, and more are expected to do so in the future. With so many consumers browsing and buying in different environments, few companies limit their marketing programs exclusively

dual distribution
Arrangement whereby a firm reaches buyers by using two or more different types of channels for the same basic product.

to the traditional marketplace or to the online marketspace. Today, it is commonplace for companies to maintain a presence in both market environments. This dual presence is called *multichannel marketing*.

Integrating Multiple Channels with Multichannel Marketing

Companies often employ multiple marketing channels for their products and services. Multichannel marketing bears some resemblance to dual distribution. For example, different communication and delivery channels are used, such as catalogues, kiosks, retail stores, and websites. However, the resemblance ends at this point. **Multichannel marketing** is the *blending* of different communication and delivery channels that are *mutually reinforcing* in attracting, retaining, and building relationships with consumers who shop and buy in the traditional marketplace and in the online marketspace. Multichannel marketing seeks to integrate a firm's communication and delivery channels, not differentiate them. In doing so, consumers can browse and buy any time, anywhere, any way, expecting that the experience will be similar regardless of channel.

Multichannel marketing is essential to success. Allowing business to measure results and make changes rapidly is one benefit, while ensuring a seamless customer experience is another benefit. At Eddie Bauer, for example, every effort is made to make the apparel shopping and purchase process for its customers the same in its retail stores, through its catalogues, and at its website. According to an Eddie Bauer marketing manager, "We don't distinguish between channels because it's all Eddie Bauer to our customers."[5]

Multichannel marketing can also leverage the value-adding capabilities of different channels. For example, retail stores leverage their physical presence by allowing customers to pick up their online orders at a nearby store, or return or exchange non-store purchases at the store if they wish. For instance, a consumer can purchase a laptop computer on the Staples website and pick up the computer at any Staples store.

Another example of multichannel marketing is the **cross-channel shopper**, who researches products online and then purchases them at a retail store. These shoppers represent both genders equally. Cross-channel shoppers want the right product at the best price, and they don't want to wait several days for delivery. The top reasons these shoppers look online before buying in stores include (1) the desire to compare products among different retailers, (2) the need for more information than is available in stores, and (3) the ease of comparing options without having to trek to multiple retail locations.

The evolution of how individuals make purchases leads us to the trend of omni-channel retailing. Omni-channel retailing creates a seamless experience among all available shopping channels. Since technology has made it difficult to distinguish between online and physical retail opportunities, the next step for retailers is to make the process seamless and potentially more engaging. Unfortunately, not all experiences can be engaging, and retailers have been facing challenges of slower growth as shown in the Marketing NewsFlash box, "Closing the Channel Gap."[6] Both online and offline retailers need to be ready for the changes in the competitive landscape. It will become an expectation for them to invest resources toward omni-channel retailing to meet the demand of consumers.[7]

Implementing Multichannel Marketing It should not be surprising to you that not all companies use websites for multichannel marketing the same way. Different companies apply the value-creation capabilities

The Gap generates more sales volume from its website than any one of its stores, except for one.

©McGraw-Hill Education/Andrew Resek

Closing the Channel Gap

Retailers are facing many challenges with slower growth and competing channels. Once a thriving clothing and accessories retailer, The Gap, Inc. made an announcement in early 2019 to close stores in Canada. These closures were part of a global strategy to close almost half of Gap's locations in the next two years.

Closing stores will reduce annual sales, eliminating the fixed and variable costs from low-profit stores; however, these cost reductions will also lead to multimillion-dollar savings for the organization. The Gap, Inc. also announced it would split its brands into two companies: one with Old Navy and the other with Gap, Banana Republic, Athleta, Intermix, and Hill City.

Although Gap created an iconic clothing brand spanning across over 70 countries, the 2019 closures were not the first time The Gap revised its distribution strategy. In 2015, Gap announced closures of over 175 stores in the United States and Canada, bringing its total number of stores in North America to approximately 800. ●

Store closures are in Gap's future.
©Francesco Losenno/Shutterstock

Questions

1. Knowing that iconic brands like Gap are closing retail stores, what distribution strategy would you consider if you were a new retailer?

2. Other than customers, what organizations in the supply chain are impacted by Gap's store closures?

---

of Internet/web technology differently depending on their overall marketing program. Websites can play multiple roles in multichannel marketing because they can serve as either a communication or delivery channel, or as both. There are two general types of websites, classified based on their intended purpose: transactional websites and promotional websites.

Transactional websites are essentially electronic storefronts. They focus mainly on converting an online browser into an online, catalogue, or in-store buyer using website design elements. Transactional websites are most common among store and catalogue retailers such as Lee Valley. The Gap, for instance, generates more sales volume from its website than from any one of its stores, except for one. The company has built on its online success and prepared for the future by forming an innovation and digital strategy group to take advantage of growing e-tailing in Canada.[8]

Transactional websites are used less frequently by manufacturers of consumer products, but a recurring issue for manufacturers is the threat of channel conflict by harming their relationships with their retailing intermediaries. Hudson's Bay, for instance, would not be very happy if a brand of jeans it carries is being sold online directly from the manufacturer to the consumer; however, Ethan Allen, the furniture manufacturer,

markets its product line at **www.ethanallen.com** whenever feasible. Ethan Allen has attempted to address channel conflict by having retailers fill online orders and receive 25 percent of the sales price. For items shipped directly from the Ethan Allen factory, the store nearest the customer receives 10 percent of the sales price.[9]

Promotional websites have a different purpose than transactional sites: No actual selling takes place on them, but they showcase products and services and provide information.

Global Channel Strategy

Distribution is of critical importance in global marketing. The availability and quality of retailers and wholesalers as well as transportation, communication, and warehousing facilities are often determined by a country's economic infrastructure. Figure 10–7 outlines the channel through which a product manufactured in one country must travel to reach its destination in another country. The first step involves the seller; its headquarters is responsible for the successful distribution to the ultimate consumer.

The next step is the channel between two nations, moving the product from one country to another.

Figure 10–7
Channels of distribution in global marketing

Seller → Seller's international marketing headquarters → Channels between nations → Channels within foreign nations → Final consumer

vertical marketing systems

Professionally managed and centrally coordinated marketing channels designed to achieve channel economies and maximum marketing impact.

Intermediaries that can handle this responsibility include resident buyers in a foreign country, independent merchant wholesalers who buy and sell the product, and agents who bring buyers and sellers together.

Once the product is in the foreign nation, that country's distribution channels take over. These channels can be very long or surprisingly short, depending on the product line. In Japan, fresh fish can go through three intermediaries before getting to a retail outlet. Conversely, shoes go through only one intermediary. The sophistication of a country's distribution channels increases as its economic infrastructure develops. Supermarkets are helpful in selling products in many nations, but they are not popular or available in many others where culture and a lack of refrigeration dictate shopping on a daily rather than a weekly basis. For example, when Coke and Pepsi entered China, both

had to create direct distribution channels, investing in refrigerator units for small retailers.

Vertical Marketing Systems

The traditional marketing channels described so far represent a network of independent producers and intermediaries brought together to distribute goods and services. However, channel arrangements have emerged for the purpose of improving efficiency in performing channel functions and achieving greater marketing effectiveness. These arrangements are called vertical marketing systems. **Vertical marketing systems** are professionally managed and centrally coordinated marketing channels designed to achieve channel economies and maximum marketing impact. They encourage collaboration, shared responsibility, and partnership between the manufacturers and retailers in a system.[10] Figure 10–8 depicts the major types of vertical marketing systems: corporate, contractual, and administered.

Figure 10–8
Types of vertical marketing systems

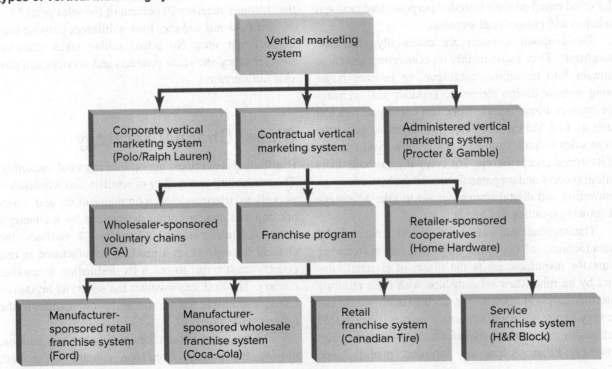

Vertical marketing system

- Corporate vertical marketing system (Polo/Ralph Lauren)
- Contractual vertical marketing system
- Administered vertical marketing system (Procter & Gamble)

Contractual vertical marketing system:
- Wholesaler-sponsored voluntary chains (IGA)
- Franchise program
- Retailer-sponsored cooperatives (Home Hardware)

Franchise program:
- Manufacturer-sponsored retail franchise system (Ford)
- Manufacturer-sponsored wholesale franchise system (Coca-Cola)
- Retail franchise system (Canadian Tire)
- Service franchise system (H&R Block)

Tiffany & Co. and H&R Block represent two different types of vertical marketing systems.

(left) ©Allstar Picture Library/Alamy Stock Photo; (right) Used with permission of H&R Block

Corporate Systems

Under a *corporate vertical marketing system*, a firm at one level of a channel owns the firm at the next level or owns the entire channel. For example, a producer might own the intermediary at the next level down in the channel. This practice, called *forward integration*, is exemplified by Polo/Ralph Lauren, which manufactures clothing and also owns apparel shops. Another example of forward integration is Goodyear, which distributes its tires not only through preferred stores but also through its own retail stores. Alternatively, a retailer might own a manufacturing operation, a practice called *backward integration*. For example, Tiffany & Co., the exclusive jewellery retailer, manufactures about half of the fine jewellery items for sale through its 150 stores and boutiques worldwide.

Companies seeking to reduce distribution costs and gain greater control over supply sources or resale of their products pursue forward and backward integration. Many companies favour contractual vertical marketing systems to achieve channel efficiencies and marketing effectiveness.

Contractual Systems

Under a *contractual vertical marketing system*, independent production and distribution firms combine their efforts on a contractual basis to obtain greater functional economies and marketing impact than they could achieve alone. Contractual systems are the most popular among the three types of vertical marketing systems. They account for about 40 percent of all retail sales.

Three variations of contractual systems exist. The first contractual system, *wholesaler-sponsored* *voluntary chains*, involves a wholesaler that develops a contractual relationship with small, independent retailers to standardize and coordinate buying practices, merchandising programs, and inventory management efforts. With the organization of a large number of independent retailers, economies of scale and volume discounts can be achieved to compete with chain stores. Independent Grocers Alliance (IGA) was the largest group of independent grocers in Canada and pursued this strategy. The group garnered the interest of Sobeys, which purchased the stores and incorporated a different business model.

Retailer-sponsored cooperatives exist when small, independent retailers form an organization that operates a wholesale facility cooperatively. Member retailers then concentrate their buying power through the wholesaler and plan collaborative promotional and pricing activities. Home Hardware is an example of a retailer-sponsored cooperative. The Marketing NewsFlash box, "Putting the Right Tools in Place," explains the benefits of this structure.[11]

The most visible variation of contractual systems is **franchising**, a contractual arrangement between a parent company (a franchiser) and an individual or firm (a franchisee) that allows the franchisee to operate a certain type of business under an established name and according to specific rules set by the franchiser.

Four types of franchise arrangements are most popular. *Manufacturer-sponsored retail franchise systems*

franchising
Contractual arrangement in which a parent company (the franchiser) allows an individual or firm (the franchisee) to operate a certain type of business under an established name and according to specific rules set by the franchiser.

Putting the Right Tools in Place

Home Hardware is an example of a retail-sponsored cooperative. Small independent retailers work together to concentrate their resources. This allows for collaboration and builds economies of scale for promotions and pricing activities.

Home Hardware stores are proudly 100 percent Canadian-owned. Approximately 1,100 independent small business operators across Canada operate under the store names Home Hardware, Home Hardware Building Centre, Home Building Centre, and Home Furniture.

Home Hardware facilitates the supply chain through distributions centres in St. Jacobs, Ontario; Elmira, Ontario; Debert, Nova Scotia; and Wetaskiwin, Alberta. The distributions centres hold over 100,000 products across 2.5 million square feet, and Home Hardware's fleet of over 400 yellow trucks, trailers, and vans deliver to stores across the country.

With new leadership overseeing Home Hardware, the organization is evolving into a "fully integrated retailer." What initially started as a wholesaling function supporting independent retailers across the country, Home Hardware is building a leadership team to be a repair and renovations chain that can be consistent among all of its marketing touch points.

Home Hardware believes its success comes from its dealers. The entrepreneurial spirit of the men and women that listen to and meet the needs of customers are the core of this organization. With the changing landscape of retailing, Home Hardware executives want to prepare their dealers for competition across Canada and around the world. As customers interact with the Home Hardware brand in-person and digitally, the organization needs to meet and exceed expectations in all those touch points.

As more and more consumers interact digitally with brands, companies like Home Hardware will continue to build marketing campaigns with digital and social strategies to connect with them. Connecting with new homeowners or young

Small businesses can operate under Home Hardware Building Centre and Home Furniture as well as Home Hardware and Home Hardware Building Centre.
©Kevin Brine - Editorial/Alamy Stock Photo

families digitally will reinforce Home Hardware's brand of being a helping hand. Its brand taglines of "Home of the Handyman," "Help Is Close to Home," and "Homeowners Helping Homeowners," have developed into a "Here's How," message. ●

Questions

1. Why is it important for Home Hardware to have a digital and social strategy?

2. What other touch points could Home Hardware create in-store or out-of-store to reinforce its "Here's How" message?

---

are prominent in the automobile industry, where a manufacturer such as Ford licenses dealers to sell its cars subject to various sales and service conditions. *Manufacturer-sponsored wholesale franchise systems* appear in the soft-drink industry, where Pepsi-Cola licenses wholesalers (bottlers) that purchase concentrate from Pepsi-Cola and then carbonate, bottle, promote, and distribute its products to supermarkets and restaurants. *Retail franchise systems* are provided by firms that have designed a unique approach for selling merchandise to consumers. Canadian Tire and McDonald's represent this franchising approach.

Service franchise systems exist when franchisers license individuals or firms to dispense a service under a trade name and specific guidelines. An example is H&R

Block tax services. Service franchise arrangements are the fastest-growing type of franchise.

Administered Systems   Ownership of a marketing system is not always necessary to achieve desired results. *Administered vertical marketing systems* achieve coordination at successive stages of production and distribution by the size and influence of one channel member. Procter & Gamble, given its broad product assortment ranging from disposable diapers to detergents, is able to obtain cooperation from supermarkets in displaying, promoting, and pricing its products. Given its position as the world's largest retailer, Walmart can obtain cooperation from manufacturers in terms of product specifications, price levels, and promotional support.

ask YOURSELF

1. What is the difference between a direct and an indirect channel?

2. What is the major distinction between a corporate vertical marketing system and an administered vertical marketing system?

Channel Choice and Management

LO 3 Marketing channels not only link a producer to its buyers but also provide the means through which a firm executes various elements of its marketing strategy. Therefore, choosing a marketing channel is a critical decision.

Factors Affecting Channel Choice

The final choice of a marketing channel by a producer depends on a number of market, product, and company factors. Providing convenience to retail consumers may provide advantages in certain industries, like Canada's $6.2 billion coffee industry.

Convenient Coffee Options

Canadians have plenty of options when choosing their morning brew.

Tim Hortons	Over 3,600 locations
McDonald's	Over 1,400 locations
Starbucks	Over 1,200 locations
Second Cup	Over 300 locations

Market Factors

- **Geographic concentration of the market:** When most of a firm's customers are concentrated in a few geographic areas, a direct sale to customers is practical. When customers are geographically dispersed, a direct sale is likely to be impractical due to high travel costs. Sellers may establish sales branches in densely populated markets and use intermediaries in less-concentrated markets.

- **Number of potential customers:** A manufacturer with few potential customers may use its own sales force to sell directly to ultimate consumers or business users. Bombardier uses this approach in selling its jet aircrafts and subway cars. For a large number of customers, the manufacturer would probably use intermediaries. For example, Tim Hortons relies on numerous franchisee outlets to reach the large number of consumers buying coffee.

- **Type of market:** Consumer products are made available through retailers, while business products are sold either direct to customers or through intermediaries.

- **Order size:** Direct distribution makes sense when an order size is large. For example, Campbell's delivers its soups directly to large grocery chains. On the other hand, Campbell's uses wholesalers to reach small independent grocery and convenience stores, whose orders are usually too small to justify a direct sale.

> *It would not make sense for Hershey Canada to call on households to sell an Oh Henry! chocolate bar.*

Product Factors

- **Technical factors:** In general, highly sophisticated products, such as custom-built machinery and scientific computers, are distributed direct to buyers. The producer's sales force must provide considerable pre-purchase and post-purchase service for these types of products, and typically, wholesalers do not do these tasks.

- **Perishability:** Some goods, such as milk and bread, deteriorate fairly quickly. As a result, these types of products go directly from the producer to the retailer, no matter the size of the order.

- **Unit value:** The price attached to each unit of a product affects the amount of funds available for distribution. For example, a company like Bombardier can afford to use its own employees to sell aircraft costing millions of dollars. But it would not make sense for Hershey Canada to call on households to sell an Oh Henry! chocolate bar. That's why intermediaries such as convenience stores, vending machines, and gasoline service stations carry low unit-value products.

- **Product life cycle:** Over time, some products, such as the Apple iPad, become very popular, easy to operate, and available in more mainstream channels such as Walmart and Best Buy.

Tim Hortons is an example of a retail franchise system.
©eye35.pix/Alamy Stock Photo

clientele enjoys buying products that are not available everywhere. The retailer may command a premium price for the jam because of its perceived quality and limited distribution.

- **Desire for channel control:** Some producers establish direct channels because they want to control their product's distribution, even though a direct channel may be more costly than an indirect channel. For example, Gap Inc. employs designers to come up with the styles that consumers want. Instead of selling Gap products to independent retailers, Gap Inc. assures distribution with its more than 3,000 Gap stores. Having its own stores assures Gap that its products are marketed properly and merchandised prominently.

Channel Design Considerations

Marketing executives consider three questions when choosing a marketing channel and intermediaries:

1. Which channel and intermediaries will best reach the target market?
2. Which channel and intermediaries will best serve the needs of the target market?
3. Which channel and intermediaries will lead to the most cost-efficient and profitable results?

Target Market Coverage Achieving the best coverage of the target market requires attention to the density—that is, the number of stores in a given geographical area—and type of intermediaries to be used at the retail level of distribution. Three degrees of distribution intensity exist: intensive, exclusive, and selective.

Intensive distribution means that a firm tries to place its products and services in as many outlets as possible. Intensive distribution is usually chosen for convenience products or services, such as candy, newspapers, and soft drinks. For example, Coca-Cola's retail distribution objective is to place its products "within an arm's reach of desire."

Exclusive distribution is the extreme opposite of intensive distribution because only one retail outlet in a specified geographical area carries the firm's products. Exclusive distribution is typically chosen for specialty products or services such as specialty automobiles, some women's fragrances, men's and women's apparel and accessories, and yachts. Sometimes, retailers sign exclusive distribution agreements with manufacturers and suppliers.

Selective distribution lies between these two extremes and means that a firm selects a few retail

intensive distribution

A firm tries to place its products or services in as many outlets as possible.

exclusive distribution

Only one retail outlet in a specific geographical area carries the firm's products.

selective distribution

A firm selects a few retail outlets in a specific geographical area to carry its products.

Company Factors

- **Financial resources and ability of management:** A business with limited financial resources may be unable to employ its own salespeople, and thus resorts to using intermediaries such as selling agents or manufacturer's agents to reach customers. Also, businesses that have limited or no marketing know-how may elect to use intermediaries.

    A manufacturer of jams and marmalades may face limited markets for its products because it cannot afford the listing fees that supermarkets demand for the privilege of carrying the product. The manufacturer chooses instead to sell to small fruit and vegetable markets, who do not demand a listing fee and whose

outlets in a specific geographical area to carry its products. Selective distribution combines some of the market coverage benefits of intensive distribution with the control measures possible with exclusive distribution. For this reason, selective distribution is the most common form of distribution intensity. It is usually associated with products such as Rolex watches, Levi's jeans, and Samsung flat-panel TVs.

Satisfying Buyer Requirements A second objective in channel design is gaining access to channels and intermediaries that satisfy at least some of the interests buyers might have when they purchase a firm's products or services. These requirements fall into four categories: information, convenience, variety, and pre- or post-sale services.

Information is an important requirement when buyers have limited knowledge or desire specific data about a product or service. Properly chosen intermediaries communicate with buyers through in-store displays, demonstrations, and personal selling. Electronics manufacturers such as Apple and Sony have opened their own retail outlets, with highly trained personnel to inform buyers about their products and how they can meet the buyers' needs.

Convenience has multiple meanings for buyers, such as proximity or driving time to a retail outlet or hours of operation. For example, Mac's convenience stores, with outlets nationwide, many of which are open 24 hours a day, satisfy this interest for buyers. Candy and snack food firms benefit by gaining display space in these stores.

For other consumers, convenience means a minimum of time and hassle. Jiffy Lube and Mr. Lube, which promise to change engine oil and filters quickly, appeal to this aspect of convenience. Another example of convenience is Tim Hortons®, which has locations in Esso service stations across Canada.

Variety reflects buyers' interest in having numerous competing and complementary items from which to choose. Variety is seen in both the breadth and depth of products carried by intermediaries, which enhances their attractiveness to buyers. Thus, manufacturers of pet food and supplies seek distribution through pet stores such as PetSmart and PJ's Pets.

Services provided by intermediaries are an important buying requirement for products such as large household appliances that require delivery, installation, and credit. Therefore, Whirlpool seeks dealers that provide such services.

The late Steve Jobs, formerly Apple's CEO, was one person who believed that computer retailers have failed to satisfy the buying requirements of today's consumer. Believing that "buying a car is no longer the worst purchasing experience; buying a computer is number one," he launched Apple Stores.[12]

Profitability The third consideration in designing a channel is profitability, which is determined by the

Tim Hortons® has added convenient locations to Esso service stations across Canada.
©JHVEPhoto/Shutterstock

revenues earned minus cost for each channel member and for the channel as a whole. Cost is the critical factor of channel profitability. These costs include distribution, advertising, and selling expenses. The extent to which channel members share these costs determines the profitability of each member and of the channel as a whole.

Channel Relationships: Conflict and Cooperation

Unfortunately, because channels consist of independent individuals and firms, there is always potential for disagreements concerning who performs which channel functions, how profits are distributed, which products and services will be provided by whom, and who makes critical channel-related decisions. These channel conflicts necessitate measures for dealing with them.

Conflict in Marketing Channels

Channel conflict arises when one channel member believes another channel member is engaged in behaviour that prevents it from achieving its goals. Two types of conflict occur in marketing channels: vertical conflict and horizontal conflict. Although channel conflict may have a negative effect on channel performance, it can also encourage channels to find better efficiencies to deliver results.[13]

Vertical conflict occurs between different levels in a marketing channel—for example, between a manufacturer and a wholesaler or between a manufacturer and a retailer. An example of vertical conflict was when Coke and Costco had a disagreement on price. Costco claimed that Coke's selling price to Costco was too high. As a result, Costco stopped carrying Coke products. It took a month for the two channel members to resolve their differences before Coke once again was made available at Costco.[14]

Another type of vertical conflict arises when a channel member bypasses another member and sells directly to consumers, a practice called **disintermediation**. Apple is an excellent example of how disintermediation works. Before

Vertical conflict occurred between Coke and Costco.
©John Lee/Aurora Photos/ Getstock.com

Apple Stores existed, Apple products were sold through independent retailers. When Apple started opening its own stores, its retailers began to complain. In 2005, independent Apple retailers filed a lawsuit against Apple, accusing the company of giving preferential treatment to its own stores and harming their sales. The lawsuit claimed that Apple had favoured Apple Stores by providing significant discounts that were unavailable to independent retailers. It also claimed that Apple was holding back product from the independent retailers.

Horizontal conflict occurs between intermediaries at the same level in a marketing channel, such as between two or more retailers or two or more wholesalers that handle the same manufacturer's brands. For instance, one Toyota dealer might complain to Toyota that another Toyota dealer has located too close to its dealership and is affecting its business.

Cooperation in Marketing Channels

Conflict can have disruptive effects on the workings of a marketing channel, so it is necessary to secure cooperation among channel members. One means is through a *channel captain*, a dominant channel member that coordinates, directs, and supports other channel members. Channel captains can be producers, wholesalers, or retailers. Procter & Gamble assumes this role because it has a strong consumer following in brands such as Crest, Tide, and Pampers. Therefore, it can set policies or terms that supermarkets will follow. Walmart and Home Depot are retail channel captains because of their strong consumer image, number of outlets, and purchasing volume.

A firm becomes a channel captain because it is the channel member with the ability to influence the behaviour of other members.[15] Influence can take four

> ❝ *Conflict can have disruptive effects on the workings of a marketing channel.*

channel conflict
Arises when one channel member believes another channel member is engaged in behaviour that prevents it from achieving its goals.

disintermediation
Vertical channel conflict that arises when a channel member bypasses another member and sells directly to consumers.

forms. First, economic influence arises from the ability of a firm to reward other members because of its strong financial position. Microsoft Corporation and Toys "R" Us have such influence. Expertise is a second source of influence. Third, identification with a particular channel member creates influence for that channel member. For example, retailers may compete to carry the Ralph Lauren line, or clothing manufacturers may compete to be carried by Hudson's Bay or Holt Renfrew. In both instances, the desire to be associated with a channel member gives that firm influence over others. Finally, influence can arise from the legitimate right of one channel member to direct the behaviour of other members. This situation occurs under contractual vertical marketing systems where a franchiser can legitimately direct how a franchisee behaves.

ask YOURSELF

1. What are the three degrees of distribution intensity?

2. What are the three questions marketing executives consider when choosing a marketing channel and intermediaries?

Logistics and Supply Chain Management

LO 4 A marketing channel relies on logistics to make products available to consumers and industrial users. **Logistics** involves those activities that focus on getting the right amount of the right products to the right place at the right time at the lowest possible cost. The performance of these activities is *logistics management*, the practice of organizing the cost-effective flow of raw materials, in-process inventory, finished goods, and related information from point of origin to point of consumption to satisfy *customer requirements*. Although logistics primarily provide distribution services, there is underlying value to the supply chain.[16]

Three elements of this definition deserve emphasis. First, logistics deals with decisions from the source of raw materials to consumption of the final product—that is, the *flow* of the product. Second, those decisions have to be *cost-effective*. Third, while it is important to drive down logistics costs, there is a limit: A firm needs to drive down logistics costs as long as it can deliver

expected *customer service*, while satisfying customer requirements. The role of management is to see that customer needs are satisfied in the most cost-effective manner. When properly done, the results can be spectacular. Procter & Gamble is a case in point. Beginning in the 1990s, the company set out to meet the needs of consumers more effectively by collaborating and partnering with its suppliers and retailers to ensure that the right products reached store shelves at the right time and at a lower cost. The effort was judged a success when, during an 18-month period, Procter & Gamble's retailers recorded a US$65-million savings in logistics costs while customer service increased.[17]

The Procter & Gamble experience is not an isolated incident. Companies now recognize that getting the right items needed for consumption or production to the right place at the right time in the right condition at the right cost is often beyond their individual capabilities and control. Instead, collaboration, coordination, and information sharing among manufacturers, suppliers, and distributors are necessary to create a seamless flow of goods and services to customers. This perspective is represented in the concept of a supply chain and the practice of supply chain management.

Supply Chains versus Marketing Channels

A **supply chain** is a series of firms that perform activities required to create and deliver a good or service to consumers or industrial users. It differs from a marketing channel in terms of the firms involved. A supply chain is longer and includes suppliers that provide raw material inputs to a manufacturer as well as the wholesalers and retailers that deliver finished goods to you. The management process is also different. **Supply chain management** is the integration and organization of information and logistics activities across firms in a supply chain for the purpose of creating and delivering goods and services that provide value to consumers. The relation among marketing channels, logistics management, and supply chain management is shown in Figure 10–9. An important feature of supply chain management is its use of sophisticated information technology that allows companies to share and

logistics
Activities that focus on getting the right amount of the right products to the right place at the right time at the lowest possible cost.

supply chain
Sequence of firms that perform activities required to create and deliver a product to consumers or industrial users.

supply chain management
Integration and organization of information and logistics activities across firms in a supply chain for the purpose of creating and delivering goods and services that provide value to consumers.

Figure 10-9
How distribution channels work: the relationships between supplier networks, marketing channels, logistics management, and supply chain management

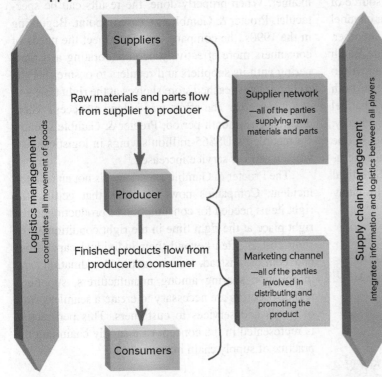

operate systems for order processing, transportation scheduling, and inventory and facility management.

Sourcing, Assembling, and Delivering a New Car: The Automotive Supply Chain

All companies are members of one or more supply chains. A supply chain is essentially a series of linked suppliers and customers in which every customer is, in turn, a supplier to another customer until a finished product reaches the ultimate consumer. Even a simplified

supply chain diagram for carmakers shown in Figure 10–10 illustrates how complex a supply chain can be.[18] A carmaker's supplier network includes thousands of firms that provide the 5,000 or so parts in a typical automobile. They provide items ranging from raw materials such as steel and rubber to components, including transmissions, tires, brakes, and seats, to complex sub-assemblies and assemblies such as in chassis and suspension systems that make for a smooth, stable ride. Coordinating and scheduling material and component flows for their assembly into actual automobiles by carmakers is heavily dependent on logistical activities, including transportation, order processing, inventory control, materials handling, and information technology. A central link is the carmaker supply chain manager, who is responsible for translating customer requirements into actual orders and arranging for delivery dates and financial arrangements for automobile dealers.

Logistical aspects of the automobile marketing channel are also an important part of the supply chain. Major responsibilities include transportation (which involves the selection and management of external carriers—trucking, airline, railroad, and shipping companies—for cars and parts to dealers), the operation of distribution centres, the management of finished goods inventories, and order processing for sales. Supply chain managers also play an important role in the marketing channel. They work with extensive car dealer networks to ensure that the right mix of automobiles is delivered to each location. In addition, they make sure that spare and service parts are available so that dealers can meet the car maintenance and repair needs of consumers. All of this is done with the help of information technology that links the entire automotive supply chain. What does all of this cost? It is

Figure 10-10
The automotive supply chain

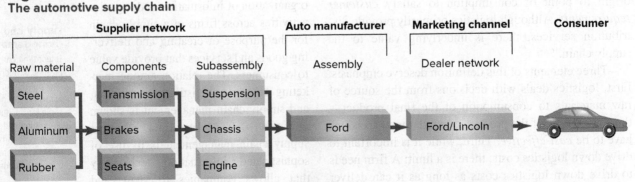

estimated that logistics costs represent 25 to 30 percent of the retail price of a typical new car.

Supply Chain Management and Marketing Strategy

The automotive supply chain illustration shows how logistics activities are interrelated and organized across firms to create and deliver a car for you. What's missing from this illustration is the linkage between a specific company's supply chain and its marketing strategy. Just as companies have different marketing strategies, they also manage supply chains differently. The goals to be achieved by a firm's marketing strategy determine whether its supply chain needs to focus on being more responsive or more efficient in meeting customer requirements.

Aligning a Supply Chain with Marketing Strategy

There are a variety of supply chain configurations, each of which is designed to perform different tasks well. Marketers today recognize that the choice of a supply chain follows from a clearly defined marketing strategy. With the globalization of the world economy and increased competition, see the importance of integrating supply chain management with their marketing strategy through the following three steps:[19]

1. *Understand the customer.* To understand the customer, a company must identify the needs of the customer segment being served. These needs, such as a desire for a low price or convenience of purchase, help a company define the relative importance of efficiency and responsiveness in meeting customer requirements.

2. *Understand the supply chain.* A company must understand what a supply chain is designed to do well. Supply chains range from those that emphasize being responsive to customer requirements and demand to those that emphasize efficiency with a goal of supplying products at the lowest possible delivered cost.

3. *Harmonize the supply chain with the marketing strategy.* A company needs to ensure that what the supply chain is capable of doing well is consistent with the targeted customer's needs and its marketing strategy. If a mismatch exists between what the supply chain does particularly well and a company's marketing strategy, the company will either need to redesign the supply chain to support the marketing strategy or change the marketing strategy. The bottom line is that a poorly designed supply chain can do serious damage to an otherwise brilliant marketing strategy.

How are these steps applied and how are efficiency and response considerations built into a supply chain? Let's briefly look at how two market leaders—Dell Computer Corporation and Walmart, Inc.—have harmonized their supply chain and marketing strategy.

Dell Computer Corporation: A Responsive Supply Chain

The Dell marketing strategy targets customers who want to have the most up-to-date personal computer equipment customized to their needs. These customers are also willing to wait to have their customized personal computer delivered in a few days, rather than picking out a pre-packaged model at a retail store, and they pay a reasonable, though not the lowest, price in the marketplace. Given Dell's market segments, the company has the option of choosing either an efficient or a responsive supply chain.

An efficient supply chain may use inexpensive but slower modes of transportation, emphasize economies of scale in its production process by reducing the variety of PC configurations offered, and limit its assembly and inventory storage facilities to a single location, say Austin, Texas, where the company is headquartered. If Dell opted only for efficiency in its supply chain, it would be difficult if not impossible to satisfy its target customer's desire for rapid delivery and a wide variety of customizable products. Dell instead has opted for a responsive supply chain. It relies on more expensive express transportation for receipt of components from suppliers and delivery of finished products to customers. The company achieves product variety and manufacturing efficiency by designing common platforms across several products and using common components. Dell also has invested heavily in information technology to link itself with suppliers and customers.

Dell has a responsive supply chain.
©The McGraw-Hill Companies, Inc./Jill Braaten

Walmart Stores Inc.: An Efficient Supply Chain Walmart's marketing strategy is to be a reliable, lower-price retailer for a wide variety of mass-consumption consumer goods. This strategy favours an efficient supply chain designed to deliver products to consumers at the lowest possible cost. By competing on price, Canadians are considering Walmart for some of their grocery needs.

Walmart's efficient supply chain allows it to keep relatively low inventory levels; that is, most inventory is stocked in stores available for sale, not in warehouses gathering dust. The low inventory arises from Walmart's use of *cross-docking*—a practice that involves unloading products from suppliers, sorting products for individual stores, and quickly reloading products onto its trucks for a particular store. No warehousing or storing of products occurs, except for a few hours or, at most, a day. Cross-docking allows Walmart to operate only a small number of distribution centres to service its vast network of stores and supercentres, which contributes to efficiency. It also uses fleet-management software to enhance operations.

This does increase cost and investment, but the benefits in terms of responsiveness justify the cost in Walmart's case. Walmart has invested significantly more than its competitors in information technology to operate its supply chain. The company feeds information about customer requirements and demand from its stores back to its suppliers, which manufacture only what is being demanded. This large investment has improved the efficiency of Walmart's supply chain and made it responsive to customer needs.

Walmart's strategy allows for availability of product. When renovating stores, Walmart ensures any construction is performed during off-hours. When reviewing its supply chain, Walmart continues to enhance its program by diligently assessing associated risks; that is, it reviews the countries it sources from, and assesses the compliance of its potential suppliers.

> *Walmart keeps relatively low inventory levels, and most inventory is stocked in stores available for sale, not in warehouses gathering dust.*

Walmart operates with an efficient supply chain.

©Niloo/Shutterstock

The SmartWay

The impact of vehicle emissions on our environment is concerning, and many companies are taking the initiative to address the issue. Some businesses have used the reduction of greenhouse emissions in their practices as a key focus of their corporate social responsibility.

In 2013, the SmartWay program was introduced in Canada. Natural Resources Canada and the Supply Chain Management Association partnered to bring this program across the border from the U.S. The U.S. Environmental Protection Agency originally launched the program, which shares industry best practices on supply chain transportation with its members.

The SmartWay Transport Partnership is a voluntary program that helps businesses transport goods efficiently. This free program keeps fuel costs and the impact on the environment low. Together,

organizations boost one another's environmental performance and accountability.

The SmartWay Transport Partnership tools help truck carriers to benchmark operations and track fuel consumption. This year-over-year analysis provides feedback to transportation companies and elicits accountability of each company's carbon footprint. Now, program members that can potentially have a negative impact on our environment can work together to create a greener process within the supply chain.

SmartWay helps its partners find SmartWay shippers, reduce operating costs, and reduce their companies' carbon footprint. By joining SmartWay as a SmartWay Partner, organizations send a message to stakeholders that their company is committed to clean freight and see environmental performance as a key business metric. ●

The SmartWay Transport Partnership helps boost environmental performance and accountability.
©Rouzes/E+/Getty Images

Questions

1. What are the main benefits that organizations receive from being members of SmartWay?

2. What Canadian companies do you believe need to join Smart-Way if they have not already?

In the United States, Walmart uses technology to efficiently run its supply chain. *RFID,* which stands for *radio frequency identification,* is a tag that is incorporated in a product for tracking purposes. RFID improves the efficiency of inventory tracking and management. Walmart has already asked its suppliers to use RFID. Walmart says that RFID will result in a 30 percent reduction of out-of-stock items and less excess inventory in the supply chain.[20] Some suppliers have complied, but many to date have not. The cost of using this new technology is the reason for them not going ahead.

Three lessons can be learned from these two examples. First, there is no one best supply chain for every company. Second, the best supply chain is the one that is consistent with the needs of the customer segment being served and complements a company's marketing strategy. And finally, supply chain managers are often called upon to make trade-offs between efficiency and responsiveness on various elements of a company's supply chain.

For a discussion of linking supply chain management with corporate social responsibility, review the Focus on Ethics box, "The SmartWay."[21]

Reverse Logistics

The flow of products in a supply chain does not end with the ultimate consumer or industrial user. Companies today recognize that a supply chain can work in reverse. **Reverse logistics** is a process of reclaiming recyclable and reusable materials, returns, and reworks from the point of consumption or use for repair, remanufacturing, redistribution, or disposal. The effect of reverse logistics can be seen in the reduced waste in landfills and lowered operating costs for companies.

reverse logistics
A process of reclaiming recycling recyclable and reusable materials, returns, and reworks from the point of consumption or use for repair, remanufacturing, redistribution, or disposal.

Key Logistics Functions in a Supply Chain

The four key logistics functions in a supply chain are transportation, order processing, inventory management, and warehousing. These functions have become so complex that many companies are outsourcing them to third-party logistics providers. Ultimately, successful logistics management minimize the total costs to logistics while delivering the appropriate level of customer service factors of time, dependability, communication, and convenience.

Transportation

There are five basic modes of transportation—railroads, motor carriers, air carriers, water carriers, and pipelines—as combinations involving two or more modes, such as highway trailers on a rail flatcar. Although many manufacturers pay transportation expenses, some retailers negotiate with their vendors to absorb this expense. The transportation modes can be evaluated on six basic service criteria:

- **Cost:** Charges for transportation
- **Time:** Speed of transit
- **Capability:** What can be realistically carried with this mode, such as controlled temperatures and humidity levels
- **Dependability:** Reliability of service regarding time, loss, and damage
- **Accessibility:** Ability to move products over a specific route or network; for example, some destinations, such as remote areas in northern parts of Canada, may be unavailable by truck or water
- **Frequency:** Refers to how often a marketer can ship products by a specific transportation mode. Pipelines provide continuous shipments whereas railways and water carriers follow specific schedules for moving products from one location to another.

Order Processing

Order processing is much more sophisticated these days with the use of **electronic data interchange (EDI)**. EDI is the computer-to-computer exchange of business documents from a retailer to a supplier and back. Purchase orders and invoices can be transmitted back and forth electronically, replacing manual processing. Walmart is a pioneer in using EDI. Now, many other retailers also use this system. The use of EDI increases the speed, accuracy, and streamlining of operations between retailer and supplier.

Inventory Management

Inventory management entails maintaining the delicate balance between keeping too little and too much inventory. For example, a retailer that carries too much inventory ends up with a lot of capital tied up in storing products in a warehouse. Too little inventory means that there is an increased risk for being out of stock and having unhappy customers.

A solution to this problem is the **just-in-time (JIT) inventory system**, which is designed to deliver less merchandise on a more frequent basis than traditional inventory systems. This system requires fast on-time delivery. The firm gets the merchandise "just-in-time" for it to be used in production of another product, or for sale when the customer wants it, in the case of consumer products.

Inventory management helps companies maintain optimal levels of inventory.

©Cultura Creative (RF)/Alamy Stock Photo

Although firms achieve great benefits from a just-in-time system, it is not without its costs. The logistics function becomes more complicated with more frequent deliveries. Greater order frequencies result in smaller orders, which are more expensive to transport and more difficult to coordinate.

Warehousing

There are two types of warehouses: a public warehouse offering storage for small companies or individuals, and a private warehouse is used usually by large firms. Most storage warehouses are located in the outskirts of the city where rail and truck transportation are easily available. Warehouses are places to store products, whereas distribution centres described below receive, store, and redistribute goods to customers.

Distribution centres can be divided into three types: traditional, cross-docking, and combination. In a traditional distribution centre, merchandise is unloaded from trucks and placed on shelves for storage. When the merchandise is required in stores, a worker goes to the shelf, picks up the item, and places it in a bin. A conveyer transports the merchandise to a staging area, where it is consolidated and made ready for shipment to stores.

The second type of distribution centre is called cross-docking. For example, Heinz ships ketchup pre-packaged in the quantity required for each Walmart store. It is then sent to a staging area rather than into storage. When all the merchandise going to a particular Walmart store has arrived in the staging area, it is loaded onto a Walmart truck that goes directly to the store.

The third type of distribution centre consists of a combination of the two types explained above. Most modern distribution centres are comprised of the third type. It is difficult for a company to operate without some storage facilities, even if merchandise is stored for only a few days.

ask YOURSELF

1. *Explain the concept of cross-docking.*
2. *Describe a just-in-time inventory system.*

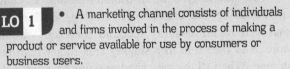

LO 1 • A marketing channel consists of individuals and firms involved in the process of making a product or service available for use by consumers or business users.

• Intermediaries make possible the flow of products and services from producers to buyers by performing transactional, logistical, and facilitating functions, thereby creating time, place, form, information, and possession utility.

LO 2 • Multichannel marketing is the blending of different communication and delivery channels that are mutually reinforcing in attracting, retaining, and building relationships with consumers.

• When consumers shop and buy in the traditional marketplace as well as in the online marketspace, marketers reinforce the consumer benefits of time, place, form, information, and possession utility.

• Vertical marketing systems are channels designed to achieve channel function economies and marketing impact. A vertical marketing system may be one of three types: corporate, contractual, or administered.

• Corporate systems display ownership of the next level or the entire channel.

• Contractual systems benefit from functional economies and marketing impact by combining efforts on a contractual basis.

• Administered systems achieve coordination through size and influence rather than ownership.

LO 3 • The final choice of a marketing channel by a producer depends on a number of factors.

They are market factors, product factors, and company factors.

• Channel design considerations are based on the target market coverage sought by producers, the buyer requirements to be satisfied, and the profitability of the channel.

• Target market coverage comes about through one of three levels of distribution density: intensive, exclusive, or selective distribution.

• Buyer requirements are evident in the amount of information, convenience, variety, and service sought by consumers.

• Profitability—of each channel member and the channel as a whole—is largely affected by costs and whether or not costs can be shared by members.

LO 4 • A supply chain is a sequence of firms that perform activities required to create and deliver a good or service to consumers or industrial users.

• Supply chain management is the integration and organization of information and logistics across firms for the purpose of creating value for consumers.

• The goals to be achieved by a firm's marketing strategy determine whether its supply chain needs to be more responsive or efficient in meeting customer requirements. Marketers today recognize that the choice of a supply chain involves three steps: (1) understand the customer, (2) understand the supply chain, and (3) harmonize the supply chain with the marketing strategy.

---

key terms and concepts... **A REFRESHER**

channel conflict
cross-channel shopper
disintermediation
dual distribution
electronic data interchange (EDI)
electronic marketing channels
exclusive distribution

franchising
intensive distribution
intermediaries
just-in-time (JIT) inventory system
logistics
marketing channel
multichannel marketing

reverse logistics
selective distribution
supply chain
supply chain management
vertical marketing systems

---

hands-on... **APPLY YOUR KNOWLEDGE**

The Importance of Supply Chain in Marketing The opening vignette describes the reliance companies have on intermediaries performing a logistical function. Review Figures 10–1 and 10–3 and create a list of companies that could potentially work with Fuzion Flooring to perform the transactional and facilitating function of the marketing channel.

In the opening vignette, a Fuzion Flooring executive describes the role of the company's supply chain to produce and deliver exceptional products to consumers across Canada. Considering the comments in the vignette, as well as the figures describing intermediaries and the marketing functions they perform, set out at least three expectations that Fuzion Flooring would have of its dealers.

The Infographic in this chapter outlines detail of the Purolator Shipping Centre locations. Consider the number of individuals working at each location. Now consider the different individuals and business being served. What would be the impact on business productivity if hours of these locations needed to be reduced?

Retailing and Wholesaling

Playing sports brings enjoyment to players, coaches, and spectators. Professional leagues like the National Basketball Association (NBA) surged in popularity and not only brought enjoyment to fans but also created opportunities in retailing and wholesaling.

©EPA/LARRY W. SMITH/The Canadian Press

CHAPTER OUTLINE

- Cap off a strong season
- The value of retailing
- Forms of ownership
- Target market selection and positioning
- Retailing mix
- Non-store retailing
- Online retailing
- Retailer's usage of the mobile channel
- Wholesaling

During the 2019 NBA Finals, the Eastern Conference champion Toronto Raptors won game six to win the first NBA championship in its franchise's history. The historic NBA championship galvanized a nation and brought a lot of excitement to Canadians coast-to-coast.

Canadians interviewed after the Raptors' first NBA championship could vividly remember where they watched the game. Some were in neighbours' homes while others were in restaurants that stayed open later than usual.

At the end of game six, instead of rushing onto the streets and celebrating with the rest of Canada, Ken Haqq and the New Era "Hot Market" team were busy coordinating the shipment of several thousand championship caps. After all, Canadians who supported a team to win its first NBA championship would want memorabilia to commemorate the occasion. "Manufacturers need intermediaries to meet the needs of consumers," shares Haqq. "Intermediaries create selection and availability for retailers as the needs of consumers change."

As the Canadian national director of sales and planning for the New Era Cap Company, Haqq has witnessed the evolution of the cap market segment. "It changed from a fan-based segment to a fashioned-based segment," explains Haqq. "When Spike Lee ordered the first red Yankees hat in 1996, it changed the industry. Sport and culture collided!"

In the business of capturing historic moments through its fashionable caps, New Era Cap Company has its fair share of history. The fourth-generation family-owned business began in manufacturing by producing 60,000 Gatsby-style hats in its first year. In 1934, the first New Era professional baseball cap was produced for the Cleveland Indians' uniforms. In the 1950s, New Era was one of only a few independent cap makers supplying caps to many of the 16 teams in Major League Baseball.

In the 1980s, New Era offered authentic Major League Baseball on-field player caps to fans through mail order. In 1996, New Era collaborated with Spike Lee in its first venture in fashion headwear. In the following millennium, New Era evolved into a global marketing company as influencers like rappers and filmmakers began representing their teams.

Ninety-five percent of New Era Cap Company's business is headwear. It is the official on-field cap of Major League Baseball, the official sideline cap of the National Football League, the official on-court cap of the NBA, and the official uniform and headwear provider for the Canadian Football League. The vision that marked New Era's growth in the 1920s and 1930s proved to be alive and well in the early part of the new millennium. The company's globalization efforts continued with offices in 18 international regions and sales in 125 countries worldwide. In 2001, Chris Koch was named CEO after serving as the company's president since 1993. And in 2006, the company moved its corporate offices from Derby back to downtown Buffalo, where it all started 86 years earlier.[1]

CHAPTER FEATURES

Cap Off a Strong Season
Discover what sales executives at New Era Cap Co., Inc. do to celebrate a championship.

What's Trending?
Led by a technology disruption, learn about five trends affecting Canadian retailers.

It's Not Easy Going Green
Greentailing in Canada is led by Roots.

Overcoming the Channel Gap
Learn about the challenges retailers are facing and their strategies to address their challenges.

Canadian Responsible Reputation
Do these 10 Canadian companies have a good reputation according to you?

Kiosks in Good Taste
McDonald's uses kiosks to create a customized experience.

Pedestrian Pandemic
A Canadian shoe chain files for bankruptcy during the COVID-19 pandemic.

Online Presents
Discover the top 10 sites where Canadians shop.

reality CHECK ⊘

As you read Chapter 11, refer back to the New Era vignette to answer the following questions:

- Why do you think the orders for merchandise items like baseball caps need to made as soon as possible?
- What is the value of retailers having championship merchandise in their stores the day after a championship?

The Value of Retailing

LO 1   **Retailing** includes all activities involved in selling, renting, and providing goods and services to ultimate customers for personal, family, or household use. Distribution involves creating a place where the customer can access a product. It is a key and evolving component of the marketing mix. As technology enables customers to access multiple channels of distribution, the challenge of retailers becomes anticipating customer needs and providing them with favourable purchasing options.

Retailing is an important marketing activity that engages consumers by offering a place for showcasing products that creates interest and excitement. Shopping is not only a way to acquire necessities but also a social activity and often an adventure—retailing makes this possible. Producers and consumers are brought together through retailing actions, and retailing also creates customer value and has a significant impact on the economy. Retailing's economic value is represented by the number of people employed in retailing as well as by the total amount of money exchanged in retail sales. As shown in the Infographic titled "5 Trends Canadian Retailers Need To Prepare For," technology is disrupting the retailing landscape.

Consumer Utilities Offered by Retailing

The utilities provided by retailers create value for consumers. Time, place, form, information, and possession utilities are offered by most retailers in varying degrees, but one utility is often emphasized more than others. Look at Figure 11–1 to find out how well you can match the retailer with the utility being emphasized in the description.

Placing minibanks in supermarkets puts the bank's products and services close to the consumer, providing place utility. Retail kiosks continue to grow in supermarkets and drugstores as this self-source technology is meant to improve service.[2] Hudson's Bay makes the purchase easier by offering different ways to pay for the purchase, providing possession utility. Form utility—production or alteration of a product—is offered by Ralph Lauren through its online "Create Your Own" program, which offers shirts that meet each customer's specifications. Finding well-stocked

retailing
All activities involved in selling, renting, and providing goods and services to ultimate consumers for personal, family, or household use.

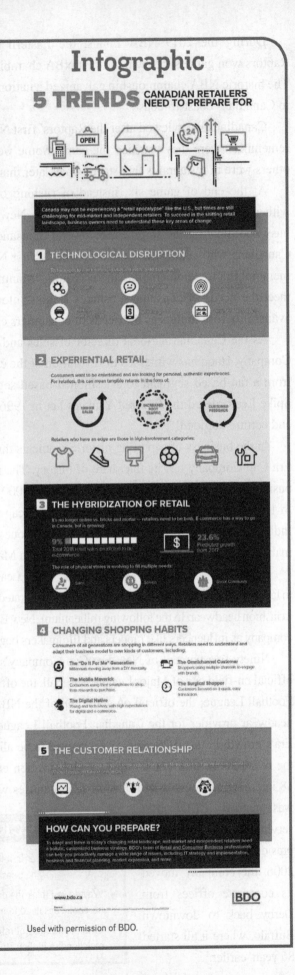

Infographic

5 TRENDS CANADIAN RETAILERS NEED TO PREPARE FOR

Canada may not be experiencing a "retail apocalypse" like the U.S., but times are still challenging for mid-market and independent retailers. To succeed in the shifting retail landscape, business owners need to understand these key areas of change.

1 TECHNOLOGICAL DISRUPTION

2 EXPERIENTIAL RETAIL

Consumers want to be entertained and are looking for personal, authentic experiences. For retailers, this can mean tangible returns in the form of:

Retailers who have an edge are those in high-involvement categories:

3 THE HYBRIDIZATION OF RETAIL

It's no longer online vs. bricks and mortar — retailers need to have both. E-commerce has a way to go in Canada, but is growing.

9% Total 2018 retail sales predicted to be e-commerce.

$ 23.6% Predicted growth from 2017

The role of physical stores is evolving to fill multiple needs:

4 CHANGING SHOPPING HABITS

Consumers of all generations are shopping in different ways. Retailers need to understand and adapt their business model to new kinds of customers, including:

- **The "Do It For Me" Generation** Millennials moving away from a DIY mentality.
- **The Mobile Maverick** Consumers using their smartphone to shop, from research to purchase.
- **The Digital Native** Young and tech-savvy, with high expectations for digital and e-commerce.
- **The Omnichannel Customer** Shoppers using multiple channels to engage with brands.
- **The Surgical Shopper** Customers focused on a quick, easy transaction.

5 THE CUSTOMER RELATIONSHIP

HOW CAN YOU PREPARE?

To adapt and thrive in today's changing retail landscape, mid-market and independent retailers need a holistic, customized business strategy. BDO's team of Retail and Consumer Business professionals can help you proactively manage a wide range of issues, including IT strategy and implementation, business and financial planning, market expansion, and more.

www.bdo.ca   **BDO**

Used with permission of BDO.

Figure 11–1
Which company best represents which utilities?

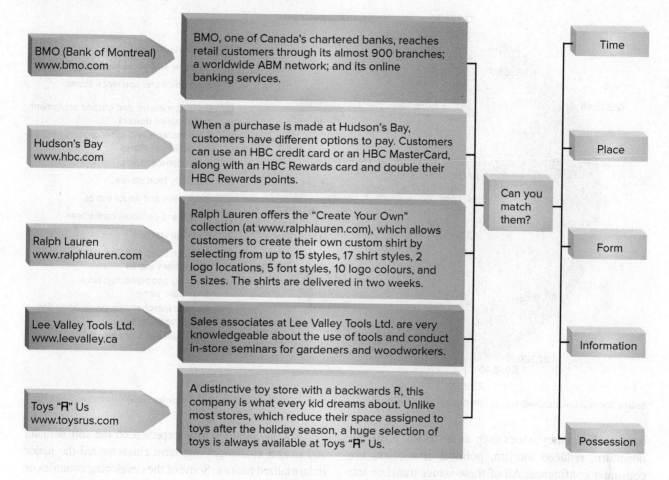

BMO (Bank of Montreal)
www.bmo.com

BMO, one of Canada's chartered banks, reaches retail customers through its almost 900 branches; a worldwide ABM network; and its online banking services.

Hudson's Bay
www.hbc.com

When a purchase is made at Hudson's Bay, customers have different options to pay. Customers can use an HBC credit card or an HBC MasterCard, along with an HBC Rewards card and double their HBC Rewards points.

Ralph Lauren
www.ralphlauren.com

Ralph Lauren offers the "Create Your Own" collection (at www.ralphlauren.com), which allows customers to create their own custom shirt by selecting from up to 15 styles, 17 shirt styles, 2 logo locations, 5 font styles, 10 logo colours, and 5 sizes. The shirts are delivered in two weeks.

Lee Valley Tools Ltd.
www.leevalley.ca

Sales associates at Lee Valley Tools Ltd. are very knowledgeable about the use of tools and conduct in-store seminars for gardeners and woodworkers.

Toys "Я" Us
www.toysrus.com

A distinctive toy store with a backwards R, this company is what every kid dreams about. Unlike most stores, which reduce their space assigned to toys after the holiday season, a huge selection of toys is always available at Toys "Я" Us.

Can you match them?

Time

Place

Form

Information

Possession

---

toy shelves year-round is the time utility dreamed about by every child (and many parents) who enters a retailer's toy section. Many retailers offer a combination of the four basic utilities. Some supermarkets, for example, offer convenient locations (place utility) and are open 24 hours (time utility). In addition, consumers may seek additional utilities such as entertainment, recreation, or information.

The Canadian Retail Scene

Retail is a vibrant and important part of the Canadian economy as retailers develop strong ties with Canadians throughout their everyday lives.

In 2016, Canadian retailers had revenues of over $532 billion.[3] In Canada, Loblaw Companies Limited, Empire Company Limited, and Metro Inc. are the top three in terms of sales, while Wal-Mart Stores Inc., Costco Wholesale Corporation, and The Kroger Co. are the top three globally.[4]

Figure 11–2 tells us that $115 billion was spent on food and drink in 2016. Supermarkets make up the majority of that retail spend, so it follows logically that the three largest retailers in Canada in terms of sales are predominantly in the food business.

There is a growing trend for American retailers to open locations in Canada. However, entering the Canadian retail scene is not easy. HBC sold the bulk of its weakest chain Zellers Inc. to the U.S. retail giant Target. The chain assumed control of up to 220 Zellers stores. The move, which came after years of rumours and discussion about Target's desire to acquire space in Canada, dramatically reshaped the domestic retail landscape. It underscored the growing demand by foreign retailers for Canadian locations to take advantage of the country's relatively healthy economy as well as the importance of Canadian retailers to be competitive to keep Canadians shopping at home. Unfortunately, two years after it opened its first stores in Canada, Target closed down its Canadian retail operations.[5]

The Global Retail Picture

Retailing is also a very important factor in the global economy, and it is a difficult retail climate for store owners. In the past few years, the worldwide economy has

Figure 11–2
Retail sales ($ millions) for 2016 in Canada by industry

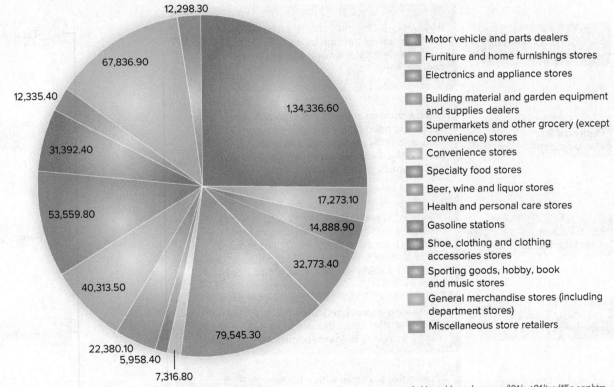

Legend:
- Motor vehicle and parts dealers
- Furniture and home furnishings stores
- Electronics and appliance stores
- Building material and garden equipment and supplies dealers
- Supermarkets and other grocery (except convenience) stores
- Convenience stores
- Specialty food stores
- Beer, wine and liquor stores
- Health and personal care stores
- Gasoline stations
- Shoe, clothing and clothing accessories stores
- Sporting goods, hobby, book and music stores
- General merchandise stores (including department stores)
- Miscellaneous store retailers

Pie chart values: 12,298.30; 67,836.90; 12,335.40; 31,392.40; 53,559.80; 40,313.50; 22,380.10; 5,958.40; 7,316.80; 79,545.30; 32,773.40; 14,888.90; 17,273.10; 1,34,336.60

Source: Statistics Canada, CANSIM, table 080-0020, February 22, 2017, accessed at http://www.statcan.gc.ca/tables-tableaux/sum-som/l01/cst01/trad15a-eng.htm.

been challenged by issues such as terrorism, economic downturn, reduced tourism, political crises, and low consumer confidence. All of these issues translate into lower sales for retail. At the same time, consumers are empowered, and it is more difficult to gain and maintain their loyalty. Profits have to be worked at very diligently. Technology is making the industry more sophisticated and streamlined, and consolidation makes some competitors large and very powerful. It is a demanding and thorny business.

Not all countries have experienced the soft demand and market challenges that have characterized the major industrialized nations. Some of the developing countries or emerging markets in Asia and Eastern Europe are experiencing solid growth and are developing modern types of retailing. China, India, and Russia are seen as some of the biggest growth opportunities for retail in the next few years.

A study of the top 250 global retailers by Deloitte ranks the world's biggest retailers. The chart accompanying Figure 11–3 shows that most of the top ten global

Figure 11–3
Where do we find the top retailers in the world? Who are they?

Rank	Country of Origin	Name of Company	FY2018 Retail Revenue (US$ Millions)
1	US	Wal-Mart Stores, Inc.	$514,405
2	US	Costco Wholesale Corporation	$141,576
3	US	Amazon.com Inc.	$140,211
4	Germany	Schwarz Group	$121,581
5	US	The Kroger Co.	$117,527
6	US	Walgreens Boots Alliance Inc.	$110,673
7	US	The Home Depot, Inc.	$108,203
8	Germany	Aldi Einkauf GmbH & Co. oHG	$106,175
9	US	CVS Health Corporation	$83,989
10	UK	Tesco PLC	$82,799

retailers have sought opportunities to serve consumers outside their country of origin.

ask YOURSELF

1. When Ralph Lauren makes shirts to a customer's exact preferences, what utility is provided?

2. The customer has different ways to pay for a purchase at Hudson's Bay. What utility is provided?

Forms of Ownership

LO 2 For manufacturers, consumers, and the economy, retailing is an important component of marketing that has several variations. Because of the large number of alternative forms of retailing, it is easier to understand the differences among retail institutions by recognizing that outlets can be classified by ownership. **Form of ownership** distinguishes retail outlets on the basis of whether individuals, corporate chains, or contractual systems own or control the outlet. Each form has its own benefits and challenges.

Independent Retailer

One of the most common forms of retail ownership is the independent business, owned by an individual. Small independent retailers account for more than 60 percent of the total retail trade in Canada. They tend to be retailers such as bakeries, sporting goods stores, jewellery stores, or gift stores. Other types of small independent retailers include restaurants, automotive supply stores, bookstores, paint stores, flower shops, and women's accessories outlets. The advantage of this form of ownership for the owner is that he or she can be his or her own boss. For customers, the independent store can offer convenience, quality personal service, and lifestyle compatibility. This is mainly due to the smaller organization being able to adapt and to be more efficient than its larger competitors.[6]

Corporate Chain

A second form of ownership, the corporate chain, involves multiple outlets under common ownership. If you've ever shopped at Hudson's Bay or Real Canadian Superstore, you've shopped at a chain outlet.

In a chain operation, centralization of decision-making and purchasing is common. Chain stores have advantages in dealing with manufacturers, particularly as the size of the chain grows. A large chain can bargain with a manufacturer to obtain good service or volume discounts on orders. Loblaw's large volume makes it a strong negotiator with manufacturers of most products. The buying power of chains is obvious to consumers who compare prices at chain stores with other types of stores. Consumers also benefit in dealing with chains because there are multiple outlets with similar merchandise and consistent management policies.

Retailing has become a high-tech business for many large chains. Walmart, for example, has developed a sophisticated inventory-management and cost-control system that allows rapid price changes for each product in every store. In addition, stores such as Walmart are implementing pioneering new technologies such as radio frequency identification (RFID) tags to improve the quality of information available about products. RFID is a tag that is incorporated in a product for tracking purposes, which improves the efficiency of inventory tracking and management.

Contractual System

Contractual systems involve independently owned stores that use leverage to act like a chain. Contractual systems include retailer-sponsored cooperatives, wholesaler-sponsored voluntary chains, and franchises. One retailer-sponsored cooperative is Home Hardware, which is a collection of independent hardware and home-renovation stores across Canada. Home Hardware actually created its own wholesale operation to take full advantage of dealings with manufacturers and suppliers. As a cooperative, members can take advantage of volume discounts commonly available to chains and also give the impression of being a large chain, which may be viewed more favourably by some consumers. Wholesaler-sponsored voluntary chains such as Independent Grocers' Association (IGA) try to achieve similar benefits.

In a franchise system, an individual or firm (the franchisee) contracts with a parent company (the franchisor) to set up a business or retail outlet. McDonald's,

form of ownership
Distinguishes retail outlets on the basis of whether individuals, corporate chains, or contractual systems own the outlet.

McDonald's offers franchising opportunities.

©David Cooper/Toronto Star via Getty Images

Holiday Inn, and Subway all offer franchising opportunities. The franchisor usually assists in selecting the store location, setting up the store, advertising, and training personnel. In addition, the franchisor provides step-by-step procedures for major aspects of the business and guidelines for the most likely decisions a franchisee will confront. The franchisee pays a one-time franchise fee and an annual royalty, usually tied to the store's sales. By selling franchises, an organization reduces the cost of expansion, although they lose some control. To ensure mutual benefits to all parties involved, a good franchisor concentrates on enhancing the image and reputation of the franchise name.[7]

Target Market Selection and Positioning

LO 3 Retailing involves many decisions and considerations. In this section, we look at the issues in selecting a target market and the concept of retail positioning.

Selecting a Target Market

The first task in developing a retail strategy is to define a target market, describing it in detail. Without customers, even the best-conceived retail concept is nothing, so focusing on customers is the guiding principle of successful retail businesses. This focus involves understanding wants and needs, knowing customer preferences, analyzing behaviour, and deciding how to craft all of the dimensions of the retail concept to appeal to the targeted customer. Look at any mall or shopping district, and you will see the varied selection of retail offerings the customer has to choose from. This provides a challenge to retailers. It is no longer enough to appeal to customers; now the retailer has to interest, engage, and delight customers in order to foster loyalty.

> *McDonald's and Subway look at demographics—population, family, and age characteristics—to determine where new restaurants should be located and what formats to offer.*

How do we define target markets? The most common descriptors are geographic, demographic, psychographic, and behaviouristic. Retailers study these factors and adjust their retail mix accordingly. McDonald's and Subway look at demographics—population, family, and age characteristics—to determine where new restaurants should be located and what formats to offer. Retailers such as Canadian Tire look at consumers' trends and tastes and adjust their product offerings and store composition to match customer preferences. Staples and Shoppers Drug Mart have adjusted their store hours to respond to the behaviour of consumers; many now prefer to shop and do errands in the evening after working during the day. In fact, some retailers are open 24 hours a day.

Retail Positioning

Just as marketers of packaged goods position their products to differentiate themselves from competitors, so do retailers. For example, Harry Rosen is a high-end men's clothing retailer. It would be a mistake in times of recession for Harry Rosen to start carrying lower-quality, low-priced suits. Larry Rosen, CEO and chairman of Harry Rosen Inc., and son of founder Harry Rosen, says, "The customer who is used to the quality and calibre of our product is not looking for a cheaper product. Maybe

Harry Rosen, a high-end men's clothing retailer, provides a good example of retail positioning.
Used by permission of Harry Rosen Inc.

he'll buy slightly less this year but it's not about reducing quality. It's about sticking to your guns, to who you are." The confidence to be able to do so comes from a deep understanding of your customers and their buying habits.[8]

Shopper Marketing

Shopper marketing is a hot trend in marketing today. It is a discipline designed to understand how consumers behave as shoppers in different channels and formats. Consequently, shopper-marketing practices extend well outside of the store, to the place and time when a consumer first thinks about purchasing a product. That might be on a treadmill at the gym, at home reading a magazine, or in the car while driving to work. That means that shopper marketing is by necessity a multichannel practice that makes use of traditional media, new media, direct marketing, loyalty, trade promotion, and innumerable other marketing techniques.

Underneath it all is one area that is largely alien to traditional marketers, whose focus has been almost exclusively on understanding *consumers*—that is, the consumption of goods and services. What's been ignored is understanding *shoppers*—that is, consumers when they are in the shopping mode. Shopper marketing is new to Canada, but the distinction in understanding shoppers is important.[9]

Retailing Mix

LO 4 The marketing mix, or the 4 Ps (product, price, place, and promotion), is used in retail just as it is in other businesses, but with some unique considerations. In this section, we look at the retailing mix, which includes product and service considerations, retail pricing, physical location factors, and communications, as shown in Figure 11–4. All of these components of the

Figure 11–4
The retailing mix

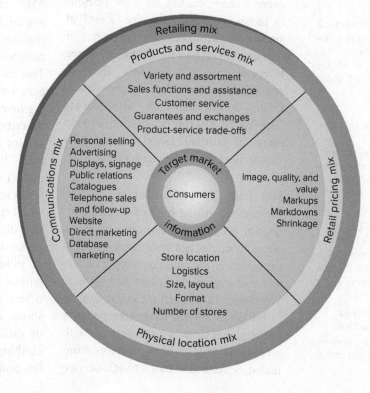

mix focus on the consumer. In retail, it is often said that the consumer is king, and treating consumers that way is a winning idea for successful retailing.

The positioning of a retail store must be consistent with the store's **retailing mix**. The four elements must be coordinated so that they portray a clear position to consumers. For example, Winners is positioned as a store providing upscale designer clothing at a discount price. If prices suddenly rose and consumers came to the conclusion that they were not getting a bargain, Winners' positioning would not be effective.

Products and Services

One of the first decisions that retailers make is what they are going to sell. Usually, both services and products are offered. McDonald's offers a hamburger, which is the tangible product, but the smiles, thank yous, and clean washrooms make up some of the service components. A department store such as Hudson's Bay sells many products—from clothing to housewares—and also provides services such as bridal registries. First Choice Hair Cutters provides services such as haircuts, colouring, and styling, but also sells hair care products. The balance between products and services involves a trade-off between costs and customer satisfaction.

Level of Service
Most customers perceive little variation in retail outlets by form of ownership. Rather, differences among retailers are more obvious in terms of level of service. **Level of service** is used to describe the degree of service provided to the customer. Three levels of service include self-, limited-, and full-service retailers. Stores such as Costco do not offer bags, while outlets such as Holt Renfrew provide a wide range of customer services from gift wrapping to wardrobe consultation.

SELF-SERVICE Self-service is at the extreme end of the level-of-service continuum because the customer performs many functions and little is provided by the outlet. Home building-supply outlets and gas stations are often self-service. Warehouse stores such as Costco, usually in buildings several times larger than a conventional store, are self-service, with all non-essential customer services eliminated. Several new forms of self-service

include FedEx's placement of self-service package shipping stations in retail stores and office buildings, and self-service scanning systems currently in use in Loblaw stores, Home Depot, Walmart, and other retailers.

LIMITED SERVICE Limited-service outlets provide some services, such as credit and merchandise return, but not others, such as alterations to clothes. General merchandise stores such as Shoppers Drug Mart and Ikea are usually considered limited-service outlets. Customers are responsible for most shopping activities, although salespeople are available in departments such as cosmetics at Shoppers Drug Mart.

FULL SERVICE Full-service retailers, which include most specialty stores and department stores, provide many services to their customers. Holt Renfrew, a Canadian specialty fashion retailer with nine stores across the country, is very committed to exemplary customer service. Its stores feature more salespeople on the floor than other similarly sized stores, and Holt Renfrew offers a national concierge service, as well as personal shopping in each store. Employees are trained in customer follow-up, and many call their clients to advise them of new merchandise and send thank-you notes after purchase. With an eye kept fixed on customers and their evolving needs, Holt Renfrew is a leader in merchandise assortments and in innovations in customer services demonstrated by its previous successes and future expansion plans.[10]

Merchandise Mix
Merchandise selection is one of the major attracting factors for customers, so choices and combinations must be made carefully and continually updated to reflect current trends and tastes. This involves finding sources of supply of the products, or having them manufactured, as well as managing inventory and warehousing. The **merchandise mix** describes how many different types of products a store carries and in what assortment. The Focus on Ethics box, "It's Not Easy Going Green," suggests that the move to carrying eco-friendly products is another factor in retailers' merchandise mix decisions.[11]

Retail outlets vary by their merchandise mix, the key distinction being the breadth and depth of the items offered to customers (see Figure 11–5). **Depth of product line** means the assortment of products within each product line, such as a shoe store that offers running shoes, dress shoes, and children's shoes. **Breadth of product line** refers to the variety of different lines a store carries, such as women's clothing, men's clothing, children's clothing, cosmetics, and housewares.

retailing mix
The goods and services, pricing, physical distribution, and communications tactics chosen by a store.

level of service
The degree of service provided to the customer by self-, limited-, and full-service retailers.

merchandise mix
How many different types of products a store carries and in what assortment.

depth of product line
The assortment of products within each product line.

breadth of product line
The variety of different items a store carries.

It's Not Easy Going Green

According to the Environmental Careers Organization (ECO) Canada, the green economy includes "inputs, activities, outputs, and outcomes as they relate to the production of green products and services." In essence, by "reducing resource consumption, harmful emissions, and minimizing all forms of environment impact," a new economy is created that can not only save money and our world but also create career opportunities. ECO Canada is a non-profit organization whose vision is to build the world's leading environmental workforce. It does this by creating online resources for careers and training.

Since consumers are becoming more and more aware of the impact of their purchases on the environment, green products have become increasingly available, and more emphasis is being placed on marketing these strategies. For example, apparel companies have begun to produce environmentally friendly clothing. For example, Roots employs sustainable practices through using eco-friendly materials and manufacturing clothes out of organic or recycled cottons. The company continues to develop more eco-friendly products each year.

Roots has made protecting the environment a core value. It believes the environment is one of the most critical issues of our time. Along with some of the world's leading environmentalists, Roots demonstrates its commitment through its actions and financial support of environmental organizations. A partial list of environmental organizations that Roots works with includes the David Suzuki Foundation, the Canadian Wildlife Federation, and the Jane Goodall Institute of Canada.

The larger strategy being considered in Canadian retailing and business is corporate social responsibility (CSR), where companies voluntarily conduct business in a manner that is sustainable from an economic, social, and environmental standpoint. Not only is CSR important locally, but Canadian companies see the value of incorporating their practices on an international scale. Considering what Roots is doing with its stores and apparel, it is surprising not to see them recognized in lists of reputable companies in corporate

©Jill Morgan/Alamy Stock Photo

social responsibility. Furthermore, seeing Roots' competitors, such as Adidas, Nike, and Gap, get recognized helps confirm the importance of CSR in Canadian retailing. ●

Questions

1. Describe the target market that retailers such as Roots are trying to reach by adopting green practices.

2. Considering a retailer you have made a purchase from, identify three changes it can make to its practices that would support a green economy.

Figure 11–5
Breadth versus depth of merchandise lines

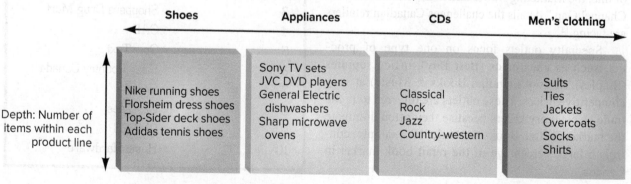

Breadth: Number of different product lines

	Shoes	Appliances	CDs	Men's clothing
Depth: Number of items within each product line	Nike running shoes Florsheim dress shoes Top-Sider deck shoes Adidas tennis shoes	Sony TV sets JVC DVD players General Electric dishwashers Sharp microwave ovens	Classical Rock Jazz Country-western	Suits Ties Jackets Overcoats Socks Shirts

Overcoming the Channel Gap

Retailers are facing many challenges with slower growth and competing channels. Once a thriving clothing and accessories retailer, The Gap, Inc. made an announcement in early 2019 to close stores in Canada. These closures were part of a global strategy to close almost half of Gap's locations in the next two years.

Although closing stores will reduce annual sales, eliminating the fixed and variable costs from low profit stores is predicted to lead to multi-million dollar savings for the company. The Gap, Inc. also announced it would split its brands into two companies: one with Old Navy and the other with Gap, Banana Republic, Athleta, Intermix and Hill City.

The 2019 closures were not the first time The Gap revised its distribution strategy. In 2015, The Gap announced closures of over 175 stores in the United States and Canada bringing its total number of stores in North America to approximately 800. Follow that up with the COVID-19 global pandemic in 2020 and retailers like the Gap struggled with the costs associated with their bricks and mortar strategy. ●

Questions

1. Knowing iconic brands like the Gap are closing stores, what would your distribution strategy be as a new retailer?

2. Other than customers, what other organizations are impacted by Gap's store closures?

©Tupungato/Shutterstock

DEPTH OF LINE Stores that carry a large assortment (depth) of a related line of items are limited-line stores. Sport Chek sporting goods stores carry considerable depth in sports equipment, ranging from golf accessories to running shoes. Stores that carry tremendous depth in one primary line of merchandise are single-line stores. Victoria's Secret, a nationwide chain, carries great depth in women's lingerie. Both limited- and single-line stores are often referred to as *specialty outlets*. Despite depth of line, the Marketing NewsFlash box, "Overcoming the Channel Gap," details the challenges Canadian retailers are facing.[12]

Specialty outlets focus on one type of product, such as electronics (Best Buy), office supplies (Staples), or books (Indigo Books & Music) at very competitive prices. These outlets are referred to in the trade as category killers because they often dominate the market. Indigo Books & Music, for example, controls a large percentage of the retail book market in Canada.

Canadian Responsible Reputation

The top 10 most reputable companies for corporate social responsibility in Canada:

Rank	Brand
1	MEC
2	Canadian Tire
3	Shoppers Drug Mart
4	CAE
5	OpenText
6	Sleep Country Canada
7	Roots
8	Cascades
9	OMERS
10	Home Hardware

!ndigo
Enrich your life

Indigo Books & Music is the largest book retailer in Canada and is a category killer.

Used with permission from Indigo

BREADTH OF LINE Stores that carry a variety of product lines, with limited depth, are referred to as *general merchandise stores*. For example, large department stores such as Hudson's Bay carry a wide range of different lines of products but not unusual sizes. The breadth and depth of merchandise lines are important decisions for a retailer. Traditionally, outlets carried related lines of goods. Today, however, **scrambled merchandising**, offering several unrelated product lines in a single store, is common. The modern drugstore carries food, cosmetics, camera equipment, magazines, paper products, toys, small hardware items, and pharmaceuticals. Supermarkets rent carpet-cleaning equipment, operate pharmacy departments, and sell flowers.

Scrambled merchandising makes it convenient for consumers because it eliminates the number of stops required in a shopping trip. However, for the retailer, this merchandising policy means that there is competition between very dissimilar types of retail outlets, or **intertype competition**. A local bakery may compete with a department store, discount outlet, or even a local gas station. Scrambled merchandising and intertype competition make retailing more challenging.

Planograms A planogram is a visual diagram or drawing of fixtures and products that illustrates how and where retail products should be placed on a store shelf. It also illustrates how many facings should be allocated for each stock-keeping unit (SKU). The planogram is arranged so that the fastest-moving high-margin products get the most space on the shelf. For example, Procter & Gamble works closely with Walmart by providing the retailer with planograms, which lead to higher profits than if products were placed indiscriminately on the shelf.

As competition increases, we're seeing suppliers and retailers becoming more aware of the importance of correctly merchandising their products. Some retailers produce their own planograms while others, such as Walmart, receive planograms from suppliers such as Procter & Gamble.

Store Atmosphere Store atmosphere is related to the positioning of a store. For example, Costco has a warehouse appearance that is consistent with the low prices that it offers. Store atmosphere refers to the physical characteristics of a store that provide an overall impression to the consumer. These characteristics consist of the exterior and interior appearance and physical layout of the store. The Apple Store's customer-friendly layout encourages consumers to mingle and sample the products. Apple successfully trademarked its store design, and continues to trademark the distinctive design and layout of its retail store in Canada. It filed an application with the Canadian Intellectual Property Office and received a trademark for its distinctive design and layout.[13]

The Apple Store is usually quite crowded. This frenetic atmosphere draws in even more people who want to be part of the "event." Every Apple Store offers a range of services designed to help customers get the most out of their Apple products, including face-to-face support and advice at the Genius Bar, hands-on workshops, and special programs for kids.

> **scrambled merchandising**
> Offering several unrelated product lines in a single retail store.
>
> **intertype competition**
> Competition between very dissimilar types of retail outlets.

Apple offers a store atmosphere allowing consumers to engage with Apple products.

©Piero Cruciatti/Alamy Stock Photo

Retail Pricing

In setting prices for merchandise, retailers must decide on the markup. The markup refers to how much should be added to the cost the retailer paid for a product to reach the final selling price. We discussed the calculation of markup in Chapter 9. The difference between the final selling price and retailer cost is called the gross margin.

Discounting a product, or taking a *markdown*, occurs when the product does not sell at the original price and an adjustment is necessary. Often, new models or styles force the price of existing models to be marked down. Discounts may also be used to increase demand for related products.[14] For example, retailers might take a markdown on DVD players to increase sales of DVDs or reduce the price of cake mix to generate frosting purchases. The *timing* of a markdown can be important. Many retailers take a markdown as soon as sales fall off, to free up valuable selling space and obtain cash. However, other stores delay markdowns to discourage bargain hunters and maintain an image of quality. There is no clear answer, but retailers must consider how the timing might affect future sales.

> *What is surprising is that more than 50 percent of thefts are made not by consumers but by employees.*

Although most retailers plan markdowns, many retailers use price discounts as a part of their regular merchandising policy. In Canada, retailers such as Walmart and Bed, Bath & Beyond emphasize consistently low prices and eliminate most markdowns with a strategy often called *everyday low pricing*.[15] Consumers often use price as an indicator of product quality; however, the brand name of the product and the image of the store become important decision factors in these situations.[16]

A special issue for retailers trying to keep prices low is **shrinkage**, or breakage and theft of merchandise by customers and employees. What is surprising is that more than 50 percent of thefts are made not by consumers but by employees.

Off-price retailing is a retail pricing practice that is used by retailers such as Winners. **Off-price retailing** involves selling brand-name merchandise at lower than regular prices. The difference between the off-price retailer and a discount store is that off-price merchandise is bought by the retailer from manufacturers with excess inventory at prices below wholesale prices, whereas the discounter buys at full wholesale price but takes less of a markup than do traditional department stores. Because of this difference in the way merchandise is purchased by the retailer, selection at an off-price retailer is unpredictable, and searching for bargains has become a popular activity for many consumers. Savings to the consumer at off-price retailers are reported as high as 70 percent off the prices of a traditional department store.

Physical Location

Another aspect of the retailing mix involves deciding where to locate the store and how many stores to have. Department stores, which started downtown in most cities, have followed customers to the suburbs, and in recent years, more stores have been opened in large regional malls. Most stores today are near several others in one of five settings: the central business district, the regional centre, the community shopping centre, the strip, or the power centre.

The **central business district** is the oldest retail setting, the community's downtown area. Until the regional outflow to suburbs, it was the major shopping area, but the suburban population has grown at the expense of the downtown shopping area.

Regional shopping centres consist of 50 to 150 stores that typically attract customers who live or work within a 5- to 15-km range. These large shopping areas often contain two or three anchor stores, which are

Power centres are unenclosed shopping centres.

©David Cooper/Toronto Star via Getty Images

well-known national or regional stores such as Hudson's Bay. One of the largest variations of a regional centre is the West Edmonton Mall in Alberta. The shopping centre is a conglomerate of over 800 stores, 7 amusement centres, 110 restaurants, and a 355-room Fantasyland hotel.[17]

A more limited approach to retail location is the **community shopping centre**, which typically has one primary store (usually a department store branch) and often about 20 to 40 smaller outlets. Generally, these centres serve a population of consumers who are within a 2- to 5-km drive.

Not every suburban store is located in a shopping mall. Many neighbourhoods have clusters of stores, referred to as a **strip location**, to serve people who are within a 5- to 10-minute drive. Gas station, hardware, laundry, grocery, and pharmacy outlets are commonly found in a strip location. Unlike the larger shopping centres, the composition of these stores is usually unplanned. A variation of the strip shopping location is called the **power centre**, which is a large shopping strip with many national stores. Power centres are seen as having the convenient location found in many strip centres and the added power of national stores. These large strips often have two to five anchor stores plus a supermarket, which brings the shopper to the power centre on a weekly basis.[18]

Communications

The elements of the retailing communication mix described in Figure 11–4 represent an exciting menu of choices for creating customer value in the marketplace. Each format allows retailers to offer unique benefits and meet particular needs of various customer groups.

Today, retailers combine many of the formats to offer a broader spectrum of benefits and experiences. These **multichannel retailers** utilize and integrate a combination of traditional store and non-store formats such as catalogues and online retailing. Indigo Books & Music, for example, created **chapters.indigo.ca** to compete with Amazon.

Integrated channels can make shopping simpler and more convenient. A consumer can research choices online or in a catalogue and then make a purchase online, over the telephone, or at the closest store. In addition, the use of multiple channels allows retailers to reach a broader profile of customers. While online retailing may cannibalize catalogue business to some degree, a web transaction costs about half as much to process as a catalogue order. Multichannel retailers also benefit from the synergy of sharing information among the different channel operations.

community shopping centre

Retail location that typically has one primary store and 20 to 40 smaller outlets, serving a population of consumers within a 2- to 5-km drive.

strip location

A cluster of stores serving people who live within a 5- to 10-minute drive.

power centre

Large shopping strip with multiple anchor stores, a convenient location, and a supermarket.

multichannel retailers

Use a combination of traditional store formats and non-store formats such as catalogues and online retailing.

ask YOURSELF

1. Explain how shrinkage impacts retailers.
2. A large shopping strip with multiple anchor stores is a _____ centre.
3. How do multichannel retailers make shopping simpler and more convenient?

Non-Store Retailing

LO 5 Most of the retailing examples discussed earlier in the chapter, such as corporate chains, department stores, and limited- and single-line specialty stores, involve the consumer physically being in the store. Many retailing activities today, however, are not limited to sales in a store. Non-store retailing occurs outside a retail outlet through activities that involve varying levels of customer and retailer involvement. Forms of non-store retailing include automatic vending, television home shopping, and direct marketing (direct mail and catalogue retailing, telemarketing, direct selling, and online buying). Many traditional bricks-and-mortar

Kiosks in Good Taste

©Roberto Machado Noa/LightRocket via Getty Images

The Canadian restaurant industry has a number of home-grown chains, including St-Hubert, Tim Hortons, and Pizza Pizza. Restaurants such as Harvey's, Wimpy's, and The Works are established hamburger chains that are creating more competition for U.S.-based firms such as McDonald's.

For an organization that has built its brand on consistency, McDonald's is also an innovator. In 2016, McDonald's Canada ventured into customized burgers to enhance the retail experience of its customers. Some customers described the experience as upscale and personalized.

Following Australia and the U.K., the in-restaurant experience involves a kiosk, a 100 percent Canadian angus beef patty, and the choice of 30 quality ingredients. Individuals are different, and although many enjoy a Big Mac®, many Canadians would rather make their own burger.

McDonald's Canada installed electronic ordering kiosks in its restaurants. According to John Betts, chief executive of McDonald's Restaurants of Canada Ltd., there is a lot of interest from Canadians in personalizing a premium burger order. McDonald's Canada has developed the customization strategy because its customers want it and the market is demanding it.

The key to McDonald's Canada's strategy is to enhance the retail experience, not replace roles or automate it. In fact, it plans to hire 15,000 new restaurant employees to assist customers with the ordering kiosks. Furthermore, the company will invest $280 million to establish the kiosks across its 1,400 Canadian locations. ●

Questions

1. How do you feel the customization strategy will affect McDonald's Canada's brand perception?

2. What other changes could McDonald's Canada make in order to address the personalization and customization that the marketplace is asking for?

---

stores are involved in non-store retailing, making them "click and mortar" concepts; for example, Indigo Books & Music has developed **chapters.indigo.ca**, its online store. Dell Computers, in contrast, relies mainly on non-store retailing for its consumer sales.

Automatic Vending and Kiosks

Non-store retailing includes vending machines, which make it possible to serve customers when and where stores cannot. Maintaining and operating vending machines is expensive, so product prices in vending machines tend to be higher than those in stores. Typically, small convenience products are available in vending machines. In Japan, products available in vending machines include dried squid, hair tonic, boxers, green tea, beer, CDs, books, clothing, and even music downloaded from a satellite transmission system. Best Buy uses automated vending kiosks in select airports across Canada. Furthermore, the Marketing NewsFlash box, "Kiosks in Good Taste," discusses how

McDonald's uses kiosk technology to help enhance its customer experience.[19]

Improved technology will soon make vending machines easier to use by reducing the need for cash. In Europe, for example, Marconi Online Systems has installed 6,000 vending machines that allow consumers to pay for products using a cellphone. Similarly, the world's largest vending machine company, Canteen Services Inc., is testing a cashless system called FreedomPay, which allows consumers to wave a small wand in front of a sensor to make a purchase.

Another improvement in vending machines—the use of wireless technology to notify retailers when their machines are empty—is one reason automatic merchandising sales are expected to increase in the future.[20]

Television Home Shopping

Television home shopping is possible when consumers watch a shopping channel on which products are displayed; orders are then placed over the telephone or the

Internet. One popular network is The Shopping Channel, which has 24-hour programming and calls itself a broadcast retailer. A limitation of TV shopping has been the lack of buyer-seller interaction. New Internet technologies, however, now allow consumers to explore different possibilities.

Direct Marketing from a Retailing Perspective

We talk in detail about direct marketing in Chapter 12; here we introduce the idea, as it is an important form of retailing. In its simplest terms, direct marketing is an interactive process of marketing that uses advertising media or direct consumer contact to offer products or services. When a direct communication to a consumer or a business market is intended to generate a response from the recipient, direct marketing is the tactic being used.

Direct Mail and Catalogues Direct mail and catalogue retailing is attractive because it eliminates the cost of a store and clerks. It costs a traditional retail store more than twice the amount to acquire a new customer than it costs a catalogue retailer. Why? Because catalogues improve marketing efficiency through segmentation and targeting. In addition, they create customer value by providing a fast and convenient means of making a purchase. In Canada, the amount spent on direct mail catalogue

IKEA delivers over 210 million copies of its catalogue.
©Inter IKEA Systems B.V. 2017.

merchandise continues to increase; internationally, spending is also increasing. IKEA delivers over 210 million copies of its catalogue to 48 countries in 28 languages, including over 7 million in Canada.[21]

One reason for the growth in catalogue sales is that traditional retailers are adding catalogue operations. Another reason is that many Internet retailers, such as Amazon, have also added catalogues. As consumers' direct mail purchases have increased, the number of catalogues and the number of products sold through catalogues have increased. A typical Canadian household now receives dozens of catalogues every year, and there are billions circulated around the world. The competition and recent increases in postal rates, however, have combined to cause catalogue retailers to focus on proven customers rather than "prospects." Another successful new approach used by many catalogue retailers is to send specialty catalogues to market niches identified in their databases. L.L. Bean, a longstanding catalogue retailer, has developed an individual catalogue for fly-fishing enthusiasts. Lee Valley Tools Ltd. sends out specialized catalogues for hardware, woodworking, gardening, and Christmas.

Telemarketing Another form of non-store retailing, called **telemarketing**, involves using the telephone to interact with and sell directly to consumers. Compared with direct mail, telemarketing is often viewed as a more efficient means of targeting consumers, although the two techniques are often used together. Sears Canada utilizes telemarketing to increase sales of extended warranty programs and other services. Communications companies such as Bell Mobility telemarket new potential customers, and financial institutions such as HSBC and MBNA use telemarketing for customer follow-up and cross-selling. Telemarketing has grown in popularity as companies search for ways to cut costs but still provide convenient access to their customers. Twenty-five years ago, the telemarketing industry generated $3.1 billion in sales and planned to employ one million Canadians by the year 2000. By 2007, there were approximately 250,000 Canadians employed by the industry, and it generated $17 billion in sales annually.[22]

> *IKEA delivers over 210 million copies of its catalogue to 48 countries in 28 languages, including over 7 million in Canada.*

As the use of telemarketing grows, consumer privacy has become a topic of discussion among consumers, governments, and businesses. Issues such as industry standards, ethical guidelines, and new privacy laws are evolving to provide a balance between the varying perspectives. The Canadian Radio-television and Telecommunications Commission (CRTC) instituted a national Do Not Call List (DNCL), which was created to enable Canadian consumers to reduce the number of unsolicited telemarketing calls they receive. Every year, thousands of Canadians raise concerns about receiving unwanted telemarketing calls, despite being on the DNCL list.

Direct Selling   Direct selling, sometimes called door-to-door retailing, involves direct sales of goods and services to consumers through personal interactions and demonstrations in their home or office. A variety of companies, including familiar names such as Avon, Tupperware, and Mary Kay Cosmetics, have created an industry with billions in sales by providing consumers with personalized service and convenience. However, sales have been declining as retail chains begin to carry similar products at discount prices and as the increasing number of dual-career households reduces the number of potential buyers who can be found at home.

In response to change, many direct-selling retailers are expanding online and into other markets. Avon, for example, already has over six million sales representatives in over 100 countries, with over 10,000 reps trained to sell online. In Canada, the Avon sales force is 65,000 strong.[23] Direct selling is likely to continue to grow in markets where the lack of effective distribution channels increases the importance of door-to-door convenience and where the lack of consumer knowledge about products and brands will increase the need for a person-to-person approach. Furthermore, it will help maximize growth and customer loyalty.[24]

Online Retailing

LO 6   Online retailing allows customers to search for, evaluate, and order products through the Internet. For many consumers, the advantages of this form of retailing are the 24-hour access, the ability to comparison-shop, and the in-home privacy. Four in ten Canadians aged 16 and over use the Internet to purchase products and services. This is a space that can no longer be ignored by Canadian retailers, as reported by a Forrester Research study. Canadians may

bestbuy.ca and ebay.ca are two examples of online retailers.

(left): Best Buy Canada. (right): eBay Inc.

marketing NewsFlash

Pedestrian Pandemic

During the COVID-19 pandemic, Canadians practised physical distancing and adapted to new, abnormal ways of interacting with their retailers. The Canadian government provided guidance to manage a critical infrastructure, which included businesses in the following sectors:

- Energy and utilities
- Information and communication technologies
- Finance
- Health
- Food
- Water
- Transportation
- Safety
- Government
- Manufacturing

In May 2020, luxury retailer Neiman Marcus, U.S. retailer J.Crew, and Montreal-based Aldo shoes were all in financial difficulty. Aldo shoes began a business-restructuring process as the COVID-19 pandemic forced the almost 50-year-old business to close stores.

Aldo was founded in 1972 as a dress shoe company focused on style. Its challenge over time has been its ability adapt to a world that is evolving more towards casual footwear. When it declared its financial challenges, Aldo was selling shoes and accessories in 3,000 stores over 100 countries.

COVID-19's negative impact on the Canadian economy saw almost 2 million jobs lost in April 2020. Court filings suggest that Aldo will be closing stores and laying off people to add to the number of jobs lost to the pandemic. ●

©JHVEPhoto/Shutterstock

Questions

1. What retailers are at risk to downturns in the economy?

2. What are some practices and strategies retailers can implement today to protect themselves from future downturns in the economy?

---

begin foregoing their loyalty to Canadian retailers if prices are cheaper online from non-Canadian retailers. Furthermore, Forrester Research believes that the online retail sales market will increase from $20 billion to $34 billion by 2018, creating a huge opportunity cost for Canadian retailers who have not ventured into an online retailing strategy.[25]

Studies of online shoppers indicated that men were initially more likely than women to buy something online. As the number of online households increased to more than 50 percent, however, the profile of online shoppers changed to include all shoppers. In addition, the number of online retailers grew rapidly for several years but then declined as many stand-alone, Internet-only businesses failed or consolidated. Today, there has been a melding of traditional and online retailers—"bricks and clicks"—that are using experiences from both approaches to create better value and experiences for customers.

In 2020, amongst the COVID-19 global pandemic, the melding became more of a necessity. Technology companies flourished as retailers relied more on online retailing to provide products to consumers. Companies like Skip The Dishes and Door Dash helped feed Canadians, while businesses rethought innovative ways to provide service in a contactless environment. Unfortunately, not all retailer models could adapt as easily as seen in the Marketing NewsFlash box, "Pedestrian Pandemic," which discusses how retailers coped during this challenging time.[26]

Online buying is getting a boost from the comments that consumers are leaving on social media sites such as Facebook and Twitter. These sites are having an influence on what consumers are buying online. Research shows that Facebook and Twitter influences online buying decisions.[27]

Mobile Banking and Cashless Future

One of the biggest problems that online retailers face is that nearly two-thirds of online shoppers make it to "checkout" and then leave the website to compare shipping costs and prices on other sites. Of the shoppers who leave, 70 percent do not return. One way online retailers are addressing this issue is to offer consumers a comparison of competitors' offerings. Online retailers are also trying to improve the online retailing experience by adding experiential, or interactive, activities to their websites. Montreal-based My Virtual Model Inc. develops software for apparel stores so that consumers can create models of themselves online to assist with the purchase process and help with product selection.[28] Car manufacturers such as BMW and Toyota encourage website visitors to build a vehicle by selecting interior and exterior colours, packages, and options and then view the customized virtual car.

Why Consumers Shop and Buy Online

Consumers typically offer six reasons why they shop and buy online: convenience, choice, communication, customization, cost, and control.

- **Convenience:** Online shopping and buying is *convenient*, so websites must be easy to locate and navigate, and image downloads must be fast.
- **Choice:** There are two dimensions to choice: *selection*—numerous websites for almost anything consumers want—and *assistance*—interactive capabilities of Internet/web-enabled technologies assist customers to make informed choices.
- **Communication:** Communication can take three forms: marketer-to-consumer e-mail notification, consumer-to-marketer buying and service requests, and consumer-to-consumer chat rooms and instant messaging.[29]
- **Customization:** Internet/web-enabled capabilities make possible a highly interactive and individualized information and exchange environment for shoppers and buyers. Consumers get what they want and feel good about the experience. An example is Dell, which allows consumers to choose the components of their computer rather than purchase a computer off the shelf at a bricks-and-mortar retailer.
- **Cost:** Many popular items bought online can be purchased at the same price or cheaper than in retail stores. Lower prices also result from Internet/web-enabled software that permits *dynamic pricing*, the practice of changing prices for products and services in real time in response to supply and demand conditions. *Showrooming* refers to the practice of consumers visiting stores to physically examine products before purchasing them online at a lower price.
- **Control:** Online shoppers and buyers are empowered consumers. They readily use Internet/web-enabled

technology to seek information, evaluate alternatives, and make purchase decisions on their own time, terms, and conditions.

When and Where Online Consumers Shop and Buy

Shopping and buying also happen at different times in the online marketspace than in the traditional marketplace. Though most online retail sales occur Monday through Friday, the busiest shopping day is Monday. Canadians are the world's heaviest Internet users, spending on average 34 hours online monthly. However, Canadians are not the heaviest online consumers, with one in five stating they have never purchased anything online.[30]

Online Presents	
The top 10 e-commerce sites in Canada:	
Rank	**Retailer**
1	Amazon Canada
2	eBay Canada
3	Walmart Canada
4	Best Buy Canada
5	Canadian Tire
6	Costco Canada
7	Home Depot Canada
8	Etsy Canada
9	Hudson's Bay
10	Newegg Canada

Describing the Online Consumer

Research indicates that more than 80 percent of Canadians over the age of 16 are now connected to the Internet. Ninety-four percent of Canadians say they use the Internet to compare prices, and 60 percent go online to read or write reviews. As a result, consumers are becoming smarter, increasingly informed, and more demanding. This trend will continue as more and more Canadians are now embracing mobile technologies from smartphones to iPads.[31]

Many consumers are spending online time at social media sites such as Facebook and Twitter as well as purchasing products and services on company websites.

Social media can impact consumer purchases.
©Alex Segre/Alamy Stock Photo

The following points describe the effects of social media on the online consumer:

- Research suggests that social media recommendations tend to increase the chances of people buying products or services. For instance, a study found that 50 percent of people under 35 followed the recommendations of their social media friends, compared to only 17 percent who bought because of celebrity endorsements.

- Another study reveals that while, on average, 7 percent of visitors to an online store make a purchase, if directed to the retailer via a social media site, the percentage of visitors who will make a purchase goes up to 71 percent. This means that people accessing an online retailer via social media are ten times more likely to buy something than other users.[32]

- Research has also shown that becoming a follower of a brand on Twitter or a fan on Facebook has a positive impact on the possibility of buying and recommending a product or service.

> *The influence of word of mouth on consumer purchases is still strong, be it face to face or on social media sites.*

Recommendations from personal acquaintances or opinions posted by consumers online are the most trusted forms of advertising, according to a Nielsen global online consumer survey of over 25,000 Internet consumers from 50 countries. Ninety percent of consumers surveyed noted that they trust recommendations from people they know, while 70 percent trusted consumer opinions posted online. The influence of word of mouth on consumer purchases is still strong, be it face to face or on social media sites.[33]

Finally, consumers are also beginning to leverage cashback sites to save money while shopping.

As consumers aspire to pursues their different wants, the rising costs of necessities can be a challenge to their day-to-day budget. Over the years, coupons and discounts have been the part of the promotional strategy of many companies. As technology has become interlaced in the lives of the consumer, cashback sites like Rakuten have added another element to the consumer decision-making process.

Using Rakuten and a disciplined approach to shopping can allow you to plan your purchases and receive rewards. Not every product on sites qualify for your ideal rewards; however, in our fast-paced environment of consumer decision-making, taking a little bit of extra time to save money will serve consumers well in the long run.

Rakuten has over 70 businesses, including digital content and communications. With over 1.3 billion members worldwide and a growing presence in the Canadian marketplace, Rakuten is helping Canadians shop smarter. In Canada, Rakuten has over 750 stores in its partnership and over 5 million members.[34]

What Online Consumers Buy

There is a lot marketers have to learn about online consumer purchase behaviour. Although research has documented the most frequently purchased products and services bought online, marketers also need to know why these items are popular in the digital marketplace.

Retailer Usage of the Mobile Channel

LO 7 Retailers are becoming increasingly aware of the value of smartphone-equipped customers. Like they did with the emergence of the Internet, many retailers initially approached the mobile channel with a bit of trepidation. Today, retailers are looking at mobile as another important customer touch point. Cellphones, smartphones, and other handheld devices are a convenient way for customers to gather more information about a retailer's products or even conduct transactions on a mobile basis. In-store shoppers can research products and prices on their handsets using cameras, barcode scanners, QR codes, and other mobile applications. QR (quick response) codes are two-dimensional images that look like blobs of black on a white background. They are similar to standard barcodes but have much more functionality. QR codes are encoded with information ranging from text to photos to website addresses and are scanned by smartphones. They can be used to send consumers who scan the codes to places online and are very effective marketing tools.[35]

Retailers can provide immediate incentives by knowing the specific in-store location of the shopper via GPS technology. The customer can make the purchase in-store or over a mobile cellphone or smartphone. The key is to provide methods to retain customer interest and loyalty via a consistent shopping and branding experience across channels. Smartphones are being used to engage consumers and help them make better shopping choices.

The following scenarios demonstrate how mobile can be used:[36]

- Riding the chairlift of a major western ski resort, a customer of a ski apparel retailer pulls out a smartphone and clicks on the retailer's specialty application. The mobile software uses GPS technology to determine the skier's location, and the customer sees feedback on this specific mountain's terrain and recommendations on how to approach its trails.

- Walking through the pet food section of a major discount chain, a customer receives a text message with a digital coupon good for 20 percent off Iams dog food. The store has detected the shopper's presence in the pet food aisle, and knows that this particular shopper generally purchases the competitor's product, Purina. For the retailer's suppliers, this provides a chance to encourage a brand switch. For the retailer, it enhances loyalty from a customer who has opted in to participate in the mobile program.

-  Two teenage girls rifle through the racks of tops in a major department store chain's juniors section. Stopping on one she likes, one girl takes out her phone and scans a QR code on the shelf next to the shirt. On the screen of her phone, she sees product reviews from other shoppers, and also gets a special offer on a pair of shoes to complete the outfit.

- As he jockeys to make his flight at Calgary International Airport, a Montreal-bound traveller realizes he's forgotten to pack his laptop's power

Smartphones are being integrated into the shopping experience.
©Jeffrey Blackler/Alamy Stock Photo

cord. He turns to his cellphone and brings up Best Buy's wireless website. He orders a replacement cord, finds the store location closest to his hotel, and picks it up on his way to check in.

The above are examples of just a handful of customer interactions taking place today in the mobile commerce (*m-commerce*) channel. In each instance, a retailer uses mobile as a way to enhance customer engagement and loyalty. And it is the pervasiveness of cellphones, smartphones, and other mobile devices that is leading a growing number of retailers to explore what additional opportunities await in the mobile space.

Here's an example of how Sephora, the beauty products retailer, uses mobile strategy. It created a specific mobile website with thousands of product reviews intended to help shoppers evaluate and compare items on their smartphones when they are in the stores. All the shopper has to do to retrieve the reviews is type in the SKU number or the name of the product in their smartphone.

Sephora, the beauty products retailer, uses mobile strategy.

The increasing number of shoppers arriving at stores with smartphones can also pose a threat for retailers. The threat comes from in-store shoppers using their phones to check prices at other retailers. Retailers that ignore the growing number of mobile Internet users will see their customers defect to competitors. A retailer's best defence for maintaining customer loyalty is to develop a mobile website, with information on the site that differentiates itself from competitors. This can take the form of such intangibles as product reviews, warranty information, customer service, product knowledge, and return policy.

Retailers should take note that their websites might have to be adapted for smartphones. Regular websites are not configured for mobile, which may lead to frustration as a shopper, for example, tries to read words that are too tiny to read on a phone. By providing mobile access to their extensive online product information, retailers can help customers feel more comfortable about making a purchase at that store as opposed to fleeing to another store solely for the low price.[37]

Wholesaling

LO 8 Many retailers rely on intermediaries to provide them with selection and availability of the products sold in their retail operations. Many other businesses also use intermediaries to provide them with selection and availability, plus value-added services for products that they need to operate their businesses. Those intermediaries are commonly called wholesalers and agents (described briefly in Chapter 10), according

to the functions that they fulfill in the distribution process. In addition, there are manufacturers' sales offices operated by the original manufacturers of the products. All of these wholesaling intermediaries play an important role in the retailing process and in helping other businesses get the products they need.

Merchant Wholesalers

Merchant wholesalers are independently owned firms that take title to—that is, they buy—the merchandise they handle. They go by various names, described in detail below. About 83 percent of the firms engaged in wholesaling activities are merchant wholesalers.

Merchant wholesalers are classified as either full-service or limited-service wholesalers, depending on the number of functions performed. Two major types of full-service wholesalers exist. General merchandise (or full-line) wholesalers carry a broad assortment of merchandise and perform all channel functions. This type of wholesaler is most prevalent in the hardware, drug, and clothing industries. However, these wholesalers do not maintain much depth of assortment within specific product lines. Specialty merchandise (or

merchant wholesalers Independently owned firms that take title to the merchandise they handle.

Truck jobbers are small wholesalers that have a small warehouse from which they stock their trucks for distribution to retailers.

©Digital Vision/Punchstock

limited-line) wholesalers offer a relatively narrow range of products but have an extensive assortment within the product lines carried. They perform all channel functions and are found in the health foods, automotive parts, and seafood industries.

Four major types of limited-service wholesalers exist. Rack jobbers furnish the racks or shelves that display merchandise in retail stores and perform all channel functions. They sell on consignment to retailers, which means they retain the title to the products displayed and bill retailers only for the merchandise sold. Familiar products such as hosiery, toys, housewares, and health and beauty aids are sold by rack jobbers. Cash and carry wholesalers take title to merchandise but sell only to buyers who call on them, pay cash for merchandise, and furnish their own transportation for merchandise. They carry a limited product assortment and do not make deliveries, extend credit, or supply market information. This wholesaler commonly deals in electric supplies, office supplies, hardware products, and groceries. Drop shippers, or desk jobbers, are wholesalers that own the merchandise they sell but do not physically handle, stock, or deliver it. They simply solicit orders from retailers and other wholesalers and have the merchandise shipped directly from a producer to a buyer. Drop shippers are used for bulky products such as coal, lumber, and chemicals, which are sold in large quantities. Truck jobbers are small wholesalers that have a small warehouse from which they stock their trucks for distribution to retailers. They usually handle limited assortments of fast-moving or perishable items that are sold for cash directly from trucks in their original packages. Truck jobbers handle products such as bakery items, dairy products, and meat.

<dl>
<dt>manufacturers' agents</dt>
<dd>Work for several producers and carry non-competitive, complementary merchandise in an exclusive territory.</dd>
<dt>selling agents</dt>
<dd>Represent a single producer and are responsible for the entire marketing function of that producer.</dd>
<dt>brokers</dt>
<dd>Independent firms or individuals whose main function is to bring buyers and sellers together to make sales.</dd>
</dl>

Agents and Brokers

Unlike merchant wholesalers, agents and brokers do not take title to merchandise and typically provide fewer channel functions. They make their profit from commissions or fees paid for their services, whereas merchant wholesalers make their profit from the sale of the merchandise they have bought and resold.

Manufacturers' agents and selling agents are the two major types of agents used by producers. **Manufacturers' agents**, or manufacturers' representatives, work for several producers and carry non-competitive, complementary merchandise in an exclusive territory. Manufacturers' agents act as a producer's sales arm in a territory and are principally responsible for the transactional channel functions, primarily selling. They are used extensively in the automotive supply, footwear, and fabricated steel industries. By comparison, **selling agents** represent a single producer and are responsible for the entire marketing function of that producer. They design promotional plans, set prices, determine distribution policies, and make recommendations on product strategy. Selling agents are used by small producers in the textile, apparel, food, and home furnishing industries.

Brokers are independent firms or individuals whose main function is to bring buyers and sellers together to make sales. Brokers, unlike agents, usually have no continuous relationship with the buyer or seller but negotiate a contract between two parties and then move on to another task. Brokers are used extensively in the real estate industry.

A unique broker that acts in many ways like a manufacturer's agent is a food broker, representing buyers and sellers in the grocery industry. Food brokers differ from conventional brokers because they act on behalf of producers on a permanent basis and receive a commission for their services. For example, food giant Nabisco uses food brokers to sell its candies, margarine, and Planters peanuts, but it sells its line of cookies and crackers directly to retail stores.

Manufacturer's Branches and Offices

Unlike merchant wholesalers, agents, and brokers, manufacturer's branches and sales offices are wholly owned extensions of the producer that perform wholesaling activities. Producers assume wholesaling functions when there are no intermediaries to perform these activities, customers are few in number and geographically concentrated, orders are large or require significant attention, or they want to control the distribution of their products. A *manufacturer's branch office* carries a producer's inventory and performs the functions of a full-service wholesaler. A *manufacturer's sales office* does not carry inventory, typically performs only a sales function, and serves as an alternative to agents and brokers.

ask YOURSELF

1. *Describe how smartphones are being used by retailers to engage consumers and help them make better shopping choices.*

2. *What is the difference between merchant wholesalers and agents?*

©New Era Cap 2020

1. *What do you think the strategy behind this ad is?*
2. *What is the main message you take away from this ad?*
3. *What would you change in the ad to make it more effective?*

• Retailing provides customer value in the form of various utilities: time, place, form, information, and possession.

• Economically, retailing is important in terms of the people employed and money exchanged in retail sales.

 • Retailing outlets can be classified by forms of ownership, such as independent retailer, corporate chain, and contractual system.

 • The first task in developing a retail strategy is to define the target market and positioning of the retail store.

 • The retailing mix consists of goods and services, retail pricing, physical location, and communications.

• In retailing, the product P (of the 4 Ps of the marketing mix) includes level of service, merchandise mix, and store atmosphere.

• Stores vary in the level of service they provide. Three levels are self-service, limited service, or full service.

• Retail outlets vary in terms of the breadth and depth of their merchandise lines. Breadth refers to the number of different items carried, and depth refers to the assortment of each item offered.

• In retail pricing, retailers must decide on the markup. Off-price retailers offer brand-name merchandise at lower than regular prices.

• Retail store location is an important retail mix decision. The common alternatives are the central business district, regional shopping centre, community shopping centre, or strip location.

A variation of the strip location is the power centre, which is a strip location with multiple national anchor stores.

 • Non-store retailing includes automatic vending, television home shopping, online retailing, and direct marketing (direct mail and catalogue retailing, telemarketing, and direct selling).

 • Online retailing allows consumers to search for, evaluate, and purchase products and services online. The increasing sales and number of people purchasing online suggest that the profile of the online consumer is becoming more and more like the profile of the consumer of the traditional marketplace.

• Consumers refer to six reasons they shop and buy online: convenience, choice, communication, customization, cost, and control.

 • Retailers are becoming increasingly aware of the value of smartphone-equipped customers:

– Retailers are looking at mobile as another important customer touch point.

– Cellphones, smartphones, and other handheld devices are a convenient way for customers to gather more information about a retailer's products or even conduct transactions on a mobile basis.

– Many retailers depend on the numerous types of intermediaries that engage in wholesaling activities.

 • The main difference between the various types of wholesalers lies in whether they take title to the items they sell.

breadth of product line
brokers
central business district
community shopping centre
depth of product line
form of ownership
intertype competition
level of service

manufacturers' agents
merchandise mix
merchant wholesalers
multichannel retailers
off-price retailing
power centre
regional shopping centres
retailing

retailing mix
scrambled merchandising
selling agents
shrinkage
strip location
telemarketing

Online Retailing Assignment A number of retailers will supply New Era caps. Online retailing is a key component to its strategy. Interview an employee of a sports equipment retailer in your local community to determine the benefits and challenges of providing an online retailing offering to the organization's clientele.

In the opening vignette of this chapter, the national director of sales and planning at New Era discusses how different retailers need to distribute its products. In groups, research different potential retailers in Canada and identify the top three you would want New Era to distribute through.

The Infographic, "5 Trends Canadian Retailers Need To Prepare For," identifies technology disruption as a major trend. List three companies that have recently used technology to disrupt business models.

Outbound Marketing Communications

LEARNING OBJECTIVES

LO 1 Describe the integrated marketing communication process

LO 2 Understand the differences between outbound and inbound communication

LO 3 Describe the process of promotional program planning and evaluation

LO 4 Describe the promotional mix and the uniqueness of each component

LO 5 Evaluate the different forms of advertising and the advantages and disadvantages of each

LO 6 Outline the different consumer and trade sales promotional approaches

LO 7 Assess the role of personal selling as a marketing tool

LO 8 Explain current trends affecting marketing communications

LO 9 Outline the compositions of the marketing communications industry

The marketing communications tools available to marketers have evolved significantly over the last decade. This chapter looks at the marketing communications tools that are used to communicate with target audiences: advertising, sales promotion, personal selling, and direct marketing. These inform and persuade and cover the top of the communication funnel in Figure 12–1. Chapter 13 focuses on the public relations, event marketing, and social media marketing communication tools that build brand and community. Both approaches need to work in an integrated fashion to ensure maximum impact of marketing communication.

TM & © Tim Hortons, 2020

CHAPTER OUTLINE

- Tim Hortons Roll Up the Rim integrated marketing campaign
- Integrated marketing communication
- Planning and evaluating the promotional mix
- Outbound versus inbound communication

- Advertising
- Sales promotion
- Product placement and branded entertainment
- Personal selling
- Recent developments in marketing communications

Tim Hortons has maintained the largest market share in the increasingly competitive and ever-changing coffee market in Canada.

Tim Hortons was started by its namesake in 1964, in Hamilton, Ontario, initially selling coffee and two types of doughnuts. Tim Horton, an NHL defenceman who played from 1949 to 1974 for the Toronto Maple Leafs and other NHL teams, was an entrepreneur who started numerous restaurants. In 1967, he partnered with Ron Joyce to assist him in more closely managing the three doughnut shop locations Tim owned at that time. The business grew quickly with Ron Joyce at the helm, and innovative product introductions were utilized to continue to invigorate the brand. Some of the most successful new product introductions were the Timbit in 1976, the Iced Capp in 1999, and dark roast coffee in 2014. Tim Hortons went digital in 2014 with the TimmyMe app allowing consumers to pay with their smartphone. In 1995, it merged with Wendy's International to increase locations. In 2000, Tim's opened its 2,000th store. In 2006, it became a separate company again, publicly trading on the stock exchange. In 2014, it sold to Burger King for $11.4 billion, and the fight for market share continues. Today, Tim Hortons locations are in 14 countries with 4,646 stores.

Tim Hortons' target market is predominantly baby boomers, and it has identified that there is not as much loyalty with the under-40 market. Consequently, many of its recent promotions have targeted millennials and Gen Z.

In 1986, Tim Hortons was looking for a way to increase sales in the dreary dark days of the Canadian winter. The company decided to create a sales promotion in the form of a contest, naming it Roll Up the Rim. Customers would roll up the rim of their cup and win various prizes. In the first year, the top prize was a box of Timbits, but as the popularity of the contest grew, so did the range of possible prizes, including cars and computers along with the drinks and doughnuts. Tim Hortons created a complete integrated marketing communication (IMC) strategy for the very popular promotion, including television advertising, print advertising, billboards and posters, press releases announcing the contest and the winners, and eventually, social media posts on Facebook and Instagram in more recent years. Since the contest has been running for over 30 years, the campaign objective has been to remind customers about the contest, as everyone knows how it works. There was even a tool made for rolling up the rim so no one had to break a nail. For years, the contest was successful, but as attitudes around waste changed, decisions were made to change the contest to reduce the waste created by the takeaway cups used to roll up the rim.

In 2020, to make Roll Up the Rim more sustainable, Tim Hortons created a new version of the contest that used an app, allowed people to use reusable cups, and had a limited supply of the actual rims. This new version of the contest also leveraged technology to appeal to a younger demographic market. However, this change presented a whole new set of challenges for the marketing team as instead of an IMC to remind customers to play, the team had to inform the customers and introduce a new and more complicated process for this brand-building sales promotion. The updated IMC strategy included the following:

- **Advertising:** A significant investment was made in paid media advertisements to explain the new and improved system, including television ads in prime time as well as on TSN during the Tim Hortons Brier curling champinship, radio ads, print ads in newspapers, Google and Facebook ads, outdoor billboards and posters, and electronic boards and posters at actual Tim Hortons locations.

- **Sales Promotion:** The Roll Up the Rim contest allowed customers to roll up the rim on a disposable cup or get additional "rolls" by bringing a reusable cup and using the app that was associated with the Tim Hortons loyalty card.

- **Public Relations:** Numerous press releases were dispatched to provide information about the new contest and explain the new rules and the reason for the changes. Using its owned media, Tim Hortons' marketing team created a video to explain the new contest and posted it on its website and on social media platforms Instagram, Facebook, and Twitter.

It wasn't long before the PR team had to go into crisis management mode as social media was inundated with negative opinions about the new contest. There was a feeling that it was not going "green" if the contest still used paper cups, and that the new online contest was too complicated for consumers to participate in.

So the contest was deemed a bit of a marketing disaster, sales were down, and customers were really unhappy feeling like their brand had completely lost touch. Then things got much more complicated with the 2020 lockdown during the COVID-19 pandemic and the subsequent inability to complete the contest as it was designed. The Roll Up the Rim fiasco was overshadowed by much more important news.

This story still has a happy ending as the Tim Hortons' marketing team turned on a dime and started a completely new program, supporting front-line workers by dropping off coffee and doughnuts and using social media platforms and advertising to reassure customers that the brand had not completely lost its way.

Tim Hortons has always been community focused, and it found renewed success by returning to the origin of the brand that had it opening up a Tim Hortons in Afghanistan to support our troops; outfitting thousands of hockey, baseball, and soccer players in Timbits uniforms; and attending local events in communities all over the country.

It will be interesting to see if this ship can get turned around and find its way back to being the iconic Canadian brand—one large double-double, please![1]

---

reality CHECK ⊘

As you read Chapter 12, refer back to this Tim Hortons vignette to answer the following questions:

- Why is the use of hockey and brand ambassadors a good choice for Tim Hortons?
- Why do you think that Tim Hortons growth into the United States market is slower than anticipated?

Marketing Communications— Promotion

The next two chapters provide readers with a realistic view of marketing communications, bringing to the forefront the approaches that are used by marketers to reach consumers. Chapter 12 focuses on the elements of the promotional mix—advertising, sales promotion, direct marketing, and personal selling—that marketers use to reach out to consumers or send outbound communication. It also includes trends currently impacting marketing communications and details the planning and evaluation of marketing communications programs. Chapter 13 examines the remaining elements of the promotional mix—public relations, event sponsorship, and social media—that pull in and create community, considered more inbound communication. Of utmost importance is the fact that all marketing communications must work together, in an integrated fashion, to reach consumers in their worlds, relying on metrics and analytics to measure and evaluate success and to make improvements.

Today, consumers are bombarded with marketing messages. With the use of tags, bookmarks, opt-ins, and selective feeds, consumers can determine whether they receive marketing communication messages, and if so, when, where, and on what device. The lines are blurred between reality, entertainment, self-expression, and marketing communications.

> *The lines are blurred between reality, entertainment, self-expression, and marketing communications.*

Developing the Promotional Mix

A successful marketing campaign demonstrates the opportunity for engaging potential customers and the importance of integrating the various elements of a marketing communication program. Promotion represents the fourth element in the marketing mix. The promotional element consists of six communication tools, including advertising, personal selling, sales promotion, public relations, event sponsorship, and direct marketing. The combination of one or more of these communication tools is called the promotional mix.

Integrated Marketing Communications

LO 1 In putting together the promotional mix, a marketer must consider two issues. First, the balance of the elements must be determined. Should advertising be emphasized more than personal selling? Should a promotional rebate be offered? Would public relations activities be effective? Several factors affect such decisions: the target audience for the promotion, the stage of the product's life cycle, the characteristics of the product, the decision stage of the buyer, and even the channel of distribution. Second, because the various promotional elements are often the responsibility of different departments, coordinating a consistent promotional effort is necessary. A promotional planning process designed to ensure integrated marketing communications (IMC) can facilitate this goal.

The Target Audience Promotional programs are directed to the ultimate consumer, to an intermediary (retailer, wholesaler, or industrial distributor), or to both. Promotional programs directed to buyers of consumer products often use mass media because the number of potential buyers is large. Personal selling is used at the place of purchase, generally the retail store. Direct marketing may be used to encourage first-time or repeat purchases. Combinations of many media alternatives are a necessity for some target audiences today.

The concept of designing a marketing communications program that coordinates all promotional activities to provide a consistent message to a target audience is referred to as **integrated marketing communications (IMC)**.

The key to developing successful IMC programs is to use a process that makes it easy to design and evaluate. In an IMC program, each element has a distinct role as well as a purpose in the overall campaign. For example, TV ads and Internet display advertising might be used to build awareness and to drive consumers to a website; print advertising may be used to provide details on technical specifications; social media interactions may be used to encourage engagement; sales promotional offers may be needed to encourage product trial; e-mail marketing approaches may be required to create a database of the target market; and personal selling might be needed to complete a transaction. Each tool is used for a different reason and needs to be evaluated against that purpose and its contribution to the overall success of the marketing communications program.

The Customer Advocacy Funnel

Marketers use integrated marketing communications approaches to ensure that all communication elements speak with the same messaging and use a shared visual platform. This approach involves developing, executing, and evaluating each element of a promotional program so that it encourages customers to become loyal supporters that spread positive messages. We call this *advocacy*.

The **Customer Advocacy Funnel** (Figure 12–1) demonstrates how, over time, the positive connections that customers make with brands encourage them to become brand advocates who recommend the brand to others. This funnel has consumers moving from an initial awareness stage through to interest, engagement, trial, purchase, loyalty, and advocacy.

Let's try to understand how marketers can use specific tools in an integrated fashion to drive customers through the funnel:

- **Awareness:** A company trying to raise brand awareness may use a website, search engine, traditional, and online advertising to maximize consumer exposure to the product.

Figure 12–1
The Customer Advocacy Funnel

- **Awareness**: A company trying to raise online product awareness may use a website, search engine optimization, online video, and display ads to drive consumers to an online destination.
- **Interest:** Interesting product attributes are highlighted to entice potential customers to learn more.
- **Engagement**: Potential customers are invited to participate in the product experience and interact with its marketing.
- **Trial**: Customers obtain free samples or purchase the product as a limited trial or download.
- **Purchase**: Positive product experiences lead to product purchase.
- **Loyalty**: Ongoing positive product experiences lead to repeat purchases.
- **Advocacy**: Loyal customers are rewarded with additional experiences and become advocates who recommend the product to others.

- **Interest:** A company may use online video to increase interest in the product, this time using experts to demo the product and add credibility.
  - **Engagement:** Social media can be added to the mix to encourage engagement by consumers.
  - **Trial:** Contests, samples, and limited trials can be communicated through direct mail, product microsites, and social media networks.
  - **Purchase:** Follow-up on product trial can be done through e-mail to reinforce a positive product experience, which can lead to product purchase.
  - **Loyalty:** Customer loyalty can be encouraged through programs that reward continued purchases, such as loyalty programs. Social media can help encourage interaction with the brand.
  - **Advocacy:** Ongoing communications, often one-to-one, through e-mail newsletters, social networks, branded

communities, and blogs can solidify connections with loyal customers, providing them with information and experiences to share with others.

Outbound and Inbound Marketing Communications

LO 2 There are two terms that we need to understand in marketing communications: outbound marketing and inbound marketing. **Outbound marketing** refers to the traditional marketing approach where marketers seek out consumers by widely broadcasting messages using advertising, direct mail, e-mail marketing, telemarketing, and personal selling approaches. It includes advertising methods that consumers increasingly avoid, such as ads on TV and radio, ads in newspapers and magazines, and Internet display ads. **Inbound marketing** is when interested consumers find the product and its messaging by using online techniques that marketers facilitate. It involves search engine optimization, pay-per-click ads, and the use of social media to connect with consumers through social networks, blogs, social bookmarks, social media releases, and microsites.

These two approaches often work together to communicate with consumers in ways they prefer. Smaller businesses may rely more on inbound marketing, which is cheaper, while larger businesses, depending on the target market, may use a combination of both techniques.

Designing Marketing Communication Programs

LO 3 Marketing communications can be a fun yet daunting task for marketers. Its subjective nature can make it unnerving. However, the creativity required to pull it together, and the ability of metrics to measure success, can make it very rewarding.

Marketers turn to marketing communication experts to navigate this terrain. Communication agencies provide expertise on communication approaches with access to insights on new opportunities, consumer trends, and media research. They help guide strategy development, creative development, and media planning and buying, as well as program evaluation. Marketers shape the backdrop by providing company, product, and target market information, as well as insights into

outbound marketing
Marketers seek out consumers by widely broadcasting messages using advertising, direct mail, e-mail marketing, telemarketing, and personal-selling approaches.

inbound marketing
When consumers find a product and its messaging by using online techniques that marketers facilitate, including search engine optimization, pay-per-click ads, and the use of social media to connect with consumers.

product positioning, previous campaigns, the competition, and the competition, and budgetary constraints. They explain the balance between consumer and trade promotion, as well as how push and pull strategies are used. They are also involved in program creation and evaluation.

A **push strategy** is when marketers focus communication efforts on the distribution channel to gain support from retailers, distributors, and wholesalers through listings, sales, merchandising, featured pricing, and the inclusion in flyers. A **pull strategy** is when marketers focus communication efforts on ultimate consumers to build awareness, trial, and demand for a product. These approaches should work together (see Figure 12–2).

Steps in the Marketing Communications Process

Today, with the multitude of communication tools available, and consumers fragmented over a wide array of touch points, marketers follow an integrated approach to marketing communications, making sure all elements work together to reach specific target audiences. The steps in this process, outlined in Figure 12–3, require a marketer to (1) specify the IMC objectives, (2) identify the target audience, (3) set the promotional budget, (4) design the promotional program, (5) schedule and run the IMC elements, and (6) evaluate the program and recommend changes. These steps are explained below.

Step 1: Specify the IMC Objectives
The first step formalizes the purpose of the promotional program, such as building brand awareness, creating customer engagement, or increasing brand loyalty. Specific numerical targets are often included at this point and used later to evaluate the program. The Customer Advocacy

push strategy
When marketers focus communication on the distribution channel to gain support from retailers, distributors, and wholesalers.

pull strategy
When marketers focus communication efforts on ultimate consumers to build awareness, trial, and demand for a product.

Figure 12–2
Push and pull communication strategies
Push and pull strategies need to work together.

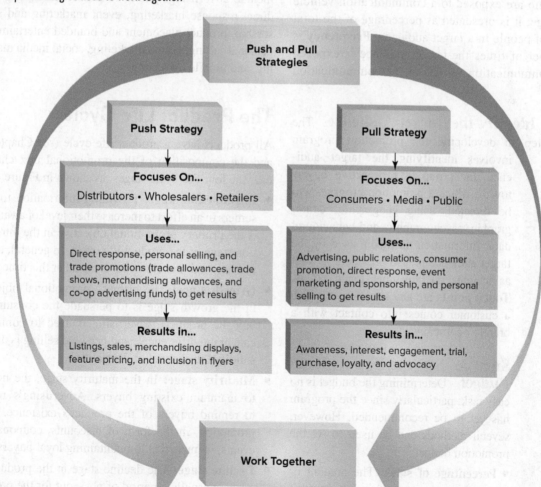

Push and Pull Strategies

Push Strategy

Focuses On...
Distributors • Wholesalers • Retailers

Uses...
Direct response, personal selling, and trade promotions (trade allowances, trade shows, merchandising allowances, and co-op advertising funds) to get results

Results in...
Listings, sales, merchandising displays, feature pricing, and inclusion in flyers

Pull Strategy

Focuses On...
Consumers • Media • Public

Uses...
Advertising, public relations, consumer promotion, direct response, event marketing and sponsorship, and personal selling to get results

Results in...
Awareness, interest, engagement, trial, purchase, loyalty, and advocacy

Work Together

Figure 12–3
Steps in the marketing communications process

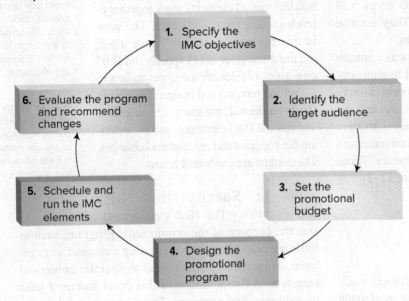

Funnel noted earlier may help determine these objectives. Often a promotional plan includes objectives such as reach and frequency. **Reach** is the number of people who are exposed to a communication vehicle or message; it is presented as percentage of the total number of people in a target audience. **Frequency** is the number of times the target audience is exposed to the communication vehicle or the communication message.[2]

Step 2: Identify the Target Audience
The second step in developing the promotion program involves identifying the target audience, the group of prospective buyers toward which a promotion program will be directed, using geographic, demographic, psychographic, and behavioural data. Information on media used by the target audience is also provided, as well as insights on consumer touch points. **Touch points** are any situation in which a customer comes into contact with a brand or company.

Step 3: Set the Promotional Budget
Determining the budget is no easy task, particularly since the program has yet to be recommended. However, several methods can be used to set the promotion budget:[3]

- **Percentage of sales:** The amount of money spent on promotion is a percentage of past or anticipated sales.

- **Competitive parity:** Matches the competitor's absolute levels of spending or a proportion of their spend based on market shares.

- **All you can afford:** Allows money to be spent on promotion only after all other budget items—such as manufacturing costs—are covered.

- **Objective and task:** The company determines the promotion objectives, outlines the tasks to accomplish those objectives, and determines the promotion cost of performing those tasks.

Step 4: Design the Promotional Program
The key component of a promotional program is its messaging. It needs to be visible, resonate with its target audience, and be memorable. One of the major challenges of IMC is to design each promotional activity to communicate the same message.

It can encompass online and offline approaches and include advertising, public relations, sales promotion, direct response marketing, event marketing and sponsorship, product placement and branded entertainment, personal selling, online marketing, social media marketing, and mobile marketing.

The Product Life Cycle

All products have a product life cycle (see Chapter 8), and the composition of the promotional mix changes over the four life-cycle stages, as shown in Figure 12–4.

- **Introduction stage:** Providing information to consumers in an effort to increase their level of awareness is the primary promotional objective in the introduction stage of the product life cycle. In general, all the promotional mix elements are used at this time.

- **Growth stage:** The primary promotional objective in the growth stage is to persuade the consumer to buy the product. Advertising is used to communicate brand differences, and personal selling is used to solidify the channel of distribution.

- **Maturity stage:** In the maturity stage, the need is to maintain existing buyers. Advertising's role is to remind buyers of the product's existence. Sales promotion, in the form of discounts, coupons, and events, is important in maintaining loyal buyers.

- **Decline stage:** The decline stage in the product life cycle is usually a period of phaseout for the product, and little money is spent on the promotional mix.

reach
The number of people who are exposed to a communication vehicle or message; is presented as percentage of the total number of people in a target audience.

frequency
The number of times the target audience is exposed to the communication vehicle or the communication message.

touch points
Any situation in which a customer comes into contact with a brand or company.

Figure 12–4
Product life cycle considerations for promotional programs

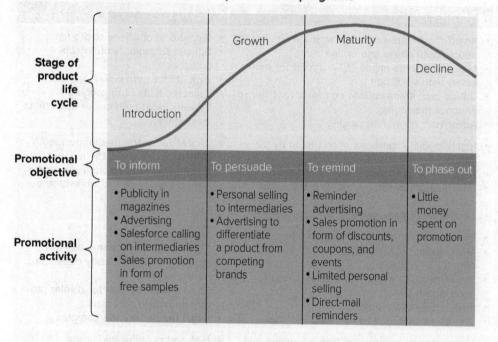

Step 5: Schedule and Run the IMC Elements

The promotion schedule describes the order in which each promotional tool is introduced and the frequency of its use during a specified time frame. The order of promotional elements is carefully planned so that individual aspects seamlessly work together to communicate with target audiences. Throughout the campaign, marketers carefully monitor developments, particularly in social media, to immediately answer questions, respond to comments, and carefully deal with negative feedback.

Step 6: Evaluate the Program and Recommend Changes

Promotional programs are evaluated on four levels. First, messaging is often evaluated before a program is fully developed to gauge responses so that adjustments can be made before launch.

Second, once the program is live, research may be fielded to measure campaign awareness and messaging elements such as *likability, message comprehension,* and *attitude changes* toward the brand.

Third, upon completion, each individual element will be evaluated against expectations. Online programs may look at page views and time on site. Public relations efforts may be measured on publicity mentions and return on investment (ROI).

Fourth, the promotional program will be evaluated against its objectives. This will look at business results such as sales, profitability, market share, and expected ROI.

All of these metrics will be used to determine campaign success and what elements can be strengthened in the future.

Promotional Mix

LO 4 In this diverse media environment, a wide range of marketing communication tools is available. **Marketing communication tools**, also referred to as the **promotional mix**, consist of advertising, public relations, sales promotion, direct response marketing, event marketing and sponsorship, product placement and branded entertainment, personal selling, online marketing, social media marketing, and mobile marketing. Figure 12–5 summarizes the relative strengths and weaknesses of these elements.

Figure 12–5
Strengths and weaknesses of communication tools

Communication Tool	Strengths	Weaknesses
Advertising	• An efficient means of reaching large numbers of people both online and offline • Many affordable online options exist for marketers with small budgets • Online and offline options can work together to enhance messaging • Advertisers control messaging	• Higher cost of offline approaches • Difficult to evaluate offline approaches • High clutter both online and offline • Low credibility of messaging • Viewers avoid both online and offline messaging
Public relations (discussed in Chapter 13)	• Highly credible messages when spread by the media • Inexpensive, particularly when using social media • New measurable tools available due to social media • Can be well-integrated into IMC programs	• Unable to control media messaging • Difficult to influence the number of messages spread through the media • Results can be difficult to evaluate
Sales promotion	• Effective at increasing short-term sales • Many options are available both online and offline • Social media provides an affordable way to disseminate offers • Results are measurable • Can be well-integrated into IMC programs	• Fraud can occur • Can lead to promotional wars • Promotions can be easily duplicated by competitors • Consumers may wait for a sales promotion before purchasing • Legal regulations are complex
Direct response marketing	• Messages can be targeted through online and offline approaches • Facilitates customer relationships • Results are measurable	• High cost of offline and online approaches • Negative customer reactions • Clutter • Requires a well-constucted database to be done properly
Event marketing and sponsorship (discussed in Chapter 13)	• Small branded events can be used to create a buzz and spread viral messages • Major event sponsorships can reach large audiences and create positive associations • Can be integrated into IMC programs • Sponsorships can be carried into the online environment • Buzz can be affordably created through microsites and social media	• Large event sponsorships can be limited to awareness-building messages • Sponsorships can be costly and difficult to evaluate • Results can be difficult to measure
Product placement and branded entertainment	• Seamless product integration into programming • Can create a positive association for the brand with a particular movie or TV show	• Can be expensive • Product placement is becoming ubiquitous
Personal selling	• Personal interactions can build lasting relationships with consumers • Online approaches can be used to enhance relationships • An important approach for expensive products • Can be used in large and small businesses • Can be a strong form of product differentiation	• Can become expensive when large salesforces are involved • Consistency in approach and messaging is difficult to achieve • People may not want to engage
Online marketing (discussed in Chapter 13)	• Allows for two-way communication • Can be used to implement most forms of marketing communication • Can be relatively inexpensive	• Online message clutter • Dependence on technology
Social media marketing (discussed in Chapter 13)	• Allows for two-way communication • Can be relatively inexpensive • Many platforms to select from	• Online message clutter • Dependence on technology • Potential immediate negative feedback
Mobile marketing	• Number of mobile users is increasing rapidly • Can integrate mobile marketing programs with other promotion tools quite easily	• Mobile message clutter • Dependence on technology • Formatting challenges

Advertising

LO 5 **Advertising** is a paid form of media used for non-personal communication to consumers about an organization, good, service, or idea. The *paid* aspect of this definition is important because advertising space is normally purchased, with the exception of some public service announcements, which may use donated media. The *non-personal* component of advertising is also important since advertising involves mass media (such as TV, radio, magazines, and online), which are non-personal and do not have an immediate feedback loop available as does direct marketing or personal selling.

> *Marketers have a number of media options from which to choose. Selection is based on campaign objectives as well as the product, the target market, and budget constraints.*

Advertising can be very expensive. A one-time, national rate for a full-page, four-colour ad in the hard copy of *Maclean's* magazine, for example, costs $42,264.[4] Television ads are even more expensive, with average production costs running at approximately $200,000 and media prices running over $150,000 to run a 30-second spot during a top, prime-time, highly viewed TV broadcast. Media prices will vary, depending on when and where an advertiser wishes to run the spot.

Designing the Advertisement

An advertising message usually focuses on the key benefits of the product that are important to a prospective buyer in making trial and adoption decisions. The message depends on the general form or appeal used in the ad and the actual words included in the ad.

MESSAGE CONTENT Most advertising messages are made up of both informational and persuasive elements. These two elements are so intertwined that it is sometimes difficult to tell them apart. For example, basic information such as the product name, benefits, features, and price can be presented in a way that tries to attract attention and encourage purchase. On the other hand, even the most persuasive advertisements have to contain at least some basic information to be successful.

Information and persuasive content can be combined in the form of an appeal to provide a basic reason for the consumer to act. Although the marketer can use many different types of appeals, common advertising appeals include fear, sex, and humour.

Fear appeals suggest to the consumer that he or she can avoid some negative experience through the purchase and use of a product or service, a change in behaviour, or a reduction in the use of a product. Examples with which you may be familiar include automobile safety ads that depict an accident or injury; political candidate endorsements that warn against the rise of other, unpopular ideologies; or social cause ads warning of the serious consequences of drug and alcohol use. Insurance companies often try to show the negative effects on the relatives of those who die prematurely without carrying enough life or mortgage insurance. Food producers encourage the purchase of low-carb, low-fat, and high-fibre products as a means of reducing weight, lowering cholesterol levels, and preventing a heart attack. MADD advertisements are an example of fear appeal.

When using fear appeals, the advertiser must be sure that the appeal is strong enough to get the audience's attention and concern but not so strong that it will lead them to tune out the message.

advertising
Paid form of media used for non-personal communication to consumers about an organization, good, service, or idea.

Maclean's offers marketers a variety of advertising options.

Research suggests that overly threatening messages have a negative effect on the intention to adapt behaviour. In fact, research on anti-smoking ads indicates that stressing the severity of long-term health risks may actually enhance smoking's allure among youth.[5]

In contrast, *sex appeals* suggest to the audience that the product will increase the attractiveness of the user. Sex appeals can be found in almost any product category, from automobiles to toothpaste. Consumers, however, are redefining what is acceptable use of sex appeals. There is growing interest in positive messages about female and male roles, and views on gender identity are changing. Abercrombie & Fitch, for example, has moved away from overly "sexualized" campaigns, and brands such as Zara, Guess, and Mattel's Barbie are using gender-neutral ads. The contemporary lifestyle brand AG designs its advertising to communicate its "chic, sophisticated, classic" positioning for men and women. Studies indicate that sex appeals generate a greater response than other appeals, and they increase attention by helping advertising stand out in today's cluttered media environment. Unfortunately, sexual content does not always lead to changes in recall, recognition, or purchase intent. Experts suggest that sexual content is most effective when there is a strong fit between the use of sex appeal in the ad and the image and positioning of the brand.[6]

Humorous appeals imply either directly or subtly that the product is more fun or exciting than competitors' offerings. As with fear and sex appeals, the use of humour is widespread in advertising and can be found in many product categories. You may have smiled at the popular Geico ads that use a talking gecko, or a group of robbers ordering a getaway car with an app, or a group of pigeons on a wire talking about Geico. These ads use humour to differentiate the company from its competitors. Geico has also created viral videos and posted them on video-sharing websites such as YouTube, where millions of viewers watch them within days.[7] You may have a favourite humorous ad character, such as the Energizer battery bunny, the Old Spice man, the AFLAC duck, or Travelocity's gnome. Advertisers believe that humour improves the effectiveness of their ads, although some studies suggest that humour wears out quickly, losing the interest of consumers. Another problem with humorous appeals is that their effectiveness may vary across cultures if used in a global campaign.[8]

Advertising Media Choices Marketers have a number of media options from which to choose. Selection is based on campaign objectives as well as the product, the target market, and budget constraints. Figure 12–6 summarizes the advantages and disadvantages of the major forms of advertising: Internet, TV,

Figure 12–6
Advertising options—advantages and disadvantages

Medium	Advantages	Disadvantages
Television	Reaches extremely large audience, uses picture, print, sound, and motion for effect, and can target specific audiences.	High cost to prepare and run ads, short exposure time and perishable message, and difficult to convey complex information.
Radio	Low cost, can target specific local audiences, ads can be placed quickly, and can use sound, humour, and intimacy effectively.	No visual element, short exposure time and perishable message, and difficult to convey complex information.
Magazines	Can target specific audiences, high-quality colour, long life of ad, ads can be clipped and saved, and can convey complex information.	Long time needed to place ad, relatively high cost, and competes for attention with other magazine features.
Newspapers	Excellent coverage of local markets, ads can be placed and changed quickly, ads can be saved, quick consumer response, and low cost.	Ads compete for attention with other newspaper features, short lifespan, and poor colour.
Yellow Pages	Excellent coverage of geographic segments, long use period, and available 24 hours/365 days.	Proliferation of competitive directories in many markets and difficult to keep up-to-date.
Internet	Video and audio capabilities, animation can capture attention, and ads can be interactive and link to advertiser.	Animation and interactivity require large files and more time to load and effectiveness is still uncertain.
Outdoor	Low cost, local market focus, high visibility, and opportunity for repeat exposures.	Message must be short and simple, low selectivity of audience, and criticized as a traffic hazard.
Direct Mail	High selectivity of audience, can contain complex information and personalized messages, and high-quality graphics.	High cost per contact and poor image (junk mail).

Figure 12–7
Television, direct mail, and Internet account for more than 75 percent of all advertising expenditures ($ in millions).

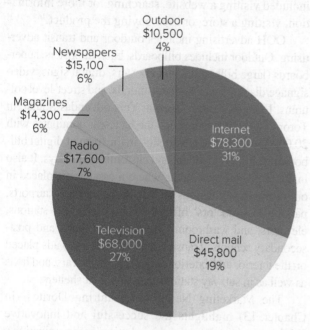

Outdoor
$10,500
4%

Newspapers
$15,100
6%

Magazines
$14,300
6%

Radio
$17,600
7%

Internet
$78,300
31%

Television
$68,000
27%

Direct mail
$45,800
19%

newspaper, magazine, radio, and out-of-home. These media choices are described in more detail in the following pages.

Media choice is an important decision for a marketer to make. Figure 12–7 shows where the majority of advertising spending is currently focused.

TELEVISION Television is a valuable medium because it communicates with sight, sound, and motion and gets attention from large target audiences. Digital technology now allows TV viewing to be flexible, whether this means watching it on the go on a smartphone or tablet, time-shifting to watch it in a different time zone, or using a digital recording device to watch a program at a more convenient time. The rapid adoption of Internet-based services such as Netflix offers consumers more choices. Canadian Netflix subscriptions have now surpassed 7 million, and it is changing how consumers view TV-type programming and how marketers view TV as an advertising platform.[9]

When TV ads are well-designed and appropriately placed in the media, this tool can deliver very impactful and effective messages. Many TV advertisers complement their ads with other advertising options that meet target audiences online through online display ads or with pre-roll video ads that play before an online broadcast of a TV program. Marketers are aware that consumer behaviour is placing the effectiveness of stand-alone TV advertising into question. TV viewers frequently change channels when ads appear during commercial breaks, and many use digital recording devices to watch programs at a later date. Sometimes, people prefer to watch TV programs online where fewer ads exist, or catch a show at another time through on-demand digital programming. It is estimated that approximately 420,000 Canadians annually are "cord cutters," people who decide to cancel TV cable or satellite and focus on online viewing. Between 2012 and 2019 over 2.5 million Canadians cut their TV subscriptions.[10]

NEWSPAPERS The Canadian newspaper industry has undergone significant change over the last few years, with a decline in circulation rates and a concerted move to digital formats. In addition, newspapers are challenged with lower advertising revenues in this digital age where the news is accessible through multiple avenues.

However, newspapers are still an important advertising medium that are well-recognized in the market for providing reliable information. There are three types of newspapers: daily paid-circulation newspapers, free daily newspapers, and free community newspapers. The highest daily circulation of a paid newspaper in Canada is the *Globe and Mail*, followed in order by the *Toronto Star*, *Hamiton Spectator*, and *Montreal Gazette*. Two free daily newspapers, *Metro* (in Quebec only) and *24 Hours*, are enjoying high circulation numbers that rival some of the traditional paid-circulation newspapers.[11] Community newspapers are published either weekly or monthly and are an excellent media choice for local retailers and for community events.

MAGAZINES Magazines provide advertisers with a high-quality media environment and provide an excellent opportunity for advertisers to match magazines to their target market profile. Vividata readership and circulation figures show that 63 percent of Canadians read exclusively print magazines, while 17 percent read print in combination with more than one digital device.[12]

Magazines have adapted well to the online environment by providing added online content such as searchable databases, blogs, contests, and polls, as well as mobile versions that can be accessed on tablets and other mobile devices. As a result, almost half of all magazine readers are reading on a digital platform.

Agility PR Solutions identified the top 10 Canadian magazines in 2020 by circulation (see Figure 12–8).[13]

RADIO Canadians over the age of 18 listen to the radio for 14.6 hours per week on average, supplemented by an additional 8.1 hours of audio streaming content. But listeners are utilizing different methods for listening to radio programming. Almost one quarter (23 percent) stream radio online. In addition, it is estimated that

Figure 12–8
Top magazines (readership in Canada)

Ranking	Magazine
1	Chatelaine
2	Maclean's
3	Flare
4	enRoute
5	Toronto Life
6	Zoomer Magazine
7	NOW Magazine
8	Realscreen
9	Elle Canada
10	The Kit Magazine

16 percent of adult Canadians subscribe to satellite radio. The main characteristics of radio are that it is local and has a relatively low production cost. This makes it affordable for both small and large advertisers. There are 720 private commercial radio stations in Canada, many of which focus on specific listener interests, including news and talk, or music genres such as adult contemporary, country, contemporary hits, rock, classical, and the oldies. Stations also exist for specific ethnic groups that broadcast content in foreign languages. Radio stations have responded to the Internet with online broadcasts, downloadable podcasts, apps, and blogs.[14]

OUT-OF-HOME **Out-of-home (OOH) advertising** reaches consumers outside the home in outdoor locations using media such as billboards, posters, bus shelter ads, transit ads, washroom ads, and a variety of non-conventional methods such as aerial advertising, closed-circuit TV, electronic signage, and street furniture.

Since consumers spend 70 percent of their time outside of their homes, OOH advertising is an effective medium for generating reach quickly to build awareness and interest in a product.[15] It is also an excellent reminder for current products. Over the last few years, this media has experienced slight increases due to its participation in IMC programs and the realization by marketers that this media cannot be turned off. The Out-of-Home Marketing Association of Canada's latest Canadian shopper habits survey reported 78 percent of shoppers aged 18 to 64 said they pay attention to OOH advertising.

out-of-home (OOH) advertising
Casually referred to as *outdoor*; reaches consumers outside the home in outdoor locations, in transit, or in commercial or business locations.

In a survey completed by TNS Canada, 57 percent of adults indicated that they had taken action after seeing OOH advertising within the last six months. Actions included visiting a website, searching for more information, visiting a store, or even buying the product.[16]

OOH advertising includes outdoor and transit advertising. Outdoor includes billboards, back-lit posters, superboards (large billboards), mall posters, digital signs, video signage/displays, wall banners, murals, and street-level columns. Examples can be seen at Yonge-Dundas Square in Toronto where Canada's first media tower dominates with 20,000 square feet of advertising in the form of digital billboards, full-motion video, and customized displays. It also includes place-based media where messages are placed in out-of-home destinations such as shopping malls, airports, parking lots, doctors' offices, health clubs, gas stations, elevators, and washrooms in restaurants, bars, and post-secondary schools. Transit advertising refers to ads placed on the interior and exterior of buses, subway cars, and taxis as well as in subway stations and on transit shelters.

The Marketing NewsFlash featuring Doritos (in Chapter 13) highlights the successful and innovative IMC campaign (integrated marketing communication), including OOH advertising, combined with online advertising, event sponsorship, influencer marketing, and social media to attract the younger gen Z customer.

INTERNET The Internet represents a relatively new medium for many advertisers, although it has already attracted a wide variety of industries and is the largest medium in terms of advertising expenditures. Online advertising is similar to print advertising in that it offers a visual message. It has additional advantages, however, because it can also use the audio and video capabilities of the Internet. There are a variety of online advertising options. The most popular options are paid search, display (banner) ads, classified ads, and video. Online advertising also has the unique feature of being

KitchenAid Matches This Mixer billboard with the shifting colour of Toronto's CN Tower.

KitchenAid/Zulu Alpha Kilo

comScore's service can provide an assessment of the effectiveness of a website by measuring its impact on the digital audience.

Courtesy of comScore, Inc.; (tape measure): ©Kim Hall/Getty Images

interactive. Called *rich media*, these interactive ads have drop-down menus, built-in games, or search engines to engage viewers. Online advertising also offers an opportunity to reach younger consumers who have developed a preference for online communication.

Classified ads, such as those on Craigslist, and video ads also contribute to the growth of online advertising by providing many of the advantages and characteristics of other media such as yellow pages, magazines, newspaper, and television. Video ads also have the benefit of "going viral" when people share the ads with friends. The widespread availability of Internet access and the popularity of smartphones means that online advertising also provides the unique characteristic of being mobile. In fact, *mobile marketing*, defined in Chapter 1, now includes the broad set of interactive messaging options that enable organizations to communicate and engage with consumers through any mobile device. Recent research indicates that the location data available from mobile devices can substantially increase the effectiveness of mobile marketing efforts.[17]

Another disadvantage to online advertising is the difficulty of measuring impact. Several companies are testing methods of tracking where viewers go on their computer in the days and weeks after seeing an ad. Nielsen's online rating service, for example, measures actual Internet use through meters installed on the computers of 500,000 individuals in 20 countries. Measuring the relationship between online and offline behaviour is also important. Research by comScore, which studied 139 online ad campaigns, revealed that online ads didn't always result in a "click," but they increased the likelihood of a purchase by 17 percent and increased visits to the advertiser's website by 40 percent.[18]

When it comes to online advertising, companies can create display ads that can be placed on various online destinations such as websites, web portals, blogs, social networks, e-mail platforms, and online gaming sites. Pay-per-click ads can also be placed on search engines, content networks, and social networks such as Facebook, LinkedIn, or YouTube.

MOBILE Advertising that renders on mobile devices is a rapidly growing area of mobile marketing, and it represents more than one-third of overall Internet advertising spending in Canada. Over half of the mobile advertising spend was for mobile search, followed by mobile display ads and mobile streaming video. Rather than cannibalizing other more traditional media formats, the spend on mobile seems to be an incremental spend.[19]

Research tells us that mobile ads are most effective in increasing brand awareness and purchase consideration. The next most common outcome when consumers click on mobile ads is that they are likely to make a purchase, followed by saving a page to their device and adding to a product to their shopping list. While consumers indicate that they are most likely to pay attention to TV advertisements, mobile is second, with desktop, print, and radio far behind. This fact also reinforces the importance of implementing a multi-device marketing program, since a large number of consumers use mobile devices at the same time that they are watching television.[20]

Advertising options on mobile devices include placing displays ads on highly trafficked mobile-optimized websites or placing ads within third-party apps such as the Weather Network app, which delivers ads for many companies such as the OLG lottery. Pay-per-click mobile ads can also be placed around mobile search results and takeover ads, and mobile video ads can be created to appear as pre-roll video ads that are seen before watching a video on a mobile device.

> *Research tells us that mobile ads are most effective in increasing brand awareness and purchase consideration.*

An example of how marketers design ads for each device to maximize their impact is the Weather Network website properties:

- The Weather Network desktop site at **www.theweathernetwork.com/ca** hosts display ads for companies such as BMO, Keurig, and Pampers that appear as banners, leaderboards, and vertical ads in various sizes. The display ads change regularly and reflect the customer's views, browsing history, and interests.

- The Weather Network mobile site for smartphones can be downloaded from one of the app stores and is available in multiple formats. It has ads on its home page, but only as you scroll further down the page. This ensures that ads do not interfere with the ability to quickly obtain current weather conditions.

- The Weather Network tablet site focuses on weather information that needs to be communicated and has less space for any type of display advertising

The Weather Network app is very popular in Canada.

©2020 The Weather Network Pelmorex Weather Networks

compared to the mobile and desktop versions. Small square display ads are interspersed with weather-related videos, and leaderboard-style ads are placed at the very bottom of the page.

What is consistent across all platforms is a focus on functionality and consistent branding. However, the Weather Network offers a variety of advertising opportunities that best fit the format.

Scheduling the Advertising There is no correct schedule to advertise a product, but three factors must be considered. First is the issue of *buyer turnover*, which is how often new buyers enter the market to buy the product. The higher the buyer turnover, the greater the amount of advertising required. A second issue in scheduling is the *purchase frequency*; the more frequently the product is purchased, the less repetition is required. Finally, companies must consider the *forgetting*

rate, the speed with which buyers forget the brand if advertising is not seen.

Setting schedules requires an understanding of how the market behaves. Most companies tend to follow one of three basic approaches:

1. *Continuous (steady) schedule.* When seasonal factors are unimportant, advertising is run at a continuous or steady schedule throughout the year.

2. *Flighting (intermittent) schedule.* Periods of advertising are scheduled between periods of no advertising to reflect seasonal demand.

3. *Pulse (burst) schedule.* A flighting schedule is combined with a continuous schedule because of increases in demand, heavy periods of promotion, or introduction of a new product.

For example, products such as breakfast cereals have a stable demand throughout the year and would typically use a continuous schedule of advertising. In contrast, products such as snow skis and suntan lotions have seasonal demands and receive flighting-schedule advertising during the seasonal demand period. Some products such as toys or automobiles require pulse-schedule advertising to facilitate sales throughout the year and during special periods of increased demand (such as holidays or new car introductions). Some evidence suggests that pulsing schedules are superior to other advertising strategies.[21] In addition, research indicates the effectiveness of a particular ad wears out quickly; therefore, many alternative forms of a commercial may be more effective.[22]

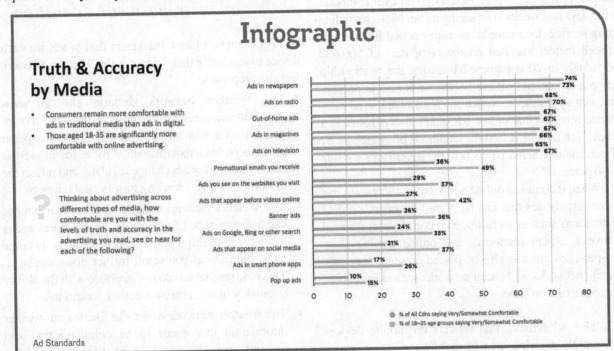

Infographic

Truth & Accuracy by Media

- Consumers remain more comfortable with ads in traditional media than ads in digital.
- Those aged 18-35 are significantly more comfortable with online advertising.

? Thinking about advertising across different types of media, how comfortable are you with the levels of truth and accuracy in the advertising you read, see or hear for each of the following?

Media	% of All Cdns	% of 18–35
Ads in newspapers	74%	73%
Ads on radio	68%	70%
Out-of-home ads	67%	67%
Ads in magazines	67%	66%
Ads on television	65%	67%
Promotional emails you receive	36%	49%
Ads you see on the websites you visit	29%	37%
Ads that appear before videos online	27%	42%
Banner ads	26%	36%
Ads on Google, Bing or other search	24%	35%
Ads that appear on social media	21%	37%
Ads in smart phone apps	17%	26%
Pop up ads	10%	15%

● % of All Cdns saying Very/Somewhat Comfortable
● % of 18–35 age groups saying Very/Somewhat Comfortable

Ad Standards

Product Placement and Branded Entertainment

The fact that consumers avoid TV ads by muting the sound, changing the channel, or leaving the room is encouraging marketers to include products in TV shows and movies. This can be done through **product placement**, the inclusion of a product such as a soft drink in a movie or TV program, or the creation of an entire movie or TV episode around a brand, which is referred to as **branded entertainment**. When Ikea pays to have its furniture featured in a scene of *Deadpool*, this is an example of product placement. *The Lego Movie* and the Marvel franchise of movies are examples of branded entertainment. The Marketing NewsFlash box, "The Evolution of Product Placement," looks at the one of the initial most valuable instances of product placement, Reese's Pieces in *E.T.*, through to current product placement in Netflix programming.[23]

ask YOURSELF

1. What types of advertising opportunities are available on the Internet?

2. How are newspapers in Canada dealing with the decline in advertising revenues?

3. Why is out-of-home advertising so effective?

Sales Promotion

LO 6 Sales promotion is a communications tool that provides short-term incentives to generate interest in a product or cause and encourages purchase or support.

There are two basic types of sales promotion: (1) consumer promotions and (2) trade promotions. **Consumer promotions** are short-term marketing tools used to encourage immediate consumer purchase. They include incentives such as coupons, premiums, contests, sweepstakes, samples, loyalty programs, rebates, bonus packs, and point-of-purchase materials, which are outlined in Figure 12–9.

Consumer Promotions

McDonald's "Monopoly" game has been one of Canada's most successful consumer promotions for over 30 years. The promotion is a result of a partnership between McDonald's and Hasbro, building on the popularity of the Monopoly board game. Consumers collect Monopoly properties as they purchase McDonald's products and use the properties to win prizes. Despite the promotion tarnished with

product placement
The inclusion of a product in a movie or TV program in return for payment.

branded entertainment
The creation of an entertainment program, such as a TV episode, that is highly focused on a brand in exchange for payment.

sales promotion
A communications tool that provides short-term incentives to generate interest in a product or cause and encourages purchase or support.

consumer promotions
Short-term marketing tools used to encourage immediate consumer purchase.

Figure 12–9
Consumer promotions
Consumer promotions are an effective way to increase short-term sales.

Consumer Promotions	Promotional Tools	Explanation
Short-term marketing tools used to encourage immediate consumer purchase	Coupons	Price reductions offered in exchange for electronic or paper documents. Can be distributed online, on-pack, through flyers, or on shelf.
	Premiums	Offers that provide merchandise for free or at a significant savings in exchange for proof-of-purchase of a product.
	Contests	Offers where participants require a skill to win a prize such as creative submissions.
	Sweepstakes	Offers which are pure games-of-chance and where consumers often participate by completing an entry form and, if selected as a winner, answering a skill-testing question.
	Samples	The provision of free products to encourage consumers to try and purchase a product.
	Loyalty programs	Programs that encourage and reward customers for ongoing purchases with points that can be redeemed for rewards.
	Rebates	A price reduction supplied via mail in exchange for proof-of-purchase.
	Bonus packs/special packs	The provision of oversized packs or bonus items attached to the original product.
	Point-of-purchase materials	The use of in-store merchandising such as display materials, banners, floor decals, and posters to draw attention.

The Evolution of Product Placement

In 1981, when Steven Speilberg was making the movie *E.T.*, the producers were looking for a candy brand to use in the scene where Elliott lures E.T. out with small candies. The Mars company with M&Ms was originally approached and turned down the opportunity. Luckily for them, the Reese's company was approached instead. *E.T.* was released in 1982 and outperformed *Star Wars*. Sales of Reese's Pieces increased due to the successful collaboration in which Reese's agreed to include *E.T.* in $1 million worth of advertising to promote the movie. For this investment, it is estimated that Reese's Pieces received over $15 million worth of exposure. This story marks the beginning of the modern era of product placement.

One of the benefits of subscribing to a streaming video service is the lack of commercial interruptions during viewing. Netflix has seen increased viewership, especially in the millennial segment. Viewers have moved away from traditional broadcast television to a monthly subscription to Netflix. The competition is increasing with Amazon Prime Video and Disney Plus entering the market. Netflix has been very successful in producing original content, but this creativity requires additional revenue to fund growth. According to Greg Isaacs, chief product and marketing officer at Branded Entertainment Network, more than 70 percent of Netflix shows contain some product placement for which Netflix receives between $50,000 and $500,000, depending on the program. Netflix also uses other cross-promotions with companies like Subway, which

they partnered with on the Green Eggs and Ham sandwich to promote and extend the life cycle of the movie by the same name.

Stranger Things, one of Netflix's most popular shows, has deals with over 75 companies to have product placements and cross-promotions for its 2020 season, including Baskin-Robbins ice cream flavour called Eleven Heaven, named after a character in the show, and a reboot of New Coke. In these cases, Netflix does not necessarily get paid by these companies but rather creates connections with brands that are meaningful to their audience. Netflix executives claim that the *Stranger Things* promotions are designed to get people excited about the show so they join Netflix and tell their friends.

Another cool development is tech that provides on-demand product placements targeted at individuals in the audience. A company called Ryff would provide each viewer with a unique experience, where the placements can be tailored to the audience, show, time of day, and geographic location and would run seamlessly throughout the streamed video.

Have you noticed a proliferation of Pop-Tarts in the shows that you have been watching? Or seen oddly flavoured Pop-Tart memes show up in your Instagram? Even *Deadpool 2* had a scene with the dreaded unfrosted Pop-Tart. This is all part of the constantly evolving Pop-Tart strategy to appeal to its teenage audience by being integrated into

pop culture. Pop-Tarts have a long history of being in TV shows like *Seinfeld*, movies like *Elf*, and more recently in the Netflix original show *Daybreak*. Like the other brands that we are seeing embedded in streaming videos, Pop-Tarts marketing understands the importance of reaching the right people in order for the brand to have relevance and success.

The mutual benefit to the streamers and the brands using product placement is evident in the increased sales and positive brand attitudes that are created. ●

Questions

1. What is the benefit of product placement for both the company selling the product and producers who are being approached to use it?

2. What other product placement opportunities are there for Pop-Tarts?

McDonald's Monopoly game has been a successful consumer promotion in Canada for 30 years.

©CoCo Jones/Alamy Stock Photo

fraud exposed in a Netflix documentary, and the 2020 promotion postponed due to the coronavirus, the promotion is still going strong. It now has a stronger online component and leverages social media and YouTube to highlight real-time winners of prizes to consumers.[24]

Mobile Sales Promotional Tools

Mobile Sales Promotional Tools Sales promotions provide short-term incentives for people to interact with brands whether through a discount, an offer, or another form of engagement. These elements can be communicated through the advertising approaches mentioned above, but in the mobile space, other more direct tools can encourage engagement and interaction. In the sales promotion space, mobile marketers can use mobile messaging, matrix 2D barcodes, and proximity marketing approaches. Common examples include text message alerts, app notifications, and various mobile downloads (mobile coupons, wallpapers, ringtones, and games).

MOBILE MESSAGING **Mobile messaging** comes in four main forms. There are (1) common short codes (CSC), (2) short messaging services (SMS), (3) multimedia messaging services (MMS), and (4) e-mail messaging.

Common short codes (CSC) are dedicated short messaging codes of typically five to six digits that trigger subscriptions, donations, alerts, downloads, or the ability to access promotional content. Mobile marketers often use these codes in conjunction with keywords to involve consumers in a program. CSC numbers are provided by the Canadian Wireless Telecommunications Association (CWTA). There are numerous examples of CSC programs in Canada, such as BMO, which offers mobile alerts for any abnormal transactions on your bank account. Many charitable foundations also use CSC programs in Canada to raise funds. For example, a person can text the word "SUPPORT" to the number 45678 to donate $10

to March of Dimes Canada, and this amount is then added to his or her mobile phone bill.

> *CSC programs in Canada must abide by the Canadian Wireless Telecommunications Association guidelines.*

In terms of guidelines, all CSC programs in Canada must abide by the Canadian Wireless Telecommunications Association guidelines, which are discussed later in this chapter.

Short messaging services (SMS) and **multimedia messaging services (MMS)** are mobile communication approaches that allow marketers to send text messages or multimedia messages that contain graphics, video, or audio to an opted-in customer's mobile device. Customers must opt in to SMS/MMS programs to receive ongoing communication that might include, among other things, text message alerts, offers, discounts, or coupons. Airlines, such as Air Canada, regularly communicate flight information and check-in options to customers via SMS text.

Mobile e-mail is an important tool in a mobile marketer's arsenal. Mobile devices are personal communication gadgets, and retrieving and sending e-mails is widely used on these devices. As mentioned earlier in the chapter, while the overall use of apps has stagnated, app use for reading e-mails is still growing. When designing e-mails, marketers must consider that an e-mail may be viewed on a desktop, a laptop, a tablet, or a cellphone, which may render e-mails differently. E-mail marketing communications can be deployed by using e-mail service providers that provide analytics on open rates, forward rates, bounce rates, and clicks. These metrics allow marketers to test different subject lines, headlines, and content so that, over time, the most effective e-mail campaigns are deployed. When using e-mail campaigns, marketers must adhere to Canada's Anti-Spam Legislation and other marketing regulations as outlined in Chapter 2.

MATRIX 2D BARCODES A **matrix 2D barcode** is a two-dimensional square

mobile messaging
Comes in the form of common short codes (CSC), short messaging services (SMS), multimedia messaging services (MMS), e-mail messaging, in-person voice phone calls, and voice messaging.

common short codes (CSC)
Dedicated short messaging codes of typically five to six digits that are used to trigger subscriptions, donations, alerts, or downloads, or to access promotional content.

short messaging services (SMS)
Standard text messaging that uses protocols of 160 characters per message.

multimedia messaging services (MMS)
Standard text messaging services that include audio, video, or images.

mobile e-mail
E-mail sent and/or received using a mobile device.

matrix 2D barcode
A two-dimensional response code that, when scanned by a mobile barcode reader or app, provides additional information, launches websites, prompts downloads, sends text messages, or deploys messages.

or rectangular response code that, when scanned by a mobile barcode reader or app, provides additional information, launches websites, prompts downloads, or sends SMS or e-mail messages. A popular brand of matrix 2D barcode is the QR code.

Yelp is a popular mobile discovery app.
©dennizn/Shutterstock

> ## A popular brand of matrix 2D barcode is the QR code.

Bluetooth
Low-power radio waves that are transmitted though beacons and wirelessly transfer text, images, and audio or video data through a local hotspot to Bluetooth-enabled and -activated devices.

near field communications (NFC)
The two-way radio communication between smartphones and smartphone-type devices to transfer images, documents, or monetary transactions when the two devices touch or are within a few inches of each other.

geofencing
Uses global positioning system (GPS) to trigger an event to happen when a device enters a certain geographic area.

WiFi hotspots
Areas set up with free Internet access in which once customers log in to use the free WiFi, they can be sent location-specific content.

mobile check-in services
When consumers check into locations using apps to post their whereabouts and to receive offers from local merchants on their mobile device.

Matrix 2D barcodes can be placed on flat surfaces such as print ads, posters, business cards, or even at the bottom of TV screens so that they can be scanned by mobile devices. The use of QR codes was ubiquitous when smartphones were first brought to market. Currently, they are used less frequently but can be very effective tools for the marketer. Spotify launched a program whereby the customer could create a customized greeting card with a QR code printed on the card. When the recipient scanned the QR code with a mobile device, he or she would be able to enjoy a mixtape playlist selected by the card giver. Columbia Sportswear integrated QR codes into its corporate social responsibility campaign by including a QR code on reused or recycled packaging. When customers purchased a Columbia product online, they were asked whether they would like a new or reused box. If the customer selected reused, the product was delivered in a box with a QR code that has compiled all of the information regarding where this box had been, creating an interesting historical narrative in words and pictures. Eco-conscious customers loved the program, and it gained international attention.[25]

PROXIMITY MARKETING *Proximity marketing* is the local distribution of marketing content to mobile devices that have opted in at a specific geolocation. A shopping mall may use proximity marketing to provide mobile coupons to shoppers who are using its free WiFi network. A local coffee shop may use Bluetooth

Near field communications.
©Artur Marciniec/Alamy Stock Photo

technology to invite people in the immediate vicinity to come in and try a new coffee. In research conducted by Unacast in 2016, retail, shopping malls, hotels/tourism, airports, stadiums/sports, and restaurants were the industries most likely to use proximity marketing.[26]

Proximity marketing can be implemented using a number of different technologies such as Bluetooth beacons, near field communications (NFC), geofencing, and WiFi.

- **Bluetooth** or low-power radio waves are transmitted though beacons and wirelessly transfer text, images, and audio or video data through a local hotspot to Bluetooth-enabled and -activated devices. The Unacast research also estimated that there were 8.3 million beacons activated worldwide in 2016, a growth of over eight times the number of beacons deployed one year earlier.

- **Near field communications (NFC)** is the two-way radio communication between smartphones and smartphone-type devices that can transfer images, documents, or monetary transactions when the two devices touch or are within a few inches of each other. Unlike beacons, you cannot send push notifications with NFC, and it has a short range. The mobile wallet app Android Pay is an example of NFC. NFC approaches are used at industry events and conferences where NFC-enabled mobile devices can tap a centrally located hotspot to download complementary white papers, research studies, or speaker information.

- **Geofencing** uses global positioning systems (GPS) to trigger an event to happen when a device enters a certain geographic area.

- **WiFi hotspots** can be set up with free Internet access, and once customers log in to use the free WiFi, they can be sent location-specific content.[27]

Proximity marketing also includes mobile check-in services and mobile discovery apps that provide consumers with offers from local merchants. **Mobile check-in services** are when consumers check into locations using apps such as Foursquare or Yelp to post their whereabouts and then receive offers from local merchants on their mobile devices. **Mobile discovery** refers to the use of mobile apps such as Google Maps, Yelp, or Zomato to find local services that are rated in the area.

Trade Promotions **Trade promotions** are short-term promotional tools used to generate support with wholesalers, distributors, or retailers. Common approaches include trade shows, trade allowances and discounts, and cooperative advertising (see Figure 12–10).

Personal selling plays a central role in many industries.
©Rob Melnychuk/Getty Images

mobile discovery
The use of mobile apps to help find local businesses, services, and attractions.

trade promotions
Short-term promotional tools used to generate support with wholesalers, distributors, or retailers.

personal selling
The two-way flow of communication between a buyer and seller, often face-to-face or facilitated through communication devices, to influence an individual and group purchase decision.

ask YOURSELF

1. *What types of consumer promotions are available to marketers?*

2. *How do trade promotions differ from consumer promotions?*

3. *What trade promotional tools are available to marketers?*

Personal Selling

LO 7 | **Personal selling** involves the two-way flow of communication between a buyer and seller, often face-to-face or facilitated through communication devices, to influence an individual or group purchase-decision. Unlike advertising, personal selling is usually face-to-face communication, although telephone and electronic communication is also used.

Sales positions include account management positions, manufacturing sales personnel, real estate brokers, stockbrokers, and salesclerks who work in retail stores. In reality, virtually every occupation that involves customer contact has an element of personal selling with the salespeople representing the company.

The personal selling process consists of six stages: prospecting, pre-approach, approach, presentation, close, and follow-up, as detailed in Figure 12–11.

Figure 12–10
Trade promotions
Trade promotions are often required to encourage retail support.

Trade Promotions	Promotional Tools	Explanation
Short-term promotional tools given to wholesalers, distributors, or retailers	Trade shows	Participation in industry events that showcase new products and initiatives.
	Off-invoice allowances	A price reduction taken off the invoice of a purchase that is made within a specific time frame.
	Merchandising allowances	A price reduction taken off a purchase in return for displaying the product.
	Co-op advertising	The contribution of funds for inclusion in a wholesaler, distributor, or retailer advertising program such as a flyer.

Figure 12–11
Stages and objectives in the personal selling process

Stage	Objective	Comments
1. Prospecting	Search for and qualify prospects	Start of the selling process; prospects generated through advertising, referrals, and cold canvassing
2. Pre-approach	Gather information and decide how to approach the prospect	Information sources include personal observation, other customers, and company salespeople
3. Approach	Gain prospect's attention, stimulate interest, and make transition to the presentation	First impression is critical; gain attention and interest through references to common acquaintances, a referral, or product demonstration
4. Presentation	Begin converting a prospect into a customer by creating a desire for the product or service	Different presentation formats are possible; involving the customer is critical; responding to objections is key; a professional ethical approach is needed
5. Close	Obtain a purchase commitment from the prospect and secure a customer	Salesperson asks for the order; different approaches include the trial close and assumptive close; trial close can be used at any stage
6. Follow-up	Ensure that the customer is satisfied with the product or service	Resolve any problems faced by the customer to ensure customer satisfaction and future sales possibilities

Trends in Marketing Communications

A Changing Landscape

LO 8 We start by looking at the current trends impacting marketing communications.

Connected Consumers Affordable Internet technology and some of the fastest download times, provides consumers in Canada with easy-to-use services and devices that facilitate marketing communications. Free online services such as e-mail, search engines, and social media have made media more accessible so that two-way communication now exists between marketers and consumers, and between consumers and their friends. Many individuals multitask with the media, spending time on the Internet while watching TV, and using tablets and smartphones interchangeably, depending on the circumstance.[28]

The use of mobile devices in Canada (smartphones, tablets, e-readers, handheld gaming devices, and portable MP3 players) continues to grow. In 2019, there were over 32 million mobile subscribers in Canada.[29] Smartphone penetration in Canada has reached 90 percent, with one-third of households relying exclusively on wireless services. Smartphones are used for everything on the go, with usage including taking photos, messaging, social networking, listening to music, conducting searches, using apps, playing games, and shopping.[30] Chapter 13 reviews mobile marketing in more detail.

Research studies tell us that consumers in Canada are among the most connected in the world. Nearly three in four Canadians report spending three to four hours per day online. Online video viewing is particularly high, with 73 percent watching video on the Internet. Social networking is a popular online activity, with people in Canada increasingly accessing social networks on their mobile devices.[31] **Social networks** are online websites that allow members to create a network of friends and contacts to share messages, comments, videos, and images as a form of self-expression.

The most popular social networking sites in Canada are Facebook, LinkedIn, Instagram, Twitter, and Snapchat.[32] Chapter 13 provides an in-depth look at social media in Canada.

Media Usage The amount of time consumers spend with the media has changed significantly over

social networks
Online websites that allow members to create a network of friends and contacts to share messages, comments, videos, and images as a form of self-expression.

the last few years, prompting marketers to take note and adapt marketing communications approaches. Adults in Canada spent 10 hours and 24 minutes per day using some form of media. Figure 12–12 illustrates that time spent on digital forms of media, including mobile and computer, is expected to continue increasing, whereas time spent on all other forms of media is decreasing.[33]

> The most popular social networking sites in Canada are Facebook, LinkedIn, Instagram, Twitter, and Snapchat.

Advertising Expenditures Marketers are shifting advertising dollars online to respond to changing media habits. The Internet is now the largest recipient of advertising dollars in Canada, ahead of TV and newspaper. The latest data on advertising expenditures show that the overall advertising spend in Canada in 2019 will reach the equivalent of US$12 billion (see Figures 12–13 and 12–14).[34]

Evolving Media The digital reality sees consumers spending more time online. Even the television industry is changing. Content is being produced strictly for streaming, and many television networks have made their content available online. Traditional media such as television, magazines, newspapers, and radio are creating their own online assets to remain competitive and relevant. News organizations, such as the CBC, use YouTube channels and apps to deliver content, despite having websites and TV channels of their own. Radio stations stream content online, create podcasts, and write articles for their websites, and there has been an influx in Internet and satellite radio services such as Sirius. Magazines create content specifically for online reading, and in this new media universe, we see newspapers such as the *Globe and Mail* undergo digital redesigns to compete with online news and the 24/7 news cycle. Out-of-home advertising, such as billboards and transit advertising, are being replaced with digital boards, which provide the opportunity for video and interactive touchscreens. Digital advertising has also seen a shift from desktop- and laptop-formatted ads to mobile advertising.[35]

Figure 12–12
Average time spent on traditional versus digital media in Canada

Traditional* vs. Digital Media: Average Time Spent in Canada, 2018–2022 (hrs:mins per day among population)		
	Digital	**Traditional***
2018	4:50	5:02
2019	4:58	4:54
2020	5:32	4:51
2021	5:23	4:37
2022	5:28	4:29

Note: Ages 18+; time spent with each medium includes all time spent with that medium, regardless of device or multitasking; for example, 1 hour of multitasking on Facebook while using Snapchat is counted as 1 hour for Snapchat and 1 hour for Facebook.

*Includes time spent on TV, newspapers, magazines, and radio.

Figure 12–13
Cost to reach audiences in traditional versus digital media in Canada

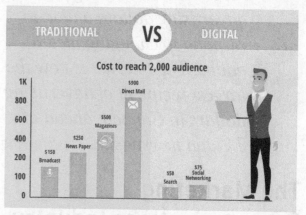

© 2020 Asset Digital Communications

Figure 12–14
Trends—advertising expenditures in Canada (C$ billions)

Total Media Ad Spending in Canada, Traditional* vs. Digital**, 2018–2023 (forecasted data)			
	Traditional*	**Digital****	**Total**
2018	$7.66	$7.72	$15.37
2019	$7.64	$8.80	$16.43
2020	$7.56	$9.90	$17.46
2021	$7.51	$10.94	$18.44
2022	$7.47	$11.92	$19.39
2023	$7.48	$12.75	$20.24

* Includes directories, magazines, newspapers, out-of-home, radio, and TV.

** Includes advertising that appears on desktop and laptop computers as well as mobile phones, tablets, and other Internet-connected devices. Also includes all the various formats of advertising on those platforms, including SMS, MMS, and P2P messaging-based advertising.

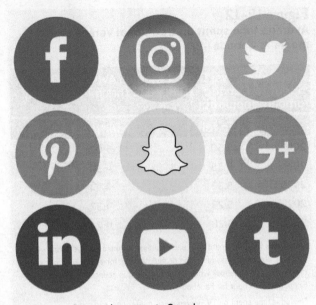

Popular social networking sites in Canada.

©Brilliantist Studio/Shutterstock

> *Marketers are shifting advertising dollars online to respond to changing media habits. The Internet is now the largest recipient of advertising dollars in Canada, ahead of TV and newspaper.*

The Marketing Communications Industry

LO 9 The marketing communications industry consists of five main areas that work together to form an industry that is ethical, trustworthy, cohesive, and measurable. These areas include the following: (1) the media, (2) marketing communication agencies, (3) media research companies, (4) associations, and (5) regulatory bodies. Let's look at these areas in more detail.

The Media

The main forms of media are Internet (including mobile), TV, newspaper, magazine, radio, and out-of-home (including billboards and transit).

Paid media is the media time that is purchased so that messages can be disseminated through channels that are controlled by others—TV advertising is an example. **Owned media** refers to the media channels that a company controls, either fully or partially, such as a website, microsite, or social media page that is used to directly communicate with consumers. **Earned media**, a term with origins in the public relations industry, refers to the free publicity secured through unpaid media mentions and consumers who spread the word through word of mouth or the Internet.

Marketing Communication Agencies

Marketing communication agencies provide marketers with expertise on how best to communicate messages to their audiences. Agencies can be broad-spectrum and offer a variety of services to their clients, or they can be specialty agencies providing expertise in media, creative, public relations, event marketing, digital, product placement, direct marketing, or sales promotion. These terms are discussed in more detail later in this chapter.

Media Research Companies

Metrics are central to the smooth functioning of the marketing communications industry. Data on audience measurement, readership, consumer trends, and the quality of communication messages is needed to provide transparent and reliable information to the media, agencies,

---

Looking for Media Data?

Alliance for Audited Media (AAM)	auditedmedia.com
Numeris	www.numeris.ca
Canadian Out-of-Home Marketing & Measurement Bureau (COMMB)	www.commb.ca
comScore	www.comscore.com
Forrester Research	www.forrester.com
Interactive Advertising Bureau of Canada (IAB)	www.iabcanada.com
Canadian Media Directors' Council	www.cmdc.ca
Nielsen Company	www.nielsen.com/ca
ThinkTV (formerly Television Bureau of Canada)	www.thinktv.ca
Vividata (amalgamation of NADbank and the Print Measurement Bureau [PMB])	www.vividata.ca

and clients. Most major media sectors publish third-party data for the industry, which is used to determine advertising rates and trends. In addition, other media research companies, such as comScore and the Nielsen Company, provide data to keep the industry apprised on the latest developments.

Associations

The marketing communications industry has a number of active associations that provide data and host informative events and educational workshops for the industry. Here are just a few that are active in keeping the industry:

- Canadian Marketing Association (**www.the-cma.org**)
- Institute of Communications Agencies (**theica.ca**)
- Interactive Advertising Bureau of Canada (**www.iabcanada.com**)
- Association of Canadian Advertisers (**www.acaweb.ca/en/**)

It is worth your time to investigate the resources and support available from each association.

Regulatory Bodies

Prior to embarking on a marketing communications program, marketers need to be well-versed on the limitations and restrictions placed on them by regulatory bodies. Marketers are well-advised to become familiar with their specific industry associations and to stay up-to-date on marketing regulations, business restrictions, and best practices. Chapter 2 provides details on these regulatory bodies and the regulations that guide marketing communications in Canada. It is advisable at this point for you to re-visit these pages to obtain details. The following is only a brief reminder.

This Ad Standards ad encourages truthful communications.

Ad Standards

In Canada, there are six main regulatory groups that work toward limiting intentional and unintentional deceptive marketing practices: (1) Advertising Standards Canada (Ad Standards), (2) the Competition Bureau, (3) the Canadian Radio-television and Telecommunications Commission (CRTC), (4) the Canadian Marketing Association (CMA), (5) the Canadian Wireless Telecommunications Association (CWTA), and (6) the Mobile Marketing Association (MMA). Specialist areas and industry groups such as the public relations and health care industries also have regulatory bodies or associations that provide codes of ethics and guidelines on best practices to assist members.

- **Advertising Standards Canada (Ad Standards)** is the national, independent, not-for-profit advertising self-regulatory body that sets and regulates advertising standards. It uses a consumer-complaint process to review questionable ads that are withdrawn from the media if they contravene its guidelines and are not fixed. Ad Standards provides advice and pre-clearance services for advertisers but has no legal jurisdiction and does not levy fines. Detailed guidelines can be found at **www.adstandards.ca**. The magnitude of communication in social media provides a whole other challenge for marketers. This topic is discussed further in the Focus on Ethics box, "Advertising Standards in Social Media."[36]

- The **Competition Bureau** is an independent law-enforcement agency with jurisdiction in many areas. In the marketing communications area, it looks at fraudulent advertising and misleading representation to sell products, including price and warranty claims. Deceptive price claims and contests that do not publish the required terms and conditions are illegal and heavily scrutinized. To see more about the Competition Bureau, visit its website at **http://competitionbureau.gc.ca**.

- The **Canadian Radio-television and Telecommunications Commission (CRTC)** is another government agency. It regulates the broadcast and telecommunications industry in Canada, including the licensing of stations. It also provides guidelines

Advertising Standards in Social Media

With over 1.69 billion users worldwide, does Facebook have an ethical responsibility to ensure that advertising published on its site is truthful?

Facebook CEO Mark Zuckerburg says no as he defends his company's reluctance to take down political advertising that contains false information, likening it to censorship and saying, "What I believe is that in a democracy, it's really important that people can see for themselves what politicians are saying, so they can make their own judgments."

Many of the other online social media platforms have recognized the challenges with trying to monitor political advertising, and Twitter, for example, responded by banning all political advertising. Google put limits on some political advertising but stopped short of an outright ban. Zuckerberg cites freedom of speech as his reason for accepting ads that contain false information.

In Canada and the United States, there are clear guidelines for advertising products or services such as Trident Gum or Weight Watchers. These acts were put in place to protect consumers from false or misleading claims. In Canada, the *Competition Act* contains "criminal and civil provisions to address false or misleading representations and deceptive marketing practices in promoting the supply or use of a product or any business interest." Even Facebook has clear guidelines about misinformation in product advertising on the platform, which states that advertisers who repeatedly post false information may have restrictions on their ability to advertise on Facebook.

The guidelines for political advertising have become less clear, and those guidelines seem to be more concerned with who is sponsoring the ads and less with the truthfulness of the content. This is becoming even more important as outside forces try to impact the democratic process and as social media platforms become a greater source of news. Since the guidelines for political advertising are less clear, social media platforms are left to determine their own policies. These policies are based on the principle that people should be able to hear from those who wish to lead them, and what they say should be debated in public.

Since four out of ten people admit to getting their news from Facebook, Facebook has put into place a system of fact-checking that uses both in-house and third-party accredited fact-checkers to validate stories that are posted in newsfeeds. This action recognizes that the platform is a source of news and thus has a responsibility to ensure that false news is not reported on the site. This same fact-checking is not used when accepting political advertisements for the site, which can be particularly disconcerting due to the extensive analytics available to advertisers that enables them to target particularly vulnerable market segments with messages that are not verified to be true.

This is an interesting dilemma as there are two ways of looking at the ethics of this issue. You could see Facebook as a source of news and

©Jason O. Watson (USA: California photographs)/ Alamy Stock Photo

therefore expect it to fall under the same ethical guidelines as a newspaper or other legitimate news source. You would then feel that taking money for false advertising would be unethical. On the other hand, you could take Facebook's perspective as a social media platform and publicly traded corporation where it is ethical to defend the rights of free speech, avoid censorship, and create value for its shareholders.

As social media evolves to an ever-important source of news, democratic governments will have to decide how both political and market advertising will be treated under competition laws so that companies like Facebook or Twitter will not be left to decide what is "ethical." ●

Questions

1. Do you think Facebook should ban all political advertising?

2. Should social media platforms like Facebook be responsible for fact-checking to ensure information posted is accurate?

on Canadian content and sets limitations on the amount of advertising permitted during broadcasts. It oversees the advertising of alcoholic beverages and works with the Ad Standards on advertising to children. It also has jurisdiction over the national Do Not Call List (DNCL), which provides parameters for telemarketing in Canada. Find more about the CRTC at **www.crtc.gc.ca**.

- The **Canadian Marketing Association (CMA)** uses a code of ethics and standards of practice to guide the marketing industry in Canada on telemarketing, e-mail marketing, mobile marketing, Internet marketing, promotional contests, fundraising, database marketing, and marketing to children and teenagers. It also provides guidelines on privacy issues and anti-spam practices. Visit **www.the-cma.org** for more information.

- The Canadian Wireless Telecommunications Association (CWTA) administers the CWTA short code guidelines, a strict set of guidelines on pricing and practices for mobile text messaging. This includes pricing guidelines, the use of keyword protocols, opt-in rules, privacy requirements, and terms and conditions. To find out more about the CWTA, go to **www.cwta.ca**.

- The Mobile Marketing Association (MMA) is a global association that sets standards and guidelines for mobile messaging, advertising, and promotion. It liaises with the Canadian Marketing Association to bring the best practices and ethical approaches in mobile marketing to marketers in Canada. For more information on the MMA, visit **http://www.mmaglobal.com/**.

Failure to abide by marketing communication regulations can have dire consequences for marketers—campaigns may be forced off air, companies and individuals may be fined, and legal action can result in jail time.

ask YOURSELF

1. *How much time do you spend weekly searching the Internet, on mobile apps, listening to the radio, watching television, streaming video, and reading magazines or newspapers?*

2. *What are the most impactful trends in marketing communications?*

3. *How is marketing communications regulated in Canada?*

LO 1 • Integrated marketing communications (IMC) approaches coordinate all elements of the promotional mix to provide a consistent message to a target audience.

LO 2 • Marketing communications approaches can include inbound and outbound approaches, with marketers commonly using an IMC approach.

LO 3 • The promotional planning process requires marketers to (1) specify the IMC objectives, (2) identify the target audience, (3) set the promotional budget, (4) design the promotional program, (5) schedule and run the IMC elements, and (6) evaluate the program and recommend changes.

• Evaluation approaches look at the program in general as well as each individual element.

LO 4 • The promotional mix or marketing communication tools include advertising, public relations, sales promotion, direct response marketing, event marketing and sponsorship, and personal selling.

LO 5 • Advertising media choices include Internet/mobile, TV, newspaper, magazine, radio, and out-of-home.

LO 6 • Consumer promotional tools include coupons, contests, sweepstakes, samples, premiums, loyalty programs, rebates, bonus packs, and point-of-sale materials.

• Trade promotions include trade shows, off-invoice allowances, merchandising allowances, and co-op advertising.

LO 7 • The personal selling process consists of six stages: prospecting, pre-approach, approach, presentation, close, and follow-up.

LO 8 • The current trends impacting marketing communications include a more connected consumer, which has resulted in a shift to digital media from more traditional forms.

LO 9 • The marketing communications industry consists of the media, marketing communications agencies, research companies, associations, and regulatory bodies.

• The marketing communications industry is regulated by Advertising Standards Canada (Ad Standards), the Competition Bureau, the Canadian Radio-television and Telecommunications Commission (CRTC), the Canadian Marketing Association (CMA), the Canadian Wireless Telecommunications Association (CWTA), and the Mobile Marketing Association (MMA).

---

key terms and concepts... **A REFRESHER**

advertising
Bluetooth
branded entertainment
common short codes (CSC)
consumer promotions
customer advocacy funnel
earned media
frequency
geofencing
inbound marketing
integrated marketing communications (IMC)
marketing communication agencies

marketing communication tools
matrix 2D barcode
mobile check-in services
mobile discovery
mobile e-mail
mobile messaging
multimedia messaging services (MMS)
near field communications (NFC)
outbound marketing
out-of-home (OOH) advertising
owned media
paid media
personal selling

product placement
promotional mix
pull strategy
push strategy
reach
sales promotion
short messaging services (SMS)
social networks
touch points
trade promotions
WiFi hotspots

---

hands-on... **APPLY YOUR KNOWLEDGE**

Promotion Assignment. Using the information in the Marketing NewsFlash box regarding product placement, choose a popular product from a movie or TV show you have watched and determine the following for a promotional campaign for that product: (1) IMC objectives, (2) target market profile, (3) central promotional idea, (4) recommended promotional mix, and (5) methods to evaluate the campaign.

This chapter's opening vignette examines Tim Hortons' integrated marketing campaign for the Roll Up the Rim sales promotion. Brainstorm other elements that you would add to the campaign to create additional touch points with the target audience.

infographic... **DATA ANALYSIS**

Review the Infographic that details information on an Advertising Standards Canada (Ad Standards) study indicating the truth and accuracy level of trust that individuals have with each media format. Why do you believe that some media formats are trusted more than others?

13

LEARNING OBJECTIVES

LO 1 Explain the concept of public relations and the tools used by the industry

LO 2 Explain direct response marketing

LO 3 Explain event marketing and sponsorship

LO 4 Explain the unique online approaches used in marketing communications

LO 5 Describe social media marketing

LO 6 Outline the main social networks and tools used in social media marketing

LO 7 Summarize the best practices associated with the creation and monitoring of social media programs

LO 8 Explain mobile marketing and its approaches

LO 9 Describe the tools involved in mobile marketing

LO 10 List the best practices and regulations that guide mobile marketing

Inbound Marketing Communications

As discussed in the opening vignette for Chapter 12, Tim Hortons leveraged all elements of the promotional mix to implement a successful IMC campaign for its sales promotion, Roll Up the Rim. The company invested in a strategic promotional plan with outbound communications to successfully gain awareness and participation in the promotion. In this chapter, we are focusing on the inbound elements of the promotional mix used to create community and build brands. We look at Hub Town Brewery, an innovative small business in a niche market who successfully leverages social media and community building with limited financial resources to build its brand. In both cases, the key is an integrated marketing communications (IMC) program.

Hub Town Brewing Company

CHAPTER OUTLINE

- Hub Town Brewery
- The online marketing landscape
- Social media marketing tools
- Social media marketing best practices

- The mobile marketing landscape
- Mobile marketing tools
- Mobile marketing regulations and best practices

Recent changes to liquor laws and changing consumers tastes has fuelled the growth in the craft brewery market in Canada. According to Alberta Gaming, Liquor and Cannabis, the number of breweries in Alberta shot up to 123 from 27 between October 2015 and January 2020. According to the Alberta Small Brewers Association, one of the biggest challenges facing craft brewers is attracting repeat customers and getting a foothold in the expanding marketplace. The challenge is for them to create a unique brand experience that helps them stand out from the competition. These entrepreneurs hire locally, process local agriculture, and contribute to the economy. It is now estimated that Alberta brewers employ over 3,000 people and represent 10 percent of the market share in Alberta, with plans for further growth.

New business owners are always challenged with how to create awareness and build their brand while completing all of the other tasks involved with starting a new venture. Hub Town Brewing Company in Okotoks, Alberta, is no exception. Owners Lisa and Mark Watts spent years developing the concept for their microbrewery, finding space, securing permits, crowdfunding, outfitting the brewery and tap room, learning how to scale up production, and the list goes on. So no one would be surprised if these brewmasters from the oil and gas industry were unfamiliar with an integrated marketing communication strategy and how to implement it in a new venture. But implement it they did, and in the first year of business, Hub Town has become a go-to place for beer and community. Here is a little more of the story.

With a slice of life appeal, Mark and Lisa used a variety of IMC tools to create a thriving craft brewery and taproom in downtown Okotoks, opening in the fall of 2019, and then overnight pivoted to a craft brew and local food delivery business when the COVID-19 shutdown was imposed in April 2020. What the Watts have demonstrated is that having a clear marketing vision and using an integrated strategy, even a start-up small business with a limited budget can leverage time and money to create a successful venture.

Using professional photography, regular social media posts, and customer-generated content, Hub Town Brewing Company regularly sells out of tickets to events and the various beers that they have brewed on-site. In doing so, it has created relationships with other local businesses and community organizations to increase the organic reach of its campaign. The IMC tools being employed are public relations, direct marketing, event marketing, and sponsorships. The Hub Town team uses the social media platforms of Instagram, Facebook, and Twitter as the communication vehicles to drive customers to its transactional website or to the brewery itself.

Public relations: Mark and Lisa Watts have developed a good relationship with local media, including a local newspaper and radio station. When Hub Town finally received approval for its location, the brew team put together a crowdfunding campaign, creating much-needed capital and a VIP community. Alerting local news outlets with press releases resulted in radio reports and newspaper and online articles being published. The local community newspaper, the *Okotoks Western Wheel*, has a circulation of 14,000, and combined with radio and online, the publicity generated enough interest that crowdfunding enabled the business to order equipment and start renovations.

Direct marketing: To build on the crowdfunding community long before the brewery opened, social media accounts were set up and posts on the brewery's progress were updated regularly. Over 2,000 followers on Facebook and 3,200 on Instagram received regular updates on the progress, ups and downs, and anticipated opening dates. This strategy has continued since the opening, with professionally photographed posts being used to announce events and then portray the various successful events. The Hub Town community is also encouraged to post about their own experiences with the product, and these are often followed up with compiled Instagram stories of customer-generated content.

Event marketing: The Hub Town team has encouraged local groups to have events on slower week nights in the pub. Events like paint nights, karaoke, and mixers have been organically staged along with the sold-out Flames and Oilers hockey nights, movie trivia contests, Oktoberfest and Halloween events. Each event creates interest and an interesting story line for the regular social media posts.

Sponsorships: Hub Town has been a major supporter and participant in local Town of Okotoks events like Enchanted Okotoks. Early in 2020, Hub Town was the major beer sponsor for the Okotoks Oilers Casino Fundraiser, supporting the hockey community and creating new fans for Hub Town brews.

A perfect example of the slice of life appeal and the effective implementation of the Hub Town strategy happened when the Tap Room was closed due to the 2020 pandemic. Mark and Lisa switched overnight to beer delivery service and created beautiful photographs for the accompanying PR, social media, and blog communications. This program has been so successful that Hub Town has run out of cans and jugs a couple of times.

True to the community roots and ideals, Hub Town joined forces with other local businesses to deliver food and created a weekly subscription service. This transition would not have been possible without the foundation of excellent communication that had been laid over the previous year.

Hub Town illustrates that effective IMC is not just for big brands like Tim Hortons, but thoughtful implementation can help every brand leverage its promotional resources to build the trust and awareness that it needs to become an integral and successful member of the community. Even when faced with a pandemic and a complete change in business model, Hub Town has been able to grow organically, adding followers and sales month over month through the strategic use of professional creative material, interesting stories, posting without fail, and using customer-created content.[1]

---

reality **CHECK** ⊘

As you read Chapter 13, refer back to the Hub Town Brewing Company opening vignette on building community with IMC to answer the following questions:

- Why is social media such a powerful communication tool for building community?
- What other digital tools would you recommend that Hub Town Brewing Company integrate into its campaigns?

Promotional Mix, Continued

This chapter focuses on the remaining areas of the promotional mix—public relations, direct response marketing, and event sponsorship—along with more detail in the mediums of social media and mobile to build community. This chapter is designed to provide students with an understanding of how digital communication tools are used for marketing purposes and how they can be integrated with offline marketing tools to create a truly integrated brand message. Recent data shows that Canadians spend over nine hours per day on digital media, making it an important tool for any marketer.[2]

Public Relations

LO 1 Public relations is an area that is increasingly used by marketers to deliver messages to consumers. While advertising may be viewed with suspicion, messages that come through a third party, such as the media, are often seen as more reliable and credible. In addition, for marketers with small budgets, public relations efforts can be a more affordable way to communicate with a wide audience.

Public relations is a communications tool that seeks to influence the opinions and attitudes of target groups through the use of unpaid media exposure. Public relations professionals build relationships with the media and stakeholders and use tools such as press releases, social media releases, press kits, news conferences, and events to spread the word. Public relations specialists target the media in an attempt to generate positive publicity for a company, product, or individual. Public relations can also take the form of crisis management and image management.

Crisis management can be an important aspect of public relations, as seen with various incidents over the last few years that have severely impacted people's lives and forced companies to answer to the public outcry. Public relations professionals, well-versed in crisis management, help companies navigate these difficult circumstances by advising on what strategies should be followed to rectify situations and salvage a company's image.

An example worth noting is that of Coca-Cola, which came under fire when it was uncovered that it had funded research downplaying the role that diet plays in obesity. As part of a partnership with the Global Energy Balance Network, funded by Coca-Cola, research was conducted that attempted to attribute obesity to lack of exercise. After this partnership was exposed by the media in Canada and the United States, Coca-Cola needed to deal with this corporate crisis by responding to its critics. When a crisis occurs within an organization, response must be rapid, with the CEO leading the charge. The organization needs to take responsibility and acknowledge any wrongdoing with transparency. It is also very important for the organization to present an action plan of next steps to confirm its commitment to rectifying the situation. Coke did all of these things. Within a couple days, the chief technical officer at Coca-Cola responded with a letter to the editor of *USA Today*, and this was followed by an editorial in the *Wall Street Journal* by Coca-Cola's CEO Muhtar Kent. Coca-Cola acknowledged that some of the decisions it had made to fund research and health programs were confusing to the public and created mistrust. In future,

the company committed to more transparency and reinforced that both diet and exercise play an important role in combating obesity. Coca-Cola also committed to establishing an oversight committee of external experts to review any future research activities. By all accounts, Coca-Cola managed to handle this crisis in a professional manner, which reinforced its commitment to its customers.[3]

> *Crisis management can be an important aspect of public relations.*

It is important to understand that while public relations efforts can yield positive results, ultimately the media decides if, what, and when it may spread a message about a company, brand, or individual. **Publicity** is a non-personal form of communication that appears in the media and is not paid for directly by the organization. The publicity is not controlled by the company itself, and the company has no control over what is discussed.

Public Relations Tools Public relations activities need to be ethical and integrated into marketing communications efforts. Several tools and tactics are available for marketers, including press releases, press conferences, special events, and company reports. Social media releases and social media initiatives are relatively new tools that can come under the guise of public relations. Let's look at the tools.

PRESS RELEASES One of the most frequently used public relations tools is the **press release**, an announcement written by the organization and sent to the media.

PRESS CONFERENCES Another commonly used publicity tool is the **press conference**, when representatives of the media are invited to an informational meeting with the company. Advanced materials and press releases are often distributed ahead of time and external experts and/or executives from the company are present. This tool is often used during crisis management situations.

---

public relations
A communications tool that seeks to influence the opinions and attitudes of target groups through the use of unpaid media exposure; targets the media in an attempt to generate positive publicity for a company, product, or individual.

publicity
A non-personal form of communication that appears in the media and is not paid for directly by the organization.

press release
An announcement written by an organization and sent to the media.

press conference
A planned event where representatives of the media are invited to an informational meeting with the company.

SPECIAL EVENTS This growing area of public relations involves the creation, support, or sponsorship of special events such as company-sponsored seminars, conferences, and sporting or entertainment events. The goal of these events is to create a forum to disseminate company information and to create positive brand associations for participants or viewers.

COMPANY REPORTS Formal company information that is published in annual reports, brochures, newsletters, or videos are also public relations tools that help spread positive messages.

SOCIAL MEDIA RELEASES A **social media release** is a tool available for marketers to efficiently and effectively communicate information to the media and the public. Unlike press releases, which exist online and offline with mainly text-based information, social media releases use online multimedia to communicate with recipients. Video, images, and text are included in online releases, with comment areas and share buttons so that readers can easily share the release on blogs or social networks such as Twitter and Facebook.

Direct mail pieces often include a call to action for the consumer, and when integrated with other marketing communication vehicles, they can help a brand build a long-term relationship with the customer.

Source: Banana Republic

response marketing program is multifaceted and designed with short-term communication blasts to build long-term relationships with the company and brand loyalty.

Offline approaches include direct mail, catalogues, telemarketing, and direct-response advertising on TV, radio, or print, where telephone numbers or web addresses drive an immediate call to action. Online approaches look to the Internet to facilitate one-on-one interactions and use tools such as e-mail campaigns and social media interactions to drive consumers to landing pages, websites, or microsites. In many instances, offline and online direct response approaches work together to encourage consumers to go to a store or an e-commerce site to complete a transaction.

Direct response marketing programs use metrics to evaluate success, such as business leads, traffic generation, and direct orders. **Lead generation** is the resultant request for additional information. **Traffic generation** is the resultant visit to a location or website.

A successful direct mail campaign was launched by BMW to mark the 40th anniversary of the M series vehicle. BMW sent existing and prospective customers an actual print of the wheel tread of an M series vehicle. In addition, the customer received a personalized URL to a YouTube video documenting the creation of the direct mail piece. The video itself received 500,000 hits and was shared extensively on social media. Owners of M series vehicles even started to post their own M series tire treads on social media.[5]

E-mail Marketing **E-mail marketing** includes the use of opt-in e-mail lists where consumers register and give permission to receive online communications. The Canadian Marketing Association (CMA) strictly

Direct Response Marketing

LO 2 **Direct response marketing** is a tool designed to communicate with consumers in a targeted and personalized way using either traditional or online approaches. In addition, unique to direct response marketing is the inclusion of a call to action for consumers.[4] In many instances, a direct

advises members not to use spam. **Permission-based e-mail** is when a recipient chooses to receive e-mail from a marketer, while *spam* is unsolicited e-mail that clutters the Internet. The usage of e-mail marketing by Canadian marketers continues to grow. It was initially thought that the introduction of tougher anti-spam laws would severely limit the use of e-mail communication. However, marketers are finding that they have better quality e-mail lists to work with, and according to an Ipsos study, 80 percent of customers are willing to receive e-mails from companies.[6]

Event Marketing and Sponsorship

LO 3 **Event marketing** refers to the creation or involvement of a brand in an experience or occasion that heightens its awareness, creates positive associations, and generates a desired response. *Experiential marketing*, introduced in Chapter 1, can be based around an event, but it often combines public relations, event marketing, and promotions to break through the clutter of competing marketing messages. Event marketing and sponsorship often go hand-in-hand with brands lending their names to established events. Companies often weave event marketing into integrated campaigns to make connections with consumers and create a buzz.

Sponsorship involves a company paying a fee in exchange for inclusion in an event, involvement in its advertising opportunities, or exposure within the event itself. Sponsorship programs can encompass a multitude of approaches that range from placing ads or logos in brochures, to setting up banners at events, to the naming of the event itself.

An example of sponsorship can be seen with the annual Toronto International Film Festival, or TIFF. The lead sponsor of TIFF is Bell. The 530,000 attendees at the event are only the tip of the iceberg. Over 2 million people interact in some way with TIFF each year. In addition, TIFF is able to provide a very clear description of its audience. Attendees are overwhelmingly younger individuals with a post-secondary education and an average household income of $91,000. For companies like Bell, the Royal Bank, and L'Oréal Paris, they can be sure that they will gain significant exposure with key target groups before, during, and after the event. TIFF not only offers opportunities for companies to entertain and host clients at the event, but there are a multitude of branding and promotional opportunities for sponsors as well, depending on the negotiated package. Media impressions hit 3.3 billion worldwide with over 1,000 media outlets.[7]

Over 2 million people interact with the Toronto International Film Festival each year, providing valuable sponsorship opportunities.
©Roberto Machado Noa/Getty Images

> *Companies often weave event marketing into integrated campaigns.*

Digital Marketing Communication

Digital marketing communication tools are the most rapidly evolving areas in marketing, and a marketer needs to understand how consumers and marketers use them to stay connected and engaged. One of the first touch points that a brand may have with a consumer is through its website, where a consumer may go to find out more about a product or company. Consumers connect with each other and with brands using social media, whether this is with Facebook to locate an offer or with Twitter to lodge a complaint. Mobile platforms are often used by consumers to reach out on social networks, checking statuses and posting updates to share with friends throughout the day and on the go. Marketers in turn connect brands with consumers on these networks and use mobile marketing approaches to reach consumers on their mobile devices.

Online Marketing Tools

LO 4 The Internet has a number of unique online tools that marketers use to engage individuals—namely, websites and microsites, search

permission-based e-mail
When a recipient chooses to receive e-mail from a marketer.

event marketing
The creation or involvement of a brand in an experience or occasion that will heighten its awareness, create positive associations, and generate a desired response.

sponsorship
When an advertiser pays a fee in exchange for inclusion in an event, involvement in its advertising opportunities, or exposure within the event itself.

transactional websites

Electronic storefronts focused on converting an online browser into an online buyer.

promotional websites

Promotional websites focus on showcasing products and services.

microsites

Promotional websites created for short-term promotional purposes, often allowing consumers to enter contests and access promotional information.

corporate websites

Websites that provide company and brand information to consumers and the media.

search engine marketing (SEM)

Includes the use of search engine optimization and pay-per-click advertising to market on search engines.

search engine optimization (SEO)

Ensuring that websites are written, indexed, and coded so that they are highly rated and ranked by the search engines.

pay-per-click advertising (PPC)

Ads that appear in response to keyword triggers on search engines, as well as on some websites, blogs, and social media sites, where the advertiser pays only when the ad is clicked.

engine marketing, influencer marketing, word-of-mouth marketing, social media marketing, and mobile marketing.

Websites When it comes to websites, their design and content is central to successful ranking on search engines, which facilitates discovery by consumers. Content needs to be fresh and frequently updated. Many websites include blogs as a means of routinely adding fresh new content. Visual website appeal is also important. Consumers decide to click on a web page within seconds; therefore, content and visual appeal need to work together to present an appealing proposition. Websites can be transactional, promotional, or both. **Transactional websites** were discussed in Chapter 10. They are essentially electronic storefronts focused on converting an online searcher into an online buyer. **Promotional websites** focus on showcasing products and services.

Microsites are promotional websites created to showcase a specific brand or for short-term promotional purposes, often providing consumers with the ability to enter contests and access promotional offers. McCain Foods used a microsite to promote its #Modifry contest, encouraging customers to submit

their innovative recipes using McCain French fries. **Corporate websites** are important destination sites for consumers and the media that want to quickly access company and product information.

Websites often form the foundation of a company or brand's digital marketing strategy, providing links to social media as well as sign-up pages for newsletter and e-mail communications.

> ❞ *Microsites are promotional websites created to showcase a specific brand or for short-term promotional purposes.*

Search Engine Marketing **Search engine marketing (SEM)** is an Internet marketing approach that includes two areas: (1) search engine optimization and (2) pay-per-click advertising. **Search engine optimization (SEO)** looks at website design, technical coding, written content, incoming links, and website updates to ensure that websites are highly rated and properly indexed by search engines such as Google and Bing. Marketers often work with specialists to maximize search engine optimization.

An Internet advertising approach pioneered by search engines and now also used by a few websites, blogs, and social media sites is called **pay-per-click advertising (PPC)**. It is often referred to as *search advertising*

The Walmart website has a focus on transactions.
©Ed Endicott/Alamy Stock Photo

because it primarily appears on search engines in the form of mini-text ads that are served during keyword searches on either the top or right-hand side of the search page. The search engine is paid by the PPC advertiser only when the ads are clicked. Pay-per-click image ads also exist on some blogs and social media sites.

Influencer Marketing Social media have changed how marketing communications are targeted and have spurred the emergence of influencer marketing. **Influencer marketing** is the practice of focusing on the identification and recruitment of influencers to advocate a company's products, services, and brands rather than focusing exclusively on prospective buyers.

Influencer marketing is based on the concept of personal influence; namely, a consumer's purchases are often influenced by the views, opinions, or behaviour of others (see Chapter 3). Influencer marketing applies this behavioural concept to social media in the presence of social networks and user-generated content. A perfect marriage!

Kendall Jenner has close to 100 million Instagram followers. Read the text to learn how many followers she, her sisters, and her mother likely have on social media.

Source: Instagram

The identification of influencers on social media is based, in large part, on the number of followers an influencer has on social networking sites such as Facebook, Instagram, and Twitter as well as content community sites such as YouTube.[8] The number of followers, in turn, is often attributed to an influencer's *perceived* credibility, knowledge, authenticity, and reliability in providing relevant content to his or her audience. In short, social media influencers are trusted by their followers.

The recruitment of social media influencers involves partnering with individuals who are willing and able to effectively engage their followers with a product, service, or brand. These influencers are often compensated. They are paid outright, given free products or services, and reimbursed for their expenses in creating and posting content. It is estimated that 75 percent of large U.S. companies will spend $101 billion on influencer marketing initiatives in 2020.[9]

Social media influencers exist within specific categories. For example, the Kardashians (Kim, Kourtney, and Khloe) and Jenners (Kris, Kylie, and Kendall) are prominent influencers in the fashion, fitness, entertainment, beauty, and pop culture categories. Their combined worldwide social media followers likely exceed 500 million people. The Marketing NewsFlash, "Two Canadian Influencers," introduces a couple of prominent influencers in Canada.[10]

Word-of-Mouth Marketing **Word-of-mouth marketing** is based on the spread of positive messages about a product by listening to consumers, identifying influential individuals who can spread the word, and making it easier for them to do so. Research by the Word of Mouth Marketing Association shows the impact that word of mouth can exert, with 72 percent of respondents claiming that reviews from friends and family influence their decisions.[11]

Word-of-mouth communication works on several levels. On a viral level, it tries to create buzz through social media that seeds fun and interesting messages, many times with influential people who spread the word. On an influencer level, it identifies key communities, opinion leaders, and product advocates who get personally involved with the brand and have the ability to influence others.[12] On a professional level, official referral programs may be put in place to reward satisfied customers who refer the brand to friends and contacts.

influencer marketing
The practice of focusing on the identification and recruitment of influencers to advocate a company's products, services, and brands rather than focusing exclusively on prospective buyers.

word-of-mouth marketing
The spread of positive messages about a product by listening to consumers, identifying influential individuals that can spread the word, and making it easier for them to do so.

Two Canadian Influencers

Indigenous fashion lovers Gabrielle Fayant and Dani Lanouette.

Courtesy of Gabrielle Fayant and Dani Lanoueutte

With all of the changes in the media land-scape, an interesting trend has emerged in the social media arena, and that is the power of influencers on both a macro and micro level. So you might be wondering what exactly is an influencer and how one can help build a brand. According to *Marketing Hub*, an influencer is someone who has:

- The power to affect the purchasing decisions of others because of his or her authority, knowledge, position, or relationship with his or her audience; and

- A following in a distinct niche, with whom he or she actively engages, the size of which depends on the size of his/her topic of the niche.

It is important to note that these individuals are not merely marketing tools, but rather social relationship assets with which brands can collaborate to achieve their marketing objectives.

The great thing about influencers is that they already have a following of people who like and trust them, and with the right relationship, that trust can be also connected to brands that they like and promote. It is difficult to create a large following on social media from scratch aligning with like-minded influencers can help you reach your target audience more effectively. The online marketing metrics are driven by the conversion rate of customers, which basically means how we persuade our potential customers to move from being interested in our product or service to actually purchasing. To be successful in driving conversions, you must have a combination of brand awareness, brand trust, and urgency. The right influencers help to create brand awareness and trust in their loyal followers; arming those influencers with a promo code or information about upcoming events provides the urgency. Influencers also help with the heavy lifting of having an online presence as they provide the brand with additional unique content, improve the search engine rankings, expose them to new markets, and increase lead generation. In order to get these benefits from this emerging marketing tool, it is vital that brands partner with influencers that strongly align with the brand image and target market.

Matt R Edwards (@mattredwards) is a fashion and lifestyle influencer in the Greater Toronto area market. Matt is a media communications graduate from Humber College and blogs about lifestyle and fashion for men. He has a large following on Instagram, close to 20,000, and has worked with a variety of brands, showcasing his unique style and providing "how to" blogs for today's men. Matt's content is topical and current, with professionally designed photography on all of his platforms. His blogs are thoughtful and helpful, answering questions many of his followers might have about fitness, fashion, and fun, with titles like "20 things to help you get through 2020."

Another interesting use of influencers and collaboration is demonstrated with the @indigistyle initiative created by Indigenous fashion lovers Gabrielle Fayant and Dani Lanouette. Being really interested in fashion, they created @ indigistyle as a platform to encourage and support Indigenous designers and help them create a greater online presence. They also work alongside another Indigenous fashion blogger Andrea Deleeuw, working together as a collective to make space for Indigenous values, community, and bloggers.

"It's almost like a fan page to hype up the artists and brands that we buy from and that we really love," said Gabrielle Fayant.

To create buzz, the #Indigistyle Challenge was created to lift spirits and showcase Indigenous style. Participants were encouraged to post different types of fashion items on different days through the seven-day challenge period. Future plans

Matt R Edwards, fashion and lifestyle influencer.

Courtesy of Matt Edwards

have the platform showcasing specific designers, having contests, and providing intel on special designer drops happening throughout the year. Working together to create trust, interest, and buzz around Indigenous fashion and the @indigistyle brand will also create opportunities for the team to widen their sphere of influence into the wider fashion market, improving the reach and creating more opportunities for buyers and sellers of these unique items.

Thoroughly investigating the content of any interesting influencer to check on alignment with your brand values and audience is much more important than just picking the person with the most followers or likes on their sites. With a well-aligned choice of social media influencers on your brand's side, you can build trust, content, and urgency with new markets that find your networks and optimize searches. ●

Questions

1. What is an influencer?

2. What are important considerations when choosing an influencer for your brand?

The Social Media Landscape

LO 5 Defining *social media* is challenging, but it's necessary to help a brand or marketing manager select the right platform. This section defines social media, classifies social media, and describes why and how social media have transformed marking communications.

What Are Social Media?

This section defines social media and classifies the countless social media available to assist marketing managers in choosing among them.

Defining Social Media Social media represent a unique blending of technology and social interaction to create a communal experience and personal value for users. Social media are online media where users submit comments, photos, and videos—often accompanied by a feedback process to identify "popular" topics. Most social media involve a genuine online conversation among people about a subject of mutual interest, one built on their personal thoughts and experiences. However, other social media sites involve games and virtual worlds in which the online interaction includes playing a game, completing a quest, controlling an avatar, and so on. Business firms also refer to social media as *consumer-generated media*. A single social media site with millions of users interacting with each other, like Facebook, Twitter, and LinkedIn, is referred to as a *social network*.

The term "social media" is sometimes used interchangeably with the terms "Web 2.0" and "Web 3.0" and "user-generated content"—concepts that are the foundation of today's social media. Web 2.0 and Web

The next-generation Web, Web 3.0, will be customized to each individual. Read the text to learn how!
©Wright Studio/Shutterstock

3.0 identify technological functionalities that make possible today's high degree of interactivity among users. Web 2.0 includes functionalities that permit people to collaborate and share information online. Web 3.0, now in its early application stages, includes additional functionalities that allow personalization and customization to each individual based on location, interests, and needs. It integrates new features such as cloud computing, big data, the Internet of Things, security solutions, and privacy protection.[13]

User-generated content (UGC) refers to any form of online media content that is publicly available and created by consumers or end users. The term *user-generated content* (also referred to as consumer-generated content) includes video, blogs, discussion forum posts, digital images, audio files, and related content. To qualify as UGC, content must satisfy three basic criteria:[14]

1. It is published either on a publicly accessible website or on a social media site, so it is not simply an e-mail.

user-generated content (UGC)
Original online content that has been created by users in the form of blogs, posts, images, audio, or video.

2. It shows a significant degree of original or creative effort, so it is more than simply posting a newspaper article on a personal blog without editing or comments.

3. It is consumer generated by an individual outside of a professional or commercial organization.

Today, about 80 percent of the content appearing on social media is user generated.[15]

Classifying Social Media Most of us would probably say that Facebook, Twitter, LinkedIn, and YouTube are well-known social media platforms. But marketing managers trying to reach potential customers need a system to classify the more than 400 specialized and diverse social media networks to select the best among them. Kaplan and Haenlein have proposed a classification system for marketers based on two factors:[16]

1. *Media richness.* This involves the degree of acoustic, visual, and personal contact between two communication partners—face-to-face communications, say, being higher in media richness than telephone or e-mail communications. The higher the media richness and quality of presentation, the greater the social influence that communication partners have on each other's behaviour.

2. *Self-disclosure.* In any type of social interaction, individuals want to make a positive impression to achieve a favourable image with others. This favourable image is affected by the degree of self-disclosure about a person's thoughts, feelings, likes, and dislikes—where greater self-disclosure is likely to increase one's influence on those reached.

Coca-Cola's #ShareaCoke generated thousands of shared images of friends and their Cokes.
©vadimguzhva/iStock/Getty Images Plus

Figure 13–1 uses these two factors of media richness and self-disclosure to position a number of social media sites in two-dimensional space. For example, Wikipedia is a collaborative project that is low on both self-disclosure and media richness. LinkedIn, on the other hand, contains detailed career and resumé information for business networking and is high in self-disclosure but only moderate in media richness.

Marketing managers look carefully at the positioning of the social media shown in Figure 13–1 when selecting those to use in their plans. For example, LinkedIn, positioned in the Social Networking Sites segment in Figure 13–1, is a professional networking service with 500 million members in 200 countries. LinkedIn recently generated $2.3 billion in annual revenue from advertising, recruiter fees, and subscriptions. LinkedIn's customers include companies such as Citigroup, Microsoft, Chevron, Hewlett-Packard, and Volkswagen, which promote their companies' career opportunities to people with specific job titles and individuals who are seeking a job or building a professional network.[17]

Why and How Social Media Transformed Marketing Communications

Consumers receive information, news, and education from print (newspapers, magazines) and electronic (radio, television) media. These traditional media remain important elements in a company's marketing communications effort. As discussed in Chapter 12, social media can complement and augment these traditional media when they are focused on brand-building, customer acquisition, and customer advocacy.

How do marketing managers choose the best social media sites to reach their target markets? As a first step, the text describes how social media can be classified and how they differ from traditional media.
©Anatolii Babii/Alamy Stock Photo

Figure 13–1

A sample of social media, classified by media richness and self-disclosure. Note that in moving from words to photos, videos, and animation, media richness increases. Also, in moving from very impersonal messages to highly personal ones, self-disclosure increases.

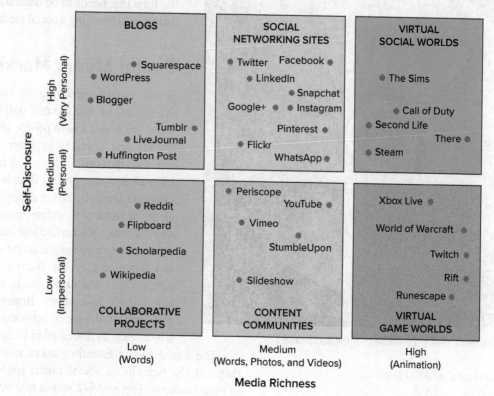

Content marketing is when brands or companies reach out by creating and sharing expertise and brand information that is designed to inform and engage with tools such as research papers, infographics, e-books, how-to videos, blogs, webinars, e-newsletters, case studies, and events. This information can be readily found by search engines. In the business-to-business market, the virtual meeting service provider GoToMeeting shares its own content around productive meetings, working from home, and other relevant topics to its business customers. It also shares other people's content to provide additional value to its followers.[18] Tangerine, the Canadian bank formerly known as ING, considers content marketing a core means of communicating with customers. Unlike its competitors, Tangerine doesn't have any bricks-and-mortar locations. Tangerine provides information that answers the questions and concerns that people have regarding banking and investing. Using tools such as social listening, Google search trends, and inbound inquiries, Tangerine has been able to provide valuable content such as "How I got over the intimidation of investing" and the "Return on investment of going back to school."[19] Check out the "Forward Thinking" section of the Tangerine website at **www.tangerine.ca** for some insightful articles.

Another form of user-generated content is a **blog**. Blog, a short form for "web log," is a web page in the form of an online diary that is used by organizations and individuals to post updates that include personal opinions, activities, and experiences. Readers can subscribe to blogs, post comments, and share content. A **vlog**, short form for a "video blog," is a blog that is posted in a video format. A **wiki** is a collaborative website (such as Wikipedia) that uses an application with which multiple users can create, add, edit, or delete content.

Brian Solis developed the Conversation Prism to visually demonstrate the vastness of the social media landscape and all that it has to offer. It tracks dominant, niche, and promising new social networks. It shows that social media is much larger than the popular sites that we hear about every day—Facebook, Twitter, LinkedIn, and YouTube. It shows that social media includes blogs and wikis as well as countless other social networks, such as Quora for asking questions, last.fm for listening to music, SlideShare for sharing presentations, Goodreads for book lovers, Foodspotting for food enthusiasts, Telfie for TV buffs, and so many more.

blog
A website in the form of an online diary that is used by organizations and individuals to post updates that include personal opinions, activities, and experiences with readers able to subscribe and post comments.

vlog
A blog posted in video format.

wiki
A collaborative website that uses an application with which multiple users can create, add, edit, or delete content.

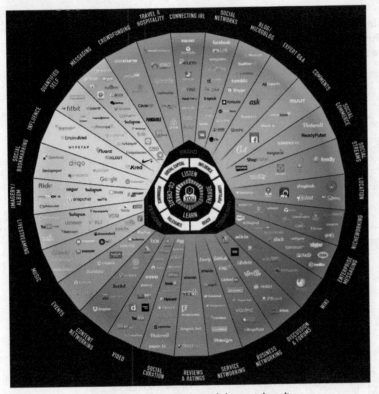

The Conversation Prism shows the vastness of the social media landscape.

©Brian Solis (briansolis.com) and JESS3 (jess3.com)

The Conversation Prism is a useful tool for marketers as it may point to social networks that may be useful for their brands. You can see more about this tool at **www.conversationprism.com.**

Comparing Social Media with Traditional Media

In Chapter 12, traditional media such as print, television, and radio were discussed. While both the more traditional forms of media and social media are effective at communicating brand messages, there are several inherent differences:[20]

- Social media is flexible and can be changed even after it is published.
- Social media is available immediately.
- Social media creates a conversation, and so marketers do not have full control over the messaging.
- Social media can have less reliable demographic data about its audiences.
- Social media can be produced inexpensively.
- Social media needs dedicated attention.

There is the misconception that social media is free. While it is less expensive to produce, a company also needs to consider the time that needs to be dedicated to monitoring and managing a social media program.

Social Media Marketing

Social media marketing is when brands reach out to consumers online through social networks where people connect with friends and contacts to share comments, articles, opinions, videos, and images as a form of self-expression. Brands engage on these platforms by hiring experts and social media managers to create brand pages on social media platforms, to join online conversations, to monitor and respond to questions and comments, to use metrics to measure performance and engagement, and to send out updates and offers. Brands may also place ads on the social networks that accept advertising, as discussed in Chapter 12.

The Social Media Examiner asked marketers what they felt the benefits of social media marketing were to their business. Figure 13–2 shows that 93 percent of marketers believe that social media marketing generates brand exposure, and 87 percent indicate increased traffic is a major benefit. Interestingly, 71 percent mentioned that social media helped them develop loyal fans, and 58 percent believed that social media was responsible for providing market insights. All of these benefits can have a significant impact on a brand.[21]

On average, Canadians spend 18 percent of their social media time interacting with brands. The most common interactions include visiting corporate or brand websites; talking about companies with friends and family; reading permission-based content; following companies on Facebook, Twitter, Instagram, and/or LinkedIn; and posting comments on the same sites.[22]

Social media is a public venue, and marketers need to delicately deal with detractors and negative interactions, understanding that vehemently defending a brand in the court of public opinion can rapidly escalate on social media with negative repercussions. Unhappy consumers are most likely to take to Facebook or Twitter with their complaints.[23] In order to avoid negative situations on social media, companies create social media policies and guidelines to help guide programs and interactions.

Managing customers' comments, reviews, and complaints can be a very time-consuming process. Customers expect answers quickly. A recent study found

Figure 13–2
Benefits of social media marketing

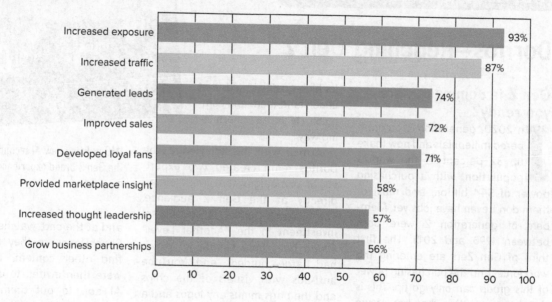

Benefit	Percentage
Increased exposure	93%
Increased traffic	87%
Generated leads	74%
Improved sales	72%
Developed loyal fans	71%
Provided marketplace insight	58%
Increased thought leadership	57%
Grow business partnerships	56%

that 72 percent of consumers expressing a complaint on Twitter expected an answer within an hour. However, only 11 percent of companies responded within an hour. The risk is that if companies aren't meeting customer expectations, they are likely to feel negatively about the brand. And this negativity is expressed in a very public social media forum.[24]

Doritos did an excellent job at engaging a new younger target audience with its brand and revitalizing the Doritos brand with two successful and innovative IMC campaigns involving social media. The Marketing NewsFlash box, "Doritos—Reaching Gen Z" discusses these two campaigns in more detail.[25]

Social Media Marketing Networks and Tools

LO 6 Social media marketing requires knowledge of the social networks that can be used to drive engagement as well as an understanding of the tools that exist to help manage and measure these programs.

Social Media Networks in Canada

Social media is used by marketers in many ways to help connect consumers with a brand. For example, Facebook can send out offers, updates, and contests; Twitter can post newsworthy updates and answer customer service questions; Pinterest and Instagram can post inspiring images and contests; YouTube can be used for storytelling, how-to content, and engaging videos; and LinkedIn can profile a company's expertise. The most developed social media programs use multiple social media sites to profile a brand in creative, engaging, and imaginative ways. Before creating social media marketing programs, marketers need to check any restrictions that these social media sites may have for running elements such as contests, which should also always adhere to the marketing regulations in Canada that were outlined in Chapter 2.

In 2019, the most popular social networks for Canadians were Facebook, LinkedIn, Instagram, Twitter, Snapchat, and Pinterest.[26] The life cycle of social media sites can be rather fickle since these sites grow and die based on public perceptions. The databox on page 329, "Comparing Social Media Networks," shows how social network usage compares globally.

While social media network usage is important, marketers tend to focus the majority of their time on specific networks: Facebook, Twitter, Instagram, Pinterest, Snapchat, and LinkedIn.[27] Next, we look at five mainstream social media networks to understand how they

marketing NewsFlash

Doritos—Reaching Gen Z

Gen Z is coming . . . are you ready?

In 2020, generation Z outnumbered millennials and now make up 32 percent of the world's population, with a purchasing power of $44 billion, and most of them don't even have jobs yet. Members of generation Z were born between 1995 and 2015. The first third of Gen Zers are entering the workforce, and the purchasing power of this group can only go up. This is the first generation that has grown up completely online, and they spend up to an hour more than their older millennial counterparts connected to the Internet.

The PepsiCo marketing team responsible for the Doritos brand noticed a number of things that set generation Z consumers apart from older segments. The marketing team noticed that Gen Z consumers aren't fond of overt brand advertising and are more likely to choose ad-free experiences such as Netflix and other subscription services. Generation Z consumers also do not have the patience to sit through broadcast media ads as their attention span of eight seconds is a good four seconds less than that of the millennials. This generation is looking

for high-quality brands that understand them and communicate in an entertaining way.

Armed with this knowledge, the Doritos team created two experiential campaigns that were aimed directly at the Gen Z audience. The first was Doritos' largest digital investment in the "Another Level" @logo_goes_here campaign, which had large outdoor and YouTube anti-ads with visuals of the chips and the bags minus any logos and a message that the consumer "knows what goes here." Over the course of the campaign, which ran in conjunction with the MTV Awards, all of the brand symbols were removed from social media platforms in an effort to create a relationship with Gen Z Doritos consumers. This "anti-marketing" campaign objective was to create a feeling of belongingness in the intended market where the name is unnecessary due to the iconic nature of the product. Followers could even get a Snapchat lens that turned their face into a triangle. The brand is betting that the tagline "Another Level" will resonate with followers in all platforms for future campaigns.

The second interesting idea was launched in conjunction with the 2020 Super Bowl and the new Cool Ranch Doritos. Using pop cultural references, Lil Nas X and Sam Elliott teamed up for a dance-off to the surprise viral hit song "Old Town Road." The YouTube video has over 13 million views,

IMC utilizing new AI technology to personaliz the Gen Z brand experience
PepsiCo Inc.

and at the end, watchers saw #CoolRanchDance so they could go and find other content. The audience were then invited to use the SWAY AI app to put themselves into a video doing the dance moves. This was the first time this technology was used for this purpose. Pretty soon, fans were joining the TikTok hashtag challenge and creating dances to the song clip and posting on YouTube. This created an abundance of user-generated content and also created more fans for the brand. The dance videos aligned really well with generation Z's perception of themselves as highly creative individuals who participate in creative endeavours in their off-line time. Using influencers in this campaign also seemed to increase the number of participants.

These are two examples of IMC using current and innovative technology to reach Gen Z when and how they want to receive it. ●

Questions

1. Who are other potential influencers or celebrity endorsements that Doritos has used to reach Gen Z?

2. Other than influencers, event sponsorship, social media, and outdoor advertising, what other elements of the promotional mix could Doritos have used to reach Gen Z?

Doritos' Another Level campaign
PepsiCo Inc.

Comparing Social Media Networks - Global Users

Facebook	2,375,000,000
WhatsApp	1,600,000,000
Messenger	1,300,000,000
WeChat	1,112,000,000
Instagram	1,000,000,000
QQ	823,000,000
Qzone	572,000,000
TikTok	500,000,000
Weibo	465,000,000
Reddit	330,000,000
Twitter	330,000,000

are used for marketing purposes. Figure 13–3 compares these major networks based on their usage and the ways they can be used for marketing.

Facebook   With over 2.3 billion users, Facebook is a free social network that is the top choice for people wanting to share photos, videos, and stories with their connections.[28] Facebook is the most used social networking site by marketers, with 93 percent indicating that they have a Facebook account.[29] Due to its dominance and well-developed platform, Facebook is usually the centre of a brand's social media program, and it accounts for most of its social media audience.

Facebook is a social network with three tracks. First, there is the *personal track*, which is how Facebook started, where users create a personal profile; add other users as friends; exchange comments, photos, videos, and "likes"; and receive updates through notifications in the News Feed feature. Private messages can also be sent, a popular feature that is used to quickly message people without using e-mail. Second, there is the *group track*, which uses Facebook Groups to allow Facebook members to create public or private groups where members are focused on a particular interest, such as a high school reunion group or a group on pets, fitness, marketing, or an educational course. Facebook Groups allow members to post comments to everyone in the group at once. Facebook Groups provide members with notifications and have the added benefit of allowing people to upload documents. Third, there is the commercial

Figure 13–3
A comparison of social networks

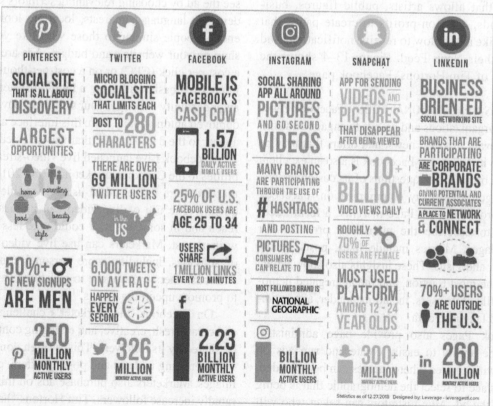

Figure 13–4
Tim Hortons' Facebook page

TM & © Tim Hortons, 2020

page track that allows artists, public figures, businesses, brands, and non-profits to create pages that people can like and follow to receive notifications and updates in their News Feed. Figure 13–4 shows the components of Tim Hortons' Facebook page.

FACEBOOK AS A PROMOTIONAL TOOL   Facebook Pages are used by organizations and brands to engage consumers with relevant updates, news, and offers that may be of interest to its followers. Facebook is also an excellent vehicle for a brand to ask questions of its customers and to allow ongoing two-way communication. Facebook Pages are provided with Page *insights*, a term Facebook uses to describe the metrics it provides for Facebook Pages. Metrics include likes, posts, reach, engagement, and visits. These insights also show which posts have the most traction, and the aggregated demographic profile of its users, including gender, age, country, city, and language data.

Facebook Pages also provide page administrators with the ability to easily create and run ads on Facebook, with an area where images can be uploaded, and an interface to select the demographic that is being targeted by the ad. Administrators can select who will

see the ad by choosing relevant descriptors such as gender, age, language, interests, location, lookalike audiences (people similar to those who like your page or shop on your website), and budget. Ads are paid for by a cost per click (CPC) or on a cost-per-thousand (CPM) impression basis, and using a bidding system, you have an opportunity to budget your spend per day. Ads can be deployed automatically from this interface and will only appear to the demographic that was selected.[30]

Facebook Live launched live video-streaming capabilities to the Canadian market in spring 2016, and many marketers are interested in using live video more frequently. The use of live video can increase a brand's reach and in some cases, it could take less time than a written post. Marketers can use live video for a range of activities, including more personal communication with customers in response to questions or postings, or to promote upcoming events.[31]

On Facebook, the marketer's challenge is to post and create fresh, creative, and engaging content that will be shared by its followers. This is often done by providing interesting updates and posting offers, contests, and images. Marketers also purchase ads on this network to rapidly increase followers. Tim Hortons® has the largest

Canadian fan base on Facebook with over 3 million total fans, including 2.2 million Canadian fans.[32] Marketers can use some of the following tips to maximize consumer engagement (comments, shares, and likes) with their brand on Facebook:[33]

- *Post when engagement is the highest*, not when the most users are logged in.

- *Learn about your customers* and share content that your customers want to see, not just what you want them to see.

- *Learn from the past* which content perform strongest and create more.

- *Use photos*, which are still the most posted and shared content. To make it even easier, post your Instagram photos to Facebook.

- *Engage by replying to comments.*

- *Create share-worthy content* with a headline that will grab attention.

- *Include a call to action* in your post by asking for a share, comment, or like.

- *Keep posts short*, between 0 and 50 words.

In order to promote its movie *Straight Outta Compton*, Universal Pictures and Beats by Dre launched the #StraightOutta campaign. This campaign started with over 100 celebrities from movies, music, and sports sharing their hometown using #StraightOutta and letting people know how their background influenced where they are today. An app was created to maximize engagement. People could upload a picture to the app and create their own custom #StraightOutta meme, highlighting their hometown and posting it to their Facebook timeline. Not only did celebrities get on board, but other companies jumped in to create their own meme. It became a true phenomenon, with Beat by Dre receiving 10 million shares. It was also the number one trending topic on Facebook and Instagram—a feat that hadn't been achieved by any other brand.[34]

Twitter Twitter is a free social media site for individuals and organizations to post and receive short newsworthy text updates—*tweets*—and links in 280 characters from accounts of interest, whether this be from friends, journalists, media outlets, brands, or experts that are followed. Its advantage is the speed with which people can scan updates and decide whether they warrant additional reading. In this way, people

The #StraightOutta campaign was a partnership between Universal Pictures and Beats by Dre. It was the number one trending topic on Facebook and Instagram.

©Artem Kovalenco/Shutterstock

are updated on developments in areas of interest, whether this be for business purposes or related to a passion or hobby. Twitter users can create lists, *favourite* tweets, send out other people's tweets through a *retweet*, and receive notifications recommending whom to follow. The platform encourages users to use hashtags (#) so that topics and conversations are searchable in the Twitter database. Twitter is home to 330 million global users, and it is supported in 40+ languages.[35]

TWITTER AS A PROMOTIONAL TOOL Organizations use Twitter for customer service and marketing purposes. While Facebook is the platform of choice for unhappy customers, Twitter is in second place, with 23 percent of consumers expressing their complaints with a company using Twitter.[36] Companies can use analytics platforms such as Hootsuite to monitor the Twitter landscape for brand and company mentions, to answer questions, and to respond to comments and suggestions in real time.

On Twitter, brands post newsworthy content related to areas of expertise and engage brand advocates that have influential social networks. Seventy-eight percent of Canadian brands have indicated a presence on Twitter.[37] Brand tweets may be pre-planned and pre-approved to coincide with marketing events and integrated into marketing communication programs, while others may task social media managers with the responsibility to deploy real-time tweets that respond to opportunities and buzz. Some marketers also use Twitter chats to profile their expertise and to build their following on social media platforms. These pre-scheduled chats revolve around a certain topic and occur on Twitter by using a pre-determined hashtag to monitor the conversations. These chats are hosted by a brand that could pose a few questions for discussion or bring an influencer into the chat to engage customers.

Marketers can use some of the following tips to make their tweets stand out in the crowd:[38]

- Develop an *editorial calendar* and schedule events throughout the year.

- Create and reuse *graphic templates*.

- Use *videos and images* for Twitter promotion.

- Use *Twitter ads* that take the form of promoted accounts or promoted tweets. The advertiser pays only when followers are added or tweets are clicked, retweeted, or favourited, or when they result in a reply. Ads can be targeted by interest or by using your own e-mail contact list.

Real-time marketing is a planned tactical approach where brands make themselves relevant online during events or newsworthy occurrences by diving into conversations as they occur with aligned short-term messaging that takes advantage of the current buzz. This concept was introduced in Chapter 1. The best-known example of real-time marketing surfaced during the 2013 Super Bowl, when, during a lengthy power outage, Oreo cookies posted a tweet, "Power out? No problem," with a link to a visual showing an Oreo cookie with the caption, "You can still dunk in the dark." This real-time marketing tweet was retweeted almost 16,000 times, and generated over 20,000 likes on Facebook. This effort was not a fluke, Oreo had identified the Super Bowl as a focus and had a "command centre" set up, complete with marketers and advertising experts—with senior managers on call for approvals. In this manner, Oreo was ready and poised to respond to whatever situation presented itself.[39]

Twitter has its own live-streaming service called Periscope. Similar to Facebook Live, it is available using the Periscope app or the Twitter app. It can be used to release brand videos, to talk directly to your customers, or for a regular weekly live broadcast. Given the large audiences available to marketers on Facebook, it makes sense to use Facebook Live as a live video-streaming platform, but Periscope is a great vehicle to reach out to a new audience using the base of Twitter.[40]

YouTube

YouTube is a free video-sharing social network owned by Google, used by people to discover and be inspired by interesting, entertaining, and informative videos. Today it has more than 1 billion global users who collectively watch billions of hours of video per month. YouTube has been launched in more than 130 countries globally. The platform allows users to create their own YouTube channels, subscribe to other channels, and to upload, watch, and share videos. The platform also allows users to post comments and share videos across other social media sites, such as Facebook, Twitter, and LinkedIn. YouTube is widely used by marketers who upload short films, how-to videos, and video ads on their products, relying on the platform to engage with storytelling. Marketers can also purchase advertising on this site.[41]

Globally, YouTube is the second-largest social media network.
©TP/Alamy Stock Photo

YOUTUBE AS A PROMOTIONAL TOOL Marketers understand that YouTube provides a robust marketing tool: Brands can create YouTube channels, upload videos, access YouTube analytics, and purchase advertising. Marketers target ads on YouTube in the form of **banner ads**, sponsored/featured videos, or in-stream video ads. They can also optimize their YouTube channels and videos for the search engines through the use of keywords.

> *Marketers understand that YouTube provides a robust marketing tool.*

Red Bull has one of the most popular brand YouTube channels. Its main YouTube channel strives to represent what it calls the "Red Bull lifestyle"; it is joined by a range of channels, including Red Bull Music, Red Bull Snow, Red Bull Surfing, Red Bull Skateboarding, Red Bull Bike, Red Bull Gaming, Red Bull Motorsports, Red Bull Music and Wings for Life World Run. Red Bull seeks to engage its subscribers by capturing exciting lifestyle-related programming, including ongoing series with key influencers and athletes.[42]

In a few instances, marketers use YouTube to upload videos that are designed to go *viral*. This is generally a carefully orchestrated approach that involves creating catchy content that is often humorous or very creative to appeal to a wide audience that will quickly view, share, and rate the video, sending it to the top of YouTube's recommended videos, which will immediately boost its popularity. Building on its "Red Bull gives you wings" slogan, Red Bull orchestrated the Red Bull Stratos Project. The Stratos videos are thought to be the most successful viral videos in history. Eight million viewers tuned in to watch Felix Baumgartner jump from a capsule 24 miles (38.6 km) in space, breaking the sound barrier and a world record for the highest jump. Not only did YouTube views break records, but longer term, the Red Bull YouTube channel subscriber base jumped. Social media engagement included over 900,000 Facebook interactions, and 83,000 shares. With Twitter, @redbullstratos received over 20,000 mentions in two days. It is estimated that the video could have reached up to 50 million people.[43]

Instagram Instagram is a free social network that is owned by Facebook. It is a mobile app that is the

banner ads
Online ads that can stretch across the top of a web page or be formatted in various sizes, such as leaderboards, rectangles, big boxes, and skyscrapers.

Red Bull has one of the most popular brand YouTube channels.

(both): ©EvrenKalinbacak/Shutterstock

world's largest photo-sharing site, with over 1 million active users who quickly and easily share their lives through photos and short videos that are taken with a mobile device, instantly adding filters and captions to customize the image before it is shared. Instagram's interface is very simple and allows users to add comments and likes, as well as use hashtags for easy search. Users can connect accounts to other social media sites so that images seamlessly appear on Facebook or

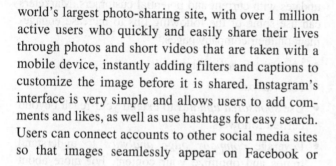

Interesting images work for SportChek on Instagram.

Used with permission of FGL Sports

Twitter—an element that makes Instagram very popular. Instagram is quickly being recognized by marketers as an essential tool to share visual content. It is estimated that 82 percent of brands in Canada use Instagram.[44]

INSTAGRAM AS A MARKETING TOOL Instagram can be used by marketers to post interesting behind-the-scenes footage from events, as well as stunning product shots and contests. Hashtags and captions can be added that invite people to engage with the brand by adding comments, liking the image, and posting their own images of the brand. Visual brands do well on Instagram: GoPro uses Instagram to showcase the adventures that can be captured on the GoPro camera. It posts stunning images of sand dunes, underwater vistas, and off-road adventures.[45] Marketers can build a more engaged Instagram following by observing these tips:[46]

- Include a *call to action*. Coca-Cola could ask their followers which flavour of Coke they prefer of the Coca-Cola Freestyle choices.

- *Leverage hashtags* that are already relevant to your audience. For example, #photooftheday is a commonly used hashtag on Instagram, Facebook, and Twitter. You may also consider using hashtags familiar to a particular interest. The #thesweatlife, is commonly utilized by a variety of fitness companies and fitness enthusiasts.

- *Share your Instagram* posts on Twitter, Facebook, and Snapchat.

- *Post at the right time*. Post when your audience can engage with your content. The use of Instagram tends to peak during off-work hours.

LinkedIn LinkedIn is a freemium (some services are free, and others require payment) business networking social media site for professionals that was launched in 2003. It has over 690 million global members and over 100 million active users, and is used in over 200 countries.[47]

LinkedIn is free for its basic usage, which allows members to create professional profiles, connect to their network of business people, join business-oriented groups on particular interests, and use its job-search function to see recent job postings and company profiles. A free membership also allows members to post and share updates, endorse individuals, write recommendations, add comments, like articles, answer questions, contribute to discussions, follow companies, view profiles of individuals in their network, and see basic information on other LinkedIn members.

Premium LinkedIn services are offered for a monthly or annual fee and include upgraded services that range in price for recruiters, job seekers, and business professionals. These services include, among others, advanced search, increased e-mail capacity, and extended profile access. A premium service for job seekers moves a person to the top of a recruiter's list, provides comparisons with other applicants, and gives advice through its job seekers' group where webinars can be accessed. For a fee, companies on LinkedIn can post job openings and receive real-time analytics on who has viewed the posting as well as profiles on the applicants.

LinkedIn is widely used by businesses to establish credibility.

PRNewsFoto/PwC/AP Images

> *LinkedIn services include upgraded services that range in price for recruiters, job seekers, and business professionals.*

LINKEDIN AS A PROMOTIONAL TOOL In the business-to-business market, LinkedIn can be used as a successful marketing tool. It is used by organizations to profile their expertise and to target individuals, companies, and sectors who may be interested in their services. On the marketing front, LinkedIn allows companies to create company pages, access visitor analytics, and create groups that profile certain areas of interest or expertise. Companies can also run ads on LinkedIn with razor-sharp targeting, whether this is a job posting, a branded display ad, or a sponsored story. LinkedIn has the advantage of having fewer distractions than the other social networks as it is focused on business and work-related

topics. LinkedIn display ads and sponsored stories are on a cost-per-click or a cost-per-impression basis. These ads can target by location, keyword, and interest. They stand out for business-to-business marketers in that they also target by company, job title, job function, and group, which can result in very high-quality responses and business leads.

It is estimated that 35 percent of Canadian brands have a presence on LinkedIn and use their LinkedIn company page to drive engagement.[48] These organizations recognize the opportunity to use LinkedIn to share company values, expertise, and updates with current and potential customers. Marketers can use some of the following tips to increase engagement on their company pages:[49]

- Make the *headline* stand out.
- Post *videos*.
- Use *sponsored updates* to extend your reach beyond current followers.
- Leverage *company page analytics* to understand trends and optimize your content. For more about how keeping up with trends can impact marketers, see the Infographic on "Social Media Content Trends in 2020 and Beyond."
- Include your logo and an *impactful banner image* on your company page.

Social Media Marketing Example: Game of Thrones*

Facebook	"Like" if you're addicted to *Game of Thrones.*
Twitter	HBO releases season 7 #gameofthrones.
YouTube	See HBO trailer for *Game of Thrones,* season 7.
LinkedIn	Spruce up your networking skills by joining the LinkedIn group for *Game of Thrones* addicts.
Instagram	Post a selfie watching #gameofthrones.
Pinterest	Find a map showing all the major land holdings from the houses on *Game of Thrones.*

* This is a hypothetical example.

Infographic

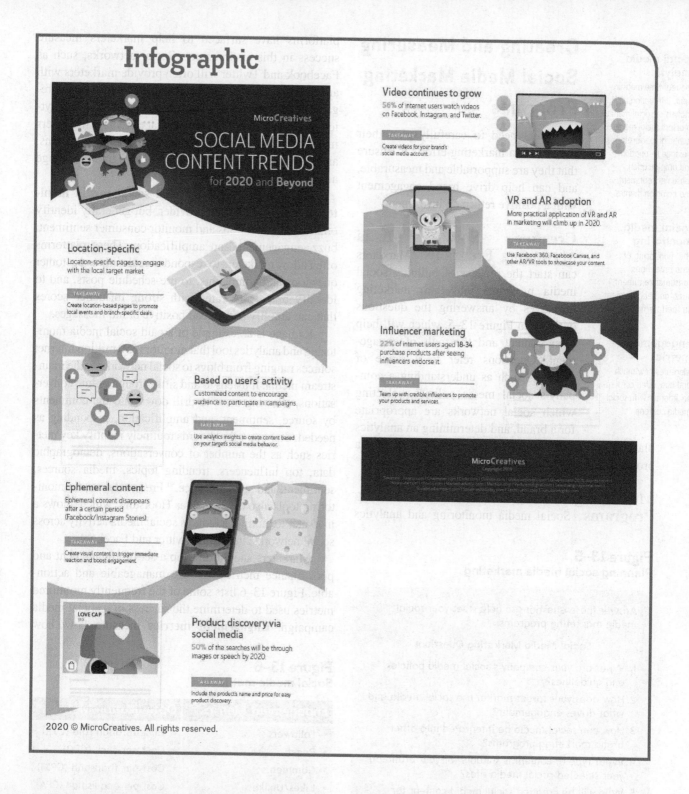

MicroCreatives

SOCIAL MEDIA CONTENT TRENDS
for 2020 and Beyond

Location-specific
Location-specific pages to engage with the local target market.

TAKEAWAY
Create location-based pages to promote local events and branch-specific deals.

Based on users' activity
Customized content to encourage audience to participate in campaigns.

TAKEAWAY
Use analytics insights to create content based on your target's social media behavior.

Ephemeral content
Ephemeral content disappears after a certain period (Facebook/Instagram Stories).

TAKEAWAY
Create visual content to trigger immediate reaction and boost engagement.

Product discovery via social media
50% of the searches will be through images or speech by 2020.

TAKEAWAY
Include the product's name and price for easy product discovery.

Video continues to grow
56% of internet users watch videos on Facebook, Instagram, and Twitter.

TAKEAWAY
Create videos for your brand's social media account.

VR and AR adoption
More practical application of VR and AR in marketing will climb up in 2020.

TAKEAWAY
Use Facebook 360, Facebook Canvas, and other AR/VR tools to showcase your content.

Influencer marketing
22% of internet users aged 18-34 purchase products after seeing influencers endorse it.

TAKEAWAY
Team up with credible influencers to promote your products and services.

MicroCreatives
Copyright 2019

Best Practices in Social Media Marketing

LO 7 The rapid adoption of digital technology and social media provides a great opportunity for marketers to develop strong customer relationships, improve their brand image, and help give customers the ability to engage with the brand.

Creating and Measuring Social Media Marketing Programs

Marketers need to carefully plan their social media marketing efforts to ensure that they are supportable and measurable, and can help drive brand engagement with a positive return on investment.

Creating Social Media Marketing Programs Marketers can start the process of building social media programs into their marketing initiatives by answering the questions outlined in Figure 13–5, which will help steer content and the tools of engagement. Questions refer to a range of elements such as understanding a company's social media policies, selecting which social networks are appropriate for a brand, and determining an analytics platform to monitor, measure, and deploy social media programs, as well as many other important elements.

Measuring Social Media Marketing Programs Social media monitoring and analytics platforms have surfaced to help marketers measure success in this environment. Social networks, such as Facebook and Twitter will often provide marketers with analytics on their accounts, but these cannot be aggregated across platforms. Third-party social media analytics and monitoring tools have surfaced to help marketers measure and manage multiple social media platforms, an important consideration since many brands engage across multiple platforms.

Social media analytics and **social media monitoring** software vary by provider, but generally identify online brand mentions and monitor consumer sentiment, buzz, engagement, and amplification. These platforms often allow marketers to respond in real-time to customer questions and complaints, to pre-schedule posts, and to identify brand advocates with strong influence scores that can amplify and spread positive brand messages.

Radian6 is an example of a paid social media monitoring and analytics tool that monitors 650 million Internet sources ranging from blogs to social networks to the mainstream media. It listens to and sifts through online conversations, allowing users to drill down into the comments by source, sentiment, and amplification, responding as needed. Summary dashboards routinely identify key metrics such as the number of conversations, demographic data, top influencers, trending topics, media sources, sentiment, and share of voice.[50] Free social media monitoring tools also exist, such as Hootsuite, which allows a marketer to monitor a brand's social media activity across social networks, including Twitter and Facebook.

Marketers should develop a set of engagement and performance metrics that are manageable and actionable. Figure 13–6 lists some of the frequently monitored metrics used to determine the success of a social media campaign. **Engagement metrics** measure how, how

Figure 13–5
Planning social media marketing

Answer these questions to help steer your social media marketing programs:

Social Media Marketing Questions

1. What are your company's social media policies and guidelines?
2. How does your target market use social media and what drives engagement?
3. How can social media be integrated into other brand marketing programs?
4. What type of content is suitable for your brand on your selected social media sites?
5. Who will be creating social media content for your brand and what is the budget?
6. What are your daily/weekly targets for social media posts and interactions?
7. Who will be running and monitoring the social media programs?
8. What analytics platforms will be used to monitor, measure, and evaluate social media programs?
9. What social media networks are appropriate for your brand and target group?

Figure 13–6
Social media metrics

Engagement Metrics	Optimization Metrics
• Followers	• Click through rate (CTR)
• Reach	• Cost per click (CPC)
• Comments	• Cost per thousand (CPM)
• Likes/Unlikes	• Cost per acquisition (CPA)
• Shares	• Cost per conversion
• Views	• Conversion rate
• Clicks	• Retention rate
• Sentiment	
• Buzz	
• Engagement	
• Brand awareness	
• Share of voice	

much, and how often consumers interact with social media content. Marketers can fairly easily track measures such as followers, likes, comments, shares, clicks, and views. Much of this data is available on the social media platform being utilized.

Optimization metrics provide data that can point to adjustments or changes that should be made to your social media program. Generally, marketers will look at **cost per thousand (CPM)**, the cost of reaching 1,000 people; **cost per acquisition (CPA)**, the cost of acquiring a new follower or sale; and **cost per click (CPC)**, the cost of getting someone to click on a link, image, or ad.

Best Practices

Brands need to be seen as a trusted source of information on all platforms, and they need to use social media to connect. Organizations and brands are advised to use the following best practices when starting to use social media:

- Obtain senior management commitment.
- Set company-wide governance for social media.
- Create detailed social media policies, guidelines, and rules of engagement.
- Set clearly defined and measurable social media marketing objectives.
- Select a platform that will be used to deploy, monitor, and measure social media activity.
- Identify the social networks that will be used.
- Establish metrics that will be used to evaluate approaches.
- Dedicate, train, and hire social media marketing experts.
- Understand that negative comments will surface on social networks and plan to handle them.
- Realize that mistakes will be made.
- Integrate social media programs into marketing practices.

> *Brands need to be seen as a trusted source of information on all platforms, and they need to use social media to connect.*

These best practices will help organizations and brands reflect brand images and authentically communicate through multiple social networks. These best practices will also help organizations plan for negative situations that may surface and flag when scenarios

should be escalated to a senior level. Social media marketing should be integrated into paid, owned, and earned media programs so that it positively impacts on the consumers' path-to-purchase.

ask YOURSELF

1. *What two type of metrics are used to measure social media marketing programs?*
2. *Which five of the best practices outlined would you prioritize for any organization?*

The Mobile Marketing Landscape

The Mobile Market

LO 8 Mobile has become a driving force in marketing, a central connector to other forms of media. It is used by consumers to communicate, to gather information, and to be entertained. It is a pillar in a multi-screen era where consumers connect in and out of home using portable devices such as tablets and smartphones, and use them to complement desktop/laptop usage and TV viewing. Mobile devices are no longer accessories, but tools that help manage daily lives.

Global data tell us that in 2020, there were 5.1 billion unique mobile subscribers and that this number is expected to grow to 5.8 billion by 2025. When focusing on devices, there are more mobile connections globally than the entire population.[51] Unlike other platforms, mobile devices are personal, portable, and usually on. They accompany us in the home, at work, and into our social spaces. They help manage our lives in real time, letting us access messages, set reminders, e-mail, text, and update calendars. They entertain us with photo apps, video viewing, and social networking. They help us find local restaurants, read product reviews, and shop for products.

Importantly, people use mobile devices to help in the path-to-purchase. People check mobile devices multiple times a day, providing numerous touch points for marketers to engage on this journey. Whether comparing product prices, looking for a store location, researching product features,

optimization metrics
Data that can point to adjustments or changes that should be made to your social media program.

cost per thousand (CPM)
The cost of reaching 1,000 people.

cost per acquisition (CPA)
The cost of acquiring a new follower or sale.

cost per click (CPC)
The cost of getting someone to click on a link or ad.

or purchasing products and services, mobile devices have become relevant in the consumer path-to-purchase. Unlike other marketing tools, mobile marketing allows marketers to communicate directly with consumers at the point-of-purchase, which can be persuasive and compelling.

Mobile marketing is defined by the Mobile Marketing Association (MMA) as "a set of practices that enables organizations to communicate and engage with their audiences in an interactive and relevant manner through any mobile device or network."[52]

Mobile Devices

The mobile industry is complex due to the wide range of handsets, screen sizes, operating systems, browsers, and products that exist in this space. Devices include feature phones, smartphones, tablets, wearables, Internet-enabled handheld gaming devices, Internet-enabled MP3 players, and e-readers. Growth is currently driven by smartphones and tablets, but wearable devices are expected to increase in popularity once privacy issues are overcome.

> " *Mobile devices are used by over 5.1 billion unique subscribers worldwide.*

A **feature phone** is a cellphone that is Internet-enabled and that allows for e-mailing, texting, and browsing, but unlike smartphones, it cannot download or use apps.[53] Feature phones tend to be cheaper and make the mobile landscape more complex as they are often built with their own unique technology, which makes consistent viewing across all devices difficult.

A **smartphone** is a more advanced cellphone that has similar functionality to a personal computer in addition to taking pictures, playing music and movies, offering GPS navigation, and using apps to enhance its features and capabilities.[54]

Smartwatches and other wearables are becoming very popular due the number of brands entering the market and the ease of use. The wearable electronics market in Canada has been growing rapidly, with 3.8 million units being worn by a variety of customer segments.[55] **Wearables** are devices that can be worn, either on clothes or on the body. They include smartwatches, health care monitors such as the Fitbit, smart clothing, and augmented reality devices such as Google Glass.[56]

From a platform perspective, the main mobile device platforms in Canada, iOS (Apple, 49.95 percent) and Android (Google, 49.69 percent), are almost evenly split market share in Canada as of May 2020. Two other platforms are Samsung at 0.22 percent and Blackberry at 0.07 percent.[57]

In 2019, there were over 33 million mobile subscribers in Canada, with numbers expected to continue to climb, ad ownership in Canada has reached over 90 percent.[58] Figure 13–7 highlights the percentage of Canadians

Figure 13–7
Mobile subscribers—Canada (millions)
The number of mobile subscribers is growing rapidly in Canada.

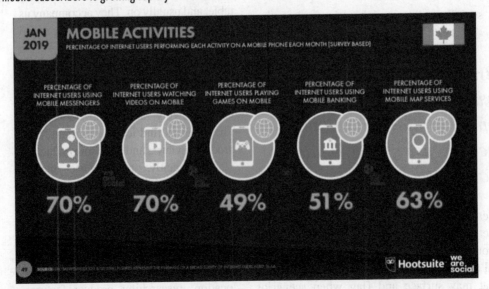

A wide range of mobile devices are available to keep consumers connected.

©Monicaodo | Dreamstime.com

performing activities on their mobile phone, compiled by Hootsuite. The majority of Canadians use their mobile devices for mobile messenger and watching videos, while mobile map services comes a close second.[59]

Consumers and Mobile Devices

Mobile spending represented one-third of e-commerce sales in Canada in 2019, growing at +27 percent from

Top Ten Activities on Mobile Devices for Canadians

Smartphone
1. Send or receive e-mail
2. Send or receive a text/instant message
3. Check weather
4. Search the Internet
5. Social networking
6. Watch a video
7. Access a map
8. Listen to music
9. Post photos
10. Play a game

Tablet
1. Search the Internet
2. Watch a video
3. Social networking
4. Send or receive e-mail
5. Check weather
6. Listen to music
7. Access a map
8. Watch TV online
9. Read reviews for products or services
10. Send or receive a text/instant message

Figure 13–8
E-commerce sales in Canada

	Retail e-commerce sales	% of total retail sales	% change
Retail e-commerce sales in Canada, 2017–2023 (CAD$ billions, % change, and % of total retail sales)			
2017	$45.10	7.5	29.9
2018	$53.31	8.6	18.2
2019	$64.56	10.0	21.1
2020	$75.57	11.4	17.1
2021	$87.51	12.9	15.8
2022	$98.10	14.1	12.1
2023	$108.10	15.1	10.2

Note: Includes products or services ordered using the Internet via any device, regardless of the method of payment or fulfillment; excludes travel and event tickets, payments such as bill pay, taxes or money transfers, food services and drinking place sales, gambling, and other vice good sales.

> *Mobile devices have become relevant in the consumer path-to-purchase.*

What is "showrooming"?

©Eva Katalin Kondoros/E+/Getty Images

the previous year. According to Figure 13–8 from eMarketers, retail e-commerce sales will continue to be a larger part of total retail sales, with growth continuing to 2023. This report also identifies Amazon as the top online shopping destination for consumers in Canada. E-commerce sales currently represent 10 percent of overall retail sales.[60]

The widespread use of smartphones at retail is prompting a new consumer shopping habit known as *showrooming*, the practice of using mobile devices in-store to check competitive online product reviews and prices and to then purchase the cheaper product online. Marketers note that mobile devices are taking the store out of the store and making shopping accessible on the go, all hours of the day, and every day of the week.

ask YOURSELF

1. What is mobile marketing?
2. How does consumer behaviour differ on mobile devices throughout the day?
3. What is the importance of mobile commerce to a brand?

mobile web
A website designed for the smaller screens of mobile devices.

mobile applications (apps)
Software programs that can be downloaded on a smartphone or tablet to engage consumers with information, entertainment, or interactivity.

Mobile Marketing Tools

LO 9 Mobile marketing provides marketers with a platform for one-to-one personalized communications where targeting can be more precise, not only demographically but also by device, by interest, and in real time by exact location. Marketers note that consumers carefully guard their mobile devices and are cautious about inviting marketers in. Marketers are therefore advised to follow best practices, provide added value, show respect for the privacy of the mobile user, and in all instances, follow regulatory guidelines and ethical approaches. Remember that in most instances, consumers need to opt in to receive mobile messaging, so unless a mobile marketer can provide exceptional value and interest, a marketer will not want to opt in to your messages.

Here we examine the mobile marketing tools that are used to engage consumers: mobile web and mobile applications (apps).

> "*Consumers carefully guard their mobile devices and are cautious about inviting marketers in.*

Mobile Web

Websites that render on mobile devices need to be fast and functional and easier to use than a brand's desktop website. People do not want to scroll across screens on small mobile devices or pinch and zoom to read content. Mobile websites are created and designed for the smaller mobile screen with screens that load quickly, display clearly, and offer unique mobile features that satisfy the goal-oriented mobile user. **Mobile web** is when a website is designed for the smaller screens of mobile devices.

Research conducted by Nielsen showed that mobile users visit websites an average of six times before making a purchase, and 83 percent of those who use mobile to research a product want to make the purchase within one day.[61] These results highlight the importance of having a mobile website that is functional, engaging, and user-friendly.

It has been shown that companies use one of three approaches with mobile web. They either optimize a desktop website for the mobile web by using responsive design platforms that offer flexible layouts, flexible images, and flexible file options so that websites automatically adjust and resize to render on mobile devices. Alternatively, they can design separate mobile websites with streamlined content and finger- and thumb-friendly navigation. The third option uses a combination of these approaches. Some companies will create three different interfaces: one for a desktop site, which is information rich; one for tablets, which has heavy image-based content; and one for smartphones, which has less content and fewer images. Booking.com has a mobile site that is a variation of its desktop website, focused on providing the tools necessary for a customer to search for a hotel immediately upon landing on the page. Information is plentiful while the functionality and visual appeal is still strong.[62]

Mobile Applications (Apps)

Mobile applications (apps) are software programs designed for mobile devices so that with a quick tap or click, they engage with information, entertainment, or other forms of interactivity. It is estimated that Google Play has 2.6 million apps available for the Android platform, the Apple App Store has 1.9 million, Windows has 670,000, and Amazon offering over 500,000 apps each.[63] While there has been significant growth in the number of apps available to users, Canadians are more selective about which apps they use. In fact, app usage has started to decline overall. In 2019, people had an average of 80 apps on their phones, with only 9 of those apps seeing daily use. The exceptions to this trend are online banking and e-mail apps. While Canadians are downloading apps at a slower pace, they are uninstalling them at a rapid rate.[64] Competition is fierce for the mobile consumer, reinforcing the need to provide value and quality to ensure app retention.

Booking.com has a functional, yet appealing mobile website, mobile app, and tablet interface.

Used with permission of Booking.com B.V.

The most popular apps are for social networking, weather, maps, music, TV/movie, gaming, YouTube, and banking.[65]

Apps are most likely to be downloaded when they are recommended by friends and family, if they sound interesting and fun, if the user is familiar with the company or brand, and if they have an exclusive offer. Most consumers expect apps to be free.[66]

> *The most popular apps are for social networking, weather, maps, gaming, YouTube, and banking.*

Apps can be free or paid, and can also host ads, sell products, or just provide content. They are downloaded from online device-specific app stores. App developers pay small annual fees to these app stores, and typically

pay a commission to the app stores from the revenues generated from the app (downloads, product sales, or ad revenues).

Technically, three types of apps can be created for marketing programs: (1) native apps, (2) web apps, or (3) hybrid apps. Depending on the choice, the app creation can become more or less expensive for marketers. For the end user, it is the app functionality that is important, and most users will not understand the nuances between these types of apps. Marketers, however, need to understand the differences:

- **Native apps** are created specifically to be hosted and run on a mobile device. They are downloaded from app stores and reside on mobile devices. They can provide a rich experience by interacting with mobile features such as the device's GPS, camera, or notification system. They can also work offline. Technology differences dictate that separate native apps need to be designed for iOS, Android, Windows, and BlackBerry devices. This can be an expensive undertaking.

- **Mobile web apps** are websites designed to simulate a native app experience. They run off browsers rather than the actual mobile device, and ask users to add a shortcut to the home screen. They can therefore run on any platform, making them cheaper to develop. The user experience is not as rich as on a native app, as these apps do not interact with the mobile device features. These apps do not pay app store developer fees, do not require app store approval, and do not share revenue with the app store.

- **Hybrid apps** combine the superior functionality of a native app with the flexibility of a web app. They can interact with mobile features, but render in a browser and so can be used across mobile platforms with minimal changes and therefore lower costs. Hybrid apps are generally cheaper to develop than native apps as they require minimal development changes for cross-platform use. Typically, hybrid apps do not provide the same rich experience as native apps, but they are becoming increasingly popular.[67]

Marketers use apps in various ways to engage with users. For example, Booking.com created an app to allow customers to research their destination, search for accommodations, and book hotel rooms; Facebook created an app to conveniently provide its service on the go; and Loblaws has an app for its PC Optimum loyalty

Top 10 Mobile App Rankings in Canada (by monthly active users)

1. Facebook
2. Facebook Messenger
3. Instagram
4. WhatsApp Messenger
5. Snapchat
6. Weather Network
7. Netflix
8. Spotify
9. Amazon
10. Pinterest

Starbucks is seen to have the premier branded mobile app.
©BestStockFoto/Shutterstock

push notifications
Any content sent to a mobile device that a customer must opt in to receive from a marketer.

program. Other marketers use apps to provide functionality and to also generate revenue. For example, the Weather Network and the CTVNews apps both sell advertising space on their apps to marketers.

Starbucks is seen to have the premier branded mobile app. Starbucks was one of the first brands to initiate a mobile loyalty and payment system for its customers. With its "Mobile Order and Pay" system, a customer can open the app, decide on an order from the hundreds of options at Starbucks, pay for the order, and even tip the barista before arriving at the store. Once the customer arrives at the store, he or she can fast-track past the line and pick up the order without delay. The mobile payment system has been so successful that it is expected the app will account for 50 percent of all Starbucks transactions in the next few years.[68]

The functionality exists on many apps for consumers to be sent push notifications on their mobile phone. **Push notifications** are content that is sent to a mobile device. For example, the Weather Network allows users to select what type of weather notifications they would like to have sent to their phone. According to Canada's Anti-Spam Legislation (CASL), consumers must opt in to consent to receive push notifications, and marketers must provide a clear method for consumers to unsubscribe or opt out.

> *The functionality exists on many apps for consumers to be sent push notifications on their mobile phone.*

Mobile Marketing Regulations and Best Practices

Mobile Marketing Regulations

LO 10 The mobile marketing industry is regulated by the same guidelines that apply to the marketing industry in general, but with the addition of further regulations for mobile marketing practices. In this manner, the regulations, guidelines, and policies discussed in Chapter 2 all need to be followed. Mobile marketers need to be keenly aware of Canada's privacy legislation as well as Canada's anti-spam legislation (CASL).

In the mobile space, the Canadian Radio-television and Telecommunications Commission (CRTC), the Canadian Wireless Telecommunications Association (CWTA), and the Mobile Marketing Association (MMA) have additional regulations and codes of conduct to protect consumers and to help standardize the industry. The mobile marketing industry is rapidly changing, and so, in all instances, marketers are strongly advised to obtain regulatory updates and to consult with marketing lawyers and mobile marketing experts to ensure that approaches adhere to regulatory and legislative updates.

The Wireless Code In mobile marketing, the CRTC regulates the Wireless Code. This was introduced in 2013 as a mandatory code of conduct for all wireless service providers. It ensures that wireless contracts are easy to understand and that contracts can be cancelled after two years.[69]

For more details on the CRTC Wireless Code, navigate to **www.crtc.gc.ca/eng/phone/mobile/code.htm**. Complaints against wireless service providers can be lodged at the website for the Commissioner for Complaints for Telecommunications Services at **www.ccts-cprst.ca**.

Common Short Code (CSC) Guidelines These guidelines are administered by the CWTA to provide direction on CSC pricing and marketing

The CRTC Wireless Code helps protect consumers.
CRTC

practices. Mobile marketers must provide participants with mandatory keyword protocols (STOP/ARRET to stop participation, HELP/AIDE to access information on terms of use and privacy policies, and INFO to retrieve company and customer service information). In addition, consumers must double opt-in to some premium subscription CSC programs and be informed of its terms, conditions, and pricing.[70] Updates on CSC regulations can be found at **www.cwta.ca** and **www.txt.ca**.

The MMA Global Code of Conduct

The MMA Global Code of Conduct is administered by the Mobile Marketing Association, which guides the industry with standards, guidelines, and best practices. The MMA has over 800 members and is represented in nearly 50 countries. The MMA Global Code of Conduct specifically notes that privacy policies and terms and conditions must be clear, and opt-in and opt-out protocols must be used. Messaging should be limited to its initial purpose, personal data must be protected, and all MMA members must demonstrate compliance with the code.[71] You can find out more about the MMA and its code of conduct at **www.mmaglobal.com**.

Mobile Marketing Best Practices

The mobile marketing industry is rapidly changing, with new technologies, devices, and regulations. Best practices start with marketers abiding by marketing regulations and using a mobile-first approach to make connections. A mobile-first approach means that mobile becomes a central element in a marketing program and is integrated throughout the consumer path-to-purchase.

Mobile is not added as an afterthought, but instead it is integrated into marketing programs from the start.

> *A mobile-first approach means that mobile becomes a central element in a marketing program.*

Best practices also use market research to stay abreast of how technology impacts consumer behaviour and to learn how mobile devices are integrated into daily lives. Changes in shopping habits are noted and mobile analytics programs are used to glean insights on how best to approach, engage, and connect with consumers.

The Mobile Marketing Association (MMA) advises mobile marketers to keep the following best practices in mind:[72]

- Think *mobile first* and start with a mobile perspective.
- Generate *creative specifically for mobile*.
- *Communicate across multiple screens* to create a seamless experience as consumers switch between devices.
- *Target your audiences* more specifically using the rich dataset available from mobile interaction, including location.
- *Utilize a full spectrum of mobile tools* to interact with consumers.
- *Integrate mobile marketing programs* into traditional marketing campaigns.
- *Offer great service*, functionality, and benefits.
- *Leverage every stage of the path-to-purchase*, understanding that mobile is used for search and discovery as well as connecting and purchasing.
- Test your way to success by *tracking, measuring, and making adjustments* to improve results and ROI.

ask **YOURSELF**

1. *Which associations and commissions regulate mobile marketing in Canada?*

2. *What best practices have surfaced in mobile marketing?*

LO 1
• Public relations initiatives include press releases, press conferences, special events, company reports, and the use of social media releases.

LO 2
• Direct response marketing tools include direct mail, catalogues, telemarketing, and direct response advertising on TV, radio, and print, as well as e-mail marketing and social media interactions.

LO 3
• Event marketing and sponsorship refers to the involvement of a brand in an event through either an advertising package or on-site involvement.

LO 4
• The Internet has a number of unique online tools including websites and microsites, search engine marketing, influencers, and word-of-mouth marketing.

 LO 5
• Social media marketing is when brands reach out to consumers online through social networks where people connect with friends and contacts to share comments, articles, opinions, videos, and images as a form of self-expression.

• On social media networks, brands post updates and offers, join online conversations, respond to questions and comments, and use metrics to measure performance and engagement.

• Brands can place ads on social networks that accept advertising.

LO 6
• The main social networks used in Canada for marketing purposes are Facebook, Twitter, YouTube, Instagram, and LinkedIn.

LO 7
• The best social media marketing practices include obtaining senior management commitment, setting company-wide governance,

creating detailed social media policies, setting clearly defined and measurable social media marketing objectives, selecting social networks that will be used, establishing metrics, utilizing social media marketing experts, planning to handle negative comments, realizing that mistakes will be made, and integrating social media programs into marketing practices.

 LO 8
• Mobile marketing is a set of practices that enables organizations to communicate and engage with audiences in an interactive and relevant manner through any mobile device or network.

• Mobile marketing provides marketers with an additional platform to communicate with consumers one-to-one. It can target by location, by device, by interest, and by demographic.

• Mobile platforms are changing consumers' path-to-purchase with mobile devices used to gather information, to engage with brands, to make decisions, and to purchase products.

LO 9
• Mobile marketing uses a variety of tools, including the mobile web and mobile apps.

LO 10
• Best practices for mobile marketing advise marketers to think mobile first, and to plan programs across devices and screens by using multiple mobile tools that can integrate offline and online approaches.

• Standard marketing regulations in Canada also apply to mobile marketing.

• Specific mobile marketing regulations are administered by the Canadian Radio-television and Telecommunications Commission (CRTC), the Canadian Wireless Telecommunications Association (CWTA), and the Mobile Marketing Association (MMA).

banner ads	leaderboards	search engine marketing (SEM)
blog	microsites	search engine optimization (SEO)
corporate websites	mobile applications (apps)	smartphone
cost per acquisition (CPA)	mobile web	social media analytics
cost per click (CPC)	mobile web apps	social media monitoring
cost per thousand (CPM)	native apps	social media release
direct response marketing	optimization metrics	sponsorship
display advertising	pay-per-click advertising (PPC)	traffic generation
e-mail marketing	permission-based e-mail	transactional websites
engagement metrics	press conference	user-generated content (UGC)
event marketing	press release	vlog
feature phone	promotional websites	wearables
hybrid apps	public relations	wiki
influencer marketing	publicity	word-of-mouth marketing
lead generation	push notifications	

Social Media Marketing Assignment Pick your favourite brand and conduct a digital media audit for that brand. This involves monitoring which networks the brand is active on, the types of content posted on each network, and the level of consumer engagement. Based upon your research, do you believe that your favourite brand has a strong social media presence? Why or why not?

This chapter's opening vignette outlined Hub Town Brewery's IMC campaign utilizing public relations, event sponsorship, and social media. Brainstorm additional social media and mobile elements that you would add to the campaign to create more touch points with the target audience.

Review the Infographic on "Social Media Content Trends in 2020 and Beyond" created by MicroCreatives. Choose one of the organizations discussed in this chapter and evaluate its current social media strategy and how and if it follows these trends.

Customer Relationship Management

LEARNING OBJECTIVES

LO 1 Define the concepts of customer relationship management (CRM) and customer experience management (CEM)

LO 2 Discuss the role of social media in CRM

LO 3 Describe customer acquisition and customer retention, as well as examples of various loyalty programs

LO 4 Define database marketing, data mining, and customer lifetime value, and explain why each is important

LO 5 Explain the worth of retaining marginal customers and outline the process of customer reacquisition

As technology continues to provide efficiency in business, small to mid-sized businesses prefer a more personal touch. Although all meetings and communications do not need to be in-person, a good customer relationship management strategy offers a variety of options for a business to connect with its clientele. In fact, the COVID-19 pandemic has caused businesses to rethink how relationships are maintained.

The Paint Channel

CHAPTER OUTLINE

- The importance of relationships
- Customer relationship management (CRM)
- Social media and CRM
- Customer acquisition and retention
- Database marketing
- CRM and customer reacquisition

Founded in 2005 and based in the Greater Toronto Area (GTA), The Paint Channel Corporation is one of Canada's leading manufacturer's representative firms (sales agency) catering to the Canadian paint and hardware markets. The Paint Channel's president, Dennis Kwasnicki, is the primary contact of support sales for his clients.

As an intermediary, Kwasnicki needs to manage relationships with both the customers he serves and the manufacturers he represents. Being a critical part of the supply chain, Kwasnicki's customer relationship management skills need to be at their best.

"Everyone wants your time," explains Kwasnicki, "You are juggling relationships, and you don't want to let anyone down." With the importance of Kwasnicki's business being on the end consumer, one might think that is where all his time in spent. "Losing a product line or two teaches you to keep strong manufacturing relationships as well." The manufacturers hire The Paint Channel to represent them, and Kwasnicki ensures they are represented well.

The Paint Channel's mission is "understand the meaning of quality." It prides itself on representing brands that are "world class" and leaders in their respective categories. The Paint Channel's objective is to represent all major paint-related categories by supplying brands that are identified with and appreciated by their end users.

In 2005, The Paint Channel began with one line: 3M Canada (abrasives, adhesives, and safety). Over the next eight years, the company grew to five category-leading product lines, and The Paint Channel established itself as a major player in the Ontario paint market. In 2014, 18-year paint industry veteran Dennis Kwasnicki purchased The Paint Channel and developed a customer relationship management culture. Existing product lines were cultivated by deepening relationships, and new complementary lines have been added as The Paint Channel enters into a new decade serving the Canadian paint and hardware markets.

A lot of the product lines Dennis represents do not warrant a dedicated sales representative due to their gross sales. An agency like The Paint Channel can allow a more cost-effective sales approach. The current and future distribution opportunities of the company were established through the strong relationships that Kwasnicki has built over the years.

To represent quality and keep his customers and suppliers happy, Kwasnicki developed a basket of products from different manufacturers that complement, but do not compete with one another. From ladders to paint shakers to wallpaper paste, The Paint Channel is responsible for product placement, promotions, and training store staff on new products.

"Relationships are the most important facet of a business," explains Kwasnicki. Since Kwasnicki maintains relationships from continually contacting his customers, the COVID-19 pandemic forced him to rethink his relationship management strategy.

In a pre-pandemic world, Dennis built new relationships by attending contractor events and national trade shows on behalf of manufacturers. "Managing new

CHAPTER FEATURES

The Importance of Relationships
Learn how The Paint Channel manages relationships with both manufacturers and customers to enhance the customer experience.

Managing Relationships in a Crisis
How business leaders lobbied the Canadian government to put the needs of Canadians first.

Banking On Customer Satisfaction
How do Canadian banks fare when it comes to satisfying customers?

Brewing New Strategies
How Starbucks Canada managed to serve members during a pandemic.

Landing Aeroplan
How loyalty marketing drives business strategy and improves customer relationships.

Facilitating Purchases
Understand the online spending habits of Canadians and the importance of privacy.

business relationships can be challenging," explains Kwasnicki. "There are always other representatives and competition trying to meet your customers." Kwasnicki staves off the competition by connecting with business contacts on a personal level. Once conversations go beyond the business solution, relationships are further cemented.

Building a connection is the goal of customer relationship management. Most of Kwasnicki's success is being present for his customers. Although Dennis understands the Pareto's Rule, he recommends organizations make time to stay connected with the 80 percent of customers that generate 20 percent of the business. That relationship can lead to additional opportunities and stronger relationships over time.

The Paint Channel's customer relationship management process prioritizes customers into monthly, bi-monthly, quarterly, and semi-annual categories. Call frequency is influenced by geographic location or categorized by potential revenue opportunity. Of the manufacturers Kwasnicki represents, six out of eight lines are members of the CanPro buying group. This buying group creates buying power for independent paint stores, including discounted pricing with manufacturers, yearly rebates, and annual shows for manufacturers to connect with these members to show new products. All contacts and next steps are part of a customer relationship management strategy that has served The Paint Channel and its customers well for years.[1]

Customer Relationship Management (CRM)

LO 1 *Customer relationship management* (CRM) is the overall process of building and maintaining profitable customer relationships by delivering superior customer value and satisfaction. Executing CRM may involve technology, business rules, and operational processes, as well as the cooperation of key stakeholders within the organization.[2] This involves many aspects within an organization, including how consumers become customers, how they are retained as customers, and how well a company manages information on customers. The strategies that companies put into place around how they manage data will help them be successful in the customer relationship management discipline.[3]

After consumers have initiated and completed their purchase decision, they become customers. Customer relationship management (CRM) considers the purchase decision from the point of view of the business. It engages three interactions with customers, including customer acquisition, customer retention, and customer reacquisition. To be executed effectively, CRM requires support from the company's top management.

Over time, businesses have used technology to leverage time connecting with customers. Knowing when to contact members maximizes effort. In a post-COVID-19 pandemic world, face-to-face interactions may become less and less of a practice, giving businesses more time to reach more people. Consider the Marketing NewsFlash, "Managing Relationships in a Crisis," that discusses CEO responses to COVID-19.[4]

Customer relationship management (CRM) strives to build and maintain profitable customer relationships.
©Andres Rodriguez/Alamy Stock Photo

Managing Relationships in a Crisis

©fizkes/Shutterstock

Whether they were lobbying the federal government, communicating directly with their customers, or sharing best practices with one another, Canadian CEOs displayed leadership during the COVID-19 pandemic.

In March 2020, a group of 30 executives from Canada's largest industries collaborated so the country could stop the spread of COVID-19. In an open letter asking other business leaders to take notice, they suggested that government measures would only be effective if businesses did their part.

Stopping non-essential travel, promoting physical distancing, and arranging for employees to work from home were just some recommended steps. During this time, business leaders sent e-mails directly to their customers explaining the steps they were taking to keep their employees and customers safe. These communications from the leaders of some of our favourite brands was well received by customers who found different ways to interact in this new reality.

With the traditional face-to-face meeting with handshakes being inappropriate during the pandemic, companies found other ways to keep connected to their loyal client base. CRM systems were vital to ensure companies did not miss opportunities to market to and service members through online and other contactless means. Although business etiquette was evolving during this challenging time, the importance of maintaining relationships was still key to the success of a business. ●

Questions

1. Think of a brand you are particularly loyal to and research what the company did to keep in contact with customers during the COVID-19 crisis. Choose one that resonates with you and explain why.

2. What are some unique ways companies can communicate with customers?

Customer Satisfaction

Information about customers can be used to create marketing programs that result in customer satisfaction. Information technology and database systems are a great starting point for CRM; however, for CRM to be successful, there must be attitude changes in the organization. CRM started out as a tool to help the sales force keep track of customers and prospects, but it has evolved into so much more. A large corporation may spend tens of millions of dollars on a CRM system. Among the big suppliers are Oracle, SAP, and IBM; dozens of other companies specialize in components such as telephone call centre technology, database software, and Internet systems. The whole idea is to customize each system to a specific company's needs. Funnelling information to one place that otherwise would be dispersed in a big company allows all employees to access one customer profile instead of bits and pieces of information about the customer scattered throughout the company.

Call your local bank about your chequing account and you may discover that the person on the phone is looking at a screen that summarizes your previous calls and displays information about your mortgage and credit card as well. Visit your local bank and you may be surveyed about your experiences and your likelihood to recommend the branch.

Apple knows that customers dislike the touch point that consists of impersonal technical support calls, so it has created the Genius Bar in its retail stores.

©david pearson/Alamy Stock Photo; ©Cliff Hide News/Alamy Stock Photo

Customer Experience Management

A concept similar to CRM is a process called **customer experience management (CEM)**. CEM involves managing customer interactions to build brand equity and improve long-term profitability.

It requires strategy to manage all points of the customer experience, as keeping customers satisfied will be more important than simply making a sale.[5] CEM focuses on customer interactions, or touch points. A *touch point* describes any customer interaction with the brand or company.

Customer interactions include every point in which the customer interacts with a business, product, or service. In the case of MacBooks, Apple ascertained that its customers disliked the touch point of impersonal technical support calls. Instead, Apple resolves this issue by creating Genius Bar touch points that offer face-to-face help at the Apple Store. Your banking touch points include experiences with automatic bank machines (ABMs), online banking, and customer service representatives. For the Starbucks customer, this may include the anticipation of going to Starbucks, walking up to a shop, opening the door, ordering and paying for the coffee, talking to the server, getting the coffee, and sitting down in the relaxed atmosphere of the shop to enjoy the coffee. Understanding the importance of each touchpoint is how Starbucks was able to manage customer expectations during a pandemic. Read the Marketing NewsFlash box, "Brewing New Strategies," for more details.[6]

Companies should measure and improve customer interactions on an ongoing basis. Levels of customer satisfaction at each touch point can be a better measure of customer loyalty than just measuring overall customer satisfaction. It starts by understanding and listing each individual interaction or touch point that influences customer satisfaction. Whether human (such as sales staff or a call centre), interactive (such as websites, e-mail, or Twitter), or static (such as radio or newspaper ads), each touch point is an opportunity to improve customer experience.[7]

CEM and touch points are used to maintain profitable relationships with customers and are used in various industries to enhance customer satisfaction. Canadian Pacific Hotels (CP Hotels) was not well-regarded by business travellers, a notoriously demanding and diverse group to serve, but also very lucrative and much coveted by other hotel chains. By investing time and money in learning what would most satisfy this segment, the company discovered that customers wanted recognition of their individual preferences and lots of flexibility with check-ins and check-outs. CP Hotels mapped each step of customer interactions from check-in to check-out, and set a standard of performance for each activity. Along the way, the management structure was revamped so that each hotel had a champion with broad cross-functional ability to ensure that the hotel lived up to its ambitious goals.[8]

Ideally, CEM information is analyzed to gain insight into each customer's needs and behaviour, and then it is used to improve the customer's dealings with the company. This can be as simple as freeing the customer from having to repeat his mailing address every time he places an order, to something like being able to instantly tell the customer the status of a shipment. The analysis might guide promotion efforts so that the customer receives mailings, calls, e-mails, or website advertising tailored to his or her likes.

Brewing New Strategies

R etailers were faced with trying times when the COVID-19 pandemic forced stores to close in 2020. Governments prioritized essential services and protected and supported of Canadian workers and consumers. These initiatives created a new normal that threatened the continuation of past habits and indulgences. Fortunately, for some companies, their customer relationship management strategies allowed them to engage with customers in a different way that maintained connectivity and engagement.

Companies like Starbucks Canada kept connected to their suppliers and customers in innovative ways. Open communication was key to their strategy, as was a stage-by-stage approach that promoted protection and safety. Social channels that promoted store hours kept consumers engaged and informed.

Starbucks has been a leader in innovative concepts like mobile apps and pickup-only stores. As consumer behaviours changed and decisions had to be made, Starbucks knew enough about its member habits through its omnichannel options to allow it to continue to do business where it made the most sense. Furthermore, the digital channels that Starbucks opened up to Canadians not only tracked behaviour, but also changed behaviour. Why wait for a beverage after ordering when you can pre-order and pick it up when you are ready?

In 2017, three in ten Starbucks orders were placed through its mobile app. The circumstances placed on coffee lovers during COVID-19 will change that statistic in the future. Canadians' expectations on retail interactions have changed. Starbucks Canada has experimented with alternative interactive strategies and has been ready for this change. The global pandemic, which forced the company to change locations to to-go only, also created new behaviours and expectations for consumers with respect to how they enjoy their beverages.

©BestStockFoto/Shutterstock

Friendly staff, letters from the CEO, and an overall focus on the customer experience allowed Starbucks Canada to survive and thrive during COVID-19. The pandemic drove increases to online sales to counteract the slowing demand of its retail stores. For Starbucks Canada, it understood what customers needed pre-and-post COVID-19, allowing for continued success. ●

Questions

1. Describe the attributes of a Canadian retailer that keeps a consumer engaged. Explain why.

2. How do customer expectations affect customer relationship management and the future success of companies?

Banking On Customer Satisfaction

J.D. Power creates a customer satisfaction index ranking based on a 1,000-point scale. The big 5 banks are ranked as follows:

RBC Royal Bank	794
TD Canada Trust	790
Segment Average	788
CIBC	787
BMO Bank of Montreal	784
Scotiabank	782

Cultural Changes

CRM databases allow companies to get closer to their customers to establish a mutually beneficial relationship. A company's failure with CRM is often the result of approaching CRM as a software project rather than an overall company strategy. A company may spend millions of dollars on software, but doesn't bother changing the cultural attitudes of the organization. A company may be looking for a quick fix for its problems. Companies feel that if they purchase CRM software, their problems will disappear. Collecting and managing data is just one component of CRM. A more important component is the organizational culture and support from top management.

A hotel that is suffering from poor employee customer-service skills cannot use software alone to solve the issue. CRM requires a top-down long-run commitment and attitude change by management. If the hotel employees see that management treats them with respect and rewards customer satisfaction, there is a larger incentive for employees to treat customers with respect.

> *A company's failure with CRM is often the result of approaching CRM as a software project rather than an overall company strategy.*

Organizations like BLUERUSH create personalized digital customer experiences that generate leads, build loyalty, and increase sales. As an integral part of a customer lifecycle management program, INDIVIDEO™ and ActivDialog, two proprietary BLUERUSH products, are significantly transforming online experiences and delivering real value to clients and their customers. These tools not only need to be adopted by client-facing individuals, they need to be driven by management.

In 1997, Xerox Canada refocused a 5,100-person organization with annual revenues over $1.1 billion and underwent a change in structure and compensation incentives to ensure that its employees focused on customer satisfaction. Although the change was not an easy one, it was necessary to achieve the result of customers being more satisfied with the company's service offerings.[9]

Although not always noticed by customers, the cultural change that organizations undergo requires an investment of time and resources. In the same year that Xerox Canada underwent its cultural change, the 407 ETR opened in the Greater Toronto Area, allowing an all-electronic tolling feature for drivers on this highway. Customer loyalty is increasing for this service due to a lack of competition and the additional convenience offered by the highway. Unfortunately, more resources should be allocated to understanding customer complaints from this organization.[10]

CRM at Four Seasons Hotels and Resorts

Four Seasons Hotels and Resorts grew from a modest hotel in downtown Toronto to a luxury hotel chain consisting of 91 hotels in 38 countries around the world. Founder Isadore Sharp spent decades developing a culture in which all employees are empowered to take responsibility and make decisions, rather than exclusively relying on orders from management. Mr. Sharp says that culture has to start from the top, the person who really is able to control and make the decisions to reinforce the culture in a meaningful way. "The Golden Rule guides our interactions with our guests, our business partners and investors, but most importantly, with each other," says Sharp. "We also believe in investing in our employees and promoting from within. Many of our senior managers began their careers with Four Seasons and continue to be culture ambassadors." CRM involves tracking guest information and preferences, such as extra pillows, into a database. This information should be used by employees the next time the guest returns to the hotel. Satisfied employees will take this extra step to make guests feel important and recognized. However, if hotel employees are not feeling engaged or appreciated themselves, they may not take that extra step and may fail to enhance the guest experience. It has been estimated that in a 200- to 300-room luxury hotel, there are as many as 5,000 interactions between guests and staff per day; in other words, thousands of opportunities for high performance or for mishaps. Four Seasons Hotels and Resorts excels in making its interactions with guests very positive.[11]

The cultural attitudes of the organization must change internally to what is called a CRM culture if the company is really interested in instituting positive customer service. Management must understand the customer and drive its company to developing the best experience. Top-management support to align internal processes toward a company's CRM strategy is critical to a CRM program's success.[12]

CRM at WestJet

WestJet is an excellent example of a company that has embraced CRM from the top management down. Every employee literally takes ownership in what they do. As shareholders of the company, WestJet employees have a heightened sense of customer service responsibility uncharacteristic of many employees. Seeing this as a differentiator, WestJet launched a series of ads that focused on WestJet's theme of ownership.

The average business executive goes into CRM thinking it's only about technology, but if cultural attitudes don't change, employees won't benefit from the information collected and analyzed. Without employees using the system, the software becomes useless. The most senior levels of management need to embrace the business strategy of CRM and move the message and tactics of CRM throughout the organization. CEOs need

Employees who take ownership in what they do have a heightened sense of customer service responsibility.

©Sean Locke/iStock.com

to get the message out to their VPs and have them get it out to their managers, down to supervisors, and down to the front line.

Gaining loyal customers is critical to a successful CRM strategy. In that strategy, you can ask questions similar to these below:

- Who are your most profitable customers?

- Why do your customers buy from you and not the competition?

- What percentage of your customers are profitable?

- How can you make profitable customers do more business with you?

- How do you plan on managing less profitable customers?

Ultimately, a company should consider the answers to these questions to evaluate the state of the firm's CRM strategy and what culture changes need to be made in order to effectively execute the strategy. In the end, technology is an enabler of CRM, but a successful CRM strategy is executed by high-performing employees.[13]

CRM at TD Canada Trust

TD Canada Trust leads Canada's five big banks in customer satisfaction. Its customer relationship management involves building and maintaining profitable customer relationships. After the merger of TD and Canada Trust banks, the newly formed organization invested $15 million in informing its clients of what to expect of the new company. The investment was part of its strategy of client retention and profitability. In TD Canada Trust customer loyalty polls, customers are expecting a higher level of customer service and are receiving it.[14]

But if they don't receive positive customer service, they may not be coming back. Businesses are constantly looking for ways to show customers that they care, such as through reward programs. Many customers appreciate the perks, but according to the findings of the TD Canada Trust loyalty poll, customers want to be treated well. When asked which form of appreciation they are most interested in, 49 percent ranked "just good customer service" as number one. This was followed by just 18 percent who cited reward programs. According to the results, respondents' definition of good service was friendly staff followed by quick and helpful service.

Social Media and CRM

LO 2 A growing number of companies are keeping track of what's said about their brands on social media platforms such as Facebook and Twitter. This activity falls in line with the process of CRM because it's an excellent way to build and maintain a relationship with customers. Dell, General Motors, H&R Block, Kodak, and Whole Foods Market are among a growing number of companies monitoring Twitter to see what people are saying about their brands as well as to provide solutions to customers' concerns. With the ability to create a conversation between companies and customers, social media provides an excellent platform for the consumer voice and a great resource for marketers. The attention to Twitter reflects the power of new social media tools in letting consumers shape public discussion over brands.[15] A single Twitter message—known informally as a tweet—sent in frustration over a product or a service's performance, can be read by hundreds or thousands of people. Similarly, positive interaction with a representative of the company can help turn an unhappy customer into a more loyal one.

Some companies are hiring social media analytics consultants to monitor social media sites such as Facebook and Twitter in order to digest and understand what consumers are saying about their brands. These consultants have developed specialized software for their clients to scour these sites in real time and to provide actionable insights for smarter business decisions.

Tourism and Social Media

Hotels and airlines were among the first industries to recognize the value of social media platforms such as Twitter and Facebook, and to monitor them to respond to angry customers. Increasingly, companies are taking the tactic to a new level, trying to listen in on every mention of their brands for a real-time gauge of what people think of their offerings, competitors, and industry trends.[16]

Dave Carroll got his revenge when United Airlines broke his guitar.
©Christian Laforce/Halifax Chronicle Herald/The Canadian Press

©Ingvar Björk/Alamy Stock Photo

Consumers are increasingly using tools such as Twitter to contact an airline as opposed to the old way of phoning the company. For flyers who have lost luggage or missed a flight, the immediacy of social media–based feedback could render toll-free numbers and website feedback forms obsolete in the near future. In an industry where every airline essentially sells the same commoditized service, airlines that use social media to turn disappointed customers into happy ones, or to simply enhance the travel experience, are already setting themselves apart and building loyalty.

Consider this scenario, which actually took place at Porter Airlines. When an unhappy passenger found herself waiting in a check-in line that wasn't moving quickly enough, she tweeted her dissatisfaction from her smartphone. At the same time that this was occurring, Porter Airlines employees were scanning Twitter traffic

and came across the woman's complaint. By the time that passenger got to the front of the line, Porter staff were on hand to directly deal with her complaint.[17]

The engagement created by social media cannot be ignored as it may have consequences. United Airlines baggage handlers damaged Halifax songwriter David Carroll's $3,500 custom-made bass guitar on a flight from Halifax to Chicago. Carroll spent nine months seeking compensation by sending e-mails, writing letters, and calling airline representatives, all to no avail. Carroll, deeply frustrated and out of options, wrote a song entitled "United Breaks Guitars" and uploaded it to YouTube. The catchy song went viral, with 150,000 views the day it went live and nearly 10 million since then. United Airlines finally relented and, at Carroll's request, donated the $1,200 he paid for repairs to charity. It's interesting to note that within four days of the song going online, the bad PR caused United Airlines' stock price to suffer a plunge of 10 percent, costing shareholders $180 million. After the incident, United Airlines created a Twitter presence, but approaches social media with a more controlled strategy.[18]

Porter Airlines employees scanned social media sites to help identify and resolve a customer complaint.
©Mary Claire/Shutterstock

Ford used social media to promote its Fiesta subcompact car.
©Paceman/Shutterstock

Credibility Issues of Social Media

One of the temptations for a company is to encourage consumers to say positive things about its brand on a social media platform. In 2009, Ford promoted its new Fiesta subcompact by letting 100 consumers drive the car for free for six months, gas included. All they had to do was blog, tweet, and post about the car. There exists the possibility that they were more likely to say good things about the car as a result of the freebie, instead of truly giving their unbiased opinions. Although credibility may have suffered as a result of this campaign, the underlying strategy for Ford was engagement. Even though there are not a lot of Fiestas on the road, Ford believes in social media as a means to attract the tech-savvy consumer, and it relaunched a similar social media campaign in 2014.[19]

ask YOURSELF

1. What is customer relationship management all about?

2. Describe how companies are using social media in their relationships with customers.

Customer Acquisition and Retention

LO 3 CRM starts by building customer relationships. Data-driven programs can examine the profiles of a company's most-popular customers and use these characteristics to find prospective customers.

After a company has found commonalities among profitable customers, it can use this information to accurately target potential customers with the same profile.

Once customer relationships are established, CRM shifts to maintaining profitable customer relationships. A company that builds strong relationships with customers will retain these customers, resulting in more sales and profits than the company would have if it focused only on getting new customers. It's important to note that making a sale to a current customer is way less expensive than making a sale to a new customer.

> ❝ Listening to customers is as important as—if not more important than—talking to them.

Listening to customers is as important as—if not more important than—talking to them. Some business-to-business (B2B) companies are now making a special effort to ask customers when and how they would like to be contacted by the company. This information is placed in a database so that it is readily available. This practice shows respect for loyal customers' time and allows companies to direct the brand communication in a way that is appropriate. Moreover, communicating with customers is a key strategy for businesses to ensure they are thought of and retained.

The increased profitability that is associated with customer retention is due to several factors that occur after a relationship has been established with a customer. Furthermore, by choosing the right customer, nurturing the right customer, and allocating resources to the right customer, profitability can be further enhanced. Among Canadian respondents in the financial services industry, more than three out of five say that the greatest benefit of CRM is in understanding, acquiring, and retaining customers. Why CRM can help increase profitability through customer retention is explained by the following factors:[20]

- The cost of acquiring a customer occurs only at the beginning of a relationship, so the longer the relationship, the lower the amortized cost.

- Long-term customers tend to be less inclined to switch, and also tend to be less price-sensitive.

- Long-term customers may initiate word-of-mouth activity and referrals.

Loyalty Programs

One way to retain customers is through **loyalty programs**. In Canada, customers have created emotional connections

> **loyalty programs**
> Programs specifically designed for customer retention.

Landing Aeroplan

Loyalty cards are normally associated with rewards. One of the more recognizable loyalty cards in Canada is Aeroplan. This consumer-facing brand allows travellers to collect points for travel rewards with Air Canada and its strategic alliances. Owned now by Air Canada, Aeroplan is considered Canada's premier coalition loyalty program since it has over 75 world-class partners and represents over 150 brands in the retail, travel, and financial industries.

With over 30 years in the loyalty business, Aeroplan has more than 4.6 million active members, making it a sought-after partner in a variety of industries. Well-known Canadian companies such as Esso, Home Hardware, and Sobeys were added as partners in 2005. In the financial services industry, Aeroplan partnered with American Express® and CIBC to offer rewards credit cards. Aeroplan's relationship with CIBC began in 1991 when Aeroplan and CIBC partnered to launch the CIBC Aerogold® VISA Card, considered one of the most popular credit cards in Canada.

Although the 20-year-plus partnership had been successful, Aeroplan had another suitor. In 2013, TD Bank entered into the Aeroplan loyalty business by becoming the primary credit card issuer for the Aeroplan loyalty rewards program. For a few months, this caused friction between all parties involved, including existing Aeroplan credit card holders. Fortunately, TD Bank Group and Canadian Imperial Bank of Commerce were able to reach an agreement.

With half of the Aeroplan card portfolio shifting from CIBC to TD, over 550,000 cardholder accounts were changing banks. As compensation for this change, CIBC received over $312.5 million from TD and Aimia, with Aimia paying $150 million of that figure.

The challenges placed on the travel industry by COVID-19 forced

©Hemis/Alamy Stock Photo

Aeroplan to allow members cancel flight rewards free of charge up to the end of April 2020. Full refunds were also provided on related taxes, fees and surcharges on the unused value of your travel. The key message that Aeroplan was sending was that customer loyalty was not a unilateral relationship. Aeroplan appreciated its members, and did the right thing during a challenging time. •

Questions

1. In terms of customer loyalty, why do you believe TD was so interested in becoming an Aeroplan partner?

2. Why do you believe Aeroplan was so flexible with its membership during the pandemic crisis?

---

to loyalty programs such as the Air Miles Reward Program.[21] Air Miles is Canada's largest loyalty program; Air Miles can be earned through more than 100 different sponsors, and there are almost 1,000 different rewards that can be redeemed. BMO Bank of Montreal offers an Air Miles–sponsored program, and TD offers an Aeroplan program (see the Marketing NewsFlash box, "A Safe Landing for Aeroplan," for more detail).[22] Loyalty programs were not always as advanced as Air Miles. In fact, the oldest and best-known loyalty program in Canada is Canadian Tire Money.

Loblaw offered the President's Choice Financial MasterCard, with which consumers can get PC points that can be redeemed for groceries. And the Shoppers Drug Mart Optimum card was a very successful loyalty program. When Loblaw bought Shoppers Drug Mart, it merged the two popular loyalty programs into a single PC Optimum program. Loyalty programs have become a way for one company to differentiate itself from another, but these differentiations have high expectations from Canadians.[23]

Although businesses appreciate all their customers, CRM practices allow them to distinguish between the loyalty habits of their customers. In most product categories, a small number of heavy users accounts for a large percentage of a brand's sales and profits. Heavy users are customers who buy an above-average amount of a given brand. According to **Pareto's Rule**, a marketing rule of thumb named after Italian economist Vilfredo Pareto, 80 percent of a brand's sales come from 20 percent of its customers. Heavy users should be rewarded differently than light users. The implication here is to take special care of the 20 percent by offering them better rewards than the remaining 80 percent. Databases allow companies to do more than merely recognize their customers. Companies that surprise and delight their

Pareto's Rule
The concept that 80 percent of a brand's sales come from 20 percent of its customers.

high-profit customers with reward programs are more likely to keep these customers in the long run.

Consider the loyalty program at Starwood Hotels & Resorts, which has such brands as Sheraton and Westin. The chain offers a different twist on personalizing a loyalty program. As well as the usual system of accumulating points that can be redeemed for free rooms, Starwood Preferred Guest program members can use their points to bid for special experiences. The Moments program allows members to take part in online auctions to bid for "insider access" to red-carpet premieres, closed rehearsals with top musicians, private dinners with celebrity chefs, or rounds of golf with PGA Tour pros.

Members of the Moments program can hone their golf skills with a hands-on clinic led by PGA TOUR Professional Jason Gore. Members learn golfing techniques from Gore and then test out their new skills with 18 holes of challenging play, where Jason joins the member for several holes and offers tips along the way.[24]

Canadian banks have unique loyalty offerings as well. These can take the form of multiproduct rebates, as well as credit cards offering rewards programs. The rewards from these cards can be redeemed for travel and other incentives.[25]

In addition to rewarding customers, loyalty programs provide businesses with a wealth of information about their customers. This information is the raw material for data mining, which is discussed in the next section.

Privacy

With technology becoming more pervasive in our culture and companies having access to more and more consumer information, the Canadian government has extended the responsibilities of the Office of the Privacy Commission of Canada to the private sector. This office acts as an advocate for Canadians on their rights to privacy. The *Personal Information Protection and Electronic Documents Act (PIPEDA)* established rules for how personal information is handled during the course of business.

Personal information can be collected only through lawful means. Consumers need to consent to the information being collected, while companies need to protect the information and cannot use it for purposes other than what was originally intended. The Infographic, "How Are Canadians Spending Online?" illustrates how prevalent this is and that one in five Canadians have privacy concerns.

Furthermore, in 2014, the Canadian government introduced anti-spam legislation. Given the ease of accessibility to consumer information, this legislation is intended to protect Canadians from unwanted communications and threats.[26]

> *In addition to rewarding customers, loyalty programs provide businesses with a wealth of information about their customers.*

Database Marketing

LO 4 **Database marketing** is an essential practice for enhancing the customer experience. It is significant to a company's success in identifying its customers and customizing its service offerings. Over time, company's collect, process, and analyze information on their customers, potential customers, and competitors. Through careful analysis, companies can better recognize customer needs and adjust accordingly to meet and exceed expectations. Whether through traditional means or social networks, database marketing can help companies improve customer loyalty.[27]

Data Mining

How does a company use the reams of information in its databases? One answer is data mining. *Data mining* is an efficient way to sort through large amounts of data to find relationships between variables. It is a process of analyzing customer patterns and insights to make better marketing decisions. By spotting trends and relationships among the reams of information, data mining can help specifically target customer segments to meet their needs. Since data mining is growing in its impact to customer satisfaction and developing business opportunities, companies need to place more emphasis in getting customer information in the hands of sales and support staff to make a difference. Effective integration of data mining in a company's CRM strategy will allow for improved customer service and sales performance.[28]

Loyalty programs supply a lot of information that can be used for data mining purposes. Information that customers supply when they apply for a loyalty program can be tied to their purchase behaviour. Data mining can then be used to find patterns in consumer

database marketing
The use of databases to customize communications to customers and potential customers for the purpose of promoting a product or service.

Infographic

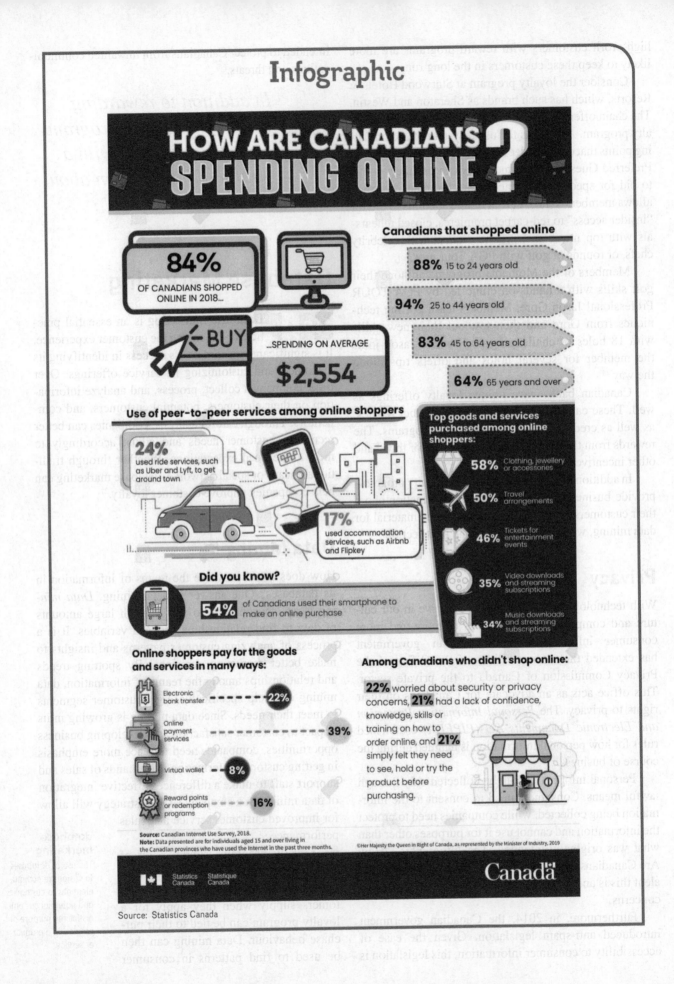

HOW ARE CANADIANS SPENDING ONLINE?

84% OF CANADIANS SHOPPED ONLINE IN 2018...

BUY

...SPENDING ON AVERAGE **$2,554**

Canadians that shopped online

88% 15 to 24 years old

94% 25 to 44 years old

83% 45 to 64 years old

64% 65 years and over

Use of peer-to-peer services among online shoppers

24% used ride services, such as Uber and Lyft, to get around town

17% used accommodation services, such as Airbnb and Flipkey

Did you know?

54% of Canadians used their smartphone to make an online purchase

Top goods and services purchased among online shoppers:

58% Clothing, jewellery or accessories

50% Travel arrangements

46% Tickets for entertainment events

35% Video downloads and streaming subscriptions

34% Music downloads and streaming subscriptions

Online shoppers pay for the goods and services in many ways:

Electronic bank transfer — **22%**

Online payment services — **39%**

Virtual wallet — **8%**

Reward points or redemption programs — **16%**

Among Canadians who didn't shop online:

22% worried about security or privacy concerns, **21%** had a lack of confidence, knowledge, skills or training on how to order online, and **21%** simply felt they need to see, hold or try the product before purchasing.

Source: Canadian Internet Use Survey, 2018.
Note: Data presented are for individuals aged 15 and over living in the Canadian provinces who have used the Internet in the past three months.

©Her Majesty the Queen in Right of Canada, as represented by the Minister of Industry, 2019

Statistics Canada   Statistique Canada

Canadä

Source: Statistics Canada

behaviour and also help marketers with customer segmentation.

All the data about customers is stored in a central place, called the **data warehouse**. A data warehouse can be thought of as an electronics library where all the information is indexed. Once the data warehouse brings the data together, the company uses data mining techniques to find insights about customers.

There are multiple examples of how CRM and data mining techniques positively impact retail organizations in Canada. For example, Royal Bank of Canada has invested in its CRM strategy. It considers CRM a core strategy and attributes it having a positive impact to its revenue growth and profitability. The deeper the data can be analyzed, the better insights that can be made.[29]

A second example is Canadian Tire. Data mining enabled the retailer's credit card division to create psychological profiles of its cardholders that were built upon alarmingly precise correlations. Data mining revealed that cardholders who purchased carbon-monoxide detectors, premium birdseed, and felt pads for the bottoms of their chair legs rarely missed a payment. On the other hand, those who bought cheap motor oil and visited a Montreal pool bar called "Sharx" were a higher risk. Canadian Tire leveraged these learnings and is now quite an innovator in digital marketing.[30]

A third example of data mining involves Metro, a chain of supermarkets in Ontario and Quebec. Its bottled juices traditionally were placed on the shelves by brand. But data mining information showed that consumers preferred the juices to be shelved by flavour. Metro made the change and sales of juices increased, and the chain continues to be flexible in its offer to the evolving consumer.[31]

Carl Sewell, a successful car dealer-owner and author of a book called *Customers for Life*, looks at each customer as an investment. If he can provide each customer with excellent customer service, that customer will likely remain loyal to Carl's dealership in the future. In a sense, that customer may have a lifetime value to Carl of hundreds of thousands of dollars. Knowing this, Carl keeps an insightful perspective in dealing with customers.[32]

data warehouse
A central repository of an organization's electronically stored data.

An example of Carl's insight involved a customer who came to pick up his car after servicing and noticed that his tennis racquet, which he had left in the car, was gone. Under normal circumstances, a dealer would say that it is not responsible for items left in a car. Carl Sewell, on the other hand, went over to the customer and apologized for the mishap. He then proceeded to write a cheque for replacement of the racquet. Carl surmised that it was not worth jeopardizing an investment of hundreds of thousands of dollars over the price of a tennis racquet.

A concept very close to customer lifetime value is *share of wallet*. CRM techniques can help marketers get a larger share of a customer's purchases from that company. Here's an example of how a bank can increase its share of wallet. The bank that holds a customer's mortgage and chequing account may learn at some point that the customer has children and may then try to sell the customer a registered education savings plan. Another example of a company increasing share of wallet is Shoppers Drug Mart. A customer with a PC Optimum card who purchases cosmetics may receive subsequent communications from Shoppers that offer coupons for related cosmetic products.

---

ask YOURSELF

1. *What is Pareto's Rule?*
2. *Give some examples of loyalty programs.*
3. *What is data mining?*

ask YOURSELF

1. *Why is customer lifetime value important for companies to calculate?*
2. *What does share of wallet mean?*

Customer Lifetime Value

In customer relationship management, a company focuses on its relationship with customers with the ultimate goal of creating an unbreakable bond with its customers. Companies are starting to focus on the value of a customer if that customer remains loyal to the firm over the customer's lifetime. This is referred to as *customer lifetime value*.

CRM and Customer Reacquisition

LO 5 Companies are realizing that losing a customer means more than losing a sale. It means losing the entire future stream of purchases that the customer would make over a lifetime of patronage.

Customers stop buying from a company for a variety of reasons. Very often, the reason can be poor customer service as opposed to something inherently wrong with the brand. The first step in customer recovery is to find the customer who is in jeopardy of being lost to the company. The longer customers stay away from a business, the less likely they are to return. Because customer databases capture purchases, computers can be programmed to periodically examine transaction frequencies and create a list of all customers who have not made a purchase within a set period of time. Because each customer generally has a certain purchase frequency, software can determine when each customer's purchase frequency has been broken. After lapsed customers are identified, the second step is to contact them to determine why they have stopped buying and potentially prepare an appropriate offer.[33] If the problem is resolved, the lapsed customer may become a very loyal customer because the firm has shown interest in the customer.

Retaining Marginal Customers

CRM allows firms to use information technology to quantify the value of individual customers in terms of sales and profits. High-value customers are provided with better privileges, discounts, or other inducements. CRM analysis shows that a small proportion of customers contribute to a large percentage of profits, and that many customers are unprofitable. Many firms are beginning to jettison or fire their low-value customers and are focusing their time on their high-valued customers. In 2007, CNN reported that Sprint had dropped about 1,000 customers who were calling the customer-care centre too frequently—40 to 50 times more than the average customer every month over an extended period.[34]

Firing low-value customers seems to be a common-sense approach, but in some cases there is a danger. If a company is left with only high-value customers, this leaves the company open to poaching by competitors if they are aware of its customer base.

ask YOURSELF

1. What does firing a customer mean?
2. Describe the two steps in customer recovery.

1 • Customer relationship management (CRM) focuses on using information about customers to build and maintain profitable customer relationships.

• Customer experience management (CEM) involves managing customer interactions to build brand equity and improve long-term profitability.

 2 • A growing number of companies are keeping track of what's said about their brands on social media platforms such as Facebook and Twitter. This activity falls in line with the process of CRM, because it's an excellent way to build a relationship with customers.

 3 • One way to retain customers is through loyalty programs. It should be noted that all customers should be rewarded, but not all customers are the same. In most product categories, a small number of heavy users account for a large percentage of a brand's sales and profits.

 4 • Companies use database marketing to collect, process, and analyze information on their customers, potential customers, and competitors with a goal to improve customer loyalty.

• Data mining is an efficient way to sort through large amounts of data to find relationships between variables.

• Companies are starting to focus on the value of a customer if that customer remains loyal to the firm over the customer's lifetime.

LO 5 • Many firms are beginning to jettison or fire their low-value customers and are focusing their time on their high-value customers.

• Companies are instituting customer reacquisition programs to prevent losing customers.

key terms and concepts... A REFRESHER

customer experience management (CEM)
data warehouse

database marketing
loyalty programs

Pareto's Rule

hands-on... APPLY YOUR KNOWLEDGE

Online Assignment on Building Relationships Visit the The Paint Channel website at **https://thepaintchannel.com /brands**. Choose two brands and research their websites.

Now, determine how you would continue to maintain a long-term business relationship with these organizations.

chapter vignette... ACTIVITY

In the opening vignette, customer relationship management is discussed. Answer the questions at the end of the vignette by reviewing the vignette as well as the Marketing NewsFlash boxes, "Brewing New Strategies" and "Landing Aeroplan."

infographic... DATA ANALYSIS

Review the Infographic in this chapter and take note of the online spending habits of Canadians. Using this data and additional research, propose a new online business venture to promote to Canadians and gain some of their online spending share of wallet.

CHAPTER

15

LEARNING OBJECTIVES

LO 1 Describe how strategy is developed at the corporate, business unit, and functional levels in an organization

LO 2 Define the concepts of business, mission, and goals, and explain why they are important in organizations

LO 3 Explain why managers use marketing dashboards and marketing metrics

LO 4 Discuss how organizations formulate strategies

LO 5 Outline the strategic marketing process

Strategic Marketing Planning

anadians interact with multiple businesses daily. Whether as employees, consumers, or partners, the connections that individuals create are the result of strategic marketing plans companies are executing.

©UPI/Alamy Stock Photo

CHAPTER OUTLINE

- Building long-term business relationships
- Organizational structure and strategy
- Setting strategic directions
- The strategic marketing process

As a marketing strategist with experience in sports entertainment, Denis Cordick understands the importance of building relationships. As vice president, marketing and business development for AMJ Campbell, Cordick can see clear connections between the businesses, sports celebrities, and people he works with. "The strategies used in sports like curling apply to business," explains Cordick. Constantly looking for opportunities and taking advantage of them is how Denis approaches his role. "When I see a business opportunity, I try to determine the best way to create a solution."

Strategic marketing planning involves making good business decisions as well as creative marketing decisions. "Some of the mutually rewarding relationships we have built over the years were created simply because they made good business sense," shares Cordick. Cordick is referring to AMJ Campbell's growth into Canada's largest moving company while strategically investing in sponsoring sports properties with Tennis Canada, Soccer Canada, and Curling Canada.

Cordick has years of experience in creating win-win situations through sponsorship negotiations. Generally, finding value for both parties through key connections. "Not only should your marketing strategy be a good marketing decision," shares Cordick, "it should also be a good business decision." Cordick has observed companies spending a lot of marketing on advertising, but not executing on all the different integrated marketing components.

Aside from moving, AMJ Campbell has a specialized products division where it diversifies its service offering. The goal of the division is to ensure on-time delivery of goods to their destination. Many times, the company's expertise in logistics and special care of the merchandise delivered leads to exceptional client experiences from manufacturers, retailers, and the end customer.

"We are a diverse business," says Cordick, "so we have multiple touch points with the Canadian public." AMJ Campbell is important to the supply chain of many of its business partners, and it also works directly with consumers.

By creating strategic partnerships that are good business and marketing decisions, Cordick has created relationships that have lasted for years. As a young marketer for a professional hockey team, Cordick observed the team invested a lot in courier and moving costs. He then identified an opportunity with AMJ Campbell to sponsor the team's "Move of the Game" that allowed fans to move from less expensive seats to premium seats in the arena. When he joined AMJ Campbell, he proactively worked with sports organizations to make further connections. These initiatives were all part of a marketing plan.

Creating a marketing plan requires goals or objectives. One of the key objectives Cordick implements is integrated marketing into multiple touch points. For example, not only does AMJ Campbell sponsor Curling Canada events through TV, online, and signage, the company also moves all the teams when they travel for tournaments. "There are a lot of logistics involved in managing an event with professional athletes," explains Cordick, "and you get the opportunity to create great business relationships." Not only is AMJ Campbell the official mover of Curling

Canada, the company also sponsors the Homan and Tirinzoni curling teams.

Cordick reminisces about presenting some of his innovative ideas in board of directors meetings. "Strategic business units need to be accountable," explains Cordick. "If you can complement your experience-driven recommendations with strong data, then you can garner the support for your strategies."[1]

Organizational Structure and Strategy

LO 1 This chapter describes how organizations set their mission and overall direction and link these activities to marketing strategies. As consumers become more concerned about a company's impact on society, marketing strategy may need to be linked to the social goals of the company's mission statement. This chapter also focuses on strategic planning and the role it plays in the marketing process.

Kinds of Organizations

Today's organizations can be divided into business firms and not-for-profit organizations. A *business firm* is an organization that serves its customers in order to earn a profit. **Profit** is the excess of revenues over costs, the reward to a business for the risk it undertakes in offering a product for sale. In contrast to business firms, a *not-for-profit organization* is an organization that serves its customers but does not have profit as an organizational goal. For simplicity, however, we use the terms *firm, company, corporation,* and *organization* to cover both business and not-for-profit operations.

profit
The excess of revenues over costs, the reward to a business for the risk it undertakes in offering a product for sale.

Marketing and the Three Organizational Levels

All organizations should have a strategic direction—that is, they should have an idea of what they hope to achieve and how they plan to achieve it. Marketing not only helps set the direction but also helps the organization get there. Large organizations are complex and may consist of three organizational levels whose strategies are linked to marketing. Figure 15–1 illustrates the three levels of strategy in an optimal organization.

At the *corporate level*, top management directs overall strategy for the entire organization. Multimarket, multiproduct firms such as General Electric or Unilever really manage a group of different businesses, variously termed strategic business units (SBUs), strategic business segments, or product-market units (PMUs).[2] Each of these units markets a set of related products to a clearly defined group of customers. Management at the corporate level focuses on the interests of the shareholders of the firm, as measured by stock performance and profitability.

The *business unit level* has business unit managers set the direction for individual products and markets. Strategic direction is more specific at the business unit level of an organization. For less complex firms with a single business focus, the corporate and business unit strategies may merge. Unilever has provided products such as Sunlight and Vaseline to Canadians for over 100 years. Another example of one of its strategic business units is Ben & Jerry's, a premium ice cream company with fun flavour names.[3]

At the *functional level*, each business unit has marketing and other specialized activities such as finance,

Similar to adjusting trajectory in the game Angry Birds, marketers make slight adjustments after executing their strategy.

©Ian Dagnall/Alamy Stock Photo

manufacturing, or human resources. The name of a *department* generally refers to its specialized function, such as the marketing department or information systems department. At the functional level, the strategic direction becomes very specific and focused.

In a large corporation with multiple business units, marketing may be called on to assess consumer trends as an aid to corporate planning. At the business unit level, marketing may be asked to provide leadership in developing a new, integrated customer service program across all business units. At the functional level, marketing may implement an advertising campaign.

Strategy Issues in Organizations

LO 2 Organizations need a reason for their existence—and a direction. This is where their business, mission, and goals converge. We'll discuss each below. Figure 15–1 illustrates the different organizational levels in a business. Business and mission apply to the corporate and business unit levels, while goals relate to all levels.

Strategy Defined for Business Plans and Marketing Plans

As discussed earlier, an organization has limited resources available to produce and market its offerings. Since it cannot possibly do everything, it must develop strategies to focus and direct the resources it has to achieve its goals. Unfortunately, the definition of strategy is debated among management and marketing theorists, so for our purposes, we will define **strategy** as an organization's long-term course of action designed to deliver a unique customer experience while achieving its goals.[4] Once the strategy of an organization or an organizational initiative is defined, business leaders collaborate to develop a marketing plan.

Getting ideas and goals down on paper is the first step to making them into reality. The business plan becomes a valuable tool for organizations to do this. It is a document that can help convey the value of your company to investors, employees, and future partners. Business plans help identify the strengths, weaknesses, opportunities, and threats of a business, as well as help develop accurate financial forecasts. Essential to the overall business plan, a marketing plan helps a business develop the right products to address customer needs, establish the best way to promote the business, and determine where the product will be distributed. Advertising and communications are also important components of the marketing plan.[5]

The Business Organizations such as Canadian Blood Services and your college or university exist for a purpose—to accomplish something for someone. At the beginning, most organizations have clear ideas about what "something" and "someone" mean. But as the organization grows over time, often its purpose becomes fuzzy and continually unclear.

This is where the organization repeatedly asks some of the most difficult questions it ever faces: What business are we in? Who are our customers? What offerings should we provide to give these customers value? One guideline in defining the company's business is to

Figure 15–1
The three levels of strategy in organizations: corporate, business unit, and functional

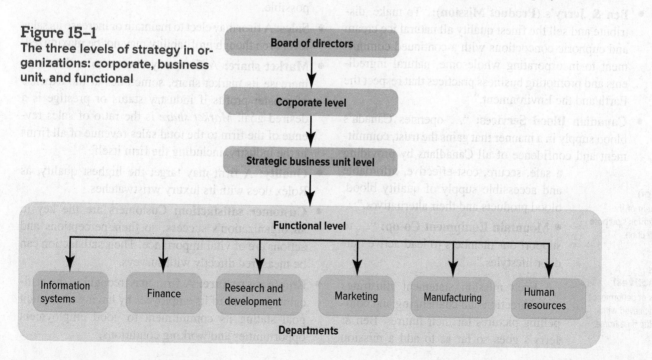

Board of directors

Corporate level

Strategic business unit level

Functional level

| Information systems | Finance | Research and development | Marketing | Manufacturing | Human resources |

Departments

try to understand the people served by the organization and the value they receive, which emphasizes the critical customer-driven focus that successful organizations have.

In a now-famous article entitled "Marketing Myopia," Harvard professor Theodore Levitt cited railroads as organizations that had a narrow, production-oriented statement of their business: "We are in the railroad business!" This narrow definition of their business lost sight of who their customers were and what their needs were. Railroads saw only other railroads as competitors and failed to design strategies to compete with airlines, barges, pipelines, trucks, bus lines, and cars and may have fared better over the past century by recognizing they are in "the transportation business." Examining business from a broader perspective allows you apply this concept to companies such as Disney. Disney is *not* in the movie and theme park business, but rather it *is* in the business of entertainment, creating fun and fantasy for customers.

The Mission

By understanding its business, an organization can take steps to define its **mission**, a statement of the organization's scope, often identifying its customers, markets, products, technology, and values. Today often used interchangeably with *vision*, the *mission statement* frequently has an inspirational theme—something that can ignite the loyalty of customers, employees, and others with whom the organization comes in contact.

Inspiration and focus appear in the mission statements of business and non-profit organizations. Even if the businesses are different, their mission statements can exhibit similar qualities:

- **Ben & Jerry's (Product Mission):** "To make, distribute and sell the finest quality all natural ice cream and euphoric concoctions with a continued commitment to incorporating wholesome, natural ingredients and promoting business practices that respect the Earth and the Environment."
- **Canadian Blood Services:** "… operates Canada's blood supply in a manner that gains the trust, commitment and confidence of all Canadians by providing a safe, secure, cost-effective, affordable and accessible supply of quality blood, blood products and their alternatives."
- **Mountain Equipment Co-op:** "… to support our members to lead active outdoor lifestyles."

Each mission statement illustrates clear direction and challenging and compelling pictures for their futures. Ben & Jerry's goes so far as to add a mission

mission
Statement of the organization's purpose and direction.

goals (objectives)
Targets of performance to be achieved within a specific time frame.

focused on social responsibility as well as a mission for its product. IBM has put strategy in place to create a "smarter planet." It is driven by three core values that help it create its mission statement.

Organizations must connect not just with their customers but with all their *stakeholders*. Stakeholders are the people who are affected by what the company does and how well it performs. This group includes employees, owners, and board members, as well as suppliers, distributors, unions, local communities, governments, society in general, and, of course, customers. Communicating the mission statement is an important corporate-level marketing function. Some companies publish their mission statement on their website or in their annual reports. One British Columbia company has its mission statement on a huge wall poster in its manufacturing facility, and every employee reads and signs it! The Focus on Ethics box, "Board Diversity," discusses the value to a company of adhering to corporate values, in this case promoting diversity.[6]

Goals

Goals or **objectives** take an organization's mission and translate it into targeted levels of performance to be achieved within a specific time frame. These goals measure how well the mission is being accomplished. Goals exist at the corporate, business unit, and functional levels, which were shown in Figure 15–1. All lower-level goals must contribute to achieving goals at the next highest level.

Business firms can pursue several different types of goals:

- **Profit:** Most firms seek to maximize profits—to get as high a financial return on investment (ROI) as possible.
- **Sales:** A firm may elect to maintain or increase its sales level even though profitability may not be maximized.
- **Market share:** A firm may choose to maintain or increase its market share, sometimes at the expense of greater profits if industry status or prestige is a desired goal. *Market share* is the ratio of sales revenue of the firm to the total sales revenue of all firms in the industry, including the firm itself.
- **Quality:** A firm may target the highest quality, as Rolex does with its luxury wristwatches.
- **Customer satisfaction:** Customers are the key to an organization's success, so their perceptions and actions are of vital importance. Their satisfaction can be measured directly with surveys.
- **Employee welfare:** A firm may recognize the critical importance of its employees by having an explicit goal stating its commitment to good employment opportunities and working conditions.

Board Diversity

The correlation between the diversity of a board of directors and the financial performance of an organization is a good argument to establish diverse boards. In the U.S., the state of California introduced a law stating that publicly traded companies must have at least one female director by 2020. Canada has a different approach to promoting diversity, which has created challenging situations in the past.

An organization's success depends on many factors. The strategic direction helps identify an organization's goals and its actions to achieve them. Marketing may play a role in setting direction as well as executing plans.

As organizations increase in size, their organizational structure may increase in complexity. Large organizations normally have a board of directors that holds the top management accountable for the strategic direction set by the organization as well as the results achieved.

Canada's diverse population is not always represented in the diversity of corporate boards. Gender diversity on corporate boards has become a contentious issue between companies and their shareholders. In 2016, Restaurant Brands International, the parent company of Tim Hortons and Burger King, turned down a proposal to increase the number of women on its board of directors. At the time, there were no women on the board.

Before Tim Hortons merged with Burger King in 2014, a quarter of the Tim Hortons board were women. The combined company Restaurant Brands International (RBI) rolled out a ten-person all-male board of directors. Although RBI had two women in senior management, some shareholders believed formal board diversity was required to ensure appropriate representation.

Gender is one point of diversity, as are race, background, and experience. Tim Hortons may be the most recognizable brand in Canada where tension on gender diversity is apparent; however, other Canadian companies, such as BCE and Dollarama, have shareholders that also raise diversity issues.

There is a correlation between diverse boards of directors and financial performance.

©bowdenimages/iStock/Getty Images Plus

Canada encourages companies to adopt a diverse board model rather than mandate them. As more and more companies comply, the Canadian economy should reap the benefits. ●

Questions

1. Other than financial performance, what other benefits are there to having a diverse board of directors in an organization?

2. If you do not agree with a company's strategy on governance or operations, what can you as a consumer do "voice" your opinion?

- **Social responsibility:** A firm may seek to balance conflicting goals of stakeholders to promote overall welfare, even at the expense of profits. (See, for example, the discussion of the emphasis on corporate social responsibility at Mountain Equipment Co-op in the Focus on Ethics box, "MEC Believes Accountability Is Key to Corporate Social Responsibility.")[7]

Goals keep organizations focused and achieving goals help companies grow. Many organizations (for example, museums, symphony orchestras, and private schools) do not seek profits as a primary goal. These organizations strive to serve consumers as efficiently as possible. Government agencies also perform marketing activities in trying to achieve their goal of serving the public good.

Canada's Most Profitable Companies

1. Royal Bank of Canada
2. Bank of Nova Scotia
3. Toronto Dominion Bank
4. Bank of Montreal
5. Online Casino Companies
6. Suncor Energy
7. Canadian National Railway
8. BCE Inc.
9. Husky Energy
10. The Woodbridge Company Limited

MEC Believes Accountability Is Key to Corporate Social Responsibility

Used with permission of Mountain Equipment Co-op (MEC)

In 2013, Mountain Equipment Co-op (MEC) set challenging goals for itself. When sourcing its apparel materials, it focused on using facilities with environmental management systems and products with environmentally preferred materials. The additional steps MEC made for the benefit of the environment were not in vain. It surpassed its targets with respect to how it designs its products, how it operates as an organization, and how it supports the community.

In 2020, MEC's accountability translated into a focused effort to assist front-line health care workers during the COVID-19 pandemic. MEC donated products to health care workers and designed Canada's first Fair Trade Certified non-surgical mask. It also created the MEC Outdoor Partner Relief Fund to support trail organizations. Although its stores were closed, members continued to make purchases online.

Through the high standards set and accountability report shared with the public, MEC has been recognized alongside Canadian Tire as one of the most reputable brands for corporate social responsibility. The accountability report highlighted where it succeeded and where it needed to improve.

Furthermore, to ensure that results were conveyed in an unbiased yet fair manner, MEC looked to its stakeholders to form an accountability review panel to help compile and submit the findings.

Mountain Equipment Co-op is not the only company focused on corporate social responsibility. Not only does applying socially responsible practices makes good business sense, it also adds to the bottom line of many Canadian companies. ●

Questions

1. Give some examples of other companies practising corporate social responsibility.

2. Would you pay more for more environmentally friendly apparel? Discuss.

Marketing Budgets and Financials Clearly stating goals in a marketing plan is important. Aligning marketing objectives and financial objectives of a company is also important since discrepancies between chief marketing officer (CMO) and chief financial officer (CFO) activities can have a negative impact on financial results.[8]

The break-even analysis and profit equation, discussed in Chapter 9, help develop a pricing strategy for products and services. With key assumptions, marketing plans need to generate sales forecasts to determine the amount of money or sales that will be generated. These sales help the business's finance team forecast a company's cash flow and profit and loss for its overall business plan. Marketers rely on historical information, emerging trends, and assumptions to look forward, and then suggest the potential impact that marketing will have on the company's success.[9]

Determining how marketing spending impacts company profitability is an ongoing challenge for CMOs.[10] With this challenge looming, marketers need to be able to prepare accurate budgets for their marketing plans. Since forecasts in marketing plans may be relied upon for other decisions, it is important for marketers to ensure that more than one forecast is created. Considering realistic, optimistic, and pessimistic forecasts helps decision makers see expected, best-case, and worst-case scenarios. Preparing forecasts and budgets provides an opportunity for companies to predict future revenues and expenses while looking for ways to cut costs. To help improve accuracy in budgeting and forecasting for marketing, marketers may review past sales, consider upcoming contracts, and propose predictions to potential changes in the market.[11]

Tracking Strategic Performance

LO 3 Although marketing managers can set strategic directions for their organizations, how do they know if they are making progress in getting there? One answer is to measure performance by using marketing dashboards.

Once the marketing plan is put into practice, it is immediately evaluated. Measuring the results of a marketing plan is a key step in achieving client satisfaction. As we review marketing metrics and dashboards, the tools and technology we are discussing today, may be obsolete in a few years. Notwithstanding, technology has added value to measuring the results from the investments made in marketing research and creative. When describing the importance of metrics, we can relate it to Angry Birds, the video game by Rovio. Before metrics and dashboards, marketing plans would be executed with a ready-aim-fire approach. That is, marketers would not receive feedback until the campaign was complete. The digital age we are in right now allows us to execute marketing plans with an aim-fire-adjust approach. After we execute a part of the recruitment marketing plan, we use the metrics to quickly adjust our plan and get closer to our desired result.

Marketing Dashboards

A **marketing dashboard** is the visual display of the essential information related to achieving a marketing objective. Often, it is a computer-based display with real-time information and active hyperlinks to provide further detail. For example, a CMO may want to see daily what the effect of a new TV advertising campaign is on a product's sales in order to allocate future marketing resources effectively. Dashboards can track other parts of an organization's business, including the impact of its corporate social responsibility endeavours. Similar to a dashboard in a car, marketing dashboards can give feedback at a quick glance.

What the marketing dashboard shows are the key marketing metrics that the organization believes will drive it to success.

Marketing Metrics

Most companies keep their marketing dashboards and metrics proprietary, as the information in the dashboard gives an indication as to the organization's strategy. Marketing dashboards are similar to the accountability report dashboard shown in Figure 15–2. The graphic displays of marketing dashboards are key performance measures of a product category, such as sales versus cost of sales. Each variable in a marketing dashboard is a **marketing metric**, which is a measure of the quantitative value or trend of a marketing activity or result. The choice of which marketing

Figure 15–2
Example of a marketing dashboard

An effective dashboard, like this one from Mountain Equipment Co-op, helps managers assess their corporate social responsibility impact at a glance.

Used with permission of Mountain Equipment Co-op (MEC)

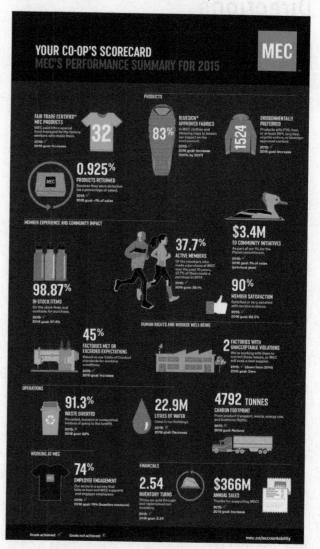

metrics to display is critical for a busy marketing manager, who can be overwhelmed with too much or inappropriate information.

Dashboard designers take great care to show graphs and tables in easy-to-understand formats to enable clear interpretation at a glance. What the marketing dashboard shows are the key marketing metrics that the organization believes will drive it to success.

Setting Strategic Directions

LO 4 Setting strategic direction for drawing employees or consumers closer to an organization involves answering challenging questions: Where are we now? Where do we want to go? How will we get there?

A Look Around: Where Are We Now?

Asking an organization where it is at the present time involves identifying its customers, competencies, and competitors. More-detailed approaches of assessing "where are we now?" include SWOT analysis, discussed later in this chapter, and environmental scanning (Chapter 2). It is important for an organization to look internally and externally to assess its starting point. These approaches may be carried out at each of the three levels in the organization.

Customers Tilley Endurables is a Canadian retailer that knows that its customers appreciate the fine hats and travel clothing that Tilley makes. Tilley provides an example of a clear focus on customers. Its stores and website give a remarkable statement about its commitments to customer relationships and the quality of its products. The Tilley guarantee for its legendary hats has always been an unconditional one: "Tilley Hats will be replaced free if they ever wear out, mildew, or shrink." The same guarantee applies to some of their shorts, vests, jackets, pants, and skirts. They are replaced free if they ever wear out.[12]

Mountain Equipment Co-op distributes Garmin products, another company committed to being a good corporate citizen.
©OvuOng/Shutterstock

Competencies "What do we do best?" asks about an organization's competencies—an organization's special capabilities, including skills, technologies, and resources that distinguish it from other organizations. Exploiting these competencies can lead to success.[13] In Tilley's case, its competencies include an obsession with quality. To quote the founder Alex Tilley, "I'll make travel clothing! I'll make it the best in the world! And then I'll make it even better!" Tilley Endurables is one of the last remaining companies to manufacture all its products in Canada.[14]

Competitors After understanding your business internally, it is important to set your analysis externally. In today's global competition, the lines among competitive sectors are increasingly blurred. This may not be as evident in the apparel industry, but consider Loblaws. Loblaws competes directly with other supermarkets such as Sobeys. At the same time, it also competes against mass merchandisers such as Walmart Supercentres, which also carry groceries, and it competes with warehouse clubs such as Costco. Loblaws also carries many pharmacy items, which puts it into direct competition with pharmacies such as Shoppers Drug Mart and Pharma Plus. Shoppers Drug Mart carries many lines of cosmetics, which puts it in direct competition with department stores such as Hudson's Bay, which traditionally carries cosmetics.

The crucial point: Strategic directions must be customer-focused and provide genuine value and benefits to existing and prospective customers. There should be clear competency for the organization and a good understanding of competition.

Competitive sports even has issues vying for the attention of viewers. The Marketing NewsFlash, "Marketing Rocks," discusses how Curling Canada is promoting the sport to try to gain more interest and engagement from Canadians.[15]

Marketing Rocks

©PCN Photography/Alamy Stock Photo

Centuries ago, curling was introduced in Canada by Scottish immigrants and has become more popular in recent years. The sport involves players sliding stones down a sheet of ice to score in a target area of concentric circles.

With some televised curling games gaining more Canadian viewers than hockey, Curling Canada saw an opportunity to raise further awareness of the sport. It found a strategic partner in Cosette, a marketing and communications agency, to help elevate awareness of the sport and attract younger fans. The resulting advertising campaign was launched to reach existing fans who enjoy the social and strategic game.

Curling Canada is the national governing body responsible for the development, promotion, and organization of all levels of curling across Canada. Using a light-hearted approach in its advertising allows also Curling Canada to attract more Canadians to this social, welcoming sport. ●

Questions

1. From what you know about the sport of curling, do you think humour was the appropriate strategy to use in Curling Canada's advertising campaign?

2. What brands do you recall use humour to reach their target audience?

Growth Strategies: Where Do We Want to Go?

Knowing where the organization is at the present time enables managers to set a direction for the firm and commit resources to move in that direction. Two techniques to aid in these decisions are the business portfolio analysis and the market-product analysis.

Business Portfolio Analysis Developed by the Boston Consulting Group (BCG), *business portfolio analysis* uses quantified performance measures and market growth rates to analyze a firm's strategic business units as though they were a collection of separate investments.[16] While used at the business unit level here, the BCG analysis has also been applied at the product line or individual product or brand level. This kind of portfolio analysis is very popular; most large firms have used it in some form.

BCG, a leading management consulting firm, advises its clients to locate the position of each of its SBUs on a growth-share matrix (Figure 15–3). The vertical axis is the *market growth rate*, which is the annual rate of growth of the specific market or industry in which a given SBU is competing. The horizontal axis is the *relative market share*, defined as the sales of the SBU divided by the sales of the largest firm in the industry.

BCG has given specific names and descriptions to the four resulting quadrants in its growth-share matrix

Figure 15–3
Boston Consulting Group's growth-share matrix for a strong, diversified firm showing some strategic plans

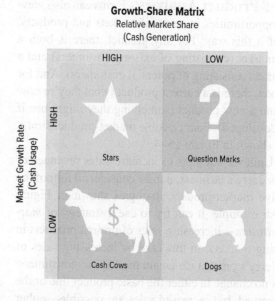

based on the amount of cash they generate for or require from the firm:

● *Cash cows* are SBUs that typically generate large amounts of cash, far more than they can invest profitably in their own product line. They have a dominant share of a slow-growth market and provide cash to

Figure 15–4
Four market-product strategies: Alternative ways to expand sales revenues for Ben & Jerry's

	Products	
Markets	**Current**	**New**
Current	**Market penetration** Selling more Ben & Jerry's super premium ice cream in North America	**Product development** Selling a new product such as frozen yogurt under the Ben & Jerry's brand in North America
New	**Market development** Selling Ben & Jerry's super premium ice cream in Brazil for the first time	**Diversification** Selling a new product such as breakfast cereal in China for the first time

pay large amounts of company overhead and to invest in other SBUs.

- *Question marks* or *problem children* are SBUs with a low share of high-growth markets. They require large injections of cash just to maintain their market share, and even more to increase it. Their name implies management's dilemma for these SBUs: choosing the right ones to invest in and phasing out the rest.

- *Dogs* are SBUs with a low share of low-growth markets. Although they may generate enough cash to sustain themselves, they do not hold the promise of ever becoming real winners for the firm. Dropping SBUs that are dogs may be required, except when relationships with other SBUs, competitive considerations, or potential strategic alliances exist.[17]

Market-Product Analysis Firms can also view growth opportunities in terms of markets and products. Think of it this way: For any product, there is both a current market (consisting of existing customers) and a new market (consisting of potential customers). And for any market, there is a current product (what they're now using) and a new product (something they might use if it were developed). Four possible market-product strategies are shown in Figure 15–4.

As Unilever attempts to increase sales revenues of its Ben & Jerry's business, it must consider all four of the alternative market-product strategies shown in Figure 15–4. For example, it can try to use a strategy of *market penetration*—increasing sales of present products in its existing markets, in this case by increasing sales of Ben & Jerry's present ice cream products to consumers. There is no change in either the basic product line or the market served, but increased sales are possible—either by selling more ice cream (through better promotion or distribution) or by selling the same amount of ice cream at a higher price to its existing customers.

Market development is a marketing strategy to sell current products to new markets. For Ben & Jerry's, Brazil is an attractive new market. There is good news and bad news for this strategy: As household incomes of Brazilians increase, consumers can buy more ice cream; however, the Ben & Jerry's brand may be unknown to Brazilian consumers.

An expansion strategy using *product development* involves selling a new product to existing markets. When Ben and Jerry's launched sorbet and frozen yogurt products, the firm was following a product development strategy. Figure 15–4 shows that the firm could try leveraging the Ben & Jerry's brand by selling its own frozen yogurt in North America.

Diversification involves developing new products and selling them in new markets. This is a potentially high-risk strategy for Ben & Jerry's—and for most firms—because the company has neither previous production experience nor marketing experience on which to draw. For example, in trying to sell a Ben & Jerry's brand of breakfast cereal in China, the company has expertise neither in producing cereals nor in marketing to consumers in China. Fast-food giant McDonald's has implemented diversification strategies to gauge success prior to introducing new product development in an established market. An example of this is its McCafé launch in Australia in 1993, many years before it came to North America.

Diversification can take different forms to open a company to new opportunities and threats. When Rogers purchased the Toronto Blue Jays, it got into a completely new area of business. Diversification can also consist of

McDonald's introduced McCafé in Australia, as well as the Veg McMuffin and the McVeggie in India, all examples of its diversification strategy.

©Alex Segre/Alamy Stock Photo

a company introducing a variation of a product to a new market. For example, McDonald's introduced product variations in India including the Veg McMuffin™ and the McVeggie™ to appeal to the high population of vegetarians.

The Strategic Marketing Process

LO 5 The Marketing NewsFlash box, "The Netflix Launch and Its Continually Changing Business Model," describes how Netflix changed its business model to benefit from the digital age.[18] It is a great example of the strategic marketing process in action. In

general, after an organization assesses where it's at and where it wants to go, it must work out how it will get there. Specifically, it must decide the following:

- How to allocate resources
- How to convert plans into actions
- How results compare with plans, and whether deviations (results that differ from expectations) require new plans and actions

This approach is used in the **strategic marketing process**, whereby an organization allocates its marketing mix resources to reach its target markets and achieve its goals. The strategic marketing process is so central to the activities of most organizations that they formalize it as a **marketing plan**, which is a road map for the marketing activities of an organization for a specified future period of time, such as one year or five years. The marketing plan is divided into three phases: planning, implementation, and evaluation (Figure 15–5). See Appendix A for an example of a marketing plan, which also includes an executive summary.

strategic marketing process
Approach whereby an organization allocates its marketing mix.

marketing plan
Road map for the marketing activities of an organization for a specified future period of time.

Figure 15–5
Outline of a marketing plan

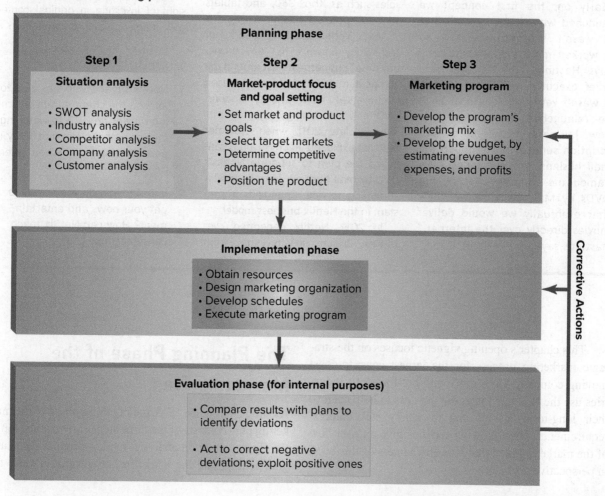

Planning phase

Step 1
Situation analysis
- SWOT analysis
- Industry analysis
- Competitor analysis
- Company analysis
- Customer analysis

Step 2
Market-product focus and goal setting
- Set market and product goals
- Select target markets
- Determine competitive advantages
- Position the product

Step 3
Marketing program
- Develop the program's marketing mix
- Develop the budget, by estimating revenues expenses, and profits

Implementation phase
- Obtain resources
- Design marketing organization
- Develop schedules
- Execute marketing program

Evaluation phase (for internal purposes)
- Compare results with plans to identify deviations
- Act to correct negative deviations; exploit positive ones

Corrective Actions

The Netflix Launch and Its Continually Changing Business Model

©Ian Dagnall/Alamy Stock Photo

I f in 1997 a customer had been charged a late fee of $40 for a VHS tape of *Apollo 13,* what might she or he have done? Maybe just grumble and pay it?

In the case of Reed Hastings, he was embarrassed, apparently paid the $40 late fee, and—this is where he's different—got to thinking that there's a big market out there. "So I started to investigate the idea of how to create a movie-rental business by mail," he told a *Fortune* magazine reviewer.

The Original Business Model

"Early on, the first concept we launched was rental by mail, but it wasn't subscription-based so it worked more like Blockbuster," says Hastings, the founder and chief executive officer of Netflix. It wasn't very popular. So in 1999, he relaunched his idea with a new business model—as a subscription service, pretty much the mail business you see today. "We named the company Netflix, not DVDs by Mail, because we knew that eventually we would deliver movies directly over the Internet," Hastings says.

Netflix's Changing Business Model

The Netflix DVDs-by-mail model delivered movies on DVD to customers for a fixed monthly fee—and drove Blockbuster to seek bankruptcy protection. But the Netflix business model changed over eight months in 2008: from "Watch Now," enabling subscribers to watch any of 1,000 streaming movies on a PC, to partnering with TiVo, Xbox, and others to enable their systems to let you see one of about 12,000 movies on your television.

The movie distribution channel has also expanded with web-ready TVs such as Sony's Bravia, game consoles such as Xbox 360, and tablets such as Apple's iPad.

With Netflix breaking a series of technology barriers, its "any movie, any time" business was just around the corner. In mid-2011, Netflix introduced controversial new pricing options: DVD only, streaming only, or both. Then in late 2011, when customer reaction exploded, Reed Hastings cancelled the plan to separate Netflix's DVD-by-mail business from its movie-streaming service. Change is a constant in the Netflix business model.

In 2019, Netflix generated over US$20 billion in revenue from domestic DVD sales, domestic streaming, and international streaming lines of business. By altering its business model to respond to changing consumer demand and technologies, Netflix keeps itself flexible to respond to market demand. During the COVID-19 global pandemic, the company's strategic marketing planning saw double the demand of new subscribers. Furthermore, the organization's foresight of investing in original content gave it an edge over its competitors. ●

Questions

1. Netflix's leadership was able to foresee the change from watching movies on DVD to watching movies over the Internet. Why is foresight important when determining strategy?

2. What media do you access to get your news and entertainment? How can Netflix reach consumers like you?

This chapter's opening vignette focuses on the strategic marketing process for the largest coast-to-coast moving company. Both profit and not-for-profit industries use the strategic marketing process to help achieve their long-term visions and to satisfy stakeholders' requirements. The following sections give an overview of the marketing plan that puts all chapters of this book in perspective.

The Planning Phase of the Marketing Plan

As shown in Figure 15–5, the planning phase of the marketing plan consists of the three steps shown at the top of the figure: situation analysis, market-product focus and goal setting, and the marketing program. Let's use the

Figure 15–6
Ben & Jerry's: A SWOT analysis

Location of Factor	Type of Factor	
	Favourable	Unfavourable
Internal	**Strengths** • Prestigious, well-known brand name among North American consumers • Major share of the super premium ice cream market • Can complement Unilever's existing ice cream brands • Widely recognized for its social responsibility actions	**Weaknesses** • Danger that B&J's social responsibility actions may add costs, reduce focus on core business • Need for experienced managers to help growth • Flat sales and profits in recent years
External	**Opportunities** • Growing demand for quality ice cream in overseas markets • Increasing demand for frozen yogurt and other low-fat desserts • Success of many firms in extending successful brand in one product category to others	**Threats** • Consumer concern with fatty desserts; B&J customers are the type who read new government-ordered nutritional labels • Competes with Haagen-Dazs brand • Increased competition in international markets

recent marketing planning experiences of several companies to look at each of these steps.

Step 1: Situation Analysis

The essence of a *situation analysis* is taking stock of the firm's or product's past performance, where it is now, and where it is headed in light of the organization's plans and the external factors and trends affecting it. The situation analysis box in Figure 15–5 is the first of the three steps in the planning phase.

Step 1 starts with a *SWOT analysis*, which describes an organization's appraisal of its internal Strengths and Weaknesses and its external Opportunities and Threats. Both the situation and SWOT analyses can be done at the level of the entire organization, the business unit, the product line, or the specific product. As an analysis moves from the level of the entire organization to the specific product, it, of course, gets far more detailed. For small firms or those with basically a single product line, an analysis at the firm or product level is really the same thing.

> *A SWOT analysis helps a firm identify the strategy-related factors that can have a major effect on the firm.*

Let's assume you are the Unilever vice president responsible for integrating Ben & Jerry's into Unilever's business. You might do the SWOT analysis shown in

Figure 15–6. Note that your SWOT table has four cells formed by the combination of internal versus external factors (the rows) and favourable versus unfavourable factors (the columns) that summarize Ben & Jerry's strengths, weaknesses, opportunities, and threats.

A SWOT analysis helps a firm identify the strategy-related factors in these four cells that can have a major effect on the firm. The goal is not simply to develop the SWOT analysis but to translate the results of the analysis

One of Ben & Jerry's 75 flavours of ice cream.
©Keith Homan/Shutterstock

into specific actions to help the firm grow and succeed. The ultimate goal is to identify the critical factors affecting the firm and then build on vital strengths, correct glaring weaknesses, exploit significant opportunities, and avoid or prepare for disaster-laden threats. That is a big order.

The Ben and Jerry's SWOT analysis in Figure 15–6 can be the basis for these kinds of specific actions. An action in each of the four cells might be as follows:

- **Build on a strength.** Find specific efficiencies in distribution with Unilever's existing ice cream brands.
- **Correct a weakness.** Recruit experienced managers from other consumer product firms to help stimulate growth.
- **Exploit an opportunity.** Develop a new line of low-fat yogurts to respond to consumer health concerns.
- **Avoid or prepare for a disaster-laden threat.** Focus on less risky international markets, such as Mexico.

The next areas to consider in step 1 are as follows:

- The *industry analysis* section focuses on the industry and trends.

competitive advantages

Those characteristics of a product or service that make it superior to competing substitutes.

- The *competitor analysis* section looks at the firm's competitors.
- The *company analysis* section provides details of the company itself.
- The *customer analysis* section addresses the question: Who are the customers of the firm's products?

Step 2: Market-Product Focus and Goal Setting
Determining which products will be directed toward which customers (step 2 of the planning phase in Figure 15–5) is essential for developing an effective marketing program (step 3). This decision is often based on *market segmentation*, which involves considering prospective buyers in terms of groups, or segments. These groups have common needs and will respond similarly to a marketing program. Ideally, a firm can use market segmentation to identify the segments on which it will focus its efforts—its target market segments—and develop one or more marketing programs to reach them.

Goal setting involves setting measurable marketing objectives to be achieved. For organizations launching recruitment marketing campaign, the objective is applications and hires. Entertainment companies such as Netflix measure the number of members as well as the number of hours of television shows and movies that are downloaded. An organization selling apparel, such as Tilley Endurables, sets objectives for its product categories and offerings. When viewing the entire marketing program, objectives are often a series of actions to be implemented over several years.

Using the marketing plan outline shown in Figure 15–5, step 2 can be illustrated using Sleep Country Canada as an example:

- **Set market and product goals.** Based on listening to what is important to customers, Sleep Country Canada offers lots of choice in mattresses. It also makes each experience before, during, and after the sale an enjoyable one for the customer. One of its market goals may be to increase its market share by a certain percentage in the retailing mattress business in Canada. It's important to quantify the percentage so that the company can measure whether it successfully meets its goals.
- **Select target markets.** Sleep Country Canada targets consumers who want a quality mattress as well as a positive customer service experience.
- **Determine competitive advantages. Competitive advantages** are those characteristics of a product that make it superior to competing substitutes. Sleep Country Canada offers the mattress purchaser an enjoyable customer service experience unparalleled in this market. It offers clean, bright stores; sleep experts who put the customer's comfort and budget needs first; and courteous delivery people.
- **Position the product.** Sleep Country Canada is positioned as a mattress specialist that offers quality products with the added benefit of courteous and knowledgeable staff, an attractive in-store setting, and a convenient delivery service.

Details in these four elements of step 2 provide a solid foundation to use in developing the marketing program—the next step in the planning phase of the marketing plan.

Ben & Jerry's Non-dairy Debut

In Canada, Ben & Jerry's debuted three new non-dairy, almond-based frozen treats in order to adapt to the changing dietary needs of consumers. There are additional flavours available in the United States.

1. Chocolate Fudge Brownie
2. P.B. Cookies
3. Coffee Caramel Fudge

Step 3: Marketing Program
Activities in step 2 tell the marketing manager which customers to target and which customer needs the firm's product offerings can satisfy—the *who* and *what* aspects of the marketing

Figure 15–7
Elements of the marketing mix that comprise a cohesive marketing program

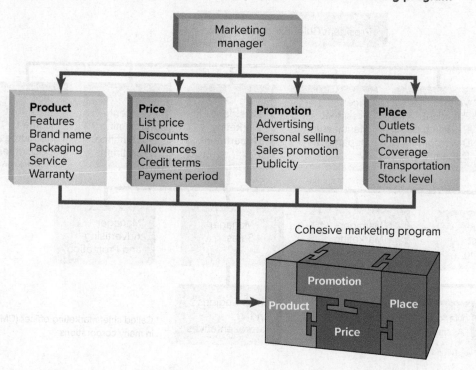

plan. The *how* aspect—step 3 in the marketing plan—involves developing the program's marketing mix and its budget.

Figure 15–7 shows components of each marketing mix element that are combined to provide a cohesive marketing program. For Sleep Country Canada, the marketing mix activities can include the following:

- **Product strategy:** Offer consumers one of the largest selections of top, name-brand mattresses.

- **Price strategy:** Offer consumers a low-price guarantee. If consumers find a comparable product at a competitor that is equal to or lower than Sleep Country Canada's price, the company will beat that figure by 5 percent.

- **Promotion strategy:** Sleep Country Canada uses mass media advertising to communicate its unique retail experience to prospective and current customers.

- **Place (distribution) strategy:** Sleep Country Canada is conveniently located in six Canadian provinces with 240 stores in total.

Putting a marketing program into effect requires that the firm commit time and money to it, prepare a sales forecast, and establish a budget that must be approved by top management. In some organizations, this is referred to as financial data and projections.

The Implementation Phase of the Marketing Plan

A firm's marketing plan is the result of the many hours spent in the planning phase of the strategic marketing process. Implementation, the second phase of the marketing plan, involves implementing the marketing program that emerges from the planning phase. An organization needs to invest time and resources into the planning phase of the marketing plan, but just as is important is the implementation phase. The implementation phase is the part of the process that executes the individual tactics that support the marketing strategy. Figure 15–5 shows the four components of the implementation phase: obtaining resources, designing the marketing organization, developing schedules, and actually executing the marketing program designed in the planning phase.

Figure 15–8

Organization of a typical manufacturing firm, showing a breakdown of the marketing department

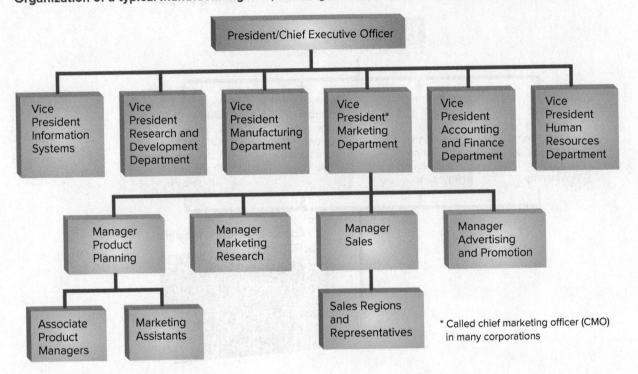

* Called chief marketing officer (CMO) in many corporations

Obtaining Resources Most companies have numerous options for growth. But such growth requires an investment. Corporate leadership within an organization determines the best options for growth and how they should be funded. Tying back to the three levels within an organization, it can sometimes be challenging to get support from all stakeholders. Ideally, this part of the process is already introduced during the planning phase and is more of a formality at this point.

Designing the Marketing Organization A marketing program needs marketing staff to implement it. Figure 15–8 shows the organization chart of a typical manufacturing firm, giving some details of the marketing department's structure. Four managers of marketing activities are shown to report to the vice president of marketing. Several regional sales managers and an international sales manager may report to the manager of sales. This marketing organization is responsible for converting marketing plans to reality.

Developing Schedules Effective implementation requires developing appropriate schedules and determining specific deadlines for the creation and execution of marketing activities. For example, if a company wants to place an ad in the *Globe and Mail's Report on*

Business magazine, it must reserve space a month prior to the date that the ad appears in the magazine. Also, the company must allow time for creating and producing the ad. Digital advertising allows for shorter advanced notice and tweaks to the creative process.

Executing the Marketing Program Marketing plans are meaningless unless they are put into action. This requires attention to detail to both marketing strategies and marketing tactics. A **marketing strategy** is the means by which a marketing goal is to be achieved, usually characterized by a specified target market and a marketing program to reach it. Although the term strategy is often used loosely, it implies both the end sought (target market) and the means to achieve it (marketing program).

To implement a marketing program successfully, hundreds of detailed decisions are often required, such as writing ads or setting prices. These decisions, called **marketing tactics**, are detailed day-to-day operational decisions essential to the overall success of marketing strategies.

The Evaluation Phase of the Marketing Plan

The evaluation phase of the marketing plan is used to determine if the plan is moving in the right direction. The marketing manager compares the results of the marketing activities with the goals laid out in the marketing

marketing strategy
Means by which a marketing goal is to be achieved.

marketing tactics
Detailed day-to-day operational decisions essential to the overall success of marketing strategies.

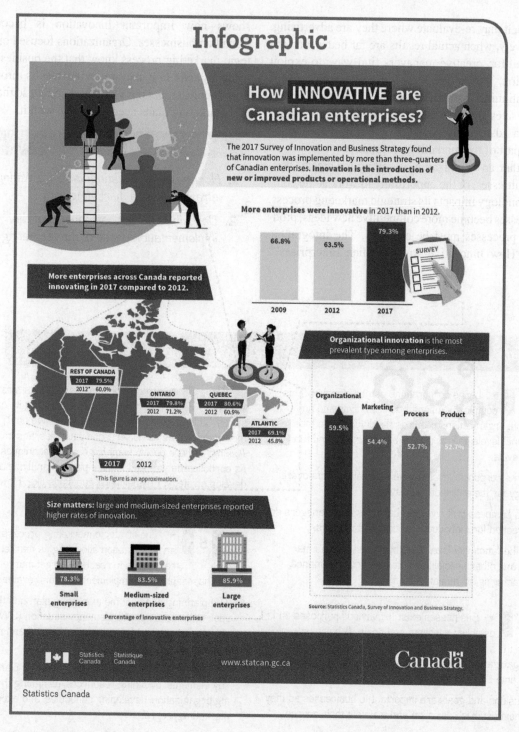

Infographic

How **INNOVATIVE** are Canadian enterprises?

The 2017 Survey of Innovation and Business Strategy found that innovation was implemented by more than three-quarters of Canadian enterprises. **Innovation is the introduction of new or improved products or operational methods.**

More enterprises were innovative in 2017 than in 2012.

- 2009: 66.8%
- 2012: 63.5%
- 2017: 79.3%

More enterprises across Canada reported innovating in 2017 compared to 2012.

REST OF CANADA
- 2017: 79.5%
- 2012*: 60.0%

ONTARIO
- 2017: 79.8%
- 2012: 71.2%

QUEBEC
- 2017: 80.6%
- 2012: 60.9%

ATLANTIC
- 2017: 69.1%
- 2012: 45.8%

2017   2012

*This figure is an approximation.

Size matters: large and medium-sized enterprises reported higher rates of innovation.

- Small enterprises: 78.3%
- Medium-sized enterprises: 83.5%
- Large enterprises: 85.9%

Percentage of innovative enterprises

Organizational innovation is the most prevalent type among enterprises.

- Organizational: 59.5%
- Marketing: 54.4%
- Process: 52.7%
- Product: 52.7%

Source: Statistics Canada, Survey of Innovation and Business Strategy.

Statistics Canada / Statistique Canada   www.statcan.gc.ca   Canada

Statistics Canada

---

plan to identify deviations and to act on these deviations—correcting negative deviations and exploiting positive ones. Dashboards displaying marketing metrics will allow decisions makers to determine the next step.

Identifying Deviations
At this point of the marketing plan, dashboards and marketing metrics help evaluate the marketing plan. When a company sets goals and then compares them to actual results, it needs to research the reasons for the differences. Where plans are exceeded, the company determines the drivers of this success and identifies ways to build on them as it moves forward. When there is a shortfall (actual results less than planned—often referred to as the *planning gap*), the company has to "fill in" this planning gap with a revised marketing program and possibly revised goals.

Acting on Deviations
Generally speaking, results of a marketing plan will not be exactly as anticipated. Sometimes, the marketing program falls short of its goals. When this occurs, managers need to take corrective action. This is called *correcting a negative deviation*. For example, if Sleep Country Canada is experiencing less-than-desired sales from an Internet

campaign, it may re-evaluate where they are advertising. Alternatively, when actual results are far better than the plan called for, creative managers find ways to exploit the situation. This is called *exploiting a positive deviation*. Continuing with the example, if Sleep Country Canada's sales are more than expected from certain digital media ads, it may consider investing more money into that part of the marketing program.

Whether an organization is selling ice cream, box-spring mattresses, or the opportunity to work at the company, technology impacts its strategic marketing process. As businesses become more competitive new ideas, products and processes must be explored. The Infographic entitled "How Innovative Are Canadian Enterprises?" shows how important innovation is becoming for Canadian businesses. Organizations focused on the strategic marketing process know that the business world is changing. Not only can we review results through dashboards quicker, but our world is changing so that strategy and marketing plans need to change with it.

ask YOURSELF

1. *How would you distinguish a marketing strategy from a marketing tactic?*

2. *Describe the four components of the implementation phase of the marketing plan.*

summary... JUST THE FACTS

LO 1
- Large corporations can be complex. This complexity among business firms and not-for-profit organizations requires the division into three functional levels: the corporate, business unit, and functional levels.
- At the *corporate level*, top management directs overall strategy for the entire organization.
- The *business unit level* has business unit managers set the direction for individual products and markets.
- At the *functional level*, each business unit has marketing and other specialized activities such as finance, manufacturing, or human resources.

LO 2
- Businesses exist for various purposes and establish missions and goals. A business's mission is the statement of its direction. Goals are the targets the organization has set to be achieved within a specific time frame.
- Missions and goals are important to businesses as they help them establish direction and maintain their course.

LO 3
- In order to gauge the success of a marketing program, managers use marketing dashboards and marketing metrics to determine the performance of various elements of the marketing plan.

LO 4
- An organization develops its strategy and direction by first understanding its current status. This involves asking "Where are we now?" to assess the organization's customers, competencies, and competitors. Asking "Where do we want to go" with techniques such as portfolio analysis and market-product analysis also help develop strategy. Furthermore, questions like "How will we get there?" helps create the marketing plan.

LO 5
- The strategic marketing process involves an organization allocating its marketing mix resources to reach its target markets using three phases: planning, implementation, and evaluation.
- The planning phase of the marketing plan has three steps, each with more specific elements: situation (SWOT) analysis, market-product focus and goal setting, and marketing program.
- The implementation phase of the marketing plan has four key elements: obtaining resources, designing the marketing organization, developing schedules, and executing the marketing program.
- The evaluation phase of the marketing plan is used for internal purposes and involves comparing results with the planned targets to identify deviations and take actions to correct negative deviations and exploit positive ones.

key terms and concepts... A REFRESHER

competitive advantages
goals (objectives)
marketing dashboard
marketing metric

marketing plan
marketing strategy
marketing tactics
mission

profit
strategic marketing process
strategy

Strategic Marketing Planning Assignment. AMJ Campbell built long-term strategic partnerships through strategic planning and marketing. Review the components of the strategic planning process. Create a new business in an industry that interests you. Using the ideas from the vignette and Figure 15–5 as a guide, outline a strategic marketing plan to gain more businesses as clients.

chapter vignette... **ACTIVITY**

In this chapter's opening vignette, we learn how companies may partner with outside organizations to create strategic marketing partnerships. Answer the Reality Check questions at the end of the vignette by reviewing the strategic marketing process in detail throughout the chapter.

infographic... **DATA ANALYSIS**

The Infographic entitled "How Innovative Are Canadian Enterprises?" illustrates the focus companies have on organizational and marketing innovation. Companies need to be able to adjust to the changing market environments with new ideas, products, and processes. Identify more recent data on the subject of innovation to project what companies will be focused on in the next few years.

Building an Effective Marketing Plan

Personal finances can be challenging for Canadians. Whether it is managing on a fixed budget in college or university, or living on a fixed income in retirement, valuable advice from experts in the investment industry can help Canadians achieve their financial goals.

Courtesy of SeeWhyLearning

Decades ago, the Canadian banking industry designed services focused specifically on the future of Canada. By cultivating a youth market, banks began to reap the rewards from post-secondary graduates. With Canadians facing a challenge with growing household debt, teaching students the fundamentals of personal finances at an early age continues to be a key strategy.

SeeWhy Learning partners with financial services organizations to train talented individuals that require industry licensing. The team is engaged when an organization needs expertise outside of its employee and executive base. The delivery strategy that SeeWhy Learning employs is primarily allowing the effects of the COVID-19 pandemic to have minimal impact on its delivery channels.

The desire for Canadians to learn about personal finances has created a number of opportunities for advisory roles in the Canadian financial services industry. Moreover, this desire for knowledge and support in learning has also created opportunities for companies like SeeWhy Learning to thrive.

SeeWhy Learning offers online study tools to prepare future financial industry professionals for their qualification examinations. "We don't aim to sell our client's a product," explains director of training Andre Samuels. "We want to help them achieve a result." Similar to many organizations, SeeWhy Learning's initial marketing plan involved completing a situation analysis. Once it understood its strengths and weaknesses, the organization began developing and positioning its product. It set goals and developed a marketing program that would allow it to achieve profits. It continues to execute and evaluate its marketing success as it acquires new clients and grows as an organization.

Since 2008, See Why Learning set a simple strategy to grow the number of corporate clients it works with.

This required the company to increase the number of retail customers who independently purchase SeeWhy's tools via its online delivery channels. "Early on, we realized that large financial institutions were not receptive to cold calls," explains Cory Snyder, director of sales and service. "We needed a different strategy."

Today, SeeWhy Learning is well-known for offering quality training solutions and has obtained credibility in the marketplace. Nonetheless, the organization continues to use marketing plans to plan and structure growth for the organization.[1]

When reviewing marketing plans of organizations, there are noticeable variations in strategy from company to company. Sustainability and greening are important to many, while market share are the priority of others.

A marketing plan is an excellent document to capture the marketing strategies and tactics of this organization. In this example, we illustrate each component of the strategic marketing process, including potential examples of corrective actions. Although plans may deviate from this outline, generally there is a planning phase, an implementation phase, and an evaluation phase. In planning, marketers complete a situation analysis, decide on a market-product focus and goal setting, and then create a marketing program.

Small to medium-size businesses may be constrained by human and financial resources. Creating an effective marketing plan can allow the business to see more results in an efficient and effective manner. Following the marketing plan outline presented in Chapter 15, this section suggests some guidelines for creating an effective marketing plan.

Sample Marketing Plan for SeeWhy Learning

This is a **hypothetical** illustration of what SeeWhy Learning's marketing plan could look like. This plan is brief, given the hypothetical scenario and is not SeeWhy Learning's actual marketing plan, although it does identify key elements that are required to provide clear direction to an organization. Marketing plans can be more robust so long as the information provided enhances the strategy for the reviewer.

1. Executive Summary

The following marketing plan outlines strategies for SeeWhy Learning, a company that provides distance learning training solutions to individuals and firms in the financial services industry.

SeeWhy Learning is located outside of Toronto's financial district but is able to service clients across Canada (or even globally) since most of its training solutions are offered remotely via online deliverables. The company has bricks-and-mortar locations in Milton and Huntsville, Ontario, and also offers its employees the opportunity to work remotely. This flexibility is a competitive advantage for SeeWhy Learning in the wake of the COVID-19 health crisis.

SeeWhy uses a blended approach to learning with many of its study packages, including video lessons, a condensed study guide, key concept flash cards, and exam preparation questions. It has had success offering training and development solutions to financial services organizations with preparatory study tools for over 20 different industry examinations, including securities, insurance, and even real estate licensing exams. SeeWhy Learning also ramped up training resources to some of the larger advisory companies in the investment

SeeWhyLearning.com

industry by offering full-service solutions that include webinars and access to a dedicated study coach.

As the organization grows, profits are reinvested into the company's infrastructure. SeeWhy Learning's goal is to reach its target client businesses in a cost-effective manner.

SeeWhy Learning is certain that financial advisory businesses in Canada will continue to have challenges with training recruits in challenging industry examinations. Regulatory requirements and exams tend to become more difficult with time, not easier.

Whether it is an entry-level examination or one with more complex concepts, the SeeWhy Learning offering addresses the business issues by clearly understanding the clients' needs. Its comprehensive and flexible solution allows customers to focus on their strengths and expertise while receiving access to exceptional training.

2. Company Description

Established in 2008, SeeWhy Learning began offering preparation tools to the financial services industry, and a few years later, it expanded to also support the real estate licensing exams in Ontario. As industry examinations become more challenging, with annual updates to content, more organizations are deciding to outsource the examination preparation process. SeeWhy Learning is able to win more business with a client-centric service approach and added-value ancillary services.

According to the Government of Canada, Canada has one of "the strongest financial services sectors in the world." Target companies for SeeWhy Learning to partner with include banks, credit unions, securities dealers, and independent insurance agencies and brokers. SeeWhy Learning has expanded its team to service its growing client base. The staff is known for being able to provide support to new industry registrants in a consultative and collaborative fashion. Team members are experts in their field, but they make technical and non-technical clients alike feel comfortable with their approach.

This hypothetical marketing plan describes how SeeWhy Learning can expand its presence within the financial services industry. It involves marketing strategies and tactics appropriate for an organization needing to maximize its resources.

3. Strategic Focus and Plan

CORE VALUES   The core values of SeeWhy Learning are as follows:

1. To provide a continuously improving and learning environment for clients and team members.

2. To offer exceptional advice and service to its clients.

3. To align the success of SeeWhy Learning with its students by focusing on exam results.

MISSION   The mission of SeeWhy Learning is to become the training partner for financial services advisory businesses, tailoring training solutions to the size of the business it is working with. This involves creating a collaborative and social environment among the company and the organizations that SeeWhy Learning serves.

NON-FINANCIAL OBJECTIVES

1. SeeWhy aspired to open a satellite office in Western Canada by December 2022 to gain a greater visual presence in that market. However, this initiative will be reconsidered in light of the COVID-19 impact on the business structure and an even greater migration to distance-learning solutions. (Note: SeeWhy Learning already services these clients quite well by scheduling client meetings in Western Canada on a regular and as needed basis.)

2. Be recognized as the top training partner in the financial services industry.

FINANCIAL OBJECTIVES

1. Increase revenues by a stated percentage on an annual basis.

2. Retain a stated percentage of annual profits within the business to finance future growth. Historically, SeeWhy Learning has grown using internally generated funds instead of taking on corporate debt.

COMPETENCIES AND COMPETITIVE ADVANTAGE   The core competency of SeeWhy Learning is the expertise of its founders and the talent that they have hired. Essentially, its people are on the cutting edge of the financial services industry and are able to provide innovative, cost-effective training solutions for its clients. Given its size, SeeWhy Learning has mobility and flexibility in decision-making.

4. SWOT and Market Analysis

SWOT ANALYSIS   The SWOT analysis is summarized in Figure A–1. It shows internal and external factors that can affect the organization's success. The following statements help summarize the organization's situation:

- **SeeWhy Learning has an unmatched service offering.** Unlike its competitors, SeeWhy Learning offers a success guarantee on many of its training programs.

Figure A–1
SeeWhy Learning SWOT Analysis

Location of Factor	Type of Factor	
	Favourable	**Unfavourable**
Internal	**Strengths** • Established brand. • Superior product when compared to other training organizations. • Able to grow the client base and employees in line with corporate culture.	**Weaknesses** • Ability to grow and hire talent as demand increases. • Competitive market.
External	**Opportunities** • Thousands of prospective corporate and retail clients. • Continued growth in Canada. • Additional products to supplement post-secondary educators. • Early indications during the COVID-19 health crisis show companies embracing distance learning at an ever-increasing rate.	**Threats** • Clients' needs may become more demanding, requiring video conference training.

- **SeeWhy Learning is in a competitive marketplace.** Start-up sole proprietors offering inferior training materials on sites like Kijiji continually enter the marketplace as there is a low barrier to entry in terms of cost. SeeWhy Learning's biggest threat is that these companies could attempt to compete on price with an inferior product. To guard against this, SeeWhy provides potential clients with samples of its high-quality training materials by offering many complimentary training videos on its YouTube channel.

- **SeeWhy Learning has implemented a full-time social and multimedia team.** This allows the company to gain even more market exposure.

- **SeeWhy Learning has the opportunity to grow nationally.** With well-established customers and academic partners such as the IFSE Institute, the organization has the opportunity to expand its client base across Canada and find more target customers.

INDUSTRY ANALYSIS According to the Toronto Financial Services Alliance, "The Toronto region is home to over 40 percent of all financial services headquarters employment in Canada, including two of the world's largest life insurers."

SeeWhy Learning can continue to build its network in the Toronto area, understanding that there are more opportunities across Canada for expansion.

COMPETITIVE ANALYSIS SeeWhy Learning has several competitors, ranging from "Mom-and-Pop" type training outfits to larger organizations. Given the nature of the solutions, competitors outside of Canada may also come into play. In order to compete in this marketplace, SeeWhy Learning needs to keep each proposal client-centric. It also has to perform nimbly enough to adjust to the competitive proposals. By focusing on its local clientele, SeeWhy Learning can definitely offer the benefit of more on-site presence than some of the larger, global organizations that may begin targeting its client base.

CUSTOMER ANALYSIS The ideal clients of SeeWhy Learning are financial services advisory businesses that either are growing the number of advisors or need to recruit and train replacement advisors. A company's stage in its life cycle will help determine the breadth of services sought from SeeWhy Learning. Businesses that are in the growth stage of their life cycle are prime targets for SeeWhy Learning's services. These businesses have begun to generate income for their organization, and they need to focus on their core competencies for continued growth. By engaging SeeWhy Learning as a partner, they can expand their training expertise without having to invest as much to build their own training infrastructure.

5. Market-Product Focus and Goal Setting

ONE-YEAR MARKETING OBJECTIVES

1. Improve brand awareness, specifically within the Greater Toronto Area as well as in Western Canada.

2. Increase market share, specifically in Toronto, where the majority of target customers have head office locations.

MARKETING AND PRODUCT OBJECTIVES SeeWhy Learning plans to take full advantage of its market potential in Canada while also considering expansion into the U.S. market. This plan is outlined in three areas below:

- **Established markets:** SeeWhy Learning will service and grow its existing client base with the intent of expanding its offering into new leading-edge training services.
- **New markets:** SeeWhy Learning will build the foundation for expansion into the U.S. This will involving building out prospective client lists while servicing its existing client base.
- **New services:** SeeWhy Learning will expand its exam preparatory service offering to include mobile technology.

POINTS OF DIFFERENCE SeeWhy Learning will have three distinguishing characteristics when compared to its competitors:

1. A training partnership philosophy.
2. A success-based guarantee on specific training packages.
3. Easy access to the co-founders and/or senior staff.

POSITIONING In the exam preparatory marketplace, there are three areas that add value to clients: (1) operational excellence (cost-effective training solutions); (2) product leadership (best product); and (3) customer intimacy (truly customized service, based on deep customer knowledge). While it is imperative to be competent in all three disciplines, it is impossible to be viewed as superior in all three, since the market inherently distinguishes among all three. SeeWhy Learning is positioning itself to offer more customer intimacy than the larger consulting firms, while having greater operational excellence and product leadership than other consulting firms of its size. The company's ability to be nimble, while still offering advice at the same level of expertise of large consulting firms, positions it perfectly to the businesses it wants to serve.

6. Marketing Program

PRODUCT STRATEGY SeeWhy Learning will service and grow its existing client base with the intent of expanding its training offering into new leading-edge digital services.

PRICE STRATEGY SeeWhy Learning plans to offer at-market pricing for its services. It will not price-match

firms of similar or smaller size and instead will continue to focus on quality along with its unprecedented "If you don't pass, you don't pay" guarantee. For bids against larger firms, the pricing strategy is to provide value-added services while maintaining a firm price. This is especially true when pursuing medium-size businesses with reasonable brand recognition. SeeWhy is able to offer more competitive pricing for corporate clients that represent significant volume.

PROMOTION STRATEGY There are a number of initiatives that SeeWhy Learning can undertake to promote its business. These initiatives include pull and push marketing strategies that will enhance personal selling. Below are four initiatives to focus on:

1. Website upgrade
2. High-quality video production
3. YouTube channel
4. LinkedIn

PLACE STRATEGY SeeWhy Learning is online, and in a post-COVID-19 world, it will continue to thrive with its online distribution strategy.

7. Sales Forecast

As a privately held corporation, SeeWhy Learning does not publicly report sales and profitability figures. However, it reportedly strives to grow annual sales by a stated percentage per annum.

8. Implementation Plan

MARKETING ORGANIZATION Each quarter, in his capacity as sales director, Cory Snyder will lead his sales team to identify and reach out to five prospective corporate clients, with the goal of building a client relationship with at least one of them. These are usually warm leads as the sales team identifies companies whose employees are already purchasing SeeWhy Learning tools through its retail delivery channels. It turns the contact from a "sales call" to an opportunity to save the company's employees money through corporate pricing. During these sales calls, academic director Andre Samuels is responsible for listening to the client's needs and then working with the training team to offer an effective solution.

MARKETING BUDGET Figure A–2 presents the marketing budget for year one of the plan implementation.

Figure A–2
Marketing Budget
The marketing budget for year one is limited to $82,500.

Marketing Costs	Budget
Website upgrade	$20,000
Content production costs (e.g., video)	$40,000
Advertising - print	$ 5,000
Advertising - online	$ 7,500
Give-away items	$ 5,000
Entertainment	$ 5,000
Marketing Budget - Year One	$82,500

MARKETING ACTIVITIES PLAN The marketing activities plan will consist of the various activities outlined in the promotion strategy and the personal selling activities of the sales team. All marketing materials and media placements need to be ready by December 2021.

9. Evaluation Plan

SeeWhy Learning will prepare an annual budget. Actual sales and expenses will be compared to the figures, and variances will be investigated and identified. Weekly sales activities and successes will also be tracked.

Glossary

actual product   The physical good or the services that a consumer purchases.

adoption curve   The sequential diffusion and acceptance of an innovation into the market by consumers.

advertising   Paid form of media used for non-personal communication to consumers about an organization, good, service, or idea.

analytics   The process of taking metrics data and applying smart thinking and technology to gain actionable insights that can help make better business decisions.

attitude   Tendency to respond to something in a consistently favourable or unfavourable way.

augmented product   The additional features and attributes that accompany a product.

baby boomers   Generation of people born between 1946 and 1965.

back translation   Retranslating a word or phrase back into the original language by a different interpreter to catch errors.

banner ads   Online ads that can stretch across the top of a web page or be formatted in various sizes, such as leaderboards, rectangles, big boxes, and skyscrapers.

behaviouristics   How and why consumers buy and use a product, including the desired product benefits, how frequently they buy, where they buy, and whether consumers are brand loyal in their purchase behaviour.

beliefs   Consumer's perceptions of how a product or brand performs.

binge viewing   Watching complete or partial seasons of TV shows over a few days.

blog   A website in the form of an online diary that is used by organizations and individuals to post updates that include personal opinions, activities, and experiences with readers able to subscribe and post comments.

Bluetooth   Low-power radio waves that are transmitted though beacons and wirelessly transfer text, images, and audio or video data through a local hotspot to Bluetooth-enabled and -activated devices.

brand   A name, phrase, symbol, or design uniquely given by a company to a product to distinguish it from the competition.

brand development index (BDI)   An index that shows how well a brand's sales are developed in a region relative to the region's population size.

brand equity   The value of a brand that results from the favourable exposure, interactions, associations, and experiences that consumers have with a brand over time.

brand extension   When new goods or services are introduced under an existing flagship brand name.

brand loyalty   Favourable attitude toward and consistent purchase of a single brand over time; the degree of target market commitment toward a brand over time that results in varying levels of purchase commitment.

brand personality   A set of human characteristics associated with a brand.

branded entertainment   The creation of an entertainment program, such as a TV episode, that is highly focused on a brand in exchange for payment.

breadth of product line   The variety of different items a store carries.

break-even analysis   Examines the relationship between total revenue and total cost to determine profitability at different levels of output.

brokers   Independent firms or individuals whose main function is to bring buyers and sellers together to make sales.

business analysis   Financial projections on the impact of bringing the new product to market and selling it in the future.

business market   Products that are purchased either to run a business or to be used as a component in another product or service.

business marketing   Marketing to firms, governments, or non-profit organizations.

business products   Products that are purchased either to run a business or to be used as a component in another product or service.

buy classes   Three types of organizational buying situations: straight rebuy, modified rebuy, or new buy.

buying centre   Group of people in an organization who participate in the buying process.

central business district   The oldest retail setting, the community's downtown area.

channel conflict   Arises when one channel member believes another channel member is engaged in behaviour that prevents it from achieving its goals.

commercialization   When the new product is brought to market with full-scale production, sales, and marketing support.

common short codes (CSC)   Dedicated short messaging codes of typically five to six digits that are used to trigger subscriptions, donations, alerts, or downloads, or to access promotional content.

community shopping centre   Retail location that typically has one primary store and 20 to 40 smaller outlets, serving a population of consumers within a 2- to 5-km drive.

competitive advantages   Those characteristics of a product or service that make it superior to competing substitutes.

competitive forces Alternative products that can satisfy a specific market's needs.

concept tests External evaluations of a new product idea, rather than the actual product itself.

consumer behaviour Actions a person takes when purchasing and using products and services.

consumer market Goods, services, and ideas that a person can purchase, use, or support for personal use.

consumer products Products purchased for their personal use by the ultimate consumer.

consumer promotions Short-term marketing tools used to encourage immediate consumer purchase.

content marketing Creating and sharing expertise, information, or branded content that is designed to inform and engage with tools such as research papers, e-books, infographics, how-to videos, blogs, webinars, e-newsletters, case studies, and events that can readily be found with search engines.

continuous innovations New products with more than just a minor product improvement, but that do not require radical changes by the consumer.

convenience products Items purchased frequently that are inexpensive and require minimum risk and shopping effort.

copyrights Used to legally protect original written works, sound recordings, or forms of communication from being copied by others.

core product The fundamental benefit that a consumer derives from having the product.

corporate social responsibility (CSR) When organizations voluntarily consider the well-being of society by taking responsibility for how their businesses impact consumers, customers, suppliers, employees, shareholders, communities, the environment, and society in general.

corporate websites Websites that provide company and brand information to consumers and the media.

cost per acquisition (CPA) The cost of acquiring a new follower or sale.

cost per click (CPC) The cost of getting someone to click on a link or ad.

cost per thousand (CPM) The cost of reaching 1,000 people.

cross-channel shopper An online consumer who researches products online and then purchases them at a retail store.

cross-cultural analysis Study of similarities and differences among consumers in two or more societies.

cultural symbols Objects, ideas, or processes that represent a particular group of people or society.

culture A set of values, ideas, and attitudes that are learned and shared among the members of a group.

Customer Advocacy Funnel A communications approach that takes consumers from initial product awareness through to brand advocacy.

customer experience management (CEM) Managing customer interactions with the goal of increasing satisfaction and loyalty.

customer lifetime value The potential sales that will be generated by a customer if that customer remains loyal to that company for a lifetime.

customer relationship management (CRM) The overall process of building and maintaining profitable customer relationships by delivering superior customer value and satisfaction.

customer value proposition The unique combination of benefits received by targeted buyers that will satisfy their needs; includes quality, price, convenience, delivery, and both before-sale and after-sale service.

customs Norms and expectations about the way people do things in a specific country or culture.

dashboards The visualization of data and key performance indicators using graphs, charts, and numbers so that numerical information tells a story that is insightful and easy to use and understand.

data The facts and figures related to the project that are divided into two main parts: secondary data and primary data.

data mining The processing of large amounts of data using sophisticated software to find insightful correlations and patterns that lead to better business decisions.

data warehouse A central repository of an organization's electronically stored data.

database marketing The use of databases to customize communications to customers and potential customers for the purpose of promoting a product or service.

delete When a company discontinues a product.

demand curve Graph relating quantity sold and price, which shows how many units will be sold at a given price.

demographics The statistical data on a population according to characteristics such as gender, age, ethnicity, income, education, and occupation.

depth of product line The assortment of products within each product line.

derived demand Demand for industrial products and services driven by demand for consumer products and services.

descriptive analytics A type of analytics that focuses on *what has happened*.

development The new product idea is turned into a prototype for further consumer research and manufacturing tests.

digital marketing Using digital technology to reach consumers through computers, gaming devices, out-of-home electronic screens, or mobile devices such as smartphones and tablets.

direct competitors Similar products sold in the same category.

direct response marketing A tool designed to communicate with consumers in a targeted and personalized way using either traditional or online approaches.

discretionary income Money that consumers have left after paying taxes and buying necessities.

disintermediation Vertical channel conflict that arises when a channel

member bypasses another member and sells directly to consumers.

display advertising The use of online ads with graphics or animation that are placed on websites.

disposable income Balance of income left after paying taxes; income that is used for spending and savings.

Do Not Call List (DNCL) Gives customers the ability to elect to not receive telemarketing calls on cellphones and landline phones by registering the numbers of their communication devices.

dual distribution Arrangement whereby a firm reaches buyers by using two or more different types of channels for the same basic product.

dumping Occurs when a firm sells a product in a foreign country below its domestic prices or below its actual cost.

durable good An item that lasts over an extended number of uses.

earned media The free publicity secured through unpaid media mentions and consumers who spread the word through word of mouth or the Internet.

economy The collective income, expenditures, and resources that affect the cost of running a business or a household.

electronic data interchange (EDI) A computer-to-computer exchange of business documents from a retailer to a supplier and back.

electronic marketing channels Channels that use the Internet to make goods and services available to consumers or business buyers.

e-mail marketing The use of e-mail to market products.

e-marketplaces Online trading communities that bring together buyers and supplier organizations.

engagement metrics Measures how much and how often consumers interact with social media content.

environmental scan The process of continually acquiring information on events occurring outside an organization to identify trends, opportunities, and threats to a business.

event marketing The creation or involvement of a brand in an experience or occasion that will heighten its

awareness, create positive associations, and generate a desired response.

exchange The trade of things of value between buyers and sellers so that each benefits.

exclusive distribution Only one retail outlet in a specific geographical area carries the firm's products.

experiential marketing Creating opportunities for consumers to directly interact with brands.

experiment In marketing, changing a variable involved in a customer purchase to find out what happens.

fad Novelty products with very short product life cycles that experience immediate rapid growth, followed by an equally rapid decline.

family brand When a company uses a brand name to cover a number of different product categories.

family life cycle A family's progression from formation to retirement, with each phase bringing distinct needs and purchasing behaviours.

fashion product The life cycle for fashion is relatively short and cyclical, going from introduction to decline within two to three years, only to resurface again a few years later.

feature phone Cellphone that is Internet-enabled and that allows for e-mailing, texting, and browsing but cannot download or use apps.

fixed cost Firm's expenses that are stable and do not change with the quantity of product that is produced and sold.

fluctuating demand Demand for business products and services fluctuates more than demand for consumer products and services.

focus group A qualitative research technique where a small group of people (usually six to ten) meet for a few hours with a trained moderator to discuss predetermined areas.

form of ownership Distinguishes retail outlets on the basis of whether individuals, corporate chains, or contractual systems own the outlet.

franchising Contractual arrangement in which a parent company (the franchiser) allows an individual or firm (the franchisee) to operate a certain type of

business under an established name and according to specific rules set by the franchiser.

frequency The number of times the target audience is exposed to the communication vehicle or the communication message.

generation X People born between 1966 and 1980.

generation Y People born between 1981 and 2000. This generation is also referred to as *millennials*.

generation Z People born in 2001 and beyond.

generic brand A product that has no branding and is produced as a cheap alternative to a manufacturer's brand and to branded private-label products.

geofencing Uses global positioning system (GPS) to trigger an event to happen when a device enters a certain geographic area.

geographics Where a target market lives, using variables such as country, region, province, city size, and population density, such as urban, suburban, or rural.

global brands Brands that are sold in a variety of international markets and that enjoy wide recognition in these markets.

goals (objectives) Targets of performance to be achieved within a specific time frame.

good A product you can touch and own.

greenwashing The deceptive use of marketing practices to give the impression that a good, service, or organization is environmentally friendly.

grey market Situations where products are sold through unauthorized channels of distribution.

gross domestic product (GDP) The total dollar value of all goods and services produced in a country within a specified time period.

gross income Total amount of money made in one year by a person, household, or family unit, including taxes.

harvest When a company keeps a product but reduces marketing support in an attempt to reap some minor profits.

high-learning product Significant consumer education is required for these products, which have an extended introductory period.

hybrid apps Apps that combine the functionality of native apps with the flexibility of web apps.

idea A concept that typically looks for support.

idea generation Developing a pool of new product ideas.

idle production capacity When the supply of a service exceeds its demand.

inbound marketing When consumers find a product and its messaging by using online techniques that marketers facilitate, including search engine optimization, pay-per-click ads, and the use of social media to connect with consumers.

in-depth interviews Detailed interviews where a researcher questions an individual at length in a free-flowing conversational style in order to discover information that may help solve a marketing problem.

indirect competitors Products competing for the same buying dollar in a slightly different but related category.

individual brand When a company uses a brand name solely for a specific product category.

individualized marketing One-to-one marketing that involves customizing offers and, in some cases, products to fit individual needs.

inelastic demand Demand for products does not change because of increases or decreases in price.

inflation When the cost to produce and buy products and services gets higher as prices rise.

influencer marketing The practice of focusing on the identification and recruitment of influencers to advocate a company's products, services, and brands rather than focusing exclusively on prospective buyers.

information technology Includes all of the computing resources that collect, store, and analyze data.

integrated marketing communications (IMC) A communications approach that coordinates all promotional activities to provide a consistent message to a target audience.

intensive distribution A firm tries to place its products or services in as many outlets as possible.

interest rates The amount charged as a fee for borrowing money, normally expressed as a percentage per year.

intermediaries Individuals or firms performing a role in the marketing channel, involved in making a product available.

Internet of Things (IoT) The network of products embedded with connectivity-enabled electronics.

intertype competition Competition between very dissimilar types of retail outlets.

involvement Personal, social, and economic significance of a purchase to the consumer.

just-in-time (JIT) inventory system A system designed to deliver less merchandise on a more frequent basis than traditional inventory systems.

key performance indicators (KPIs) Types of metric that are used to evaluate performance.

lead generation The requests for additional information that result from direct response marketing.

leaderboards Banner ads that stretch across the top of a web page.

learning Behaviours that result from repeated experience or reasoning.

level of service The degree of service provided to the customer by self-, limited-, and full-service retailers.

line extension The addition of a new item to an already existing product line.

logistics Activities that focus on getting the right amount of the right products to the right place at the right time at the lowest possible cost.

low-learning product Little consumer education is required, resulting in a short introductory stage for the product.

loyalty programs Programs specifically designed for customer retention.

macroeconomic forces The state of a country's economy as a whole as indicated by its growth rates, inflation rates, unemployment rates, and consumer confidence indexes.

manufacturer's brand A brand owned and produced by the manufacturer.

manufacturers' agents Work for several producers and carry non-competitive, complementary merchandise in an exclusive territory.

market Potential consumers with both the willingness and the ability to buy.

market segmentation The aggregation of prospective buyers into groups that have common needs and respond similarly to marketing programs.

market share The percentage of sales volume for a product, relative to the entire sales volume of the category in which it competes; ratio of a firm's sales to the total sales of all firms in the industry.

marketing The process of planning and managing goods, services, or ideas to meet consumer needs and organizational objectives. It includes the conception of these products and the pricing, promotion, and distribution programs designed to make a profit and generate revenue or support for an organization.

marketing channel The set of individuals or firms involved in the process of making a product available.

marketing communication agencies Broad-spectrum integrated agencies or specialist agencies that provide marketers with expertise on how best to communicate messages to their audiences.

marketing communication tools Advertising, public relations, sales promotion, direct response marketing, event marketing and sponsorship, product placement and branded entertainment, personal selling, online marketing, social media marketing, and mobile marketing.

marketing dashboard A visual computer display of essential marketing information.

marketing metric A measure of the value or trend of a marketing activity or result.

marketing mix The 4 Ps—product, price, place, and promotion.

marketing orientation   Focusing organizational efforts to collect and use information about customers' needs to create customer value.

marketing plan   Road map for the marketing activities of an organization for a specified future period of time.

marketing process   The process of (1) identifying consumer needs, (2) managing the marketing mix to meet these needs, and (3) realizing profits.

marketing research   The process of defining a marketing problem and opportunity, systematically collecting and analyzing information, and recommending actions.

marketing strategy   Means by which a marketing goal is to be achieved.

marketing tactics   Detailed day-to-day operational decisions essential to the overall success of marketing strategies.

markup   The difference between selling price and cost, usually expressed as a percentage of cost.

mass marketing   Marketing a product with broad appeal to the entire market without any product or marketing differentiation.

matrix 2D barcode   A two-dimensional response code that, when scanned by a mobile barcode reader or app, provides additional information, launches websites, prompts downloads, sends text messages, or deploys messages.

measures of success   Criteria or standards used in evaluating proposed solutions to the problem.

merchandise mix   How many different types of products a store carries and in what assortment.

merchant wholesalers   Independently owned firms that take title to the merchandise they handle.

metrics   Numeric data that are collected and grouped to track performance, often presented in spreadsheets and dashboards.

microeconomic forces   The supply and demand of goods and services and how this is impacted by individual, household, and company decisions to purchase.

microsites   Promotional websites created for short-term promotional purposes, often allowing consumers to enter contests and access promotional information.

millennials   People born between 1981 and 2000. This generation is also referred to as *generation Y*.

minor innovations   Minor product modifications that require no adjustments on behalf of the consumer.

mission   Statement of the organization's purpose and direction.

mobile applications (apps)   Software programs that can be downloaded on a smartphone or tablet to engage consumers with information, entertainment, or interactivity.

mobile check-in services   When consumers check into locations using apps to post their whereabouts and to receive offers from local merchants on their mobile device.

mobile discovery   The use of mobile apps to help find local businesses, services, and attractions.

mobile e-mail   E-mail sent and/or received using a mobile device.

mobile marketing   A set of practices that enables organizations to communicate and engage with their audiences in an interactive and relevant manner through any mobile device or network.

mobile messaging   Comes in the form of common short codes (CSC), short messaging services (SMS), multimedia messaging services (MMS), e-mail messaging, in-person voice phone calls, and voice messaging.

mobile web   A website designed for the smaller screens of mobile devices.

mobile web apps   Websites designed to simulate an app experience by adding a shortcut that runs off a browser on a mobile device.

monopolistic competition   Type of competition where a large number of sellers compete with each other, offering customers similar or substitute products

monopoly   When only one company sells in a particular market.

motivation   Energizing force that stimulates behaviour to satisfy a need.

multichannel marketing   Blending of different communication and delivery channels that are mutually reinforcing in attracting, retaining, and building relationships with customers.

multichannel retailers   Use a combination of traditional store formats and non-store formats such as catalogues and online retailing.

multimedia messaging services (MMS)   Standard text messaging services that include audio, video, or images.

native apps   Apps downloaded from app stores that are specifically created to be hosted and run on a mobile device.

near field communications (NFC)   The two-way radio communication between smartphones and smartphone-type devices to transfer images, documents, or monetary transactions when the two devices touch or are within a few inches of each other.

need   Occurs when a person feels deprived of basic necessities.

new product development process   Sequence of steps that a firm takes to develop a new product idea and take it to market.

new product development strategy   Setting the new product strategic direction for the company as a whole, and the precise objectives for the project at hand.

niche marketing   Marketing a limited product line to a narrow but profitable segment of the market that is of marginal interest to major competitors.

non-durable good   An item that does not last and is consumed only once, or for a limited number of times.

non-probability sampling   Selecting a sample so that the chance of selecting a particular element of a population is either unknown or zero.

North American Industry Classification System (NAICS)   Provides common industry definitions for Canada, Mexico, and the United States.

objectives   Specific, measurable, and achievable goals.

observational research   Obtained by watching how people behave, in person or by using a machine to record the event.

off-price retailing   Selling brand-name merchandise at lower than regular prices.

oligopoly Type of competition that occurs when a few companies control a market.

omnibus survey The voluntary participation of respondents in routine research surveys that allow marketers to add a small number of questions to an existing survey to receive cost-effective data.

online behavioural advertising (OBA) The use of web-based programs to track consumers' online activity so as to deliver ads that correspond to browsing interests.

online research bulletin boards Private online static forums, without real-time dialogue, where respondents can post their responses to questions posed by researchers.

online research communities The use of consumer groups, brought together privately in an online environment, to answer questions, respond to ideas, and collaborate with researchers in real time.

opinion leaders Individuals who have social influence over others.

optimization metrics Data that can point to adjustments or changes that should be made to your social media program.

organizational buyers Manufacturers, wholesalers, retailers, and government agencies that buy goods and services for their own use or for resale.

organizational buying behaviour Process by which organizations determine the need for goods and then choose among alternative suppliers.

outbound marketing Marketers seek out consumers by widely broadcasting messages using advertising, direct mail, e-mail marketing, telemarketing, and personal-selling approaches.

out-of-home (OOH) advertising Casually referred to as *outdoor;* reaches consumers outside the home in outdoor locations, in transit, or in commercial or business locations.

owned media The media channels that a company controls, either fully or partially, such as a website, microsite, or social media page that is used to directly communicate with consumers.

paid media The media time purchased so that messages can be disseminated through channels that are controlled by others.

panel A large sample of respondents that voluntarily complete questionnaires on a regular basis so that researchers can assess changes in behaviour and attitudes.

Pareto's Rule The concept that 80 percent of a brand's sales come from 20 percent of its customers.

partnership marketing The creation of formal associations between brands that will result in incremental business for both brands that could not have been achieved separately.

patents Used to legally protect new technologies, unique processes, or formulations from usage by other companies.

pay-per-click advertising (PPC) Ads that appear in response to keyword triggers on search engines, as well as on some websites, blogs, and social media sites, where the advertiser pays only when the ad is clicked.

perceived risk Anxiety felt when a consumer cannot anticipate possible negative outcomes of a purchase.

perception Process by which someone selects, organizes, and interprets information to create a meaningful picture of the world

perfect competition Type of competition where there are many sellers with nearly identical products and little differentiation.

permission-based e-mail When a recipient chooses to receive e-mail from a marketer.

personal selling The two-way flow of communication between a buyer and seller, often face-to-face or facilitated through communication devices, to influence an individual and group purchase decision.

personality A person's character traits that influence behavioural responses.

personas Character descriptions of a typical customer in the form of fictional character narratives, complete with images that capture the personalities, values, attitudes, beliefs, demographics, and expected interactions with a brand.

place Distribution channels, retail formats, and merchandising used to sell a product.

positioning maps Visual representations of how products in a category are positioned in consumers' minds; also known as *perceptual maps.*

positioning statement A formalized statement that identifies the image a branded product represents in the market and what sets it apart from the competition.

power centre Large shopping strip with multiple anchor stores, a convenient location, and a supermarket.

predictive analytics The combination of data from varied sources to reveal patterns that are modelled to predict *what might happen* in the future.

predictive modelling Based on statistical models that use data mining and probability analysis to foretell outcomes.

press conference A planned event where representatives of the media are invited to an informational meeting with the company.

press release An announcement written by an organization and sent to the media.

price What is exchanged for a product, including theexpected regular retail or sale price.

pricing constraints Factors that limit the range of price a firm may set.

pricing objectives Expectations that specify the role of price in an organization's marketing and strategic plans.

primary data Data that is original and specifically collected for a project.

private-label brand Otherwise known as a store brand, a brand owned by a retailer that contracts its manufacturing to major suppliers, and then sells the product at its own retail stores, under its own store-brand name.

probability sampling Selecting a sample so that each element of a population has a specific known chance of being selected.

product Attributes that make up a good, a service, or an idea, including product design, features, colour, packaging, warranty, and service levels.

product differentiation Positioning a product to a target group so that it appears distinct from competitive offerings.

product life cycle The stages that a new product goes through, starting with introduction and evolving into growth, maturity, and decline.

product line A group of similar products that are closely related because they satisfy a similar need and are directed at the same general target market.

product line depth The assortment of different versions of each product sold within its product lines.

product line length The total number of products or brands in a product line.

product mix All the product lines marketed by a company.

product mix width The number of different product lines offered by a company.

product placement The inclusion of a product in a movie or TV program in return for payment.

product positioning The impression of the product you want to establish in consumers' minds relative to their needs and the competition.

production orientation Focusing organizational efforts on the manufacture of goods.

profit The excess of revenues over costs, the reward to a business for the risk it undertakes in offering a product for sale.

profit equation Profit = total revenue – total cost.

promotion Communication tools needed to inform consumers about a product, including advertising, public relations, sales promotion, direct response, event marketing, sponsorship, online approaches, and personal selling.

promotional mix The selection of promotional tools used to communicate with a target market.

promotional websites Promotional websites focus on showcasing products and services

psychographics Understanding consumers' attitudes to life, values, personalities, general interests, opinions, and activities.

public relations A communications tool that seeks to influence the opinions and attitudes of target groups through the use of unpaid media exposure; targets the media in an attempt to generate positive publicity for a company, product, or individual.

publicity A non-personal form of communication that appears in the media and is not paid for directly by the organization.

pull strategy When marketers focus communication efforts on ultimate consumers to build awareness, trial, and demand for a product.

purchase decision process Stages that a buyer passes through when making choices about which products or services to buy.

push notifications Any content sent to a mobile device that a customer must opt in to receive from a marketer.

push strategy When marketers focus communication on the distribution channel to gain support from retailers, distributors, and wholesalers.

questionnaire Obtaining information by posing standardized questions through surveys that can be conducted in person, through the mail, on the telephone, or through the Internet.

radical innovations New products that involve the introduction of a product that is entirely new and innovative to the market.

reach The number of people who are exposed to a communication vehicle or message; is presented as percentage of the total number of people in a target audience.

recession A time of slow economic activity with two consecutive periods of negative growth.

reference group A group of people who influence a person's attitudes, values, and behaviour.

regional shopping centres Consist of 50 to 150 stores that typically attract customers who live within a 5- to 15-km range; often containing two or three anchor stores.

regulations Restrictions placed on marketing practices by government and industry associations.

relationship marketing When organizations create long-term links with customers, employees, suppliers, and other partners to increase loyalty and customer retention.

repositioning Changing the place a product occupies in consumers' minds relative to competitive products to more accurately meet consumer needs.

retailing All activities involved in selling, renting, and providing goods and services to ultimate consumers for personal, family, or household use.

retailing mix The goods and services, pricing, physical distribution, and communications tactics chosen by a store.

reverse auction Occurs when a buyer communicates a need for something and would-be suppliers bid in competition with each other.

reverse logistics A process of reclaiming recyclable and reusable materials, returns, and reworks from the point of consumption or use for repair, remanufacturing, redistribution, or disposal.

RFM analysis The rating of customers on the basis of how recently products were purchased (recency), how often products were purchased (frequency), and the dollar value of the transactions (monetary value)

sales orientation Focusing organizational efforts on selling as many products as possible.

sales promotion A communications tool that provides short-term incentives to generate interest in a product or cause and encourages purchase or support.

sampling The process of gathering data from a subset of the total population rather than from all members of that particular group.

scrambled merchandising Offering several unrelated product lines in a single retail store.

screening and evaluation Reduces the list of ideas down to a list of promising concepts.

search engine marketing (SEM) Includes the use of search engine optimization and pay-per-click advertising to market on search engines.

search engine optimization (SEO) Ensuring that websites are written, indexed, and coded so that they are highly rated and ranked by the search engines.

secondary data Facts and figures that have already been recorded by a third party.

selective distribution A firm selects a few retail outlets in a specific geographical area to carry its products.

selling agents Represent a single producer and are responsible for the entire marketing function of that producer.

service A product that is intangible; an activity, benefit, or satisfaction that you cannot touch.

service continuum A range from tangible goods to intangible services.

share of wallet The percentage of a customer's purchases that a company has in a specific product category.

shopping products Items that require comparison-shopping between different brands and an investment of shopping time.

short messaging services (SMS) Standard text messaging that uses protocols of 160 characters per message.

showrooming Using mobile devices in-store to check online competitive product reviews and prices, which results in the online purchase of a cheaper product.

shrinkage Breakage and theft of merchandise by customers and employees.

situation analysis Taking stock of a firm's or product's past performance, where it is now, and where it is headed.

smartphone An advanced cellphone that has similar functionality to a personal computer in addition to taking pictures, playing music and movies, navigating with GPS, and using apps to enhance its features and capabilities.

social analytics The real-time measurement, interaction, and analysis of social media to assess social media campaign performance, message resonation and amplification, consumer sentiment, and common themes.

social listening Research that monitors public online consumer conversations on social media sites such as social networks, blogs, and forums.

social media A form of online media that allows members to create their own network of friends and contacts to share comments, articles, opinions, videos, and images as a form of self-expression.

social media analytics The real-time measurement, interaction, and analysis of social media to assess social media campaign performance, message resonation and amplification, consumer sentiment, and common themes.

social media marketing Reaching out to consumers online through social media networks.

social media monitoring The monitoring of brand mentions, consumer sentiment, buzz, and engagement on the Internet.

social media release A multimedia, online press-release platform that includes video, text, and images, as well as social media buttons for sharing on social networks and comment areas where viewers can leave comments.

social networks Online websites that allow members to create a network of friends and contacts to share messages, comments, videos, and images as a form of self-expression.

social TV Watching TV programming while adding comments on social networks.

societal marketing concept Marketing programs that focus on the consumer *and* the well-being of society.

socio-cultural forces Cultural values, ideas, and attitudes, as well as society's morals and beliefs.

spam The dissemination of unsolicited electronic messages to recipients.

specialty products Items for special occasions that require a specific product or brand and require considerable time and effort to purchase.

sponsorship When an advertiser pays a fee in exchange for inclusion in an event, involvement in its advertising opportunities, or exposure within the event itself.

strategic alliance Long-term arrangement between companies with similar values and marketing objectives that extends beyond short-term promotional offers into long-term formal business agreements.

strategic marketing process Approach whereby an organization allocates its marketing mix.

strategy An organization's long-term course of action that delivers a unique customer experience while achieving its goals.

strip location A cluster of stores serving people who live within a 5- to 10-minute drive.

sub-brand A brand that uses the family brand name as well as its own brand name and identity so that it can take on the strengths of the parent brand but also differentiate itself.

subcultures Subgroups within a larger culture that have unique values, ideas, and attitudes.

supply chain Sequence of firms that perform activities required to create and deliver a product to consumers or industrial users.

supply chain management Integration and organization of information and logistics activities across firms in a supply chain for the purpose of creating and delivering goods and services that provide value to consumers.

supply partnership Relationship between a buyer and supplier that adopt mutually beneficial objectives, policies, and procedures.

SWOT analysis The assessment of how well an organization or brand is servicing its businesses and target markets by evaluating its internal strengths and weaknesses, andits external opportunities and threats.

syndicated studies A hybrid of primary and secondary research whereby the cost of a research study is shared among clients and made available at a price to interested parties.

target market The specific group or segment(s) of existing and potential consumers to which marketers direct their marketing efforts.

target market profile A description of the target market that contains specific information about the target group in four areas: geographics, demographics, psychographics, and behaviouristics.

technological forces Inventions from science or engineering research.

telemarketing   Using the telephone to interact with and sell directly to consumers.

test market   An in-market localized approach, or short-term online destination, used to test the success of promotional offers, new services, or new product launches.

test marketing   Offering a new product for sale on a limited basis in a defined geographic area to assess its success.

total cost   Total expenses incurred by a firm in producing and marketing a product; total cost is the sum of fixed cost and variable costs.

total revenue   Total money received from the sale of a product.

touch points   Any situation in which a customer comes into contact with a brand or company.

trade promotions   Short-term promotional tools used to generate support with wholesalers, distributors, or retailers.

trademarks   Used by people or organizations to protect brand images, names, slogans, and designs from usage by others.

traditional auction   Occurs when a seller puts an item up for sale and would-be buyers bid in competition with each other.

traffic generation   The visits to a location or website that result from direct response marketing.

transactional websites   Electronic storefronts focused on converting an online browser into an online buyer.

unemployment rate   Measures the share of the labour force that is not working.

unsought products   Unknown items or those of no interest to the purchaser.

user-generated content (UGC) Original online content that has been created by users in the form of blogs, posts, images, audio, or video.

value   The ratio of perceived benefits to price.

variable cost   Sum of the expenses of the firm that vary directly with the quantity of products that is produced and sold.

vertical marketing systems Professionally managed and centrally coordinated marketing channels designed to achieve channel economies and maximum marketing impact.

virtual services   Services that exist only online and have no person-to-person interaction.

vlog   A blog posted in video format.

want   A need that is shaped by a person's knowledge, culture, and personality.

wearables   Devices that can be worn on the body or on clothes.

web analytics   The measurement and analysis of website data, looking at elements such as page views, time on site, bounce rate, new visitors, returning visitors, and referral traffic.

WiFi hotspots   Areas set up with free Internet access in which once customers log in to use the free WiFi, they can be sent location-specific content.

wiki   A collaborative website that uses an application with which multiple users can create, add, edit, or delete content.

word of mouth   People influencing each other in personal conversations.

word-of-mouth marketing   The spread of positive messages about a product by listening to consumers, identifying influential individuals that can spread the word, and making it easier for them to do so.

Chapter Sources

Chapter 1

Data Box: Loblaw Community Giving in 2018

Source: *Our Purpose: Live Life Well: 2018 Corporate Social Responsibility Report*, Loblaw Companies Limited, accessed September 2019 at http://www.loblaw.ca/en/responsibility/reports.html.

Data Box: Device Reach in Canada, US, and UK

Source: "2018 Canada Digital Future in Focus," comScore, March 25, 2020, https://www.comscore.com/Insights/Presentations-and-Whitepapers/2018/Global-Digital-Future-in-Focus-2018-Canada-Edition.

Chapter 2

Marketing NewsFlash: Chinese Consumers in Canada

Source: Toneguzzi, Mario, "Chinese Consumers Drive Luxury Retail Growth in Canada," *Retail Insider*, December 2019, https://www.retail-insider.com/retail-insider/2019/12/chinese-consumers-drive-luxury-retail-growth-in-canada-study.

Data Box: Five Largest Countries (population in millions)

Source: World Population Review, "2020 World Population," accessed January 2020, http://worldpopulationreview.com/.

Chapter 4

Chapter Opening Vignette

Source: Paul Schumlich personal interview, 2019; "Aquaponics Market worth $1.4 billion by 2025-Exclusive Report by Meticulous Research." (2019). Meticulous Research. Retrieved from https://www.globenewswire.com/news-release/2019/07/13/1882266/0/en/Aquaponics-Market-worth-1-4-billion-by-2025-Exclusive-Report-by-Meticulous-Research.html; Hesterman, O., & Horan, D. (2017). "The demand for 'local' food is growing - here's why investors should pay attention." Retrieved from https://www.businessinsider.com/the-demand-for-local-food-is-growing-2017-4; Report on local food demand in the Calgary region. (2015). Alberta Agriculture and Forestry. Retrieved from https://www1.agric.gov.ab.ca/$Department/deptdocs.nsf/all/explore16031/$FILE/LocalFoodDe mand-CalgaryFINAL.pdf.

Figure 4–6: Mistakes to avoid when writing survey questions

Source: Sam Lloyd, "The 10 Commandments for Writing Outstanding Survey Questions," Qualtrics, January 28, 2013, https://www.qualtrics.com/blog/good-survey-questions/; Tara Wildt, "Marketing Research 101: Six Common Mistakes in Survey Questionnaire Design," Lightspeed GMI, September 21, 2015, http://blog.lightspeedgmi.com/marketing-research-101-six-commons-mistakes-in-survey-questionnaire-design.

Figure 4–7: Rules of marketing metrics

Source: Linda J. Popky, "Identify the Marketing Metrics That Actually Matter," *Harvard Business Review*, July 14, 2015, https://hbr.org/2015/07/identify-the-marketing-metrics-that-actually-matter.

Chapter 5

Data Box: Helping Feed the World

Source: "World Trade Statistical Review: 2018," *World Trade Organization*. Retrieved from https://www.wto.org/english/res_e/statis_e/wts2018_e/wts2018_e.pdf.

Data Box: Part of Our World

Source: "Global Top 100 Companies by market capitalization," pwc, May 2020, accessed at pwc.com/gx/en/services/audit-assurance/publications/global-top-100-companies-2020.html.

Chapter 6

Data Box: Demographic and Geographic Profile: *Canadian Living* Magazine

Source: "Canadian Living Media Kit 2020," Quebecor Media Sales, accessed April 2020 at http://quebecormediasales.ca/content/media/pdf/2020/CanadianLiving-MediaKit2020.pdf.

Figure 6–4: Identifying consumer clusters

Source: Amira El Deeb, "Class 5/1 Segmentation, Targeting, Differentiation & Positioning," Marketers' Magazine [blog], July 14, 2010, http://mmauc.blogspot.ca/2010/07/class51-segmentation-targeting.html.

Chapter 7

Figure 7–3: Reviewing the Procter & Gamble Canada product mix

Source: "All Brands," Procter & Gamble website, accessed April 2020 at http://www.pg.ca/en-CA/our-brands.

Data Box: Interbrand's Top 10 Global Brands

Source: "Best Global Brands 2019 Rankings" Interbrand website, accessed April 2020 at https://www.interbrand.com/best-brands/best-global-brands/2019/ranking/.

Chapter 8

Figure 8–2: Apple iPhone product life cycle

Source: Montgomery, April and Mingis, Ken, "The evolution of Apple's iPhone," *Computerworld*, September 10, 2019, accessed April 2020 at https://www.computerworld.com/article/2604020/the-evolution-of-apples-iphone.html#slide15; "How Apple's iPhone has evolved since launch," *USA Today*, March 21, 2016, http://www.usatoday.com/story/tech/news/2016/03/21/how-apples-iphone-has-evolved-since-launch/82071340/; "Compare iPhone models," Apple website, accessed April 2020 at http://www.apple.com/ca/iphone/compare/; "Compare [Apple iPhones]," GSM Arena website, accessed July 2016 at http://www.gsmarena.com/compare.php3?idPhone1=4910&sSearch2=iphone+5s&idPhone2=5685&idPhone3=5690; Matt Rosoff, "The end of iPhone's amazing eight-year run," *Business Insider*, April 25, 2016, http://www.businessinsider.com/apple-iphone-sales-by-year-2016-4; Scott Stein, "Jet-black Apple iPhone 7 is here," *CNET*, September 7, 2016, http://www.cnet.com/products/apple-iphone-7/preview/.

Data Box: Best New Product Award Winners

Source: "BrandSpark International's 2020 Best New Product Award Winners Announced," Cision, February 27, 2020, accessed April 2020 at https://www.newswire.ca/news-releases/brandspark-international-s-2020-best-new-product-award-winners-announced-895852042.html.

Figure 8–7: Avoiding new product failure

Source: Barbara Thau, "The Five Biggest Reasons Why Consumer Products Fail," *Forbes*, June 3, 2014, http://www.forbes.com/sites/barbarathau/2014/06/03/the-five-biggest-reasons-why-consumer-products-fail-according-to-a-retail-insider/print/; Joan Schneider and Julie Hall, "Why Most Product Launches Fail," *Harvard Business Review*, April 2011, https://hbr.org/2011/04/why-most-product-launches-fail.

Chapter 9

Data Box: Tipping Etiquette

Source: "Canada: Tipping & Etiquette," Trip Advisor, accessed at http://www.tripadvisor.com/Travel-g153339-s606/Canada:Tipping.And.Etiquette.html.

Chapter 10

Data Box: Convenient Coffee Options

Source: "Fresh Facts," Tim Hortons corporate website, accessed at https://www.timhortons.com/ca/en/corporate/fresh-facts.php#!open_flyout; "Our History," Second Cup corporate website, accessed at http://www.secondcup.com/our-story;jsessionid=B8EB02561075E87B516B57B6A8869977; "Our Canadian Story," Starbucks website, accessed at https://www.starbucks.ca/careers/our-canadian-story; "Corporate Info," McDonald's Canada corporate website, accessed at http://www.mcdonalds.ca/ca/en/our_story/corporate_info.html.

Chapter 11

Figure 11–3: Where do we find the top retailers in the world? Who are they?

Source: Deloitte, *Global Powers of Retailing 2020*, accessed at https://www2.deloitte.com/global/en/pages/consumer-business/articles/global-powers-of-retailing.html.

Data Box: Canadian Responsible Reputation

Source: Justin Dallaire, "MEC, Canadian Tire most reputable brands for CSR," *Strategy*, October 26, 2018, accessed at http://strategyonline.ca/2018/10/26/mec-canadian-tire-among-most-reputable-brands-for-csr/.

Data Box: Online Presents

Source: "Top 10 e-commerce sites in Canada 2019," Disfold, October 18, 2019, accessed at https://disfold.com/top-e-commerce-sites-canada/.

Chapter 12

Figure 12–8: Top magazines (readership in Canada)

Source: "Top 10 Canadian Magazines by Circulation," updated January 2020, accessed in May 2020 at https://www.agilitypr.com/resources/top-media-outlets/top-10-canadian-magazines/.

Figure 12–12: Average time spent on traditional versus digital media in Canada

Source: https://www.emarketer.com/content/canada-time-spent-with-media-2020

Figure 12–14: Trends—advertising expenditures in Canada (C$ billions)

Source: https://www.emarketer.com/content/canada-time-spent-with-media-2020

Chapter 13

Figure 13–2 Benefits of social media marketing

Source: https://medium.com/@JBBC/10-key-findings-from-the-2019-social-media-marketing-industry-report-9ffb95b33926.

Data Box: Comparing Social Media Networks - Global users

Source: https://www.statista.com/chart/5194/active-users-of-social-networks-and-messaging-services/.

Figure 13–5 Social media metrics

Source: Adapted from Jay Shemenski, "The 3 Types of Social Media Metrics that Matter to You," SimplyMeasured [blog], December 1, 2016, http://simplymeasured.com/blog/the-3-types-of-social-media-metrics-that-matter-to-you/#sm.00000k61g84uecztxyp1birlwcur0.

Figure 13–6 Mobile Activities in Canada 2019

Source: https://www.slideshare.net/DataReportal/digital-2019-canada-january-2019-v01.

Data Box: Top Ten Activities on Mobile Devices for Canadians

Source: "Mobile Device Activities," Media Technology Monitor website, accessed December 2016 at https://mtm-otm.ca/Download.ashx?req=18-2-1.

Figure 13–7 Mobile User Behaviour

Source: https://www.emarketer.com/content/canada-ecommerce-2019.

Data Box: Top 10 Mobile App Rankings in Canada - by monthly active users

Source: https://www.slideshare.net/DataReportal/digital-2019-canada-january-2019-v01.

Chapter 14

Data Box: Banking On Customer Satisfaction

Source: "Canadian Banks Face Untimely Digital Banking Headwinds Since Pandemic Began, J.D. Power Finds" [news release], May 7, 2020, accessed at https://canada.jdpower.com/press-releases/2020-canada-retail-banking-satisfaction-study.

Chapter 15

Data Box: Canada's Most Profitable Companies

Source: "10 of the biggest Canadian companies," *Canada Telecommunications*, January 8, 2020, https://www.ctca.ca/10-of-the-biggest-canadian-companies/.

Data Box: Ben & Jerry's Non-Dairy Debut

Source: "Non-Dairy Pints," Ben & Jerry's website, accessed February 2017 at http://www.benjerry.com/flavors/non-dairy; "Ben & Jerry's Canada Debuts 3 New Non-Dairy Frozen Treat Flavors," *Canadify*, February 22, 2017, http://canadify.com/2017/02/22/ben-jerrys-canada-debuts-3-new-non-dairy-frozen-treat-flavors/.

Chapter Notes

Chapter 1

1. Written input and interview with Richard Bartrem, vice president, marketing of WestJet Airlines, December 2019.
2. Richard Robinson, "It's Time for Marketers to Start a Bonfire of the Legacies," *Marketing Week*, January 26, 2017, p. 13; David Z. Morris, "Elon Musk Is the Most Admired Leader in Technology," *Fortune*, September 8, 2016, p. 1; and "Microsoft Joins Forces with Musk on Artificial-Intelligence Deal," *Investors Business Daily*, November 15, 2016, p. 1.
3. Joe Morsello, "Google: Online Consumer Touchpoints Range Between 20–500 Depending on Purchase," *LSA Insider*, February 5, 2019, https://www.lsainsider.com/google-online-consumer-touchpoints-range-between-20-500-depending-on-purchase/archives.
4. National Retail Foundation, "Top 100 Retailers 2018," *Stores*, July 2018, http://stores.org/stores-top-retailers-2018/.
5. "2017 Annual Report," Amazon, http://www.annualreports.com/Company/amazoncom-inc.
6. "Amazon Prime," Amazon.ca, accessed September 2019 at www.amazon.ca/gp/prime.
7. Heather MacMullin, "Halo Top, The Low-Cal Ice Cream Americans Are Obsessed With, Is Here–But How Does It Taste?" *Chatelaine*, March 5, 2018, https://www.chatelaine.com/food/trends/halo-top-ice-cream-canada/.
8. Debra Kelly, "The Untold Truth of Halo Top Ice Cream," Mashed.com, February 12, 2018, https://www.mashed.com/109187/untold-truth-halo-top-ice-cream/.
9. Jessica Wohl, "How Halo Top Is Conquering the Ice Cream Biz–Without Ads," *AdAge*, March 6, 2017, https://adage.com/article/print-edition/halo-top-conquering-ice-cream-biz-ads/308177.
10. Lauren Johnson, "Halo Top Ice Cream and FX Are the First Brands to Back Gay Dating App Grindr's New Digital Magazine," *AdWeek*, August 15, 2017, https://www.adweek.com/digital/halo-top-and-fx-are-the-first-brands-to-back-dating-app-grindrs-new-digital-magazine/.
11. "Amazon Prime," Amazon.ca, accessed September 2019 at www.amazon.ca/gp/prime.
12. CPA Canada, "Average annual amount spent on online purchases according to digital shoppers in Canada as of February 2018" [Graph], in Statista, March 7, 2018, accessed September 2019 at https://www.statista.com/statistics/468627/online-shopping-consumer-spending-canadians/.
13. Patrick Seitz, "Online Shoppers Rank Free Shipping As Most Important," *Investor's Business Daily*, July 28, 2015.
14. "Amazon Prime," Amazon.ca, accessed September 2019 at www.amazon.ca/gp/prime.
15. 2017 Amazon Annual Report, Amazon, http://www.annualreports.com/Company/amazoncom-inc.
16. Adapted from "Marketing," *Business Dictionary* website, accessed September 2019 at www.businessdictionary.com/definition/marketing.html.
17. "Join," SCENE.ca, accessed September 2019 at https://www.scene.ca/en-ca/enrollment.
18. "History and Impact," MADD Canada, accessed September 2019 at http://madd.ca/pages/about-us/what-we-do/history-and-impact/; and "Information for Parents," MADD Canada, accessed September 2019 at http://madd.ca/pages/programs/youth-services/information-for-parents/.
19. Blair Sanderson, "Movember Canada trying to move beyond the moustache," CBC News, November 5, 2017, https://www.cbc.ca/news/canada/nova-scotia/movember-canada-fundraising-men-s-health-1.4387768; Matt Campbell, "Movember - Whatever you grow, will save a bro," CampaignLive, October 2, 2019, https://www.campaignlive.co.uk/article/movember-whatever-grow-will-save-bro-matta/1661259.
20. Brendan Sinclair, "Nintendo targeting Wii U marketing to kids, families," gamesindustry.biz, December 18, 2013, http://www.gamesindustry.biz/articles/2013-12-18-nintendo-targeting-wii-u-marketing-to-kids-families.
21. Frederick Crane, Roger Kerin, Steven Hartley, and William Rudelius, *Marketing*, Ninth Canadian Edition (Toronto: McGraw-Hill, 2014).
22. Benevity.com, accessed April 2020 at https://www.benevity.com/why-benevity; Benevity, "Benevity Expands Market-Leading CSR Platform to Mobile, Enabling More Inclusive, In-the-Moment Giving [News release]", December 5, 2019, accessed April 2020 at https://www.globenewswire.com/news-release/2019/12/05/1956735/0/en/Benevity-Expands-Market-Leading-CSR-Platform-to-Mobile-Enabling-More-Inclusive-In-the-Moment-Giving.html; Certified B Corporation, "About B Corps," accessed August 2020 at https://bcorporation.net/about-b-corps.
23. *Our Purpose: Live Life Well: 2018 Corporate Social Responsibility Report*, Loblaw Companies Limited, accessed September 2019 at http://www.loblaw.ca/en/responsibility/reports.html; "Our CSR Pillars [Infographic]," Loblaw Companies Limited, accessed June 2020 at https://www.loblaw.ca/content/dam/lclcorp/pdfs/Responsibility/Reports/CSR_digital_English.pdf.
24. *Telus Sustainability Report 2015*, Telus, accessed May 2016 at https://telusdigital-sustainability-production.s3.amazonaws.com/uploads/2017/04/2015_Sustainability_Report-EN.pdf.
25. Julie Smyth, "Canada's top 50 socially responsible corporations: 2015," *Maclean's*, June 8, 2015, http://www.macleans.ca/economy/business/canadas-top-50-most-socially-responsible-companies/.
26. "Pampers and Unicef: A powerful partnership and a decade of achievement," Pampers.ca, accessed June 2017 at https://www.pampers.ca/en-ca/about-pampers/pampers-unicef-partnership/article/pampers-and-unicef-the-journey-so-far-a-decade-of-achievement.
27. "10 worst household products for greenwashing," CBC News, September 14, 2012, http://www.cbc.ca/news/canada/10-worst-household-products-for-greenwashing-1.1200620.
28. "Our Commitments," The Body Shop, accessed May 2016 at http://www.thebodyshop.ca/enrich-not-exploit/.
29. "Facts & Figures: 2019," Canadian Wireless and Telecommunications Association, accessed March 2020 at http://www.cwta.ca/facts-figures/.
30. Bryan Segal, "Global Digital Future in Focus 2018 Canada Edition," comScore, June 26, 2018, accessed September 2019 at https://www.comscore.com/Insights/Presentations-and-Whitepapers/2018/Global-Digital-Future-in-Focus-2018-Canada-Edition; "Daily time spent using the internet in Canada from 2010 to 2018 (in minutes)," Statista, accessed June 2020 at https://www.statista.com/statistics/237502/daily-time-spent-using-the-internet-among-adults-in-canada/.
31. "My Starbucks Idea," Starbucks, accessed March 2020 at http://mystarbucksidea.force.com/.

32. Roberto Torres, "Starbucks' digital strategy is working. Now it wants to dive deeper," *CIO Dive*, July 26, 2019, https://www.ciodive.com/news/starbucks-digital-strategy-is-working-now-it-wants-to-dive-deeper/559602/.

33. "8 Content Marketing Examples That Turn Heads and Spark Engagement [Blog post]," Lyfe Marketing, October 2, 2019, accessed June 2020 at https://www.lyfemarketing.com/blog/content-marketing-examples/.

34. "The State of the Industry: Mobile Marketing in North America," WARC and the Mobile Marketing Association, May 2017, accessed March 2020 at https://www.mmaglobal.com/documents/state-mobile-marketing-north-america.

35. Ibid.

36. Ibid.

37. "2019 Canadian Social Media Insights," Insights West, June 2019, accessed March 2020 at https://insightswest.com/wp-content/uploads/2019/06/Rep_IW_CDNSocialMediaInsights_June2019.pdf.

38. "Most popular Facebook fan pages as of April 2016, based on number of fans (in millions)," Statista, accessed May 2016 at http://www.statista.com/statistics/269304/international-brands-on-facebook-by-number-of-fans/; David Moth, "How Coca-Cola uses Facebook, Twitter, Pinterest and Google+," *Econsultancy*, April 17, 2013, https://econsultancy.com/blog/62548-how-coca-cola-uses-facebook-twitter-pinterest-and-google/.

39. David Moth, "How Nike uses Facebook, Twitter, Pinterest and Google+," *Econsultancy*, March 27, 2013, https://econsultancy.com/blog/62412-how-nike-uses-facebook-twitter-pinterest-and-google; Nike Football Facebook page, accessed May 2016 at www.facebook.com/nikefootball/.

40. Kayla Matthews, "The 6 Best Augmented Reality Marketing Campaigns We've Seen So Far [Blog post]," MarTech Advisor, March 19, 2019, accessed March 2020 at https://www.martechadvisor.com/articles/interactive-marketing/the-6-best-augmented-reality-marketing-campaigns-weve-seen-so-far/.

41. Christopher Ratcliff, "Six inspiring new examples of experiential marketing," *Econsultancy*, May 13, 2015, https://econsultancy.com/blog/66431-six-inspiring-new-examples-of-experiential-marketing/.

42. Val Maloney, "Spotted! Nike's baller weekend," *Media in Canada*, February 16, 2016, http://mediaincanada.com/2016/02/16/spotted-nikes-baller-weekend/.

43. Joss Davidge, "The force is strong with Lego's brand experience," *BEcause Experiential Marketing*, November 25, 2015, https://www.becausexm.com/blog/the-force-is-strong-with-legos-brand-experience.

44. Lauren Johnson, "Nestlé Will Be the First Brand to Run a Sponsored Periscope Stream," *Adweek*, June 19, 2015, http://www.adweek.com/news/technology/nestl-will-be-first-brand-run-sponsored-periscope-stream-165443; "Periscope case study: Nestle turns camera on customers to generate social buzz," Digital Training Academy, accessed May 2016 at http://www.digitaltrainingacademy.com/casestudies/2016/04/periscope_case_study_nestle_turns_camera_on_customers_to_generate_social_buzz.php.

45. Allie Decker, "The Ultimate Guide to Marketing Trends in 2020 [Blog post]," HubSpot.com, August 8, 2019, accessed March 2020 at https://blog.hubspot.com/marketing/marketing-trends.

46. Jo Coughlin, "Creating the perfect blend in partnership marketing," *The Drum*, April 29, 2016, http://www.thedrum.com/opinion/2016/04/29/creating-perfect-blend-partnership-marketing.

47. Harmeet Singh, "Brand Partner of the Year: Nutella's pairings," *Strategy*, October 16, 2015, http://strategyonline.ca/2015/10/16/brand-partner-of-the-year-nutellas-pairings/.

48. "Benefits of the Program," SCENE.ca, accessed June 2016 at https://www.scene.ca/programbenefits.aspx; Matt Semansky, "Scotiabank Takes Scene-ic Route to Youth," *Marketing*, July 27, 2008, http://www.marketingmag.ca/brands/scotiabank-takes-scene-ic-route-to-youth-16881.

49. Samuel Wich, "Is 2020 the Year of Sustainable Business in Hospitality?", *HospitalityNet*, February 24, 2020, https://www.hospitalitynet.org/opinion/4097111.html; Siobhan O'Neill,

"Amazing Hotels – Canadian sustainability at Fogo Island," *Green Hotelier*, April 24, 2017, https://www.greenhotelier.org/destinations/americas/amazing-hotels-canadian-sustainability-at-fogo-island/; "Entrepreneur Zita Cobb's social conscience lands her in the Business Hall of Fame," CBC News, January 05, 2020, https://www.cbc.ca/news/canada/newfoundland-labrador/zita-cobb-business-hall-of-fame-1.5414055.

50. Lisa Quast, "Personal Branding 101," *Forbes*, April 22, 2013, http://www.forbes.com/sites/lisaquast/2013/04/22/personal-branding-101/#158f0cd615fa.

Chapter 2

1. Canada Post, *2018 Annual Report*, accessed July 2020 at https://www.canadapost.ca/cpc/en/our-company/about-us/financial-reports/2018-annual-report/story-of-2018.page; personal interview with Jon Hamilton, general manager, communications strategy, Canada Post, May 2016; personal communication with Rob Linke, director, writing services, Canada Post, June 2016; Ian Lee, "Is the Cheque Still in the Mail?" Macdonald-Laurier Institute, July 2015, www.macdonaldlaurier.ca/files/pdf/MLI_PostOffice_F_web.pdf; Canada Post, *What's in the Truck? 2015 Annual Report*," accessed at https://www.canadapost.ca/web/en/pages/aboutus/details.page?article=annual_report; "Housing starts by province," Statistics Canada, CANSIM, table 027-0008, April 22, 2016, http://www.statcan.gc.ca/tables-tableaux/sum-som/l01/cst01/manuf05-eng.htm; "Homeownership and Shelter Costs in Canada: National Household Survey, 2011," Statistics Canada, Catalogue no. 99-014-X2011002 (Ottawa: Minister of Industry, 2013), http://www12.statcan.gc.ca/nhs-enm/2011/as-sa/99-014-x/99-014-x2011002-eng.pdf; "Retail sales, by industry," Statistics Canada, CANSIM, table 080-0020, March 2016, http://www.statcan.gc.ca/tables-tableaux/sum-som/l01/cst01/trad42a-eng.htm; Murad Hemmadi, "Why Canada has a serious e-commerce problem, in one infographic," *Canadian Business*, November 27, 2014, http://www.canadianbusiness.com/innovation/canada-serious-e-commerce-problem-infographic/; Accenture Consulting, "Accenture Technology Vision for Postal Organizations: Five trends shaping the future" (Toronto: Author, 2015), https://www.accenture.com/us-en/insight-five-trends-shaping-future; David James Friend, "76% of Canadians shopped online last year, Canada Post says," Canadian Press, May 12, 2015, http://www.cbc.ca/news/business/76-of-canadians-shopped-online-last-year-canada-post-says-1.3070651; Canadian Internet Registration Authority (CIRA), "The State of e-Commerce in Canada: CIRA Internet Factbook," March 2016, https://cira.ca/sites/default/files/public/ecommerce-factbook-march-2016_0.pdf; Statistics Canada, "Digital technology and Internet use, 2013," *The Daily*, June 11, 2014, http://www.statcan.gc.ca/daily-quotidien/140611/dq140611a-eng.htm; Qasim Mohammad, "After years in the slow lane, Canada's e-commerce ecosystem is booming," *Canadian Business*, February 22, 2016, http://www.canadianbusiness.com/innovation/canada-ecommerce-innovators/; "Digital Canada 150 2.0," Industry Canada, December 2015, http://www.ic.gc.ca/eic/site/028.nsf/eng/home.

2. T. J. Kiely, "5 Digital Marketing Trends That Will Shape Your 2018," *thedrum.com*, January 12, 2018; Patricia Odell, "Top 10 Trends to Transform Digital Marketing in 2017," *Promotional Marketing*, January 20, 2017, p. 1; Hal Conick, "2017 Marketing Trends from CES," *Marketing News*, February 2017, pp. 3–4; Verne Harnish, "5 Trends to Ride in 2017," *Fortune.com*, p. 32; and Patricia Odell, "10 Disruptive Marketing Trends All Marketers Should Consider," *Promotional Marketing*, February 2, 2017, p. 1.

3. Statistics Canada, "Population size and growth in Canada: Key results from the 2016 Census," *The Daily*, February 8, 2017, http://www.statcan.gc.ca/daily-quotidien/170208/dq170208a-eng.htm?HPA=1.

4. Statistics Canada, "Age and sex, and type of dwelling data: Key results from the 2016 Census," *The Daily*, May 3, 2017, http://www.statcan.gc.ca/daily-quotidien/170503/dq170503a-eng.htm?HPA=1.

5. Statistics Canada, *The Daily*, "Canada's Population Estimates: Age and sex, July 1, 2019," September 30, 2019, https://www150.statcan.gc.ca/n1/daily-quotidien/190930/dq190930a-eng.htm.

6. Ibid.

7. Ellen Samek, "Move over, millennials - baby boomers are the ultimate untapped market," April 2, 2019, *Financial Post*, https://business.financialpost.com/news/retail-marketing/move-over-millennials-baby-boomers-re-the-ultimate-untapped-market;Doug Norris, "Don't call us seniors: The Baby Boomers at 65 [Blog post]," Environics Analytics, July 23, 2014, accessed July 2020 at https://environicsanalytics.com/resources/blogs/ea-blog/2014/07/23/dont-call-us-seniors-the-baby-boomers-at-65.

8. Sonya Fatah, "How boomers are consuming media," *Strategy*, January 25, 2016, http://strategyonline.ca/2016/01/25/diving-deep-into-boomers-media-consumption-habits/; Catherine Phillips, "Are brands missing opportunities with the 50+ cohort? [Blog post]," Media in Canada, August 22, 2019, accessed July 2020 at http://mediaincanada.com/2019/08/22/are-brands-missing-opportunities-with-the-50-cohort/#.

9. Statistics Canada, "Population Estimates on July 1st, by age and sex," Table 17-10-0005-01, accessed July 2020 at https://www150.statcan.gc.ca/t1/tbl1/en/tv.action?pid=1710000501; Doug Norris, "Millennials: The Generation Du Jour [Blog post]," Environics Analytics, January 22, 2016, accessed July 2020 at https://environicsanalytics.com/resources/blogs/ea-blog/2016/01/22/millennials-the-generation-du-jour.

10. Doug Norris, "Millennials."

11. Bree Rody, "Gen X : Affluent, Connected and Traditional [Blog post]," Media in Canada, February 13, 2019, accessed July 2020 at https://mediaincanada.com/2019/02/13/gen-x-affluent-connected-and-traditional/;Ellie Williams, "Generation X Consumer Behavior," *AZCentral*, Business and Entrepreneurship, accessed May 2016, http://yourbusiness.azcentral.com/generation-x-consumer-behavior-9585.html.

12. Statistics Canada, "Population Estimates on July 1st, by age and sex"; Doug Norris, "Millennials."

13. Doug Norris, "Millennials."

14. Arti Patel, "Generation Z: Make room for Canada's connected, open and optimistic generation," Global News, June 18, 2018, https://globalnews.ca/news/4211788/generation-z/; Ernst and Young, *Rise of Gen Z, a new challenge for retailers* (London: Author, 2015), accessed at http://www.ey.com/Publication/vwLUAssets/EY-rise-of-gen-znew-challenge-for-retailers/$FILE/EY-rise-of-gen-znew-challenge-for-retailers.pdf.

15. Doug Norris, "Millennials"; Statistics Canada, "Population by sex and age group."

16. Statistics Canada, "Canada's Population, July 1 2019."

17. Statistics Canada, "Population size and growth in Canada: Key results from the 2016 Census."

18. Statistics Canada, "Canada's population estimates: Age and sex, July 1, 2019."

19. Statistics Canada, "Study: A look at immigration, ethnocultural diversity and languages in Canada up to 2036, 2011 to 2036," *The Daily*, January 25, 2017, http://www.statcan.gc.ca/daily-quotidien/170125/dq170125b-eng.htm.

20. Statistics Canada, "An increasingly diverse linguistic landscape: Highlights from the 2016 Census," *The Daily*, August 2, 2017, http://www.statcan.gc.ca/daily-quotidien/170802/dq170802b-eng.htm.

21. Susan Krashinsky, "More Companies taking multicultural marketing to mainstream levels," *Globe and Mail*, October 8, 2015, http://www.theglobeandmail.com/report-on-business/industry-news/marketing/more-companies-taking-multicultural-marketing-to-mainstream-levels/article26727716/.

22. Mario Toneguzzi, "Chinese Consumers Drive Luxury Retail Growth in Canada: Study," *Retail Insider*, December 6, 2019, https://www.retail-insider.com/retail-insider/2019/12/chinese-consumers-drive-luxury-retail-growth-in-canada-study.

23. World Population Review, "Country Population 2020" and "Continent Population 2020," accessed January 2020 at http://worldpopulationreview.com/.

24. Statistics Canada, "Families, households, and marital status: Key results from the 2016 Census," *The Daily*, August 2, 2017, http://www.statcan.gc.ca/daily-quotidien/170802/dq170802a-eng.htm.

25. "Reflecting Canadian values," Canadian Index of Wellbeing, accessed May 2016 at https://uwaterloo.ca/canadian-index-wellbeing/about-canadian-index-wellbeing/reflecting-canadian-values.

26. Sarah Radwanic, "An Average Monday in the UK: PCs for Lunch, Tablets for Dinner," comScore, February 17, 2013, http://www.comscore.com/Insights/Data-Mine/An-Average-Monday-in-the-UK-PCs-for-Lunch-Tablets-for-Dinner.

27. Rob Young, "Canada's Media Landscape," PHD Canada (prepared for Interactive Advertising Bureau), December 2015, https://iabcanada.com/content/uploads/2017/02/1.-CMUST-2015-V3-Total-Canada-Exec-Summary-Dec-2-2015.pdf.

28. Ellen Chang, "Showrooming Remains Unpopular With the Majority of Customers," *TheStreet*, May 26, 2016, https://www.thestreet.com/story/13587093/1/showrooming-remains-unpopular-with-the-majority-of-customers.html.

29. Larry Simmons, "Social Media & Consumer Behavior," *Houston Chronicle*, accessed May 2016 at http://smallbusiness.chron.com/social-media-consumer-behavior-45733.html.

30. Insights West, "2019 Canadian Social Media Insights," June 2019, accessed January 2020 at https://www.insightswest.com/wp-content/uploads/2019/06/Rep_IW_CDNSocialMediaInsights_June2019.pdf, p. 9.

31. Canadian Radio-television and Telecommunications Commission (CRTC), *Communications Monitoring Report 2016* (Ottawa: Author, 2016), http://www.crtc.gc.ca/eng/publications/reports/policymonitoring/2016/cmrs.htm#exii.

32. Sophia Harris, "Cable cord-cutting numbers soar in Canada thanks to Netflix, high prices, says report," CBC News, April 8, 2016, http://www.cbc.ca/news/business/cable-costs-cord-cutting-canada-netflix-1.3525949.

33. Paul Rich, Ben Martin, and Leah Jenkins, "2015 Canada Digital Future in Focus," comScore, March 27, 2015, https://www.comscore.com/Insights/Presentations-and-Whitepapers/2015/2015-Canada-Digital-Future-in-Focus.

34. Emily Jackson, "Netflix lands over a million new Canadian subscribers in less than one year: report," *Financial Post*, June 14, 2016, http://business.financialpost.com/technology/netflix-lands-over-a-million-new-canadian-subscribers-in-less-than-one-year-report/wcm/db9ff8aa-414d-41cb-8414-23bd49a38943.

35. "To Binge or Not to Binge, That is the Question," Solutions Research Group Consultants Inc., March 7, 2013, www.srgnet.com/index.php/2013/03/07/to-binge-or-not-that-is-the-question/.

36. Lu Ann Williams, "The 2015 Trends Impacting the Food Industry," *Canadian Food Business*, December 17, 2014, http://canadianfoodinsights.com/2014/12/17/2015-trends-impacting-food-industry/.

37. Pete Evans, "Kraft Dinner to remove synthetic colours from macaroni and cheese," CBC News, April 20, 2015, http://www.cbc.ca/news/business/kraft-dinner-to-remove-synthetic-colours-from-macaroni-and-cheese-1.3040324.

38. Lu Ann Williams, "The 2015 Trends Impacting the Food Industry."

39. "Mapping Your Future Growth: Five Game-Changing Consumer Trends," Business Development Bank of Canada, October 2013, https://www.bdc.ca/consumertrend.

40. "Food Intolerance in Canada," Euromonitor International, April 2016, http://www.euromonitor.com/food-intolerance-in-canada/report.

41. Hollie Shaw, "Beyond chicken and fries: Loblaw seeks bigger bite of restaurant sales with new fresh-food offerings," *Financial Post*, August 2, 2014, http://business.financialpost.com/news/retail-marketing/loblaw-fresh-food.

42. Tanya Dua, "From Coca-Cola to Barbie: The Fierce Rise of Gender-Neutral Advertising," *Digiday*, March 29, 2015; Kristina

Monllos, "Brands Are Throwing Out Gender Norms to Reflect a More Fluid World," *Adweek*, October 17, 2016; Kelvin Claveria, "Ungendered: Why Forward-Thinking Marketers Are Embracing Gender Fluidity," *Visioncritical*, October 24, 2016; Sam Frizell, "Here's How Pinterest Is Trying to Attract More Men," *Time.com*, January 23, 2015, p. 1; Gillian Rich, "Can Female-Focused Lululemon Sell Yoga Pants to Men?" *Investors Business Daily*, June 14, 2013, p. 1; Elizabeth Sweet, "Guys and Dolls No More?" *The New York Times*, December 23, 2012, p. 12; and Patricia Odell, "UGG VP Marketing on Tom Brady's Impact on the Brand," *Chief Marketer*, November 29, 2012.

43. Statistics Canada, *Population Projections for Canada, Provinces and Territories, 2009 to 2036*, Catalogue no. 91-520-X (Ottawa: Minister of Industy, 2010), http://www.statcan.gc.ca/pub/91-520-x/2010001/aftertoc-aprestdm1-eng.htm.

44. Jonah Comstock, " IMS: Half of Android health apps have fewer than 500 downloads," *MobiHealthNews*, October 30, 2013, http://mobihealthnews.com/26836/ims-half-of-android-health-apps-have-fewer-than-500-downloads.

45. "Mapping Your Future Growth: Five Game-Changing Consumer Trends," Business Development Bank of Canada.

46. "More than 52,000 Canadians travelled abroad for medical care in 2014: study," CTV News, March 17, 2015, http://www.ctvnews.ca/health/more-than-52-000-canadians-travelled-abroad-for-medical-care-in-2014-study-1.2283121.

47. Advertising Standards Canada, *The Canadian Children's Food and Beverage Advertising Initiative: 2014 Compliance Report*, (Toronto: Author, 2015, http://www.adstandards.com/en/childrensinitiative/2014ComplianceReport.pdf; "Canadian Families Making Healthier Choices," H & K Perspectives, July 2014, http://www.adstandards.com/en/childrensinitiative/consumerResearch.html.

48. "Greendex 2014: Consumer Choice and the Environment," National Geographic, accessed May 2016, http://images.nationalgeographic.com/wpf/media-live/file/Greendex-Canadians_FINAL-cb1409255133.pdf.

49. "Mapping Your Future Growth: Five Game-Changing Consumer Trends," Business Development Bank of Canada.

50. "Understanding Green Claims," Industry Canada, Office of Consumer Affairs, accessed May 2016 at https://www.ic.gc.ca/eic/site/oca-bc.nsf/eng/ca02523.html.

51. "Mapping Your Future Growth: Five Game-Changing Consumer Trends," Business Development Bank of Canada.

52. "Corporate Citizenship: Environmental Sustainability," Canadian Tire, accessed May 2016 at http://corp.canadiantire.ca/EN/Corporate Citizenship/EnvironmentalSustainability/Pages/default.aspx.

53. "Canadian Lifestyles 2017: Pride and Purse Strings," Mintel, accessed July 2017 at http://store.mintel.com/canadian-lifestyles-pride-and-purse-strings-canada-april-2017.

54. Rick Newman, "10 Products That Boomed During the Recession, *U.S. News & World Report*, October 20, 2009, http://money.usnews.com/money/blogs/flowchart/2009/10/20/10-products-that-boomed-during-the-recession.

55. Mark Koba, "Gross Domestic Product: CNBC Explains," CNBC, November 3, 2011, http://www.cnbc.com/id/44505017.

56. J.B. Maverick, "How do changes in interest rates affect the spending habits in the economy?" *Investopedia*, July 17, 2015, http://www.investopedia.com/ask/answers/071715/how-do-changes-interest-rates-affect-spending-habits-economy.asp.

57. Nidhi Singal, "Tech Trends 2017," *Business Today*, January 29, 2017, pp. 106–09; "5 CES Tech Trends to Look Out for in 2017," *Design Week*, January 5, 2017, p. 4; Lucy Handley, "Artificial Intelligence: A Genuine Opportunity," *Marketing Week*, May 19, 2016, pp. 33–35; Jay Greene and Ted Greenwald, "IBM, Salesforce Agree to Partner on Artificial Intelligence," *The Wall Street Journal*, March 6, 2017; Elizabeth Weise, "Amazon Delivered Its First Customer Package by Drone," *USA Today*, December 14, 2016; Adi Robertson, "LG Put WebOS and Amazon Alexa on a Fridge," *The Verge*, January 4, 2017; and Alex Davies, "Google's Self-Driving Car Company Is Finally Here," www.wired.com, December 13, 2016.

58. Hal Conick, "Turning Big Data into Big Insights," *Marketing News*, January 2017, pp. 12–13; Ralph Finos, "2016–2026 Worldwide Big Data Market Forecast," www.wikibon.com, March 30, 2016; Marco Vriens and Patricia Kidd, "The Big Data Shift," *Marketing Insights*, November–December 2014, pp. 22–29; and Cliff Saran, "Big Data Technology Has Its Work Cut Out to Harness Web Analytics," *Computer Weekly*, May 13–19, 2014, p. 12.

59. Sarah Radwanic, "An Average Monday in the UK."

60. Paul Rich et al., "2015 Canada Digital Future in Focus."

61. Karen J. Bannan, "Cross-Device Advertising: How to Navigate Mobile Marketing's Next Big Thing," Criteo, presented by Ad Age Content Strategy Studio, September 2014, http://www.criteo.com/resources/cross-device-advertising-how-to-navigate-the-next-big-opportunity-in-mobile-marketing/.

62. "Number of internet users in Canada from 2000 to 2019," statista, accessed July 2020 at https://www.statista.com/statistics/243808/number-of-internet-users-in-canada/.

63. Canada Post, "The 2020 Canadian E-commerce Report," accessed July 2020 at https://www.canadapost.ca/cpc/en/business/marketing/campaign/ecommerce-report.page?gclid=EAIaIQobChMI74nXmYjQ6AIVhqDsCh15RgbUEAAYAiAAEgLK2vD_BwE.

64. K. Neilsen, "Deciphering Cloud Services for Consumers," November 21, 2011, accessed May 2016, http://cloud-services-review.toptenreviews.com/confused-about-the-cloud-deciphering-cloud-services-for-consumers.html; Kenneth Hess, "10 Cloud-Based Services You Can't Live Without," *ServerWatch*, January 13, 2011, http://www.serverwatch.com/trends/article.php/3920691/10-CloudBased-Services-You-Cant-Live-Without.htm.

65. Office of the Privacy Commissioner of Canada, "The 2018-19 Survey of Canadians on Privacy," March 2019, accessed July 2020 at https://www.priv.gc.ca/en/opc-actions-and-decisions/research/explore-privacy-research/2019/por_2019_ca/.

66. Alan Cross, "Canadians continue to adopt streaming music, and there's no going back: Alan Cross," Global News, April 21, 2019, https://globalnews.ca/news/5176580/canadians-streaming-music/.

67. "Music Streaming," statista, accessed July 2020 at https://www.statista.com/outlook/209/108/music-streaming/canada

68. Paul Briggs, "Canada Digital Video 2019," *eMarketer*, September 2019, https://www.emarketer.com/content/canada-digital-video-2019.

69. "2019 Canada's Internet Factbook," Canadian Internet Registration Authority, accessed July 2020 at https://www.cira.ca/resources/corporate/factbook/canadas-internet-factbook-2019.

70. CRTC, *Communications Monitoring Report 2019*, https://crtc.gc.ca/pubs/cmr2019-en.pdf ; Paul Rich et al., "2019 Canada Digital Future in Focus."

71. Paul Briggs, "Canada Mobile Payment Users 2019," *eMarketer*, October 2019, https://www.emarketer.com/content/canada-mobile-payment-users-2019.

72. Competition Bureau Canada website, accessed February 2017, https://www.canada.ca/en/competition-bureau.html; Amy Judd, "Top 10 scams of 2016 reveal Canadians lost more than $90M last year," Global News, March 1, 2017, http://globalnews.ca/news/3280609/top-10-scams-of-2016-reveal-canadians-lost-more-than-90m-last-year/; Mike Laanela, "Canada's top 10 scams earned crooks $1.2B last year, says BBB," CBC News, March 1, 2016, http://www.cbc.ca/news/canada/british-columbia/canada-s-top-10-scams-earned-crooks-1-2b-last-year-says-bbb-1.3471279; Canadian Competition Bureau, *The Little Black Book of Scams* (Ottawa: Author, 2012), http://www.competitionbureau.gc.ca/eic/site/cb-bc.nsf/vwapj/Little-Black-Book-Scams-e.pdf/$file/Little-Black-Book-Scams-e.pdf.

73. Advertising Standards Canada, "The Canadian Code of Advertising Standards," accessed May 2016 at http://www.adstandards.com/en/Standards/canCodeOfAdStandards.aspx.

74. "Report on the Operation of the National Do Not Call List (DNCL) for the period April 1, 2014 to March 31, 2015," Canadian Radio-television and Telecommunications Commission (CRTC), September 30, 2015, http://www.crtc.gc.ca/eng/DNCL/rpt150930.htm.

75. "CMA Guides and Mini-Guides," Canadian Marketing Association, accessed May 2016 at https://www.the-cma.org/regulatory/code-and-guidelines.

76. Canadian Wireless Telecommunications Association (CWTA) website, accessed May 2016 at http://cwta.ca.

77. "Why Use Short Codes" CWTA, accessed May 2016 at http://www.txt.ca/why-use-short-codes/.

78. "About Us," Mobile Marketing Association, accessed June 2016 at http://www.mmaglobal.com/about.

79. "Fact Sheets, Privacy Legislation in Canada," Office of the Privacy Commissioner of Canada, accessed May 2016 at www.priv.gc.ca/resource/fs-fi/02_05_d_15_e.asp; Minister of Justice, *Privacy Act* as amended April 2016, accessed May 2016 at http://laws-lois.justice.gc.ca/PDF/P-21.pdf and http://laws-lois.justice.gc.ca/eng/acts/P-21/index.html.

80. Office of the Privacy Commissioner of Canada, *Personal Information Protection and Electronic Document Act*, accessed May 2016 at https://www.priv.gc.ca/en/privacy-topics/privacy-laws-in-canada/the-personal-information-protection-and-electronic-documents-act-pipeda/pipeda-compliance-help/guide_org/.

81. "Canada's Anti-Spam Legislation, Fast Facts," Government of Canada, accessed June 2017 at http://fightspam.gc.ca/eic/site/030.nsf/eng/h_00039.html; "Canada's Anti-Spam Law Casts a Wide Net – Requires All Organizations to Take Action," Osler, Hoskin & Harcourt LLP, January 2014, https://www.osler.com/osler/media/Osler/reports/privacy-data/CASL-Canada-s-Anti-Spam-Law-Casts-a-Wide-Net.pdf.

82. "CMA Guide to Canada's Anti-Spam Law (CASL)," Canadian Marketing Association, April 2015, http://www.the-cma.org/regulatory/code-and-guidelines/cma-guide-to-canada-anti-spam-law.

83. "Online Behavioural Advertising," Office of the Privacy Commissioner of Canada, accessed May 2016 at https://www.priv.gc.ca/resource/topic-sujet/oba-pcl/index_e.asp.

84. "Understanding Online Advertising," Digital Advertising Alliance of Canada, accessed May 2016 at http://youradchoices.ca/understanding-online-advertising/.

Chapter 3

1. Personal Interview with Dustin Wright, senior director, marketing communications, Arbor Memorial, July 2019; "Canada's Best Managed Companies," Deloitte, accessed August 2020 at https://www2.deloitte.com/ca/en/pages/canadas-best-managed-companies/topics/best-managed.html.

2. Alan Walks, "Mapping the urban debtscape: The geography of household debt in Canadian cities," *Urban Geography*, April 29, 2013, *34*(2), 153–187, doi:10.1080/02723638.2013.778647; Chris Sorensen, "Living beyond our means," *Maclean's*, March 22, 2014; Bryan Borzykowski, "Managing your debt-to-income ratio," *Maclean's*, November 19, 2012; Canada Country Profile, 2013, 1–82.

3. Jonathan Law, *A Dictionary of Business and Management* (5th ed.) (New York: Oxford University Press, 2009); Gordon C. Bruner II and Richard J. Pomazal, "Problem Recognition: The Crucial First Stage of the Consumer Decision Process," *Journal of Consumer Marketing 5* (1988), pp. 53–63; and James F. Engel, Roger D. Blackwell, and Paul Miniard, *Consumer Behavior*, 9th ed. (Fort Worth, TX: Dryden Press, 1998).

4. For a thorough description of consumer expertise, see Joseph W. Alba and J. Wesley Hutchinson, "Knowledge Calibration: What Consumers Know and What They Think They Know," *Journal of Consumer Research 27* (2000), pp. 123–156. For in-depth studies on external information search patterns, see Sridhar Moorthy, Brian T. Ratchford, and Debabrata Tulukdar, "Consumer Information Search Revisited: Theory and Empirical Analysis," *Journal of Consumer Research 23* (1997), pp. 263–277; and Joel E. Urbany, Peter R. Dickson, and William L. Wilkie, "Buyer Uncertainty and Information Search," *Journal of Consumer Research 16* (1989), pp. 208–215.

5. Patricia F. Phalen, Richard V. Ducey, "Audience Behavior in the Multi-Screen 'Video-Verse'," *International Journal on Media Management 14* (2012), pp. 141–156; Ginny Marvin, "Microsoft Study: Multi-Screen Behaviour and What It Means for Marketers," *Marketing Land*, March 18, 2013; and Philip Webb, "The New Multi-Screen World: Understanding Consumer Behaviour," *Mobify*, September 17, 2012.

6. Kristin Laird, "Reinventing retail," *Marketing*, March 28, 2013; "GroupM Next and Catalyst Release 'Showrooming in Canada' Report [news release]," *Wireless News*, March 8, 2013; Megan Haynes, "Who's showrooming, and how?" *Strategy*, May 15, 2013, http://strategyonline.ca/2013/05/15/whos-showrooming-and-how/.

7. For an extended discussion on evaluative criteria, see Del J. Hawkins, Roger J. Best, and Kenneth A. Coney, *Consumer Behavior*, 8th ed. (New York: Irwin/McGraw-Hill, 2001), pp. 566–83.

8. Caroline Rouen-Mallet, Pascale Ezan, and Stéphane Mallet, "Toward a deeper understanding of the choice process in child consumers through the concept of the evoked set," *Recherche et Applications en Marketing* (English Edition), 29(4) (2014), pp. 60–88, doi:10.1177/2051570714558169; Jochen Wirtz and Anna S. Mattila, "The effects of consumer expertise on evoked set size and service loyalty," *Journal of Services Marketing 17* (2003), pp. 649–665; John A. Howard, *Buyer Behavior in Marketing Strategy*, 2nd ed. (Englewood Cliffs, NJ: Prentice Hall, 1994), pp. 101, 128–89.

9. Pantea Foroudi, T.C. Melewar, and Surashka Gupta, "Linking corporate logo, corporate image, and reputation: An examination of consumer perceptions in the financial setting," *Journal of Business Research 67* (2014), 2269–2281; Elyria Kemp, Carla Y. Childers, and Kim H. Williams, "Place branding: creating self-brand connections and brand advocacy," *Journal of Product & Brand Management 21* (2012), 508–515; Jesse Ferreras, "Canada real estate: Millennials aren't rushing to buy, BMO says," *Huffington Post*, April 28, 2016, http://www.huffingtonpost.ca/2016/04/28/canada-real-estate-millennial_n_9801542.html; Jason Heath, "Are Millenials better off renting? Why young Canadians may want to put off home ownership," *Financial Post*, August 7, 2015, http://business.financialpost.com/personal-finance/mortgages-real-estate/are-millennials-better-off-renting-why-young-canadians-may-want-to-put-off-home-ownership; Mike Valenti, "Welcome to the new breed of consumers," Glance Marketing, November 29, 2015, http://glancemarketing.ca/welcome-to-the-new-breed-of-consumers; Russ Martin, "What do Millennials value? Spotify's ad VP explains," *Marketing*, January 14, 2015, http://www.marketingmag.ca/brands/what-do-millennials-value-spotifys-ad-vp-explains-134882; Josh Fromm, "Secrets to win with affluent Millenials: Uber, Bose and brands getting traction," *Forbes*, November 2, 2015, http://www.forbes.com/sites/jefffromm/2015/11/02/secrets-to-win-with-affluent-millennials-uber-bose-and-brands-getting-traction/2/#3e924d2e47f8.

10. Peter Weill and Stephanie L. Woerner, "Optimizing your digital business model," *MIT Sloan Management Review*, March 19, 2013, pp. 71–78; Joerg Koenigstorfer and Andrea Groeppel-Klein, "Consumer acceptance of the mobile Internet," *Marketing Letters*, August 31, 2012, pp. 917–928; Sheena Leek and George Christodoulides, "Next-Generation Mobile Marketing: How Young Consumers React to Bluetooth-Enabled Advertising," *Journal of Advertising Research 49* (2009), pp. 44–53.

11. Nicole Fallon, "Why 'Webrooming' Could Bring Customers Back Into Stores," *Business News Daily*, June 9, 2014, http://www.businessnewsdaily.com/6565-webrooming-retail-stores.html; Adam Rapp, Thomas L. Baker, Daniel G. Bachrach, Jessica Ogilvie, and Lauren Skinner Beitelspacher, "Perceived customer showrooming behavior and the effect on retail salesperson self-efficacy and performance," *Journal of Retailing 91* (2015), 358–369; and Alan Wolf, "Best Buy Besting Walmart, Target at Showrooming," *TWICE*, July 7, 2013, http://www.twice.com/news/news/best-buy-besting-walmart-target-showrooming/42595.

12. Isabelle Goyette et al., "E-WOM Scale: Word-of-Mouth Measurement Scale for e-Services Context," *Canadian Journal of Administrative Sciences 27* (2010), pp. 5–23; Sun-Jung Moon, John P.

Costello, and Dong-Mo Koo, "The impact of consumer confusion from eco-labels on negative WOM, distrust, and dissatisfaction," *International Journal of Advertising 36* (2016), pp. 246–271; Jagdish N. Sheth, Banwari Mitral, and Bruce Newman, *Consumer Behavior* (Fort Worth, TX: Dryden Press, 1999), p. 22.

13. Moti Salti, Imen El Karoui, Mathurin Maillet, and Lionel Naccache, "Cognitive Dissonance Resolution is Related to Episodic Memory," *PLoS One 9.9* (2014), e108579; Monika Koller and Thomas Salzberger, "Heterogeneous development of cognitive dissonance over time and its effect on satisfaction and loyalty," *Journal of Customer Behaviour 11* (2012), pp. 261–280; Thomas Salzberger and Monika Koller, "Investigating the impact of cognitive dissonance and customer satisfaction on loyalty and complaint behaviour," *REMark 9* (2010), pp. 5–16.

14. For an overview of research on involvement, see John C. Mowen and Michael Minor, *Consumer Behavior*, 6th ed. (Upper Saddle River, NJ: Prentice Hall, 2001), pp. 64–68; and Frank R. Kardes, *Consumer Behavior* (Reading, MA: Addison-Wesley, 1999), pp. 256–58.

15. For an overview on the three problem-solving variations, see Hawkins, Best, and Coney, *Consumer Behavior*, pp. 506–7; and Howard, *Buyer Behavior*, pp. 69–162.

16. Nelson Barber, Tim Dodd, and Natalia Kolyesiknova, "Gender differences in information search: implications for retailing," *Journal of Consumer Marketing 26* (2009), pp. 415–426; Kenneth C. Gehrt and Ruoh-Nan Yan, "Situational, consumer, and retailer factors affecting internet, catalog, and store shopping," *International Journal of Retail & Distribution Management 32* (2004), pp. 5–18; Sydney Roslow, Tiger Li, and J.A.F. Nicholls, "Impact of situational variables and demographic attributes in two seasons on purchase behaviour," *European Journal of Marketing 34* (2000), pp. 1167–1180; Russell Belk, "Situational Variables and Consumer Behavior," *Journal of Consumer Research 2* (1975), pp. 157–163.

17. "Shopping As Therapy: Good Health Comes in Small Packages," *Discover Fit & Health*, accessed June 2011 at http://health.howstuffworks.com/wellness/women/general/shopping-as-therapy.htm.

18. A. H. Maslow, *Motivation and Personality* (New York: Harper & Row, 1970).

19. "Brand Papers: Challenging Maslow," *Brand Strategy*, 2003; Francis Buttle, "The social construction of needs," *Psychology & Marketing*, September 15, 2006, p. 197.

20. Arthur Koponen, "The Personality Characteristics of Purchasers," *Journal of Advertising Research 1* (1960), pp. 89–92; Joel B. Cohen, "An Interpersonal Orientation to the Study of Consumer Behavior," *Journal of Marketing Research 4* (1967), pp. 270–78; and Rena Bartos, *Marketing to Women Around the World* (Cambridge, MA: Harvard Business School, 1989).

21. Michael R. Solomon, *Consumer Behavior*, 5th ed. (Upper Saddle River, NJ: Prentice Hall, 2002), p. 61.

22. "BMW Service and Warranties," BMW Canada website, accessed at www.bmw.ca/ca/en/owners/service/warranty/warranty_1.html.

23. Martin Fishbein and I. Aizen, *Belief, Attitude, Intention and Behavior: An Introduction to Theory and Research* (Reading, MA: Addison-Wesley, 1975), p. 6.

24. Richard J. Lutz, "Changing Brand Attitudes through Modification of Cognitive Structure," *Journal of Consumer Research 1* (1975), pp. 49–59; "Pepsi's Gamble Hits Freshness Dating Jackpot," *Advertising Age*, September 19, 1994, p. 50; and "Every Which Way to Color, Whiten, Brighten," *Brandweek*, June 17, 2002, p. 558.

25. "How many hours of sleep are enough?" Mayo Clinic website, accessed September 2014 at www.mayoclinic.com/health/how-many-hours-of-sleep-are-enough/AN01487.

26. "The VALS™ Types," www.strategicbusinessinsight.com, accessed July 2013.

27. Personal interview with Michael Weiss, chief marketing officer, Environics Analytics, July 2013.

28. "Maximizing the Market with Influentials," *American Demographics*, July 1995, p. 42; also see, "I'll Have What He's Having," *American Demographics*, July 2000, p. 22.

29. Representative recent work on positive and negative word of mouth can be found in Geok Theng Lau and Sophia Ng, "Individual and Situational Factors Influencing Negative Word-of-Mouth Behaviour," *Canadian Journal of Administrative Sciences 18* (2001), pp. 163–178; Robert E. Smith and Christine A. Vogt, "The Effects of Integrating Advertising and Negative Word-of-Mouth Communications on Message Processing and Response," *Journal of Consumer Psychology 4* (1995), pp. 133–151; Paula Bone, "Word-of-Mouth Effects on Short-Term and Long-Term Product Judgments," *Journal of Business Research 32* (1995), pp. 213–23; Chip Walker, "Word of Mouth," *American Demographics*, July 1995, pp. 38–45; and Dale F. Duhan, Scott D. Johnson, James B. Wilcox, and Gilbert D. Harrell, "Influences on Consumer Use of Word-of-Mouth Recommendation Sources," *Journal of the Academy of Marketing Science 25* (1997), pp. 283–295.

30. Weng Marc Lim, "The Influence of Internet Advertising and Electronic Word of Mouth on Consumer Perceptions and Intention: Some Evidence from Online Group Buying," *Journal of Computer Information Systems 55*(4) (2015), 81–89; Megan Haynes, "Hey brands, millennials want you to help out," *Strategy*, September 19, 2014, http://strategyonline.ca/2014/09/19/hey-brands-millennials-want-you-to-help-out/; Marta Tsimicalis, "Ethical consumerism is rampant amongst Canada's younger generation," *St. Joseph Communications* (n.d.), http://stjoseph.com/ethical-consumerism-and-youth/; and "Sowing the seeds of business success," *Globe and Mail* (Ottawa/Quebec Edition), September 30, 2015.

31. For an extended discussion on reference groups, see Wayne D. Hoyer and Deborah J. MacInnis, *Consumer Behavior*, 2nd ed. (Boston: Houghton Mifflin, 2001), chap. 15.

32. For an extensive review on consumer socialization of children, see Deborah Roedder John, "Consumer Socialization of Children: A Retrospective Look at Twenty-Five Years of Research," *Journal of Consumer Research 26* (1999), pp. 183–213.

33. This discussion is based on "The American Family in the 21st Century," *American Demographics*, August 2001, p. 20; and J. Paul Peter and Jerry C. Olson, *Consumer Behavior and Marketing Strategy*, 5th ed. (New York: Irwin/McGraw-Hill, 1999), pp. 341–43.

34. "Canadian households in 2011: Type and growth," Statistics Canada, September 2012, http://www12.statcan.gc.ca/census-recensement/2011/as-sa/98-312-x/98-312-x2011003_2-eng.pdf.

35. Diane Crispell, "Dual-Earner Diversity," *American Demographics*, July 1995, pp. 32–37.

36. "There She Is . . . ," *American Demographics*, August 2001, p. 6; "Wearing the Pants," *Brandweek*, October 20, 1997, pp. 20, 22; "Look Who's Shopping," *Progressive Grocer*, January 1998, p. 18.

37. Bridget Brennan, "Top 10 Things Everyone Should Know About Women Consumers," *Forbes*, January 21, 2015, http://www.forbes.com/sites/bridgetbrennan/2015/01/21/top-10-things-everyone-should-know-about-women-consumers/#7f28a29f2897; "Call It 'Kid-fluence,'" *U.S. News & World Report*, July 30, 2001, pp. 32–33; "Special Report: Superstars of Spending," *Advertising Age*, February 20, 2001, pp. S1, S10; Teen Research Unlimited, www.teenresearch.com, September 4, 2001.

38. "I.AM.Canadian by Molson," CBC Digital Archives, www.cbc.ca/archives/categories/economy-business/business/selling-suds-the-beer-industry-in-canada/i-am-canadian.html; and Susan Krashinsky, "I am Canadian, and so are they: Molson's new nationalist pitch," *Globe and Mail*, February 6, 2013, www.theglobeandmail.com/report-on-business/industry-news/marketing/i-am-canadian-and-so-are-they-molsons-new-nationalist-pitch/article8280376/.

39. "French and the francophonie in Canada," Statistics Canada, October 2012, www12.statcan.gc.ca/census-recensement/2011/as-sa/98-314-x/98-314-x2011003_1-eng.cfm.

40. Danny Kucharsky, "French Lessons," *Marketing*, March 27, 2006, p. 8.

41. Ed Crain, "Say 'Oui' to the Quebec Market," *Electronic Retailer*, August 2010, www.electronicretailermag.com/er0810_quebec.

42. Rebecca Harris, "Embrace and Prosper," *Marketing*, January 23, 2006.

43. For comprehensive references on cross-cultural aspects of marketing, see Paul A. Herbig, *Handbook of Cross-Cultural Marketing* (New York: Halworth Press, 1998); and Jean-Claude Usunier, *Marketing across Cultures*, 2nd ed. (London: Prentice Hall Europe, 1996). Unless otherwise indicated, examples found in this section appear in these excellent sources.

44. "McDonald's Adapts Mac Attack to Foreign Tastes with Expansion," *Dallas Morning News*, December 7, 1997, p. 3H; and "Taking Credit," *The Economist*, November 2, 1996, p. 75.

45. Patricia Adams, "Foreign aid corruption case puts Canada on trial," *National Post*, August 20, 1999.

46. These examples appear in Del I. Hawkins, Roger J. Best, and Kenneth A. Coney, *Consumer Behavior*, 8th ed. (Burr Ridge, IL: McGraw-Hill/Irwin, 2001), chap 2.

47. "Greeks Protest Coke's Use of Parthenon," *Dallas Morning News*, August 17, 1992, p. D4.

48. Valentina Vescovi, "In Spain, Pepsi Becomes 'Pesi,'" *Advertising Age*, February 4, 2010, http://adage.com/article/global-news /marketing-spain-pepsi-pesi/141916/; and Valentina Vescovi and Aixa Rocca, "In Argentina, Pepsi Becomes 'Pecsi,'" *Advertising Age*, July 15, 2009, http://adage.com/globalnews/article?article _id=137946.

49. "Global Thinking Paces Computer Biz," *Advertising Age*, March 6, 1995, p. 10.

50. "If only Krispy Kreme makes you smarter," *Business 2.0*, August 2005, p. 108.

51. Anca Bucuta, "A review of the specific characteristics of the generation Y consumer," *The Proceedings of the International Conference, Marketing - from Information to Decision 8* (2015): 38; "The 'compassion effect,'" *USA Today*, Dec. 2015; Jeff Fromm, "Think Tank," *WWD*, July 22, 2015; "McDonald's Canada introduces self-serve ordering," *Toronto Star*, September 30, 2015, http://www .thestar.com/business/2015/09/30/mcdonalds-canada-introduces -self-serve-ordering.html; Brian Sozzi, "McDonald's rolling out self-ordering kiosks in Europe: Will the U.S. be next?" *The Street*, April 13, 2016, https://www.thestreet.com/story/13511123/1 /mcdonald-s-rolling-out-self-ordering-kiosks-in-europe-will-u-s-be -next.html.

Chapter 4

1. Personal interview with Paul Shumlich, co-founder, Deepwater Farms, 2019; Food and Agriculture Organization of the United Nations, *The State of World Fisheries and Aquaculture: 2016*, accessed August 2020 at http://www.fao.org/3/a-i5555e.pdf; Oran B. Hesterman and Daniel Horan, "The demand for 'local' food is growing—here's why investors should pay attention," *Business Insider*, April 25, 2017, https://www.businessinsider.com /the-demand-for-local-food-is-growing-2017-4; Meticulous Market Research, "Aquaponics Market worth $1.4 billion by 2025- Exclusive Report by Meticulous Research [News release]," July 13, 2019, accessed August 2020 at https://www.globenewswire.com /news-release/2019/07/13/1882266/0/en/Aquaponics-Market-worth -1-4-billion-by-2025-Exclusive-Report-by-Meticulous-Research .html; Alberta Agriculture and Forestry, "Report on local food demand in the Calgary region," August 2015, accessed August 2020 at https://open.alberta.ca/publications/report-on-local-food-demand -in-the-calgary-region.

2. A lengthier, expanded definition is found on the American Marketing Association's website. See https://www.ama.org/AboutAMA /Pages/Definition-of-Marketing.aspx; and for a researcher's comments on this and other definitions of marketing research, see Lawrence D. Gibson, "Quo Vadis, *Marketing Research?*" *Marketing Research*, Spring 2000, pp. 36–41.

3. "Loyalty and Behaviour Among Younger Fans [Case study]," Insightrix, accessed August 2020 at https://insightrix.com /saskatchewan-roughriders-case-study/;Insightrix, https://insightrix .com/; "CRM Programmer Analyst [Job order detail]," SaskJobs.ca, accessed August 2020 at https://www.saskjobs.ca/jsp/joborder/detail .jsp?job_order_id=902363; SaskWatch, www.saskwatch.ca.

4. Lawrence D. Gibson, "Defining Marketing Problems," *Marketing Research*, Spring 1998, pp. 4–12; and Martin Meister, "How to Define a Marketing Research Problem," *Business Insights Review*, July 11, 2012.

5. David A. Aaker, V. Kumar, George S. Day, and Robert P. Leone, *Marketing Research*, 10th ed. (Hoboken, NJ: Wiley, 2010), pp. 114–16.

6. Anand Rao, "Social listening: How market sensing trumps market research," PwC, June 13, 2016, accessed August 2020 at https://www.pwc.com/gx/en/governance-risk-compliance -consulting-services/resilience/publications/pdfs/social-listening. pdf.

7. Matthew Klein, "Selling Pies, Driving ROI: Pizza Hut's Solid Social Listening Strategy," Falcon.IO, January 27, 2016, https:// www.falcon.io/insights-hub/case-stories/cs-social-media-roi/pizza- hut-social-listening-case-study/.

8. "Homescan," Nielsen Canada, accessed June 2016 at https://www .homescan.ca/panel/CA/EN/Login.htm.

9. "What Is Online Research?" Marketing Research Association, accessed at http://www.marketingresearch.org/?q=node/221. See also *www.surveymonkey.com*.

10. For more discussion on wording questions effectively, see Gilbert A. Churchill Jr., Tom J. Brown, and Tracy A. Suter, *Basic Marketing Research*, 7th ed. (Mason, OH: South-Western, Cengage Learning, 2010), pp. 289–307.

11. Kira Vermond, "Why London, Ontario is the perfect test market," *Globe and Mail*, October 19, 2015, http://www.theglobeandmail .com/report-on-business/small-business/sb-managing/london-test -market/article26846284/.

12. "Population by year, by province and territory, 2015," Statistics Canada, CANSIM, table 051-0001, accessed June 2016 at http:// www.statcan.gc.ca/tables-tableaux/sum-som/l01/cst01/demo02a -eng.htm.

13. Janakiraman Moorthy, Rangin Lahiri, Neelanjan Biswas, Dipyaman Sanyal, Jayanthi Ranjan, Krishnadas Nanath, and Pulak Ghosh, "Big Data: Prospects and Challenges," *Vikalpa*, January–March, 2015, pp. 74–96; Karthik Kambatla, Giorgos Kollias, Vipin Kumar, and Ananth Grama, "Trends in Big Data Analytics," *Journal of Parallel and Distributed Computing*," January 2014, pp. 2561–73; Steve LaValle, Eric Lesser, Rebecca Shockley, Michael S. Hopkins, and Nina Kruschwitz, "Big Data, Analytics and the Path from Insights to Value," *Sloan Management Review*, Winter 2011, pp. 21–31; and "Big Data: Before You Start Restricting It, Be Aware of All the Opportunities," *The Wall Street Journal*, November 19, 2012, p. R10.

14. Hal Conick, "The Past, Present and Future of AI in Marketing," *Marketing News*, January 2017, pp. 26-35.

15. "Target Using Predictive Analytics to Increase Value Capture," HBS Digital Innovation and Transformation," November 22, 2015, https://digit.hbs.org/submission/target-using-predictive-analytics -to-increase-value-capture/.

16. "How Social Media Data Mining Could Shape the Products of Tomorrow," *www.phys.org*, February 15, 2017; Joni R. Jackson, "Big Data: Goldmine or Minefield," *AMA Winter Conference Proceedings*, 2016, p. 41; Joel Stein, "Your Data, Yourself," *Time*, March 21, 2011, pp. 39–46; Ryan Flinn, "The Big Business of Sifting through Social Media Data," *Bloomberg Businessweek*, October 25–October 31, 2010, pp. 20–22; and Michael Lev-Ram, "The Hot New Gig in Tech," *Fortune*, September 5, 2011, p. 29.

17. Bala Deshpande, "How to use RFM analysis for customer segmentation and classification," Simafore, December 3, 2013, http://www.simafore.com/blog/bid/159575/How-to-use -RFM-analysis-for-customer-segmentation-and -classification.

18. "RFM Analysis," IBM Knowledge Center, November 30, 2015, http://www.ibm.com/support/knowledgecenter/SSLVMB_20.0.0 /com.ibm.spss.statistics.help/rfm_intro.xml.htm.

Chapter 5

1. Personal interview with Chris Venter, project director, IFS, July 2019.

2. Peter LaPlaca, "From the Editor," *Journal of Business and Industrial Marketing* 3 (1992); D. Lawin, "Business-to-business marketing: A defined strategy," *Franchising World* 36 (2004), pp. 24–25; Nicole E. Coviello and Roderick J. Brodie, "Contemporary marketing practices of consumer and business-to-business firms: How different are they?" *Journal of Business & Industrial Marketing* 16 (2001), pp. 382–400.

3. This figure is based on *Statistical Abstract of the United States: 2002*, 122nd ed. (Washington, DC: U.S. Census Bureau, 2002).

4. "10 things you (probably) didn't know about Canadian SMEs," BDC, accessed at https://www.bdc.ca/en/articles-tools/business -strategy-planning/manage-business/pages/10-things-didnt-know -canadian-sme.aspx; and "Key Small Business Statistics - January 2019," Government of Canada, January 31, 2019, accessed at https://www.ic.gc.ca/eic/site/061.nsf/eng/h_03090.html#point1-1.

5. "Federal Budget 2013: Government stays the course on cuts, 2015 balanced budget," Canadian Press, March 21, 2013, www .huffingtonpost.ca/2013/03/21/federal-budget-2013_n_2883904 .html; Joel Eastwood, "New database will allow Canadians to track government spending data," Canadian Press, April 22, 2013, http:// globalnews.ca/news/502224/new-database-will-allow-canadians -to-track-government-spending-data/; "Expenditure database," Treasury Board of Canada Secretariat, April 12, 2013, www.tbs-sct .gc.ca/ems-sgd/edb-bdd/edb-bdd-eng.asp.

6. Lee Berthiaume, "Feds offer $15.8B in new ships to Vancouver, Halifax while opening door to Davie," *National Post*, May 22, 2019, https://nationalpost.com/pmn/news-pmn/canada-news-pmn /feds-offer-15-8b-in-new-ships-to-vancouver-halifax-while-opening -door-to-davie; Jane Seyd, "Seaspan to build 16 more Coast Guard ships says Trudeau," *North Shore News*, May 22, 2019, https://www.nsnews.com/news/seaspan-to-build-16-more-coast -guard-ships-says-trudeau-1.23830777; Katya Slepian, "16 Coast Guard ships to be built in $15.7B 'fleet renewal' plan in B.C.: Trudeau," *Saanich News*, May 22, 2019, https://www.saanichnews .com/news/16-coast-guard-ships-to-be-built-in-15-7b-fleet-renewal -plan-in-b-c-trudeau/.

7. "Charities Listings," Canada Revenue Agency, April 4, 2013, accessed at www.cra-arc.gc.ca/tax/charities/online_listings/canreg _interim-e.html; "Charities Program Update," Canada Revenue Agency, April 18, 2013, accessed at www.cra-arc.gc.ca/chrts-gvng /chrts/bt/chrtsprgrm_pdt-eng.html.

8. North American Industry Classification System (NAICS) Canada 2012, Statistics Canada, October 24, 2013, accessed at www23.statcan .gc.ca/imdb/p3VD.pl?Function=getVDPage1&TVD=118464.

9. Tessa Wegert, "Contently Case Story: How Content is helping Xerox Rebrand," *Contently*, October 6, 2015, https://contently.com /strategist/2015/10/06/contently-case-story-how-content-is-helping -xerox-rebrand/; Chima Adiele, "Towards promoting interactivity in a B2B web community," *Information Systems Frontiers 13* (2011), pp. 237–249; Umberto Miletti, "B2B Companies Must Keep Pace with the Customer 2.0." *Social Media B2B*, June 7, 2010, http:// socialmediab2b.com/2010/06/b2b-company-customer; "About," HealthBiz Decoded (n.d.), http://healthbizdecoded.com /about/; Kate Maddox, "BMA conference focuses on content, innovation," *B to B*, June 13, 2011; "2013 Content Marketing Awards," *B to B*, September 30, 2013, www.btobonline.com /article/20130930/CONTENTMARKETING01/309269992/xerox -corp?template=CMAprofile.

10. Joe Pulizzi, "The transformation of content marketing," *EContent*, December 2012, pp. 20–21; Joe Pulizzi, "2013 B2B Content Marketing Benchmarks, Budgets and Trends," Content Marketing Institute, October 24, 2012, http://contentmarketinginstitute. com/2012/10/2013-b2b-content-marketing-research/; "What is content marketing?" Content Marketing Institute (n.d.), http:// contentmarketinginstitute.com/what-is-content-marketing/; Sarah Johnson and Laura Sparks, "How to launch a content marketing strategy," *CPA Practice Management Forum* 9 (2013), pp. 5–7.

11. This listing and portions of the following discussion are based on F. Robert Dwyer and John F. Tanner, Jr., *Business Marketing*, 2nd ed. (Burr Ridge, IL: McGraw-Hill/Irwin, 2002); and Edward G. Brierty, Robert W. Eckles, and Robert R. Reeder, *Business Marketing*, 3rd ed. (Upper Saddle River, NJ: Prentice Hall, 1998); and Dominic F. Wilson, "Why divide consumer and organizational buyer behaviour?" *European Journal of Marketing* 34 (2000), pp. 780–796.

12. "TTC and Bombardier sign contract to build 204 new street cars" [News release], Toronto Transit Commission, June 30, 2009, accessed at www.ttc.ca/News/2009/June/TTC_and_Bombardier _sign_contract_to_build_204_new_streetcars.jsp; J. T. Connelly, "Bombardier: 186 Subway Cars Ordered for Toronto Transit," *Business Review Canada*, May 13, 2010, www.businessreviewcanada .ca/news/transportation/bombardier-186-subway-cars-ordered -toronto-transit; Tess Kalinowski, " TTC unveils Toronto's new streetcars," *Toronto Star*, November 15, 2012, www.thestar.com/news /city_hall/2012/11/15/ttc_unveils_torontos_new_streetcars.html.

13. "The Changing B2B Buyer," Marketo (n.d.), accessed September 2014 at www.marketo.com/cheat-sheets/the-changing-b2b-buyer/; "What makes business-to-business marketing different," Proteus Marketing (n.d.), accessed September 2014 at www.proteusb2b .com/b2b-marketing/difference.php; R. B. Ferguson, "The uh-oh factor: Fundamental shifts in social business and what to do about it," *MIT Sloan Management Review* 54 (2012), pp. 1–4.

14. "Environmental labels and claims," Innovation, Science and Economic Development Canada, April 1, 2019, accessed September 2020 at http://www.ic.gc.ca/eic/site/oca-bc.nsf/eng/ca02523.html; "Selling to the Government of Canada," Public Works and Government Services Canada; "The Procurement Process," Public Works and Government Services; and "Key Small Business Statistics – August 2013," Innovation, Science and Economic Development Canada.

15. S. Andersson and p. Servais, "Combining industrial buyer and seller strategies for international supply and marketing management," *European Business Review* 22 (2010), pp. 64–81, doi:http:// dx.doi.org/10.1108/09555341011009016; J. H. Bantham, "An exploratory study of satisfaction in buyer-seller partnerships," *Journal of Consumer Satisfaction, Dissatisfaction and Complaining Behavior* 23 (2010), p. 130; definitions adapted from F. E. Webster and Y. Wind, *Organizational Buying Behavior* (Englewood Cliffs, NJ: Prentice Hall, 1972).

16. T. V. Bonoma, "Major Sales: Who Really Does the Buying?" *Harvard Business Review*, July 2006, http://hbr.org/2006/07/major -sales-who-really-does-the-buying/ar/1.

17. Ibid.

18. Ibid.

19. Webster and Wind, *Organizational Buying Behavior*; F.E. Webster Jr. and Y. Wind, "A General Model for Understanding Organizational Buying Behavior," *Journal of Marketing* 36 (1972), pp. 12–19.

20. "Contract awarded for St. Lawrence project bridge," *Purchasing B2B*, October 21, 2013, www.canadianmanufacturing.com /purchasing-and-procurement/news/contract-awarded-for-st-lawrence -project-bridge-120780; "Government of Canada awards contract for engineering and coordination services for the new bridge for the St. Lawrence project" [Press release], Transport Canada, October 18, 2013, www.tc.gc.ca/eng/mediaroom/releases-2013-h139e-7388.html.

21. Representative studies on the buy-class framework that document its usefulness include E. Anderson, W., Chu, and B. Weitz, "Industrial purchasing: An empirical exploration of the buy-class framework," *Journal of Marketing 51* (1987), pp. 71–86; M. Ghingold, "Testing the 'buy-grid' buying process model," *Journal of Purchasing and Materials Management 22* (1986), pp. 30–36; p. Matthyssens and W. Faes, "OEM buying process for new components: Purchasing and marketing implications," *Industrial Marketing Management 14* (1985), pp. 147–157; and T.W. Leight and A.J. Ethans, "A script-theoretic analysis of industrial purchasing

behavior," *Journal of Marketing 48* (1984), pp. 22–32. Studies not supporting the buy-class framework include J.A. Bellizi and p. McVey, "How valid is the buy-grid model?" *Industrial Marketing Management 12* (1983), pp. 57–62; and D.W. Jackson, J.E. Keith, and R.K. Burdick, "Purchasing agents' perceptions of industrial buying center influences: A situational approach," *Journal of Marketing 48* (1984), pp. 75–83.

22. N. Weinberg, "Evolution, Not Revolution," *Forbes*, May 21, 2001, www.forbes.com/best/2001/0521/038.html; "Business connections: The wired way we work," *Newsweek*, April 30, 2001; V. Vijayasri, "Arriving at a systems paradigm: Measuring and managing the complexity of organizations and consumers online," Order No. 3019131, Syracuse University, ProQuest Dissertations and Theses (2001).

23. This discussion is based on M. Roberti, "General Electric's Spin Machine," *The Industry Standard* (2001), pp. 74–83; "Grainger lightens its 'digital load,'" *Industrial Distribution 90* (2001), pp. 21–24; and K. Kuryllowicz, "The future of the net: We called up the smartest internet users we know to ask where the net is headed next," *Profit*, May 1, 2001.

24. "Surprise upturn for online trading," *Supply Management 6* (2001), p. 9; T. Gignac, "E-barter exchanges play matchmaker: Businesses are using online trading networks to swap services, save money and discover new customers," *Calgary Herald*, May 28, 2001; J.O. Soo and S.W. Kim, "The effect of B2B e-marketplace type on buyer-supplier relational advantages of e-marketplace and firm performance," *Asian Journal on Quality* 12 (2011), pp. 189–203, doi: http://dx.doi.org/10.1108/15982681111158742

25. "Our Story," Ariba website, n.d., www.ariba.com/ourstory.

26. "Etiquette guide to japan; know the rules that make the difference," rev. ed., *Reference and Research Book News 24* (2009); L. Laroche and S. Morey, "Minding your manners: Business etiquette and gift-giving are part and parcel of conducting business abroad," *CMA Management 74* (2000), pp. 38–41; B. Bradley, "Best behaviour: Business etiquette in Japan," *Report on Business Magazine*, March 2001; G. Cotton, "Do this, not that when doing business overseas," CNBC, April 6, 2013, www.cnbc.com/id/100588894; Chad Brooks, "Lost in Translation: 8 International Marketing Fails," *Business News Daily*, October 7, 2013, http://www.businessnewsdaily.com /5241-international-marketing-fails.html; Neil Kokemuller, "Marketing Blunders & Global Culture," *AZCentral* (n.d.), http:// yourbusiness.azcentral.com/marketing-blunders-global-culture -13505.html; "Nike tattoo leggings pulled after deemed exploitative of Samoan culture," *Huffington Post*, August 15, 2013, www .huffingtonpost.com/2013/08/15/nike-tattoo-leggings_n_3763591. html; V. Tapaleao, "Nike commits cultural faux pas," *New Zealand Herald*, August 14, 2013, www.nzherald.co.nz/business/news /article.cfm?c_id=3&objectid=10912088; "Nike debuts athletic ware, offends all of Samoa, pulls athletic wear," MSN, August 14, 2013, http://now.msn.com/nike-apologizes-for-using-samoan -tattoo-as-inspiration-for-running-tights.

27. Christian McIntosh, "Online auctions push E-commerce," *PC World Online*, April 29, 1999; R. Bray, "Reverse auctions going full speed ahead," *Summit* 6 (2003); Olivia Korostelina, "Online reverse auctions: a cost-saving inspiration for businesses," *Dartmouth Business Journal*, March 17, 2012, http://dartmouthbusinessjournal .com/2012/03/online-reverse-auctions-a-cost-saving-inspiration-for -businesses/.

28. Mary Kwak, "Potential pitfalls of e-auctions: smart ideas on reverse auctions," *Working Knowledge for Business Leaders*, Harvard Business School, September 9, 2002, http://hbswk.hbs.edu/archive /3086.html; Bob Tedeschi, "GE has a bright idea," *Smart Business*, September 25, 2001.

29. Sandy Jap, "Going, Going, Gone," *Harvard Business Review*, November 2000, http://hbr.org/2000/11/going-going-gone/ar/1; L. Wichmann, "Avoiding the pitfalls of e-procurement: Seminar lays down the pros and cons of internet commerce," *Plant* 59 (2000), p. 16; G. Cameron, "Reverse auctions remain high on OGCA hit list," *Daily Commercial News and Construction Record* 76 (2003), p. 5.

Chapter 6

1. Personal interview and correspondence with Dion Red Gun, founder of River Ranche Lodge, February 2020; "From carpentry to tourism: entrepreneur builds a dream [Blog post]," Alberta Culture, November 6, 2017, accessed at https://albertaculture.wordpress. com/2017/11/06/from-carpentry-to-tourism-entrepreneur-builds-a -dream/; Colleen Schmidt, "Restart for Siksika's River Ranche," CTV News, November 18, 2015, https://calgary.ctvnews.ca/restart -for-siksika-s-river-ranche-1.2665041; Ian Bickis, "Indigenous tourism helps keep stories alive as international interest grows," CBC News Calgary, January 2, 2018, https://www.cbc.ca/news/canada /calgary/indigenous-tourism-international-siksika-alberta-1.4469848.

2. "Development of Tide Synthetic Detergent," American Chemical Society, October 25, 2006, accessed April 2020 at https://www.acs .org/content/acs/en/education/whatischemistry/landmarks/tidedetergent .html; "IGain," P&G Canada website, accessed April 2020 at https://www.pgeveryday.ca/brands/gain; "Ivory Snow," P&G Canada website, accessed April 2020 at https://www.pgeveryday.ca /brands/ivory-snow; "Tide laundry detergent," P&G Canada website, accessed April 2020 at https://www.pgeveryday.ca/brands/tide.

3. "Packaging product specs," French's Flavor Ingredients, accessed April 2020 at https://www.frenchsflavoringredients.com/products /frenchs; "Frenchs Tomato Ketchup Packet," McCormick for Chefs, accessed April 2020 at https://www.mccormickforchefs.com /products/frenchs/frenchs-tomato-ketchup-packet.

4. Adapted from the American Marketing Association's dictionary, accessed July 2016 at https://www.ama.org/resources/Pages /Dictionary.aspx?dLetter=N.

5. "Model S," Tesla Canada, accessed April 2020 at https://www.tesla .com/en_ca/models.

6. "About us," Eco-Max website, accessed April 2020 at https://eco-max .com/about-us/.

7. "About Us," Crown Outdoor & Tactical website, accessed April 2020 at https://www.armysurplus.com/service/about/.

8. Philip T. Kotler and Kevin Lane Keller, *Marketing Management*, 15th ed. (New York: Pearson Education, 2016).

9. Chris Powell, "Canadians can have a Keith and a smile with the second iteration of Coca-Cola Canada's popular 'Share a Coke' campaign," *Canadian Grocer*, July 20, 2015.

10. Meagan Campbell, "E-scooter abandonment issues have cities scrambling to get problem under control," *National Post*, August 28, 2019, https://nationalpost.com/news/canada/e-scooter-abandonment- issues-have-cities-scrambling-to-get-problem-under-control; "Scooters In Calgary: Lime's First Gen 3 Launch In Canada Sees Surprising Results [Blog post]," 2nd Street Lime, July 26, 2019, https:// www.li.me/second-street/scooters-calgary-lime-first-gen-3-launch -canada-surprising-results; Stephanie Babych, "E-scooters taking the winter off while city assesses pilot data," *Calgary Herald*, October 30, 2019, https://calgaryherald.com/news/local-news/e-scooters -taking-the-winter-off-while-city-assesses-pilot-data/; Thomas Daigle, "Why an image problem is slowing e-scooter rollout in Canada," CBC News, September 7, 2019, https://www.cbc.ca/news /technology/escooters-canada-analysis-1.5273793.

11. "Centrum Products," Centrum website, accessed April 2020 at http://www.centrum.ca/products.

12. "About us," Euromonitor website, accessed April 2020 at www .euromonitor.com/.

13. "PRIZM5," Environics Analytics website.

14. *Canadian Millennial Social Values Study*, Environics Institute, February 28, 2017, https://www.environicsinstitute.org/projects /project-details/canadian-millennial-social-values-study.

15. PSYTE HD, Pitney Bowes Canada website, accessed April 2020 at http://www.pitneybowes.com/us/location-intelligence/gis-data-sets /psyte-hd-canada.html.

16. SuperDemographics website, accessed July 2016 at www .superdemographics.com.

17. Rohit Bhisey, "Prospects of Pickleball Equipment Market Continue to be Optimistic, Growth Remains Consolidated in North America

& Europe" [News release], Fact.MR, June 6, 2018, accessed April 2020 at https://www.globenewswire.com/news-release/2018/06/06/1517453/0/en/Prospects-of-Pickleball-Equipment-Market-Continue-to-be-Optimistic-Growth-Remains-Consolidated-in-North-America-Europe.html; Amanda Loudin, "Pickleball: The fastest growing sport you've never heard of," April 21, 2019, NBC News, accessed April 2020 at https://www.nbcnews.com/better/lifestyle/pickleball-fastest-growing-sport-you-ve-never-heard-ncna992106; Amanda Kolson Hurley, "Why Your Grandma Loves Pickleball," October 26, 2015, Bloomberg CityLab, accessed April 2020 at https://www.bloomberg.com/news/articles/2015-10-26/why-your-grandma-and-other-seniors-love-pickleball; "About Us," PickleBallDepot.ca, accessed April 2020 at https://www.pickleballdepot.ca/pages/about-us.

18. Chris Powell, "TSN introduces 'Champions Live Here' positioning," *Marketing*, February 11, 2016, http://www.marketingmag.ca/advertising/tsn-introduces-champions-live-here-positioning-167838.

19. Sam Oches, "Inside the Plan to Fix McDonald's," *QSR* magazine, May 2018, https://www.qsrmagazine.com/reports/inside-plan-fix-mcdonalds; "McDonald's® Canada will be the first company to serve Canadian beef from farms and ranches certified sustainable by leading industry experts" [Press release], McDonald's Canada, July 11, 2018, accessed August 2020 at https://www.newswire.ca/news-releases/mcdonalds-canada-will-be-the-first-company-to-serve-canadian-beef-from-farms-and-ranches-certified-sustainable-by-leading-industry-experts-687955591.html.

20. "A&W brings Beyond Meat's Revolutionary Plant-Based Burger to Canada" [Press release], A&W Food Services of Canada, June 21, 2018, accessed August 2020 at https://www.newswire.ca/news-releases/aw-brings-beyond-meats-revolutionary-plant-based-burger-to-canada-686152231.html; Harmeet Singh, "2017 Brands of the Year: A&W Stays Rooted in Real," September 26, 2017, *Strategy*, https://strategyonline.ca/2017/09/26/2017-brands-of-the-year-aw-stays-rooted-in-real/.

21. Brenda Bouw, "Powerful Questrade ads putting advisors on the hot seat," *Globe and Mail*, August 12, 2019, https://www.theglobeandmail.com/investing/globe-advisor/advisor-news/article-powerful-questrade-ads-putting-advisors-on-the-hot-seat/; Jordann Brown, "Best Online Brokerage Accounts in Canada for 2020 [Blog post]," Young and Thrifty, April 9, 2020, https://youngandthrifty.ca/the-ultimate-guide-to-canadas-discount-brokerages/; "Questrade profile," Ivey/Scotiabank Digital Banking Lab, September 24, 2018, accessed April 2020 at https://www.ivey.uwo.ca/cmsmedia/3783799/questrade-profile.pdf.

Chapter 7

1. "Our Story," Hillberg & Berk website, accessed April 2020 at https://hillbergandberk.com/pages/our-story; personal communication with Brittany Mattick, Hallie Bolen (director, purpose & engagement, Hillberg & Berk), and Katie Smith (community engagement partner, Calgary Hillberg & Berk); Craig Patterson, "Canadian Jewellery Brand 'Hillberg & Berk' Announces Retail Store Expansion into British Columbia and Manitoba," *Retail Insider*, September 3, 2019, https://www.retail-insider.com/retail-insider/2019/9/canadian-jewellery-brand-hillberg-amp-berk-announces-retail-store-expansion-into-british-columbia-and-manitoba; Rick Spence, "The story behind Canadian jewellery retailer Hillberg & Berk's impressive growth," *Financial Post*, March 20, 2015, https://business.financialpost.com/entrepreneur/regina-jewellery-retailer-hillberg-berk-has-a-method-to-pulling-off-one-of-the-toughest-acts-going-national; Michelle Magnan, "Meet Hillberg & Berk founder Rachel Mielke," *Feverish News*, May 10, 2019, https://feverishnews.com/meet-hillberg-berk-founder-rachel-mielke/; "Rachel Mielke (HS'98)," Luthor College High School website, accessed April 2020 at https://www.luthercollege.edu/high-school/alumni-friends/alumni/the-luther-story/springsummer-2017-alumni-profiles/rachel-mielke-hs98.

2. "Gross domestic product (GDP) by industry sector," Statistics Canada website, table 379-0031, accessed April 2020 at http://www.statcan.gc.ca/tables-tableaux/sum-som/l01/cst01/gdps04a-eng.htm.

3. George Guidoni, "The Straw Poll," *Canadian Packaging*, February 25, 2020, https://www.canadianpackaging.com/features/the-straw-poll/.

4. "Trends and Opportunities in the Canadian Packaging Industry" [News release], Cision PR Newswire, December 19, 2019, https://www.prnewswire.com/news-releases/trends-and-opportunities-in-the-canadian-packaging-industry-300971239.html; Tristanne Davis, "5 Sustainable Packaging Trends to Look Out for in 2020," *Packaging Digest*, February 21, 2020, https://www.packagingdigest.com/sustainable-packaging/5-sustainable-packaging-trends-to-look-out-for-in-2020-2020-02-21; "11 inspiring packaging design trends for 2020," 99 Designs, accessed September 2020 at https://99designs.ca/blog/trends/packaging-design-trends/; Brittany Giles, "17 Packaging Designs That Put Other Packages to Shame [Blog post]" TPH – The Printing House Blog, October 21, 2014, https://blog.tph.ca/2014/10/21/creative-unique-packaging-design/; Kristen Kazarian, "Latest Packaging Innovations Changing the Rules," *Packaging Strategies*, February 11, 2020, https://www.packagingstrategies.com/articles/95355-latest-packaging-innovations-changing-the-rules.

5. "All Brands Canada," Coca-Cola Canada website, accessed April 2020 at https://www.coca-cola.ca/brands.

6. "Google Ads - Reach customers when it matters," Google website, accessed April 2020 at https://www.google.com/ads/.

7. "All Brands," Procter & Gamble website, accessed April 2020 at http://www.pg.ca/en-CA/our-brands; "Dawn," Procter & Gamble website, accessed April 2020 at https://dawn-dish.com/en-us/coupons-and-offers/canada.

8. Steve Levy, "Ipsos Announces Ninth Annual Top 10 Most Influential Brands in Canada" [News release], Ipsos, February 5, 2020, Ipsos, accessed April 2020 at https://www.ipsos.com/en-ca/news-polls/Ipsos-announces-ninth-annual-Top-10-Most-Influential-Brands-in-Canada.

9. Ibid.

10. "2019 Global Best Global Brands," Interbrand website, accessed April 2020 at https://www.interbrand.com/best-brands/best-global-brands/2019/ranking/.

11. "What is a patent?" Canadian Intellectual Property Office website, accessed April 2020 at https://www.interbrand.com/best-brands/best-global-brands/2019/ranking/.

12. "What is copyright?" Canadian Intellectual Property Office website, accessed April 2020 at https://www.ic.gc.ca/eic/site/cipointernet-internetopic.nsf/eng/wr03719.html.

13. "What is a trademark?" Canadian Intellectual Property Office website, accessed April 2020 at https://www.ic.gc.ca/eic/site/cipointernet-internetopic.nsf/eng/wr03718.html.

14. Maryam Mohsin, "10 Facebook Statistics Every Marketer Should Know in 2020 [Infographic]," Oberlo, December 3, 2019, https://www.oberlo.com/blog/facebook-statistics; Ying Lin, "10 Twitter Statistics Every Marketer Should Know in 2020 [Infographic]," Oberlo, November 30, 2019, https://www.oberlo.ca/blog/twitter-statistics; "How Many Domains Are There? – Domain Name Stats for 2020," Make a Website Hub website, accessed April 2020 at https://makeawebsitehub.com/how-many-domains-are-there/; Joe Styler, "The top 25 most expensive domain names [Blog post]," GoDaddy, June 18, 2019, https://www.godaddy.com/garage/the-top-20-most-expensive-domain-names/; Twubs.com, accessed April 2020 at https://twubs.com/; Laura MacFarlane and Richard Stobbe, "#Hashmarks: Can a Hashtag be a Trademark?" Field Law, October 2018, accessed April 2020 at https://www.fieldlaw.com/portalresource/can-a-Hashtag-be-a-Trademark?utm_source=Mondaq&utm_medium=syndication&utm_campaign=LinkedIn-integration; "What Is Cybersquatting? Examples and What You Need to Know," *University Herald*, January 15, 2020, https://www.universityherald.com/articles/77157/20200115/what-is-cybersquatting-examples-and-what-you-need-to-know.htm; Canadian Intellectual Property Office, Trademarks Examination Manual, September 2017 update.

15. "Brand Glossary - Brand Personality," Brandchannel website, accessed April 2020 at http://brandchannel.com/brand-glossary/?ap=b.

16. "Why Brand Personality Matters: Aligning Your Brand to Cultural Drivers of Success" Millward Brown, accessed April 2020 at http://www.millwardbrown.com/docs/default-source/insight-documents/points-of-view/Millward_Brown_POV_Brand_Personality.pdf.

17. "How Many Domains Are There? – Domain Name Stats for 2020."

18. Zachary Crockett, "Microsoft vs. MikeRoweSoft," January 21, 2014, http://priceonomics.com/microsoft-vs-mikerowesoft/.

19. "2018: Record Number of UDRP Cybersquatting Complaints Filed with WIPO," March 20, 2019, IPzen, accessed April 2020 at https://www.ipzen.com/3383-2/.

20. Carman Allison, "Canadian Private Label: The Value Alternative," Nielsen, accessed April 2020 at https://www.nielsen.com/wp-content/uploads/sites/3/2019/04/Canadian-Private-Label-White-Paper.

21. Brad Tuttle, "Brand Names Don't Mean as Much Anymore, *Time*, November 1, 2012, http://business.time.com/2012/11/01/brand-names-just-dont-mean-as-much-anymore/.

Chapter 8

1. Personal correspondence with J.R. Brooks, co-owner of True Buch Kombucha; A.Amir, "Soda Production in the US," *IBIS World*, May 2019, https://clients1.ibisworld.com/reports/us/industry/default.aspx?entid=285; "Keeping It Raw. Why We Don't Pasteurize Our Kombucha," Bootleg Bucha, February 16, 2018, https://bootlegbucha.com/2018/02/16/keeping-raw-dont-pasteurize-kombucha/; "Top Five Kombucha Brands [Blog post]," Brew Your Bucha, April 21, 2018, https://brewyourbucha.com/ca/2018/04/21/kombucha-brands/; "Canada's Soft Drink, Bottled Water and Ice Industry," Agriculture and Agri-Food Canada website, n.d., accessed November 2019 at http://www.agr.gc.ca/eng/industry-markets-and-trade/canadian-agri-food-sector-intelligence/processed-food-and-beverages/profiles-of-processed-food-and-beverages-industries/canada-s-soft-drink-bottled-water-and-ice-industry/?id=1172167862291; Samantha Cassetty, "Diet and nutrition trends to keep (and toss) in 2019," NBC News, December 27, 2018, https://www.nbcnews.com/better/pop-culture/diet-nutrition-trends-keep-toss-2019-ncna952286; Joe Leech, "8 Evidence-Based Health Benefits of Kombucha Tea," *Healthline*, August 29, 2018, https://www.healthline.com/nutrition/8-benefits-of-kombucha-tea; Rachael Link, "Kombucha SCOBY: What It Is and How to Make One," *Healthline*, October 22, 2018, https://www.healthline.com/nutrition/kombucha-scoby; Joseph V. Micallef, "How The Cannabis Industry Is Revolutionizing The Beverage Sector," *Forbes*, May 22, 2019, https://www.forbes.com/sites/joemicallef/2019/05/22/how-the-cannabis-industry-is-revolutionizing-the-beverage-sector/#3ad455815673; M. Shahbandeh, "Soft drinks in Canada-statistics & facts," Statista, June 5, 2019, https://www.statista.com/topics/4259/soft-drinks-in-canada/; Kate Taylor, "People are drinking less Pepsi and Coke than ever — and it reveals the power of the 'biggest marketing trick of the century,'" *Business Insider*, May 7, 2018, https://www.businessinsider.com/pepsi-coke-decline-while-bottled-water-grows-2018-5; Christina Troitino, "Kombucha 101: Demystifying the Past, Present and Future of The Fermented Tea Drink," *Forbes*, February 1, 2017, https://www.forbes.com/sites/christinatroitino/2017/02/01/kombucha-101-demystifying-the-past-present-and-future-of-the-fermented-tea-drink/; "FAQs," True Büch, n.d. Accessed November 2019 at http://truebuch.com/faq; (2018). "Cannabis Industry Leader Zenabis Ltd. Signs LOI With Hillsboro Corp Inc., Maker of True Buch Kombucha" [Press release], True Büch News, October 16, 2018, https://truebuch.com/news/2018/10/17/zenabis-true-buch; Laura Unger, "Tea's health benefits boost its popularity," *Washington Post*, April 1, 2013, https://www.washingtonpost.com/national/health-science/teas-health-benefits-boost-its-popularity/2013/04/01/be818cfe-6ef5-11e2-aa58-243de81040ba_story.html; Larissa Zimberoff, "Why Kombucha May Never Make It Really Big," Bloomberg, October 5, 2018, https://www.bloomberg.com/news/articles/2018-10-05/can-big-soda-take-kombucha-mainstream.

2. John Kirk, "Android's Penetration Vs. Apple's Skimming Marketing Strategies," Tech.pinions, March 21, 2013, https://techpinions.com/androidss-penetration-vs-apples-skimming-marketing-strategies/15255.

3. Tom Huddleston Jr, "How Instant Pot became a kitchen appliance with a cult following and a best-seller on Amazon," CNBC, November 26, 2018, https://www.cnbc.com/2018/11/26/how-instant-pot-became-a-kitchen-appliance-with-a-cult-following.html.

4. Megan Poinski, Christopher Doering, and Lillianna Byington, "6 trends to impact the food industry in 2019 [Blog post]," Food Dive, January 7, 2019, https://www.fooddive.com/news/6-trends-to-impact-the-food-industry-in-2019/544677/.

5. "P&G Everyday: Tide," P&G website, accessed April 2020 at https://www.pgeveryday.ca/tag/tide.

6. "Canadian Brand Top 40 Ranking," *Canadian Business*, n.d., accessed April 2020 at https://www.canadianbusiness.com/canadian-brand-top-40-ranking/; Joe Castaldo, "McCain Foods: An old favourite freshens up," *Canadian Business*, April 28, 2013, https://www.canadianbusiness.com/lists-and-rankings/mccain-foods-an-old-favourite-freshens-up/.

7. Courtney Greenberg, "Knixwear's teen line aims to make girls the bosses of their periods," *Toronto Star*, May 26, 2017, https://www.thestar.com/life/2017/05/26/knixwears-teen-line-aims-to-make-girls-the-bosses-of-their-periods.html; Elizabeth Segran, "Can Knix win the 12 billion underwear wars?" *Fast Company*, October 15, 2018, https://www.fastcompany.com/90249128/can-knix-win-the-12-billion-underwear-wars; Sarah Kelsey, "How Joanna Griffiths took Knixwear from an idea to a million dollar company in just five years," *Women of Influence*, February 25, 2019, https://www.womenofinfluence.ca/2019/02/25/how-joanna-griffiths-took-knixwear-from-an-idea-to-a-million-dollar-company-in-just-five-years/; "Top 5 Highest Grossing Businesses on Dragons' Den," CBC, March 6, 2019, accessed April 2020 at https://www.cbc.ca/dragonsden/m_blog/top-successful-businesses; Tom Lorenzo, "Support the Front Line: Front-line Workers Get 30% Off At SAXX Underwear," *Men's Journal*, n.d., accessed April 2020 at https://www.mensjournal.com/style/support-the-front-line-front-line-workers-get-30-off-at-saxx-underwear/; McCann Worldgroup, "Premium Underwear Brand SAXX Partners With McCann To Push Into US Market" [Press release], Cision, July 26, 2019, accessed April 2020 at https://www.newswire.ca/news-releases/premium-underwear-brand-saxx-partners-with-mccann-to-push-into-us-market-894543022.html; "8-in-1 Evolution Bra: The World's Most Advanced Bra," Kickstarter website, accessed April 2020 at https://www.kickstarter.com/projects/evolutionbra/8-in-1-evolution-bra-the-worlds-most-advanced-bra; Hallie Cotnam, "Ottawa lab thinking outside the boxers to build better briefs," CBC News, January 14, 2020, https://www.cbc.ca/news/canada/ottawa/design-lab-hackathon-underwear-design-invent-makerspace-1.5420843.

8. Chaim Gartenberg, "Mobile Motorola Resurrects the Razr as a Foldable Android Smartphone," *The Verge*, November 13, 2019, https://www.theverge.com/2019/11/13/20963294/motorola-razr-new-foldable-smartphone-android-hands-on-flip-phone-photos-video.

9. Josh Kolm, "What drives Canadian purchase behaviour?" *Strategy*, August 24, 2016, http://strategyonline.ca/2016/08/24/what-drives-canadian-purchase-behaviour/?utm_source=rss&utm_medium=rss&utm_campaign=what-drives-canadian-purchase-behaviour.

10. "BrandSpark International's 2020 Best New Product Award Winners Announced" [News release], Cision, February 27, 2020, accessed April 2020 at https://www.newswire.ca/news-releases/brandspark-international-s-2020-best-new-product-award-winners-announced-895852042.html.

11. Leslie Hayward, "Overcoming Barriers To Electric Vehicle Adoption," *The Fuse*, May 30, 2015, http://energyfuse.org/overcoming-barriers-to-electric-vehicle-adoption/.

12. Arthur Thomas, "Drones could be the next disruptive technology," *Milwaukee Business News*, April 4, 2016, https://www

.biztimes.com/2016/04/04/drones-could-be-the-next-disruptive
-technology/; John Patrick Pullen, "This is how drones work,"
Time, April 3, 2015, http://time.com/3769831/this-is-how-drones
-work/; Peter Diamandis, "The top 10 reasons drones are
disruptive," *Forbes*, August 11, 2014, http://www.forbes.com
/sites/peterdiamandis/2014/08/11/top-10-reasons-drones-are
-disruptive/#7300470728bd/.

13. Everett Rogers, *Diffusion of Innovations*, 5th ed. (New York: Free
    Press, 2003).

14. Jagdish Sheth and Banwari Mittal, *Consumer Behavior: A Manage-
    rial Perspective*, 2nd ed. (Mason, OH: South-Western College
    Publishing, 2003).

15. "Canada Electric Car Sales Face A Roadblock In 'Range Anxiety.'
    But What's That?" Canadian Press, June 20, 2016, accessed at
    http://www.huffingtonpost.ca/2016/06/20/canada-electric-car
    -sales-range-anxiety_n_10581332.html; Christina Rogers, "De-
    mand Ebbs for Electric, Hybrid Cars," *Wall Street Journal*, Septem-
    ber 3, 2014, http://www.wsj.com/articles/electric-hybrid
    -car-demand-stalls-1409785123.

16. Jonah Comstock, "IMS: Half of Android health apps have fewer
    than 500 downloads," *MobiHealthNews*, October 29, 2013, http://
    mobihealthnews.com/26836/ims-half-of-android-health-apps
    -have-fewer-than-500-downloads; "Technology-based Client Care,"
    Equinoxe website, accessed August 2016 at http://equinoxelifecare
    .com/technology-based-care/; "Equinoxe Relaunches the EQ Vir-
    tual Clinic to Improve Access to Health Care," Equinoxe LifeCare
    [press release], February 23, 2016 accessed at PRNewswire (http://
    www.prnewswire.com/news-releases/equinoxe-relaunches-the-eq
    -virtual-clinic-to-improve-access-to-health-care-569797371.html);
    Jocelyn Aspa, "EQ Virtual works to make online health services
    accessible to the Downtown Eastside," *Georgia Straight*, March 21,
    2016, http://www.straight.com/life/662386/eq-virtual-works-make
    -online-health-services-accessible-downtown-eastside; "Virtual
    Healthcare App Akira Launches to Give Canadians a Doctor in
    Their Pocket," Akira [press release], May 18, 2016, http://www
    .newswire.ca/news-releases/virtual-healthcare-app-akira-launches
    -to-give-canadians-a-doctor-in-their-pocket-579937431.html;
    "How It Works" Askthedoctor website, accessed August 2016 at
    https://www.askthedoctor.com/ask-a-doctor; "Making care mobile:
    A roadmap to the virtualization of care," PwC website, accessed
    August 2016 at http://www.pwc.com/ca/en/industries/healthcare
    /publications/virtual-health-making-care-mobile-canada.html.

17. Elaine Watson, "Why do 85% of new CPG products fail within
    two years?" Food Navigator USA, July 31, 2014, http://www
    .foodnavigator-usa.com/Markets/Why-do-85-of-new-CPG-products
    -fail-within-two-years; Mike Collins, "Reducing the Failure Rate
    Of New Products," *Forbes*, April 30, 2015, http://www.forbes.com
    /sites/mikecollins/2015/04/30/reducing-the-failure-rate-of-new
    -products/#633f363361a4.

18. Michael E. Ross, "It seemed like a good idea at the time," NBC
    News, April 22, 2005, http://www.nbcnews.com/id/7209828/ns
    /us_news/t/it-seemed-good-idea-time/#.V8xgQ4-cHIU.

19. "Hoverboards Recalled for Fire Risk," *Wall Street Journal*, July 7,
    2016, p. B3.

20. "Innovation Process," Stage-Gate website, accessed August 2016 at
    http://www.stage-gate.com/resources_stage-gate_full.php.

21. Robert Safian, "Why Apple Is The World's Most Innovative
    Company," *Fast Company*, February 21, 2018, https://www
    .fastcompany.com/40525409/why-apple-is-the-worlds-most
    -innovative-company.

22. Personal correspondence with J.R. Brooks, co-owner of True Büch
    Kombucha, April 2020.

23. Jack Neff, "Tide Pods Winning $7 Billion Detergent Wars by
    Defining Value," *Advertising Age*, December 18, 2012; Dale Buss,
    "P&G Awash in Success of Tide Pods Despite Wrinkles Along the
    Way," *Brandchannel*, December 18, 2012; Emily Glazer, "Tide
    Rides Convenience Wave," *Wall Street Journal*, February 23, 2012;
    and Emily Glazer, "P&G to Alter Tide Pods Packaging," *Wall
    Street Journal*, May 26–27, 2012, p. B3.

24. Personal correspondence with J.R. Brooks, co-owner of True Büch
    Kombucha, April 2020.

25. Kira Vermond, "Why London, Ontario is the perfect test market,"
    Globe and Mail, October 19, 2015, http://www.theglobeandmail.
    com/report-on-business/small-business/sb-managing/london-test
    -market/article26846284/.

Chapter 9

1. Personal interview with Nick Sano, owner, The Barber's Chair,
   December 2019.

2. Michael Gauthier, "Bugatti has announced the Veyron Grand Sport
   Vitesse has officially become the fastest convertible in the world.
   The company will celebrate the event by introducing a World
   Record Car (WRC) Edition at the Shanghai Motor Show," Motor1.
   com, April 11, 2013, http://www.motor1.com/news/38024/bugatti
   -veyron-grand-sport-vitesse-world-record-car-edition/; Juergen
   Zoellter, "2013 Bugatti Veyron 16.4 Grand Sport Vitesse," *Car and
   Driver*, April 2012, http://www.caranddriver.com/bugatti/veyron;
   Aaron Robinson, "2011 Bugatti Veyron 16.4 Super Sport— First
   Drive Review," *Car and Driver*, October 2010, www.caranddriver.
   com/reviews/car/10q4/2011_bugatti_veyron_16.4_super_sport
   -first_drive_review.

3. Adapted from Kent B. Monroe, *Pricing: Making Profitable
   Decisions*, 3rd ed. (New York: McGraw-Hill, 2003); Krish-
   nakumar Davey, Paul Markowitz, and Nagi Jonnalagadda,
   "The pricing opportunity: Discovering what customers actually value," *Strategy & Leadership* 34 (2006), pp. 23–30,
   doi:10.1108/10878570610660573

4. Roger A. Kerin and Robert A. Peterson, "Throckmorten Furniture
   (A)," *Strategic Marketing Problems: Cases and Comments*, 9th
   ed. (Englewood Cliffs, NJ: Prentice Hall, 1998), pp. 235–245;
   Jukti K. Kalita, Sharan Jagpal, and Donald R. Lehmann, "Do high
   prices signal high quality? A theoretical model and empirical results," *Journal of Product and Brand Management* 13 (2004),
   pp. 279–288.

5. "H&R Block Leads the Way with 100% Free Tax Software," H&R
   Block Canada [press release], February 2016, https://www.hrblock
   .ca/uploads/our_company-media_centre-press_releases/2016/100
   FreePersonalDownloadandOnlineTaxSoftware.pdf; Rob Carrick,
   "Save money this tax season by filing for free," *Globe and Mail*,
   March 11, 2015, http://www.theglobeandmail.com/globe-investor
   /personal-finance/taxes/save-money-at-tax-time-by-filing-for-free
   /article23412438/; "Filing online? A guide to the latest tax software,"
   CBC News, February 21, 2013, http://www.cbc.ca/news/business
   /taxes/filing-online-a-guide-to-the-latest-tax-software-1.1285455.

6. For the classic description of skimming and penetration pricing, see
   Joel Dean, "Pricing Policies for New Products," *Harvard Business
   Review*, November–December 1976, pp. 141–53. See also, Reed
   K. Holden and Thomas T. Nagle, "Kamikaze Pricing," *Marketing
   Management*, Summer 1998, pp. 31–39.

7. Jean-Noel Kapferer, "Managing Luxury Brands," *Journal of Brand
   Management*, July 1997, pp. 251–60.

8. "Why That Deal Is Only $9.99," *BusinessWeek*, January 10, 2000,
   p. 36. For further reading on odd-even pricing, see Robert M.
   Schindler and Thomas M. Kilbarian, "Increased Consumer Sales
   Response through Use of 99-Ending Prices," *Journal of Retailing*,
   Summer 1996, pp. 187–99; Mark Stiving and Russell S. Winer, "An
   Empirical Analysis of Price Endings with Scanner Data," *Jour-
   nal of Consumer Research*, June 1997, pp. 57–67; and Robert M.
   Schindler, "Patterns of Rightmost Digits Used in Advertised Prices:
   Implications for Nine-Ending Effects," *Journal of Consumer
   Research*, September 1997, pp. 192–201.

9. Thomas T. Nagle and Reed K. Holden, *The Strategy and Tactics of
   Pricing*, 3rd ed. (Englewood Cliffs, NJ: Prentice Hall, 2002),
   pp. 243–49.

10. Ibid., pp. 237–39.

11. Peter M. Noble and Thomas S. Gruca, "Industrial Pricing: Theory
    and Managerial Practice," *Marketing Science* 18, no. 3 (1999),
    pp. 435–54.

12. George E. Belch and Michael A. Belch, *Introduction to Advertising and Promotion*, 5th ed. (New York: Irwin/McGraw-Hill, 2001), p. 93.

13. S. Makridakis, "Forecasting: Issues challenges for marketing management," *Journal of Marketing* 41 (1977), p. 24.

14. S. Doyle, "Business application of forecasting with a campaign management content," *Journal of Database Marketing & Customer Strategy Management* 12 (2004), pp. 87–93.

15. M. Man and L. Gadau, "The profit and loss account in different approaches: Advantages and disadvantages," *Annales Universitatis Apulensis: Series Oeconomica* 12 (2010), pp. 152–160.

16. D. Peppers and M. Rogers, "Return on customer: A new metric of value creation—return on investment by itself is not good enough," *Journal of Direct, Data and Digital Marketing Practice* 7 (2006), pp. 318–331.

17. Frank Bruni, "Price of Newsweek? It Depends," *Dallas Times Herald*, August 14, 1986, pp. S1, S20.

18. Elizabeth Weise and Roger Yu, "'Newsweek' sold to 'International Business Times,'" *USA Today*, August 5, 2013, www.usatoday.com /story/money/business/2013/08/03/newsweek-sold-to-international -business-times/2615727/.

19. "Despite a strong preference for paper books, older readers actually have an easier time reading electronic tablets." *Review of Optometry*, March 2013.

20. CB Insights, "How Uber makes – and loses – money," n.d., accessed September 2020 at https://www.cbinsights.com/research /report/how-uber-makes-money/; Oliver Moore. "UberX will be allowed to operate legally in Toronto, city council decides," *Globe and Mail*, May 3, 2016, http://www.theglobeandmail.com/news /toronto/divided-toronto-council-seeks-middle-ground-as-uber -debate-begins/article29835110/; Matt Elliot, "Toronto's taxi debate points to issues far bigger than Uber," *Metro*, May 9, 2016, http://www.metronews.ca/views/toronto/torys-toronto-matt -elliott/2016/05/09/toronto-taxi-debate-points-to-issues-far-bigger -than-uber.html; "What is Uber and what should I think about the controversies?" *The Telegraph*, May 16, 2016, http://www .telegraph.co.uk/better/technology/what-is-uber-and-what-should-i -think-about-the-controversies/; Laura Perez. "The Uber controversy reveals the rottenness of the taxi industry," *In Defence of Marxism*, January 5, 2016, http://www.marxist.com/uber-controversy-reveals -rottenness-of-taxi-industry.htm.

21. "Henderson jersey coming back to Canada: Buyer," CBC News, June 23, 2010, www.cbc.ca/canada/story/2010/06/23/henderson -hockey-canada.html.

22. "Will Tablets Close the Book on e-Readers?" *Knowledge @ Wharton*, July 7, 2010, accessed at http://knowledge.wharton .upenn.edu/printer_friendly.cfm?articleid=2539.

23. Hollie Shaw, "Hershey Canada pleasds guilty to chocolate price-fixing," *Financial Post*, June 21, 2013, http://business.financialpost .com/legal-post/hershey-canada-pleads-guilty-to-chocolate-price -fixing; Brent Jang, "Airlines fined $1.1-billion over price-fixing," *Globe and Mail*, November 9, 2010, www.theglobeandmail.com /globe-investor/air-canada-others-fined-for-price-fixing/article 1791755.

24. "New court docs outline what Competition Bureau says happened in bread price-fixing scheme," CBC News, June 29, 2018, https:// www.cbc.ca/news/business/bread-price-fixing-1.4728360; Andrew Russell, "7 Canadian companies committed indictable offences in bread-price fixing scandal: Competition Bureau," Global News, January 31, 2018, https://globalnews.ca/news/3998023/bread -price-fixing-scandal-competition-act-crimes/; and Geoff Zochodne, "Bread price-fixing scandal may have originated with PowerPoint presentation: court documents," *Financial Post*, June 29, 2018, https://business.financialpost.com/news/retail-marketing/bread -price-fixing-scandal-may-have-originated-with-powerpoint -presentation-court-documents.

25. "Grafton-Fraser to pay $1.2M in misleading ads case," CBC News, July 27, 2016, http://www.cbc.ca/news/business/grafton-fraser -to-pay-1-2m-in-misleading-ads-case-1.623251; Marina Strauss,

"Grafton-Fraser fined for misleading sale prices," *Globe and Mail*, July 28, 2006, http://www.theglobeandmail.com/report-on-business /grafton-fraser-fined-for-misleading-sale-prices/article18168771/.

26. "Stores Told to Lift Prices in Germany," *Wall Street Journal*, September 11, 2000, pp. A27.

27. "Rotten Apples," *Dallas Morning News*, April 7, 1998, p. 14A.

28. "When Grey Is Good," *The Economist*, August 22, 1998, p. 17; Neil Belmore, "Parallel Imports and Grey Market Issues," The Canadian Institute, December 5–6, 2001.

29. "How Dell Fine-Tunes Its PC Pricing to Gain Edge in a Slow Market," *Wall Street Journal*, June 8, 2001, pp. A1, A8.

30. For an extensive discussion on discounts, see Kent B. Monroe, *Pricing: Making Profitable Decisions*, 2nd ed. (New York: McGraw Hill, 1990), chaps. 14 and 15.

Chapter 10

1. Personal interview with Chris Wilson, vice president, operations, Fuzion Flooring, June 2019.

2. Patrick Gillespie, "Pepsi has a Venezuela problem: $1.4 billion," CNN, October 8, 2015, http://money.cnn.com/2015/10/06/investing /pepsi-hit-hard-in-venezuela/; Thomas T. Vogel Jr., "Pepsi Finds Bottler in Venezuela After Old Firm Defected to Coke," *Wall Street Journal*, November 14, 1996, https://www.wsj.com/articles /SB84792428752932500; Glenn Collins, "A Coke Coup in Venezuela Leaves Pepsi High and Dry," *New York Times*, August 17, 1996, www.nytimes.com/1996/08/17/business/a-coke-coup-in-venezuela -leaves-pepsi-high-and-dry.html; Elizabeth Fuhrman, "Bottler of the year: Pepsi bottling ventures," *Beverage Industry* 100 (2009), pp. 24–26, 28, 30, 34.

3. This discussion is based on Bert Rosenbloom, *Marketing Channels: A Management View*, 6th edition. (Fort Worth: Dryden Press, 1999).

4. J. K. Johansson, "International alliances: Why now?" *Journal of the Academy of Marketing Science* (1995), pp. 301–304.

5. Allan J. Magrath, "Channel Vision: Getting Your Channels Right," *Ivey Business Journal*, November/December 2002, www .iveybusinessjournal.com/topics/innovation/channel-vision-getting -your-channels-right#.Uh6XMxbvzR1; Adrienne Mand, "Eddie Bauer's banner time of year," *Advertising Age*, October 1, 2001, http://adage.com/article/focus-design/databank-retail-eddie-bauer -s-banner-time-year/53693/; D.L. Duffy, "Case study: Multi-channel marketing in the retail environment," *Journal of Consumer Marketing* 21 (2004), pp. 356–359.

6. Canadian Press, "Gap Canada stores to be included in North American closures: parent company," CTV News, March 1, 2019, https://windsor.ctvnews.ca/gap-canada-stores-to-be-included-in -north-american-closures-parent-company-1.4318768; Nathaniel Meyersohn, "Gap's plan to save itself: Shrink," CNN Business, November 21, 2018, https://www.cnn.com/2018/11/21/business /gap-old-navy-banana-republic-retail/index.html; Nathaniel Meyer-sohn, "Athleta may be the new Gap's best hope for survival," CNN Business, March 7, 2019, https://www.cnn.com/2019/03/07/business /athleta-hill-city-lululemon-gap/index.html.

7. E. Brynjolfsson, Y. J. Hu, and M. S. Rahman, "Competing in the age of omnichannel retailing," *MIT Sloan Management Review* 54 (2013), pp. 23–29.

8. Andrea Stairs, "More and more shoppers are online, so where are the retailers?" *Globe and Mail*, June 24, 2015, http://www .theglobeandmail.com/report-on-business/rob-commentary/more -and-more-shoppers-are-online-so-where-are-the-retailers/article 25078686/; Marina Strauss, "Gap expands Web shopping, eyes growth in Canada," *Globe and Mail*, August 23, 2012, http://www .theglobeandmail.com/globe-investor/gap-expands-web-shopping -eyes-growth-in-canada/article1378654/; Michael Krantz, "Click Till You Drop," *Time*, July 20, 1998, pp. 34–39; "Gap Inc. Creates Global Brand Management Structure to Drive the Company's Long-Term Growth," Gap Inc. [press release], October 16, 2012, www .gapinc.com/content/gapinc/html/media/pressrelease/2012/med _pr_GPS_Global_Brand_Management_Structure101612.html.

9. Darrell Rigby and Michael O'Sullivan, *Fighting Fire with Water—From Channel Conflict to Confluence* (Cambridge, MA: Bain & Company); D. Peppers and M. Rogers, "'Tis the season for E-retailing," *Sales and Marketing Management* 151 (1999), pp. 30–32.

10. For an overview of vertical marketing systems, see Lou E. Pelton, David Strutton, and James R. Lumpkin, *Marketing Channels*, 2nd ed. (Burr Ridge, IL: McGraw-Hill/Irwin, 2003); and Peter R.J. Trim and L. Yang-Im, "Vertically integrated organisational marketing systems: A partnership approach for retailing organisations," *Journal of Business & Industrial Marketing* 21 (2006), p. 151.

11. "History of Home Hardware," Home Hardware website, n.d., accessed September 2020 at https://www.homehardware.ca/history -of-home-hardware; Justin Dallaire, "View from the C-Suite: Home Hardware sticks to its strengths," *Strategy*, May 14, 2019, http:// strategyonline.ca/2019/05/14/view-from-the-c-suite-home -hardware-sticks-to-its-strengths/; Michael McLarney, "Home Hardware unveils hip, new marketing plan," Hardlines.ca, April 3, 2017, https://hardlines.ca/gp_dailynews/home-hardware-unveils -hip-new-marketing-plan/.

12. "Apple to Open 25 Retail Stores in 2001," Apple Computer [press release], May 15, 2001, www.apple.com/pr/library/2001 /05/15Apple-to-Open-25-Retail-Stores-in-2001.html; Kevin Anderson, "Apple unveils its offline strategy," BBC NewsOnline, May 19, 2001, http://news.bbc.co.uk/2/hi/business/1339150.stm; Dennis Sellers, "Apple 'manifesto': 5 down, 95 to go," *Macworld*, May 15, 2001, www.macworld.com/article/1017497/manifesto.html.

13. For an extensive discussion on channel conflict, see Anne T. Coughlan, Erin Anderson, Louis W. Stern, and Adel I. El-Ansary, *Marketing Channels*, 6th ed. (Upper Saddle River, NJ: Prentice Hall, 2001); K.L. Webb and J.E. Hogan, "Hybrid channel conflict: Causes and effects on channel performance," *Journal of Business & Industrial Marketing* 17 (2002), pp. 338–356.

14. Sara Zucker, "Coke Returns to Costco with its Dignity Intact," *BrandChannel*, December 11, 2009, www.brandchannel.com/home /post/2009/12/11/Coke-Returns-To-Costco-With-Its-Dignity-Intact .aspx; Martinne Geller, "Costco to resume stocking Coca-Cola drinks," Reuters, December 10, 2009, www.reuters.com/article /2009/12/10/cocacola-costco-idUSN1020190520091210.

15. For an extensive discussion on power and influence in marketing channels, see Coughlan, et al., *Marketing Channels*.

16. *What's It All About?* (Oakbrook, IL: Council of Logistics Management, 1993); S.M. Rutner and C.J. Langley, "Logistics value: Definition, process and measurement," *International Journal of Logistics Management* 11 (2000), pp. 73–82.

17. This example is described in David Simchi-Levi, Philip Kaminsky, and Edith Simchi-Levi, *Designing and Managing the Supply Chain* (Burr Ridge, IL: McGraw-Hill/Irwin, 2000).

18. This discussion is based on Robyn Meredith, "Harder than the Hype," *Forbes*, April 16, 2001, pp. 188–194; R.M. Monczka and J. Morgan, "Supply Chain Management Strategies," *Purchasing*, January 15, 1998, pp. 78–85; Robert B. Handfield and Ernest L. Nichols, *Introduction to Supply Chain Management* (Upper Saddle River, NJ: Prentice Hall, 1998); and p Charan, "Supply chain performance issues in an automobile company: A SAP-LAP analysis," *Measuring Business Excellence* 16 (2012), pp. 67–86.

19. Major portions of this discussion are based on Sunil Chopra and Peter Meindl, *Supply Chain Management: Strategy, Planning, and Operations* (Upper Saddle River, NJ: Prentice Hall, 2001); Marshall Fisher, "What Is the Right Supply Chain for Your Product?" *Harvard Business Review*, March 1997, pp. 105–117; and Pankaj M. Madhani, "Value creation through integration of supply chain management and marketing strategy," *IUP Journal of Business Strategy* 9 (2012), pp. 7–26.

20. Sophia Harris, "Walmart quest to be Canada's No. 1 grocer," CBC News, August 13, 2016, http://www.cbc.ca/news/business /walmart-grocery-store-1.3717480; Don Pitts, "Why Walmart hit the bulls-eye Target missed: Don Pitts," CBC News, http://www.cbc.ca /news/business/why-walmart-hit-the-bull-s-eye-target-missed-don -pittis-1.2953293; "Managing Risk in Our Supply Chain," Walmart, accessed at http://www.walmartcanada.ca/product-sourcing /responsible-sourcing/managing-risk; "Case Study: Why Walmart implemented cross-docking for supply chain success," Crossdock Manitoba, December 13, 2012, http://www.crossdock.mb.ca/blog /case-study-why-wal-mart-implemented-cross-docking-for-supply -chain-success/; "Walmart selects Isotrak to improve fleet visibility," *Isotrak*, March 14, 2015, http://isotrak.com/walmart-canada -selects-isotrak-to-improve-fleet-visibility/; Rebecca Walberg, "Never Lose Inventory Again," *Financial Post*, July 6, 2010, www .financialpost.com/Never+lose+inventory+again/3239772/story .html; Miguel Bustillo, "Wal-Mart Radio Tags to Track Clothing," *Wall Street Journal*, July 23, 2010, https://www.wsj.com/articles /SB10001424052748704421304575383213061198090.

21. "About SmartWay," Natural Resources Canada, January 2, 2020, accessed September 2020 at https://www.nrcan.gc.ca/energy -efficiency/energy-efficiency-transportation/greening-freight -programs/smartway-fuel-efficient-freight/about-smartway/21052; "Join SmartWay," Natural Resources Canada website, July 4, 2019, accessed September 2020 at http://www.nrcan.gc.ca/energy /efficiency/transportation/commercial-vehicles/smartway/trucks /7649; "SmartWay Comes to Canada," Supply Chain & Logistics Association of Canada website, accessed September 2014 at www .scmanational.ca/en/tools-a-resources/smartway.

Chapter 11

1. Personal interview with Ken Haqq, national director of sales and planning, New Era Cap Co., Inc., July 2019.

2. K. Cline, "The devil in the details," *Banking Strategies* 24 (1997); R. Trap, "Design your own jeans," *The Independent*, October 18, 1998, p. 22; H. Cho and S.S. Fiorito, "Self-service technology in retailing: The case of retail kiosks," *Symphonya* 1 (2010), pp. 42–54.

3. "Retail sales, by industry (unadjusted)," Statistics Canada, August 19, 2016, accessed at http://www.statcan.gc.ca/tables-tableaux/sum-som/ l01/cst01/trad15a-eng.htm.

4. Deloitte, *Global Powers of Retailing 2016*, accessed at http://www2. deloitte.com/global/en/pages/consumer-business/articles/global- powers-of-retailing.html.

5. "Target Canada closing, ending 2-year foray," CTV News, April 12, 2015, http://www.ctvnews.ca/business/target-canada-closing- ending-2-year-foray-1.2323222; Marina Strauss and Jacquie McNish, "With Target, Canada's retail landscape set for massive makeover," *Globe and Mail*, January 13, 2011, www.theglobeandmail.com /globe-investor/with-target-canadas-retail-landscape-set-for-massive -makeover/article1868308; Duncan Hood, "Target won't kill Canadian retail: It will save it," *Canadian Business*, October 15, 2012, p. 4.

6. "Retail Trade-Establishments, Employees, and Payroll," *Statistical Abstract of the United States*, 120th ed. (Washington, DC: U.S. Department of Commerce, Bureau of the Census, 2000); G. Koretz, "Those Plucky Corner Stores," *Bloomberg Businessweek*, December 5, 1994, www.businessweek.com/stories/1994-12-04 /those-plucky-corner-stores; J. Fraser, "Mapping out the treasure hunt," *Canadian Grocer* 122 (2008), p. 73.

7. "Foundations of Franchising," International Franchise Association (n.d.), accessed at www.franchise.org/code.aspx.

8. Alexandra Lopez-Pacheco, "Customers expect quality even in recession," *National Post*, January 27, 2008, p. FP7; Carol Stephenson, "Thriving in turbulent times," *Ivey Business Journal*, May/June 2009, http://iveybusinessjournal.com/publication/thriving-in-turbulent- times/; Hollie Shaw, "Online sales complement brick-and-mortar retail, Harry Rosen CEO says," *Financial Post*, August 1, 2013, http://business.financialpost.com/2013/08/01/online-sales -complement-brick-and-mortar-retail-harry-rosen-ceo-says/.

9. Tim Manners, "Shopper Marketing," *Fast Company*, June 14, 2008, accessed at https://www.fastcompany.com/890025/shopper-marketing; "With U.S. consumers watching their wallets more than ever, tuning into shoppers' mindsets key to warding off brand switching," Nielsen [news release], October 16, 2008, www.nielsen.com/content/dam /corporate/us/en/newswire/uploads/2008/10/press_release18.pdf; "Shopper marketing," *Marketing*, 116 (2011), p. 29.

10. Marina Strauss, "Holt's opens doors a little more widely," *Globe and Mail*, September 1, 2010, www.theglobeandmail.com/report -on-business/holts-opens-doors-a-little-more-widely/article 1693204/?cmpid=tgc; Hollie Shaw, "Holt Renfrew wants to make you feel welcome," *National Post*, September 2, 2010; Sarah Kelsey, "Holt Renfrew celebrates 175 years: Luxury retailer announces major expansion plans," *Huffington Post Canada*, September 7, 2012, www.huffingtonpost.ca/2012/09/07/holt -renfrew-celebrates-1_n_1864421.html.

11. R. Eagan, "The green capitalist," *Library Journal* 134 (2009); "Defining the Green Economy," ECO Canada, 2010, www.eco.ca /pdf/Defining-the-Green-Economy-2010.pdf; J.G. Hae, "Are fash-ion-conscious consumers more likely to adopt eco-friendly cloth-ing?" *Journal of Fashion Marketing and Management* 15 (2011), pp. 178–193, doi:10.1108/13612021111132627; Dixie Gong, "10 Best Canadian Eco-Shops," *Flare*, March 28, 2013, www.flare.com /fashion/10-best-canadian-eco-shops/; "Corporate Social Responsi-bility," Foreign Affairs, Trade and Development Canada, October 22, 2013, www.international.gc.ca/trade-agreements-accords-commerciaux/topics-domaines/other-autre/csr-rse.aspx?lang=eng; "The Greening of Roots," Roots (n.d.), accessed at http://about.roots. com/on/demandware.store/Sites-RootsCorporate-Site/default/Link-Page?cid=THE_ENVIRONMENT_OurCommitment.

12. Canadian Press, "Gap Canada stores to be included in North American closures: parent company," CTV News, March 1, 2019, https://windsor.ctvnews.ca/gap-canada-stores-to-be-included-in -north-american-closures-parent-company-1.4318768; Nathaniel Meyersohn, "Gap's plan to save itself: Shrink," CNN Business, November 21, 2018, https://www.cnn.com/2018/11/21/business /gap-old-navy-banana-republic-retail/index.html; Nathaniel Meyer-sohn, "Athleta may be the new Gap's best hope for survival," CNN Business, March 7, 2019, https://www.cnn.com/2019/03/07 /business/athleta-hill-city-lululemon-gap/index.html.

13. Valentina Palladino, "Apple Store receives trademark for 'distinc-tive design and layout,' " *Wired*, January 30, 2013, www.wired .com/design/2013/01/apple-store-trademark/; "Canadian Trade-Mark Data," Canadian Intellectual Property Office, October 22, 2013, www.cipo.ic.gc.ca/app/opic-cipo/trdmrks/srch/vwTrdmrk .do;jsessionid=0001aVzIlRWXB-TRtDf81OHAa5I:3UAPV7CT3?l ang=eng&status=OK&fileNumber=1503650&extension=0&starti ngDocumentIndexOnPage=1.

14. F.J. Mulhern and R.P Leon, "Implicit Price Bundling of Re-tail Products: A Multiproduct Approach to Maximizing Store Profitability," *Journal of Marketing* 55 (1991), pp. 63–76; Scott Hamilton, "U.K. retail sales increase as discounts spur consumer demand," *Bloomberg*, July 18, 2013, https://www.bloomberg.com /amp/news/articles/2013-07-18/u-k-retail-sales-increase-as-discounts -spur-consumer-demand-1-.

15. F.S. By, "The 'sale' is fading as a retailing tactic—in pricing shift, 'everyday lows' replace specials," *Wall Street Journal*, March 1, 1989; G.K. Ortmeyer, J.A. Quelch, and W.J. Salmon, "Restoring Credibility to Retail Pricing," *MIT Sloan Management Review* 33 (1991), pp. 55–66; T. Busillo, "Bed, bath & more: A Canada first," *Home Textiles Today* 19 (1998), pp. 8, 23; Andria Cheng, "Wal-Mart pitches 'everyday low prices' overseas," *MarketWatch*, June 1, 2011, www.marketwatch.com/story/wal-mart-pitches -everyday-low-prices-overseas-2011-06-01.

16. W.B. Dodds, "In Search of Value: How Price and Store Name Infor-mation Influence Buyers' Product Perceptions," *Journal of Services Marketing* 5 (1991), pp. 27–36; D. Grewal, R. Krishnan, J. Baker, and N. Borin, "The effect of store name, brand name and price discounts on consumers' evaluations and purchase intentions," *Jour-nal of Retailing* 74 (1998), pp. 331–352; N. Williams, "Profile: GM shifting gears from price to brand image," *Strategy* (2005), p. 53.

17. B. Brown, "Edmonton Makes Size Pay Off in Down Market," *Ad-vertising Age*, January 27, 1992, pp. 4–5; "Facts," West Edmonton Mall website (n.d.), accessed at www.wem.ca/about-wem/facts; R. Warnica, "Taking West Edmonton Mall to New Jersey," *Maclean's*, October 3, 2011, p. 41.

18. N. Ramage, "Edo Japan leaves the malls behind," *Marketing* 108 (2003), p. 2; A.G. Hallsworth, K.G. Jones, and R. Muncaster, "The planning implications of new retail format introductions in Canada and Britain," *Service Industries Journal* 15 (1995), p. 148; B.J. Lorch, "Big Boxes, Power Centres and the Evolving Retail Landscape of Winnipeg: A Geographical Perspective," Institute for Urban Studies, University of Winnipeg, 2004.

19. Hollie Shaw, "McDonald's Canada to add build-your-own burgers, table service," *Financial Post*, September 30, 2015, http://business. financialpost.com/news/retail-marketing/mcdonalds-canada-to-add -build-your-own-burgers-table-service; Marina Strauss, "McDon-ald's rolls out upscale options," *Globe and Mail*, September 30, 2015, http://www.theglobeandmail.com/report-on-business /mcdonalds-rolls-out-table-service-customized-burgers-in-upscale -shift/article26601464/.

20. K. Buscemi, "Vending gets smarter," *Appliance Manufacturer* 52 (2004), pp. 25–26; "Vending embraces growth and technology," *Beverage Industry* 102 (2011), pp. 118–119.

21. Christopher Brown-Humes, "Ikea creates a challenge for postmen of the world: The store catalogue is published in 36 countries and is free, writes Christopher Brown-Humes," *Financial Times*, August 14, 2003; "IKEA appoints McCann New York as global agency of record to re-invent the IKEA catalogue," *Market-ing Weekly News* [news release], August 2, 2011; "2014 IKEA Catalogue Comes to Life with Augmented Reality," IKEA Canada [press release], August 12, 2013, accessed at www.newswire.ca/en /story/1209085/2014-ikea-catalogue-comes-to-life-with -augmented-reality.

22. "Knockout strategies of the 90s: Telemarketing and direct market-ing," *Canadian Business*, advertising supplement, March 1993, pp. 45–54; "Canada's Do Not Call Registry," *The Gazette*, December 29, 2007.

23. Nanette Byrnes, "Avon's new calling," *Bloomberg Businessweek*, September 18, 2000, accessed at www.businessweek.com/2000 /00_38/b3699001.htm; D.B. Van, "Avon calling on global ad effort to change its image," *Marketing* 105 (2000), p. 6; "About Avon," Avon website (n.d.), accessed at www.avoncompany.com /aboutavon/avonmarkets.html.

24. M. Schifrin, "Okay, big mouth," *Forbes*, October 9, 1995, p. 47; V. Byrd and W. Zellner, "The Avon Lady of the Amazon," *Business Week*, October 23, 1994, www.businessweek.com/stories /1994-10-23/the-avon-lady-of-the-amazon; D.L. Duffy, "Direct selling as the next channel," *Journal of Consumer Marketing* 22 (2005), pp. 43–45; C. Rawlins and P.R. Johnson, "Let's party: The remarkable growth in direct sales," Allied Academies International Conference, Academy of Organizational Culture, Communications and Conflict Proceedings 10 (2005), pp. 47–50.

25. Tavia Grant, "More Canadians Shopping on Net," *Globe and Mail*, September 28, 2010, www.theglobeandmail.com/report-on -business/more-canadians-shopping-on-net/article1727434; Canadian Press, "Canadian retailers running out of time on in e-commerce, report says," May 6, 2013, accessed at www.cbc.ca /news/business/canadian-retailers-running-out-of-time-in-e -commerce-report-says-1.1410261; Hollie Shaw, "Online retail sales to hit $34-billion in Canada by 2018," *Financial Post*, July 23, 2013, http://business.financialpost.com/2013/07/23/online-retail -sales-to-hit-40-billion-in-canada-by-2018/.

26. Pete Evans, "Canadian shoe chain Aldo seeks creditor protection, citing pandemic pressure," CBC News, May 7, 2020, https://www .cbc.ca/news/business/aldo-bankruptcy-1.5559810; Eliza Ronalds-Hannon and Paula Sambo, "Shoe chain Aldo seeks bankruptcy protection to restructure debt," *Financial Post*, May 7, 2020, https:// business.financialpost.com/news/retail-marketing/shoe-chain-aldo -seeks-bankruptcy-protection-to-restructure-debt; Tami Jeanneret, "A Trio of retailers file for bankruptcy protection," iHeartRADIO, May 8, 2020, https://www.iheartradio.ca/610cktb/news/a-trio-of -retailers-file-for-bankruptcy-protection-1.12360455.

27. B. Hameed, "Facebook, Twitter Influences up to 28% of Online Buying Decisions," Startup Meme [blog], December 14, 2009,

http://startupmeme.com/facebook-twitter-influences-upto-28-of-online-buying-decisions; L.p Forbes, "Does social media influence consumer buying behavior? An investigation of recommendations and purchases," *Journal of Business & Economics Research* 11 (2013), p. 107; Lara O'Reilly, "Women make friends with 'liked' brands on Facebook," *Marketing Week*, August 9, 2012, p. 6.

28. S. Casimiro, "Shop Till You Crash: Just in time for Christmas, online retailing is getting bigger, smarter, faster, and easier. You'll notice we're not calling it flawless. Yet," *Fortune*, December 21, 1998, http://money.cnn.com/magazines/fortune/fortune_archive/1998/12/21/252661/index.htm; D.A. Pitta, "Internet currency," *Journal of Consumer Marketing* 19 (2002), pp. 539–540; "Lands' end improves online profitability via my virtual model technology," *Direct Marketing* 64 (2001), p. 11.

29. Wen-Jang Jih, "Effects of consumer-perceived convenience on shopping intention in mobile commerce: An empirical study," *International Journal of E-Business Research* 3 (2007), pp. 33–40, 43–48; J. Ramaprasad, "Online social influence and consumer choice: Evidence from the music industry," (Order No. 3364967, University of California, Irvine). ProQuest Dissertations and Theses (2009); "Consumers and Changing Retail Markets," Office of Consumer Affairs, Industry Canada, July 27, 2012, www.ic.gc.ca/eic/site/oca-bc.nsf/eng/ca02096.html#a21; "5 Canadian consumer trends to shape the future of retail," CBC News, October 21, 2013, www.cbc.ca/news/business/5-canadian-consumer-trends-to-shape-the-future-of-retail-1.2129072.

30. Brad Tuttle, "Why Monday is e–retailers' favorite day of the week," *Time*, January 9, 2012, http://business.time.com/2012/01/09/why-monday-is-e-retailers-favorite-day-of-the-week/; Sean Silcoff, "What keeps online retail in Canada from clicking?" *Globe and Mail*, May 12, 2012, www.theglobeandmail.com/report-on-business/what-keeps-online-retail-in-canada-from-clicking/article4178807/?page=all; Ashante Infantry, "Not all Canadians love to shop online: study," *Toronto Star*, August 21, 2013, www.thestar.com/business/tech_news/2013/08/21/not_all_canadians_love_to_shop_online_study.html; Kevin Duong, "2014 Canada Digital Future in Focus," comScore, April 2014, www.comscore.com/Insights/Presentations_and_Whitepapers/2014/2014_Canada_Digital_Future_in_Focus.

31. Alexandra Lopez-Pacheco, "Welcome the New Consumer," *Financial Post*, October 5, 2010, www.canada.com/business/fp/money/Welcome+consumer/3551652/story.html.

32. Naresh Kumar, "Social Media Recommendations May Increase Online Purchases," PSFK.com, July 1, 2010, www.psfk.com/2010/07/social-media-recommendations-may-increase-online-purchases.html.

33. "Global Advertising: Consumers Trust Real Friends and Virtual Strangers the Most," Nielsen [news release], July 7, 2009, www.nielsen.com/us/en/newswire/2009/global-advertising-consumers-trust-real-friends-and-virtual-strangers-the-most.html.

34. Casey Bond, "Here's how Ebates/Rakuten and other cashback sites really work," *Huffington Post*, March 1, 2019, https://www.huffingtonpost.ca/entry/ebates-online-shopping-cash-back_n_5c0f1d5fe4b0edf5a3a7eec0; "About Us," Rakuten website, n.d., accessed September 2020 at https://global.rakuten.com/corp/about/; "About Rakuten Canada," Rakuten website, n.d., accessed September 2020 at https://www.rakuten.ca/static/about-rakuten.

35. J. Weidauer, "QR codes: Building a mobile loyalty program beyond key tags," Retail Customer Experience, April 20, 2010, www.retailcustomerexperience.com/article/21622/QR-codes-Building-a-mobile-loyalty-program-beyond-key-tags; C. Sherburne, "Are QR codes for real?" *Printing Impressions* 52 (2010), p. 36; M. Partee, "Everyone's going crazy for QR codes!" *Credit Union Management* 34 (2011), pp. 32–33.

36. "Retail's Mobility Imperative: A Measured Approach to the Emerging Channel," *Forbes Insight* (2010), www.forbes.com/forbesinsights/retailmobility/.

37. J. Boyd, "The web goes wireless—popular site operators set their sights on mobile users," *InternetWeek* 828 (2000), pp. 20–27; R. Shields, "Digital strategy: Are you making the most from mobile?" *Marketing Week*, November 2010, pp. 69–71; J. Wisniewski, "Mobile websites with minimum effort," *Online* 34 (2010), pp. 54–57; C. Murphy, "Mistakes," *InformationWeek* 1345 (2012), pp. 32–35.

Chapter 12

1. Jon Rumley, "Tim Hortons' Roll Up The Rim To Win Gets A Revamp, But Customers Are Not Thrilled," Huffington Post, February 19, 2020, https://www.huffingtonpost.ca/entry/tim-hortons-roll-up-the-rim-to-win_ca_5e4d400bc5b6b0f6bff26bf2; Kelly Marshall, "Tim Hortons Marketing Messaging: They're Back in the Top 10," Marketing Strategy, accessed May 2020 at https://profitworks.ca/small-business-sales-and-marketing-resources/blog/marketing-strategy/690-tim-hortons-marketing-messaging.html; Justin Dallaire, "A look at Tim Hortons' yearlong turnaround," Strategy, July 16, 2019, https://strategyonline.ca/2019/07/16/breaking-down-tim-hortons-yearlong-turnaround/; Shane McNeil, "Where did it go wrong?: A marketing expert's approach to Tim Hortons' sales slump," BNN Bloomberg, February 10, 2020, https://www.bnnbloomberg.ca/where-did-it-go-wrong-an-marketing-expert-s-approach-to-tim-hortons-sales-slump-1.1388093; Sylvian Charlebois, "Tim Hortons adds to its disastrous marketing decisions," *Toronto Sun*, February 26, 2020, https://torontosun.com/opinion/columnists/charlebois-tim-hortons-adds-to-its-disastrous-marketing-decisions; Tim Hortons Social Media - Instagram, Facebook; Emily Chung, "Nestlé, Tim Hortons named Canada's top plastic polluters again," CBC News, October 9, 2019, https://www.cbc.ca/news/technology/greenpeace-plastic-brand-audit-1.5314739; "National Sponsorships," Tim Hortons website, accessed May 2020 at http://company.timhortons.com/ca/en/corporate/national-sponsorship.php; Justin Dallaire, "Tim Hortons gets serious about Roll Up the Rim," *Strategy*, February 7, 2019, https://strategyonline.ca/2019/02/07/tim-hortons-gets-serious-about-roll-up-the-rim/.

2. Adapted from the American Marketing Association's dictionary, accessed April 2020 at https://www.ama.org/resources/Pages/Dictionary.aspx.

3. "Advertising Budget," Inc. website, accessed November 2016 at http://www.inc.com/encyclopedia/advertising-budget.html.

4. "Maclean's 2019 rate card," *Maclean's* website, accessed May 2020 at https://www.rogersmedia.com/wp-content/uploads/2018/12/Media_kit_ENGLISH_2019.pdf

5. Sarah De Meulenaer, Patrick De Pelsmacker, and Nathalie Dens, "Have No Fear: How Individuals Differing in Uncertainty Avoidance, Anxiety, and Chance Belief Process Health Risk Messages," Journal of Advertising 44, no. 2 (2015), pp. 114–25; Ioni Lewis, Barry Watson, Richard Tay, and Katherine M. White, "The Role of Fear Appeals in Improving Driver Safety," The International Journal of Behavioral Consultation and Therapy, June 22, 2007, p. 203; Cornelia Pechmann, Guangzhi Zhao, Marvin E. Goldberg, and Ellen Thomas Reibling, "What to Convey in Antismoking Advertisements for Adolescents: The Use of Protection Motivation Theory to Identify Effective Message Themes," Journal of Marketing, April 2003, pp. 1–18; and John F. Tanner Jr., James B. Hunt, and David R. Eppright, "The Protection Motivation Model: A Normative Model of Fear Appeals," Journal of Marketing, July 1991, pp. 36–45.

6. Jacob Hornik, Chezy Ofir, and Matti Rachamim, "Advertising Appeals, Moderators, and Impact on Persuasion," Journal of Advertising Research, September 2017, pp. 305–18; Doug Lloyd, "Does Sex Still Sell in 2016?" campaignlive.com, September 9, 2016; Samantha Grossman," This Video Urges the Advertising Industry to Stop Treating Women Like Objects," Time.com, January 26, 2016; Kristina Monllos, "Brands Are Throwing Out Gender Norms to Reflect a More Fluid World," adweek.com, October 17, 2016; and Sanjay Putrevu, "Consumer Responses toward Sexual and Nonsexual Appeals: The Influence of Involvement, Need for Cognition (NFC), and Gender," Journal of Advertising, Summer 2008, p. 57.

7. Rupal Parekh, "With Strong Work for Walmart and Geico, Martin Agency Is Creating a New Specialty: Making Marketers Recession-Proof," *Advertising Age*, January 19, 2009, p. 30; and Louis Llovio, "Geico Gecko's Viral Videos," *Richmond Times Dispatch*, March 28, 2009, p. B-9.

8. Thomas W. Cline and James J. Kellaris, "The Influence of Humor Strength and Humor-Message Relatedness on Ad Memorability: A Dual Process Model," *Journal of Advertising*, Spring 2007, p. 55; Yong Zhang and George M. Zinkham, "Responses to Humorous Ads," *Journal of Advertising*, Winter 2006, p. 113; and Yih Hwai Lee and Elison Ai Ching Lim, "What's Funny and What's Not: The Moderating Role of Cultural Orientation in Ad Humor," *Journal of Advertising*, Summer 2008, p. 71.

9. "Number of Netflix subscribers in Canada from 2017 to 2023," Statista, October 2018, accessed May 2020 at https://www.statista.com/statistics/685141/canada-netflix-subscribers-count/.

10. "Number of households in Canada that cut their TV subscription or never had one from 2012 to 2019," Statista, April 2020, accessed May 2020 at https://www.statista.com/statistics/258444/number-of-tv-cord-cutter-households-in-canada/.

11. "Top 10 Canadian Newspapers," Agility PR Solutions, updated August 2020, accessed September 2020 at https://www.agilitypr.com/resources/top-media-outlets/top-10-canadian-print-outlets/.

12. "Overview of Results: Winter 2019 Study," Vividata, January 2019, accessed May 2020 at https://vividata.ca/wp-content/uploads/2019/01/Vividata-Winter-2019-Overview-of-Results.pdf.

13. "Top 10 Canadian Magazines by Circulation," Agility PR, accessed May 2020 at https://www.agilitypr.com/resources/top-media-outlets/top-10-canadian-magazines/.

14. "Communications Monitoring Report 2019: Broadcasting sector overview," Canadian Radio-television and Telecommunications Commission website, accessed May 2020 at https://crtc.gc.ca/eng/publications/reports/policyMonitoring/2019/cmr5.htm.

15. "FAQ," Out-of-Home Marketing Association of Canada website, accessed November 2016 at http://www.omaccanada.ca/faq/.

16. Rody, Bree, "Millenials boast strong OOH ad recall: study", Media in Canada, July 4, 2017, accessed in May 2020 at https://mediaincanada.com/2017/07/04/millennials-boast-strong-ooh-ad-recall-study/

17. "Share of Search Queries Handled by Leading U.S. Search Engine Providers," *statista.com*, April 2017; Peter Pal Zubcsek, Zsolt Katona, and Miklos Sarvary, "Predicting Mobile Advertising Response Using Consumer Colocation Networks," *Journal of Marketing*, July 2017, pp. 109–26; Jan H. Schumann, Florian von Wangenheim, and Nicole Groene, "Targeted Online Advertising: Using Reciprocity Appeals to Increase Acceptance among Users of Free Web Services," *Journal of Marketing*, January 2014, pp. 59–75; "10 Ways to Improve the Banner Ad Design and Enhance the Click Through Rate," *Tech and Techie*, May 6, 2013; "'Banner Blindness' Now a Major Marketing Concern," *Bulldog Reporter's Daily Dog*, March 29, 2013; and Thales Teixeira, "The New Science of Viral Ads," *Harvard Business Review*, March 2012, pp. 25–27. The definition of mobile marketing is adapted from the Mobile Marketing Association definition, see *http://www.mmaglobal.com/news/mma-updates-definition-mobile-marketing*, November 17, 2009.

18. See "Guidelines, Standards & Best Practices," at the Interactive Advertising Bureau website, *http://www.iab.net/guidelines*; "IAB Releases New Standard Ad Unit Portfolio," press release, International Advertising Bureau, February 26, 2012; "Online Measurement," Nielsen website, *http://www.nielsen.com/us/en/nielsen-solutions/nielsen-measurement/nielsen-onlinemeasurement.html*; and Abbey Klaassen, "Why the Click Is the Wrong Metric for Online Ads," *Advertising Age*, February 23, 2009, p. 4.

19. "Annual Online Advertising Revenue Reports," IAB Canada, accessed December 2016 at http://iabcanada.com/annual-internet-advertising-revenue-reports/; "Canada Digital Ad Spending Forecast 2016: Mobile, Video and Social Pushing Investment to New Heights," *eMarketer*, December 21, 2015, https://www.emarketer.com/Report/Canada-Digital-Ad-Spending-Forecast-2016-Mobile-Video-Social-Pushing-Investment-New-Heights/2001706.

20. Stephen Jenkins, "What's My Worth? How Ads Appeal to Consumers," Millennial Media [blog], August 27, 2015, http://www.millennialmedia.com/mobile-insights/blog/whats-my-worth-how-ads-appeal-to-consumers.

21. Sehoon Park and Minhi Hahn, "Pulsing in a Discrete Model of Advertising Competition," Journal of Marketing Research, November 1991, pp. 397–405.

22. Peggy Masterson, "The Wearout Phenomenon," *Marketing Research*, Fall 1999, pp. 27–31; and Lawrence D. Gibson, "What Can One TV Exposure Do?" *Journal of Advertising Research*, March–April 1996, pp. 9–18.

23. "Why Reese's Pieces and Not M&M's were Featured in the Movie "E.T." " accessed in May 2020 at https://www.tvovermind.com/reeses-pieces-not-mms-featured-movie-e-t/ "Here's How Netflix Makes Monster Money with Secret Ads" accessed in May 2020 at https://learnbonds.com/news/netflix-killing-secret-ads-shows/ Shieber, Jonathan," Virtual product placement is coming for TV and movies and Ryff has raised cash to put it there", Tech Crunch, December 17, 2019, accessed May 2020 at https://techcrunch.com/2019/12/17/virtual-product-placement-is-coming-for-tv-and-movies-and-ryff-has-raised-cash-to-put-it-there/ "Netflix Is Ad Free, but It Isn't Brand Free Tide Pod shout-outs onscreen. Flirtatious exchanges with companies on Twitter. Netflix may not run ads, but it has become a coveted marketing platform." accessed in May 2020 at https://www.nytimes.com/2019/12/16/business/media/netflix-commercials.html "Pop-Tarts Product Placement" accessed in May 2020 at https://productplacementblog.com/tag/pop-tarts/ Moroney, Liam, "Pop-Tarts' Recipe for Success? A Constantly Evolving Content Marketing Strategy", accessed in May 2020 at https://insights.newscred.com/pop-tarts-content-marketing/

24. "McDonald's Monopoly Coast to Coast: McDonald's Restaurants of Canada," Media Agency of the Year 2018, *Strategy*, accessed May 2020 at https://agencyoftheyear.strategyonline.ca/winners/winner/2018/?e=66382&w=McDonald%27s+Monopoly+Coast+to+Coast; Mary Hanbury, "A former cop reportedly rigged McDonald's Monopoly game to win almost every prize for 12 years in a $24 million scheme," *Business Insider*, July 30, 2018, at https://www.businessinsider.com/mcdonalds-monopoly-game-rigged-scam-report-2018-7.

25. Lynn Bates, "Are QR Codes Still Relevant in 2016?" Mobilozophy [blog], February 2, 2016, http://blog.mobilozophy.com/are-qr-codes-still-relevant-in-2016.

26. "More Marketers Use Proximity Tech, Beacons to Get Closer to the Action," *eMarketer*, September 1, 2016, https://www.emarketer.com/Articles/Print.aspx?R=1014428.

27. Romet Kallas, "Proximity Marketing - What, How, Why?" Unacast [blog], March 23, 2016, https://unacast.com/post/proximity-marketing-what-how-why.

28. Rob Young, "Canada's 2019 Media Landscape," PHD Canada (prepared for Interactive Advertising Bureau), May 2020, https://iabcanada.com/content/uploads/2017/02/2-Exec-Summary-T-Can-Final.pdf.

29. "Facts & Figures: 2019," Canadian Wireless and Telecommunications Association website, accessed May 2020 at http://www.cwta.ca/facts-figures/.

30. "Communications Monitoring Report 2019," CRTC website, accessed May 2020 at https://crtc.gc.ca/eng/publications/reports/policymonitoring/2019/index.htm; Bryan Segal, "Global Digital Future in Focus 2018 Canada," comScore, June 26, 2018, https://www.comscore.com/Insights/Presentations-and-Whitepapers/2018/Global-Digital-Future-in-Focus-2018-Canada-Edition.

31. Rich et al., "Digital Future in Focus Canada 2019."

32. "2019 Canadian Social Media Monitor," Insights West, June 2019, accessed May 2020 at https://www.insightswest.com/wp-content/uploads/2019/06/Rep_IW_CDNSocialMediaInsights_June2019.pdf; Melody McKinnon, "2019 Report: Social Media Use in

Canada," *Online Business Canada*, June 30, 2019, https://canadiansinternet.com/2019-report-social-media-use-canada/.

33. Paul Briggs, "Canada Time Spent with Media 2020: COVID-19 Will Push Media Time to Unexpected Levels," *eMarketer*, May 11, 2020, https://www.emarketer.com/content/canada-time-spent-with-media-2020.

34. Ibid.

35. "Canadian Media Investment Trends: Where are ad budgets headed?" Canada Media Insights, February 26, 2016, http://media-corps.com/canadian-media-investments/.

36. Mike Isaac and Cecilia Kang, "Facebook says it won't back down from allowing lies in political ads," *New York Times*, January 9, 2020, https://www.nytimes.com/2020/01/09/technology/facebook-political-ads-lies.html; Zayan Guedim, "The Ethical Challenges of Facebook's Targeted Advertising," *Edgy*, December 22, 2019, https://edgy.app/the-ethical-challenges-of-facebooks-targeted-advertising?pfrom=article; Laurence Hart, "Facebook: A Case Study in Ethics," *CMSWire*, December 20, 2018, https://www.cmswire.com/digital-marketing/facebook-a-case-study-in-ethics/; Irina Raicu, "The Ethics of 'Giving People a Voice' and Political Advertising on Facebook," Markkula Center for Applied Ethics at Santa Clara University, December 5, 2019, https://www.scu.edu/ethics-spotlight/social-media-and-democracy/the-ethics-of-giving-people-a-voice-and-political-advertising-on-facebook/; Forrester Research, "Facebook's recent moves highlight the grand challenge of digital ethics," *ZDNet*, July 3, 2019, https://www.zdnet.com/article/facebooks-recent-moves-highlight-the-grand-challenge-of-digital-ethics/; Margi Murphy, "Facebook removed from S&P list of ethical companies after data scandals," *The Telegraph*, June 13, 2019, https://www.telegraph.co.uk/technology/2019/06/13/facebook-gets-boot-sp-500-ethical-index/; James Vincent, "Facebook's problems moderating deepfakes will only get worse in 2020," *The Verge*, January 15, 2020, https://www.theverge.com/2020/1/15/21067220/deepfake-moderation-apps-tools-2020-facebook-reddit-social-media; Oliver Milman, "Defiant Mark Zuckerberg defends Facebook policy to allow false ads," *The Guardian*, December 2, 2019, https://www.theguardian.com/technology/2019/dec/02/mark-zuckerberg-facebook-policy-fake-ads.

Chapter 13

1. Personal and written communication with Lisa Watts, co-owner Hub Town Brewery, April 2020; Hub Town Brewery Facebook Page, accessed April 2020 at https://www.facebook.com/hubtownbrewing; Hub Town Brewery website, accessed April 2020 at https://www.hubtownbrewing.com/our_story; Hub Town Brewery Instagram account, accessed April 2020 at https://twitter.com/hubtownbrewing; Megan Thrall, "Okotoks' Hub Town Brewing open for business this weekend," *Okotoks Today*, August 30, 2019, https://www.okotokstoday.ca/local-news/okotoks-hub-town-brewing-open-for-business-this-weekend-1667340; Remy Greer, "Okotoks small businesses delivering entrepreneurial spirit," *Okotoks Today*, April 1, 2020, https://www.okotokstoday.ca/local-news/okotoks-small-businesses-delivering-entrepreneurial-spirit-2215738.

2. Amy He, "Average Time Spent with Media in Canada," *eMarketer*, July 2, 2019, https://www.emarketer.com/content/average-time-spent-with-media-in-canada.

3. "Coca-Cola's research funding criticized by obesity expert," CBC News, August 10, 2015, http://www.cbc.ca/news/health/coca-cola-s-research-funding-criticized-by-obesity-expert-1.3186279; Ed Hays, "Coca-Cola: We stand for quality, integrity," *USA Today*, August 16, 2015, http://www.usatoday.com/story/opinion/2015/08/16/coca-cola-company-ed-hays-editorials-debates/31818829/; Muhtar Kent, "Coca-Cola: We'll Do Better," *Wall Street Journal*, August 19, 2015, http://www.wsj.com/articles/coca-cola-well-do-better-1440024365; W. Comcowich, "Case Study: Coca-Cola PR Crisis Management," August 25, 2015, accessed November 2016 at http://www.cyberalert.com/blog/index.php/case-study-coca-cola-pr-crisis-management/.

4. "What is direct marketing?" Direct Marketing Association of Canada website, accessed November 2016 at http://www.directmac.org/direct-marketing1.

5. "From zero to 60 in 4 seconds: BMW wins big with sensory cross-media marketing [Blog post]," Canada Post Corporation, August 8, 2013, https://www.canadapost.ca/web/en/blogs/business/details.page?article=2013/08/08/from_zero_to_60_in_4&cattype=business&cat=directmail; "The Making of a BMW M Print," BMW USA, November 19, 2012, https://youtu.be/aYuk64NMYLM.

6. Russ Martin, "Email marketing is on the rise in Canada," *Marketing*, March 9, 2016, http://www.marketingmag.ca/tech/email-marketing-is-on-the-rise-in-canada-169813.

7. "Corporate Partners," Toronto International Film Festival website, accessed November 2016 at http://www.tiff.net/partnerships/; "Sponsorship," Toronto International Film Festival website, accessed November 2016 at http://content.tiff.net.s3.amazonaws.com/documents/Sponsorship_Festival_2016.pdf; "Sponsorship Festival 2016," Toronto International Film Festival website, accessed November 2016 at http://content.tiff.net.s3.amazonaws.com/documents/Sponsorship_Festival_2016.pdf.

8. Duncan Brown and Nick Hayes, *Influencer Marketing: Who Really Influences Your Customers* (Oxford, UK: Elsevier/Butterworth-Heinemann, 2008).

9. "Clean Break," *Advertising Age*, October 1, 2018, p. 30; "Want to Try Influencer Marketing? Be Careful," *forbes.com*, May 22, 2018.

10. Samuel Butcher, "20 Canadian Influencers to Watch in 2020 [Blog post]," The Influence Agency, February 7, 2020, accessed June 2020 at https://theinfluenceagency.com/blog/20-canadian-influencers-to-watch-2020/; Matt R. Edwards (@mattredwards), Influence Analysis, accessed June 2020 at https://www.piwox.com/user/mattredwards/6714362; Lenard Monkman, "Indigenous fashion lovers challenge others to support artists," CBC News, May 23, 2020, https://www.cbc.ca/news/indigenous/indigenous-fashion-challenge-instagram-1.5581495, "Pros and Cons: Social Media Influencers [Blog post]," SpringWise, November 13, 2019, accessed June 2020 at https://www.springwise.com/pros-cons-social-media-influencers; Heather Hart, "6 Benefits of Partnering with Social Media Influencers [Blog post]," $99 Social, accessed June 2020 at https://www.99dollarsocial.com/6-benefits-of-partnering-with-social-media-influencers/; Kristen Baker, "What Will Influencer Marketing Look Like in 2020? [Blog post]," Hubspot, December 2, 2019, accessed June 2020 at https://blog.hubspot.com/marketing/how-to-work-with-influencers.

11. "Wommapedia: Why Word of Mouth Marketing?" Word of Mouth Marketing Association website, accessed December 2016 at http://wommapedia.org/.

12. Ibid.

13. Tuck Siong Chung, Michel Wedel, and Roland T. Rust, "Adaptive Personalization Using Social Networks," Journal of the Academy of Marketing Science, 2016, pp. 66–87; Russell Newman, Victor Chang, Robert John Walters, and Gary Brian Wills, "Web 2.0—The Past and the Future," International Journal of Information Management, April 6, 2016; and Guy Levy-Yurista, "Web 3.0 and Tomorrow's IoT: Human Identity Delivers the 'Internet of Me,'" http://insights.wired.com, December 16, 2015.

14. "Participative Web and User-Created Content: Web 2.0 and Social Networking" (Paris: Organization for Economic Co-operation and Development, 2007); and Jason Daley, "Tearing Down the Walls," Entrepreneur, December 2010, pp. 57–60.

15. "116 Amazing Social Media Statistics and Facts," brandwatch.com, June 15, 2018.

16. Andreas M. Kaplan and Michael Haenlein, "Users of the World, Unite! The Challenges and Opportunities of Social Media," *Business Horizons 53*, no. 1 (2010), pp. 62–64.

17. Annual Report 2017, Microsoft, p. 25; "LinkedIn Fact Sheet," https://press.linkedin.com/content/dam/press/docs/linkedin-company-fact-sheet-12-08-16.pdf, May 17, 2017; and Michael Sebastian, "LinkedIn Sells Nearly Half a Billion Dollars in Ads Last Year," www.adage.com, February 5, 2015.

18. Meghan Keaney Anderson, "The Best of B2B Marketing Content: 9 Examples [Blog post]," HubSpot, June 9, 2015, http://blog.hubspot.com/blog/tabid/6307/bid/33505/10-b2b-companies-that-create-exceptional-content.aspx#sm.00000k61g84uecztxyp1birlwcur0.

19. "Tangerine Dreams of Fully Integrated Content Marketing," *Marketing*, August 22, 2016, http://www.marketingmag.ca/sponsored/tangerine-dreams-of-fully-integrated-content-marketing-181688; "Forward Thinking," Tangerine website, accessed November 2016 at https://www.tangerine.ca/forwardthinking/.

20. Bailey Roy, "Social vs. Traditional Media: Has the Battle Already Ended?" *MyPRSA*, April 1, 2016, https://www.prsa.org/Intelligence/Tactics/Articles/view/11445/1124/Social_vs_Traditional_Media_Has_the_Battle_Already#.WDzXJ_krLIU.

21. Michael Stelzner, "2016 Social Media Marketing Industry Report," *Social Media Examiner*, May 24, 2016, http://www.socialmediaexaminer.com/social-media-marketing-industry-report-2016/.

22. "2016 Canadian Social Media Monitor," Insights West.

23. Ibid.

24. Iris Vermeren, "Marketing: How to Provide Great Customer Service Via Social Media [Blog post]," Brandwatch, February 25, 2015, https://www.brandwatch.com/blog/marketing-provide-great-customer-service-via-social/.

25. "Doritos Scores on Social with TikTok Hashtag Challenge during Super Bowl [Blog post]," MediaKix, n.d., accessed September 2020 at https://mediakix.com/blog/tik-tok-hashtag-challenge-case-study/; Joss Davidge, "Doritos De-brands Ads to Engage with Generation Z [Blog post]," BecauseXM, April 9, 2019, https://www.becausexm.com/blog/doritos-de-brands-ads-to-engage-with-generation-z; Aliza Polkes, "Why Doritos' Marketing Strategy Made Super Bowl History [Blog post]," Yotpo, February 3, 2020, https://www.yotpo.com/blog/how-doritos-wins-every-super-bowl-with-ugc/; Ann-Christine Diaz, "Doritos Drops Its Logo and Name in Latest Campaign," *AdAge*, August 26, 2019, https://adage.com/creativity/work/doritos-drops-its-logo-and-name-latest-campaign/2193506; Kyle O'Brien, "Doritos removes the name from its logo to appeal to Gen Z in 'Another Level' campaign," *The Drum*, August 26, 2019, https://www.thedrum.com/news/2019/08/26/doritos-removes-the-name-its-logo-appeal-gen-z-another-level-campaign; Robert Williams, "Doritos lets mobile fans create Super Bowl dance videos with AI app," *Mobile Marketer*, January 30, 2020, https://www.mobilemarketer.com/news/doritos-lets-mobile-fans-create-super-bowl-dance-videos-with-ai-app/571361/; Pamela Bump, "52 Gen Z Stats Marketers Need to Know in 2020 [Blog post]," HubSpot, February 3, 2020, https://blog.hubspot.com/marketing/gen-z-stats.

26. "2019 Canadian Social Media Monitor," Insights West, May 2020, https://www.insightswest.com/wp-content/uploads/2019/06/Rep_IW_CDNSocialMediaInsights_June2019.pdf; https://canadiansinternet.com/2019-report-social-media-use-canada/

27. Emily Wexler, "The 2015 Marketer Survey," *Strategy*, December 11, 2015, http://strategyonline.ca/2015/12/11/the-2015-marketer-survey/.

28. "Global Social Media Ranking," Statista, accessed April 2020 at https://www.statista.com/statistics/272014/global-social-networks-ranked-by-number-of-users/.

29. Wexler, "The 2015 Marketer Survey."

30. "Facebook Business – Facebook Ads Basic," Facebook website, accessed December 2016 at https://www.facebook.com/business/learn/facebook-ads-basics.

31. Christian Karasiewicz, "6 Ways to Use Facebook Live Video for Your Business," *Social Media Examiner*, July 25, 2016, http://www.socialmediaexaminer.com/6-ways-to-use-facebook-live-video-for-your-business/.

32. "Facebook Pages Stats in Canada," Socialbakers website, accessed at https://www.socialbakers.com/statistics/facebook/pages/local/canada/brands/.

33. Dominique Jackson, "10 Ways Marketers Can Increase Facebook Engagement [Blog post]," SproutSocial, March 21, 2016, http://sproutsocial.com/insights/facebook-engagement/.

34. "Facebook Awards 2016 Winners - Beats by Dre," Facebook website, accessed December 2016 at https://www.facebook-studio.com/awards/winners#/gallery/submission/beats-by-dre.

35. "Monthly active users of social media Jan 2019," Statista, n.d., accessed April 2020 at https://www.statista.com/chart/5194/active-users-of-social-networks-and-messaging-services/.

36. "2019 Canadian Social Media Monitor," Insights West. https://www.insightswest.com/wp-content/uploads/2019/06/Rep_IW_CDNSocialMediaInsights_June2019.pdf

37. Wexler, "The 2015 Marketer Survey."

38. Jenn Chen, "Twitter Tips for Your Business to Follow Into 2017 [Blog post]," SproutSocial, November 30, 2016, http://sproutsocial.com/insights/twitter-tips/.

39. Richard O'Flynn, "The Way The Social Cookie Crumbles: The Genius of Oreo's Social Media Marketing," *201:digital*, April 23, 2015, http://www.201digital.co.uk/way-social-cookie-crumbles-genius-oreos-social-media-marketing-can-learn/.

40. Steve Olenski, "What Is Periscope And How Can You Use It For Business Video Streaming?" *Forbes*, December 5, 2015, http://www.forbes.com/sites/steveolenski/2015/12/05/what-is-periscope-and-how-can-you-use-it-for-business-video-streaming/print/; Therese, "Facebook Live vs. Periscope: What's the difference?" *Social Media Hound*, September 20, 2016, http://www.socialmediahound.com/2016/09/20/facebook-live-vs-periscope/.

41. "Statistics," YouTube website, accessed April 2020 at https://www.youtube.com/yt/press/statistics.html.

42. "Red Bull YouTube channel," accessed April 2020 at https://www.youtube.com/user/redbull; "Red Bull's YouTube Presence," The Shorty Awards website, accessed December 2016 at http://shortyawards.com/7th/red-bulls-youtube-channel; "Most popular YouTube channels as of October 2016," Statista website, accessed December 2016 at https://www.statista.com/statistics/277765/most-popular-youtube-brand-channels-ranked-by-subscribers/.

43. "Socialbakers Mini-Report: Red Bull Stratos on Social Media," Socialbakers, accessed December 2016 at https://cdn.socialbakers.com/www/archive/storage/www/red-bull-stratos-case-study.pdf.

44. Jennifer Horn, "What is on the mind of Canada's marketers," *Strategy*, January 15, 2019, https://strategyonline.ca/2019/01/15/what-is-on-the-mind-of-canadas-marketers/.

45. "Official GoPro Instagram page," GoPro, accessed December 2016 at https://www.instagram.com/gopro/.

46. Neil Patel, "6 Tactics That Will Instantly Improve Your Instagram Engagement," *Forbes*, May 12, 2016, http://www.forbes.com/sites/neilpatel/2016/05/12/6-tactics-that-will-instantly-improve-your-instagram-engagement/2/#4be885fa533f; Ross Simmonds, "7 Ways to Build an Engaged Instagram Following," *Social Media Examiner*, May 25, 2015, http://www.socialmediaexaminer.com/build-an-engaged-instagram-following/.

47. "About LinkedIn," LinkedIn website, n.d., accessed April 2020 at https://about.linkedin.com/.

48. Wexler, "The 2015 Marketer Survey."

49. Danielle Thibault, "8 Ways to Increase Engagement on LinkedIn Company Pages," July 3, 2015, accessed December 2016 at https://www.linkedin.com/pulse/8-ways-increase-engagement-linkedin-company-pages-danielle-thibault.

50. "Radian6," Salesforce Marketing Cloud, accessed December 2016 at https://www.marketingcloud.com/au/products/social-media-marketing/radian6/.

51. "Mobile Economy 2020," GSMA website, accessed April 2020 at http://www.gsma.com/mobileeconomy/.

52. "MMA Glossary – Mobile Marketing," Mobile Marketing Association website, accessed December 2016 at http://www.mmaglobal.com/wiki/mobile-marketing.

53. "PC Magazine Encyclopedia – Feature Phone," PC Magazine website, accessed December 2016 at http://www.pcmag.com/encyclopedia.

54. "PC Magazine Encyclopedia – Smartphone," PC Magazine website, accessed December 2016 at http://www.pcmag.com/encyclopedia.

55. "Wearables in Canada," Statista website, accessed April 2020 at https://www.statista.com/outlook/319/108/wearables/canada

56. "PC Magazine Encyclopedia – Wearable Computing," PC Magazine website, accessed December 2016 at http://www.pcmag.com/encyclopedia.

57. "Mobile Operating System Market Share in Canada - May 2020," Statcounter Global Stats, accessed May 2020 at https://gs.statcounter.com/os-market-share/mobile/canada.

58. "Facts & Figures: Wireless phone subscribers in Canada," Canadian Wireless Telecommunications Association website, accessed May 2020 at http://cwta.ca/facts-figures; Rich et al., "2019 Canada Digital Future in Focus."

59. "Digital 2019 Canada," Hootsuite, accessed April 2020 at https://www.slideshare.net/DataReportal/digital-2019-canada-january-2019-v01.

60. Paul Briggs, "Canada Ecommerce 2019," *Emarketer*, June 27, 2019, https://www.emarketer.com/content/canada-ecommerce-2019.

61. "Mobile Path to Purchase: Five Key Findings," Google/Nielsen Company, November 2013, https://ssl.gstatic.com/think/docs/mobile-path-to-purchase-5-key-findings_research-studies.pdf.

62. Christine Austin, "8 Awesome Examples of Effective Mobile Web Design," June 26, 2017, https://www.impactbnd.com/8-awesome-examples-of-effective-mobile-website-design.

63. "Number of apps available in leading app stores as of First Quarter 2020," Statista website, accessed May 2020 at https://www.statista.com/statistics/276623/number-of-apps-available-in-leading-app-stores/.

64. Irfan Ahmad, "60+ Fascinating Smartphone Apps Usage Statistics For 2019 [Infographic]," Social Media Today, March 23, 2019, https://www.socialmediatoday.com/news/60-fascinating-smartphone-apps-usage-statistics-for-2019-infographic/550990/#:~:text=A%20key%20point%20of%20note,those%20apps%20see%20daily%20use.

65. "Digital 2019 Canada," we are social and Hootsuite, January 2019, accessed May 2020 at https://www.slideshare.net/DataReportal/digital-2019-canada-january-2019-v01.

66. "Mobile App Marketing Insights: How Consumers Really Find and Use Your Apps," Google/Ipsos, May 2015, https://think.storage.googleapis.com/docs/mobile-app-marketing-insights.pdf.

67. Raluca Budiu, "Mobile: Native Apps, Web Apps, and Hybrid Apps," Nielsen Norman Group, September 14, 2013, www.nngroup.com/articles/mobile-native-apps/.

68. Olga Kharif and Leslie Patton, "Starbucks Takes its Pioneering Mobile-Phone App to a Grande Level," *Bloomberg*, March 30, 2016, https://www.bloomberg.com/news/articles/2016-03-30/starbucks-takes-its-pioneering-mobile-phone-app-to-grande-level.

69. "The Wireless Code, Simplified," Canadian Radio-television and Telecommunications Commission website, accessed December 2016 at http://crtc.gc.ca/eng/phone/mobile/codesimpl.htm.

70. "Canadian Common Short Code Application Guidelines. Version 3.0," Canadian Wireless Telecommunications Association, March 11, 2015, http://www.txt.ca/wp-content/uploads/2015/06/Canadian-Common-Short-Code-Application-Guidelines.pdf.

71. "About Us," Mobile Marketing Association website, accessed April 2017 at http://www.mmaglobal.com/about; "Global Code of Conduct," Mobile Marketing Association, July 15, 2008, http://www.mmaglobal.com/files/codeofconduct.pdf.

72. "Winning in Mobile: 8 New Principles for Today's Marketers," Mobile Marketing Association, November 2015, http://www.mmaglobal.com/documents/winning-mobile-8-new-principles-todays-marketers; "A SMoX Executive Summary on Cross-Marketing Effectiveness," Mobile Marketing Association.

Chapter 14

1. Personal interview with Dennis Kwasnicki, president, The Paint Channel, February 2020.

2. Michael J. Cunningham, *Customer Relationship Management: Marketing*, 1st ed. (Oxford: Capstone Publishing, 2002); M.R. Ciraulo and K.S. Auman, "Insurers can unlock value via CRM," *National Underwriter* 106 (2002), pp. 27:–29; Philip Kotler et al., *Principles of Marketing*, 7th Canadian edition (Toronto: Pearson, 2008).

3. Angela Reid and Daragh O'Brien, "Case study: Creating a single view of the customer for CRM strategy," *Interactive Marketing* 6 (2005), pp. 357–365.

4. Yuki Noguchi, "Nice To Meet You, But How To Greet You? #NoHandshakes Leaves Businesspeople Hanging," NPR, March 12, 2020, https://www.npr.org/2020/03/12/814076913/nice-to-meet-you-but-how-to-greet-you-nohandshake-leaves-businesspeople-hanging; Canadian Press, "Coronavirus: Canada's top CEOs say limiting COVID-19 should be 'singular objective,'" Global News, March 16, 2020, https://globalnews.ca/news/6682640/coronavirus-canada-ceo-letter/; Gene Marks, "On CRM: How Companies Are Leveraging Their CRM To Help Navigate Through COVID-19," *Forbes*, March 20, 2020, https://www.forbes.com/sites/quickerbettertech/2020/03/20/on-crm-how-companies-are-leveraging-their-crm-systems-to-help-navigate-through-covid-19/#3d9dc924fb84.

5. Dhruv Grewal, Michael Levy, and V. Kumar, "Customer experience management in retailing: An organizing framework," *Journal of Retailing* 85 (2009), pp. 1–14. doi:10.1016/j.jretai.2009.01.001

6. Jon Azpiri, "Starbucks Canada to reopen as many stores as possible by end of May," Global News, April 29, 2020, https://globalnews.ca/news/6882017/starbucks-canada-reopen-coronavirus/; Chris Walton, "3 Ways Starbucks Will Emerge From COVID-19 Stronger Than Before," *Forbes*, April 3, 2020, https://www.forbes.com/sites/christopherwalton/2020/04/03/3-ways-starbucks-will-emerge-from-covid-19-stronger-than-before/#37db0e7a1844; "Caring for Our Partners and Customers during COVID-19," Starbucks Stories Canada, March 15, 2020, accessed at https://stories.starbucks.ca/en/stories/2020/caring-for-our-partners-and-customers-during-covid-19/.

7. Michael Hinshaw, "Customer Satisfaction Is Not Enough—Why High Satisfaction Scores May Actually Spell Danger for Your Brand," *Brandchannel*, November 19, 2010; John Ozimek, "The disloyalty ladder—two rungs further down," *Journal of Direct, Data and Digital Marketing Practice* 11 (2010), pp. 207–218. doi:10.1057/dddmp.2009.45; Lucy Kimbell, "Designing for Service as One Way of Designing Services," *International Journal of Design* 5(2) (2011), pp. 41–52.

8. "Why Some Companies Succeed at CRM (and Many Fail)," *Knowledge@Wharton*, January 15, 2003, accessed at http://knowledge.wharton.upenn.edu/article.cfm?articleid=699.

9. Susan E. Robinson, "Customer satisfaction: The Xerox Canada story," *Managing Service Quality* 7 (1997), pp. 12–15.

10. Brent McKenzie, "Customer relationship management and customer recovery and retention: The case of the 407 express toll route," *Knowledge Management Research & Practice* 6 (2008), pp. 155–163. doi:10.1057/kmrp.2008.5

11. Barbara M. Talbott, "The Power of Personal Service : Why It Matters What Makes It Possible How It Creates Competitive Advantage," The Centre for Hospitality Research, Cornell University, 2006, pp. 6–14; "The Story of the Four Seasons," Four Seasons Hotels and Resorts, August 7, 2013, http://press.fourseasons.com/trending-now/corporate/the-story-of-four-seasons/.

12. K.W. Li, "The critical success factors of customer relationship management (CRM) technological initiatives," (Order No. MQ68423, Concordia University (Canada)). ProQuest Dissertations and Theses (2002); Soumaya Ben Letaifa and Jean Perrien, "The impact of E-CRM on organisational and individual behavior: The effect of the remuneration and reward system," *International Journal of E-Business Research* 3 (2007), pp. 13–16, 18, 20–23.

13. Darrell Rigby, Frederick Reicheld, and Chris Dawson, "Winning customer loyalty is the key to a winning CRM strategy," *Ivey Business Journal*, 2003, accessed at http://iveybusinessjournal.com/topics/social-responsibility/winning-customer-loyalty-is-the-key-to-a-winning-crm-strategy#.Ujj8fhbvzR0.

14. Mario Johne, "Brand building after the merge," *CMA Management* 77 (2003), p. 32; Eric Beauchesne, "Customers Want Friendly Service Most," *Star Phoenix*, June 20, 2008.

15. A. Darling, "Social media & CRM: Conversation starter," *New Media Age*, 2010, pp. 20–21; Rachael King, "How Companies Use Twitter to Bolster Their Brands," *Bloomberg Businessweek*, September 6, 2008, www.businessweek.com/technology/content /sep2008/tc2008095_320491.htm.

16. Colin Campbell, "Tuning into Twitter," *Maclean's*, October 7. 2010, www2.macleans.ca/2010/10/07/tuning-in-to-twitter/.

17. Carmi Levy, "Airlines use Twitter, other social tools to revolutionize customer service," *Toronto Star*, October 10, 2010, www .thestar.com/business/companies/porter/article/871979--airlines -use-twitter-other-social-tools-to-revolutionize-customer-service; N. Sreenivasan, C. Lee, and D. Goh, "Tweeting the friendly skies: Investigating information exchange among Twitter users about airlines," *Program: Electronic Library & Information Systems* 46 (2012), pp. 21–42. doi:10.1108/00330331211204548

18. Ravi Sawhney, "Broken Guitar Has United Playing the Blues to the Tune of $180 Million," *Fast Company*, July 28, 2009, www .fastcompany.com/blog/ravi-sawhney/design-reach/youtube-serves -180-million-heartbreak; M. Unnikrishnan and R. Wall, "All That Twitters," *Aviation Week & Space Technology* 172 (2010), pp. 42–44.

19. K. Barry, "Ford Bets the Fiesta on Social Networking," *Wired*, April 17, 2009, www.wired.com/autopia/2009/04/how-the-fiesta /all/1; "Power to the People! Fiesta Movement: A Social Remix Gives Control of New Ford Fiesta Ad Campaign to the People," Ford, press release, February 19, 2013, http://corporate.ford.com /news-center/press-releases-detail/pr-power-to-the-people-fiesta -37706; Stephen Edelstein, "Ford relaunches Fiesta movement Social Media marketing campaign," *Digital Trends*, February 20, 2013, accessed at www.digitaltrends.com/social-media/2014-ford -fiesta-goes-viral-with-fiesta-movement-social-media-campaign/.

20. Robin W. T. Buchanan and Crawford S. Gillies, "Value Managed Relationship: The Key to Customer Retention and Profitability," *European Management Journal* 8 (1990); Vikki Spencer, "Customer relationship management: Who is your customer?" *Canadian Underwriter* 68 (2001), pp. 12–16; V. Kumar, R. Venkatesan, and B. Rajan, "Implementing profitability through a customer lifetime value management framework," *GfK Marketing Intelligence Review* 1 (2009), pp. 32–43,64.

21. Caroline Papadatos, "The art of storytelling: How loyalty marketers can build emotional connections to their brands," *Journal of Consumer Marketing* 23 (2006), pp. 382–384. doi:10.1108/07363760610712902

22. Sandy MacGregor, "Coronavirus Cancellations: Here's What Canada's Travel Loyalty Programs Are Doing About Your Points," *Forbes*, April 2, 2020, https://www.forbes.com/sites /sandramacgregor/2020/04/02/coronavirus-cancellations-heres -what-canadas-travel-loyalty-programs-are-doing-about-your -points/#4f26bf896b38; Mark Brown, "The best Aeroplan credit card in the migration from CIBC to TD," *MoneySense*, January 21, 2014, http://www.moneysense.ca/save/debt/the-best-aeroplan -credit-card-in-the-migration-from-cibc-to-td/; Tim Kiladze, "TD, CIBC battle for Aeroplan loyalty," *Globe and Mail*, June 27, 2013, www.theglobeandmail.com/report-on-business/td-to-take-over-as -aeroplan-provider-as-parent-to-split-with-cibc/article12852318/; Ross Marowits, "TD Bank wins battle for Aeroplan," *Metro*, August 12, 2013, http://metronews.ca/news/canada/763882/td -bank-wins-battle-for-aeroplan/; "About Aeroplan," Aimia website, 2013, accessed at www.aimia.com/English/About/Our-Businesses /Aeroplan/default.aspx; Canadian Press, "TD, CIBC reach deal on Aeroplan credit card migration," CBC News, September 16, 2013, www.cbc.ca/news/business/td-cibc-reach-deal-on-aeroplan-credit -card-migration-1.1855664.

23. David Friend, "Canadian companies aim for balance as customers expect more for loyalty," *Globe and Mail*, July 21, 2013, www .theglobeandmail.com/report-on-business/canadian-companies -aim-for-balance-as-customers-expect-more-for-loyalty/article 13332480.

24. "About Us," Starwood Hotels and Resorts website (n.d.), Moments, accessed at http://auction.starwoodhotels.com/cgi-bin/ncommerce3 /ExecMacro/static/aboutus.d2w/report?wl=67280009; "Loyalty is a virtue and it's rewarded when you travel," *National Post*, March 22, 2013, http://nationalpost.com/luxury-living/loyalty-is-a-virtue-and -its-rewarding-when-you-travel/wcm/6f2b32d2-ad70-4c6f-821a -7e1f53658c30.

25. "Reward yourself in style with RBC Rewards and Saks Fifth Avenue," RBC [press release], February 3, 2016, http://www.rbc.com /newsroom/news/2016/20160203-rewards-saks.html; Mark Brown, "Best retail rewards credit cards of 2016," *MoneySense*, August 24, 2016, http://www.moneysense.ca/spend/credit-cards/best -retail-rewards-credit-cards-of-2016/; and Rob Carrick, "How to rid yourself of those pesky monthly banking fees," *Globe and Mail*, April 17, 2014, http://www.theglobeandmail.com/globe-investor /personal-finance/household-finances/free-banking-options-are -there/article18045437/.

26. "A Guide for Individuals Protecting Your Privacy," Office of the Privacy Commission of Canada, 2014, accessed at www.priv.gc.ca /information/pub/guide_ind_e.asp.; Canada's Anti-Spam Legislation website, 2014, accessed at http://fightspam.gc.ca/eic/site/030 .nsf/eng/home.

27. J. Łodziana-Grabowska, "Significance of database marketing in the process of target segments identification and service," *Problems of Management in the 21st Century* (2013), pp. 640–647; I. Gregurec, T. Ević, and D. Dobrinić, "The importance of database marketing in social network advertising," *International Journal of Management Cases* 13 (2011), pp. 165–172.

28. Thomas J. Siragusa, "Implementing data mining for better CRM," *Customer Inter@ction Solutions* 19 (2001), pp. 38–41; Jayanthi Ranjan and Vishal Bhatnagar, "Role of knowledge management and analytical CRM in business: Data mining based framework," *The Learning Organization* 18 (2011), pp. 131–148. doi:10.1108/09696471111103731; Vikas Saraf, MBA, PhD., p. Thakur, and L. Yadav, "CRM with data mining & warehouse: 'Optimizes customer insight,'" *International Journal of Marketing and Technology* 3 (2013), pp. 177–187.

29. N. Sutton, "RBC creates e-marketing council to assess client data," *Computing Canada*, June 20, 2003, p. 6; Lawrence Ang and Francis Buttle, "CRM software applications and business performance," *Journal of Database Marketing & Customer Strategy Management* 14 (2006), pp. 4–16.

30. John Lorinc, "How Canadian Tire is pioneering tomorrow's retail experience now," *Canadian Business*, February 29, 2016, http:// www.canadianbusiness.com/lists-and-rankings/most-innovative -companies/canadian-tire/; Dana Flavelle, "What the data crunchers know about you," *The Toronto Star*, April 23, 2010, https://www .thestar.com/business/tech_news/2010/04/23/what_the_data _crunchers_know_about_you.html.

31. Ross Marowitz, "Metro preps for future of online grocery," *Canadian Grocer*, May 20, 2015, http://www.canadiangrocer.com /top-stories/metro-preps-for-future-of-online-grocery-53510; Peter Hadekel, "Loyalty Programs Start to Pay Off for Grocer Metro," *The Gazette*, November 24, 2010, www.montrealgazette. com/columnists/Loyalty+program+starts+grocer+Metro/3875329 /story.html.

32. Carl Sewell and Paul Brown, *Customers for Life*, Doubleday Publishing, 2002.

33. "Winning Back Lost Customers," *Harvard Business Review*, April 2016, https://hbr.org/2016/03/winning-back-lost-customers; Tom Duncan, *Principles of Advertising + IMC*, 2nd Edition (New York: McGraw-Hill/Irwin, 2005); Mert Tokman, Lenita Davis, and Katherine N. Lemon, "The WOW factor: Creating value through win-back offers to reacquire lost customers," *Journal of Retailing* 83 (2007), pp. 47–64. doi:10.1016/j.jretai.2006.10.005

34. Reuters, "Sprint hangs up on high-maintenance customers," FoxNews.com, July 9, 2007, www.foxnews.com/story/2007/07/09

/sprint-hangs-up-on-high-maintenance-customers/; "Why firing your worst customers isn't such a great idea," *Knowledge @Wharton*, December 12, 2007, http://knowledge.wharton.upenn .edu/article.cfm?articleid=1870.

Chapter 15

1. Personal interview with Denis Cordick, vice president, marketing and business development, AMJ Campbell, February 2020.

2. Roger A. Kerin, Vijay Mahajan, and Rajan Varadarajan, *Contemporary Perspectives on Strategic Marketing Planning* (Boston: Allyn & Bacon, 1990), chap 1; and Orville C. Walker, Jr., Harper W. Boyd, Jr., and Jean-Claude Larreche, *Marketing Strategy* (Burr Ridge, IL: Richard D. Irwin, 1992), chaps. 1 and 2.

3. "Ben & Jerry's," Unilever website (n.d.), accessed at www.unilever .com/brands-in-action/detail/ben-and-jerrys/291995/?WT .contenttype=view%20brands.

4. The definition of *strategy* reflects thoughts appearing in Michael E. Porter, "What Is Strategy," *Harvard Business Review*, November 1, 1996, pp. 4,8.

5. "Why do you need a business plan," Canada Business Network, 2014, accessed at www.canadabusiness.ca/eng/page/3426/; "Developing a marketing plan," Canada Business Network, 2014, accessed at www.canadabusiness.ca/eng/page/2690/.

6. Barbara Shecter, "Diverse boards tied to fewer financial 'irregularities,' Canadian study finds," *Financial Post*, February 5, 2020, https://business.financialpost.com/news/fp-street/diverse -boards-tied-to-fewer-financial-irregularities-canadian-study-finds; Stephanie J. Creary, Mary-Hunter McDonnell, Sakshi Ghai, and Jared Scruggs, "When and Why Diversity Improves Your Board's Performance," *Harvard Business Review*, March 27, 2019, https:// hbr.org/2019/03/when-and-why-diversity-improves-your-boards -performance; "Companies With More Women Board Directors Experience Higher Financial Performance, According to Latest Catalyst Bottom Line Report," *Catalyst*, n.d., accessed at http://www .catalyst.org/media/companies-more-women-board-directors -experience-higher-financial-performance-according-latest; Aleksandra Sagan, "Tim Hortons parent company shareholders reject gender diversity proposal," *Toronto Star*, June 9, 2016, https:// www.thestar.com/business/2016/06/09/tim-hortons-parent -company-shareholders-reject-gender-diversity-proposal.html; David Milstead, "With no women on its board, shareholder calls for diversity policy at Tim Hortons owner RBI," *Globe and Mail*, June 8, 2016, http://www.theglobeandmail.com/report-on-business /with-no-women-on-its-board-shareholder-calls-for-diversity -policy-at-tim-hortons-owner-rbi/article30346961/; Jesse Ferreras, "Tim Hortons owner has no women on its board. It's an easy fix," *Huffington Post Canada*, June 8, 2016, http://www .huffingtonpost.ca/2016/06/08/tim-hortons-women-board-of -directors_n_10360366.html.

7. Phil Arrata, "An open letter from our CEO," MEC website, May 19, 2020, https://www.mec.ca/en/article/an-open-letter-from -our-ceo-2; Justin Dallaire, "MEC, Canadian Tire most reputable brands for CSR," *Strategy*, October 26, 2018, https://strategyonline. ca/2018/10/26/mec-canadian-tire-among-most-reputable-brands

-for-csr/; "In it for the long run," MEC website, accessed 2020 athttps://www.mec.ca/en/p/sustainability; "Things That Matter," MEC website, accessed 2016 at www.mec.ca/AST/Content Primary/Sustainability/AccountabilityReport.jsp; Alex Ballingall, "How corporate social responsibility improved these companies' bottom lines," *Maclean's*, June 14, 2012, www2.macleans .ca/2012/06/14/how-corporate-social-responsibility-improved-these -companies-bottom-lines/.

8. "CMOs and CFOs Are Misaligned," *Investor's Business Daily*, June 9, 2014, p. A07.

9. "Writing your business plan," Canada Business Network, 2014, accessed at www.canadabusiness.ca/eng/page/2753/#toc _financial_forecasts_and_other_information.

10. Christine Moorman, "From Marketing Spend to Marketing Accountability," *Marketing News* 48 (2014), pp. 24–25, https://www .ama.org/publications/MarketingNews/Pages/from-marketing -spend-marketing-accountability.aspx.

11. "Budgeting and forecasting," Canada Business Network, 2014, accessed at www.canadabusiness.ca/eng/page/2642/.

12. Tilley Endurables website, accessed at www.tilley.com/home.asp.

13. George Stalk, Phillip Evans, and Lawrence E. Shulman, "Competing on Capabilities. The New Rules of Corporate Strategy," *Harvard Business Review*, March–April 1992, pp. 57–69.

14. Tilley Endurables website, accessed at www.tilley.com/home.asp.

15. "Cosette hurries harder to win Curling Canada" [Press release], Cosette, September 18, 2019, accessed athttp://www.cossette.com /en/news/cossette-hurries-harder-win-curling-canada; "Curling Canada hires Cossette," *AdNews*, September 11, 2018, http://www .adnews.com/38113; Justin Dallaire, "Curling Canada reaches out to enthusiastic, novice fans," *Strategy*, December 4, 2018, http:// strategyonline.ca/2018/12/04/curling-canada-reaches-out-to -enthusiastic-novice-fans/.

16. Adapted from "The Experience Curve Reviewed, IV. The Growth Share Matrix of the Product Portfolio" (Boston: The Boston Consulting Group, 1973).

17. Kerin, Mahajan, and Vardarajan, *Contemporary Perspectives*, p. 52.

18. Jon Swartz, "Netflix may have edge on competition as coronavirus keeps people looking for new shows," *MarketWatch*, April 7, 2020, https://www.marketwatch.com/story/netflix-in -the-age-of-covid-19-streaming-pioneer-may-have-new-edge-on -competition-2020-04-07; Aneri Pattani, "Why Spotify, Netflix and HBO nailed business model of the future," CNBC, October 31, 2016, http://www.cnbc.com/2016/10/31/why-spotify-netflix -and-hbo-nailed-business-model-of-the-future.html; Michelle Castillo, "Netflix plans to spend $6 billion on new shows, blowing away all but one of its rivals," CNBC, October 17, 2016, http:// www.cnbc.com/2016/10/17/netflixs-6-billion-content-budget-in -2017-makes-it-one-of-the-top-spenders.html; Peter Cohan, "How Netfix Reinvented Itself," *Forbes*, April 23, 2013, https://www .forbes.com/sites/petercohan/2013/04/23/how-netflix-reinvented -itself/#5f3907242886.

Name Index

Company/Product Index

Wikipedia, 324
Word of Mouth Marketing
    Association (WOMMA),
    78
World Advertising Research Center,
    57, 98

Subject Index

business philosophies, evolution of, 14–16, 18
business plan, 365
business portfolio analysis, 371–372
business product, **168**, 170
business unit level, 364
business-to-business (B2B) marketing, 116. *See also* business marketing
business-to-consumer marketing. *See* consumer market
buy classes, **127**
buyer requirements, 249
buyer turnover, 249, 300
buyer–seller relationships, 124–126
buying centre, **127**–128
buying committee, 127
buying situation, 127–128
buying value, 64f, 67–68
buzz marketing, 78–79

C

Canada's anti-spam legislation (CASL), 55–56, 112, 342
Canadian Anti-Fraud Centre (CAFC), 51
Canadian Code of Advertising Standards, 45, 51, 53f, 54f, 56, 224
Canadian Intellectual Property Office, 173–174
Canadian Marketing Association (CMA), **311**
  code of ethics, 25, 54
  e-mail marketing, 318–319
  online advertising, 56
  privacy regulations, 55, 112
  regulatory groups, 51
Canadian Radio-television and Telecommunications Commission (CRTC), 51, 53, 54, **309**, 311, 342
Canadian retailing scene, 263, 264f
Canadian Wireless Telecommunications Association (CWTA), 51, 54, 311
careers in marketing, 5, 27–28
cash and carry wholesalers, 282
cash cow, 371–372
cash discounts, 228
catalogue retailing, 275
central business district, **272**
channel captain, 250
channel conflict, **250**
channel control, 248
channel design, 248–250
channel gap, 270
channel relationships, 250–251
cloud-based services, 48

CMA. *See* Canadian Marketing Association (CMA)
co-branding, 23–24
code of ethics, CMA, 25–26, 54
cognitive dissonance, 68
cognitive learning, 75
collaborative projects, 325f
collection methods, 95–96
commercial electronic messages (CEMS), 55–56
commercialization, 199f, **201**
Common Short Code (CSC) Guidelines, 342–343
common short codes (CSC), 54, **303**, 342–343
communications. *See* marketing communications
communications, retailing mix, 273
community shopping centre, **273**
company factors in market channel choice, 248
company reports, 318
competition, 49–51
Competition Act, 51, 53, 205, 223, 310
Competition Bureau, 50, 51, 52, **309**
competition regulation, 51–53
competition-oriented approaches to pricing, 210f, 213–214, 222–223
competitive advantages, **376**
competitive forces, **49**–51
competitive parity, 292
computers, 48
concept tests, **199**–200
consignment, 282
consumer behaviour
  brands, 78–86
  culture/subculture influences, 81–86
  level of involvement variations, 68–70
  marketing mix influencers, 70
  mobile technology, 67–68
  post-purchase behaviour stage, 68
  psychological influences, 70e, 72–77
  purchase decision process, 64–68, 70e
  situational influences, 70, 71
  socio-cultural influences, 70e, 78–81
consumer clusters, 149–150
consumer confidence, 45
consumer goods and services marketing channels, 238–239, 240f
consumer income, 216
consumer market, **139**

marketing channel, 238–240
segmentation in. *See* market segmentation
shopper marketing, 267
Consumer Packaging and Labelling Act, 51
consumer product, **168**, 169
consumer promotions, **301**
Consumer Reports, 64, 66
consumer socialization, 80
consumer touch points, 292, 350
consumer utilities, 262–263
consumer-generated media, 323
consumption value, 64f, 68
content communities, 325f
content marketing, **20**–21, 120–121, 325
continuous (steady) schedule, 300
continuous innovation, **193**
contractual system, retailing, 265–266
contractual vertical marketing system, 244f, 245
convenience products, **170**, 249
Conversation Prism, 325
co-op advertising, 305f
copyrights, **172**
"cord cutters", 43, 297
core product, **164**
corporate chain retailing, 265
corporate citizenship, 171
corporate level, 364
corporate logo, 67
corporate social responsibility (CSR), **15**
  approaches to, 15–19
  goals and, 367
  green products, 269
  greenwashing, 18
  relationship marketing, 14
  societal marketing concept, 19
corporate vertical marketing system, 244f, 245
corporate websites, **320**
correcting a negative deviation, 379
cost per acquisition (CPA), **336**
cost per click (CPC), **336**
cost per thousand (CPM), **336**
cost-oriented approaches to pricing, 209, 210f, 211–212
cost-plus pricing, 212
COVID-19
  channel gap, 270
  customer relationship management (CRM), 347–348, 349, 351
  IMC tools, 288, 315
  loyalty programs, 356

impact of, 58–59f
regulatory forces, 51–56, 57, 59f
socio-cultural forces, 41–45, 57, 58
sources of information for, 57–58f
steps in, 56–58
technological forces, 46–49
esteem needs, 73
ethical considerations, 25–26. *See also* regulations
data mining, 109
government procurement, 125
pricing, 223–225
social listening, 100, 101
ethnic diversity, 40–41, 81–82
evaluation of alternatives, 64f, 66, 70f
evaluation of alternatives stage, 126e
evaluation phase, 373f, 379–380
evaluative criteria, 66
event marketing, 294f, **319**
event sponsorship, 294f
everyday low pricing, 272
evoked set, 66
exchange, **12**
exchange relationship, 241
exclusive distribution, **248**
experiential marketing, **22**–23, 319
experiment, 101f, **103**–104
experimental data, 97
exploiting a positive deviation, 381
exploratory research, 93, 96, 100
extended problem-solving, 69
external data, 97
external search, 64
external secondary data, 97
exurban elite, 77f
exurban middle-aged, 77f

F

Facebook, 329–331
Facebook Groups, 329
Facebook Pages, 330
face-to-face exchange relationships, 241
facilitating function of intermediaries, 237f, 238
fad, **188**
family brand, **172**
family decision-making, 81
family influence, 80–81
family life cycle, **80**–81
fashion product, **188**
fear appeals, 295–296
feature phone, **338**
final price, 226–229. *See also* pricing
fixed cost, **219**, 220f
flexible-price policy, 226–227

flighting (intermittent) schedule, 300
fluctuating demand, **123**
FOB origin pricing, 228–229
focus group, 97f, **99**
food consumption, 43–44
forecasting, 214–215
forgetting rate, 300
form of ownership, **265**
form utility, 238
forward integration, 245
four Is of service, 162, 164
4 Ps, 4, 9, 377f. *See also* marketing mix
franchising, 244f, **245**–246
free trials, 74, 161, 162
freemium, 333
frequency, **292**
full service, 268
full-line wholesalers, 281
full-service wholesalers, 281
functional discount, 227–228
functional level, 364–365

G

Gen Z. *See* generation Z
gender attitudes and roles, 367
general merchandise stores, 271
general merchandise wholesalers, 281
generation X, **37**–39, 171
generation Y, **39**
generation Z, **39**, 86, 171, 328
generic brand, **176**–177
geofencing, **304**
geographic concentration of the market, 247
geographical adjustments to pricing, 228–229
geographics, **143**
global brands, **171**
global channel strategy, 243–244
global economy, 131
global marketing channel, 243–244
global pricing strategy, 225–226
goals (objectives), **366**–367
good, **12**, 170, 238–240
government markets, 117, 124, 125
Government of Canada, 120, 125
government regulations, 25
GPS technology, 280
green consumers, 45
green economy, 269
greenwashing, **18**, 26
grey market, **225**
gross domestic product (GDP), **46**
gross income, 46, **47**
group track, 329

growth stage, 292, 293f
growth-share matrix, 371f

H

harvest, **187**
hashtags, 173
high-involvement purchase, 68–69, 70
high-learning product, **188**
horizontal conflict, channel marketing, 250
humorous appeals, 296
hybrid apps, **341**

I

idea, **12**
idea generation, **198**–199
identity theft, 52
idle production capacity, **163**
illustrations, 74
image, 151
implementation phase of the marketing plan, 373f, 377–378
inbound marketing, **290**
direct response marketing, 318–319
event marketing, 319
mobile marketing, 337–343
online marketing, 319–323
public relations, 317–318
social media, 319–326
social media marketing, 326–337
sponsorships, 319
inconsistency, 162
independent retailer, 265
in-depth interviews, 97f, **99**
indirect channels, 239, 240f
indirect competitors, **49**
individual brand, **172**
individualized marketing, 140e, **142**–143
industrial distributor, 240
industrial goods, 168
industrial markets, 116
inelastic demand, **122**–123, 218
inflation, **46**
influencer marketing, 23, **321**, 322–323
influencers
marketing mix, 70f
psychological, 70f, 72–77
situational, 70–71
socio-cultural, 70f, 77–86
information search, 64, 66, 70f, 74
information search stage, 126e
information technology, **106**
information utility, 238
in-market, 103
innovators, 193, 194, 195f

global channels, 243–244
intermediaries, 236–238
logistics and supply chain, 251
multichannel marketing, 241–243
vertical marketing systems, 244–246
marketing communication agencies, **308**
marketing communication tools, **293**. *See also* promotional mix
marketing communications
associations, 309
customer advocacy funnel, 289–290
design strategies, 290–291
inbound marketing, 290
integrated marketing communications (IMC), 289
media forms, 308
media research companies, 308–309
outbound marketing, 290
product life cycle and, 292–293
program steps, 291–292
promotional mix, 293–306
regulatory groups, 51, 309, 311
trends in, 306–308
marketing dashboard, **369**
marketing environment, 35–36. *See also* environmental scan
marketing input data, 97
marketing metric, 104, 105, **369**
marketing mix, **9**–11, 377f. *See also* 4 Ps
marketing mix influences on consumer behaviour, 70f
"Marketing Myopia", **366**
marketing orientation, **14**
marketing outcome data, 97
marketing plan, **373**. *See also* strategic marketing process
evaluation phase, 373f, 378–380
implementation phase, 373f, 377–378
planning phase, 373f, 374–377
marketing process, **11**–12. *See also* strategic marketing process
marketing program, 373f, 376–377
marketing regulation, 25, 54, 112
marketing research, **92**. *See also* market research process
challenges, 92
future of, 112
market research process, steps of, 92–111
Marketing Research and Intelligence

Association (MRIA), 112
marketing strategy, **378**. *See also* strategic marketing planning
global pricing strategy, 225–226
new product development, 199f
organizational structure, 364–368
positioning, 376
product life cycle extension strategy, 189–192
push/pull strategies, 291
strategic marketing process, **373**–380
target market, 376
marketing tactics, **378**
market-product analysis, 372
market-product focus and goal setting phase, 373f, 376
marketspace, 241
markup, **211**, 272
Maslow's hierarchy of needs, 72–73
mass marketing, **140**
matrix 2D barcodes, **303**–304
maturity stage, 189, 292, 293f
maximizing current profit objective, 221
McMillennials, 86
m-commerce, 280
measures of success, **94**
media. *See also* marketing communications; social media
advertising choice, 296–300
data, 308
earned media, 308
owned media, 308
paid media, 308
rich media, 296f
socio-cultural force, as, 41–43
media research companies, 308
media richness, 324, 325f
membership group, 80
merchandise mix, **268**–271
merchandising allowances, 305f
merchant wholesalers, **281**–282
metrics, **24**, 104–106, 369
microeconomic forces, **46**
micro-influencer, 23
microsites, **320**
millennials, **39**, 67, 79, 86, 147, 153
minor innovations, **192**
misleading pricing practices, 52
mission, **366**
mission statement, 366
MMA Global Code of Conduct, 343
mobile advertising, 299–300. *See also* mobile marketing
mobile applications (apps), **340**–341

mobile channel, 279–281
mobile check-in services, **305**
mobile commerce, 280
mobile discovery, **305**
mobile e-mail, **303**
mobile marketing, **21**–22, 337. *See also* social media; social media marketing
best practices, 343
devices, 337–339
matrix 2D barcodes, 303–304
messaging option, 299, 303
mobile applications (apps), 340–341
mobile subscribers, 338f
mobile web, 340
proximity marketing, 304–305
regulatory groups, 54, 342–343
strength and weakness, 294f
top activities, 339
Mobile Marketing Association (MMA), 51, 54, 311, 342, 343
mobile messaging, **303**
mobile payments, 48–49
mobile technology
evolution of, 307–308
mobile discovery, 305
online retailing, 279–281
purchasing behaviour, effect on, 67–68
regulation, 54, 342–343
sales promotion, 294f, 303–305
social networks, 306
usage, 306–307
WiFi hotspots, 305
mobile web, **340**
mobile web apps, **341**
modified rebuy, 128
monopolistic competition, **50**
monopoly, **50**
motivation, **72**–73
multichannel marketing, **242**–243, 267
multichannel retailers, **273**
multimedia messaging services (MMS), **303**
multiple equation methods of forecasting, 215
music, 48

N

NAICS. *See* North American Industry Classification System (NAICS)
native apps, **341**
near field communications (NFC), **304**

supply chain management, **251**–254, 255

supply partnership, **126**

surveys, 100–103
  data collection methods, 95
  mistakes to avoid, 103*f*
  quantitative research, 101*f*
  techniques, 102*f*

SWOT analysis, **36**, 373*f*, 374–376

syndicated panel, 97–98

syndicated studies, **102**–103

T

tagmark, 173

target market, **9**, 143
  behaviouristics, 144*f*, 145–146
  demographics, 144*f*, 145
  geographics, 143–144
  integrated marketing communications (IMC), 289
  marketing channel choice, 248–249
  personas, 146
  psychographics, 144*f*, 145
  retailing, 266
  selection, 149–151
  strategic marketing process, 376
  target market profile, 143–146
  WestJet, 3–4

target market profile, **143**–146

target pricing, 211

target profit pricing, 212–213

target return objective, 221

target return-on-investment pricing, 213

target return-on-sales pricing, 213

tax scams, 52

technological forces, **46**–49

teenagers, influence, 81

Telecommunications Act, 53

telemarketing, **275**–276

telephone interview, 102*f*

television advertising, 296*f*, 297

television homeshopping, 274–275

temporal effects influence, 70

test market, **103**

test marketing, 199*f*, **200**–201

Textile Labelling Act, 51

"The Little Black Book of Scams", 52

"The Six Key Tribes of Millennials", 147

threats, 375

time utility, 238

time-series methods of forecasting, 215

total cost, **219**, 220*f*

total product concept, 163–164

total revenue, **218**, 220*f*

touch points, **292**, 350

trade discounts, 227–228

trade promotions, **305**

trade shows, 305*f*

trade-in allowances, 228

trademarks, **172**, 173–174, 175

traditional auction, **130**–132

traditional distribution centre, 259

traditional marketplace, 241

traffic generation, **318**

transactional function of intermediaries, 237

transactional websites, 243, **320**

transit advertising, 298

transportation, 256

truck jobbers, 281

Twitter, 329*f*, 331–332

U

unemployment rate, **46**

uniform delivered pricing, 229

unit value, 247

unsought products, **170**

urban elite, 77*f*

urban upscale diverse, 77*f*

user-generated content (UGG), **323**–324

username, 174

utility, retail, 262–263

V

VALS system, 76

value, **208**. *See also* customer value proposition

monetary, 149

price and, 208

pricing, 208

purchase decision process, 64, 65–68

value pricing, 208

values and beliefs, 75–76, 84

variable cost, **219**, 220*f*

vending machine, 274

vertical conflict, channel conflict, 250

vertical marketing systems, **244**–246

viral marketing, 79

virtual game worlds, 325*f*

virtual services, **161**

virtual social worlds, 325*f*

vision, 366

vlog, **325**

volume objective, 222

W

want, **7**–8

warehousing, 257

warranties and guarantees, 74

wearable technology, 47, 338

wearables, **338**

web analytics, **110**

web ap, 341

websites, 106*f*, 243, 320

wholesaler-sponsored voluntary chains, 244*f*, 245

wholesaling, 281–282

WiFi hotspots, **304**, 305

wiki, **325**

Wireless Code, 53, 342

word of mouth, **78**, 79

word-of-mouth marketing, **321**

Y

yellow pages advertising, 296*f*

yield management pricing, 211

YouTube, 332